Further Praise for
Code Complete

"An excellent guide to programming style and software construction."
—Martin Fowler, *Refactoring*

"Steve McConnell's *Code Complete* . . . provides a fast track to wisdom for programmers. . . .
His books are fun to read, and you never forget that he is speaking from hard-won personal
experience."   —Jon Bentley, *Programming Pearls*, 2d ed.

"This is simply the best book on software construction that I've ever read. Every developer
should own a copy and read it cover to cover every year. After reading it annually for nine
years, I'm still learning things from this book!"
—John Robbins, *Debugging Applications for Microsoft .NET and Microsoft Windows*

"Today's software *must* be robust and resilient, and secure code starts with disciplined software
construction. After ten years, there is still no better authority than *Code Complete*."
—Michael Howard, Security Engineering, Microsoft Corporation; Coauthor, *Writing Secure Code*

"A comprehensive examination of the tactical issues that go into crafting a well-engineered
program. McConnell's work covers such diverse topics as architecture, coding standards,
testing, integration, and the nature of software craftsmanship."
—Grady Booch, *Object Solutions*

"The ultimate encyclopedia for the software developer is *Code Complete* by Steve McConnell.
Subtitled 'A Practical Handbook of Software Construction,' this 850-page book is exactly
that. Its stated goal is to narrow the gap between the knowledge of 'industry gurus and professors' (Yourdon and Pressman, for example) and common commercial practice, and 'to
help you write better programs in less time with fewer headaches.' . . . Every developer should
own a copy of McConnell's book. Its style and content are thoroughly practical."
—Chris Loosley, *High-Performance Client/Server*

"Steve McConnell's seminal book *Code Complete* is one of the most accessible works discussing in detail software development methods. . . ."
—Erik Bethke, *Game Development and Production*

"A mine of useful information and advice on the broader issues in designing and producing
good software."
—John Dempster, *The Laboratory Computer: A Practical Guide for Physiologists and Neuroscientists*

"If you are serious about improving your programming skills, you should get *Code Complete* by Steve McConnell."
—Jean J. Labrosse, *Embedded Systems Building Blocks: Complete and Ready-To-Use Modules in C*

"Steve McConnell has written one of the best books on software development independent of computer environment . . . *Code Complete*."
—Kenneth Rosen, *Unix: The Complete Reference*

"Every half an age or so, you come across a book that short-circuits the school of experience and saves you years of purgatory. . . . I cannot adequately express how good this book really is. *Code Complete* is a pretty lame title for a work of brilliance."
—Jeff Duntemann, *PC Techniques*

"Microsoft Press has published what I consider to be the definitive book on software construction. This is a book that belongs on every software developer's shelf."
—Warren Keuffel, *Software Development*

"Every programmer should read this outstanding book."   —T. L. (Frank) Pappas, *Computer*

"If you aspire to be a professional programmer, this may be the wisest $35 investment you'll ever make. Don't stop to read the rest of this review: just run out and buy it. McConnell's stated purpose is to narrow the gap between the knowledge of industry gurus and common commercial practice. . . . The amazing thing is that he succeeds."
—Richard Mateosian, *IEEE Micro*

"*Code Complete* should be required reading for anyone . . . in software development."
—Tommy Usher, *C Users Journal*

"I'm encouraged to stick my neck out a bit further than usual and recommend, without reservation, Steve McConnell's *Code Complete*. . . . My copy has replaced my API reference manuals as the book that's closest to my keyboard while I work."
—Jim Kyle, *Windows Tech Journal*

"This well-written but massive tome is arguably the best single volume ever written on the practical aspects of software implementation."
—Tommy Usher, *Embedded Systems Programming*

"This is the best book on software engineering that I have yet read."
—Edward Kenworth, *.EXE Magazine*

"This book deserves to become a classic, and should be compulsory reading for all developers, and those responsible for managing them."   —Peter Wright, *Program Now*

Code Complete, Second Edition

Steve McConnell

PUBLISHED BY
Microsoft Press
A Division of Microsoft Corporation
One Microsoft Way
Redmond, Washington 98052-6399

Library of Congress Cataloging-in-Publication Data
McConnell, Steve
    Code Complete / Steve McConnell.--2nd ed.
       p. cm.
    Includes index.
    ISBN 0-7356-1967-0
    1. Computer Software--Development--Handbooks, manuals, etc. I. Title.

    QA76.76.D47M39 2004
    005.1--dc22   2004049981

Printed and bound in the United States of America.

ISBN: 978-0-7356-1967-8

28   16

Distributed in Canada by H.B. Fenn and Company Ltd. A CIP catalogue record for this book is available from the British Library.

Microsoft Press books are available through booksellers and distributors worldwide. For further information about international editions, contact your local Microsoft Corporation office or contact Microsoft Press International directly at fax (425) 936-7329. Visit our Web site at www.microsoft.com/mspress. Send comments to *mspinput@ microsoft.com*.

Microsoft, Microsoft Press, PowerPoint, Visual Basic, Windows, and Windows NT are either registered trademarks or trademarks of Microsoft Corporation in the United States and/or other countries. Other product and company names mentioned herein may be the trademarks of their respective owners.

The example companies, organizations, products, domain names, e-mail addresses, logos, people, places, and events depicted herein are fictitious. No association with any real company, organization, product, domain name, e-mail address, logo, person, place, or event is intended or should be inferred.

Acquisitions Editors: Linda Engelman and Robin Van Steenburgh
Project Editor: Devon Musgrave
Indexer: Bill Myers
Principal Desktop Publisher: Carl Diltz

Body Part No. X10-53130

To my wife, Ashlie, who doesn't have much to do with computer programming
but who has everything to do with enriching the rest of my life
in more ways than I could possibly describe

Contents at a Glance

Table of Contents

What do you think of this book? We want to hear from you!	Microsoft is interested in hearing your feedback about this publication so we can continually improve our books and learning resources for you. To participate in a brief online survey, please visit: *www.microsoft.com/learning/booksurvey/*

Preface

The gap between the best software engineering practice and the average practice is very wide—perhaps wider than in any other engineering discipline. A tool that disseminates good practice would be important.
—Fred Brooks

My primary concern in writing this book has been to narrow the gap between the knowledge of industry gurus and professors on the one hand and common commercial practice on the other. Many powerful programming techniques hide in journals and academic papers for years before trickling down to the programming public.

Although leading-edge software-development practice has advanced rapidly in recent years, common practice hasn't. Many programs are still buggy, late, and over budget, and many fail to satisfy the needs of their users. Researchers in both the software industry and academic settings have discovered effective practices that eliminate most of the programming problems that have been prevalent since the 1970s. Because these practices aren't often reported outside the pages of highly specialized technical journals, however, most programming organizations aren't yet using them today. Studies have found that it typically takes 5 to 15 years or more for a research development to make its way into commercial practice (Raghavan and Chand 1989, Rogers 1995, Parnas 1999). This handbook shortcuts the process, making key discoveries available to the average programmer now.

Who Should Read This Book?

The research and programming experience collected in this handbook will help you to create higher-quality software and to do your work more quickly and with fewer problems. This book will give you insight into why you've had problems in the past and will show you how to avoid problems in the future. The programming practices described here will help you keep big projects under control and help you maintain and modify software successfully as the demands of your projects change.

Experienced Programmers

This handbook serves experienced programmers who want a comprehensive, easy-to-use guide to software development. Because this book focuses on construction, the most familiar part of the software life cycle, it makes powerful software development techniques understandable to self-taught programmers as well as to programmers with formal training.

Technical Leads

Many technical leads have used *Code Complete* to educate less-experienced programmers on their teams. You can also use it to fill your own knowledge gaps. If you're an experienced programmer, you might not agree with all my conclusions (and I would be surprised if you did), but if you read this book and think about each issue, only rarely will someone bring up a construction issue that you haven't previously considered.

Self-Taught Programmers

If you haven't had much formal training, you're in good company. About 50,000 new developers enter the profession each year (BLS 2004, Hecker 2004), but only about 35,000 software-related degrees are awarded each year (NCES 2002). From these figures it's a short hop to the conclusion that many programmers don't receive a formal education in software development. Self-taught programmers are found in the emerging group of professionals—engineers, accountants, scientists, teachers, and small-business owners—who program as part of their jobs but who do not necessarily view themselves as programmers. Regardless of the extent of your programming education, this handbook can give you insight into effective programming practices.

Students

The counterpoint to the programmer with experience but little formal training is the fresh college graduate. The recent graduate is often rich in theoretical knowledge but poor in the practical know-how that goes into building production programs. The practical lore of good coding is often passed down slowly in the ritualistic tribal dances of software architects, project leads, analysts, and more-experienced programmers. Even more often, it's the product of the individual programmer's trials and errors. This book is an alternative to the slow workings of the traditional intellectual potlatch. It pulls together the helpful tips and effective development strategies previously available mainly by hunting and gathering from other people's experience. It's a hand up for the student making the transition from an academic environment to a professional one.

Where Else Can You Find This Information?

This book synthesizes construction techniques from a variety of sources. In addition to being widely scattered, much of the accumulated wisdom about construction has resided outside written sources for years (Hildebrand 1989, McConnell 1997a). There is nothing mysterious about the effective, high-powered programming techniques used by expert programmers. In the day-to-day rush of grinding out the latest project, however, few experts take the time to share what they have learned. Consequently, programmers may have difficulty finding a good source of programming information.

The techniques described in this book fill the void after introductory and advanced programming texts. After you have read *Introduction to Java*, *Advanced Java*, and *Advanced Advanced Java*, what book do you read to learn more about programming? You could read books about the details of Intel or Motorola hardware, Microsoft Windows or Linux operating-system functions, or another programming language—you can't use a language or program in an environment without a good reference to such details. But this is one of the few books that discusses programming per se. Some of the most beneficial programming aids are practices that you can use regardless of the environment or language you're working in. Other books generally neglect such practices, which is why this book concentrates on them.

The information in this book is distilled from many sources, as shown below. The only other way to obtain the information you'll find in this handbook would be to plow through a mountain of books and a few hundred technical journals and then add a significant amount of real-world experience. If you've already done all that, you can still benefit from this book's collecting the information in one place for easy reference.

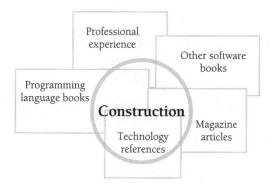

Key Benefits of This Handbook

Whatever your background, this handbook can help you write better programs in less time and with fewer headaches.

Complete software-construction reference   This handbook discusses general aspects of construction such as software quality and ways to think about programming. It gets into nitty-gritty construction details such as steps in building classes, ins and outs of using data and control structures, debugging, refactoring, and code-tuning techniques and strategies. You don't need to read it cover to cover to learn about these topics. The book is designed to make it easy to find the specific information that interests you.

Ready-to-use checklists   This book includes dozens of checklists you can use to assess your software architecture, design approach, class and routine quality, variable names, control structures, layout, test cases, and much more.

State-of-the-art information   This handbook describes some of the most up-to-date techniques available, many of which have not yet made it into common use. Because this book draws from both practice and research, the techniques it describes will remain useful for years.

Larger perspective on software development   This book will give you a chance to rise above the fray of day-to-day fire fighting and figure out what works and what doesn't. Few practicing programmers have the time to read through the hundreds of books and journal articles that have been distilled into this handbook. The research and real-world experience gathered into this handbook will inform and stimulate your thinking about your projects, enabling you to take strategic action so that you don't have to fight the same battles again and again.

Absence of hype   Some software books contain 1 gram of insight swathed in 10 grams of hype. This book presents balanced discussions of each technique's strengths and weaknesses. You know the demands of your particular project better than anyone else. This book provides the objective information you need to make good decisions about your specific circumstances.

Concepts applicable to most common languages   This book describes techniques you can use to get the most out of whatever language you're using, whether it's C++, C#, Java, Microsoft Visual Basic, or other similar languages.

Numerous code examples   The book contains almost 500 examples of good and bad code. I've included so many examples because, personally, I learn best from examples. I think other programmers learn best that way too.

The examples are in multiple languages because mastering more than one language is often a watershed in the career of a professional programmer. Once a programmer realizes that programming principles transcend the syntax of any specific language, the doors swing open to knowledge that truly makes a difference in quality and productivity.

To make the multiple-language burden as light as possible, I've avoided esoteric language features except where they're specifically discussed. You don't need to understand every nuance of the code fragments to understand the points they're making. If you focus on the point being illustrated, you'll find that you can read the code regardless of the language. I've tried to make your job even easier by annotating the significant parts of the examples.

Access to other sources of information   This book collects much of the available information on software construction, but it's hardly the last word. Throughout the chapters, "Additional Resources" sections describe other books and articles you can read as you pursue the topics you find most interesting.

cc2e.com/1234 *Book website*   Updated checklists, books, magazine articles, Web links, and other content are provided on a companion website at *cc2e.com*. To access information related to *Code Complete*, 2d ed., enter *cc2e.com/* followed by a four-digit code, an example of which is shown here in the left margin. These website references appear throughout the book.

Why This Handbook Was Written

The need for development handbooks that capture knowledge about effective development practices is well recognized in the software-engineering community. A report of the Computer Science and Technology Board stated that the biggest gains in software-development quality and productivity will come from codifying, unifying, and distributing existing knowledge about effective software-development practices (CSTB 1990, McConnell 1997a). The board concluded that the strategy for spreading that knowledge should be built on the concept of software-engineering handbooks.

The Topic of Construction Has Been Neglected

At one time, software development and coding were thought to be one and the same. But as distinct activities in the software-development life cycle have been identified, some of the best minds in the field have spent their time analyzing and debating methods of project management, requirements, design, and testing. The rush to study these newly identified areas has left code construction as the ignorant cousin of software development.

Discussions about construction have also been hobbled by the suggestion that treating construction as a distinct software development *activity* implies that construction must also be treated as a distinct *phase*. In reality, software activities and phases don't have to be set up in any particular relationship to each other, and it's useful to discuss the activity of construction regardless of whether other software activities are performed in phases, in iterations, or in some other way.

Construction Is Important

Another reason construction has been neglected by researchers and writers is the mistaken idea that, compared to other software-development activities, construction is a relatively mechanical process that presents little opportunity for improvement. Nothing could be further from the truth.

Code construction typically makes up about 65 percent of the effort on small projects and 50 percent on medium projects. Construction accounts for about 75 percent of the errors on small projects and 50 to 75 percent on medium and large projects. Any activity that accounts for 50 to 75 percent of the errors presents a clear opportunity for improvement. (Chapter 27 contains more details on these statistics.)

Some commentators have pointed out that although construction errors account for a high percentage of total errors, construction errors tend to be less expensive to fix than those caused by requirements and architecture, the suggestion being that they are therefore less important. The claim that construction errors cost less to fix is true but misleading because the cost of not fixing them can be incredibly high. Researchers have found that small-scale coding errors account for some of the most expensive software errors of all time, with costs running into hundreds of millions of dollars (Weinberg 1983, SEN 1990). An inexpensive cost to fix obviously does not imply that fixing them should be a low priority.

The irony of the shift in focus away from construction is that construction is the only activity that's guaranteed to be done. Requirements can be assumed rather than developed; architecture can be shortchanged rather than designed; and testing can be abbreviated or skipped rather than fully planned and executed. But if there's going to be a program, there has to be construction, and that makes construction a uniquely fruitful area in which to improve development practices.

No Comparable Book Is Available

In light of construction's obvious importance, I was sure when I conceived this book that someone else would already have written a book on effective construction practices. The need for a book about how to program effectively seemed obvious. But I found that only a few books had been written about construction and then only on parts of the topic. Some had been written 15 years or more earlier and employed relatively esoteric languages such as ALGOL, PL/I, Ratfor, and Smalltalk. Some were written by professors who were not working on production code. The professors wrote about techniques that worked for student projects, but they often had little idea of how the techniques would play out in full-scale development environments. Still other books trumpeted the authors' newest favorite methodologies but ignored the huge repository of mature practices that have proven their effectiveness over time.

When art critics get together they talk about Form and Structure and Meaning. When artists get together they talk about where you can buy cheap turpentine.
—Pablo Picasso

In short, I couldn't find any book that had even attempted to capture the body of practical techniques available from professional experience, industry research, and academic work. The discussion needed to be brought up to date for current programming languages, object-oriented programming, and leading-edge development practices. It seemed clear that a book about programming needed to be written by someone who was knowledgeable about the theoretical state of the art but who was also building enough production code to appreciate the state of the practice. I conceived this book as a full discussion of code construction—from one programmer to another.

Author Note

I welcome your inquiries about the topics discussed in this book, your error reports, or other related subjects. Please contact me at *stevemcc@construx.com*, or visit my website at *www.stevemcconnell.com*.

Bellevue, Washington
Memorial Day, 2004

Microsoft Learning Technical Support

Every effort has been made to ensure the accuracy of this book. Microsoft Press provides corrections for books through the World Wide Web at the following address:

http://www.microsoft.com/learning/support/

To connect directly to the Microsoft Knowledge Base and enter a query regarding a question or issue that you may have, go to:

http://www.microsoft.com/learning/support/search.asp

If you have comments, questions, or ideas regarding this book, please send them to Microsoft Press using either of the following methods:

Postal Mail:

> *Microsoft Press*
> *Attn: Code Complete 2E Editor*
> *One Microsoft Way*
> *Redmond, WA 98052-6399*

E-mail:

> *mspinput@microsoft.com*

Acknowledgments

A book is never really written by one person (at least none of my books are). A second edition is even more a collective undertaking.

I'd like to thank the people who contributed review comments on significant portions of the book: Hákon Ágústsson, Scott Ambler, Will Barns, William D. Bartholomew, Lars Bergstrom, Ian Brockbank, Bruce Butler, Jay Cincotta, Alan Cooper, Bob Corrick, Al Corwin, Jerry Deville, Jon Eaves, Edward Estrada, Steve Gouldstone, Owain Griffiths, Matthew Harris, Michael Howard, Andy Hunt, Kevin Hutchison, Rob Jasper, Stephen Jenkins, Ralph Johnson and his Software Architecture Group at the University of Illinois, Marek Konopka, Jeff Langr, Andy Lester, Mitica Manu, Steve Mattingly, Gareth McCaughan, Robert McGovern, Scott Meyers, Gareth Morgan, Matt Peloquin, Bryan Pflug, Jeffrey Richter, Steve Rinn, Doug Rosenberg, Brian St. Pierre, Diomidis Spinellis, Matt Stephens, Dave Thomas, Andy Thomas-Cramer, John Vlissides, Pavel Vozenilek, Denny Williford, Jack Woolley, and Dee Zsombor.

Hundreds of readers sent comments about the first edition, and many more sent individual comments about the second edition. Thanks to everyone who took time to share their reactions to the book in its various forms.

Special thanks to the Construx Software reviewers who formally inspected the entire manuscript: Jason Hills, Bradey Honsinger, Abdul Nizar, Tom Reed, and Pamela Perrott. I was truly amazed at how thorough their review was, especially considering how many eyes had scrutinized the book before they began working on it. Thanks also to Bradey, Jason, and Pamela for their contributions to the *cc2e.com* website.

Working with Devon Musgrave, project editor for this book, has been a special treat. I've worked with numerous excellent editors on other projects, and Devon stands out as especially conscientious and easy to work with. Thanks, Devon! Thanks to Linda Engleman who championed the second edition; this book wouldn't have happened without her. Thanks also to the rest of the Microsoft Press staff, including Robin Van Steenburgh, Elden Nelson, Carl Diltz, Joel Panchot, Patricia Masserman, Bill Myers, Sandi Resnick, Barbara Norfleet, James Kramer, and Prescott Klassen.

I'd like to remember the Microsoft Press staff that published the first edition: Alice Smith, Arlene Myers, Barbara Runyan, Carol Luke, Connie Little, Dean Holmes, Eric Stroo, Erin O'Connor, Jeannie McGivern, Jeff Carey, Jennifer Harris, Jennifer Vick, Judith Bloch, Katherine Erickson, Kim Eggleston, Lisa Sandburg, Lisa Theobald, Margarite Hargrave, Mike Halvorson, Pat Forgette, Peggy Herman, Ruth Pettis, Sally Brunsman, Shawn Peck, Steve Murray, Wallis Bolz, and Zaafar Hasnain.

Thanks to the reviewers who contributed so significantly to the first edition: Al Corwin, Bill Kiestler, Brian Daugherty, Dave Moore, Greg Hitchcock, Hank Meuret, Jack Woolley, Joey Wyrick, Margot Page, Mike Klein, Mike Zevenbergen, Pat Forman, Peter Pathe, Robert L. Glass, Tammy Forman, Tony Pisculli, and Wayne Beardsley. Special thanks to Tony Garland for his exhaustive review: with 12 years' hindsight, I appreciate more than ever how exceptional Tony's several thousand review comments really were.

Checklists

Tables

Figures

Part I
Laying the Foundation

In this part:

Chapter 1
Welcome to Software Construction

cc2e.com/0178

Contents

- 1.1 What Is Software Construction?: page 3
- 1.2 Why Is Software Construction Important?: page 6
- 1.3 How to Read This Book: page 8

Related Topics

- Who should read this book: Preface
- Benefits of reading the book: Preface
- Why the book was written: Preface

You know what "construction" means when it's used outside software development. "Construction" is the work "construction workers" do when they build a house, a school, or a skyscraper. When you were younger, you built things out of "construction paper." In common usage, "construction" refers to the process of building. The construction process might include some aspects of planning, designing, and checking your work, but mostly "construction" refers to the hands-on part of creating something.

1.1 What Is Software Construction?

Developing computer software can be a complicated process, and in the last 25 years, researchers have identified numerous distinct activities that go into software development. They include

- Problem definition
- Requirements development
- Construction planning
- Software architecture, or high-level design
- Detailed design
- Coding and debugging
- Unit testing

- Integration testing
- Integration
- System testing
- Corrective maintenance

If you've worked on informal projects, you might think that this list represents a lot of red tape. If you've worked on projects that are too formal, you *know* that this list represents a lot of red tape! It's hard to strike a balance between too little and too much formality, and that's discussed later in the book.

If you've taught yourself to program or worked mainly on informal projects, you might not have made distinctions among the many activities that go into creating a software product. Mentally, you might have grouped all of these activities together as "programming." If you work on informal projects, the main activity you think of when you think about creating software is probably the activity the researchers refer to as "construction."

This intuitive notion of "construction" is fairly accurate, but it suffers from a lack of perspective. Putting construction in its context with other activities helps keep the focus on the right tasks during construction and appropriately emphasizes important nonconstruction activities. Figure 1-1 illustrates construction's place related to other software-development activities.

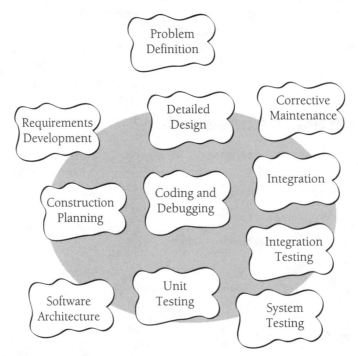

Figure 1-1 Construction activities are shown inside the gray circle. Construction focuses on coding and debugging but also includes detailed design, unit testing, integration testing, and other activities.

As the figure indicates, construction is mostly coding and debugging but also involves detailed design, construction planning, unit testing, integration, integration testing, and other activities. If this were a book about all aspects of software development, it would feature nicely balanced discussions of all activities in the development process. Because this is a handbook of construction techniques, however, it places a lopsided emphasis on construction and only touches on related topics. If this book were a dog, it would nuzzle up to construction, wag its tail at design and testing, and bark at the other development activities.

Construction is also sometimes known as "coding" or "programming." "Coding" isn't really the best word because it implies the mechanical translation of a preexisting design into a computer language; construction is not at all mechanical and involves substantial creativity and judgment. Throughout the book, I use "programming" interchangeably with "construction."

In contrast to Figure 1-1's flat-earth view of software development, Figure 1-2 shows the round-earth perspective of this book.

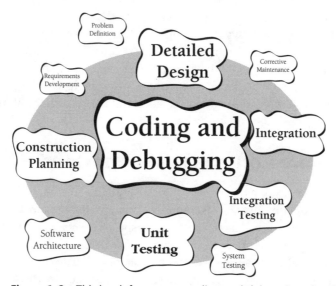

Figure 1-2   This book focuses on coding and debugging, detailed design, construction planning, unit testing, integration, integration testing, and other activities in roughly these proportions.

Figure 1-1 and Figure 1-2 are high-level views of construction activities, but what about the details? Here are some of the specific tasks involved in construction:

- Verifying that the groundwork has been laid so that construction can proceed successfully

- Determining how your code will be tested

- Designing and writing classes and routines

- Creating and naming variables and named constants

- Selecting control structures and organizing blocks of statements

- Unit testing, integration testing, and debugging your own code

- Reviewing other team members' low-level designs and code and having them review yours

- Polishing code by carefully formatting and commenting it

- Integrating software components that were created separately

- Tuning code to make it faster and use fewer resources

For an even fuller list of construction activities, look through the chapter titles in the table of contents.

With so many activities at work in construction, you might say, "OK, Jack, what activities are *not* part of construction?" That's a fair question. Important nonconstruction activities include management, requirements development, software architecture, user-interface design, system testing, and maintenance. Each of these activities affects the ultimate success of a project as much as construction—at least the success of any project that calls for more than one or two people and lasts longer than a few weeks. You can find good books on each activity; many are listed in the "Additional Resources" sections throughout the book and in Chapter 35, "Where to Find More Information," at the end of the book.

1.2 Why Is Software Construction Important?

Since you're reading this book, you probably agree that improving software quality and developer productivity is important. Many of today's most exciting projects use software extensively. The Internet, movie special effects, medical life-support systems, space programs, aeronautics, high-speed financial analysis, and scientific research are a few examples. These projects and more conventional projects can all benefit from improved practices because many of the fundamentals are the same.

If you agree that improving software development is important in general, the question for you as a reader of this book becomes, Why is construction an important focus?

Here's why:

Cross-Reference For details on the relationship between project size and the percentage of time consumed by construction, see "Activity Proportions and Size" in Section 27.5.

Construction is a large part of software development   Depending on the size of the project, construction typically takes 30 to 80 percent of the total time spent on a project. Anything that takes up that much project time is bound to affect the success of the project.

Construction is the central activity in software development   Requirements and architecture are done before construction so that you can do construction effectively. System testing (in the strict sense of independent testing) is done after construction to verify that construction has been done correctly. Construction is at the center of the software-development process.

Cross-Reference For data on variations among programmers, see "Individual Variation" in Section 28.5.

With a focus on construction, the individual programmer's productivity can improve enormously   A classic study by Sackman, Erikson, and Grant showed that the productivity of individual programmers varied by a factor of 10 to 20 during construction (1968). Since their study, their results have been confirmed by numerous other studies (Curtis 1981, Mills 1983, Curtis et al. 1986, Card 1987, Valett and McGarry 1989, DeMarco and Lister 1999, Boehm et al. 2000). This book helps all programmers learn techniques that are already used by the best programmers.

Construction's product, the source code, is often the only accurate description of the software   In many projects, the only documentation available to programmers is the code itself. Requirements specifications and design documents can go out of date, but the source code is always up to date. Consequently, it's imperative that the source code be of the highest possible quality. Consistent application of techniques for source-code improvement makes the difference between a Rube Goldberg contraption and a detailed, correct, and therefore informative program. Such techniques are most effectively applied during construction.

KEY POINT

Construction is the only activity that's guaranteed to be done   The ideal software project goes through careful requirements development and architectural design before construction begins. The ideal project undergoes comprehensive, statistically controlled system testing after construction. Imperfect, real-world projects, however, often skip requirements and design to jump into construction. They drop testing because they have too many errors to fix and they've run out of time. But no matter how rushed or poorly planned a project is, you can't drop construction; it's where the rubber meets the road. Improving construction is thus a way of improving any software-development effort, no matter how abbreviated.

1.3 How to Read This Book

This book is designed to be read either cover to cover or by topic. If you like to read books cover to cover, you might simply dive into Chapter 2, "Metaphors for a Richer Understanding of Software Development." If you want to get to specific programming tips, you might begin with Chapter 6, "Working Classes," and then follow the cross references to other topics you find interesting. If you're not sure whether any of this applies to you, begin with Section 3.2, "Determine the Kind of Software You're Working On."

Key Points

- Software construction is the central activity in software development; construction is the only activity that's guaranteed to happen on every project.
- The main activities in construction are detailed design, coding, debugging, integration, and developer testing (unit testing and integration testing).
- Other common terms for construction are "coding" and "programming."
- The quality of the construction substantially affects the quality of the software.
- In the final analysis, your understanding of how to do construction determines how good a programmer you are, and that's the subject of the rest of the book.

Chapter 2

Metaphors for a Richer Understanding of Software Development

Contents

- 2.1 The Importance of Metaphors: page 9
- 2.2 How to Use Software Metaphors: page 11
- 2.3 Common Software Metaphors: page 13

Related Topic

- Heuristics in design: "Design Is a Heuristic Process" in Section 5.1

Computer science has some of the most colorful language of any field. In what other field can you walk into a sterile room, carefully controlled at 68°F, and find viruses, Trojan horses, worms, bugs, bombs, crashes, flames, twisted sex changers, and fatal errors?

These graphic metaphors describe specific software phenomena. Equally vivid metaphors describe broader phenomena, and you can use them to improve your understanding of the software-development process.

The rest of the book doesn't directly depend on the discussion of metaphors in this chapter. Skip it if you want to get to the practical suggestions. Read it if you want to think about software development more clearly.

2.1 The Importance of Metaphors

Important developments often arise out of analogies. By comparing a topic you understand poorly to something similar you understand better, you can come up with insights that result in a better understanding of the less-familiar topic. This use of metaphor is called "modeling."

The history of science is full of discoveries based on exploiting the power of metaphors. The chemist Kekulé had a dream in which he saw a snake grasp its tail in its mouth. When he awoke, he realized that a molecular structure based on a similar ring shape would account for the properties of benzene. Further experimentation confirmed the hypothesis (Barbour 1966).

The kinetic theory of gases was based on a "billiard-ball" model. Gas molecules were thought to have mass and to collide elastically, as billiard balls do, and many useful theorems were developed from this model.

The wave theory of light was developed largely by exploring similarities between light and sound. Light and sound have amplitude (brightness, loudness), frequency (color, pitch), and other properties in common. The comparison between the wave theories of sound and light was so productive that scientists spent a great deal of effort looking for a medium that would propagate light the way air propagates sound. They even gave it a name —"ether"—but they never found the medium. The analogy that had been so fruitful in some ways proved to be misleading in this case.

In general, the power of models is that they're vivid and can be grasped as conceptual wholes. They suggest properties, relationships, and additional areas of inquiry. Sometimes a model suggests areas of inquiry that are misleading, in which case the metaphor has been overextended. When the scientists looked for ether, they overextended their model.

As you might expect, some metaphors are better than others. A good metaphor is simple, relates well to other relevant metaphors, and explains much of the experimental evidence and other observed phenomena.

Consider the example of a heavy stone swinging back and forth on a string. Before Galileo, an Aristotelian looking at the swinging stone thought that a heavy object moved naturally from a higher position to a state of rest at a lower one. The Aristotelian would think that what the stone was really doing was falling with difficulty. When Galileo saw the swinging stone, he saw a pendulum. He thought that what the stone was really doing was repeating the same motion again and again, almost perfectly.

The suggestive powers of the two models are quite different. The Aristotelian who saw the swinging stone as an object falling would observe the stone's weight, the height to which it had been raised, and the time it took to come to rest. For Galileo's pendulum model, the prominent factors were different. Galileo observed the stone's weight, the radius of the pendulum's swing, the angular displacement, and the time per swing. Galileo discovered laws the Aristotelians could not discover because their model led them to look at different phenomena and ask different questions.

Metaphors contribute to a greater understanding of software-development issues in the same way that they contribute to a greater understanding of scientific questions. In his 1973 Turing Award lecture, Charles Bachman described the change from the prevailing earth-centered view of the universe to a sun-centered view. Ptolemy's earth-centered model had lasted without serious challenge for 1400 years. Then in 1543, Copernicus introduced a heliocentric theory, the idea that the sun rather than the earth was the center of the universe. This change in mental models led ultimately to the discovery of new planets, the reclassification of the moon as a satellite rather than as a planet, and a different understanding of humankind's place in the universe.

The value of metaphors should not be underestimated. Metaphors have the virtue of an expected behavior that is understood by all. Unnecessary communication and misunderstandings are reduced. Learning and education are quicker. In effect, metaphors are a way of internalizing and abstracting concepts, allowing one's thinking to be on a higher plane and low-level mistakes to be avoided.
—*Fernando J. Corbató*

Bachman compared the Ptolemaic-to-Copernican change in astronomy to the change in computer programming in the early 1970s. When Bachman made the comparison in 1973, data processing was changing from a computer-centered view of information systems to a database-centered view. Bachman pointed out that the ancients of data processing wanted to view all data as a sequential stream of cards flowing through a computer (the computer-centered view). The change was to focus on a pool of data on which the computer happened to act (a database-oriented view).

Today it's difficult to imagine anyone thinking that the sun moves around the earth. Similarly, it's difficult to imagine a programmer thinking that all data could be viewed as a sequential stream of cards. In both cases, once the old theory has been discarded, it seems incredible that anyone ever believed it at all. More fantastically, people who believed the old theory thought the new theory was just as ridiculous then as you think the old theory is now.

The earth-centered view of the universe hobbled astronomers who clung to it after a better theory was available. Similarly, the computer-centered view of the computing universe hobbled computer scientists who held on to it after the database-centered theory was available.

It's tempting to trivialize the power of metaphors. To each of the earlier examples, the natural response is to say, "Well, of course the right metaphor is more useful. The other metaphor was wrong!" Though that's a natural reaction, it's simplistic. The history of science isn't a series of switches from the "wrong" metaphor to the "right" one. It's a series of changes from "worse" metaphors to "better" ones, from less inclusive to more inclusive, from suggestive in one area to suggestive in another.

In fact, many models that have been replaced by better models are still useful. Engineers still solve most engineering problems by using Newtonian dynamics even though, theoretically, Newtonian dynamics have been supplanted by Einsteinian theory.

Software development is a younger field than most other sciences. It's not yet mature enough to have a set of standard metaphors. Consequently, it has a profusion of complementary and conflicting metaphors. Some are better than others. Some are worse. How well you understand the metaphors determines how well you understand software development.

2.2 How to Use Software Metaphors

KEY POINT

A software metaphor is more like a searchlight than a road map. It doesn't tell you where to find the answer; it tells you how to look for it. A metaphor serves more as a heuristic than it does as an algorithm.

An algorithm is a set of well-defined instructions for carrying out a particular task. An algorithm is predictable, deterministic, and not subject to chance. An algorithm tells you how to go from point A to point B with no detours, no side trips to points D, E, and F, and no stopping to smell the roses or have a cup of joe.

A heuristic is a technique that helps you look for an answer. Its results are subject to chance because a heuristic tells you only how to look, not what to find. It doesn't tell you how to get directly from point A to point B; it might not even know where point A and point B are. In effect, a heuristic is an algorithm in a clown suit. It's less predictable, it's more fun, and it comes without a 30-day, money-back guarantee.

Here is an algorithm for driving to someone's house: Take Highway 167 south to Puyallup. Take the South Hill Mall exit and drive 4.5 miles up the hill. Turn right at the light by the grocery store, and then take the first left. Turn into the driveway of the large tan house on the left, at 714 North Cedar.

Cross-Reference For details on how to use heuristics in designing software, see "Design Is a Heuristic Process" in Section 5.1.

Here's a heuristic for getting to someone's house: Find the last letter we mailed you. Drive to the town in the return address. When you get to town, ask someone where our house is. Everyone knows us—someone will be glad to help you. If you can't find anyone, call us from a public phone, and we'll come get you.

The difference between an algorithm and a heuristic is subtle, and the two terms overlap somewhat. For the purposes of this book, the main difference between the two is the level of indirection from the solution. An algorithm gives you the instructions directly. A heuristic tells you how to discover the instructions for yourself, or at least where to look for them.

Having directions that told you exactly how to solve your programming problems would certainly make programming easier and the results more predictable. But programming science isn't yet that advanced and may never be. The most challenging part of programming is conceptualizing the problem, and many errors in programming are conceptual errors. Because each program is conceptually unique, it's difficult or impossible to create a general set of directions that lead to a solution in every case. Thus, knowing how to approach problems in general is at least as valuable as knowing specific solutions for specific problems.

How do you use software metaphors? Use them to give you insight into your programming problems and processes. Use them to help you think about your programming activities and to help you imagine better ways of doing things. You won't be able to look at a line of code and say that it violates one of the metaphors described in this chapter. Over time, though, the person who uses metaphors to illuminate the software-development process will be perceived as someone who has a better understanding of programming and produces better code faster than people who don't use them.

2.3 Common Software Metaphors

A confusing abundance of metaphors has grown up around software development. David Gries says writing software is a science (1981). Donald Knuth says it's an art (1998). Watts Humphrey says it's a process (1989). P. J. Plauger and Kent Beck say it's like driving a car, although they draw nearly opposite conclusions (Plauger 1993, Beck 2000). Alistair Cockburn says it's a game (2002). Eric Raymond says it's like a bazaar (2000). Andy Hunt and Dave Thomas say it's like gardening. Paul Heckel says it's like filming *Snow White and the Seven Dwarfs* (1994). Fred Brooks says that it's like farming, hunting werewolves, or drowning with dinosaurs in a tar pit (1995). Which are the best metaphors?

Software Penmanship: Writing Code

The most primitive metaphor for software development grows out of the expression "writing code." The writing metaphor suggests that developing a program is like writing a casual letter—you sit down with pen, ink, and paper and write it from start to finish. It doesn't require any formal planning, and you figure out what you want to say as you go.

Many ideas derive from the writing metaphor. Jon Bentley says you should be able to sit down by the fire with a glass of brandy, a good cigar, and your favorite hunting dog to enjoy a "literate program" the way you would a good novel. Brian Kernighan and P. J. Plauger named their programming-style book *The Elements of Programming Style* (1978) after the writing-style book *The Elements of Style* (Strunk and White 2000). Programmers often talk about "program readability."

HARD DATA

For an individual's work or for small-scale projects, the letter-writing metaphor works adequately, but for other purposes it leaves the party early—it doesn't describe software development fully or adequately. Writing is usually a one-person activity, whereas a software project will most likely involve many people with many different responsibilities. When you finish writing a letter, you stuff it into an envelope and mail it. You can't change it anymore, and for all intents and purposes it's complete. Software isn't as difficult to change and is hardly ever fully complete. As much as 90 percent of the development effort on a typical software system comes after its initial release, with two-thirds being typical (Pigoski 1997). In writing, a high premium is placed on originality. In software construction, trying to create truly original work is often less effective than focusing on the reuse of design ideas, code, and test cases from previous projects. In short, the writing metaphor implies a software-development process that's too simple and rigid to be healthy.

Plan to throw one away; you
will, anyhow.
—*Fred Brooks*

If you plan to throw one
away, you will throw away
two.
 —*Craig Zerouni*

Unfortunately, the letter-writing metaphor has been perpetuated by one of the most popular software books on the planet, Fred Brooks's *The Mythical Man-Month* (Brooks 1995). Brooks says, "Plan to throw one away; you will, anyhow." This conjures up an image of a pile of half-written drafts thrown into a wastebasket, as shown in Figure 2-1.

Figure 2-1   The letter-writing metaphor suggests that the software process relies on expensive trial and error rather than careful planning and design.

Planning to throw one away might be practical when you're writing a polite how-do-you-do to your aunt. But extending the metaphor of "writing" software to a plan to throw one away is poor advice for software development, where a major system already costs as much as a 10-story office building or an ocean liner. It's easy to grab the brass ring if you can afford to sit on your favorite wooden pony for an unlimited number of spins around the carousel. The trick is to get it the first time around—or to take several chances when they're cheapest. Other metaphors better illuminate ways of attaining such goals.

Software Farming: Growing a System

In contrast to the rigid writing metaphor, some software developers say you should envision creating software as something like planting seeds and growing crops. You design a piece, code a piece, test a piece, and add it to the system a little bit at a time. By taking small steps, you minimize the trouble you can get into at any one time.

KEY POINT

Sometimes a good technique is described with a bad metaphor. In such cases, try to keep the technique and come up with a better metaphor. In this case, the incremental technique is valuable, but the farming metaphor is terrible.

Further Reading For an
illustration of a different
farming metaphor, one that's
applied to software maintenance, see the chapter "On
the Origins of Designer Intuition" in *Rethinking Systems
Analysis and Design* (Weinberg 1988).

The idea of doing a little bit at a time might bear some resemblance to the way crops grow, but the farming analogy is weak and uninformative, and it's easy to replace with the better metaphors described in the following sections. It's hard to extend the farming metaphor beyond the simple idea of doing things a little bit at a time. If you buy into the farming metaphor, imagined in Figure 2-2, you might find yourself talking about fertilizing the system plan, thinning the detailed design, increasing code yields through effective land management, and harvesting the code itself. You'll talk about rotating in a crop of C++ instead of barley, of letting the land rest for a year to increase the supply of nitrogen in the hard disk.

The weakness in the software-farming metaphor is its suggestion that you don't have any direct control over how the software develops. You plant the code seeds in the spring. *Farmer's Almanac* and the Great Pumpkin willing, you'll have a bumper crop of code in the fall.

Figure 2-2   It's hard to extend the farming metaphor to software development appropriately.

Software Oyster Farming: System Accretion

Sometimes people talk about growing software when they really mean software accretion. The two metaphors are closely related, but software accretion is the more insightful image. "Accretion," in case you don't have a dictionary handy, means any growth or increase in size by a gradual external addition or inclusion. Accretion describes the way an oyster makes a pearl, by gradually adding small amounts of calcium carbonate. In geology, "accretion" means a slow addition to land by the deposit of waterborne sediment. In legal terms, "accretion" means an increase of land along the shores of a body of water by the deposit of waterborne sediment.

Cross-Reference For details on how to apply incremental strategies to system integration, see Section 29.2, "Integration Frequency—Phased or Incremental?"

This doesn't mean that you have to learn how to make code out of waterborne sediment; it means that you have to learn how to add to your software systems a small amount at a time. Other words closely related to accretion are "incremental," "iterative," "adaptive," and "evolutionary." Incremental designing, building, and testing are some of the most powerful software-development concepts available.

In incremental development, you first make the simplest possible version of the system that will run. It doesn't have to accept realistic input, it doesn't have to perform realistic manipulations on data, it doesn't have to produce realistic output—it just has to be a skeleton strong enough to hold the real system as it's developed. It might call dummy classes for each of the basic functions you have identified. This basic beginning is like the oyster's beginning a pearl with a small grain of sand.

After you've formed the skeleton, little by little you lay on the muscle and skin. You change each of the dummy classes to real classes. Instead of having your program pretend to accept input, you drop in code that accepts real input. Instead of having your program pretend to produce output, you drop in code that produces real output. You add a little bit of code at a time until you have a fully working system.

The anecdotal evidence in favor of this approach is impressive. Fred Brooks, who in 1975 advised building one to throw away, said that nothing in the decade after he wrote his landmark book *The Mythical Man-Month* so radically changed his own practice or its effectiveness as incremental development (1995). Tom Gilb made the same point in his breakthrough book, *Principles of Software Engineering Management* (1988), which introduced Evolutionary Delivery and laid the groundwork for much of today's Agile programming approach. Numerous current methodologies are based on this idea (Beck 2000, Cockburn 2002, Highsmith 2002, Reifer 2002, Martin 2003, Larman 2004).

As a metaphor, the strength of the incremental metaphor is that it doesn't overpromise. It's harder than the farming metaphor to extend inappropriately. The image of an oyster forming a pearl is a good way to visualize incremental development, or accretion.

Software Construction: Building Software

KEY POINT

The image of "building" software is more useful than that of "writing" or "growing" software. It's compatible with the idea of software accretion and provides more detailed guidance. Building software implies various stages of planning, preparation, and execution that vary in kind and degree depending on what's being built. When you explore the metaphor, you find many other parallels.

Building a four-foot tower requires a steady hand, a level surface, and 10 undamaged beer cans. Building a tower 100 times that size doesn't merely require 100 times as many beer cans. It requires a different kind of planning and construction altogether.

If you're building a simple structure—a doghouse, say—you can drive to the lumber store and buy some wood and nails. By the end of the afternoon, you'll have a new house for Fido. If you forget to provide for a door, as shown in Figure 2-3, or make some other mistake, it's not a big problem; you can fix it or even start over from the beginning. All you've wasted is part of an afternoon. This loose approach is appropriate for small software projects too. If you use the wrong design for 1000 lines of code, you can refactor or start over completely without losing much.

Figure 2-3 The penalty for a mistake on a simple structure is only a little time and maybe some embarrassment.

If you're building a house, the building process is more complicated, and so are the consequences of poor design. First you have to decide what kind of house you want to build—analogous in software development to problem definition. Then you and an architect have to come up with a general design and get it approved. This is similar to software architectural design. You draw detailed blueprints and hire a contractor. This is similar to detailed software design. You prepare the building site, lay a foundation, frame the house, put siding and a roof on it, and plumb and wire it. This is similar to software construction. When most of the house is done, the landscapers, painters, and decorators come in to make the best of your property and the home you've built. This is similar to software optimization. Throughout the process, various inspectors come to check the site, foundation, frame, wiring, and other inspectables. This is similar to software reviews and inspections.

Greater complexity and size imply greater consequences in both activities. In building a house, materials are somewhat expensive, but the main expense is labor. Ripping out a wall and moving it six inches is expensive not because you waste a lot of nails but because you have to pay the people for the extra time it takes to move the wall. You have to make the design as good as possible, as suggested by Figure 2-4, so that you don't waste time fixing mistakes that could have been avoided. In building a software product, materials are even less expensive, but labor costs just as much. Changing a report format is just as expensive as moving a wall in a house because the main cost component in both cases is people's time.

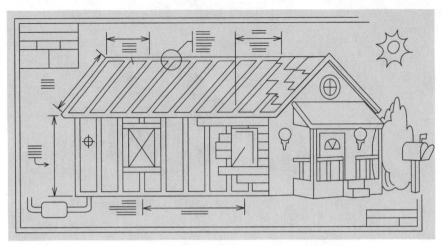

Figure 2-4   More complicated structures require more careful planning.

What other parallels do the two activities share? In building a house, you won't try to build things you can buy already built. You'll buy a washer and dryer, dishwasher, refrigerator, and freezer. Unless you're a mechanical wizard, you won't consider building them yourself. You'll also buy prefabricated cabinets, counters, windows, doors, and bathroom fixtures. If you're building a software system, you'll do the same thing. You'll make extensive use of high-level language features rather than writing your own operating-system-level code. You might also use prebuilt libraries of container classes, scientific functions, user interface classes, and database-manipulation classes. It generally doesn't make sense to code things you can buy ready-made.

If you're building a fancy house with first-class furnishings, however, you might have your cabinets custom-made. You might have a dishwasher, refrigerator, and freezer built in to look like the rest of your cabinets. You might have windows custom-made in unusual shapes and sizes. This customization has parallels in software development. If you're building a first-class software product, you might build your own scientific functions for better speed or accuracy. You might build your own container classes, user interface classes, and database classes to give your system a seamless, perfectly consistent look and feel.

Both building construction and software construction benefit from appropriate levels of planning. If you build software in the wrong order, it's hard to code, hard to test, and hard to debug. It can take longer to complete, or the project can fall apart because everyone's work is too complex and therefore too confusing when it's all combined.

Careful planning doesn't necessarily mean exhaustive planning or over-planning. You can plan out the structural supports and decide later whether to put in hardwood floors or carpeting, what color to paint the walls, what roofing material to use, and so on. A well-planned project improves your ability to change your mind later about details. The more experience you have with the kind of software you're building, the more details you can take for granted. You just want to be sure that you plan enough so that lack of planning doesn't create major problems later.

The construction analogy also helps explain why different software projects benefit from different development approaches. In building, you'd use different levels of planning, design, and quality assurance if you're building a warehouse or a toolshed than if you're building a medical center or a nuclear reactor. You'd use still different approaches for building a school, a skyscraper, or a three-bedroom home. Likewise, in software you might generally use flexible, lightweight development approaches, but sometimes you'll need rigid, heavyweight approaches to achieve safety goals and other goals.

Making changes in the software brings up another parallel with building construction. To move a wall six inches costs more if the wall is load-bearing than if it's merely a partition between rooms. Similarly, making structural changes in a program costs more than adding or deleting peripheral features.

Finally, the construction analogy provides insight into extremely large software projects. Because the penalty for failure in an extremely large structure is severe, the structure has to be over-engineered. Builders make and inspect their plans carefully. They build in margins of safety; it's better to pay 10 percent more for stronger material than to have a skyscraper fall over. A great deal of attention is paid to timing. When the Empire State Building was built, each delivery truck had a 15-minute margin in which to make its delivery. If a truck wasn't in place at the right time, the whole project was delayed.

Likewise, for extremely large software projects, planning of a higher order is needed than for projects that are merely large. Capers Jones reports that a software system with one million lines of code requires an average of 69 *kinds* of documentation (1998). The requirements specification for such a system would typically be about 4000–5000 pages long, and the design documentation can easily be two or three times as extensive as the requirements. It's unlikely that an individual would be able to understand the complete design for a project of this size—or even read it. A greater degree of preparation is appropriate.

We build software projects comparable in economic size to the Empire State Building, and technical and managerial controls of similar stature are needed.

Further Reading For some good comments about extending the construction metaphor, see "What Supports the Roof?" (Starr 2003).

The building-construction metaphor could be extended in a variety of other directions, which is why the metaphor is so powerful. Many terms common in software development derive from the building metaphor: software architecture, scaffolding, construction, foundation classes, and tearing code apart. You'll probably hear many more.

Applying Software Techniques: The Intellectual Toolbox

KEY POINT

People who are effective at developing high-quality software have spent years accumulating dozens of techniques, tricks, and magic incantations. The techniques are not rules; they are analytical tools. A good craftsman knows the right tool for the job and knows how to use it correctly. Programmers do, too. The more you learn about programming, the more you fill your mental toolbox with analytical tools and the knowledge of when to use them and how to use them correctly.

Cross-Reference For details on selecting and combining methods in design, see Section 5.3, "Design Building Blocks: Heuristics."

In software, consultants sometimes tell you to buy into certain software-development methods to the exclusion of other methods. That's unfortunate because if you buy into any single methodology 100 percent, you'll see the whole world in terms of that methodology. In some instances, you'll miss opportunities to use other methods better suited to your current problem. The toolbox metaphor helps to keep all the methods, techniques, and tips in perspective—ready for use when appropriate.

Combining Metaphors

KEY POINT

Because metaphors are heuristic rather than algorithmic, they are not mutually exclusive. You can use both the accretion and the construction metaphors. You can use writing if you want to, and you can combine writing with driving, hunting for werewolves, or drowning in a tar pit with dinosaurs. Use whatever metaphor or combination of metaphors stimulates your own thinking or communicates well with others on your team.

Using metaphors is a fuzzy business. You have to extend them to benefit from the heuristic insights they provide. But if you extend them too far or in the wrong direction, they'll mislead you. Just as you can misuse any powerful tool, you can misuse metaphors, but their power makes them a valuable part of your intellectual toolbox.

Additional Resources

cc2e.com/0285

Among general books on metaphors, models, and paradigms, the touchstone book is by Thomas Kuhn.

Kuhn, Thomas S. *The Structure of Scientific Revolutions*, 3d ed. Chicago, IL: The University of Chicago Press, 1996. Kuhn's book on how scientific theories emerge, evolve, and succumb to other theories in a Darwinian cycle set the philosophy of science on its ear when it was first published in 1962. It's clear and short, and it's loaded with interesting examples of the rise and fall of metaphors, models, and paradigms in science.

Floyd, Robert W. "The Paradigms of Programming." 1978 Turing Award Lecture. *Communications of the ACM*, August 1979, pp. 455–60. This is a fascinating discussion of models in software development, and Floyd applies Kuhn's ideas to the topic.

Key Points

- Metaphors are heuristics, not algorithms. As such, they tend to be a little sloppy.

- Metaphors help you understand the software-development process by relating it to other activities you already know about.

- Some metaphors are better than others.

- Treating software construction as similar to building construction suggests that careful preparation is needed and illuminates the difference between large and small projects.

- Thinking of software-development practices as tools in an intellectual toolbox suggests further that every programmer has many tools and that no single tool is right for every job. Choosing the right tool for each problem is one key to being an effective programmer.

- Metaphors are not mutually exclusive. Use the combination of metaphors that works best for you.

Chapter 3

Measure Twice, Cut Once: Upstream Prerequisites

cc2e.com/0309

Contents

Related Topics

Before beginning construction of a house, a builder reviews blueprints, checks that all permits have been obtained, and surveys the house's foundation. A builder prepares for building a skyscraper one way, a housing development a different way, and a dog-house a third way. No matter what the project, the preparation is tailored to the project's specific needs and done conscientiously before construction begins.

This chapter describes the work that must be done to prepare for software construction. As with building construction, much of the success or failure of the project has already been determined before construction begins. If the foundation hasn't been laid well or the planning is inadequate, the best you can do during construction is to keep damage to a minimum.

The carpenter's saying, "Measure twice, cut once" is highly relevant to the construction part of software development, which can account for as much as 65 percent of the total project costs. The worst software projects end up doing construction two or three times or more. Doing the most expensive part of the project twice is as bad an idea in software as it is in any other line of work.

Although this chapter lays the groundwork for successful software construction, it doesn't discuss construction directly. If you're feeling carnivorous or you're already well versed in the software-engineering life cycle, look for the construction meat beginning in Chapter 5, "Design in Construction." If you don't like the idea of prerequisites to construction, review Section 3.2, "Determine the Kind of Software You're Working On," to see how prerequisites apply to your situation, and then take a look at the data in Section 3.1, which describes the cost of not doing prerequisites.

3.1 Importance of Prerequisites

Cross-Reference Paying attention to quality is also the best way to improve productivity. For details, see Section 20.5, "The General Principle of Software Quality."

A common denominator of programmers who build high-quality software is their use of high-quality practices. Such practices emphasize quality at the beginning, middle, and end of a project.

If you emphasize quality at the end of a project, you emphasize system testing. Testing is what many people think of when they think of software quality assurance. Testing, however, is only one part of a complete quality-assurance strategy, and it's not the most influential part. Testing can't detect a flaw such as building the wrong product or building the right product in the wrong way. Such flaws must be worked out earlier than in testing—before construction begins.

KEY POINT

If you emphasize quality in the middle of the project, you emphasize construction practices. Such practices are the focus of most of this book.

If you emphasize quality at the beginning of the project, you plan for, require, and design a high-quality product. If you start the process with designs for a Pontiac Aztek, you can test it all you want to, and it will never turn into a Rolls-Royce. You might build the best possible Aztek, but if you want a Rolls-Royce, you have to plan from the beginning to build one. In software development, you do such planning when you define the problem, when you specify the solution, and when you design the solution.

Since construction is in the middle of a software project, by the time you get to construction, the earlier parts of the project have already laid some of the groundwork for success or failure. During construction, however, you should at least be able to determine how good your situation is and to back up if you see the black clouds of failure looming on the horizon. The rest of this chapter describes in detail why proper preparation is important and tells you how to determine whether you're really ready to begin construction.

Do Prerequisites Apply to Modern Software Projects?

The methodology used should be based on choice of the latest and best, and not based on ignorance. It should also be laced liberally with the old and dependable.
—*Harlan Mills*

Some people have asserted that upstream activities such as architecture, design, and project planning aren't useful on modern software projects. In the main, such assertions are not well supported by research, past or present, or by current data. (See the rest of this chapter for details.) Opponents of prerequisites typically show examples of prerequisites that have been done poorly and then point out that such work isn't effective. Upstream activities can be done well, however, and industry data from the 1970s to the present day indicates that projects will run best if appropriate preparation activities are done before construction begins in earnest.

KEY POINT

The overarching goal of preparation is risk reduction: a good project planner clears major risks out of the way as early as possible so that the bulk of the project can proceed as smoothly as possible. By far the most common project risks in software development are poor requirements and poor project planning, thus preparation tends to focus on improving requirements and project plans.

Preparation for construction is not an exact science, and the specific approach to risk reduction must be decided project by project. Details can vary greatly among projects. For more on this, see Section 3.2.

Causes of Incomplete Preparation

You might think that all professional programmers know about the importance of preparation and check that the prerequisites have been satisfied before jumping into construction. Unfortunately, that isn't so.

Further Reading For a description of a professional development program that cultivates these skills, see Chapter 16 of *Professional Software Development* (McConnell 2004).

A common cause of incomplete preparation is that the developers who are assigned to work on the upstream activities do not have the expertise to carry out their assignments. The skills needed to plan a project, create a compelling business case, develop comprehensive and accurate requirements, and create high-quality architectures are far from trivial, but most developers have not received training in how to perform these activities. When developers don't know how to do upstream work, the recommendation to "do more upstream work" sounds like nonsense: If the work isn't being done well in the first place, doing *more* of it will not be useful! Explaining how to perform these activities is beyond the scope of this book, but the "Additional Resources" sections at the end of this chapter provide numerous options for gaining that expertise.

cc2e.com/0316

Some programmers do know how to perform upstream activities, but they don't prepare because they can't resist the urge to begin coding as soon as possible. If you feed your horse at this trough, I have two suggestions. Suggestion 1: Read the argument in the next section. It may tell you a few things you haven't thought of. Suggestion 2: Pay attention to the problems you experience. It takes only a few large programs to learn that you can avoid a lot of stress by planning ahead. Let your own experience be your guide.

A final reason that programmers don't prepare is that managers are notoriously unsympathetic to programmers who spend time on construction prerequisites. People like Barry Boehm, Grady Booch, and Karl Wiegers have been banging the requirements and design drums for 25 years, and you'd expect that managers would have started to understand that software development is more than coding.

Further Reading For many entertaining variations on this theme, read Gerald Weinberg's classic, *The Psychology of Computer Programming* (Weinberg 1998).

A few years ago, however, I was working on a Department of Defense project that was focusing on requirements development when the Army general in charge of the project came for a visit. We told him that we were developing requirements and that we were mainly talking to our customer, capturing requirements, and outlining the design. He insisted on seeing code anyway. We told him there was no code, but he walked around a work bay of 100 people, determined to catch someone programming. Frustrated by seeing so many people away from their desks or working on requirements and design, the large, round man with the loud voice finally pointed to the engineer sitting next to me and bellowed, "What's he doing? He must be writing code!" In fact, the engineer was working on a document-formatting utility, but the general wanted to find code, thought it looked like code, and wanted the engineer to be working on code, so we told him it was code.

This phenomenon is known as the WISCA or WIMP syndrome: Why Isn't Sam Coding Anything? or Why Isn't Mary Programming?

If the manager of your project pretends to be a brigadier general and orders you to start coding right away, it's easy to say, "Yes, Sir!" (What's the harm? The old guy must know what he's talking about.) This is a bad response, and you have several better alternatives. First, you can flatly refuse to do work in an ineffective order. If your relationships with your boss and your bank account are healthy enough for you to be able to do this, good luck.

A second questionable alternative is pretending to be coding when you're not. Put an old program listing on the corner of your desk. Then go right ahead and develop your requirements and architecture, with or without your boss's approval. You'll do the project faster and with higher-quality results. Some people find this approach ethically objectionable, but from your boss's perspective, ignorance will be bliss.

Third, you can educate your boss in the nuances of technical projects. This is a good approach because it increases the number of enlightened bosses in the world. The next subsection presents an extended rationale for taking the time to do prerequisites before construction.

Finally, you can find another job. Despite economic ups and downs, good programmers are perennially in short supply (BLS 2002), and life is too short to work in an unenlightened programming shop when plenty of better alternatives are available.

Utterly Compelling and Foolproof Argument for Doing Prerequisites Before Construction

Suppose you've already been to the mountain of problem definition, walked a mile with the man of requirements, shed your soiled garments at the fountain of architecture, and bathed in the pure waters of preparedness. Then you know that before you implement a system, you need to understand what the system is supposed to do and how it's supposed to do it.

KEY POINT

Part of your job as a technical employee is to educate the nontechnical people around you about the development process. This section will help you deal with managers and bosses who have not yet seen the light. It's an extended argument for doing requirements and architecture—getting the critical aspects right—before you begin coding, testing, and debugging. Learn the argument, and then sit down with your boss and have a heart-to-heart talk about the programming process.

Appeal to Logic

One of the key ideas in effective programming is that preparation is important. It makes sense that before you start working on a big project, you should plan the project. Big projects require more planning; small projects require less. From a management point of view, planning means determining the amount of time, number of people, and number of computers the project will need. From a technical point of view, planning means understanding what you want to build so that you don't waste money building the wrong thing. Sometimes users aren't entirely sure what they want at first, so it might take more effort than seems ideal to find out what they really want. But that's cheaper than building the wrong thing, throwing it away, and starting over.

It's also important to think about how to build the system before you begin to build it. You don't want to spend a lot of time and money going down blind alleys when there's no need to, especially when that increases costs.

Appeal to Analogy

Building a software system is like any other project that takes people and money. If you're building a house, you make architectural drawings and blueprints before you begin pounding nails. You'll have the blueprints reviewed and approved before you pour any concrete. Having a technical plan counts just as much in software.

You don't start decorating the Christmas tree until you've put it in the stand. You don't start a fire until you've opened the flue. You don't go on a long trip with an empty tank of gas. You don't get dressed before you take a shower, and you don't put your shoes on before your socks. You have to do things in the right order in software, too.

Programmers are at the end of the software food chain. The architect consumes the requirements; the designer consumes the architecture; and the coder consumes the design.

Compare the software food chain to a real food chain. In an ecologically sound environment, seagulls eat fresh salmon. That's nourishing to them because the salmon ate fresh herring, and they in turn ate fresh water bugs. The result is a healthy food chain. In programming, if you have healthy food at each stage in the food chain, the result is healthy code written by happy programmers.

In a polluted environment, the water bugs have been swimming in nuclear waste, the herring are contaminated by PCBs, and the salmon that eat the herring swam through oil spills. The seagulls are, unfortunately, at the end of the food chain, so they don't eat just the oil in the bad salmon. They also eat the PCBs and the nuclear waste from the herring and the water bugs. In programming, if your requirements are contaminated, they contaminate the architecture, and the architecture in turn contaminates construction. This leads to grumpy, malnourished programmers and radioactive, polluted software that's riddled with defects.

If you are planning a highly iterative project, you will need to identify the critical requirements and architectural elements that apply to each piece you're constructing before you begin construction. A builder who is building a housing development doesn't need to know every detail of every house in the development before beginning construction on the first house. But the builder will survey the site, map out sewer and electrical lines, and so on. If the builder doesn't prepare well, construction may be delayed when a sewer line needs to be dug under a house that's already been constructed.

Appeal to Data

Studies over the last 25 years have proven conclusively that it pays to do things right the first time. Unnecessary changes are expensive.

Researchers at Hewlett-Packard, IBM, Hughes Aircraft, TRW, and other organizations have found that purging an error by the beginning of construction allows rework to be done 10 to 100 times less expensively than when it's done in the last part of the process, during system test or after release (Fagan 1976; Humphrey, Snyder, and Willis 1991; Leffingwell 1997; Willis et al. 1998; Grady 1999; Shull et al. 2002; Boehm and Turner 2004).

In general, the principle is to find an error as close as possible to the time at which it was introduced. The longer the defect stays in the software food chain, the more damage it causes further down the chain. Since requirements are done first, requirements defects have the potential to be in the system longer and to be more expensive. Defects inserted into the software upstream also tend to have broader effects than those inserted further downstream. That also makes early defects more expensive.

Table 3-1 shows the relative expense of fixing defects depending on when they're introduced and when they're found.

Table 3-1   Average Cost of Fixing Defects Based on When They're Introduced and Detected

	Time Detected				
Time Introduced	**Requirements**	**Architecture**	**Construction**	**System Test**	**Post-Release**
Requirements	1	3	5–10	10	10–100
Architecture	—	1	10	15	25–100
Construction	—	—	1	10	10–25

Source: Adapted from "Design and Code Inspections to Reduce Errors in Program Development" (Fagan 1976), *Software Defect Removal* (Dunn 1984), "Software Process Improvement at Hughes Aircraft" (Humphrey, Snyder, and Willis 1991), "Calculating the Return on Investment from More Effective Requirements Management" (Leffingwell 1997), "Hughes Aircraft's Widespread Deployment of a Continuously Improving Software Process" (Willis et al. 1998), "An Economic Release Decision Model: Insights into Software Project Management" (Grady 1999), "What We Have Learned About Fighting Defects" (Shull et al. 2002), and *Balancing Agility and Discipline: A Guide for the Perplexed* (Boehm and Turner 2004).

The data in Table 3-1 shows that, for example, an architecture defect that costs $1000 to fix when the architecture is being created can cost $15,000 to fix during system test. Figure 3-1 illustrates the same phenomenon.

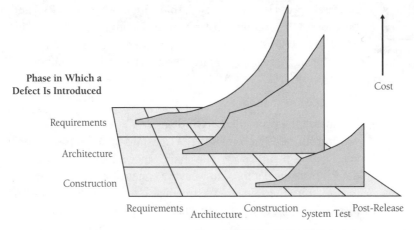

Figure 3-1   The cost to fix a defect rises dramatically as the time from when it's introduced to when it's detected increases. This remains true whether the project is highly sequential (doing 100 percent of requirements and design up front) or highly iterative (doing 5 percent of requirements and design up front).

HARD DATA

The average project still exerts most of its defect-correction effort on the right side of Figure 3-1, which means that debugging and associated rework takes about 50 percent of the time spent in a typical software development cycle (Mills 1983; Boehm 1987a; Cooper and Mullen 1993; Fishman 1996; Haley 1996; Wheeler, Brykczynski, and Meeson 1996; Jones 1998; Shull et al. 2002; Wiegers 2002). Dozens of companies have found that simply focusing on correcting defects earlier rather than later in a project can cut development costs and schedules by factors of two or more (McConnell 2004). This is a healthy incentive to find and fix your problems as early as you can.

Boss-Readiness Test

When you think your boss understands the importance of working on prerequisites before moving into construction, try the test below to be sure.

Which of these statements are self-fulfilling prophecies?

- We'd better start coding right away because we're going to have a lot of debugging to do.

- We haven't planned much time for testing because we're not going to find many defects.

- We've investigated requirements and design so much that I can't think of any major problems we'll run into during coding or debugging.

All of these statements are self-fulfilling prophecies. Aim for the last one.

If you're still not convinced that prerequisites apply to your project, the next section will help you decide.

3.2 Determine the Kind of Software You're Working On

Capers Jones, Chief Scientist at Software Productivity Research, summarized 20 years of software research by pointing out that he and his colleagues have seen 40 different methods for gathering requirements, 50 variations in working on software designs, and 30 kinds of testing applied to projects in more than 700 different programming languages (Jones 2003).

Different kinds of software projects call for different balances between preparation and construction. Every project is unique, but projects do tend to fall into general development styles. Table 3-2 shows three of the most common kinds of projects and lists the practices that are typically best suited to each kind of project.

Table 3-2   Typical Good Practices for Three Common Kinds of Software Projects

	Kind of Software		
	Business Systems	**Mission-Critical Systems**	**Embedded Life-Critical Systems**
Typical applications	Internet site	Embedded software	Avionics software
	Intranet site	Games	Embedded software
	Inventory management	Internet site	Medical devices
	Games	Packaged software	Operating systems
	Management information systems	Software tools	Packaged software
	Payroll system	Web services	
Life-cycle models	Agile development (Extreme Programming, Scrum, time-box development, and so on)	Staged delivery	Staged delivery
		Evolutionary delivery	Spiral development
		Spiral development	Evolutionary delivery
	Evolutionary prototyping		

Table 3-2 Typical Good Practices for Three Common Kinds of Software Projects

	Kind of Software		
	Business Systems	Mission-Critical Systems	Embedded Life-Critical Systems
Planning and management	Incremental project planning	Basic up-front planning	Extensive up-front planning
	As-needed test and QA planning	Basic test planning	Extensive test planning
	Informal change control	As-needed QA planning	Extensive QA planning
		Formal change control	Rigorous change control
Requirements	Informal require-ments specification	Semiformal require-ments specification	Formal requirements specification
		As-needed require-ments reviews	Formal requirements inspections
Design	Design and coding are combined	Architectural design	Architectural design
		Informal detailed design	Formal architecture inspections
		As-needed design reviews	Formal detailed design
			Formal detailed design inspections
Construction	Pair programming or individual coding	Pair programming or individual coding	Pair programming or individual coding
	Informal check-in procedure or no check-in procedure	Informal check-in procedure	Formal check-in procedure
		As-needed code reviews	Formal code inspections
Testing and QA	Developers test their own code	Developers test their own code	Developers test their own code
	Test-first development	Test-first development	Test-first development
	Little or no testing by a separate test group	Separate testing group	Separate testing group
			Separate QA group
Deployment	Informal deploy-ment procedure	Formal deployment procedure	Formal deployment procedure

On real projects, you'll find infinite variations on the three themes presented in this table; however, the generalities in the table are illuminating. Business systems projects tend to benefit from highly iterative approaches, in which planning, requirements, and architecture are interleaved with construction, system testing, and quality-assurance activities. Life-critical systems tend to require more sequential approaches—requirements stability is part of what's needed to ensure ultrahigh levels of reliability.

Iterative Approaches' Effect on Prerequisites

Some writers have asserted that projects that use iterative techniques don't need to focus on prerequisites much at all, but that point of view is misinformed. Iterative approaches tend to reduce the impact of inadequate upstream work, but they don't eliminate it. Consider the examples shown in Table 3-3 of projects that don't focus on prerequisites. One project is conducted sequentially and relies solely on testing to discover defects; the other is conducted iteratively and discovers defects as it progresses. The first approach delays most defect correction work to the end of the project, making the costs higher, as noted in Table 3-1. The iterative approach absorbs rework piecemeal over the course of the project, which makes the total cost lower. The data in this table and the next is for purposes of illustration only, but the relative costs of the two general approaches are well supported by the research described earlier in this chapter.

Table 3-3   Effect of Skipping Prerequisites on Sequential and Iterative Projects

	Approach #1: Sequential Approach Without Prerequisites		Approach #2: Iterative Approach Without Prerequisites	
Project Completion Status	**Cost of Work**	**Cost of Rework**	**Cost of Work**	**Cost of Rework**
20%	$100,000	$0	$100,000	$75,000
40%	$100,000	$0	$100,000	$75,000
60%	$100,000	$0	$100,000	$75,000
80%	$100,000	$0	$100,000	$75,000
100%	$100,000	$0	$100,000	$75,000
End-of-Project Rework	$0	$500,000	$0	$0
TOTAL	$500,000	$500,000	$500,000	$375,000
GRAND TOTAL		$1,000,000		$875,000

The iterative project that abbreviates or eliminates prerequisites will differ in two ways from a sequential project that does the same thing. First, average defect correction costs will be lower because defects will tend to be detected closer to the time they were inserted into the software. However, the defects will still be detected late in each iteration, and correcting them will require parts of the software to be redesigned, recoded, and retested—which makes the defect-correction cost higher than it needs to be.

Second, with iterative approaches costs will be absorbed piecemeal, throughout the project, rather than being clustered at the end. When all the dust settles, the total cost will be similar but it won't seem as high because the price will have been paid in small installments over the course of the project, rather than paid all at once at the end.

As Table 3-4 illustrates, a focus on prerequisites can reduce costs regardless of whether you use an iterative or a sequential approach. Iterative approaches are usually a better option for many reasons, but an iterative approach that ignores prerequisites can end up costing significantly more than a sequential project that pays close attention to prerequisites.

Table 3-4   Effect of Focusing on Prerequisites on Sequential and Iterative Projects

Project completion status	Approach #3: Sequential Approach with Prerequisites		Approach #4: Iterative Approach with Prerequisites	
	Cost of Work	Cost of Rework	Cost of Work	Cost of Rework
20%	$100,000	$20,000	$100,000	$10,000
40%	$100,000	$20,000	$100,000	$10,000
60%	$100,000	$20,000	$100,000	$10,000
80%	$100,000	$20,000	$100,000	$10,000
100%	$100,000	$20,000	$100,000	$10,000
End-of-Project Rework	$0	$0	$0	$0
TOTAL	$500,000	$100,000	$500,000	$50,000
GRAND TOTAL		$600,000		$550,000

As Table 3-4 suggested, most projects are neither completely sequential nor completely iterative. It isn't practical to specify 100 percent of the requirements or design up front, but most projects find value in identifying at least the most critical requirements and architectural elements early.

Cross-Reference For details on how to adapt your development approach for programs of different sizes, see Chapter 27, "How Program Size Affects Construction."

One common rule of thumb is to plan to specify about 80 percent of the requirements up front, allocate time for additional requirements to be specified later, and then practice systematic change control to accept only the most valuable new requirements as the project progresses. Another alternative is to specify only the most important 20 percent of the requirements up front and plan to develop the rest of the software in small increments, specifying additional requirements and designs as you go. Figures 3-2 and 3-3 reflect these different approaches.

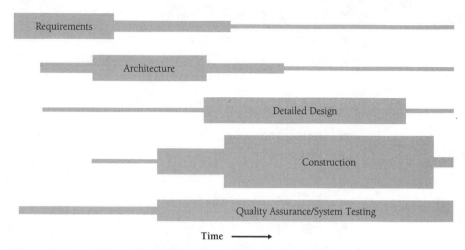

Figure 3-2 Activities will overlap to some degree on most projects, even those that are highly sequential.

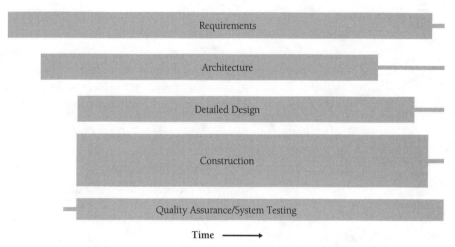

Figure 3-3 On other projects, activities will overlap for the duration of the project. One key to successful construction is understanding the degree to which prerequisites have been completed and adjusting your approach accordingly.

Choosing Between Iterative and Sequential Approaches

The extent to which prerequisites need to be satisfied up front will vary with the project type indicated in Table 3-2, project formality, technical environment, staff capabilities, and project business goals. You might choose a more sequential (up-front) approach when

- The requirements are fairly stable.
- The design is straightforward and fairly well understood.
- The development team is familiar with the applications area.

- The project contains little risk.

- Long-term predictability is important.

- The cost of changing requirements, design, and code downstream is likely to be high.

You might choose a more iterative (as-you-go) approach when

- The requirements are not well understood or you expect them to be unstable for other reasons.

- The design is complex, challenging, or both.

- The development team is unfamiliar with the applications area.

- The project contains a lot of risk.

- Long-term predictability is not important.

- The cost of changing requirements, design, and code downstream is likely to be low.

Software being what it is, iterative approaches are useful much more often than sequential approaches are. You can adapt the prerequisites to your specific project by making them more or less formal and more or less complete, as you see fit. For a detailed discussion of different approaches to large and small projects (also known as the different approaches to formal and informal projects), see Chapter 27.

The net impact on construction prerequisites is that you should first determine what construction prerequisites are well suited to your project. Some projects spend too little time on prerequisites, which exposes construction to an unnecessarily high rate of destabilizing changes and prevents the project from making consistent progress. Some projects do too much up front; they doggedly adhere to requirements and plans that have been invalidated by downstream discoveries, and that can also impede progress during construction.

Now that you've studied Table 3-2 and determined what prerequisites are appropriate for your project, the rest of this chapter describes how to determine whether each specific construction prerequisite has been "prereq'd" or "prewrecked."

3.3 Problem-Definition Prerequisite

If the "box" is the boundary of constraints and conditions, then the trick is to find the box.... Don't think outside the box—find the box.
—Andy Hunt and Dave Thomas

The first prerequisite you need to fulfill before beginning construction is a clear statement of the problem that the system is supposed to solve. This is sometimes called "product vision," "vision statement," "mission statement," or "product definition." Here it's called "problem definition." Since this book is about construction, this section doesn't tell you how to write a problem definition; it tells you how to recognize whether one has been written at all and whether the one that's written will form a good foundation for construction.

A problem definition defines what the problem is without any reference to possible solutions. It's a simple statement, maybe one or two pages, and it should sound like a problem. The statement "We can't keep up with orders for the Gigatron" sounds like a problem and is a good problem definition. The statement "We need to optimize our automated data-entry system to keep up with orders for the Gigatron" is a poor problem definition. It doesn't sound like a problem; it sounds like a solution.

As shown in Figure 3-4, problem definition comes before detailed requirements work, which is a more in-depth investigation of the problem.

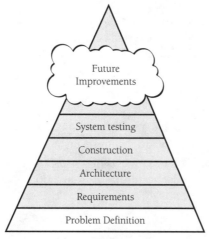

Figure 3-4   The problem definition lays the foundation for the rest of the programming process.

The problem definition should be in user language, and the problem should be described from a user's point of view. It usually should not be stated in technical computer terms. The best solution might not be a computer program. Suppose you need a report that shows your annual profit. You already have computerized reports that show quarterly profits. If you're locked into the programmer mindset, you'll reason that adding an annual report to a system that already does quarterly reports should be easy. Then you'll pay a programmer to write and debug a time-consuming program that calculates annual profits. If you're not locked into the programmer mindset, you'll pay your secretary to create the annual figures by taking one minute to add up the quarterly figures on a pocket calculator.

The exception to this rule applies when the problem is with the computer: compile times are too slow or the programming tools are buggy. Then it's appropriate to state the problem in computer or programmer terms.

As Figure 3-5 suggests, without a good problem definition, you might put effort into solving the wrong problem.

Figure 3-5   Be sure you know what you're aiming at before you shoot.

KEY POINT

The penalty for failing to define the problem is that you can waste a lot of time solving the wrong problem. This is a double-barreled penalty because you also don't solve the right problem.

3.4 Requirements Prerequisite

Requirements describe in detail what a software system is supposed to do, and they are the first step toward a solution. The requirements activity is also known as "requirements development," "requirements analysis," "analysis," "requirements definition," "software requirements," "specification," "functional spec," and "spec."

Why Have Official Requirements?

An explicit set of requirements is important for several reasons.

Explicit requirements help to ensure that the user rather than the programmer drives the system's functionality. If the requirements are explicit, the user can review them and agree to them. If they're not, the programmer usually ends up making requirements decisions during programming. Explicit requirements keep you from guessing what the user wants.

Explicit requirements also help to avoid arguments. You decide on the scope of the system before you begin programming. If you have a disagreement with another programmer about what the program is supposed to do, you can resolve it by looking at the written requirements.

KEY POINT

Paying attention to requirements helps to minimize changes to a system after development begins. If you find a coding error during coding, you change a few lines of code and work goes on. If you find a requirements error during coding, you have to alter the design to meet the changed requirement. You might have to throw away part of the old design, and because it has to accommodate code that's already written, the new design will take longer than it would have in the first place. You also have to discard code and test cases affected by the requirement change and write new code and test cases. Even code that's otherwise unaffected must be retested so that you can be sure the changes in other areas haven't introduced any new errors.

HARD DATA

As Table 3-1 reported, data from numerous organizations indicates that on large projects an error in requirements detected during the architecture stage is typically 3 times as expensive to correct as it would be if it were detected during the requirements stage. If detected during coding, it's 5–10 times as expensive; during system test, 10 times; and post-release, a whopping 10–100 times as expensive as it would be if it were detected during requirements development. On smaller projects with lower administrative costs, the multiplier post-release is closer to 5–10 than 100 (Boehm and Turner 2004). In either case, it isn't money you'd want to have taken out of your salary.

Specifying requirements adequately is a key to project success, perhaps even more important than effective construction techniques. (See Figure 3-6.) Many good books have been written about how to specify requirements well. Consequently, the next few sections don't tell you how to do a good job of specifying requirements, they tell you how to determine whether the requirements have been done well and how to make the best of the requirements you have.

Figure 3-6   Without good requirements, you can have the right general problem but miss the mark on specific aspects of the problem.

The Myth of Stable Requirements

Requirements are like water. They're easier to build on when they're frozen.
—*Anonymous*

Stable requirements are the holy grail of software development. With stable requirements, a project can proceed from architecture to design to coding to testing in a way that's orderly, predictable, and calm. This is software heaven! You have predictable expenses, and you never have to worry about a feature costing 100 times as much to implement as it would otherwise because your user didn't think of it until you were finished debugging.

It's fine to hope that once your customer has accepted a requirements document, no changes will be needed. On a typical project, however, the customer can't reliably describe what is needed before the code is written. The problem isn't that the customers are a lower life form. Just as the more you work with the project, the better you understand it, the more they work with it, the better they understand it. The development process helps customers better understand their own needs, and this is a major source of requirements changes (Curtis, Krasner, and Iscoe 1988; Jones 1998; Wiegers 2003). A plan to follow the requirements rigidly is actually a plan not to respond to your customer.

HARD DATA

How much change is typical? Studies at IBM and other companies have found that the average project experiences about a 25 percent change in requirements during development (Boehm 1981, Jones 1994, Jones 2000), which accounts for 70 to 85 percent of the rework on a typical project (Leffingwell 1997, Wiegers 2003).

Maybe you think the Pontiac Aztek was the greatest car ever made, belong to the Flat Earth Society, and make a pilgrimage to the alien landing site at Roswell, New Mexico, every four years. If you do, go ahead and believe that requirements won't change on your projects. If, on the other hand, you've stopped believing in Santa Claus and the Tooth Fairy, or at least have stopped admitting it, you can take several steps to minimize the impact of requirements changes.

Handling Requirements Changes During Construction

KEY POINT

Here are several things you can do to make the best of changing requirements during construction:

Use the requirements checklist at the end of the section to assess the quality of your requirements   If your requirements aren't good enough, stop work, back up, and make them right before you proceed. Sure, it feels like you're getting behind if you stop coding at this stage. But if you're driving from Chicago to Los Angeles, is it a waste of time to stop and look at a road map when you see signs for New York? No. If you're not heading in the right direction, stop and check your course.

Make sure everyone knows the cost of requirements changes   Clients get excited when they think of a new feature. In their excitement, their blood thins and runs to their medulla oblongata and they become giddy, forgetting all the meetings you had to discuss requirements, the signing ceremony, and the completed requirements document. The easiest way to handle such feature-intoxicated people is to say, "Gee, that sounds like a great idea. Since it's not in the requirements document, I'll work up a revised schedule and cost estimate so that you can decide whether you want to do it now or later." The words "schedule" and "cost" are more sobering than coffee and a cold shower, and many "must haves" will quickly turn into "nice to haves."

If your organization isn't sensitive to the importance of doing requirements first, point out that changes at requirements time are much cheaper than changes later. Use this chapter's "Utterly Compelling and Foolproof Argument for Doing Prerequisites Before Construction."

Cross-Reference For details on handling changes to design and code, see Section 28.2, "Configuration Management."

Set up a change-control procedure   If your client's excitement persists, consider establishing a formal change-control board to review such proposed changes. It's all right for customers to change their minds and to realize that they need more capabilities. The problem is their suggesting changes so frequently that you can't keep up. Having a built-in procedure for controlling changes makes everyone happy. You're happy because you know that you'll have to work with changes only at specific times. Your customers are happy because they know that you have a plan for handling their input.

Cross-Reference For details on iterative development approaches, see "Iterate" in Section 5.4 and Section 29.3, "Incremental Integration Strategies."

Use development approaches that accommodate changes   Some development approaches maximize your ability to respond to changing requirements. An evolutionary prototyping approach helps you explore a system's requirements before you send your forces in to build it. Evolutionary delivery is an approach that delivers the system in stages. You can build a little, get a little feedback from your users, adjust your design a little, make a few changes, and build a little more. The key is using short development cycles so that you can respond to your users quickly.

Further Reading For details on development approaches that support flexible requirements, see *Rapid Development* (McConnell 1996).

Dump the project   If the requirements are especially bad or volatile and none of the suggestions above are workable, cancel the project. Even if you can't really cancel the project, think about what it would be like to cancel it. Think about how much worse it would have to get before you would cancel it. If there's a case in which you would dump it, at least ask yourself how much difference there is between your case and that case.

Cross-Reference For details on the differences between formal and informal projects (often caused by differences in project size), see Chapter 27, "How Program Size Affects Construction."

Keep your eye on the business case for the project   Many requirements issues disappear before your eyes when you refer back to the business reason for doing the project. Requirements that seemed like good ideas when considered as "features" can seem like terrible ideas when you evaluate the "incremental business value." Programmers who remember to consider the business impact of their decisions are worth their weight in gold—although I'll be happy to receive my commission for this advice in cash.

cc2e.com/0323

Checklist: Requirements

The requirements checklist contains a list of questions to ask yourself about your project's requirements. This book doesn't tell you how to do good requirements development, and the list won't tell you how to do one either. Use the list as a sanity check at construction time to determine how solid the ground that you're standing on is—where you are on the requirements Richter scale.

Not all of the checklist questions will apply to your project. If you're working on an informal project, you'll find some that you don't even need to think about. You'll find others that you need to think about but don't need to answer formally. If you're working on a large, formal project, however, you may need to consider every one.

Specific Functional Requirements

- ❑ Are all the inputs to the system specified, including their source, accuracy, range of values, and frequency?

- ❑ Are all the outputs from the system specified, including their destination, accuracy, range of values, frequency, and format?

- ❑ Are all output formats specified for Web pages, reports, and so on?

- ❑ Are all the external hardware and software interfaces specified?

- ❑ Are all the external communication interfaces specified, including handshaking, error-checking, and communication protocols?

- ❑ Are all the tasks the user wants to perform specified?

- ❑ Is the data used in each task and the data resulting from each task specified?

Specific Nonfunctional (Quality) Requirements

- ❑ Is the expected response time, from the user's point of view, specified for all necessary operations?

- ❑ Are other timing considerations specified, such as processing time, data-transfer rate, and system throughput?

- ❑ Is the level of security specified?

- ❑ Is the reliability specified, including the consequences of software failure, the vital information that needs to be protected from failure, and the strategy for error detection and recovery?

- ❑ Are minimum machine memory and free disk space specified?

- ❑ Is the maintainability of the system specified, including its ability to adapt to changes in specific functionality, changes in the operating environment, and changes in its interfaces with other software?

- ❑ Is the definition of success included? Of failure?

Requirements Quality

- ❏ Are the requirements written in the user's language? Do the users think so?

- ❏ Does each requirement avoid conflicts with other requirements?

- ❏ Are acceptable tradeoffs between competing attributes specified—for example, between robustness and correctness?

- ❏ Do the requirements avoid specifying the design?

- ❏ Are the requirements at a fairly consistent level of detail? Should any requirement be specified in more detail? Should any requirement be specified in less detail?

- ❏ Are the requirements clear enough to be turned over to an independent group for construction and still be understood? Do the developers think so?

- ❏ Is each item relevant to the problem and its solution? Can each item be traced to its origin in the problem environment?

- ❏ Is each requirement testable? Will it be possible for independent testing to determine whether each requirement has been satisfied?

- ❏ Are all possible changes to the requirements specified, including the likelihood of each change?

Requirements Completeness

- ❏ Where information isn't available before development begins, are the areas of incompleteness specified?

- ❏ Are the requirements complete in the sense that if the product satisfies every requirement, it will be acceptable?

- ❏ Are you comfortable with all the requirements? Have you eliminated requirements that are impossible to implement and included just to appease your customer or your boss?

3.5 Architecture Prerequisite

Cross-Reference For more information on design at all levels, see Chapters 5 through 9.

Software architecture is the high-level part of software design, the frame that holds the more detailed parts of the design (Buschman et al. 1996; Fowler 2002; Bass Clements, Kazman 2003; Clements et al. 2003). Architecture is also known as "system architecture," "high-level design," and "top-level design." Typically, the architecture is described in a single document referred to as the "architecture specification" or "top-level design." Some people make a distinction between architecture and high-level design—architecture refers to design constraints that apply systemwide, whereas high-level design refers to design constraints that apply at the subsystem or multiple-class level, but not necessarily systemwide.

Because this book is about construction, this section doesn't tell you how to develop a software architecture; it focuses on how to determine the quality of an existing architecture. Because architecture is one step closer to construction than requirements, however, the discussion of architecture is more detailed than the discussion of requirements.

KEY POINT

Why have architecture as a prerequisite? Because the quality of the architecture determines the conceptual integrity of the system. That in turn determines the ultimate quality of the system. A well-thought-out architecture provides the structure needed to maintain a system's conceptual integrity from the top levels down to the bottom. It provides guidance to programmers—at a level of detail appropriate to the skills of the programmers and to the job at hand. It partitions the work so that multiple developers or multiple development teams can work independently.

Good architecture makes construction easy. Bad architecture makes construction almost impossible. Figure 3-7 illustrates another problem with bad architecture.

Figure 3-7   Without good software architecture, you may have the right problem but the wrong solution. It may be impossible to have successful construction.

HARD DATA

Architectural changes are expensive to make during construction or later. The time needed to fix an error in a software architecture is on the same order as that needed to fix a requirements error—that is, more than that needed to fix a coding error (Basili and Perricone 1984, Willis 1998). Architecture changes are like requirements changes in that seemingly small changes can be far-reaching. Whether the architectural changes arise from the need to fix errors or the need to make improvements, the earlier you can identify the changes, the better.

Typical Architectural Components

Cross-Reference For details on lower-level program design, see Chapters 5 through 9.

Many components are common to good system architectures. If you're building the whole system yourself, your work on the architecture will overlap your work on the more detailed design. In such a case, you should at least think about each architectural component. If you're working on a system that was architected by someone else, you should be able to find the important components without a bloodhound, a deerstalker cap, and a magnifying glass. In either case, here are the architectural components to consider.

Program Organization

If you can't explain something to a six-year-old, you really don't understand it yourself.
—*Albert Einstein*

A system architecture first needs an overview that describes the system in broad terms. Without such an overview, you'll have a hard time building a coherent picture from a thousand details or even a dozen individual classes. If the system were a little 12-piece jigsaw puzzle, your one-year-old could solve it between spoonfuls of strained asparagus. A puzzle of 12 subsystems is harder to put together, and if you can't put it together, you won't understand how a class you're developing contributes to the system.

In the architecture, you should find evidence that alternatives to the final organization were considered and find the reasons for choosing the final organization over its alternatives. It's frustrating to work on a class when it seems as if the class's role in the system has not been clearly conceived. By describing the organizational alternatives, the architecture provides the rationale for the system organization and shows that each class has been carefully considered. One review of design practices found that the design rationale is at least as important for maintenance as the design itself (Rombach 1990).

Cross-Reference For details on different size building blocks in design, see "Levels of Design" in Section 5.2.

The architecture should define the major building blocks in a program. Depending on the size of the program, each building block might be a single class or it might be a subsystem consisting of many classes. Each building block is a class, or it's a collection of classes or routines that work together on high-level functions such as interacting with the user, displaying Web pages, interpreting commands, encapsulating business rules, or accessing data. Every feature listed in the requirements should be covered by at least one building block. If a function is claimed by two or more building blocks, their claims should cooperate, not conflict.

Cross-Reference Minimizing what each building block knows about other building blocks is a key part of information hiding. For details, see "Hide Secrets (Information Hiding)" in Section 5.3.

What each building block is responsible for should be well defined. A building block should have one area of responsibility, and it should know as little as possible about other building blocks' areas of responsibility. By minimizing what each building block knows about the other building blocks, you localize information about the design into single building blocks.

The communication rules for each building block should be well defined. The architecture should describe which other building blocks the building block can use directly, which it can use indirectly, and which it shouldn't use at all.

Major Classes

Cross-Reference For details on class design, see Chapter 6, "Working Classes."

The architecture should specify the major classes to be used. It should identify the responsibilities of each major class and how the class will interact with other classes. It should include descriptions of the class hierarchies, of state transitions, and of object persistence. If the system is large enough, it should describe how classes are organized into subsystems.

The architecture should describe other class designs that were considered and give reasons for preferring the organization that was chosen. The architecture doesn't need to specify every class in the system. Aim for the 80/20 rule: specify the 20 percent of the classes that make up 80 percent of the system's behavior (Jacobsen, Booch, and Rumbaugh 1999; Kruchten 2000).

Data Design

Cross-Reference For details on working with variables, see Chapters 10 through 13.

The architecture should describe the major files and table designs to be used. It should describe alternatives that were considered and justify the choices that were made. If the application maintains a list of customer IDs and the architects have chosen to represent the list of IDs using a sequential-access list, the document should explain why a sequential-access list is better than a random-access list, stack, or hash table. During construction, such information gives you insight into the minds of the architects. During maintenance, the same insight is an invaluable aid. Without it, you're watching a foreign movie with no subtitles.

Data should normally be accessed directly by only one subsystem or class, except through access classes or routines that allow access to the data in controlled and abstract ways. This is explained in more detail in "Hide Secrets (Information Hiding)" in Section 5.3.

The architecture should specify the high-level organization and contents of any databases used. The architecture should explain why a single database is preferable to multiple databases (or vice versa), explain why a database is preferable to flat files, identify possible interactions with other programs that access the same data, explain what views have been created on the data, and so on.

Business Rules

If the architecture depends on specific business rules, it should identify them and describe the impact the rules have on the system's design. For example, suppose the system is required to follow a business rule that customer information should be no more than 30 seconds out of date. In that case, the impact that rule has on the architecture's approach to keeping customer information up to date and synchronized should be described.

User Interface Design

The user interface is often specified at requirements time. If it isn't, it should be specified in the software architecture. The architecture should specify major elements of Web page formats, GUIs, command line interfaces, and so on. Careful architecture of the user interface makes the difference between a well-liked program and one that's never used.

The architecture should be modularized so that a new user interface can be substituted without affecting the business rules and output parts of the program. For example, the architecture should make it fairly easy to lop off a group of interactive interface classes and plug in a group of command line classes. This ability is often useful, especially since command line interfaces are convenient for software testing at the unit or subsystem level.

cc2e.com/0393

The design of user interfaces deserves its own book-length discussion but is outside the scope of this book.

Resource Management

The architecture should describe a plan for managing scarce resources such as database connections, threads, and handles. Memory management is another important area for the architecture to treat in memory-constrained applications areas such as driver development and embedded systems. The architecture should estimate the resources used for nominal and extreme cases. In a simple case, the estimates should show that the resources needed are well within the capabilities of the intended implementation environment. In a more complex case, the application might be required to more actively manage its own resources. If it is, the resource manager should be architected as carefully as any other part of the system.

cc2e.com/0330

Security

Further Reading For an excellent discussion of software security, see *Writing Secure Code*, 2d Ed. (Howard and LeBlanc 2003) as well as the January 2002 issue of *IEEE Software*.

The architecture should describe the approach to design-level and code-level security. If a threat model has not previously been built, it should be built at architecture time. Coding guidelines should be developed with security implications in mind, including approaches to handling buffers, rules for handling untrusted data (data input from users, cookies, configuration data, and other external interfaces), encryption, level of detail contained in error messages, protecting secret data that's in memory, and other issues.

Performance

Further Reading For additional information on designing systems for performance, see Connie Smith's *Performance Engineering of Software Systems* (1990).

If performance is a concern, performance goals should be specified in the requirements. Performance goals can include resource use, in which case the goals should also specify priorities among resources, including speed vs. memory vs. cost.

The architecture should provide estimates and explain why the architects believe the goals are achievable. If certain areas are at risk of failing to meet their goals, the architecture should say so. If certain areas require the use of specific algorithms or data types to meet their performance goals, the architecture should say that. The architecture can also include space and time budgets for each class or object.

Scalability

Scalability is the ability of a system to grow to meet future demands. The architecture should describe how the system will address growth in number of users, number of servers, number of network nodes, number of database records, size of database records, transaction volume, and so on. If the system is not expected to grow and scalability is not an issue, the architecture should make that assumption explicit.

Interoperability

If the system is expected to share data or resources with other software or hardware, the architecture should describe how that will be accomplished.

Internationalization/Localization

"Internationalization" is the technical activity of preparing a program to support multiple locales. Internationalization is often known as "I18n" because the first and last characters in "internationalization" are "I" and "N" and because there are 18 letters in the middle of the word. "Localization" (known as "L10n" for the same reason) is the activity of translating a program to support a specific local language.

Internationalization issues deserve attention in the architecture for an interactive system. Most interactive systems contain dozens or hundreds of prompts, status displays, help messages, error messages, and so on. Resources used by the strings should be estimated. If the program is to be used commercially, the architecture should show that the typical string and character-set issues have been considered, including character set used (ASCII, DBCS, EBCDIC, MBCS, Unicode, ISO 8859, and so on), kinds of strings used (C strings, Visual Basic strings, and so on), maintaining the strings without changing code, and translating the strings into foreign languages with minimal impact on the code and the user interface. The architecture can decide to use strings in line in the code where they're needed, keep the strings in a class and reference them through the class interface, or store the strings in a resource file. The architecture should explain which option was chosen and why.

Input/Output

Input/output (I/O) is another area that deserves attention in the architecture. The architecture should specify a look-ahead, look-behind, or just-in-time reading scheme. And it should describe the level at which I/O errors are detected: at the field, record, stream, or file level.

Error Processing

HARD DATA

Error processing is turning out to be one of the thorniest problems of modern computer science, and you can't afford to deal with it haphazardly. Some people have estimated that as much as 90 percent of a program's code is written for exceptional, error-processing cases or housekeeping, implying that only 10 percent is written for nominal cases (Shaw in Bentley 1982). With so much code dedicated to handling errors, a strategy for handling them consistently should be spelled out in the architecture.

Error handling is often treated as a coding-convention-level issue, if it's treated at all. But because it has systemwide implications, it is best treated at the architectural level. Here are some questions to consider:

■ Is error processing corrective or merely detective? If corrective, the program can attempt to recover from errors. If it's merely detective, the program can continue processing as if nothing had happened, or it can quit. In either case, it should notify the user that it detected an error.

■ Is error detection active or passive? The system can actively anticipate errors—for example, by checking user input for validity—or it can passively respond to them only when it can't avoid them—for example, when a combination of user input produces a numeric overflow. It can clear the way or clean up the mess. Again, in either case, the choice has user-interface implications.

■ How does the program propagate errors? Once it detects an error, it can immediately discard the data that caused the error, it can treat the error as an error and enter an error-processing state, or it can wait until all processing is complete and notify the user that errors were detected (somewhere).

■ What are the conventions for handling error messages? If the architecture doesn't specify a single, consistent strategy, the user interface will appear to be a confusing macaroni-and-dried-bean collage of different interfaces in different parts of the program. To avoid such an appearance, the architecture should establish conventions for error messages.

■ How will exceptions be handled? The architecture should address when the code can throw exceptions, where they will be caught, how they will be logged, how they will be documented, and so on.

Cross-Reference A consistent method of handling bad parameters is another aspect of error-processing strategy that should be addressed architecturally. For examples, see Chapter 8, "Defensive Programming."

- Inside the program, at what level are errors handled? You can handle them at the point of detection, pass them off to an error-handling class, or pass them up the call chain.

- What is the level of responsibility of each class for validating its input data? Is each class responsible for validating its own data, or is there a group of classes responsible for validating the system's data? Can classes at any level assume that the data they're receiving is clean?

- Do you want to use your environment's built-in exception-handling mechanism or build your own? The fact that an environment has a particular error-handling approach doesn't mean that it's the best approach for your requirements.

Fault Tolerance

Further Reading For a good introduction to fault tolerance, see the July 2001 issue of *IEEE Software*. In addition to providing a good introduction, the articles cite many key books and key articles on the topic.

The architecture should also indicate the kind of fault tolerance expected. Fault tolerance is a collection of techniques that increase a system's reliability by detecting errors, recovering from them if possible, and containing their bad effects if not.

For example, a system could make the computation of the square root of a number fault tolerant in any of several ways:

- The system might back up and try again when it detects a fault. If the first answer is wrong, it would back up to a point at which it knew everything was all right and continue from there.

- The system might have auxiliary code to use if it detects a fault in the primary code. In the example, if the first answer appears to be wrong, the system switches over to an alternative square-root routine and uses it instead.

- The system might use a voting algorithm. It might have three square-root classes that each use a different method. Each class computes the square root, and then the system compares the results. Depending on the kind of fault tolerance built into the system, it then uses the mean, the median, or the mode of the three results.

- The system might replace the erroneous value with a phony value that it knows to have a benign effect on the rest of the system.

Other fault-tolerance approaches include having the system change to a state of partial operation or a state of degraded functionality when it detects an error. It can shut itself down or automatically restart itself. These examples are necessarily simplistic. Fault tolerance is a fascinating and complex subject—unfortunately, it's one that's outside the scope of this book.

Architectural Feasibility

The designers might have concerns about a system's ability to meet its performance targets, work within resource limitations, or be adequately supported by the implementation environments. The architecture should demonstrate that the system is technically feasible. If infeasibility in any area could render the project unworkable, the architecture should indicate how those issues have been investigated—through proof-of-concept prototypes, research, or other means. These risks should be resolved before full-scale construction begins.

Overengineering

Robustness is the ability of a system to continue to run after it detects an error. Often an architecture specifies a more robust system than that specified by the requirements. One reason is that a system composed of many parts that are minimally robust might be less robust than is required overall. In software, the chain isn't as strong as its weakest link; it's as weak as all the weak links multiplied together. The architecture should clearly indicate whether programmers should err on the side of overengineering or on the side of doing the simplest thing that works.

Specifying an approach to overengineering is particularly important because many programmers overengineer their classes automatically, out of a sense of professional pride. By setting expectations explicitly in the architecture, you can avoid the phenomenon in which some classes are exceptionally robust and others are barely adequate.

Buy-vs.-Build Decisions

Cross-Reference For a list of kinds of commercially available software components and libraries, see "Code Libraries" in Section 30.3.

The most radical solution to building software is not to build it at all—to buy it instead or to download open-source software for free. You can buy GUI controls, database managers, image processors, graphics and charting components, Internet communications components, security and encryption components, spreadsheet tools, text-processing tools—the list is nearly endless. One of the greatest advantages of programming in modern GUI environments is the amount of functionality you get automatically: graphics classes, dialog box managers, keyboard and mouse handlers, code that works automatically with any printer or monitor, and so on.

If the architecture isn't using off-the-shelf components, it should explain the ways in which it expects custom-built components to surpass ready-made libraries and components.

Reuse Decisions

If the plan calls for using preexisting software, test cases, data formats, or other materials, the architecture should explain how the reused software will be made to conform to the other architectural goals—if it will be made to conform.

Change Strategy

Cross-Reference For details on handling changes systematically, see Section 28.2, "Configuration Management."

Because building a software product is a learning process for both the programmers and the users, the product is likely to change throughout its development. Changes arise from volatile data types and file formats, changed functionality, new features, and so on. The changes can be new capabilities likely to result from planned enhancements, or they can be capabilities that didn't make it into the first version of the system. Consequently, one of the major challenges facing a software architect is making the architecture flexible enough to accommodate likely changes.

Design bugs are often subtle and occur by evolution with early assumptions being forgotten as new features or uses are added to a system.
—*Fernando J. Corbató*

The architecture should clearly describe a strategy for handling changes. The architecture should show that possible enhancements have been considered and that the enhancements most likely are also the easiest to implement. If changes are likely in input or output formats, style of user interaction, or processing requirements, the architecture should show that the changes have all been anticipated and that the effects of any single change will be limited to a small number of classes. The architecture's plan for changes can be as simple as one to put version numbers in data files, reserve fields for future use, or design files so that you can add new tables. If a code generator is being used, the architecture should show that the anticipated changes are within the capabilities of the code generator.

Cross-Reference For a full explanation of delaying commitment, see "Choose Binding Time Consciously" in Section 5.3.

The architecture should indicate the strategies that are used to delay commitment. For example, the architecture might specify that a table-driven technique be used rather than hard-coded *if* tests. It might specify that data for the table is to be kept in an external file rather than coded inside the program, thus allowing changes in the program without recompiling.

General Architectural Quality

Cross-Reference For more information about how quality attributes interact, see Section 20.1, "Characteristics of Software Quality."

A good architecture specification is characterized by discussions of the classes in the system, of the information that's hidden in each class, and of the rationales for including and excluding all possible design alternatives.

The architecture should be a polished conceptual whole with few ad hoc additions. The central thesis of the most popular software-engineering book ever, *The Mythical Man-Month*, is that the essential problem with large systems is maintaining their conceptual integrity (Brooks 1995). A good architecture should fit the problem. When you look at the architecture, you should be pleased by how natural and easy the solution seems. It shouldn't look as if the problem and the architecture have been forced together with duct tape.

You might know of ways in which the architecture was changed during its development. Each change should fit in cleanly with the overall concept. The architecture shouldn't look like a U.S. Congress appropriations bill complete with pork-barrel, boondoggle riders for each representative's home district.

The architecture's objectives should be clearly stated. A design for a system with a primary goal of modifiability will be different from one with a goal of uncompromised performance, even if both systems have the same function.

The architecture should describe the motivations for all major decisions. Be wary of "we've always done it that way" justifications. One story goes that Beth wanted to cook a pot roast according to an award-winning pot roast recipe handed down in her husband's family. Her husband, Abdul, said that his mother had taught him to sprinkle it with salt and pepper, cut both ends off, put it in the pan, cover it, and cook it. Beth asked, "Why do you cut both ends off?" Abdul said, "I don't know. I've always done it that way. Let me ask my mother." He called her, and she said, "I don't know. I've always done it that way. Let me ask your grandmother." She called his grandmother, who said, "I don't know why you do it that way. I did it that way because it was too big to fit in my pan."

Good software architecture is largely machine- and language-independent. Admittedly, you can't ignore the construction environment. By being as independent of the environment as possible, however, you avoid the temptation to overarchitect the system or to do a job that you can do better during construction. If the purpose of a program is to exercise a specific machine or language, this guideline doesn't apply.

The architecture should tread the line between underspecifying and overspecifying the system. No part of the architecture should receive more attention than it deserves, or be overdesigned. Designers shouldn't pay attention to one part at the expense of another. The architecture should address all requirements without gold-plating (without containing elements that are not required).

The architecture should explicitly identify risky areas. It should explain why they're risky and what steps have been taken to minimize the risk.

The architecture should contain multiple views. Plans for a house will include elevations, floor plan, framing plan, electrical diagrams, and other views of the house. Software architecture descriptions also benefit from providing different views of the system that flush out errors and inconsistencies and help programmers fully understand the system's design (Kruchten 1995).

Finally, you shouldn't be uneasy about any parts of the architecture. It shouldn't contain anything just to please the boss. It shouldn't contain anything that's hard for you to understand. You're the one who'll implement it; if it doesn't make sense to you, how can you implement it?

cc2e.com/0337

Checklist: Architecture

Here's a list of issues that a good architecture should address. The list isn't intended to be a comprehensive guide to architecture but to be a pragmatic way of evaluating the nutritional content of what you get at the programmer's end of the software food chain. Use this checklist as a starting point for your own checklist. As with the requirements checklist, if you're working on an informal project, you'll find some items that you don't even need to think about. If you're working on a larger project, most of the items will be useful.

Specific Architectural Topics

- ❑ Is the overall organization of the program clear, including a good architectural overview and justification?

- ❑ Are major building blocks well defined, including their areas of responsibility and their interfaces to other building blocks?

- ❑ Are all the functions listed in the requirements covered sensibly, by neither too many nor too few building blocks?

- ❑ Are the most critical classes described and justified?

- ❑ Is the data design described and justified?

- ❑ Is the database organization and content specified?

- ❑ Are all key business rules identified and their impact on the system described?

- ❑ Is a strategy for the user interface design described?

- ❑ Is the user interface modularized so that changes in it won't affect the rest of the program?

- ❑ Is a strategy for handling I/O described and justified?

- ❑ Are resource-use estimates and a strategy for resource management described and justified for scarce resources like threads, database connections, handles, network bandwidth, and so on?

- ❑ Are the architecture's security requirements described?

- ❑ Does the architecture set space and speed budgets for each class, subsystem, or functionality area?

- ❑ Does the architecture describe how scalability will be achieved?

- ❑ Does the architecture address interoperability?

- ❑ Is a strategy for internationalization/localization described?

- ❑ Is a coherent error-handling strategy provided?

- ❑ Is the approach to fault tolerance defined (if any is needed)?

❑ Has technical feasibility of all parts of the system been established?

❑ Is an approach to overengineering specified?

❑ Are necessary buy-vs.-build decisions included?

❑ Does the architecture describe how reused code will be made to conform to other architectural objectives?

❑ Is the architecture designed to accommodate likely changes?

General Architectural Quality

❑ Does the architecture account for all the requirements?

❑ Is any part overarchitected or underarchitected? Are expectations in this area set out explicitly?

❑ Does the whole architecture hang together conceptually?

❑ Is the top-level design independent of the machine and language that will be used to implement it?

❑ Are the motivations for all major decisions provided?

❑ Are you, as a programmer who will implement the system, comfortable with the architecture?

3.6 Amount of Time to Spend on Upstream Prerequisites

Cross-Reference The amount of time you spend on prerequisites will depend on your project type. For details on adapting prerequisites to your specific project, see Section 3.2, "Determine the Kind of Software You're Working On," earlier in this chapter.

The amount of time to spend on problem definition, requirements, and software architecture varies according to the needs of your project. Generally, a well-run project devotes about 10 to 20 percent of its effort and about 20 to 30 percent of its schedule to requirements, architecture, and up-front planning (McConnell 1998, Kruchten 2000). These figures don't include time for detailed design—that's part of construction.

If requirements are unstable and you're working on a large, formal project, you'll probably have to work with a requirements analyst to resolve requirements problems that are identified early in construction. Allow time to consult with the requirements analyst and for the requirements analyst to revise the requirements before you'll have a workable version of the requirements.

If requirements are unstable and you're working on a small, informal project, you'll probably need to resolve requirements issues yourself. Allow time for defining the requirements well enough that their volatility will have a minimal impact on construction.

Cross-Reference For approaches to handling changing requirements, see "Handling Requirements Changes During Construction" in Section 3.4, earlier in this chapter.

If the requirements are unstable on any project—formal or informal—treat requirements work as its own project. Estimate the time for the rest of the project after you've finished the requirements. This is a sensible approach since no one can reasonably expect you to estimate your schedule before you know what you're building. It's as if you were a contractor called to work on a house. Your customer says, "What will it cost to do the work?" You reasonably ask, "What do you want me to do?" Your customer says, "I can't tell you, but how much will it cost?" You reasonably thank the customer for wasting your time and go home.

With a building, it's clear that it's unreasonable for clients to ask for a bid before telling you what you're going to build. Your clients wouldn't want you to show up with wood, hammer, and nails and start spending their money before the architect had finished the blueprints. People tend to understand software development less than they understand two-by-fours and sheetrock, however, so the clients you work with might not immediately understand why you want to plan requirements development as a separate project. You might need to explain your reasoning to them.

When allocating time for software architecture, use an approach similar to the one for requirements development. If the software is a kind that you haven't worked with before, allow more time for the uncertainty of designing in a new area. Ensure that the time you need to create a good architecture won't take away from the time you need for good work in other areas. If necessary, plan the architecture work as a separate project, too.

Additional Resources

cc2e.com/0344

Following are more resources on requirements:

cc2e.com/0351

Requirements

Here are a few books that give much more detail on requirements development:

Wiegers, Karl. *Software Requirements*, 2d ed. Redmond, WA: Microsoft Press, 2003. This is a practical, practitioner-focused book that describes the nuts and bolts of requirements activities, including requirements elicitation, requirements analysis, requirements specification, requirements validation, and requirements management.

Robertson, Suzanne and James Robertson. *Mastering the Requirements Process*. Reading, MA: Addison-Wesley, 1999. This is a good alternative to Wiegers' book for the more advanced requirements practitioner.

Gilb, Tom. *Competitive Engineering*. Reading, MA: Addison-Wesley, 2004. This book describes Gilb's requirements language, known as "Planguage." The book covers Gilb's specific approach to requirements engineering, design and design evaluation, and evolutionary project management. This book can be downloaded from Gilb's website at *www.gilb.com*.

cc2e.com/0358

IEEE Std 830-1998. IEEE Recommended Practice for Software Requirements Specifications. Los Alamitos, CA: IEEE Computer Society Press. This document is the IEEE-ANSI guide for writing software-requirements specifications. It describes what should be included in the specification document and shows several alternative outlines for one.

cc2e.com/0365

Abran, Alain, et al. *Swebok: Guide to the Software Engineering Body of Knowledge.* Los Alamitos, CA: IEEE Computer Society Press, 2001. This contains a detailed description of the body of software-requirements knowledge. It can also be downloaded from *www.swebok.org.*

Other good alternatives include the following:

Lauesen, Soren. *Software Requirements: Styles and Techniques.* Boston, MA: Addison-Wesley, 2002.

Kovitz, Benjamin L. *Practical Software Requirements: A Manual of Content and Style.* Manning Publications Company, 1998.

Cockburn, Alistair. *Writing Effective Use Cases.* Boston, MA: Addison-Wesley, 2000.

cc2e.com/0372

Software Architecture

Numerous books on software architecture have been published in the past few years. Here are some of the best:

Bass, Len, Paul Clements, and Rick Kazman. *Software Architecture in Practice*, 2d ed. Boston, MA: Addison-Wesley, 2003.

Buschman, Frank, et al. *Pattern-Oriented Software Architecture, Volume 1: A System of Patterns.* New York, NY: John Wiley & Sons, 1996.

Clements, Paul, ed. *Documenting Software Architectures: Views and Beyond.* Boston, MA: Addison-Wesley, 2003.

Clements, Paul, Rick Kazman, and Mark Klein. *Evaluating Software Architectures: Methods and Case Studies.* Boston, MA: Addison-Wesley, 2002.

Fowler, Martin. *Patterns of Enterprise Application Architecture.* Boston, MA: Addison-Wesley, 2002.

Jacobson, Ivar, Grady Booch, and James Rumbaugh. *The Unified Software Development Process.* Reading, MA: Addison-Wesley, 1999.

IEEE Std 1471-2000. Recommended Practice for Architectural Description of Software-Intensive Systems. Los Alamitos, CA: IEEE Computer Society Press. This document is the IEEE-ANSI guide for creating software-architecture specifications.

cc2e.com/0379   ## General Software-Development Approaches

Many books are available that map out different approaches to conducting a software project. Some are more sequential, and some are more iterative.

McConnell, Steve. *Software Project Survival Guide*. Redmond, WA: Microsoft Press, 1998. This book presents one particular way to conduct a project. The approach presented emphasizes deliberate up-front planning, requirements development, and architecture work followed by careful project execution. It provides long-range predictability of costs and schedules, high quality, and a moderate amount of flexibility.

Kruchten, Philippe. *The Rational Unified Process: An Introduction*, 2d ed. Reading, MA: Addison-Wesley, 2000. This book presents a project approach that is "architecture-centric and use-case driven." Like *Software Project Survival Guide*, it focuses on up-front work that provides good long-range predictability of costs and schedules, high quality, and moderate flexibility. This book's approach requires somewhat more sophisticated use than the approaches described in *Software Project Survival Guide* and *Extreme Programming Explained: Embrace Change*.

Jacobson, Ivar, Grady Booch, and James Rumbaugh. *The Unified Software Development Process*. Reading, MA: Addison-Wesley, 1999. This book is a more in-depth treatment of the topics covered in *The Rational Unified Process: An Introduction*, 2d ed.

Beck, Kent. *Extreme Programming Explained: Embrace Change*. Reading, MA: Addison-Wesley, 2000. Beck describes a highly iterative approach that focuses on developing requirements and designs iteratively, in conjunction with construction. The Extreme Programming approach offers little long-range predictability but provides a high degree of flexibility.

Gilb, Tom. *Principles of Software Engineering Management*. Wokingham, England: Addison-Wesley, 1988. Gilb's approach explores critical planning, requirements, and architecture issues early in a project and then continuously adapts the project plans as the project progresses. This approach provides a combination of long-range predictability, high quality, and a high degree of flexibility. It requires more sophistication than the approaches described in *Software Project Survival Guide* and *Extreme Programming Explained: Embrace Change*.

McConnell, Steve. *Rapid Development*. Redmond, WA: Microsoft Press, 1996. This book presents a toolbox approach to project planning. An experienced project planner can use the tools presented in this book to create a project plan that is highly adapted to a project's unique needs.

Boehm, Barry and Richard Turner. *Balancing Agility and Discipline: A Guide for the Perplexed*. Boston, MA: Addison-Wesley, 2003. This book explores the contrast between agile development and plan-driven development styles. Chapter 3 has four especially revealing sections: "A Typical Day using PSP/TSP," "A Typical Day using Extreme Programming," "A Crisis Day using PSP/TSP," and "A Crisis Day using Extreme Programming." Chapter 5 is on using risk to balance agility, which provides incisive guidance for selecting between agile and plan-driven methods. Chapter 6, "Conclusions," is also well balanced and gives great perspective. Appendix E is a gold mine of empirical data on agile practices.

Larman, Craig. *Agile and Iterative Development: A Manager's Guide.* Boston, MA: Addison Wesley, 2004. This is a well-researched introduction to flexible, evolutionary development styles. It overviews Scrum, Extreme Programming, the Unified Process, and Evo.

cc2e.com/0386

Checklist: Upstream Prerequisites

❑ Have you identified the kind of software project you're working on and tailored your approach appropriately?

❑ Are the requirements sufficiently well defined and stable enough to begin construction? (See the requirements checklist for details.)

❑ Is the architecture sufficiently well defined to begin construction? (See the architecture checklist for details.)

❑ Have other risks unique to your particular project been addressed, such that construction is not exposed to more risk than necessary?

Key Points

- The overarching goal of preparing for construction is risk reduction. Be sure your preparation activities are reducing risks, not increasing them.

- If you want to develop high-quality software, attention to quality must be part of the software-development process from the beginning to the end. Attention to quality at the beginning has a greater influence on product quality than attention at the end.

- Part of a programmer's job is to educate bosses and coworkers about the software-development process, including the importance of adequate preparation before programming begins.

- The kind of project you're working on significantly affects construction prerequisites—many projects should be highly iterative, and some should be more sequential.

- If a good problem definition hasn't been specified, you might be solving the wrong problem during construction.

- If good requirements work hasn't been done, you might have missed important details of the problem. Requirements changes cost 20 to 100 times as much in the stages following construction as they do earlier, so be sure the requirements are right before you start programming.

- If a good architectural design hasn't been done, you might be solving the right problem the wrong way during construction. The cost of architectural changes increases as more code is written for the wrong architecture, so be sure the architecture is right, too.

- Understand what approach has been taken to the construction prerequisites on your project, and choose your construction approach accordingly.

Chapter 4
Key Construction Decisions

cc2e.com/0489

Contents

Related Topics

Once you're sure an appropriate groundwork has been laid for construction, preparation turns toward more construction-specific decisions. Chapter 3, "Measure Twice, Cut Once: Upstream Prerequisites," discussed the software equivalent of blueprints and construction permits. You might not have had much control over those preparations, so the focus of that chapter was on assessing what you have to work with when construction begins. This chapter focuses on preparations that individual programmers and technical leads are responsible for, directly or indirectly. It discusses the software equivalent of how to select specific tools for your tool belt and how to load your truck before you head out to the job site.

If you feel you've read enough about construction preparations already, you might skip ahead to Chapter 5, "Design in Construction."

4.1 Choice of Programming Language

By relieving the brain of all unnecessary work, a good notation sets it free to concentrate on more advanced problems, and in effect increases the mental power of the race. Before the introduction of the Arabic notation, multiplication was difficult, and the division even of integers called into play the highest mathematical faculties. Probably nothing in the modern world would have more astonished a Greek mathematician than to learn that ... a huge proportion of the population of Western Europe could perform the operation of division for the largest numbers. This fact would have seemed to him a sheer impossibility.... Our modern power of easy reckoning with decimal fractions is the almost miraculous result of the gradual discovery of a perfect notation.

—Alfred North Whitehead

The programming language in which the system will be implemented should be of great interest to you since you will be immersed in it from the beginning of construction to the end.

Studies have shown that the programming-language choice affects productivity and code quality in several ways.

Programmers are more productive using a familiar language than an unfamiliar one. Data from the Cocomo II estimation model shows that programmers working in a language they've used for three years or more are about 30 percent more productive than programmers with equivalent experience who are new to a language (Boehm et al. 2000). An earlier study at IBM found that programmers who had extensive experience with a programming language were more than three times as productive as those with minimal experience (Walston and Felix 1977). (Cocomo II is more careful to isolate effects of individual factors, which accounts for the different results of the two studies.)

HARD DATA

Programmers working with high-level languages achieve better productivity and quality than those working with lower-level languages. Languages such as C++, Java, Smalltalk, and Visual Basic have been credited with improving productivity, reliability, simplicity, and comprehensibility by factors of 5 to 15 over low-level languages such as assembly and C (Brooks 1987, Jones 1998, Boehm 2000). You save time when you don't need to have an awards ceremony every time a C statement does what it's supposed to. Moreover, higher-level languages are more expressive than lower-level languages. Each line of code says more. Table 4-1 shows typical ratios of source statements in several high-level languages to the equivalent code in C. A higher ratio means that each line of code in the language listed accomplishes more than does each line of code in C.

Table 4-1   Ratio of High-Level-Language Statements to Equivalent C Code

Language	Level Relative to C
C	1
C++	2.5
Fortran 95	2
Java	2.5
Perl	6
Python	6
Smalltalk	6
Microsoft Visual Basic	4.5

Source: Adapted from *Estimating Software Costs* (Jones 1998), *Software Cost Estimation with Cocomo II* (Boehm 2000), and "An Empirical Comparison of Seven Programming Languages" (Prechelt 2000).

Some languages are better at expressing programming concepts than others. You can draw a parallel between natural languages such as English and programming languages such as Java and C++. In the case of natural languages, the linguists Sapir and Whorf hypothesize a relationship between the expressive power of a language and the ability to think certain thoughts. The Sapir-Whorf hypothesis says that your ability to think a thought depends on knowing words capable of expressing the thought. If you don't know the words, you can't express the thought and you might not even be able to formulate it (Whorf 1956).

Programmers may be similarly influenced by their languages. The words available in a programming language for expressing your programming thoughts certainly determine how you express your thoughts and might even determine what thoughts you can express.

Evidence of the effect of programming languages on programmers' thinking is common. A typical story goes like this: "We were writing a new system in C++, but most of our programmers didn't have much experience in C++. They came from Fortran backgrounds. They wrote code that compiled in C++, but they were really writing disguised Fortran. They stretched C++ to emulate Fortran's bad features (such as gotos and global data) and ignored C++'s rich set of object-oriented capabilities." This phenomenon has been reported throughout the industry for many years (Hanson 1984, Yourdon 1986a).

Language Descriptions

The development histories of some languages are interesting, as are their general capabilities. Here are descriptions of the most common languages in use today.

Ada

Ada is a general-purpose, high-level programming language based on Pascal. It was developed under the aegis of the Department of Defense and is especially well suited to real-time and embedded systems. Ada emphasizes data abstraction and information hiding and forces you to differentiate between the public and private parts of each class and package. "Ada" was chosen as the name of the language in honor of Ada Lovelace, a mathematician who is considered to have been the world's first programmer. Today, Ada is used primarily in military, space, and avionics systems.

Assembly Language

Assembly language, or "assembler," is a kind of low-level language in which each statement corresponds to a single machine instruction. Because the statements use specific machine instructions, an assembly language is specific to a particular processor—for example, specific Intel or Motorola CPUs. Assembler is regarded as the second-generation language. Most programmers avoid it unless they're pushing the limits in execution speed or code size.

C

C is a general-purpose, mid-level language that was originally associated with the UNIX operating system. C has some high-level language features, such as structured data, structured control flow, machine independence, and a rich set of operators. It has also been called a "portable assembly language" because it makes extensive use of pointers and addresses, has some low-level constructs such as bit manipulation, and is weakly typed.

C was developed in the 1970s at Bell Labs. It was originally designed for and used on the DEC PDP-11—whose operating system, C compiler, and UNIX application programs were all written in C. In 1988, an ANSI standard was issued to codify C, which was revised in 1999. C was the de facto standard for microcomputer and workstation programming in the 1980s and 1990s.

C++

C++, an object-oriented language founded on C, was developed at Bell Laboratories in the 1980s. In addition to being compatible with C, C++ provides classes, polymorphism, exception handling, templates, and it provides more robust type checking than C does. It also provides an extensive and powerful standard library.

C#

C# is a general-purpose, object-oriented language and programming environment developed by Microsoft with syntax similar to C, C++, and Java, and it provides extensive tools that aid development on Microsoft platforms.

Cobol

Cobol is an English-like programming language that was originally developed in 1959–1961 for use by the Department of Defense. Cobol is used primarily for business applications and is still one of the most widely used languages today, second only to Visual Basic in popularity (Feiman and Driver 2002). Cobol has been updated over the years to include mathematical functions and object-oriented capabilities. The acronym "Cobol" stands for COmmon Business-Oriented Language.

Fortran

Fortran was the first high-level computer language, introducing the ideas of variables and high-level loops. "Fortran" stands for FORmula TRANslation. Fortran was originally developed in the 1950s and has seen several significant revisions, including Fortran 77 in 1977, which added block-structured if-then-else statements and character-string manipulations. Fortran 90 added user-defined data types, pointers, classes, and a rich set of operations on arrays. Fortran is used mainly in scientific and engineering applications.

Java

Java is an object-oriented language with syntax similar to C and C++ that was developed by Sun Microsystems, Inc. Java was designed to run on any platform by converting Java source code to byte code, which is then run in each platform within an environment known as a virtual machine. Java is in widespread use for programming Web applications.

JavaScript

JavaScript is an interpreted scripting language that was originally loosely related to Java. It is used primarily for client-side programming such as adding simple functions and online applications to Web pages.

Perl

Perl is a string-handling language that is based on C and several UNIX utilities. Perl is often used for system administration tasks, such as creating build scripts, as well as for report generation and processing. It's also used to create Web applications such as Slashdot. The acronym "Perl" stands for Practical Extraction and Report Language.

PHP

PHP is an open-source scripting language with a simple syntax similar to Perl, Bourne Shell, JavaScript, and C. PHP runs on all major operating systems to execute server-side interactive functions. It can be embedded in Web pages to access and present database information. The acronym "PHP" originally stood for Personal Home Page but now stands for PHP: Hypertext Processor.

Python

Python is an interpreted, interactive, object-oriented language that runs in numerous environments. It is used most commonly for writing scripts and small Web applications and also contains some support for creating larger programs.

SQL

SQL is the de facto standard language for querying, updating, and managing relational databases. "SQL" stands for Structured Query Language. Unlike other languages listed in this section, SQL is a "declarative language," meaning that it does not define a sequence of operations, but rather the result of some operations.

Visual Basic

The original version of Basic was a high-level language developed at Dartmouth College in the 1960s. The acronym BASIC stands for Beginner's All-purpose Symbolic

Instruction Code. Visual Basic is a high-level, object-oriented, visual programming version of Basic developed by Microsoft that was originally designed for creating Microsoft Windows applications. It has since been extended to support customization of desktop applications such as Microsoft Office, creation of Web programs, and other applications. Experts report that by the early 2000s more professional developers were working in Visual Basic than in any other language (Feiman and Driver 2002).

4.2 Programming Conventions

Cross-Reference For more details on the power of conventions, see Sections 11.3 through 11.5.

In high-quality software, you can see a relationship between the conceptual integrity of the architecture and its low-level implementation. The implementation must be consistent with the architecture that guides it and consistent internally. That's the point of construction guidelines for variable names, class names, routine names, formatting conventions, and commenting conventions.

In a complex program, architectural guidelines give the program structural balance and construction guidelines provide low-level harmony, articulating each class as a faithful part of a comprehensive design. Any large program requires a controlling structure that unifies its programming-language details. Part of the beauty of a large structure is the way in which its detailed parts bear out the implications of its architecture. Without a unifying discipline, your creation will be a jumble of sloppy variations in style. Such variations tax your brain—and only for the sake of understanding coding-style differences that are essentially arbitrary. One key to successful programming is avoiding arbitrary variations so that your brain can be free to focus on the variations that are really needed. For more on this, see "Software's Primary Technical Imperative: Managing Complexity" in Section 5.2.

What if you had a great design for a painting, but one part was classical, one impressionist, and one cubist? It wouldn't have conceptual integrity no matter how closely you followed its grand design. It would look like a collage. A program needs low-level integrity, too.

KEY POINT

Before construction begins, spell out the programming conventions you'll use. Coding-convention details are at such a level of precision that they're nearly impossible to retrofit into software after it's written. Details of such conventions are provided throughout the book.

4.3 Your Location on the Technology Wave

During my career I've seen the PC's star rise while the mainframe's star dipped toward the horizon. I've seen GUI programs replace character-based programs. And I've seen the Web ascend while Windows declines. I can only assume that by the time you read this some new technology will be in ascendance, and Web programming as I know it today (2004) will be on its way out. These technology cycles, or waves, imply different programming practices depending on where you find yourself on the wave.

In mature technology environments—the end of the wave, such as Web programming in the mid-2000s—we benefit from a rich software development infrastructure. Late-wave environments provide numerous programming language choices, comprehensive error checking for code written in those languages, powerful debugging tools, and automatic, reliable performance optimization. The compilers are nearly bug-free. The tools are well documented in vendor literature, in third-party books and articles, and in extensive Web resources. Tools are integrated, so you can do UI, database, reports, and business logic from within a single environment. If you do run into problems, you can readily find quirks of the tools described in FAQs. Many consultants and training classes are also available.

In early-wave environments—Web programming in the mid-1990s, for example—the situation is the opposite. Few programming language choices are available, and those languages tend to be buggy and poorly documented. Programmers spend significant amounts of time simply trying to figure out how the language works instead of writing new code. Programmers also spend countless hours working around bugs in the language products, underlying operating system, and other tools. Programming tools in early-wave environments tend to be primitive. Debuggers might not exist at all, and compiler optimizers are still only a gleam in some programmer's eye. Vendors revise their compiler version often, and it seems that each new version breaks significant parts of your code. Tools aren't integrated, and so you tend to work with different tools for UI, database, reports, and business logic. The tools tend not to be very compatible, and you can expend a significant amount of effort just to keep existing functionality working against the onslaught of compiler and library releases. If you run into trouble, reference literature exists on the Web in some form, but it isn't always reliable and, if the available literature is any guide, every time you encounter a problem it seems as though you're the first one to do so.

These comments might seem like a recommendation to avoid early-wave programming, but that isn't their intent. Some of the most innovative applications arise from early-wave programs, like Turbo Pascal, Lotus 123, Microsoft Word, and the Mosaic browser. The point is that how you spend your programming days will depend on where you are on the technology wave. If you're in the late part of the wave, you can plan to spend most of your day steadily writing new functionality. If you're in the early part of the wave, you can assume that you'll spend a sizeable portion of your time trying to figure out your programming language's undocumented features, debugging errors that turn out to be defects in the library code, revising code so that it will work with a new release of some vendor's library, and so on.

When you find yourself working in a primitive environment, realize that the programming practices described in this book can help you even more than they can in mature environments. As David Gries pointed out, your programming tools don't have to determine how you think about programming (1981). Gries makes a distinction between programming *in* a language vs. programming *into* a language. Programmers who program "in" a language limit their thoughts to constructs that the language directly supports. If the language tools are primitive, the programmer's thoughts will also be primitive.

Programmers who program "into" a language first decide what thoughts they want to express, and then they determine how to express those thoughts using the tools provided by their specific language.

Example of Programming *into* a Language

In the early days of Visual Basic, I was frustrated because I wanted to keep the business logic, the UI, and the database separate in the product I was developing, but there wasn't any built-in way to do that in the language. I knew that if I wasn't careful, over time some of my Visual Basic "forms" would end up containing business logic, some forms would contain database code, and some would contain neither—I would end up never being able to remember which code was located in which place. I had just completed a C++ project that had done a poor job of separating those issues, and I didn't want to experience déjà vu of those headaches in a different language.

Consequently, I adopted a design convention that the .frm file (the form file) was allowed only to retrieve data from the database and store data back into the database. It wasn't allowed to communicate that data directly to other parts of the program. Each form supported an IsFormCompleted() routine, which was used by the calling routine to determine whether the form that had been activated had saved its data. IsFormCompleted() was the only public routine that forms were allowed to have. Forms also weren't allowed to contain any business logic. All other code had to be contained in an associated .bas file, including validity checks for entries in the form.

Visual Basic did not encourage this kind of approach. It encouraged programmers to put as much code into the .frm file as possible, and it didn't make it easy for the .frm file to call back into an associated .bas file.

This convention was pretty simple, but as I got deeper into my project, I found that it helped me avoid numerous cases in which I would have been writing convoluted code without the convention. I would have been loading forms but keeping them hidden so that I could call the data-validity-checking routines inside them, or I would have been copying code from the forms into other locations and then maintaining parallel code in multiple places. The IsFormCompleted() convention also kept things simple. Because every form worked exactly the same way, I never had to second-guess the semantics of IsFormCompleted()—it meant the same thing every time it was used.

Visual Basic didn't support this convention directly, but my use of a simple programming convention—programming *into* the language—made up for the language's lack of structure at that time and helped keep the project intellectually manageable.

KEY POINT

Understanding the distinction between programming in a language and programming into one is critical to understanding this book. Most of the important programming principles depend not on specific languages but on the way you use them. If your language lacks constructs that you want to use or is prone to other kinds of problems, try to compensate for them. Invent your own coding conventions, standards, class libraries, and other augmentations.

4.4 Selection of Major Construction Practices

Part of preparing for construction is deciding which of the many available good practices you'll emphasize. Some projects use pair programming and test-first development, while others use solo development and formal inspections. Either combination of techniques can work well, depending on specific circumstances of the project.

The following checklist summarizes the specific practices you should consciously decide to include or exclude during construction. Details of these practices are contained throughout the book.

cc2e.com/0496

> ## Checklist: Major Construction Practices
> ### Coding
> ❑ Have you defined how much design will be done up front and how much will be done at the keyboard, while the code is being written?
>
> ❑ Have you defined coding conventions for names, comments, and layout?
>
> ❑ Have you defined specific coding practices that are implied by the architecture, such as how error conditions will be handled, how security will be addressed, what conventions will be used for class interfaces, what standards will apply to reused code, how much to consider performance while coding, and so on?
>
> ❑ Have you identified your location on the technology wave and adjusted your approach to match? If necessary, have you identified how you will program *into* the language rather than being limited by programming *in* it?
>
> ### Teamwork
> ❑ Have you defined an integration procedure—that is, have you defined the specific steps a programmer must go through before checking code into the master sources?
>
> ❑ Will programmers program in pairs, or individually, or some combination of the two?

Cross-Reference For more details on quality assurance, see Chapter 20, "The Software-Quality Landscape."

Quality Assurance

❑ Will programmers write test cases for their code before writing the code itself?

❑ Will programmers write unit tests for their code regardless of whether they write them first or last?

❑ Will programmers step through their code in the debugger before they check it in?

❑ Will programmers integration-test their code before they check it in?

❑ Will programmers review or inspect each other's code?

Cross-Reference For more details on tools, see Chapter 30, "Programming Tools."

Tools

❑ Have you selected a revision control tool?

❑ Have you selected a language and language version or compiler version?

❑ Have you selected a framework such as J2EE or Microsoft .NET or explicitly decided not to use a framework?

❑ Have you decided whether to allow use of nonstandard language features?

❑ Have you identified and acquired other tools you'll be using—editor, refactoring tool, debugger, test framework, syntax checker, and so on?

Key Points

■ Every programming language has strengths and weaknesses. Be aware of the specific strengths and weaknesses of the language you're using.

■ Establish programming conventions before you begin programming. It's nearly impossible to change code to match them later.

■ More construction practices exist than you can use on any single project. Consciously choose the practices that are best suited to your project.

■ Ask yourself whether the programming practices you're using are a response to the programming language you're using or controlled by it. Remember to program *into* the language, rather than programming *in* it.

■ Your position on the technology wave determines what approaches will be effective—or even possible. Identify where you are on the technology wave, and adjust your plans and expectations accordingly.

Part II
Creating High-Quality Code

Chapter 5
Design in Construction

cc2e.com/0578

Contents

- 5.1 Design Challenges: page 74
- 5.2 Key Design Concepts: page 77
- 5.3 Design Building Blocks: Heuristics: page 87
- 5.4 Design Practices: page 110
- 5.5 Comments on Popular Methodologies: page 118

Related Topics

- Software architecture: Section 3.5
- Working classes: Chapter 6
- Characteristics of high-quality routines: Chapter 7
- Defensive programming: Chapter 8
- Refactoring: Chapter 24
- How program size affects construction: Chapter 27

Some people might argue that design isn't really a construction activity, but on small projects, many activities are thought of as construction, often including design. On some larger projects, a formal architecture might address only the system-level issues and much design work might intentionally be left for construction. On other large projects, the design might be intended to be detailed enough for coding to be fairly mechanical, but design is rarely that complete—the programmer usually designs part of the program, officially or otherwise.

Cross-Reference For details on the different levels of formality required on large and small projects, see Chapter 27, "How Program Size Affects Construction."

On small, informal projects, a lot of design is done while the programmer sits at the keyboard. "Design" might be just writing a class interface in pseudocode before writing the details. It might be drawing diagrams of a few class relationships before coding them. It might be asking another programmer which design pattern seems like a better choice. Regardless of how it's done, small projects benefit from careful design just as larger projects do, and recognizing design as an explicit activity maximizes the benefit you will receive from it.

Design is a huge topic, so only a few aspects of it are considered in this chapter. A large part of good class or routine design is determined by the system architecture, so be sure that the architecture prerequisite discussed in Section 3.5 has been satisfied. Even more design work is done at the level of individual classes and routines, described in Chapter 6, "Working Classes," and Chapter 7, "High-Quality Routines."

If you're already familiar with software design topics, you might want to just hit the highlights in the sections about design challenges in Section 5.1 and key heuristics in Section 5.3.

5.1 Design Challenges

Cross-Reference The difference between heuristic and deterministic processes is described in Chapter 2, "Metaphors for a Richer Understanding of Software Development."

The phrase "software design" means the conception, invention, or contrivance of a scheme for turning a specification for computer software into operational software. Design is the activity that links requirements to coding and debugging. A good top-level design provides a structure that can safely contain multiple lower-level designs. Good design is useful on small projects and indispensable on large projects.

Design is also marked by numerous challenges, which are outlined in this section.

Design Is a Wicked Problem

The picture of the software designer deriving his design in a rational, error-free way from a statement of requirements is quite unrealistic. No system has ever been developed in that way, and probably none ever will. Even the small program developments shown in textbooks and papers are unreal. They have been revised and polished until the author has shown us what he wishes he had done, not what actually did happen.
—*David Parnas and Paul Clements*

Horst Rittel and Melvin Webber defined a "wicked" problem as one that could be clearly defined only by solving it, or by solving part of it (1973). This paradox implies, essentially, that you have to "solve" the problem once in order to clearly define it and then solve it again to create a solution that works. This process has been motherhood and apple pie in software development for decades (Peters and Tripp 1976).

In my part of the world, a dramatic example of such a wicked problem was the design of the original Tacoma Narrows bridge. At the time the bridge was built, the main consideration in designing a bridge was that it be strong enough to support its planned load. In the case of the Tacoma Narrows bridge, wind created an unexpected, side-to-side harmonic ripple. One blustery day in 1940, the ripple grew uncontrollably until the bridge collapsed, as shown in Figure 5-1.

This is a good example of a wicked problem because, until the bridge collapsed, its engineers didn't know that aerodynamics needed to be considered to such an extent. Only by building the bridge (solving the problem) could they learn about the additional consideration in the problem that allowed them to build another bridge that still stands.

Figure 5-1 The Tacoma Narrows bridge—an example of a wicked problem.

One of the main differences between programs you develop in school and those you develop as a professional is that the design problems solved by school programs are rarely, if ever, wicked. Programming assignments in school are devised to move you in a beeline from beginning to end. You'd probably want to tar and feather a teacher who gave you a programming assignment, then changed the assignment as soon as you finished the design, and then changed it again just as you were about to turn in the completed program. But that very process is an everyday reality in professional programming.

Design Is a Sloppy Process (Even If it Produces a Tidy Result)

The finished software design should look well organized and clean, but the process used to develop the design isn't nearly as tidy as the end result.

Further Reading For a fuller exploration of this viewpoint, see "A Rational Design Process: How and Why to Fake It" (Parnas and Clements 1986).

Design is sloppy because you take many false steps and go down many blind alleys—you make a lot of mistakes. Indeed, making mistakes is the point of design—it's cheaper to make mistakes and correct designs than it would be to make the same mistakes, recognize them after coding, and have to correct full-blown code. Design is sloppy because a good solution is often only subtly different from a poor one.

Cross-Reference For a better answer to this question, see "How Much Design is Enough?" in Section 5.4 later in this chapter. Design is also sloppy because it's hard to know when your design is "good enough." How much detail is enough? How much design should be done with a formal design notation, and how much should be left to be done at the keyboard? When are you done? Since design is open-ended, the most common answer to that question is "When you're out of time."

Design Is About Tradeoffs and Priorities

In an ideal world, every system could run instantly, consume zero storage space, use zero network bandwidth, never contain any errors, and cost nothing to build. In the real world, a key part of the designer's job is to weigh competing design characteristics and strike a balance among those characteristics. If a fast response rate is more important than minimizing development time, a designer will choose one design. If minimizing development time is more important, a good designer will craft a different design.

Design Involves Restrictions

The point of design is partly to create possibilities and partly to *restrict possibilities*. If people had infinite time, resources, and space to build physical structures, you would see incredible sprawling buildings with one room for each shoe and hundreds of rooms. This is how software can turn out without deliberately imposed restrictions. The constraints of limited resources for constructing buildings force simplifications of the solution that ultimately improve the solution. The goal in software design is the same.

Design Is Nondeterministic

If you send three people away to design the same program, they can easily return with three vastly different designs, each of which could be perfectly acceptable. There might be more than one way to skin a cat, but there are usually dozens of ways to design a computer program.

Design Is a Heuristic Process

KEY POINT

Because design is nondeterministic, design techniques tend to be heuristics—"rules of thumb" or "things to try that sometimes work"—rather than repeatable processes that are guaranteed to produce predictable results. Design involves trial and error. A design tool or technique that worked well on one job or on one aspect of a job might not work as well on the next project. No tool is right for everything.

Design Is Emergent

cc2e.com/0539

A tidy way of summarizing these attributes of design is to say that design is "emergent." Designs don't spring fully formed directly from someone's brain. They evolve and improve through design reviews, informal discussions, experience writing the code itself, and experience revising the code.

Further Reading Software isn't the only kind of structure that changes over time. Physical structures evolve, too—see *How Buildings Learn* (Brand 1995).

Virtually all systems undergo some degree of design changes during their initial development, and then they typically change to a greater extent as they're extended into later versions. The degree to which change is beneficial or acceptable depends on the nature of the software being built.

5.2 Key Design Concepts

Good design depends on understanding a handful of key concepts. This section discusses the role of complexity, desirable characteristics of designs, and levels of design.

Software's Primary Technical Imperative: Managing Complexity

Cross-Reference For discussion of the way complexity affects programming issues other than design, see Section 34.1, "Conquer Complexity."

To understand the importance of managing complexity, it's useful to refer to Fred Brooks's landmark paper, "No Silver Bullets: Essence and Accidents of Software Engineering" (1987).

Accidental and Essential Difficulties

Brooks argues that software development is made difficult because of two different classes of problems—the *essential* and the *accidental*. In referring to these two terms, Brooks draws on a philosophical tradition going back to Aristotle. In philosophy, the essential properties are the properties that a thing must have in order to be that thing. A car must have an engine, wheels, and doors to be a car. If it doesn't have any of those essential properties, it isn't really a car.

Accidental properties are the properties a thing just happens to have, properties that don't really bear on whether the thing is what it is. A car could have a V8, a turbocharged 4-cylinder, or some other kind of engine and be a car regardless of that detail. A car could have two doors or four; it could have skinny wheels or mag wheels. All those details are accidental properties. You could also think of accidental properties as *incidental*, *discretionary*, *optional*, and *happenstance*.

Cross-Reference Accidental difficulties are more prominent in early-wave development than in late-wave development. For details, see Section 4.3, "Your Location on the Technology Wave."

Brooks observes that the major accidental difficulties in software were addressed long ago. For example, accidental difficulties related to clumsy language syntaxes were largely eliminated in the evolution from assembly language to third-generation languages and have declined in significance incrementally since then. Accidental difficulties related to noninteractive computers were resolved when time-share operating systems replaced batch-mode systems. Integrated programming environments further eliminated inefficiencies in programming work arising from tools that worked poorly together.

Brooks argues that progress on software's remaining *essential* difficulties is bound to be slower. The reason is that, at its essence, software development consists of working out all the details of a highly intricate, interlocking set of concepts. The essential difficulties arise from the necessity of interfacing with the complex, disorderly real world; accurately and completely identifying the dependencies and exception cases; designing solutions that can't be just approximately correct but that must be exactly correct; and so on. Even if we could invent a programming language that used the same terminology as the real-world problem we're trying to solve, programming would still be difficult because of the challenge in determining precisely how the real world works. As software addresses ever-larger real-world problems, the interactions among the real-world entities become increasingly intricate, and that in turn increases the essential difficulty of the software solutions.

The root of all these essential difficulties is complexity—both accidental and essential.

Importance of Managing Complexity

There are two ways of constructing a software design: one way is to make it so simple that there are *obviously* no deficiencies, and the other is to make it so complicated that there are no *obvious* deficiencies.
—*C. A. R. Hoare*

When software-project surveys report causes of project failure, they rarely identify technical reasons as the primary causes of project failure. Projects fail most often because of poor requirements, poor planning, or poor management. But when projects do fail for reasons that are primarily technical, the reason is often uncontrolled complexity. The software is allowed to grow so complex that no one really knows what it does. When a project reaches the point at which no one completely understands the impact that code changes in one area will have on other areas, progress grinds to a halt.

KEY POINT

Managing complexity is the most important technical topic in software development. In my view, it's so important that Software's Primary Technical Imperative has to be *managing complexity*.

Complexity is not a new feature of software development. Computing pioneer Edsger Dijkstra pointed out that computing is the only profession in which a single mind is obliged to span the distance from a bit to a few hundred megabytes, a ratio of 1 to 10^9, or nine orders of magnitude (Dijkstra 1989). This gigantic ratio is staggering. Dijkstra put it this way: "Compared to that number of semantic levels, the average mathematical theory is almost flat. By evoking the need for deep conceptual hierarchies, the automatic computer confronts us with a radically new intellectual challenge that has no precedent in our history." Of course software has become even more complex since 1989, and Dijkstra's ratio of 1 to 10^9 could easily be more like 1 to 10^{15} today.

One symptom that you have bogged down in complexity overload is when you find yourself doggedly applying a method that is clearly irrelevant, at least to any outside observer. It is like the mechanically inept person whose car breaks down—so he puts water in the battery and empties the ashtrays.
—*P. J. Plauger*

Dijkstra pointed out that no one's skull is really big enough to contain a modern computer program (Dijkstra 1972), which means that we as software developers shouldn't try to cram whole programs into our skulls at once; we should try to organize our programs in such a way that we can safely focus on one part of it at a time. The goal is to minimize the amount of a program you have to think about at any one time. You might think of this as mental juggling—the more mental balls the program requires you to keep in the air at once, the more likely you'll drop one of the balls, leading to a design or coding error.

At the software-architecture level, the complexity of a problem is reduced by dividing the system into subsystems. Humans have an easier time comprehending several simple pieces of information than one complicated piece. The goal of all software-design techniques is to break a complicated problem into simple pieces. The more independent the subsystems are, the more you make it safe to focus on one bit of complexity at a time. Carefully defined objects separate concerns so that you can focus on one thing at a time. Packages provide the same benefit at a higher level of aggregation.

Keeping routines short helps reduce your mental workload. Writing programs in terms of the problem domain, rather than in terms of low-level implementation details, and working at the highest level of abstraction reduce the load on your brain.

The bottom line is that programmers who compensate for inherent human limitations write code that's easier for themselves and others to understand and that has fewer errors.

How to Attack Complexity

Overly costly, ineffective designs arise from three sources:

- A complex solution to a simple problem

- A simple, incorrect solution to a complex problem

- An inappropriate, complex solution to a complex problem

As Dijkstra pointed out, modern software is inherently complex, and no matter how hard you try, you'll eventually bump into some level of complexity that's inherent in the real-world problem itself. This suggests a two-prong approach to managing complexity:

KEY POINT

- Minimize the amount of essential complexity that anyone's brain has to deal with at any one time.

- Keep accidental complexity from needlessly proliferating.

Once you understand that all other technical goals in software are secondary to managing complexity, many design considerations become straightforward.

Desirable Characteristics of a Design

When I am working on a problem I never think about beauty. I think only how to solve the problem. But when I have finished, if the solution is not beautiful, I know it is wrong.
—*R. Buckminster Fuller*

A high-quality design has several general characteristics. If you could achieve all these goals, your design would be very good indeed. Some goals contradict other goals, but that's the challenge of design—creating a good set of tradeoffs from competing objectives. Some characteristics of design quality are also characteristics of a good program: reliability, performance, and so on. Others are internal characteristics of the design.

Cross-Reference These characteristics are related to general software-quality attributes. For details on general attributes, see Section 20.1, "Characteristics of Software Quality."

Here's a list of internal design characteristics:

Minimal complexity　The primary goal of design should be to minimize complexity for all the reasons just described. Avoid making "clever" designs. Clever designs are usually hard to understand. Instead make "simple" and "easy-to-understand" designs. If your design doesn't let you safely ignore most other parts of the program when you're immersed in one specific part, the design isn't doing its job.

Ease of maintenance　Ease of maintenance means designing for the maintenance programmer. Continually imagine the questions a maintenance programmer would ask about the code you're writing. Think of the maintenance programmer as your audience, and then design the system to be self-explanatory.

Loose coupling　Loose coupling means designing so that you hold connections among different parts of a program to a minimum. Use the principles of good abstractions in class interfaces, encapsulation, and information hiding to design classes with as few interconnections as possible. Minimal connectedness minimizes work during integration, testing, and maintenance.

Extensibility　Extensibility means that you can enhance a system without causing violence to the underlying structure. You can change a piece of a system without affecting other pieces. The most likely changes cause the system the least trauma.

Reusability　Reusability means designing the system so that you can reuse pieces of it in other systems.

High fan-in　High fan-in refers to having a high number of classes that use a given class. High fan-in implies that a system has been designed to make good use of utility classes at the lower levels in the system.

Low-to-medium fan-out   Low-to-medium fan-out means having a given class use a low-to-medium number of other classes. High fan-out (more than about seven) indicates that a class uses a large number of other classes and may therefore be overly complex. Researchers have found that the principle of low fan-out is beneficial whether you're considering the number of routines called from within a routine or the number of classes used within a class (Card and Glass 1990; Basili, Briand, and Melo 1996).

Portability   Portability means designing the system so that you can easily move it to another environment.

Leanness   Leanness means designing the system so that it has no extra parts (Wirth 1995, McConnell 1997). Voltaire said that a book is finished not when nothing more can be added but when nothing more can be taken away. In software, this is especially true because extra code has to be developed, reviewed, tested, and considered when the other code is modified. Future versions of the software must remain backward-compatible with the extra code. The fatal question is "It's easy, so what will we hurt by putting it in?"

Stratification   Stratification means trying to keep the levels of decomposition stratified so that you can view the system at any single level and get a consistent view. Design the system so that you can view it at one level without dipping into other levels.

Cross-Reference For more on working with old systems, see Section 24.5, "Refactoring Strategies."

For example, if you're writing a modern system that has to use a lot of older, poorly designed code, write a layer of the new system that's responsible for interfacing with the old code. Design the layer so that it hides the poor quality of the old code, presenting a consistent set of services to the newer layers. Then have the rest of the system use those classes rather than the old code. The beneficial effects of stratified design in such a case are (1) it compartmentalizes the messiness of the bad code and (2) if you're ever allowed to jettison the old code or refactor it, you won't need to modify any new code except the interface layer.

Cross-Reference An especially valuable kind of standardization is the use of design patterns, which are discussed in "Look for Common Design Patterns" in Section 5.3.

Standard techniques   The more a system relies on exotic pieces, the more intimidating it will be for someone trying to understand it the first time. Try to give the whole system a familiar feeling by using standardized, common approaches.

Levels of Design

Design is needed at several different levels of detail in a software system. Some design techniques apply at all levels, and some apply at only one or two. Figure 5-2 illustrates the levels.

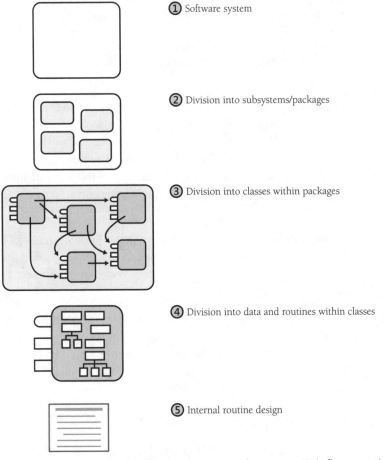

Figure 5-2   The levels of design in a program. The system (1) is first organized into subsystems (2). The subsystems are further divided into classes (3), and the classes are divided into routines and data (4). The inside of each routine is also designed (5).

Level 1: Software System

The first level is the entire system. Some programmers jump right from the system level into designing classes, but it's usually beneficial to think through higher level combinations of classes, such as subsystems or packages.

Level 2: Division into Subsystems or Packages

The main product of design at this level is the identification of all major subsystems. The subsystems can be big: database, user interface, business rules, command interpreter, report engine, and so on. The major design activity at this level is deciding how to partition the program into major subsystems and defining how each subsystem is allowed to use each other subsystem. Division at this level is typically needed on any project that takes longer than a few weeks. Within each subsystem, different methods of design might be used—choosing the approach that best fits each part of the system. In Figure 5-2, design at this level is marked with a 2.

Of particular importance at this level are the rules about how the various subsystems can communicate. If all subsystems can communicate with all other subsystems, you lose the benefit of separating them at all. Make each subsystem meaningful by restricting communications.

Suppose for example that you define a system with six subsystems, as shown in Figure 5-3. When there are no rules, the second law of thermodynamics will come into play and the entropy of the system will increase. One way in which entropy increases is that, without any restrictions on communications among subsystems, communication will occur in an unrestricted way, as in Figure 5-4.

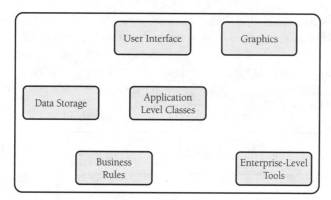

Figure 5-3   An example of a system with six subsystems.

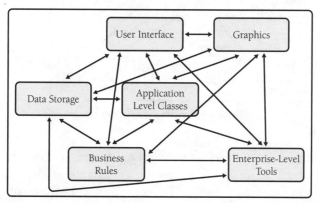

Figure 5-4   An example of what happens with no restrictions on intersubsystem communications.

As you can see, every subsystem ends up communicating directly with every other subsystem, which raises some important questions:

- How many different parts of the system does a developer need to understand at least a little bit to change something in the graphics subsystem?
- What happens when you try to use the business rules in another system?
- What happens when you want to put a new user interface on the system, perhaps a command-line UI for test purposes?
- What happens when you want to put data storage on a remote machine?

You might think of the lines between subsystems as being hoses with water running through them. If you want to reach in and pull out a subsystem, that subsystem is going to have some hoses attached to it. The more hoses you have to disconnect and reconnect, the more wet you're going to get. You want to architect your system so that if you pull out a subsystem to use elsewhere, you won't have many hoses to reconnect and those hoses will reconnect easily.

With forethought, all of these issues can be addressed with little extra work. Allow communication between subsystems only on a "need to know" basis—and it had better be a *good* reason. If in doubt, it's easier to restrict communication early and relax it later than it is to relax it early and then try to tighten it up after you've coded several hundred intersubsystem calls. Figure 5-5 shows how a few communication guidelines could change the system depicted in Figure 5-4.

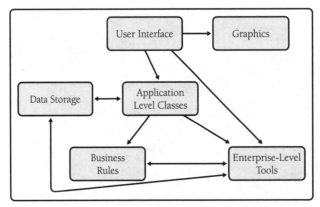

Figure 5-5   With a few communication rules, you can simplify subsystem interactions significantly.

To keep the connections easy to understand and maintain, err on the side of simple intersubsystem relations. The simplest relationship is to have one subsystem call routines in another. A more involved relationship is to have one subsystem contain classes from another. The most involved relationship is to have classes in one subsystem inherit from classes in another.

A good general rule is that a system-level diagram like Figure 5-5 should be an acyclic graph. In other words, a program shouldn't contain any circular relationships in which Class A uses Class B, Class B uses Class C, and Class C uses Class A.

On large programs and families of programs, design at the subsystem level makes a difference. If you believe that your program is small enough to skip subsystem-level design, at least make the decision to skip that level of design a conscious one.

Common Subsystems   Some kinds of subsystems appear again and again in different systems. Here are some of the usual suspects.

Cross-Reference For more on simplifying business logic by expressing it in tables, see Chapter 18, "Table-Driven Methods."

Business rules   Business rules are the laws, regulations, policies, and procedures that you encode into a computer system. If you're writing a payroll system, you might encode rules from the IRS about the number of allowable withholdings and the estimated tax rate. Additional rules for a payroll system might come from a union contract specifying overtime rates, vacation and holiday pay, and so on. If you're writing a program to quote automobile insurance rates, rules might come from government regulations on required liability coverages, actuarial rate tables, or underwriting restrictions

User interface   Create a subsystem to isolate user-interface components so that the user interface can evolve without damaging the rest of the program. In most cases, a user-interface subsystem uses several subordinate subsystems or classes for the GUI interface, command line interface, menu operations, window management, help system, and so forth.

Database access   You can hide the implementation details of accessing a database so that most of the program doesn't need to worry about the messy details of manipulating low-level structures and can deal with the data in terms of how it's used at the business-problem level. Subsystems that hide implementation details provide a valuable level of abstraction that reduces a program's complexity. They centralize database operations in one place and reduce the chance of errors in working with the data. They make it easy to change the database design structure without changing most of the program.

System dependencies   Package operating-system dependencies into a subsystem for the same reason you package hardware dependencies. If you're developing a program for Microsoft Windows, for example, why limit yourself to the Windows environment? Isolate the Windows calls in a Windows-interface subsystem. If you later want to move your program to Mac OS or Linux, all you'll have to change is the interface subsystem. An interface subsystem can be too extensive for you to implement on your own, but such subsystems are readily available in any of several commercial code libraries.

Level 3: Division into Classes

Further Reading For a good discussion of database design, see *Agile Database Techniques* (Ambler 2003).

Design at this level includes identifying all classes in the system. For example, a database-interface subsystem might be further partitioned into data access classes and persistence framework classes as well as database metadata. Figure 5-2, Level 3, shows how one of Level 2's subsystems might be divided into classes, and it implies that the other three subsystems shown at Level 2 are also decomposed into classes.

Details of the ways in which each class interacts with the rest of the system are also specified as the classes are specified. In particular, the class's interface is defined. Overall, the major design activity at this level is making sure that all the subsystems have been decomposed to a level of detail fine enough that you can implement their parts as individual classes.

Cross-Reference For details on characteristics of high-quality classes, see Chapter 6, "Working Classes."

The division of subsystems into classes is typically needed on any project that takes longer than a few days. If the project is large, the division is clearly distinct from the program partitioning of Level 2. If the project is very small, you might move directly from the whole-system view of Level 1 to the classes view of Level 3.

Classes vs. Objects   A key concept in object-oriented design is the differentiation between objects and classes. An object is any specific entity that exists in your program at run time. A class is the static thing you look at in the program listing. An object is the dynamic thing with specific values and attributes you see when you run the program. For example, you could declare a class *Person* that had attributes of name, age, gender, and so on. At run time you would have the objects *nancy*, *hank*, *diane*, *tony*, and so on—that is, specific instances of the class. If you're familiar with database terms, it's the same as the distinction between "schema" and "instance." You could think of the class as the cookie cutter and the object as the cookie. This book uses the terms informally and generally refers to classes and objects more or less interchangeably.

Level 4: Division into Routines

Design at this level includes dividing each class into routines. The class interface defined at Level 3 will define some of the routines. Design at Level 4 will detail the class's private routines. When you examine the details of the routines inside a class, you can see that many routines are simple boxes but a few are composed of hierarchically organized routines, which require still more design.

The act of fully defining the class's routines often results in a better understanding of the class's interface, and that causes corresponding changes to the interface—that is, changes back at Level 3.

This level of decomposition and design is often left up to the individual programmer, and it's needed on any project that takes more than a few hours. It doesn't need to be done formally, but it at least needs to be done mentally.

Level 5: Internal Routine Design

Cross-Reference For details on creating high-quality routines, see Chapter 7, "High-Quality Routines," and Chapter 8, "Defensive Programming."

Design at the routine level consists of laying out the detailed functionality of the individual routines. Internal routine design is typically left to the individual programmer working on an individual routine. The design consists of activities such as writing pseudocode, looking up algorithms in reference books, deciding how to organize the paragraphs of code in a routine, and writing programming-language code. This level of design is always done, though sometimes it's done unconsciously and poorly rather than consciously and well. In Figure 5-2, design at this level is marked with a 5.

5.3 Design Building Blocks: Heuristics

Software developers tend to like our answers cut and dried: "Do A, B, and C, and X, Y, Z will follow every time." We take pride in learning arcane sets of steps that produce desired effects, and we become annoyed when instructions don't work as advertised. This desire for deterministic behavior is highly appropriate to detailed computer programming, where that kind of strict attention to detail makes or breaks a program. But software design is a much different story.

Because design is nondeterministic, skillful application of an effective set of heuristics is the core activity in good software design. The following subsections describe a number of heuristics—ways to think about a design that sometime produce good design insights. You might think of heuristics as the guides for the trials in "trial and error." You undoubtedly have run across some of these before. Consequently, the following subsections describe each of the heuristics in terms of Software's Primary Technical Imperative: managing complexity.

Find Real-World Objects

Ask not first what the system does; ask WHAT it does it to!
—Bertrand Meyer

The first and most popular approach to identifying design alternatives is the "by the book" object-oriented approach, which focuses on identifying real-world and synthetic objects.

The steps in designing with objects are

Cross-Reference For more details on designing using classes, see Chapter 6, "Working Classes."

- Identify the objects and their attributes (methods and data).

- Determine what can be done to each object.

- Determine what each object is allowed to do to other objects.

- Determine the parts of each object that will be visible to other objects—which parts will be public and which will be private.

- Define each object's public interface.

These steps aren't necessarily performed in order, and they're often repeated. Iteration is important. Each of these steps is summarized below.

Identify the objects and their attributes   Computer programs are usually based on real-world entities. For example, you could base a time-billing system on real-world employees, clients, timecards, and bills. Figure 5-6 shows an object-oriented view of such a billing system.

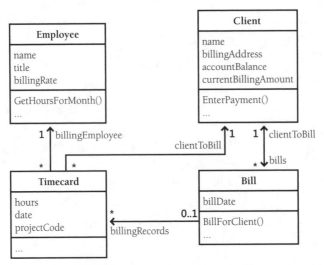

Figure 5-6   This billing system is composed of four major objects. The objects have been simplified for this example.

Identifying the objects' attributes is no more complicated than identifying the objects themselves. Each object has characteristics that are relevant to the computer program. For example, in the time-billing system, an employee object has a name, a title, and a billing rate. A client object has a name, a billing address, and an account balance. A bill object has a billing amount, a client name, a billing date, and so on.

Objects in a graphical user interface system would include windows, dialog boxes, buttons, fonts, and drawing tools. Further examination of the problem domain might produce better choices for software objects than a one-to-one mapping to real-world objects, but the real-world objects are a good place to start.

Determine what can be done to each object   A variety of operations can be performed on each object. In the billing system shown in Figure 5-6, an employee object could have a change in title or billing rate, a client object could have its name or billing address changed, and so on.

Determine what each object is allowed to do to other objects   This step is just what it sounds like. The two generic things objects can do to each other are containment and inheritance. Which objects can *contain* which other objects? Which objects can *inherit* *from* which other objects? In Figure 5-6, a timecard object can contain an employee object and a client object, and a bill can contain one or more timecards. In addition, a bill can indicate that a client has been billed, and a client can enter payments against a bill. A more complicated system would include additional interactions.

Cross-Reference For details on classes and information hiding, see "Hide Secrets (Information Hiding)" in Section 5.3.

Determine the parts of each object that will be visible to other objects   One of the key design decisions is identifying the parts of an object that should be made public and those that should be kept private. This decision has to be made for both data and methods.

Define each object's interfaces   Define the formal, syntactic, programming-language-level interfaces to each object. The data and methods the object exposes to every other object is called the object's "public interface." The parts of the object that it exposes to derived objects via inheritance is called the object's "protected interface." Think about both kinds of interfaces.

When you finish going through the steps to achieve a top-level object-oriented system organization, you'll iterate in two ways. You'll iterate on the top-level system organization to get a better organization of classes. You'll also iterate on each of the classes you've defined, driving the design of each class to a more detailed level.

Form Consistent Abstractions

Abstraction is the ability to engage with a concept while safely ignoring some of its details—handling different details at different levels. Any time you work with an aggregate, you're working with an abstraction. If you refer to an object as a "house" rather than a combination of glass, wood, and nails, you're making an abstraction. If you refer to a collection of houses as a "town," you're making another abstraction.

Base classes are abstractions that allow you to focus on common attributes of a set of derived classes and ignore the details of the specific classes while you're working on the base class. A good class interface is an abstraction that allows you to focus on the interface without needing to worry about the internal workings of the class. The interface to a well-designed routine provides the same benefit at a lower level of detail, and the interface to a well-designed package or subsystem provides that benefit at a higher level of detail.

From a complexity point of view, the principal benefit of abstraction is that it allows you to ignore irrelevant details. Most real-world objects are already abstractions of some kind. As just mentioned, a house is an abstraction of windows, doors, siding, wiring, plumbing, insulation, and a particular way of organizing them. A door is in turn an abstraction of a particular arrangement of a rectangular piece of material with hinges and a doorknob. And the doorknob is an abstraction of a particular formation of brass, nickel, iron, or steel.

People use abstraction continuously. If you had to deal with individual wood fibers, varnish molecules, and steel molecules every time you used your front door, you'd hardly make it in or out of your house each day. As Figure 5-7 suggests, abstraction is a big part of how we deal with complexity in the real world.

Figure 5-7 Abstraction allows you to take a simpler view of a complex concept.

Cross-Reference For more details on abstraction in class design, see "Good Abstraction" in Section 6.2.

Software developers sometimes build systems at the wood-fiber, varnish-molecule, and steel-molecule level. This makes the systems overly complex and intellectually hard to manage. When programmers fail to provide larger programming abstractions, the system itself sometimes fails to make it through the front door.

Good programmers create abstractions at the routine-interface level, class-interface level, and package-interface level—in other words, the doorknob level, door level, and house level—and that supports faster and safer programming.

Encapsulate Implementation Details

Encapsulation picks up where abstraction leaves off. Abstraction says, "You're allowed to look at an object at a high level of detail." Encapsulation says, "Furthermore, you aren't allowed to look at an object at any other level of detail."

Continuing with the housing-materials analogy: encapsulation is a way of saying that you can look at the outside of the house but you can't get close enough to make out the door's details. You are allowed to know that there's a door, and you're allowed to know whether the door is open or closed, but you're not allowed to know whether the door is made of wood, fiberglass, steel, or some other material, and you're certainly not allowed to look at each individual wood fiber.

As Figure 5-8 suggests, encapsulation helps to manage complexity by forbidding you to look at the complexity. The section titled "Good Encapsulation" in Section 6.2 provides more background on encapsulation as it applies to class design.

Figure 5-8   Encapsulation says that, not only are you allowed to take a simpler view of a complex concept, you are *not* allowed to look at any of the details of the complex concept. What you see is what you get—it's all you get!

Inherit—When Inheritance Simplifies the Design

In designing a software system, you'll often find objects that are much like other objects, except for a few differences. In an accounting system, for instance, you might have both full-time and part-time employees. Most of the data associated with both kinds of employees is the same, but some is different. In object-oriented programming, you can define a general type of employee and then define full-time employees as general employees, except for a few differences, and part-time employees also as general employees, except for a few differences. When an operation on an employee doesn't depend on the type of employee, the operation is handled as if the employee were just a general employee. When the operation depends on whether the employee is full-time or part-time, the operation is handled differently.

Defining similarities and differences among such objects is called "inheritance" because the specific part-time and full-time employees inherit characteristics from the general-employee type.

The benefit of inheritance is that it works synergistically with the notion of abstraction. Abstraction deals with objects at different levels of detail. Recall the door that was a collection of certain kinds of molecules at one level, a collection of wood fibers at the next, and something that keeps burglars out of your house at the next level. Wood has certain properties—for example, you can cut it with a saw or glue it with wood glue—and two-by-fours or cedar shingles have the general properties of wood as well as some specific properties of their own.

Inheritance simplifies programming because you write a general routine to handle anything that depends on a door's general properties and then write specific routines to handle specific operations on specific kinds of doors. Some operations, such as

Open() or *Close()*, might apply regardless of whether the door is a solid door, interior door, exterior door, screen door, French door, or sliding glass door. The ability of a language to support operations like *Open()* or *Close()* without knowing until run time what kind of door you're dealing with is called "polymorphism." Object-oriented languages such as C++, Java, and later versions of Microsoft Visual Basic support inheritance and polymorphism.

Inheritance is one of object-oriented programming's most powerful tools. It can provide great benefits when used well, and it can do great damage when used naively. For details, see "Inheritance ("is a" Relationships)" in Section 6.3.

Hide Secrets (Information Hiding)

Information hiding is part of the foundation of both structured design and object-oriented design. In structured design, the notion of "black boxes" comes from information hiding. In object-oriented design, it gives rise to the concepts of encapsulation and modularity and it is associated with the concept of abstraction. Information hiding is one of the seminal ideas in software development, and so this subsection explores it in depth.

Information hiding first came to public attention in a paper published by David Parnas in 1972 called "On the Criteria to Be Used in Decomposing Systems Into Modules." Information hiding is characterized by the idea of "secrets," design and implementation decisions that a software developer hides in one place from the rest of a program.

In the 20th Anniversary edition of *The Mythical Man Month*, Fred Brooks concluded that his criticism of information hiding was one of the few ways in which the first edition of his book was wrong. "Parnas was right, and I was wrong about information hiding," he proclaimed (Brooks 1995). Barry Boehm reported that information hiding was a powerful technique for eliminating rework, and he pointed out that it was particularly effective in incremental, high-change environments (Boehm 1987).

Information hiding is a particularly powerful heuristic for Software's Primary Technical Imperative because, beginning with its name and throughout its details, it emphasizes *hiding complexity*.

Secrets and the Right to Privacy

In information hiding, each class (or package or routine) is characterized by the design or construction decisions that it hides from all other classes. The secret might be an area that's likely to change, the format of a file, the way a data type is implemented, or an area that needs to be walled off from the rest of the program so that errors in that area cause as little damage as possible. The class's job is to keep this information hidden and to protect its own right to privacy. Minor changes to a system might affect several routines within a class, but they should not ripple beyond the class interface.

Strive for class interfaces that are complete and minimal.
—*Scott Meyers*

One key task in designing a class is deciding which features should be known outside the class and which should remain secret. A class might use 25 routines and expose only 5 of them, using the other 20 internally. A class might use several data types and expose no information about them. This aspect of class design is also known as "visibility" since it has to do with which features of the class are "visible" or "exposed" outside the class.

The interface to a class should reveal as little as possible about its inner workings. As shown in Figure 5-9, a class is a lot like an iceberg: seven-eighths is under water, and you can see only the one-eighth that's above the surface.

Figure 5-9   A good class interface is like the tip of an iceberg, leaving most of the class unexposed.

Designing the class interface is an iterative process just like any other aspect of design. If you don't get the interface right the first time, try a few more times until it stabilizes. If it doesn't stabilize, you need to try a different approach.

An Example of Information Hiding

Suppose you have a program in which each object is supposed to have a unique ID stored in a member variable called *id*. One design approach would be to use integers for the IDs and to store the highest ID assigned so far in a global variable called *g_maxId*. As each new object is allocated, perhaps in each object's constructor, you could simply use the *id = ++g_maxId* statement, which would guarantee a unique id, and it would add the absolute minimum of code in each place an object is created. What could go wrong with that?

A lot of things could go wrong. What if you want to reserve ranges of IDs for special purposes? What if you want to use nonsequential IDs to improve security? What if you want to be able to reuse the IDs of objects that have been destroyed? What if you want to add an assertion that fires when you allocate more IDs than the maximum number you've anticipated? If you allocated IDs by spreading $id = ++g\_maxId$ statements throughout your program, you would have to change code associated with every one of those statements. And, if your program is multithreaded, this approach won't be thread-safe.

The way that new IDs are created is a design decision that you should hide. If you use the phrase $++g\_maxId$ throughout your program, you expose the way a new ID is created, which is simply by incrementing g_maxId. If instead you put the $id = NewId()$ statement throughout your program, you hide the information about how new IDs are created. Inside the $NewId()$ routine you might still have just one line of code, $return$ ($++g\_maxId$) or its equivalent, but if you later decide to reserve certain ranges of IDs for special purposes or to reuse old IDs, you could make those changes within the $NewId()$ routine itself—without touching dozens or hundreds of $id = NewId()$ statements. No matter how complicated the revisions inside $NewId()$ might become, they wouldn't affect any other part of the program.

Now suppose you discover you need to change the type of the ID from an integer to a string. If you've spread variable declarations like $int\ id$ throughout your program, your use of the $NewId()$ routine won't help. You'll still have to go through your program and make dozens or hundreds of changes.

An additional secret to hide is the ID's type. By exposing the fact that IDs are integers, you encourage programmers to perform integer operations like >, <, = on them. In C++, you could use a simple $typedef$ to declare your IDs to be of $IdType$—a user-defined type that resolves to int—rather than directly declaring them to be of type int. Alternatively, in C++ and other languages you could create a simple $IdType$ class. Once again, hiding a design decision makes a huge difference in the amount of code affected by a change.

KEY POINT

Information hiding is useful at all levels of design, from the use of named constants instead of literals, to creation of data types, to class design, routine design, and subsystem design.

Two Categories of Secrets

Secrets in information hiding fall into two general camps:

- Hiding complexity so that your brain doesn't have to deal with it unless you're specifically concerned with it

- Hiding sources of change so that when change occurs, the effects are localized

Sources of complexity include complicated data types, file structures, boolean tests, involved algorithms, and so on. A comprehensive list of sources of change is described later in this chapter.

Barriers to Information Hiding

Further Reading Parts of this section are adapted from "Designing Software for Ease of Extension and Contraction" (Parnas 1979).

In a few instances, information hiding is truly impossible, but most of the barriers to information hiding are mental blocks built up from the habitual use of other techniques.

Excessive distribution of information   One common barrier to information hiding is an excessive distribution of information throughout a system. You might have hard-coded the literal *100* throughout a system. Using *100* as a literal decentralizes references to it. It's better to hide the information in one place, in a constant *MAX_EMPLOYEES* perhaps, whose value is changed in only one place.

Another example of excessive information distribution is interleaving interaction with human users throughout a system. If the mode of interaction changes—say, from a GUI interface to a command line interface—virtually all the code will have to be modified. It's better to concentrate user interaction in a single class, package, or subsystem you can change without affecting the whole system.

Cross-Reference For more on accessing global data through class interfaces, see "Using Access Routines Instead of Global Data" in Section 13.3.

Yet another example would be a global data element—perhaps an array of employee data with 1000 elements maximum that's accessed throughout a program. If the program uses the global data directly, information about the data item's implementation—such as the fact that it's an array and has a maximum of 1000 elements—will be spread throughout the program. If the program uses the data only through access routines, only the access routines will know the implementation details.

Circular dependencies   A more subtle barrier to information hiding is circular dependencies, as when a routine in class *A* calls a routine in class *B*, and a routine in class *B* calls a routine in class *A*.

Avoid such dependency loops. They make it hard to test a system because you can't test either class *A* or class *B* until at least part of the other is ready.

Class data mistaken for global data   If you're a conscientious programmer, one of the barriers to effective information hiding might be thinking of class data as global data and avoiding it because you want to avoid the problems associated with global data. While the road to programming hell is paved with global variables, class data presents far fewer risks.

Global data is generally subject to two problems: routines operate on global data without knowing that other routines are operating on it, and routines are aware that other routines are operating on the global data but they don't know exactly what they're doing to it. Class data isn't subject to either of these problems. Direct access to the data is restricted to a few routines organized into a single class. The routines are aware that other routines operate on the data, and they know exactly which other routines they are.

Of course, this whole discussion assumes that your system makes use of well-designed, small classes. If your program is designed to use huge classes that contain dozens of routines each, the distinction between class data and global data will begin to blur and class data will be subject to many of the same problems as global data.

Cross-Reference Code-level performance optimizations are discussed in Chapter 25, "Code-Tuning Strategies" and Chapter 26, "Code-Tuning Techniques."

Perceived performance penalties   A final barrier to information hiding can be an attempt to avoid performance penalties at both the architectural and the coding levels. You don't need to worry at either level. At the architectural level, the worry is unnecessary because architecting a system for information hiding doesn't conflict with architecting it for performance. If you keep both information hiding and performance in mind, you can achieve both objectives.

The more common worry is at the coding level. The concern is that accessing data items indirectly incurs run-time performance penalties for additional levels of object instantiations, routine calls, and so on. This concern is premature. Until you can measure the system's performance and pinpoint the bottlenecks, the best way to prepare for code-level performance work is to create a highly modular design. When you detect hot spots later, you can optimize individual classes and routines without affecting the rest of the system.

Value of Information Hiding

HARD DATA

Information hiding is one of the few theoretical techniques that has indisputably proven its value in practice, which has been true for a long time (Boehm 1987a). Large programs that use information hiding were found years ago to be easier to modify—by a factor of 4—than programs that don't (Korson and Vaishnavi 1986). Moreover, information hiding is part of the foundation of both structured design and object-oriented design.

Information hiding has unique heuristic power, a unique ability to inspire effective design solutions. Traditional object-oriented design provides the heuristic power of modeling the world in objects, but object thinking wouldn't help you avoid declaring the ID as an *int* instead of an *IdType*. The object-oriented designer would ask, "Should an ID be treated as an object?" Depending on the project's coding standards, a "Yes" answer might mean that the programmer has to write a constructor, destructor, copy operator, and assignment operator; comment it all; and place it under configuration control. Most programmers would decide, "No, it isn't worth creating a whole class just for an ID. I'll just use *ints*."

Note what just happened. A useful design alternative, that of simply hiding the ID's data type, was not even considered. If, instead, the designer had asked, "What about the ID should be hidden?" he might well have decided to hide its type behind a simple type declaration that substitutes *IdType* for *int*. The difference between object-oriented design and information hiding in this example is more subtle than a clash of explicit rules and regulations. Object-oriented design would approve of this design decision as much as information hiding would. Rather, the difference is one of heuristics—

thinking about information hiding inspires and promotes design decisions that thinking about objects does not.

Information hiding can also be useful in designing a class's public interface. The gap between theory and practice in class design is wide, and among many class designers the decision about what to put into a class's public interface amounts to deciding what interface would be the most convenient to use, which usually results in exposing as much of the class as possible. From what I've seen, some programmers would rather expose all of a class's private data than write 10 extra lines of code to keep the class's secrets intact.

Asking "What does this class need to hide?" cuts to the heart of the interface-design issue. If you can put a function or data into the class's public interface without compromising its secrets, do. Otherwise, don't.

Asking about what needs to be hidden supports good design decisions at all levels. It promotes the use of named constants instead of literals at the construction level. It helps in creating good routine and parameter names inside classes. It guides decisions about class and subsystem decompositions and interconnections at the system level.

KEY POINT

Get into the habit of asking "What should I hide?" You'll be surprised at how many difficult design issues dissolve before your eyes.

Identify Areas Likely to Change

Further Reading The approach described in this section is adapted from "Designing Software for Ease of Extension and Contraction" (Parnas 1979).

A study of great designers found that one attribute they had in common was their ability to anticipate change (Glass 1995). Accommodating changes is one of the most challenging aspects of good program design. The goal is to isolate unstable areas so that the effect of a change will be limited to one routine, class, or package. Here are the steps you should follow in preparing for such perturbations.

1. **Identify items that seem likely to change.** If the requirements have been done well, they include a list of potential changes and the likelihood of each change. In such a case, identifying the likely changes is easy. If the requirements don't cover potential changes, see the discussion that follows of areas that are likely to change on any project.

2. **Separate items that are likely to change.** Compartmentalize each volatile component identified in step 1 into its own class or into a class with other volatile components that are likely to change at the same time.

3. **Isolate items that seem likely to change.** Design the interclass interfaces to be insensitive to the potential changes. Design the interfaces so that changes are limited to the inside of the class and the outside remains unaffected. Any other class using the changed class should be unaware that the change has occurred. The class's interface should protect its secrets.

Here are a few areas that are likely to change:

Cross-Reference One of the most powerful techniques for anticipating change is to use table-driven methods. For details, see Chapter 18, "Table-Driven Methods."

Business rules   Business rules tend to be the source of frequent software changes. Congress changes the tax structure, a union renegotiates its contract, or an insurance company changes its rate tables. If you follow the principle of information hiding, logic based on these rules won't be strewn throughout your program. The logic will stay hidden in a single dark corner of the system until it needs to be changed.

Hardware dependencies   Examples of hardware dependencies include interfaces to screens, printers, keyboards, mice, disk drives, sound facilities, and communications devices. Isolate hardware dependencies in their own subsystem or class. Isolating such dependencies helps when you move the program to a new hardware environment. It also helps initially when you're developing a program for volatile hardware. You can write software that simulates interaction with specific hardware, have the hardware-interface subsystem use the simulator as long as the hardware is unstable or unavailable, and then unplug the hardware-interface subsystem from the simulator and plug the subsystem into the hardware when it's ready to use.

Input and output   At a slightly higher level of design than raw hardware interfaces, input/output is a volatile area. If your application creates its own data files, the file format will probably change as your application becomes more sophisticated. User-level input and output formats will also change—the positioning of fields on the page, the number of fields on each page, the sequence of fields, and so on. In general, it's a good idea to examine all external interfaces for possible changes.

Nonstandard language features   Most language implementations contain handy, nonstandard extensions. Using the extensions is a double-edged sword because they might not be available in a different environment, whether the different environment is different hardware, a different vendor's implementation of the language, or a new version of the language from the same vendor.

If you use nonstandard extensions to your programming language, hide those extensions in a class of their own so that you can replace them with your own code when you move to a different environment. Likewise, if you use library routines that aren't available in all environments, hide the actual library routines behind an interface that works just as well in another environment.

Difficult design and construction areas   It's a good idea to hide difficult design and construction areas because they might be done poorly and you might need to do them again. Compartmentalize them and minimize the impact their bad design or construction might have on the rest of the system.

Status variables   Status variables indicate the state of a program and tend to be changed more frequently than most other data. In a typical scenario, you might originally define an error-status variable as a boolean variable and decide later that it would be better implemented as an enumerated type with the values *ErrorType_None*, *ErrorType_Warning*, and *ErrorType_Fatal*.

You can add at least two levels of flexibility and readability to your use of status variables:

- Don't use a boolean variable as a status variable. Use an enumerated type instead. It's common to add a new state to a status variable, and adding a new type to an enumerated type requires a mere recompilation rather than a major revision of every line of code that checks the variable.

- Use access routines rather than checking the variable directly. By checking the access routine rather than the variable, you allow for the possibility of more sophisticated state detection. For example, if you wanted to check combinations of an error-state variable and a current-function-state variable, it would be easy to do if the test were hidden in a routine and hard to do if it were a complicated test hard-coded throughout the program.

Data-size constraints   When you declare an array of size *100,* you're exposing information to the world that the world doesn't need to see. Defend your right to privacy! Information hiding isn't always as complicated as a whole class. Sometimes it's as simple as using a named constant such as *MAX_EMPLOYEES* to hide a *100.*

Anticipating Different Degrees of Change

Cross-Reference This section's approach to anticipating change does not involve designing ahead or coding ahead. For a discussion of those practices, see "A program contains code that seems like it might be needed someday" in Section 24.2.

When thinking about potential changes to a system, design the system so that the effect or scope of the change is proportional to the chance that the change will occur. If a change is likely, make sure that the system can accommodate it easily. Only extremely unlikely changes should be allowed to have drastic consequences for more than one class in a system. Good designers also factor in the cost of anticipating change. If a change is not terribly likely but easy to plan for, you should think harder about anticipating it than if it isn't very likely and is difficult to plan for.

Further Reading This discussion draws on the approach described in "On the design and development of program families" (Parnas 1976).

A good technique for identifying areas likely to change is first to identify the minimal subset of the program that might be of use to the user. The subset makes up the core of the system and is unlikely to change. Next, define minimal increments to the system. They can be so small that they seem trivial. As you consider functional changes, be sure also to consider qualitative changes: making the program thread-safe, making it localizable, and so on. These areas of potential improvement constitute potential changes to the system; design these areas using the principles of information hiding. By identifying the core first, you can see which components are really add-ons and then extrapolate and hide improvements from there.

Keep Coupling Loose

Coupling describes how tightly a class or routine is related to other classes or routines. The goal is to create classes and routines with small, direct, visible, and flexible relations to other classes and routines, which is known as "loose coupling." The concept of coupling applies equally to classes and routines, so for the rest of this discussion I'll use the word "module" to refer to both classes and routines.

Good coupling between modules is loose enough that one module can easily be used by other modules. Model railroad cars are coupled by opposing hooks that latch when pushed together. Connecting two cars is easy—you just push the cars together. Imagine how much more difficult it would be if you had to screw things together, or connect a set of wires, or if you could connect only certain kinds of cars to certain other kinds of cars. The coupling of model railroad cars works because it's as simple as possible. In software, make the connections among modules as simple as possible.

Try to create modules that depend little on other modules. Make them detached, as business associates are, rather than attached, as Siamese twins are. A routine like $sin()$ is loosely coupled because everything it needs to know is passed in to it with one value representing an angle in degrees. A routine such as $InitVars(var 1, var2, var3, ..., varN)$ is more tightly coupled because, with all the variables it must pass, the calling module practically knows what is happening inside $InitVars()$. Two classes that depend on each other's use of the same global data are even more tightly coupled.

Coupling Criteria

Here are several criteria to use in evaluating coupling between modules:

Size   Size refers to the number of connections between modules. With coupling, small is beautiful because it's less work to connect other modules to a module that has a smaller interface. A routine that takes one parameter is more loosely coupled to modules that call it than a routine that takes six parameters. A class with four well-defined public methods is more loosely coupled to modules that use it than a class that exposes 37 public methods.

Visibility   Visibility refers to the prominence of the connection between two modules. Programming is not like being in the CIA; you don't get credit for being sneaky. It's more like advertising; you get lots of credit for making your connections as blatant as possible. Passing data in a parameter list is making an obvious connection and is therefore good. Modifying global data so that another module can use that data is a sneaky connection and is therefore bad. Documenting the global-data connection makes it more obvious and is slightly better.

Flexibility   Flexibility refers to how easily you can change the connections between modules. Ideally, you want something more like the USB connector on your computer than like bare wire and a soldering gun. Flexibility is partly a product of the other coupling characteristics, but it's a little different too. Suppose you have a routine that looks up the amount of vacation an employee receives each year, given a hiring date and a job classification. Name the routine *LookupVacationBenefit()*. Suppose in another module you have an *employee* object that contains the hiring date and the job classification, among other things, and that module passes the object to *LookupVacationBenefit()*.

From the point of view of the other criteria, the two modules would look loosely coupled. The *employee* connection between the two modules is visible, and there's only one connection. Now suppose that you need to use the *LookupVacationBenefit()* module from a third module that doesn't have an *employee* object but that does have a hiring date and a job classification. Suddenly *LookupVacationBenefit()* looks less friendly, unwilling to associate with the new module.

For the third module to use *LookupVacationBenefit()*, it has to know about the *Employee* class. It could dummy up an *employee* object with only two fields, but that would require internal knowledge of *LookupVacationBenefit()*, namely that those are the only fields it uses. Such a solution would be a kludge, and an ugly one. The second option would be to modify *LookupVacationBenefit()* so that it would take hiring date and job classification instead of *employee*. In either case, the original module turns out to be a lot less flexible than it seemed to be at first.

The happy ending to the story is that an unfriendly module can make friends if it's willing to be flexible—in this case, by changing to take hiring date and job classification specifically instead of *employee*.

In short, the more easily other modules can call a module, the more loosely coupled it is, and that's good because it's more flexible and maintainable. In creating a system structure, break up the program along the lines of minimal interconnectedness. If a program were a piece of wood, you would try to split it with the grain.

Kinds of Coupling

Here are the most common kinds of coupling you'll encounter.

Simple-data-parameter coupling   Two modules are simple-data-parameter coupled if all the data passed between them are of primitive data types and all the data is passed through parameter lists. This kind of coupling is normal and acceptable.

Simple-object coupling   A module is simple-object coupled to an object if it instantiates that object. This kind of coupling is fine.

Object-parameter coupling   Two modules are object-parameter coupled to each other if *Object1* requires *Object2* to pass it an *Object3*. This kind of coupling is tighter than *Object1* requiring *Object2* to pass it only primitive data types because it requires *Object2* to know about *Object3*.

Semantic coupling   The most insidious kind of coupling occurs when one module makes use not of some syntactic element of another module but of some semantic knowledge of another module's inner workings. Here are some examples:

- *Module1* passes a control flag to *Module2* that tells *Module2* what to do. This approach requires *Module1* to make assumptions about the internal workings of *Module2*, namely what *Module2* is going to do with the control flag. If *Module2* defines a specific data type for the control flag (enumerated type or object), this usage is probably OK.

- *Module2* uses global data after the global data has been modified by *Module1*. This approach requires *Module2* to assume that *Module1* has modified the data in the ways *Module2* needs it to be modified, and that *Module1* has been called at the right time.

- *Module1*'s interface states that its *Module1.Initialize()* routine should be called before its *Module1.Routine()* is called. *Module2* knows that *Module1.Routine()* calls *Module1.Initialize()* anyway, so it just instantiates *Module1* and calls *Module1.Routine()* without calling *Module1.Initialize()* first.

- *Module1* passes *Object* to *Module2*. Because *Module1* knows that *Module2* uses only three of *Object*'s seven methods, it initializes *Object* only partially—with the specific data those three methods need.

- *Module1* passes *BaseObject* to *Module2*. Because *Module2* knows that *Module1* is really passing it *DerivedObject*, it casts *BaseObject* to *DerivedObject* and calls methods that are specific to *DerivedObject*.

Semantic coupling is dangerous because changing code in the used module can break code in the using module in ways that are completely undetectable by the compiler. When code like this breaks, it breaks in subtle ways that seem unrelated to the change made in the used module, which turns debugging into a Sisyphean task.

The point of loose coupling is that an effective module provides an additional level of abstraction—once you write it, you can take it for granted. It reduces overall program complexity and allows you to focus on one thing at a time. If using a module requires you to focus on more than one thing at once—knowledge of its internal workings, modification to global data, uncertain functionality—the abstractive power is lost and the module's ability to help manage complexity is reduced or eliminated.

KEY POINT

Classes and routines are first and foremost intellectual tools for reducing complexity. If they're not making your job simpler, they're not doing their jobs.

Look for Common Design Patterns

cc2e.com/0585

Design patterns provide the cores of ready-made solutions that can be used to solve many of software's most common problems. Some software problems require solutions that are derived from first principles. But most problems are similar to past problems, and those can be solved using similar solutions, or patterns. Common patterns include Adapter, Bridge, Decorator, Facade, Factory Method, Observor, Singleton, Strategy, and Template Method. The book *Design Patterns* by Erich Gamma, Richard Helm, Ralph Johnson, and John Vlissides (1995) is the definitive description of design patterns.

Patterns provide several benefits that fully custom design doesn't:

Patterns reduce complexity by providing ready-made abstractions   If you say, "This code uses a Factory Method to create instances of derived classes," other programmers on your project will understand that your code involves a fairly rich set of interrelationships and programming protocols, all of which are invoked when you refer to the design pattern of Factory Method.

The Factory Method is a pattern that allows you to instantiate any class derived from a specific base class without needing to keep track of the individual derived classes anywhere but the Factory Method. For a good discussion of the Factory Method pattern, see "Replace Constructor with Factory Method" in *Refactoring* (Fowler 1999).

You don't have to spell out every line of code for other programmers to understand the design approach found in your code.

Patterns reduce errors by institutionalizing details of common solutions   Software design problems contain nuances that emerge fully only after the problem has been solved once or twice (or three times, or four times, or...). Because patterns represent standardized ways of solving common problems, they embody the wisdom accumulated from years of attempting to solve those problems, and they also embody the corrections to the false attempts that people have made in solving those problems.

Using a design pattern is thus conceptually similar to using library code instead of writing your own. Sure, everybody has written a custom Quicksort a few times, but what are the odds that your custom version will be fully correct on the first try? Similarly, numerous design problems are similar enough to past problems that you're better off using a prebuilt design solution than creating a novel solution.

Patterns provide heuristic value by suggesting design alternatives   A designer who's familiar with common patterns can easily run through a list of patterns and ask "Which of these patterns fits my design problem?" Cycling through a set of familiar alternatives is immeasurably easier than creating a custom design solution out of whole cloth. And the code arising from a familiar pattern will also be easier for readers of the code to understand than fully custom code would be.

Patterns streamline communication by moving the design dialog to a higher level In addition to their complexity-management benefit, design patterns can accelerate design discussions by allowing designers to think and discuss at a larger level of granularity. If you say "I can't decide whether I should use a Creator or a Factory Method in this situation," you've communicated a great deal with just a few words—as long as you and your listener are both familiar with those patterns. Imagine how much longer it would take you to dive into the details of the code for a Creator pattern and the code for a Factory Method pattern and then compare and contrast the two approaches.

If you're not already familiar with design patterns, Table 5-1 summarizes some of the most common patterns to stimulate your interest.

Table 5-1 Popular Design Patterns

Pattern	Description
Abstract Factory	Supports creation of sets of related objects by specifying the kind of set but not the kinds of each specific object.
Adapter	Converts the interface of a class to a different interface.
Bridge	Builds an interface and an implementation in such a way that either can vary without the other varying.
Composite	Consists of an object that contains additional objects of its own type so that client code can interact with the top-level object and not concern itself with all the detailed objects.
Decorator	Attaches responsibilities to an object dynamically, without creating specific subclasses for each possible configuration of responsibilities.
Facade	Provides a consistent interface to code that wouldn't otherwise offer a consistent interface.
Factory Method	Instantiates classes derived from a specific base class without needing to keep track of the individual derived classes anywhere but the Factory Method.
Iterator	A server object that provides access to each element in a set sequentially.
Observer	Keeps multiple objects in synch with one another by making an object responsible for notifying the set of related objects about changes to any member of the set.
Singleton	Provides global access to a class that has one and only one instance.
Strategy	Defines a set of algorithms or behaviors that are dynamically interchangeable with each other.
Template Method	Defines the structure of an algorithm but leaves some of the detailed implementation to subclasses.

If you haven't seen design patterns before, your reaction to the descriptions in Table 5-1 might be "Sure, I already know most of these ideas." That reaction is a big part of why design patterns are valuable. Patterns are familiar to most experienced programmers, and assigning recognizable names to them supports efficient and effective communication about them.

One potential trap with patterns is force-fitting code to use a pattern. In some cases, shifting code slightly to conform to a well-recognized pattern will improve understandability of the code. But if the code has to be shifted too far, forcing it to look like a standard pattern can sometimes increase complexity.

Another potential trap with patterns is feature-itis: using a pattern because of a desire to try out a pattern rather than because the pattern is an appropriate design solution.

Overall, design patterns are a powerful tool for managing complexity. You can read more detailed descriptions in any of the good books that are listed at the end of this chapter.

Other Heuristics

The preceding sections describe the major software design heuristics. Following are a few other heuristics that might not be useful quite as often but are still worth mentioning.

Aim for Strong Cohesion

Cohesion arose from structured design and is usually discussed in the same context as coupling. Cohesion refers to how closely all the routines in a class or all the code in a routine support a central purpose—how focused the class is. Classes that contain strongly related functionality are described as having strong cohesion, and the heuristic goal is to make cohesion as strong as possible. Cohesion is a useful tool for managing complexity because the more that code in a class supports a central purpose, the more easily your brain can remember everything the code does.

Thinking about cohesion at the routine level has been a useful heuristic for decades and is still useful today. At the class level, the heuristic of cohesion has largely been subsumed by the broader heuristic of well-defined abstractions, which was discussed earlier in this chapter and in Chapter 6. Abstractions are useful at the routine level, too, but on a more even footing with cohesion at that level of detail.

Build Hierarchies

A hierarchy is a tiered information structure in which the most general or abstract representation of concepts is contained at the top of the hierarchy, with increasingly detailed, specialized representations at the hierarchy's lower levels. In software, hierarchies are found in class hierarchies, and, as Level 4 in Figure 5-2 illustrated, in routine-calling hierarchies as well.

Hierarchies have been an important tool for managing complex sets of information for at least 2000 years. Aristotle used a hierarchy to organize the animal kingdom. Humans frequently use outlines to organize complex information (like this book). Researchers have found that people generally find hierarchies to be a natural way to organize complex information. When they draw a complex object such as a house, they draw it hierarchically. First they draw the outline of the house, then the windows and doors, and then more details. They don't draw the house brick by brick, shingle by shingle, or nail by nail (Simon 1996).

Hierarchies are a useful tool for achieving Software's Primary Technical Imperative because they allow you to focus on only the level of detail you're currently concerned with. The details don't go away completely; they're simply pushed to another level so that you can think about them when you want to rather than thinking about all the details all of the time.

Formalize Class Contracts

Cross-Reference For more on contracts, see "Use assertions to document and verify preconditions and postconditions" in Section 8.2.

At a more detailed level, thinking of each class's interface as a contract with the rest of the program can yield good insights. Typically, the contract is something like "If you promise to provide data x, y, and z and you promise they'll have characteristics a, b, and c, I promise to perform operations 1, 2, and 3 within constraints 8, 9, and 10." The promises the clients of the class make to the class are typically called "preconditions," and the promises the object makes to its clients are called the "postconditions."

Contracts are useful for managing complexity because, at least in theory, the object can safely ignore any noncontractual behavior. In practice, this issue is much more difficult.

Assign Responsibilities

Another heuristic is to think through how responsibilities should be assigned to objects. Asking what each object should be responsible for is similar to asking what information it should hide, but I think it can produce broader answers, which gives the heuristic unique value.

Design for Test

A thought process that can yield interesting design insights is to ask what the system will look like if you design it to facilitate testing. Do you need to separate the user interface from the rest of the code so that you can exercise it independently? Do you need to organize each subsystem so that it minimizes dependencies on other subsystems? Designing for test tends to result in more formalized class interfaces, which is generally beneficial.

Avoid Failure

Civil engineering professor Henry Petroski wrote an interesting book, *Design Paradigms: Case Histories of Error and Judgment in Engineering* (Petroski 1994), that chronicles the history of failures in bridge design. Petroski argues that many spectacular bridge failures have occurred because of focusing on previous successes and not adequately considering possible failure modes. He concludes that failures like the Tacoma Narrows bridge could have been avoided if the designers had carefully considered the ways the bridge might fail and not just copied the attributes of other successful designs.

The high-profile security lapses of various well-known systems the past few years make it hard to disagree that we should find ways to apply Petroski's design-failure insights to software.

Choose Binding Time Consciously

Cross-Reference For more on binding time, see Section 10.6, "Binding Time."

Binding time refers to the time a specific value is bound to a variable. Code that binds early tends to be simpler, but it also tends to be less flexible. Sometimes you can get a good design insight from asking questions like these: What if I bound these values earlier? What if I bound these values later? What if I initialized this table right here in the code? What if I read the value of this variable from the user at run time?

Make Central Points of Control

P.J. Plauger says his major concern is "The Principle of One Right Place—there should be One Right Place to look for any nontrivial piece of code, and One Right Place to make a likely maintenance change" (Plauger 1993). Control can be centralized in classes, routines, preprocessor macros, *#include* files—even a named constant is an example of a central point of control.

The reduced-complexity benefit is that the fewer places you have to look for something, the easier and safer it will be to change.

Consider Using Brute Force

When in doubt, use brute force.
—*Butler Lampson*

One powerful heuristic tool is brute force. Don't underestimate it. A brute-force solution that works is better than an elegant solution that doesn't work. It can take a long time to get an elegant solution to work. In describing the history of searching algorithms, for example, Donald Knuth pointed out that even though the first description of a binary search algorithm was published in 1946, it took another 16 years for someone to publish an algorithm that correctly searched lists of all sizes (Knuth 1998). A binary search is more elegant, but a brute-force, sequential search is often sufficient.

Draw a Diagram

Diagrams are another powerful heuristic tool. A picture is worth 1000 words—kind of. You actually want to leave out most of the 1000 words because one point of using a picture is that a picture can represent the problem at a higher level of abstraction. Sometimes you want to deal with the problem in detail, but other times you want to be able to work with more generality.

Keep Your Design Modular

Modularity's goal is to make each routine or class like a "black box": You know what goes in, and you know what comes out, but you don't know what happens inside. A black box has such a simple interface and such well-defined functionality that for any specific input you can accurately predict the corresponding output.

The concept of modularity is related to information hiding, encapsulation, and other design heuristics. But sometimes thinking about how to assemble a system from a set of black boxes provides insights that information hiding and encapsulation don't, so the concept is worth having in your back pocket.

Summary of Design Heuristics

More alarming, the same programmer is quite capable of doing the same task himself in two or three ways, sometimes unconsciously, but quite often simply for a change, or to provide elegant variation.
—*A. R. Brown and W. A. Sampson*

Here's a summary of major design heuristics:

- Find Real-World Objects
- Form Consistent Abstractions
- Encapsulate Implementation Details
- Inherit When Possible
- Hide Secrets (Information Hiding)
- Identify Areas Likely to Change
- Keep Coupling Loose
- Look for Common Design Patterns

The following heuristics are sometimes useful too:

- Aim for Strong Cohesion
- Build Hierarchies
- Formalize Class Contracts
- Assign Responsibilities
- Design for Test
- Avoid Failure
- Choose Binding Time Consciously
- Make Central Points of Control
- Consider Using Brute Force
- Draw a Diagram
- Keep Your Design Modular

Guidelines for Using Heuristics

Approaches to design in software can learn from approaches to design in other fields. One of the original books on heuristics in problem solving was G. Polya's *How to Solve It* (1957). Polya's generalized problem-solving approach focuses on problem solving in mathematics. Figure 5-10 is a summary of his approach, adapted from a similar summary in his book (emphases his).

cc2e.com/0592

1. ***Understanding the Problem.*** You have to *understand* the problem.

   What is the unknown? What are the data? What is the condition? Is it possible to satisfy the condition? Is the condition sufficient to determine the unknown? Or is it insufficient? Or redundant? Or contradictory?

   Draw a figure. Introduce suitable notation. Separate the various parts of the condition. Can you write them down?

2. ***Devising a Plan.*** Find the connection between the data and the unknown. You might be obliged to consider auxiliary problems if you can't find an intermediate connection. You should eventually come up with a *plan* of the solution.

   Have you seen the problem before? Or have you seen the same problem in a slightly different form? *Do you know a related problem?* Do you know a theorem that could be useful?

   Look at the unknown! And try to think of a familiar problem having the same or a similar unknown. *Here is a problem related to yours and solved before. Can you use it?* Can you use its result? Can you use its method? Should you introduce some auxiliary element in order to make its use possible?

   Can you restate the problem? Can you restate it still differently? Go back to definitions.

   If you cannot solve the proposed problem, try to solve some related problem first. Can you imagine a more accessible related problem? A more general problem? A more special problem? An analogous problem? Can you solve a part of the problem? Keep only a part of the condition, drop the other part; how far is the unknown then determined, how can it vary? Can you derive something useful from the data? Can you think of other data appropriate for determining the unknown? Can you change the unknown or the data, or both if necessary, so that the new unknown and the new data are nearer to each other?

   Did you use all the data? Did you use the whole condition? Have you taken into account all essential notions involved in the problem?

3. ***Carrying out the Plan.*** *Carry out* your plan.

   Carrying out your plan of the solution, *check each step*. Can you see clearly that the step is correct? Can you prove that it's correct?

4. ***Looking Back.*** *Examine* the solution.

   Can you *check the result?* Can you check the argument? Can you derive the result differently? Can you see it at a glance?

   Can you use the result, or the method, for some other problem?

Figure 5-10 G. Polya developed an approach to problem solving in mathematics that's also useful in solving problems in software design (Polya 1957).

One of the most effective guidelines is not to get stuck on a single approach. If diagramming the design in UML isn't working, write it in English. Write a short test program. Try a completely different approach. Think of a brute-force solution. Keep outlining and sketching with your pencil, and your brain will follow. If all else fails, walk away from the problem. Literally go for a walk, or think about something else before returning to the problem. If you've given it your best and are getting nowhere, putting it out of your mind for a time often produces results more quickly than sheer persistence can.

You don't have to solve the whole design problem at once. If you get stuck, remember that a point needs to be decided but recognize that you don't yet have enough information to resolve that specific issue. Why fight your way through the last 20 percent of the design when it will drop into place easily the next time through? Why make bad decisions based on limited experience with the design when you can make good decisions based on more experience with it later? Some people are uncomfortable if they don't come to closure after a design cycle, but after you have created a few designs without resolving issues prematurely, it will seem natural to leave issues unresolved until you have more information (Zahniser 1992, Beck 2000).

5.4 Design Practices

The preceding section focused on heuristics related to design attributes—what you want the completed design to look like. This section describes *design practice* heuristics, steps you can take that often produce good results.

Iterate

You might have had an experience in which you learned so much from writing a program that you wished you could write it again, armed with the insights you gained from writing it the first time. The same phenomenon applies to design, but the design cycles are shorter and the effects downstream are bigger, so you can afford to whirl through the design loop a few times.

KEY POINT

Design is an iterative process. You don't usually go from point A only to point B; you go from point A to point B and back to point A.

As you cycle through candidate designs and try different approaches, you'll look at both high-level and low-level views. The big picture you get from working with high-level issues will help you to put the low-level details in perspective. The details you get from working with low-level issues will provide a foundation in solid reality for the high-level decisions. The tug and pull between top-level and bottom-level considerations is a healthy dynamic; it creates a stressed structure that's more stable than one built wholly from the top down or the bottom up.

Many programmers—many people, for that matter—have trouble ranging between high-level and low-level considerations. Switching from one view of a system to another is mentally strenuous, but it's essential to creating effective designs. For entertaining exercises to enhance your mental flexibility, read *Conceptual Blockbusting* (Adams 2001), described in the "Additional Resources" section at the end of the chapter.

Cross-Reference Refactoring is a safe way to try different alternatives in code. For more on this, see Chapter 24, "Refactoring."

When you come up with a first design attempt that seems good enough, don't stop! The second attempt is nearly always better than the first, and you learn things on each attempt that can improve your overall design. After trying a thousand different materials for a light bulb filament with no success, Thomas Edison was reportedly asked if he felt his time had been wasted since he had discovered nothing. "Nonsense," Edison is supposed to have replied. "I have discovered a thousand things that don't work." In many cases, solving the problem with one approach will produce insights that will enable you to solve the problem using another approach that's even better.

Divide and Conquer

As Edsger Dijkstra pointed out, no one's skull is big enough to contain all the details of a complex program, and that applies just as well to design. Divide the program into different areas of concern, and then tackle each of those areas individually. If you run into a dead end in one of the areas, iterate!

Incremental refinement is a powerful tool for managing complexity. As Polya recommended in mathematical problem solving, understand the problem, devise a plan, carry out the plan, and then *look back* to see how you did (Polya 1957).

Top-Down and Bottom-Up Design Approaches

"Top down" and "bottom up" might have an old-fashioned sound, but they provide valuable insight into the creation of object-oriented designs. Top-down design begins at a high level of abstraction. You define base classes or other nonspecific design elements. As you develop the design, you increase the level of detail, identifying derived classes, collaborating classes, and other detailed design elements.

Bottom-up design starts with specifics and works toward generalities. It typically begins by identifying concrete objects and then generalizes aggregations of objects and base classes from those specifics.

Some people argue vehemently that starting with generalities and working toward specifics is best, and some argue that you can't really identify general design principles until you've worked out the significant details. Here are the arguments on both sides.

Argument for Top Down

The guiding principle behind the top-down approach is the idea that the human brain can concentrate on only a certain amount of detail at a time. If you start with general classes and decompose them into more specialized classes step by step, your brain isn't forced to deal with too many details at once.

The divide-and-conquer process is iterative in a couple of senses. First, it's iterative because you usually don't stop after one level of decomposition. You keep going for several levels. Second, it's iterative because you don't usually settle for your first attempt. You decompose a program one way. At various points in the decomposition, you'll have choices about which way to partition the subsystems, lay out the inheritance tree, and form compositions of objects. You make a choice and see what happens. Then you start over and decompose it another way and see whether that works better. After several attempts, you'll have a good idea of what will work and why.

How far do you decompose a program? Continue decomposing until it seems as if it would be easier to code the next level than to decompose it. Work until you become somewhat impatient at how obvious and easy the design seems. At that point, you're done. If it's not clear, work some more. If the solution is even slightly tricky for you now, it'll be a bear for anyone who works on it later.

Argument for Bottom Up

Sometimes the top-down approach is so abstract that it's hard to get started. If you need to work with something more tangible, try the bottom-up design approach. Ask yourself, "What do I know this system needs to do?" Undoubtedly, you can answer that question. You might identify a few low-level responsibilities that you can assign to concrete classes. For example, you might know that a system needs to format a particular report, compute data for that report, center its headings, display the report on the screen, print the report on a printer, and so on. After you identify several low-level responsibilities, you'll usually start to feel comfortable enough to look at the top again.

In some other cases, major attributes of the design problem are dictated from the bottom. You might have to interface with hardware devices whose interface requirements dictate large chunks of your design.

Here are some things to keep in mind as you do bottom-up composition:

- Ask yourself what you know the system needs to do.

- Identify concrete objects and responsibilities from that question.

- Identify common objects, and group them using subsystem organization, packages, composition within objects, or inheritance, whichever is appropriate.

- Continue with the next level up, or go back to the top and try again to work down.

No Argument, Really

The key difference between top-down and bottom-up strategies is that one is a decomposition strategy and the other is a composition strategy. One starts from the general problem and breaks it into manageable pieces; the other starts with manageable pieces and builds up a general solution. Both approaches have strengths and weaknesses that you'll want to consider as you apply them to your design problems.

The strength of top-down design is that it's easy. People are good at breaking something big into smaller components, and programmers are especially good at it.

Another strength of top-down design is that you can defer construction details. Since systems are often perturbed by changes in construction details (for example, changes in a file structure or a report format), it's useful to know early on that those details should be hidden in classes at the bottom of the hierarchy.

One strength of the bottom-up approach is that it typically results in early identification of needed utility functionality, which results in a compact, well-factored design. If similar systems have already been built, the bottom-up approach allows you to start the design of the new system by looking at pieces of the old system and asking "What can I reuse?"

A weakness of the bottom-up composition approach is that it's hard to use exclusively. Most people are better at taking one big concept and breaking it into smaller concepts than they are at taking small concepts and making one big one. It's like the old assemble-it-yourself problem: I thought I was done, so why does the box still have parts in it? Fortunately, you don't have to use the bottom-up composition approach exclusively.

Another weakness of the bottom-up design strategy is that sometimes you find that you can't build a program from the pieces you've started with. You can't build an airplane from bricks, and you might have to work at the top before you know what kinds of pieces you need at the bottom.

To summarize, top down tends to start simple, but sometimes low-level complexity ripples back to the top, and those ripples can make things more complex than they really needed to be. Bottom up tends to start complex, but identifying that complexity early on leads to better design of the higher-level classes—if the complexity doesn't torpedo the whole system first!

In the final analysis, top-down and bottom-up design aren't competing strategies—they're mutually beneficial. Design is a heuristic process, which means that no solution is guaranteed to work every time. Design contains elements of trial and error. Try a variety of approaches until you find one that works well.

Experimental Prototyping

cc2e.com/0599

Sometimes you can't really know whether a design will work until you better understand some implementation detail. You might not know if a particular database organization will work until you know whether it will meet your performance goals. You might not know whether a particular subsystem design will work until you select the specific GUI libraries you'll be working with. These are examples of the essential "wickedness" of software design—you can't fully define the design problem until you've at least partially solved it.

A general technique for addressing these questions at low cost is experimental prototyping. The word "prototyping" means lots of different things to different people (McConnell 1996). In this context, prototyping means writing the absolute minimum amount of throwaway code that's needed to answer a specific design question.

Prototyping works poorly when developers aren't disciplined about writing the *absolute minimum* of code needed to answer a question. Suppose the design question is, "Can the database framework we've selected support the transaction volume we need?" You don't need to write any production code to answer that question. You don't even need to know the database specifics. You just need to know enough to approximate the problem space—number of tables, number of entries in the tables, and so on. You can then write very simple prototyping code that uses tables with names like *Table1*, *Table2*, and *Column1*, and *Column2*, populate the tables with junk data, and do your performance testing.

Prototyping also works poorly when the design question is not *specific* enough. A design question like "Will this database framework work?" does not provide enough direction for prototyping. A design question like "Will this database framework support 1,000 transactions per second under assumptions X, Y, and Z?" provides a more solid basis for prototyping.

A final risk of prototyping arises when developers do not treat the code as *throwaway* code. I have found that it is not possible for people to write the absolute minimum amount of code to answer a question if they believe that the code will eventually end up in the production system. They end up implementing the system instead of prototyping. By adopting the attitude that once the question is answered the code will be thrown away, you can minimize this risk. One way to avoid this problem is to create prototypes in a different technology than the production code. You could prototype a Java design in Python or mock up a user interface in Microsoft PowerPoint. If you do create prototypes using the production technology, a practical standard that can help is requiring that class names or package names for prototype code be prefixed with *prototype*. That at least makes a programmer think twice before trying to extend prototype code (Stephens 2003).

Used with discipline, prototyping is the workhorse tool a designer has to combat design wickedness. Used without discipline, prototyping adds some wickedness of its own.

Collaborative Design

Cross-Reference For more details on collaborative development, see Chapter 21, "Collaborative Construction."

In design, two heads are often better than one, whether those two heads are organized formally or informally. Collaboration can take any of several forms:

- You informally walk over to a co-worker's desk and ask to bounce some ideas around.

- You and your co-worker sit together in a conference room and draw design alternatives on a whiteboard.

- You and your co-worker sit together at the keyboard and do detailed design in the programming language you're using—that is, you can use pair programming, described in Chapter 21, "Collaborative Construction."

- You schedule a meeting to walk through your design ideas with one or more co-workers.

- You schedule a formal inspection with all the structure described in Chapter 21.

- You don't work with anyone who can review your work, so you do some initial work, put it into a drawer, and come back to it a week later. You will have forgotten enough that you should be able to give yourself a fairly good review.

- You ask someone outside your company for help: send questions to a specialized forum or newsgroup.

If the goal is quality assurance, I tend to recommend the most structured review practice, formal inspections, for the reasons described in Chapter 21. But if the goal is to foster creativity and to increase the number of design alternatives generated, not just to find errors, less structured approaches work better. After you've settled on a specific design, switching to a more formal inspection might be appropriate, depending on the nature of your project.

How Much Design Is Enough?

We try to solve the problem by rushing through the design process so that enough time is left at the end of the project to uncover the errors that were made because we rushed through the design process.
—Glenford Myers

Sometimes only the barest sketch of an architecture is mapped out before coding begins. Other times, teams create designs at such a level of detail that coding becomes a mostly mechanical exercise. How much design should you do before you begin coding?

A related question is how formal to make the design. Do you need formal, polished design diagrams, or would digital snapshots of a few drawings on a whiteboard be enough?

Deciding how much design to do before beginning full-scale coding and how much formality to use in documenting that design is hardly an exact science. The experience of the team, expected lifetime of the system, desired level of reliability, and size of project and team should all be considered. Table 5-2 summarizes how each of these factors influence the design approach.

Table 5-2   Design Formality and Level of Detail Needed

Factor	Level of Detail Needed in Design Before Construction	Documentation Formality
Design/construction team has deep experience in applications area.	Low Detail	Low Formality
Design/construction team has deep experience but is inexperienced in the applications area.	Medium Detail	Medium Formality
Design/construction team is inexperienced.	Medium to High Detail	Low-Medium Formality
Design/construction team has moderate-to-high turnover.	Medium Detail	—
Application is safety-critical.	High Detail	High Formality
Application is mission-critical.	Medium Detail	Medium-High Formality
Project is small.	Low Detail	Low Formality
Project is large.	Medium Detail	Medium Formality
Software is expected to have a short lifetime (weeks or months).	Low Detail	Low Formality
Software is expected to have a long lifetime (months or years).	Medium Detail	Medium Formality

Two or more of these factors might come into play on any specific project, and in some cases the factors might provide contradictory advice. For example, you might have a highly experienced team working on safety critical software. In that case, you'd probably want to err on the side of the higher level of design detail and formality. In such cases, you'll need to weigh the significance of each factor and make a judgment about what matters most.

If the level of design is left to each individual, then, when the design descends to the level of a task that you've done before or to a simple modification or extension of such a task, you're probably ready to stop designing and begin coding.

If I can't decide how deeply to investigate a design before I begin coding, I tend to err on the side of going into more detail. The biggest design errors arise from cases in which I thought I went far enough, but it later turns out that I didn't go far enough to realize there were additional design challenges. In other words, the biggest design problems tend to arise not from areas I knew were difficult and created bad designs for, but from areas I thought were easy and didn't create any designs for at all. I rarely encounter projects that are suffering from having done too much design work.

I've never met a human being who would want to read 17,000 pages of documentation, and if there was, I'd kill him to get him out of the gene pool.
—*Joseph Costello*

On the other hand, occasionally I have seen projects that are suffering from too much design *documentation*. Gresham's Law states that "programmed activity tends to drive out nonprogrammed activity" (Simon 1965). A premature rush to polish a design description is a good example of that law. I would rather see 80 percent of the design effort go into creating and exploring numerous design alternatives and 20 percent go into creating less polished documentation than to have 20 percent go into creating mediocre design alternatives and 80 percent go into polishing documentation of designs that are not very good.

Capturing Your Design Work

cc2e.com/0506

The traditional approach to capturing design work is to write up the designs in a formal design document. However, you can capture designs in numerous alternative ways that work well on small projects, informal projects, or projects that need a lightweight way to record a design:

The bad news is that, in our opinion, we will never find the philosopher's stone. We will never find a process that allows us to design software in a perfectly rational way. The good news is that we can fake it.
—*David Parnas and Paul Clements*

Insert design documentation into the code itself Document key design decisions in code comments, typically in the file or class header. When you couple this approach with a documentation extractor like JavaDoc, this assures that design documentation will be readily available to a programmer working on a section of code, and it improves the chance that programmers will keep the design documentation reasonably up to date.

Capture design discussions and decisions on a Wiki Have your design discussions in writing, on a project Wiki (that is, a collection of Web pages that can be edited easily by anyone on your project using a Web browser). This will capture your design discussions and decision automatically, albeit with the extra overhead of typing rather than talking. You can also use the Wiki to capture digital pictures to supplement the text discussion, links to websites that support the design decision, white papers, and other materials. This technique is especially useful if your development team is geographically distributed.

Write e-mail summaries After a design discussion, adopt the practice of designating someone to write a summary of the discussion—especially what was decided—and send it to the project team. Archive a copy of the e-mail in the project's public e-mail folder.

Use a digital camera   One common barrier to documenting designs is the tedium of creating design drawings in some popular drawing tools. But the documentation choices are not limited to the two options of "capturing the design in a nicely format-ted, formal notation" vs. "no design documentation at all."

Taking pictures of whiteboard drawings with a digital camera and then embedding those pictures into traditional documents can be a low-effort way to get 80 percent of the benefit of saving design drawings by doing about 1 percent of the work required if you use a drawing tool.

Save design flip charts   There's no law that says your design documentation has to fit on standard letter-size paper. If you make your design drawings on large flip chart paper, you can simply archive the flip charts in a convenient location—or, better yet, post them on the walls around the project area so that people can easily refer to them and update them when needed.

cc2e.com/0513   *Use CRC (Class, Responsibility, Collaborator) cards*   Another low-tech alternative for documenting designs is to use index cards. On each card, designers write a class name, responsibilities of the class, and collaborators (other classes that cooperate with the class). A design group then works with the cards until they're satisfied that they've created a good design. At that point, you can simply save the cards for future reference. Index cards are cheap, unintimidating, and portable, and they encourage group interaction (Beck 1991).

Create UML diagrams at appropriate levels of detail   One popular technique for diagramming designs is called Unified Modeling Language (UML), which is defined by the Object Management Group (Fowler 2004). Figure 5-6 earlier in this chapter was one example of a UML class diagram. UML provides a rich set of formalized rep-resentations for design entities and relationships. You can use informal versions of UML to explore and discuss design approaches. Start with minimal sketches and add detail only after you've zeroed in on a final design solution. Because UML is standard-ized, it supports common understanding in communicating design ideas and it can accelerate the process of considering design alternatives when working in a group.

These techniques can work in various combinations, so feel free to mix and match these approaches on a project-by-project basis or even within different areas of a single project.

5.5 Comments on Popular Methodologies

The history of design in software has been marked by fanatic advocates of wildly con-flicting design approaches. When I published the first edition of *Code Complete* in the early 1990s, design zealots were advocating dotting every design i and crossing every design t before beginning coding. That recommendation didn't make any sense.

People who preach software design as a disciplined activity spend considerable energy making us all feel guilty. We can never be structured enough or object-oriented enough to achieve nirvana in this lifetime. We all truck around a kind of original sin from having learned Basic at an impressionable age. But my bet is that most of us are better designers than the purists will ever acknowledge.
—*P. J. Plauger*

As I write this edition in the mid-2000s, some software swamis are arguing for not doing any design at all. "Big Design Up Front is *BDUF*," they say. "BDUF is bad. You're better off not doing any design before you begin coding!"

In ten years the pendulum has swung from "design everything" to "design nothing." But the alternative to BDUF isn't no design up front, it's a Little Design Up Front (LDUF) or Enough Design Up Front—*ENUF*.

How do you tell how much is enough? That's a judgment call, and no one can make that call perfectly. But while you can't know the exact right amount of design with any confidence, two amounts of design are guaranteed to be wrong every time: designing every last detail and not designing anything at all. The two positions advocated by extremists on both ends of the scale turn out to be the only two positions that are always wrong!

As P.J. Plauger says, "The more dogmatic you are about applying a design method, the fewer real-life problems you are going to solve" (Plauger 1993). Treat design as a wicked, sloppy, heuristic process. Don't settle for the first design that occurs to you. Collaborate. Strive for simplicity. Prototype when you need to. Iterate, iterate, and iterate again. You'll be happy with your designs.

Additional Resources

cc2e.com/0520

Software design is a rich field with abundant resources. The challenge is identifying which resources will be most useful. Here are some suggestions.

Software Design, General

Weisfeld, Matt. *The Object-Oriented Thought Process*, 2d ed. SAMS, 2004. This is an accessible book that introduces object-oriented programming. If you're already familiar with object-oriented programming, you'll probably want a more advanced book, but if you're just getting your feet wet in object orientation, this book introduces fundamental object-oriented concepts, including objects, classes, interfaces, inheritance, polymorphism, overloading, abstract classes, aggregation and association, constructors/destructors, exceptions, and others.

Riel, Arthur J. *Object-Oriented Design Heuristics*. Reading, MA: Addison-Wesley, 1996. This book is easy to read and focuses on design at the class level.

Plauger, P. J. *Programming on Purpose: Essays on Software Design*. Englewood Cliffs, NJ: PTR Prentice Hall, 1993. I picked up as many tips about good software design from reading this book as from any other book I've read. Plauger is well-versed in a wide-variety of design approaches, he's pragmatic, and he's a great writer.

Meyer, Bertrand. *Object-Oriented Software Construction*, 2d ed. New York, NY: Prentice Hall PTR, 1997. Meyer presents a forceful advocacy of hard-core object-oriented programming.

Raymond, Eric S. *The Art of UNIX Programming*. Boston, MA: Addison-Wesley, 2004. This is a well-researched look at software design through UNIX-colored glasses. Section 1.6 is an especially concise 12-page explanation of 17 key UNIX design principles.

Larman, Craig. *Applying UML and Patterns: An Introduction to Object-Oriented Analysis and Design and the Unified Process*, 2d ed. Englewood Cliffs, NJ: Prentice Hall, 2001. This book is a popular introduction to object-oriented design in the context of the Unified Process. It also discusses object-oriented analysis.

Software Design Theory

Parnas, David L., and Paul C. Clements. "A Rational Design Process: How and Why to Fake It." *IEEE Transactions on Software Engineering* SE-12, no. 2 (February 1986): 251–57. This classic article describes the gap between how programs are really designed and how you sometimes wish they were designed. The main point is that no one ever really goes through a rational, orderly design process but that aiming for it makes for better designs in the end.

I'm not aware of any comprehensive treatment of information hiding. Most software-engineering textbooks discuss it briefly, frequently in the context of object-oriented techniques. The three Parnas papers listed below are the seminal presentations of the idea and are probably still the best resources on information hiding.

Parnas, David L. "On the Criteria to Be Used in Decomposing Systems into Modules." *Communications of the ACM* 5, no. 12 (December 1972): 1053-58.

Parnas, David L. "Designing Software for Ease of Extension and Contraction." *IEEE Transactions on Software Engineering* SE-5, no. 2 (March 1979): 128-38.

Parnas, David L., Paul C. Clements, and D. M. Weiss. "The Modular Structure of Complex Systems." *IEEE Transactions on Software Engineering* SE-11, no. 3 (March 1985): 259-66.

Design Patterns

Gamma, Erich, et al. *Design Patterns*. Reading, MA: Addison-Wesley, 1995. This book by the "Gang of Four" is the seminal book on design patterns.

Shalloway, Alan, and James R. Trott. *Design Patterns Explained*. Boston, MA: Addison-Wesley, 2002. This book contains an easy-to-read introduction to design patterns.

Design in General

Adams, James L. *Conceptual Blockbusting: A Guide to Better Ideas*, 4th ed. Cambridge, MA: Perseus Publishing, 2001. Although not specifically about software design, this book was written to teach design to engineering students at Stanford. Even if you never design anything, the book is a fascinating discussion of creative thought processes. It includes many exercises in the kinds of thinking required for effective design. It also contains a well-annotated bibliography on design and creative thinking. If you like problem solving, you'll like this book.

Polya, G. *How to Solve It: A New Aspect of Mathematical Method*, 2d ed. Princeton, NJ: Princeton University Press, 1957. This discussion of heuristics and problem solving focuses on mathematics but is applicable to software development. Polya's book was the first written about the use of heuristics in mathematical problem solving. It draws a clear distinction between the messy heuristics used to discover solutions and the tidier techniques used to present them once they've been discovered. It's not easy reading, but if you're interested in heuristics, you'll eventually read it whether you want to or not. Polya's book makes it clear that problem solving isn't a deterministic activity and that adherence to any single methodology is like walking with your feet in chains. At one time, Microsoft gave this book to all its new programmers.

Michalewicz, Zbigniew, and David B. Fogel. *How to Solve It: Modern Heuristics*. Berlin: Springer-Verlag, 2000. This is an updated treatment of Polya's book that's quite a bit easier to read and that also contains some nonmathematical examples.

Simon, Herbert. *The Sciences of the Artificial*, 3d ed. Cambridge, MA: MIT Press, 1996. This fascinating book draws a distinction between sciences that deal with the natural world (biology, geology, and so on) and sciences that deal with the artificial world created by humans (business, architecture, and computer science). It then discusses the characteristics of the sciences of the artificial, emphasizing the science of design. It has an academic tone and is well worth reading for anyone intent on a career in software development or any other "artificial" field.

Glass, Robert L. *Software Creativity*. Englewood Cliffs, NJ: Prentice Hall PTR, 1995. Is software development controlled more by theory or by practice? Is it primarily creative or is it primarily deterministic? What intellectual qualities does a software developer need? This book contains an interesting discussion of the nature of software development with a special emphasis on design.

Petroski, Henry. *Design Paradigms: Case Histories of Error and Judgment in Engineering*. Cambridge: Cambridge University Press, 1994. This book draws heavily from the field of civil engineering (especially bridge design) to explain its main argument that successful design depends at least as much upon learning from past failures as from past successes.

Standards

IEEE Std 1016-1998, Recommended Practice for Software Design Descriptions. This document contains the IEEE-ANSI standard for software-design descriptions. It describes what should be included in a software-design document.

IEEE Std 1471-2000. Recommended Practice for Architectural Description of Software Intensive Systems. Los Alamitos, CA: IEEE Computer Society Press. This document is the IEEE-ANSI guide for creating software architecture specifications.

cc2e.com/0527

CHECKLIST: Design in Construction

Design Practices

- ❑ Have you iterated, selecting the best of several attempts rather than the first attempt?

- ❑ Have you tried decomposing the system in several different ways to see which way will work best?

- ❑ Have you approached the design problem both from the top down and from the bottom up?

- ❑ Have you prototyped risky or unfamiliar parts of the system, creating the absolute minimum amount of throwaway code needed to answer specific questions?

- ❑ Has your design been reviewed, formally or informally, by others?

- ❑ Have you driven the design to the point that its implementation seems obvious?

- ❑ Have you captured your design work using an appropriate technique such as a Wiki, e-mail, flip charts, digital photography, UML, CRC cards, or comments in the code itself?

Design Goals

- ❑ Does the design adequately address issues that were identified and deferred at the architectural level?

- ❑ Is the design stratified into layers?

- ❑ Are you satisfied with the way the program has been decomposed into subsystems, packages, and classes?

- ❑ Are you satisfied with the way the classes have been decomposed into routines?

- ❑ Are classes designed for minimal interaction with each other?

❑ Are classes and subsystems designed so that you can use them in other systems?

❑ Will the program be easy to maintain?

❑ Is the design lean? Are all of its parts strictly necessary?

❑ Does the design use standard techniques and avoid exotic, hard-to-understand elements?

❑ Overall, does the design help minimize both accidental and essential complexity?

Key Points

■ Software's Primary Technical Imperative is *managing complexity*. This is greatly aided by a design focus on simplicity.

■ Simplicity is achieved in two general ways: minimizing the amount of essential complexity that anyone's brain has to deal with at any one time, and keeping accidental complexity from proliferating needlessly.

■ Design is heuristic. Dogmatic adherence to any single methodology hurts creativity and hurts your programs.

■ Good design is iterative; the more design possibilities you try, the better your final design will be.

■ Information hiding is a particularly valuable concept. Asking "What should I hide?" settles many difficult design issues.

■ Lots of useful, interesting information on design is available outside this book. The perspectives presented here are just the tip of the iceberg.

Chapter 6
Working Classes

cc2e.com/0665

Contents

- 6.1 Class Foundations: Abstract Data Types (ADTs): page 126
- 6.2 Good Class Interfaces: page 133
- 6.3 Design and Implementation Issues: page 143
- 6.4 Reasons to Create a Class: page 152
- 6.5 Language-Specific Issues: page 156
- 6.6 Beyond Classes: Packages: page 156

Related Topics

- Design in construction: Chapter 5
- Software architecture: Section 3.5
- High-quality routines: Chapter 7
- The Pseudocode Programming Process: Chapter 9
- Refactoring: Chapter 24

In the dawn of computing, programmers thought about programming in terms of statements. Throughout the 1970s and 1980s, programmers began thinking about programs in terms of routines. In the twenty-first century, programmers think about programming in terms of classes.

KEY POINT

A class is a collection of data and routines that share a cohesive, well-defined responsibility. A class might also be a collection of routines that provides a cohesive set of services even if no common data is involved. A key to being an effective programmer is maximizing the portion of a program that you can safely ignore while working on any one section of code. Classes are the primary tool for accomplishing that objective.

This chapter contains a distillation of advice in creating high-quality classes. If you're still warming up to object-oriented concepts, this chapter might be too advanced. Make sure you've read Chapter 5, "Design in Construction." Then start with Section 6.1, "Class Foundations: Abstract Data Types (ADTs)," and ease your way into the remaining sections. If you're already familiar with class basics, you might skim Section 6.1 and then dive into the discussion of class interfaces in Section 6.2. The "Additional Resources" section at the end of this chapter contains pointers to introductory reading, advanced reading, and programming-language-specific resources.

6.1 Class Foundations: Abstract Data Types (ADTs)

An abstract data type is a collection of data and operations that work on that data. The operations both describe the data to the rest of the program and allow the rest of the program to change the data. The word "data" in "abstract data type" is used loosely. An ADT might be a graphics window with all the operations that affect it, a file and file operations, an insurance-rates table and the operations on it, or something else.

Cross-Reference Thinking about ADTs first and classes second is an example of programming *into* a language vs. programming in one. See Section 4.3, "Your Location on the Technology Wave," and Section 34.4, "Program into Your Language, Not in It."

Understanding ADTs is essential to understanding object-oriented programming. Without understanding ADTs, programmers create classes that are "classes" in name only—in reality, they are little more than convenient carrying cases for loosely related collections of data and routines. With an understanding of ADTs, programmers can create classes that are easier to implement initially and easier to modify over time.

Traditionally, programming books wax mathematical when they arrive at the topic of abstract data types. They tend to make statements like "One can think of an abstract data type as a mathematical model with a collection of operations defined on it." Such books make it seem as if you'd never actually use an abstract data type except as a sleep aid.

Such dry explanations of abstract data types completely miss the point. Abstract data types are exciting because you can use them to manipulate real-world entities rather than low-level, implementation entities. Instead of inserting a node into a linked list, you can add a cell to a spreadsheet, a new type of window to a list of window types, or another passenger car to a train simulation. Tap into the power of being able to work in the problem domain rather than at the low-level implementation domain!

Example of the Need for an ADT

To get things started, here's an example of a case in which an ADT would be useful. We'll get to the details after we have an example to talk about.

Suppose you're writing a program to control text output to the screen using a variety of typefaces, point sizes, and font attributes (such as bold and italic). Part of the program manipulates the text's fonts. If you use an ADT, you'll have a group of font routines bundled with the data—the typeface names, point sizes, and font attributes—they operate on. The collection of font routines and data is an ADT.

If you're not using ADTs, you'll take an ad hoc approach to manipulating fonts. For example, if you need to change to a 12-point font size, which happens to be 16 pixels high, you'll have code like this:

```
currentFont.size = 16
```

If you've built up a collection of library routines, the code might be slightly more readable:

```
currentFont.size = PointsToPixels( 12 )
```

Or you could provide a more specific name for the attribute, something like

```
currentFont.sizeInPixels = PointsToPixels( 12 )
```

But what you can't do is have both *currentFont.sizeInPixels* and *currentFont.sizeInPoints*, because, if both the data members are in play, *currentFont* won't have any way to know which of the two it should use. And if you change sizes in several places in the program, you'll have similar lines spread throughout your program.

If you need to set a font to bold, you might have code like this that uses a logical *or* and a hexidecimal constant *0x02*:

```
currentFont.attribute = currentFont.attribute or 0x02
```

If you're lucky, you'll have something cleaner than that, but the best you'll get with an ad hoc approach is something like this:

```
currentFont.attribute = currentFont.attribute or BOLD
```

Or maybe something like this:

```
currentFont.bold = True
```

As with the font size, the limitation is that the client code is required to control the data members directly, which limits how *currentFont* can be used.

If you program this way, you're likely to have similar lines in many places in your program.

Benefits of Using ADTs

The problem isn't that the ad hoc approach is bad programming practice. It's that you can replace the approach with a better programming practice that produces these benefits:

You can hide implementation details   Hiding information about the font data type means that if the data type changes, you can change it in one place without affecting the whole program. For example, unless you hid the implementation details in an ADT, changing the data type from the first representation of bold to the second would entail changing your program in every place in which bold was set rather than in just one place. Hiding the information also protects the rest of the program if you decide to store data in external storage rather than in memory or to rewrite all the font-manipulation routines in another language.

Changes don't affect the whole program   If fonts need to become richer and support more operations (such as switching to small caps, superscripts, strikethrough, and so on), you can change the program in one place. The change won't affect the rest of the program.

You can make the interface more informative   Code like *currentFont.size = 16* is ambiguous because *16* could be a size in either pixels or points. The context doesn't tell you which is which. Collecting all similar operations into an ADT allows you to define the entire interface in terms of points, or in terms of pixels, or to clearly differentiate between the two, which helps avoid confusing them.

It's easier to improve performance   If you need to improve font performance, you can recode a few well-defined routines rather than wading through an entire program.

The program is more obviously correct   You can replace the more tedious task of verifying that statements like *currentFont.attribute = currentFont.attribute or 0x02* are correct with the easier task of verifying that calls to *currentFont.SetBoldOn()* are correct. With the first statement, you can have the wrong structure name, the wrong field name, the wrong operation (*and* instead of *or*), or the wrong value for the attribute (*0x20* instead of *0x02*). In the second case, the only thing that could possibly be wrong with the call to *currentFont.SetBoldOn()* is that it's a call to the wrong routine name, so it's easier to see whether it's correct.

The program becomes more self-documenting   You can improve statements like *currentFont.attribute or 0x02* by replacing *0x02* with *BOLD* or whatever *0x02* represents, but that doesn't compare to the readability of a routine call such as *currentFont.SetBoldOn()*.

HARD DATA

Woodfield, Dunsmore, and Shen conducted a study in which graduate and senior undergraduate computer-science students answered questions about two programs: one that was divided into eight routines along functional lines, and one that was divided into eight abstract-data-type routines (1981). Students using the abstract-data-type program scored over 30 percent higher than students using the functional version.

You don't have to pass data all over your program   In the examples just presented, you have to change *currentFont* directly or pass it to every routine that works with fonts. If you use an abstract data type, you don't have to pass *currentFont* all over the program and you don't have to turn it into global data either. The ADT has a structure that contains *currentFont*'s data. The data is directly accessed only by routines that are part of the ADT. Routines that aren't part of the ADT don't have to worry about the data.

You're able to work with real-world entities rather than with low-level implementation structures   You can define operations dealing with fonts so that most of the program operates solely in terms of fonts rather than in terms of array accesses, structure definitions, and *True* and *False*.

In this case, to define an abstract data type, you'd define a few routines to control fonts—perhaps like this:

```
currentFont.SetSizeInPoints( sizeInPoints )
currentFont.SetSizeInPixels( sizeInPixels )
currentFont.SetBoldOn()
currentFont.SetBoldOff()
currentFont.SetItalicOn()
currentFont.SetItalicOff()
currentFont.SetTypeFace( faceName )
```

KEY POINT

The code inside these routines would probably be short—it would probably be similar to the code you saw in the ad hoc approach to the font problem earlier. The difference is that you've isolated font operations in a set of routines. That provides a better level of abstraction for the rest of your program to work with fonts, and it gives you a layer of protection against changes in font operations.

More Examples of ADTs

Suppose you're writing software that controls the cooling system for a nuclear reactor. You can treat the cooling system as an abstract data type by defining the following operations for it:

```
coolingSystem.GetTemperature()
coolingSystem.SetCirculationRate( rate )
coolingSystem.OpenValve( valveNumber )
coolingSystem.CloseValve( valveNumber )
```

The specific environment would determine the code written to implement each of these operations. The rest of the program could deal with the cooling system through these functions and wouldn't have to worry about internal details of data-structure implementations, data-structure limitations, changes, and so on.

Here are more examples of abstract data types and likely operations on them:

Cruise Control	Blender	Fuel Tank
Set speed	Turn on	Fill tank
Get current settings	Turn off	Drain tank
Resume former speed	Set speed	Get tank capacity
Deactivate	Start "Insta-Pulverize"	Get tank status
	Stop "Insta-Pulverize"	

List	Light	Stack
Initialize list	Turn on	Initialize stack
Insert item in list	Turn off	Push item onto stack
Remove item from list		Pop item from stack
Read next item from list		Read top of stack

Set of Help Screens	**Menu**	**File**
Add help topic	Start new menu	Open file
Remove help topic	Delete menu	Read file
Set current help topic	Add menu item	Write file
Display help screen	Remove menu item	Set current file location
Remove help display	Activate menu item	Close file
Display help index	Deactivate menu item	
Back up to previous screen	Display menu	**Elevator**
	Hide menu	Move up one floor
Pointer	Get menu choice	Move down one floor
Get pointer to new memory		Move to specific floor
Dispose of memory from existing pointer		Report current floor
		Return to home floor
Change amount of memory allocated		

You can derive several guidelines from a study of these examples; those guidelines are described in the following subsections:

Build or use typical low-level data types as ADTs, not as low-level data types   Most discussions of ADTs focus on representing typical low-level data types as ADTs. As you can see from the examples, you can represent a stack, a list, and a queue, as well as virtually any other typical data type, as an ADT.

The question you need to ask is, "What does this stack, list, or queue represent?" If a stack represents a set of employees, treat the ADT as employees rather than as a stack. If a list represents a set of billing records, treat it as billing records rather than a list. If a queue represents cells in a spreadsheet, treat it as a collection of cells rather than a generic item in a queue. Treat yourself to the highest possible level of abstraction.

Treat common objects such as files as ADTs   Most languages include a few abstract data types that you're probably familiar with but might not think of as ADTs. File operations are a good example. While writing to disk, the operating system spares you the grief of positioning the read/write head at a specific physical address, allocating a new disk sector when you exhaust an old one, and interpreting cryptic error codes. The operating system provides a first level of abstraction and the ADTs for that level. High-level languages provide a second level of abstraction and ADTs for that higher level. A high-level language protects you from the messy details of generating operating-system calls and manipulating data buffers. It allows you to treat a chunk of disk space as a "file."

You can layer ADTs similarly. If you want to use an ADT at one level that offers data-structure level operations (like pushing and popping a stack), that's fine. You can create another level on top of that one that works at the level of the real-world problem.

Treat even simple items as ADTs   You don't have to have a formidable data type to justify using an abstract data type. One of the ADTs in the example list is a light that supports only two operations—turning it on and turning it off. You might think that it would be a waste to isolate simple "on" and "off" operations in routines of their own, but even simple operations can benefit from the use of ADTs. Putting the light and its operations into an ADT makes the code more self-documenting and easier to change, confines the potential consequences of changes to the *TurnLightOn()* and *TurnLight-Off()* routines, and reduces the number of data items you have to pass around.

Refer to an ADT independently of the medium it's stored on   Suppose you have an insurance-rates table that's so big that it's always stored on disk. You might be tempted to refer to it as a "rate *file*" and create access routines such as *RateFile.Read()*. When you refer to it as a file, however, you're exposing more information about the data than you need to. If you ever change the program so that the table is in memory instead of on disk, the code that refers to it as a file will be incorrect, misleading, and confusing. Try to make the names of classes and access routines independent of how the data is stored, and refer to the abstract data type, like the insurance-rates table, instead. That would give your class and access routine names like *rateTable.Read()* or simply *rates.Read()*.

Handling Multiple Instances of Data with ADTs in Non-Object-Oriented Environments

Object-oriented languages provide automatic support for handling multiple instances of an ADT. If you've worked exclusively in object-oriented environments and you've never had to handle the implementation details of multiple instances yourself, count your blessings! (You can also move on to the next section, "ADTs and Classes.")

If you're working in a non-object-oriented environment such as C, you will have to build support for multiple instances manually. In general, that means including services for the ADT to create and delete instances and designing the ADT's other services so that they can work with multiple instances.

The font ADT originally offered these services:

```
currentFont.SetSize( sizeInPoints )
currentFont.SetBoldOn()
currentFont.SetBoldOff()
currentFont.SetItalicOn()
currentFont.SetItalicOff()
currentFont.SetTypeFace( faceName )
```

In a non-object-oriented environment, these functions would not be attached to a class and would look more like this:

```
SetCurrentFontSize( sizeInPoints )
SetCurrentFontBoldOn()
SetCurrentFontBoldOff()
SetCurrentFontItalicOn()
SetCurrentFontItalicOff()
SetCurrentFontTypeFace( faceName )
```

If you want to work with more than one font at a time, you'll need to add services to create and delete font instances—maybe these:

```
CreateFont( fontId )
DeleteFont( fontId )
SetCurrentFont( fontId )
```

The notion of a *fontId* has been added as a way to keep track of multiple fonts as they're created and used. For other operations, you can choose from among three ways to handle the ADT interface:

- Option 1: Explicitly identify instances each time you use ADT services. In this case, you don't have the notion of a "current font." You pass *fontId* to each routine that manipulates fonts. The *Font* functions keep track of any underlying data, and the client code needs to keep track only of the *fontId*. This requires adding *fontId* as a parameter to each font routine.

- Option 2: Explicitly provide the data used by the ADT services. In this approach, you declare the data that the ADT uses within each routine that uses an ADT service. In other words, you create a *Font* data type that you pass to each of the ADT service routines. You must design the ADT service routines so that they use the *Font* data that's passed to them each time they're called. The client code doesn't need a font ID if you use this approach because it keeps track of the font data itself. (Even though the data is available directly from the *Font* data type, you should access it only with the ADT service routines. This is called keeping the structure "closed.")

  The advantage of this approach is that the ADT service routines don't have to look up font information based on a font ID. The disadvantage is that it exposes font data to the rest of the program, which increases the likelihood that client code will make use of the ADT's implementation details that should have remained hidden within the ADT.

- Option 3: Use implicit instances (with great care). Design a new service to call to make a specific font instance the current one—something like *SetCurrentFont* (*fontId*). Setting the current font makes all other services use the current font when they're called. If you use this approach, you don't need *fontId* as a parameter to the other services. For simple applications, this can streamline use of multiple instances. For complex applications, this systemwide dependence on state means that you must keep track of the current font instance throughout code that uses the *Font* functions. Complexity tends to proliferate, and for applications of any size, better alternatives exist.

Inside the abstract data type, you'll have a wealth of options for handling multiple instances, but outside, this sums up the choices if you're working in a non-object-oriented language.

ADTs and Classes

Abstract data types form the foundation for the concept of classes. In languages that support classes, you can implement each abstract data type as its own class. Classes usually involve the additional concepts of inheritance and polymorphism. One way of thinking of a class is as an abstract data type plus inheritance and polymorphism.

6.2 Good Class Interfaces

The first and probably most important step in creating a high-quality class is creating a good interface. This consists of creating a good abstraction for the interface to represent and ensuring that the details remain hidden behind the abstraction.

Good Abstraction

As "Form Consistent Abstractions" in Section 5.3 described, abstraction is the ability to view a complex operation in a simplified form. A class interface provides an abstraction of the implementation that's hidden behind the interface. The class's interface should offer a group of routines that clearly belong together.

You might have a class that implements an employee. It would contain data describing the employee's name, address, phone number, and so on. It would offer services to initialize and use an employee. Here's how that might look.

Cross-Reference Code samples in this book are formatted using a coding convention that emphasizes similarity of styles across multiple languages. For details on the convention (and discussions about multiple coding styles), see "Mixed-Language Programming Considerations" in Section 11.4.

C++ Example of a Class Interface That Presents a Good Abstraction

```cpp
class Employee {
public:
   // public constructors and destructors
   Employee();
   Employee(
      FullName name,
      String address,
      String workPhone,
      String homePhone,
      TaxId taxIdNumber,
      JobClassification jobClass
   );
   virtual ~Employee();
```

```
    // public routines
    FullName GetName() const;
    String GetAddress() const;
    String GetWorkPhone() const;
    String GetHomePhone() const;
    TaxId GetTaxIdNumber() const;
    JobClassification GetJobClassification() const;
    ...
private:
    ...
};
```

Internally, this class might have additional routines and data to support these services, but users of the class don't need to know anything about them. The class interface abstraction is great because every routine in the interface is working toward a consistent end.

A class that presents a poor abstraction would be one that contained a collection of miscellaneous functions. Here's an example:

CODING HORROR

C++ Example of a Class Interface That Presents a Poor Abstraction

```
class Program {
public:
    ...
    // public routines
    void InitializeCommandStack();
    void PushCommand( Command command );
    Command PopCommand();
    void ShutdownCommandStack();
    void InitializeReportFormatting();
    void FormatReport( Report report );
    void PrintReport( Report report );
    void InitializeGlobalData();
    void ShutdownGlobalData();
    ...
private:
    ...
};
```

Suppose that a class contains routines to work with a command stack, to format reports, to print reports, and to initialize global data. It's hard to see any connection among the command stack and report routines or the global data. The class interface doesn't present a consistent abstraction, so the class has poor cohesion. The routines should be reorganized into more-focused classes, each of which provides a better abstraction in its interface.

If these routines were part of a *Program* class, they could be revised to present a consistent abstraction, like so:

C++ Example of a Class Interface That Presents a Better Abstraction
```cpp
class Program {
public:
   ...
   // public routines
   void InitializeUserInterface();
   void ShutDownUserInterface();
   void InitializeReports();
   void ShutDownReports();
   ...
private:
   ...
};
```

The cleanup of this interface assumes that some of the original routines were moved to other, more appropriate classes and some were converted to private routines used by *InitializeUserInterface()* and the other routines.

This evaluation of class abstraction is based on the class's collection of public routines—that is, on the class's interface. The routines inside the class don't necessarily present good individual abstractions just because the overall class does, but they need to be designed to present good abstractions too. For guidelines on that, see Section 7.2, "Design at the Routine Level."

The pursuit of good, abstract interfaces gives rise to several guidelines for creating class interfaces.

Present a consistent level of abstraction in the class interface A good way to think about a class is as the mechanism for implementing the abstract data types described in Section 6.1. Each class should implement one and only one ADT. If you find a class implementing more than one ADT, or if you can't determine what ADT the class implements, it's time to reorganize the class into one or more well-defined ADTs.

Here's an example of a class that presents an interface that's inconsistent because its level of abstraction is not uniform:

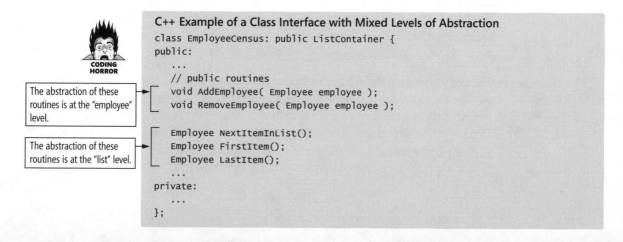

C++ Example of a Class Interface with Mixed Levels of Abstraction
```cpp
class EmployeeCensus: public ListContainer {
public:
   ...
   // public routines
   void AddEmployee( Employee employee );
   void RemoveEmployee( Employee employee );

   Employee NextItemInList();
   Employee FirstItem();
   Employee LastItem();
   ...
private:
   ...
};
```

CODING
HORROR

The abstraction of these routines is at the "employee" level.

The abstraction of these routines is at the "list" level.

This class is presenting two ADTs: an *Employee* and a *ListContainer*. This sort of mixed abstraction commonly arises when a programmer uses a container class or other library classes for implementation and doesn't hide the fact that a library class is used. Ask yourself whether the fact that a container class is used should be part of the abstraction. Usually that's an implementation detail that should be hidden from the rest of the program, like this:

C++ Example of a Class Interface with Consistent Levels of Abstraction

```cpp
class EmployeeCensus {
public:
   ...
   // public routines
   void AddEmployee( Employee employee );
   void RemoveEmployee( Employee employee );
   Employee NextEmployee();
   Employee FirstEmployee();
   Employee LastEmployee();
   ...
private:
   ListContainer m_EmployeeList;
   ...
};
```

The abstraction of all these routines is now at the "employee" level.

That the class uses the *ListContainer* library is now hidden.

Programmers might argue that inheriting from *ListContainer* is convenient because it supports polymorphism, allowing an external search or sort function that takes a *ListContainer* object. That argument fails the main test for inheritance, which is, "Is inheritance used only for "is a" relationships?" To inherit from *ListContainer* would mean that *EmployeeCensus* "is a" *ListContainer*, which obviously isn't true. If the abstraction of the *EmployeeCensus* object is that it can be searched or sorted, that should be incorporated as an explicit, consistent part of the class interface.

If you think of the class's public routines as an air lock that keeps water from getting into a submarine, inconsistent public routines are leaky panels in the class. The leaky panels might not let water in as quickly as an open air lock, but if you give them enough time, they'll still sink the boat. In practice, this is what happens when you mix levels of abstraction. As the program is modified, the mixed levels of abstraction make the program harder and harder to understand, and it gradually degrades until it becomes unmaintainable.

KEY POINT

Be sure you understand what abstraction the class is implementing Some classes are similar enough that you must be careful to understand which abstraction the class interface should capture. I once worked on a program that needed to allow information to be edited in a table format. We wanted to use a simple grid control, but the grid controls that were available didn't allow us to color the data-entry cells, so we decided to use a spreadsheet control that did provide that capability.

The spreadsheet control was far more complicated than the grid control, providing about 150 routines to the grid control's 15. Since our goal was to use a grid control, not a spreadsheet control, we assigned a programmer to write a wrapper class to hide the fact that we were using a spreadsheet control as a grid control. The programmer grumbled quite a bit about unnecessary overhead and bureaucracy, went away, and came back a couple days later with a wrapper class that faithfully exposed all 150 routines of the spreadsheet control.

This was not what was needed. We wanted a grid-control interface that encapsulated the fact that, behind the scenes, we were using a much more complicated spreadsheet control. The programmer should have exposed just the 15 grid-control routines plus a 16th routine that supported cell coloring. By exposing all 150 routines, the programmer created the possibility that, if we ever wanted to change the underlying implementation, we could find ourselves supporting 150 public routines. The programmer failed to achieve the encapsulation we were looking for, as well as creating a lot more work for himself than necessary.

Depending on specific circumstances, the right abstraction might be either a spreadsheet control or a grid control. When you have to choose between two similar abstractions, make sure you choose the right one.

Provide services in pairs with their opposites   Most operations have corresponding, equal, and opposite operations. If you have an operation that turns a light on, you'll probably need one to turn it off. If you have an operation to add an item to a list, you'll probably need one to delete an item from the list. If you have an operation to activate a menu item, you'll probably need one to deactivate an item. When you design a class, check each public routine to determine whether you need its complement. Don't create an opposite gratuitously, but do check to see whether you need one.

Move unrelated information to another class   In some cases, you'll find that half a class's routines work with half the class's data and half the routines work with the other half of the data. In such a case, you really have two classes masquerading as one. Break them up!

Make interfaces programmatic rather than semantic when possible   Each interface consists of a programmatic part and a semantic part. The programmatic part consists of the data types and other attributes of the interface that can be enforced by the compiler. The semantic part of the interface consists of the assumptions about how the interface will be used, which cannot be enforced by the compiler. The semantic interface includes considerations such as "*RoutineA* must be called before *RoutineB*" or "*RoutineA* will crash if *dataMember1* isn't initialized before it's passed to *RoutineA*." The semantic interface should be documented in comments, but try to keep interfaces minimally dependent on documentation. Any aspect of an interface that can't be enforced by the compiler is an aspect that's likely to be misused. Look for ways to convert semantic interface elements to programmatic interface elements by using *Asserts* or other techniques.

Cross-Reference For more suggestions about how to preserve code quality as code is modified, see Chapter 24, "Refactoring."

Beware of erosion of the interface's abstraction under modification As a class is modified and extended, you often discover additional functionality that's needed, that doesn't quite fit with the original class interface, but that seems too hard to implement any other way. For example, in the *Employee* class, you might find that the class evolves to look like this:

CODING HORROR

C++ Example of a Class Interface That's Eroding Under Maintenance
```cpp
class Employee {
public:
   ...
   // public routines
   FullName GetName() const;
   Address GetAddress() const;
   PhoneNumber GetWorkPhone() const;
   ...
   bool IsJobClassificationValid( JobClassification jobClass );
   bool IsZipCodeValid( Address address );
   bool IsPhoneNumberValid( PhoneNumber phoneNumber );

   SqlQuery GetQueryToCreateNewEmployee() const;
   SqlQuery GetQueryToModifyEmployee() const;
   SqlQuery GetQueryToRetrieveEmployee() const;
   ...
private:
   ...
};
```

What started out as a clean abstraction in an earlier code sample has evolved into a hodgepodge of functions that are only loosely related. There's no logical connection between employees and routines that check ZIP Codes, phone numbers, or job classifications. The routines that expose SQL query details are at a much lower level of abstraction than the *Employee* class, and they break the *Employee* abstraction.

Don't add public members that are inconsistent with the interface abstraction Each time you add a routine to a class interface, ask "Is this routine consistent with the abstraction provided by the existing interface?" If not, find a different way to make the modification and preserve the integrity of the abstraction.

Consider abstraction and cohesion together The ideas of abstraction and cohesion are closely related—a class interface that presents a good abstraction usually has strong cohesion. Classes with strong cohesion tend to present good abstractions, although that relationship is not as strong.

I have found that focusing on the abstraction presented by the class interface tends to provide more insight into class design than focusing on class cohesion. If you see that a class has weak cohesion and aren't sure how to correct it, ask yourself whether the class presents a consistent abstraction instead.

Good Encapsulation

Cross-Reference For more on encapsulation, see "Encapsulate Implementation Details" in Section 5.3.

As Section 5.3 discussed, encapsulation is a stronger concept than abstraction. Abstraction helps to manage complexity by providing models that allow you to ignore implementation details. Encapsulation is the enforcer that prevents you from looking at the details even if you want to.

The two concepts are related because, without encapsulation, abstraction tends to break down. In my experience, either you have both abstraction and encapsulation or you have neither. There is no middle ground.

> The single most important factor that distinguishes a well-designed module from a poorly designed one is the degree to which the module hides its internal data and other implementation details from other modules.
> —*Joshua Bloch*

Minimize accessibility of classes and members Minimizing accessibility is one of several rules that are designed to encourage encapsulation. If you're wondering whether a specific routine should be public, private, or protected, one school of thought is that you should favor the strictest level of privacy that's workable (Meyers 1998, Bloch 2001). I think that's a fine guideline, but I think the more important guideline is, "What best preserves the integrity of the interface abstraction?" If exposing the routine is consistent with the abstraction, it's probably fine to expose it. If you're not sure, hiding more is generally better than hiding less.

Don't expose member data in public Exposing member data is a violation of encapsulation and limits your control over the abstraction. As Arthur Riel points out, a *Point* class that exposes

```
float x;
float y;
float z;
```

is violating encapsulation because client code is free to monkey around with *Point*'s data and *Point* won't necessarily even know when its values have been changed (Riel 1996). However, a *Point* class that exposes

```
float GetX();
float GetY();
float GetZ();
void SetX( float x );
void SetY( float y );
void SetZ( float z );
```

is maintaining perfect encapsulation. You have no idea whether the underlying implementation is in terms of *floats* x, y, and z, whether *Point* is storing those items as *doubles* and converting them to *floats*, or whether *Point* is storing them on the moon and retrieving them from a satellite in outer space.

Avoid putting private implementation details into a class's interface With true encapsulation, programmers would not be able to see implementation details at all. They would be hidden both figuratively and literally. In popular languages, including

C++, however, the structure of the language requires programmers to disclose implementation details in the class interface. Here's an example:

C++ Example of Exposing a Class's Implementation Details

```
class Employee {
public:
   ...
   Employee(
      FullName name,
      String address,
      String workPhone,
      String homePhone,
      TaxId taxIdNumber,
      JobClassification jobClass
   );
   ...
   FullName GetName() const;
   String GetAddress() const;
   ...
private:
   String m_Name;
   String m_Address;
   int m_jobClass;
   ...
};
```

Here are the exposed implementation details. → (points to `String m_Name;` / `String m_Address;` / `int m_jobClass;`)

Including *private* declarations in the class header file might seem like a small transgression, but it encourages other programmers to examine the implementation details. In this case, the client code is intended to use the *JobClassification* type for job class, but the header file exposes the implementation detail that the job class is stored as an integer.

Scott Meyers describes a common way to address this issue in Item 34 of *Effective C++*, 2d ed. (Meyers 1998). You separate the class interface from the class implementation. Within the class declaration, include a pointer to the class's implementation but don't include any other implementation details.

C++ Example of Hiding a Class's Implementation Details

```
class Employee {
public:
   ...
   Employee( ... );
   ...
   FullName GetName() const;
   String GetAddress() const;
   ...
private:
   EmployeeImplementation *m_implementation;
};
```

Here the implementation details are hidden behind the pointer. → (points to `EmployeeImplementation *m_implementation;`)

Now you can put implementation details inside the *EmployeeImplementation* class, which should be visible only to the *Employee* class and not to the code that uses the *Employee* class.

If you've already written lots of code that doesn't use this approach for your project, you might decide it isn't worth the effort to convert a mountain of existing code to use this approach. But when you *read* code that exposes its implementation details, you can resist the urge to comb through the *private* section of the class interface looking for implementation clues.

Don't make assumptions about the class's users   A class should be designed and implemented to adhere to the contract implied by the class interface. It shouldn't make any assumptions about how that interface will or won't be used, other than what's documented in the interface. Comments like the following one are an indication that a class is more aware of its users than it should be:

```
-- initialize x, y, and z to 1.0 because DerivedClass blows
-- up if they're initialized to 0.0
```

Avoid friend classes   In a few circumstances such as the State pattern, friend classes can be used in a disciplined way that contributes to managing complexity (Gamma et al. 1995). But, in general, friend classes violate encapsulation. They expand the amount of code you have to think about at any one time, thereby increasing complexity.

Don't put a routine into the public interface just because it uses only public routines   The fact that a routine uses only public routines is not a significant consideration. Instead, ask whether exposing the routine would be consistent with the abstraction presented by the interface.

Favor read-time convenience to write-time convenience   Code is read far more times than it's written, even during initial development. Favoring a technique that speeds write-time convenience at the expense of read-time convenience is a false economy. This is especially applicable to creation of class interfaces. Even if a routine doesn't quite fit the interface's abstraction, sometimes it's tempting to add a routine to an interface that would be convenient for the particular client of a class that you're working on at the time. But adding that routine is the first step down a slippery slope, and it's better not to take even the first step.

> It ain't abstract if you have to look at the underlying implementation to understand what's going on.
> —*P. J. Plauger*

Be very, very wary of semantic violations of encapsulation   At one time I thought that when I learned how to avoid syntax errors I would be home free. I soon discovered that learning how to avoid syntax errors had merely bought me a ticket to a whole new theater of coding errors, most of which were more difficult to diagnose and correct than the syntax errors.

The difficulty of semantic encapsulation compared to syntactic encapsulation is similar. Syntactically, it's relatively easy to avoid poking your nose into the internal workings of another class just by declaring the class's internal routines and data *private*. Achieving semantic encapsulation is another matter entirely. Here are some examples of the ways that a user of a class can break encapsulation semantically:

- Not calling Class A's *InitializeOperations()* routine because you know that Class A's *PerformFirstOperation()* routine calls it automatically.

- Not calling the *database.Connect()* routine before you call *employee.Retrieve(database)* because you know that the *employee.Retrieve()* function will connect to the database if there isn't already a connection.

- Not calling Class A's *Terminate()* routine because you know that Class A's *PerformFinalOperation()* routine has already called it.

- Using a pointer or reference to *ObjectB* created by *ObjectA* even after *ObjectA* has gone out of scope, because you know that *ObjectA* keeps *ObjectB* in *static* storage and *ObjectB* will still be valid.

- Using Class B's *MAXIMUM_ELEMENTS* constant instead of using *ClassA.MAXIMUM_ELEMENTS*, because you know that they're both equal to the same value.

KEY POINT

The problem with each of these examples is that they make the client code dependent not on the class's public interface, but on its private implementation. Anytime you find yourself looking at a class's implementation to figure out how to use the class, you're not programming to the interface; you're programming *through* the interface *to* the implementation. If you're programming through the interface, encapsulation is broken, and once encapsulation starts to break down, abstraction won't be far behind.

If you can't figure out how to use a class based solely on its interface documentation, the right response is *not* to pull up the source code and look at the implementation. That's good initiative but bad judgment. The right response is to contact the author of the class and say "I can't figure out how to use this class." The right response on the class-author's part is *not* to answer your question face to face. The right response for the class author is to check out the class-interface file, modify the class-interface documentation, check the file back in, and then say "See if you can understand how it works now." You want this dialog to occur in the interface code itself so that it will be preserved for future programmers. You don't want the dialog to occur solely in your own mind, which will bake subtle semantic dependencies into the client code that uses the class. And you don't want the dialog to occur interpersonally so that it benefits only your code but no one else's.

Watch for coupling that's too tight   "Coupling" refers to how tight the connection is between two classes. In general, the looser the connection, the better. Several general guidelines flow from this concept:

- Minimize accessibility of classes and members.

- Avoid *friend* classes, because they're tightly coupled.

- Make data *private* rather than *protected* in a base class to make derived classes less tightly coupled to the base class.

- Avoid exposing member data in a class's public interface.

- Be wary of semantic violations of encapsulation.

- Observe the "Law of Demeter" (discussed in Section 6.3 of this chapter).

Coupling goes hand in glove with abstraction and encapsulation. Tight coupling occurs when an abstraction is leaky, or when encapsulation is broken. If a class offers an incomplete set of services, other routines might find they need to read or write its internal data directly. That opens up the class, making it a glass box instead of a black box, and it virtually eliminates the class's encapsulation.

6.3 Design and Implementation Issues

Defining good class interfaces goes a long way toward creating a high-quality program. The internal class design and implementation are also important. This section discusses issues related to containment, inheritance, member functions and data, class coupling, constructors, and value-vs.-reference objects.

Containment ("has a" Relationships)

KEY POINT

Containment is the simple idea that a class contains a primitive data element or object. A lot more is written about inheritance than about containment, but that's because inheritance is more tricky and error-prone, not because it's better. Containment is the work-horse technique in object-oriented programming.

Implement "has a" through containment   One way of thinking of containment is as a "has a" relationship. For example, an employee "has a" name, "has a" phone number, "has a" tax ID, and so on. You can usually accomplish this by making the name, phone number, and tax ID member data of the *Employee* class.

Implement "has a" through private inheritance as a last resort   In some instances you might find that you can't achieve containment through making one object a member of another. In that case, some experts suggest privately inheriting from the contained object (Meyers 1998, Sutter 2000). The main reason you would do that is to set up the containing class to access protected member functions or protected member data of the class that's contained. In practice, this approach creates an overly cozy relationship with the ancestor class and violates encapsulation. It tends to point to design errors that should be resolved some way other than through private inheritance.

Be critical of classes that contain more than about seven data members   The number "7±2" has been found to be a number of discrete items a person can remember while performing other tasks (Miller 1956). If a class contains more than about seven data members, consider whether the class should be decomposed into multiple smaller classes (Riel 1996). You might err more toward the high end of 7±2 if the data members are primitive data types like integers and strings, more toward the lower end of 7±2 if the data members are complex objects.

Inheritance ("is a" Relationships)

Inheritance is the idea that one class is a specialization of another class. The purpose of inheritance is to create simpler code by defining a base class that specifies common elements of two or more derived classes. The common elements can be routine interfaces, implementations, data members, or data types. Inheritance helps avoid the need to repeat code and data in multiple locations by centralizing it within a base class.

When you decide to use inheritance, you have to make several decisions:

- For each member routine, will the routine be visible to derived classes? Will it have a default implementation? Will the default implementation be overridable?

- For each data member (including variables, named constants, enumerations, and so on), will the data member be visible to derived classes?

The following subsections explain the ins and outs of making these decisions:

> The single most important rule in object-oriented programming with C++ is this: public inheritance means "is a." Commit this rule to memory.
> —*Scott Meyers*

Implement "is a" through public inheritance   When a programmer decides to create a new class by inheriting from an existing class, that programmer is saying that the new class "is a" more specialized version of the older class. The base class sets expectations about how the derived class will operate and imposes constraints on how the derived class can operate (Meyers 1998).

If the derived class isn't going to adhere *completely* to the same interface contract defined by the base class, inheritance is not the right implementation technique. Consider containment or making a change further up the inheritance hierarchy.

Design and document for inheritance or prohibit it   Inheritance adds complexity to a program, and, as such, it's a dangerous technique. As Java guru Joshua Bloch says, "Design and document for inheritance, or prohibit it." If a class isn't designed to be inherited from, make its members non-*virtual* in C++, *final* in Java, or non-*overridable* in Microsoft Visual Basic so that you can't inherit from it.

Adhere to the Liskov Substitution Principle (LSP)   In one of object-oriented programming's seminal papers, Barbara Liskov argued that you shouldn't inherit from a base class unless the derived class truly "is a" more specific version of the base class (Liskov 1988). Andy Hunt and Dave Thomas summarize LSP like this: "Subclasses must be usable through the base class interface without the need for the user to know the difference" (Hunt and Thomas 2000).

In other words, all the routines defined in the base class should mean the same thing when they're used in each of the derived classes.

If you have a base class of *Account* and derived classes of *CheckingAccount*, *SavingsAccount*, and *AutoLoanAccount*, a programmer should be able to invoke any of the routines derived from *Account* on any of *Account*'s subtypes without caring about which subtype a specific account object is.

If a program has been written so that the Liskov Substitution Principle is true, inheritance is a powerful tool for reducing complexity because a programmer can focus on the generic attributes of an object without worrying about the details. If a programmer must be constantly thinking about semantic differences in subclass implementations, then inheritance is increasing complexity rather than reducing it. Suppose a programmer has to think this: "If I call the *InterestRate()* routine on *CheckingAccount* or *SavingsAccount*, it returns the interest the bank pays, but if I call *InterestRate()* on *AutoLoanAccount* I have to change the sign because it returns the interest the consumer pays to the bank." According to LSP, *AutoLoanAccount* should not inherit from the *Account* base class in this example because the semantics of the *InterestRate()* routine are not the same as the semantics of the base class's *InterestRate()* routine.

Be sure to inherit only what you want to inherit A derived class can inherit member routine interfaces, implementations, or both. Table 6-1 shows the variations of how routines can be implemented and overridden.

Table 6-1 Variations on Inherited Routines

	Overridable	Not Overridable
Implementation: Default Provided	Overridable Routine	Non-Overridable Routine
Implementation: No Default Provided	Abstract Overridable Routine	Not used (doesn't make sense to leave a routine undefined and not allow it to be overridden)

As the table suggests, inherited routines come in three basic flavors:

- An *abstract overridable routine* means that the derived class inherits the routine's interface but not its implementation.

- An *overridable routine* means that the derived class inherits the routine's interface and a default implementation and it is allowed to override the default implementation.

- A *non-overridable routine* means that the derived class inherits the routine's interface and its default implementation and it is not allowed to override the routine's implementation.

When you choose to implement a new class through inheritance, think through the kind of inheritance you want for each member routine. Beware of inheriting implementation just because you're inheriting an interface, and beware of inheriting an interface just because you want to inherit an implementation. If you want to use a class's implementation but not its interface, use containment rather than inheritance.

Don't "override" a non-overridable member function   Both C++ and Java allow a programmer to override a non-overridable member routine—kind of. If a function is *private* in the base class, a derived class can create a function with the same name. To the programmer reading the code in the derived class, such a function can create confusion because it looks like it should be polymorphic, but it isn't; it just has the same name. Another way to state this guideline is, "Don't reuse names of non-overridable base-class routines in derived classes."

Move common interfaces, data, and behavior as high as possible in the inheritance tree   The higher you move interfaces, data, and behavior, the more easily derived classes can use them. How high is too high? Let *abstraction* be your guide. If you find that moving a routine higher would break the higher object's abstraction, don't do it.

Be suspicious of classes of which there is only one instance   A single instance might indicate that the design confuses objects with classes. Consider whether you could just create an object instead of a new class. Can the variation of the derived class be represented in data rather than as a distinct class? The Singleton pattern is one notable exception to this guideline.

Be suspicious of base classes of which there is only one derived class   When I see a base class that has only one derived class, I suspect that some programmer has been "designing ahead"—trying to anticipate future needs, usually without fully understanding what those future needs are. The best way to prepare for future work is not to design extra layers of base classes that "might be needed someday"; it's to make current work as clear, straightforward, and simple as possible. That means not creating any more inheritance structure than is absolutely necessary.

Be suspicious of classes that override a routine and do nothing inside the derived routine   This typically indicates an error in the design of the base class. For instance, suppose you have a class *Cat* and a routine *Scratch()* and suppose that you eventually find out that some cats are declawed and can't scratch. You might be tempted to create a class derived from *Cat* named *ScratchlessCat* and override the *Scratch()* routine to do nothing. This approach presents several problems:

- It violates the abstraction (interface contract) presented in the *Cat* class by changing the semantics of its interface.

- This approach quickly gets out of control when you extend it to other derived classes. What happens when you find a cat without a tail? Or a cat that doesn't catch mice? Or a cat that doesn't drink milk? Eventually you'll end up with derived classes like *ScratchlessTaillessMicelessMilklessCat*.

- Over time, this approach gives rise to code that's confusing to maintain because the interfaces and behavior of the ancestor classes imply little or nothing about the behavior of their descendants.

The place to fix this problem is not in the base class, but in the original *Cat* class. Create a *Claws* class and contain that within the *Cats* class. The root problem was the assumption that all cats scratch, so fix that problem at the source, rather than just bandaging it at the destination.

Avoid deep inheritance trees   Object-oriented programming provides a large number of techniques for managing complexity. But every powerful tool has its hazards, and some object-oriented techniques have a tendency to increase complexity rather than reduce it.

In his excellent book *Object-Oriented Design Heuristics* (1996), Arthur Riel suggests limiting inheritance hierarchies to a maximum of six levels. Riel bases his recommendation on the "magic number 7±2," but I think that's grossly optimistic. In my experience most people have trouble juggling more than two or three levels of inheritance in their brains at once. The "magic number 7±2" is probably better applied as a limit to the *total number of subclasses* of a base class rather than the number of levels in an inheritance tree.

Deep inheritance trees have been found to be significantly associated with increased fault rates (Basili, Briand, and Melo 1996). Anyone who has ever tried to debug a complex inheritance hierarchy knows why. Deep inheritance trees increase complexity, which is exactly the opposite of what inheritance should be used to accomplish. Keep the primary technical mission in mind. Make sure you're using inheritance to avoid duplicating code and to *minimize complexity*.

Prefer polymorphism to extensive type checking   Frequently repeated *case* statements sometimes suggest that inheritance might be a better design choice, although this is not always true. Here is a classic example of code that cries out for a more object-oriented approach:

C++ Example of a Case Statement That Probably Should Be Replaced by Polymorphism

```cpp
switch ( shape.type ) {
   case Shape_Circle:
      shape.DrawCircle();
      break;
   case Shape_Square:
      shape.DrawSquare();
      break;
   ...
}
```

In this example, the calls to *shape.DrawCircle()* and *shape.DrawSquare()* should be replaced by a single routine named *shape.Draw()*, which can be called regardless of whether the shape is a circle or a square.

On the other hand, sometimes *case* statements are used to separate truly different kinds of objects or behavior. Here is an example of a *case* statement that is appropriate in an object-oriented program:

```
C++ Example of a Case Statement That Probably Should Not Be Replaced
by Polymorphism
switch ( ui.Command() ) {
    case Command_OpenFile:
        OpenFile();
        break;
    case Command_Print:
        Print();
        break;
    case Command_Save:
        Save();
        break;
    case Command_Exit:
        ShutDown();
        break;
    ...
}
```

In this case, it would be possible to create a base class with derived classes and a polymorphic *DoCommand()* routine for each command (as in the Command pattern). But in a simple case like this one, the meaning of *DoCommand()* would be so diluted as to be meaningless, and the *case* statement is the more understandable solution.

Make all data private, not protected As Joshua Bloch says, "Inheritance breaks encapsulation" (2001). When you inherit from an object, you obtain privileged access to that object's protected routines and data. If the derived class really needs access to the base class's attributes, provide protected accessor functions instead.

Multiple Inheritance

The one indisputable fact about multiple inheritance in C++ is that it opens up a Pandora's box of complexities that simply do not exist under single inheritance.
—*Scott Meyers*

Inheritance is a power tool. It's like using a chain saw to cut down a tree instead of a manual crosscut saw. It can be incredibly useful when used with care, but it's dangerous in the hands of someone who doesn't observe proper precautions.

If inheritance is a chain saw, multiple inheritance is a 1950s-era chain saw with no blade guard, no automatic shutoff, and a finicky engine. There are times when such a tool is valuable; mostly, however, you're better off leaving the tool in the garage where it can't do any damage.

Although some experts recommend broad use of multiple inheritance (Meyer 1997), in my experience multiple inheritance is useful primarily for defining "mixins," simple classes that are used to add a set of properties to an object. Mixins are called mixins because they allow properties to be "mixed in" to derived classes. Mixins might be classes like *Displayable*, *Persistant*, *Serializable*, or *Sortable*. Mixins are nearly always abstract and aren't meant to be instantiated independently of other objects.

Mixins require the use of multiple inheritance, but they aren't subject to the classic diamond-inheritance problem associated with multiple inheritance as long as all mixins are truly independent of each other. They also make the design more comprehensible by "chunking" attributes together. A programmer will have an easier time understanding that an object uses the mixins *Displayable* and *Persistent* than understanding that an object uses the 11 more-specific routines that would otherwise be needed to implement those two properties.

Java and Visual Basic recognize the value of mixins by allowing multiple inheritance of interfaces but only single-class inheritance. C++ supports multiple inheritance of both interface and implementation. Programmers should use multiple inheritance only after carefully considering the alternatives and weighing the impact on system complexity and comprehensibility.

Why Are There So Many Rules for Inheritance?

KEY POINT

This section has presented numerous rules for staying out of trouble with inheritance. The underlying message of all these rules is that *inheritance tends to work against the primary technical imperative you have as a programmer, which is to manage complexity*. For the sake of controlling complexity, you should maintain a heavy bias against inheritance. Here's a summary of when to use inheritance and when to use containment:

Cross-Reference For more on complexity, see "Software's Primary Technical Imperative: Managing Complexity" in Section 5.2.

- If multiple classes share common data but not behavior, create a common object that those classes can contain.

- If multiple classes share common behavior but not data, derive them from a common base class that defines the common routines.

- If multiple classes share common data and behavior, inherit from a common base class that defines the common data and routines.

- Inherit when you want the base class to control your interface; contain when you want to control your interface.

Member Functions and Data

Cross-Reference For more discussion of routines in general, see Chapter 7, "High-Quality Routines."

Here are a few guidelines for implementing member functions and member data effectively.

Keep the number of routines in a class as small as possible   A study of C++ programs found that higher numbers of routines per class were associated with higher fault rates (Basili, Briand, and Melo 1996). However, other competing factors were found to be more significant, including deep inheritance trees, large number of routines called within a class, and strong coupling between classes. Evaluate the tradeoff between minimizing the number of routines and these other factors.

Disallow implicitly generated member functions and operators you don't want
Sometimes you'll find that you want to disallow certain functions—perhaps you want to disallow assignment, or you don't want to allow an object to be constructed. You might think that, since the compiler generates operators automatically, you're stuck allowing access. But in such cases you can disallow those uses by declaring the constructor, assignment operator, or other function or operator *private*, which will prevent clients from accessing it. (Making the constructor private is a standard technique for defining a singleton class, which is discussed later in this chapter.)

Minimize the number of different routines called by a class   One study found that the number of faults in a class was statistically correlated with the total number of routines that were called from within a class (Basili, Briand, and Melo 1996). The same study found that the more classes a class used, the higher its fault rate tended to be. These concepts are sometimes called "fan out."

Further Reading Good accounts of the Law of Demeter can be found in *Pragmatic Programmer* (Hunt and Thomas 2000), *Applying UML and Patterns* (Larman 2001), and *Fundamentals of Object-Oriented Design in UML* (Page-Jones 2000).

Minimize indirect routine calls to other classes   Direct connections are hazardous enough. Indirect connections—such as *account.ContactPerson().DaytimeContact-Info().PhoneNumber()*—tend to be even more hazardous. Researchers have formulated a rule called the "Law of Demeter" (Lieberherr and Holland 1989), which essentially states that Object A can call any of its own routines. If Object A instantiates an Object B, it can call any of Object B's routines. But it should avoid calling routines on objects provided by Object B. In the *account* example above, that means *account.ContactPerson()* is OK but *account.ContactPerson().DaytimeContactInfo()* is not.

This is a simplified explanation. See the additional resources at the end of this chapter for more details.

In general, minimize the extent to which a class collaborates with other classes   Try to minimize all of the following:

- Number of kinds of objects instantiated
- Number of different direct routine calls on instantiated objects
- Number of routine calls on objects returned by other instantiated objects

Constructors

Following are some guidelines that apply specifically to constructors. Guidelines for constructors are pretty similar across languages (C++, Java, and Visual Basic, anyway). Destructors vary more, so you should check out the materials listed in this chapter's "Additional Resources" section for information on destructors.

Initialize all member data in all constructors, if possible Initializing all data members in all constructors is an inexpensive defensive programming practice.

Further Reading The code to do this in C++ would be similar. For details, see *More Effective C++*, Item 26 (Meyers 1998).

Enforce the singleton property by using a private constructor If you want to define a class that allows only one object to be instantiated, you can enforce this by hiding all the constructors of the class and then providing a *static GetInstance()* routine to access the class's single instance. Here's an example of how that would work:

Java Example of Enforcing a Singleton with a Private Constructor

Here is the private constructor.

Here is the public routine that provides access to the single instance.

Here is the single instance.

```java
public class MaxId {
   // constructors and destructors
   private MaxId() {
      ...
   }
   ...

   // public routines
   public static MaxId GetInstance() {
      return m_instance;
   }
   ...

   // private members
   private static final MaxId m_instance = new MaxId();
   ...
}
```

The private constructor is called only when the *static* object *m_instance* is initialized. In this approach, if you want to reference the *MaxId* singleton, you would simply refer to *MaxId.GetInstance()*.

Prefer deep copies to shallow copies until proven otherwise One of the major decisions you'll make about complex objects is whether to implement deep copies or shallow copies of the object. A deep copy of an object is a member-wise copy of the object's member data; a shallow copy typically just points to or refers to a single reference copy, although the specific meanings of "deep" and "shallow" vary.

The motivation for creating shallow copies is typically to improve performance. Although creating multiple copies of large objects might be aesthetically offensive, it rarely causes any measurable performance impact. A small number of objects might cause performance issues, but programmers are notoriously poor at guessing which code really causes problems. (For details, see Chapter 25, "Code-Tuning Strategies.")

Because it's a poor tradeoff to add complexity for dubious performance gains, a good approach to deep vs. shallow copies is to prefer deep copies until proven otherwise.

Deep copies are simpler to code and maintain than shallow copies. In addition to the code either kind of object would contain, shallow copies add code to count references, ensure safe object copies, safe comparisons, safe deletes, and so on. This code can be error-prone, and you should avoid it unless there's a compelling reason to create it.

If you find that you do need to use a shallow-copy approach, Scott Meyers's *More Effective C++*, Item 29 (1996) contains an excellent discussion of the issues in C++. Martin Fowler's *Refactoring* (1999) describes the specific steps needed to convert from shallow copies to deep copies and from deep copies to shallow copies. (Fowler calls them reference objects and value objects.)

6.4 Reasons to Create a Class

Cross-Reference Reasons for creating classes and routines overlap. See Section 7.1.

If you believe everything you read, you might get the idea that the only reason to create a class is to model real-world objects. In practice, classes get created for many more reasons than that. Here's a list of good reasons to create a class.

Cross-Reference For more on identifying real-world objects, see "Find Real-World Objects" in Section 5.3.

Model real-world objects   Modeling real-world objects might not be the only reason to create a class, but it's still a good reason! Create a class for each real-world object type that your program models. Put the data needed for the object into the class, and then build service routines that model the behavior of the object. See the discussion of ADTs in Section 6.1 for examples.

Model abstract objects   Another good reason to create a class is to model an *abstract object*—an object that isn't a concrete, real-world object but that provides an abstraction of other concrete objects. A good example is the classic *Shape* object. *Circle* and *Square* really exist, but *Shape* is an abstraction of other specific shapes.

On programming projects, the abstractions are not ready-made the way *Shape* is, so we have to work harder to come up with clean abstractions. The process of distilling abstract concepts from real-world entities is non-deterministic, and different designers will abstract out different generalities. If we didn't know about geometric shapes like circles, squares and triangles, for example, we might come up with more unusual shapes like squash shape, rutabaga shape, and Pontiac Aztek shape. Coming up with appropriate abstract objects is one of the major challenges in object-oriented design.

KEY POINT

Reduce complexity   The single most important reason to create a class is to reduce a program's complexity. Create a class to hide information so that you won't need to think about it. Sure, you'll need to think about it when you write the class. But after it's written, you should be able to forget the details and use the class without any knowledge of its internal workings. Other reasons to create classes—minimizing code size, improving maintainability, and improving correctness—are also good reasons, but without the abstractive power of classes, complex programs would be impossible to manage intellectually.

Isolate complexity   Complexity in all forms—complicated algorithms, large data sets, intricate communications protocols, and so on—is prone to errors. If an error does occur, it will be easier to find if it isn't spread through the code but is localized within a class. Changes arising from fixing the error won't affect other code because only one class will have to be fixed—other code won't be touched. If you find a better, simpler, or more reliable algorithm, it will be easier to replace the old algorithm if it has been isolated into a class. During development, it will be easier to try several designs and keep the one that works best.

Hide implementation details   The desire to hide implementation details is a wonderful reason to create a class whether the details are as complicated as a convoluted database access or as mundane as whether a specific data member is stored as a number or a string.

Limit effects of changes   Isolate areas that are likely to change so that the effects of changes are limited to the scope of a single class or a few classes. Design so that areas that are most likely to change are the easiest to change. Areas likely to change include hardware dependencies, input/output, complex data types, and business rules. The subsection titled "Hide Secrets (Information Hiding)" in Section 5.3 described several common sources of change.

Cross-Reference For a discussion of problems associated with using global data, see Section 13.3, "Global Data."

Hide global data   If you need to use global data, you can hide its implementation details behind a class interface. Working with global data through access routines provides several benefits compared to working with global data directly. You can change the structure of the data without changing your program. You can monitor accesses to the data. The discipline of using access routines also encourages you to think about whether the data is really global; it often becomes apparent that the "global data" is really just object data.

Streamline parameter passing   If you're passing a parameter among several routines, that might indicate a need to factor those routines into a class that share the parameter as object data. Streamlining parameter passing isn't a goal, per se, but passing lots of data around suggests that a different class organization might work better.

Cross-Reference For details on information hiding, see "Hide Secrets (Information Hiding)" in Section 5.3.

Make central points of control   It's a good idea to control each task in one place. Control assumes many forms. Knowledge of the number of entries in a table is one form. Control of devices—files, database connections, printers, and so on—is another. Using one class to read from and write to a database is a form of centralized control. If the database needs to be converted to a flat file or to in-memory data, the changes will affect only one class.

The idea of centralized control is similar to information hiding, but it has unique heuristic power that makes it worth adding to your programming toolbox.

Facilitate reusable code   Code put into well-factored classes can be reused in other programs more easily than the same code embedded in one larger class. Even if a section of code is called from only one place in the program and is understandable as part of a larger class, it makes sense to put it into its own class if that piece of code might be used in another program.

HARD DATA

NASA's Software Engineering Laboratory studied ten projects that pursued reuse aggressively (McGarry, Waligora, and McDermott 1989). In both the object-oriented and the functionally oriented approaches, the initial projects weren't able to take much of their code from previous projects because previous projects hadn't established a sufficient code base. Subsequently, the projects that used functional design were able to take about 35 percent of their code from previous projects. Projects that used an object-oriented approach were able to take more than 70 percent of their code from previous projects. If you can avoid writing 70 percent of your code by planning ahead, do it!

Cross-Reference For more on implementing the minimum amount of functionality required, see "A program contains code that seems like it might be needed someday" in Section 24.2.

Notably, the core of NASA's approach to creating reusable classes does not involve "designing for reuse." NASA identifies reuse candidates at the ends of their projects. They then perform the work needed to make the classes reusable as a special project at the end of the main project or as the first step in a new project. This approach helps prevent "gold-plating"—creation of functionality that isn't required and that unnecessarily adds complexity.

Plan for a family of programs   If you expect a program to be modified, it's a good idea to isolate the parts that you expect to change by putting them into their own classes. You can then modify the classes without affecting the rest of the program, or you can put in completely new classes instead. Thinking through not just what one program will look like but what the whole family of programs might look like is a powerful heuristic for anticipating entire categories of changes (Parnas 1976).

Several years ago I managed a team that wrote a series of programs used by our clients to sell insurance. We had to tailor each program to the specific client's insurance rates, quote-report format, and so on. But many parts of the programs were similar: the classes that input information about potential customers, that stored information in a customer database, that looked up rates, that computed total rates for a group, and so on. The team factored the program so that each part that varied from client to client was in its own class. The initial programming might have taken three months or so, but when we got a new client, we merely wrote a handful of new classes for the new client and dropped them into the rest of the code. A few days' work and—voila!—custom software!

Package related operations   In cases in which you can't hide information, share data, or plan for flexibility, you can still package sets of operations into sensible groups, such as trig functions, statistical functions, string-manipulation routines, bit-manipulation routines, graphics routines, and so on. Classes are one means of combining related operations. You could also use packages, namespaces, or header files, depending on the language you're working in.

Accomplish a specific refactoring   Many of the specific refactorings described in Chapter 24, "Refactoring," result in new classes—including converting one class to two, hiding a delegate, removing a middle man, and introducing an extension class. These new classes could be motivated by a desire to better accomplish any of the objectives described throughout this section.

Classes to Avoid

While classes in general are good, you can run into a few gotchas. Here are some classes to avoid.

Avoid creating god classes   Avoid creating omniscient classes that are all-knowing and all-powerful. If a class spends its time retrieving data from other classes using *Get()* and *Set()* routines (that is, digging into their business and telling them what to do), ask whether that functionality might better be organized into those other classes rather than into the god class (Riel 1996).

Cross-Reference This kind of class is usually called a structure. For more on structures, see Section 13.1, "Structures."

Eliminate irrelevant classes   If a class consists only of data but no behavior, ask yourself whether it's really a class and consider demoting it so that its member data just becomes attributes of one or more other classes.

Avoid classes named after verbs   A class that has only behavior but no data is generally not really a class. Consider turning a class like *DatabaseInitialization()* or *StringBuilder()* into a routine on some other class.

Summary of Reasons to Create a Class

Here's a summary list of the valid reasons to create a class:

- Model real-world objects
- Model abstract objects
- Reduce complexity
- Isolate complexity
- Hide implementation details
- Limit effects of changes
- Hide global data

- Streamline parameter passing

- Make central points of control

- Facilitate reusable code

- Plan for a family of programs

- Package related operations

- Accomplish a specific refactoring

6.5 Language-Specific Issues

Approaches to classes in different programming languages vary in interesting ways. Consider how you override a member routine to achieve polymorphism in a derived class. In Java, all routines are overridable by default and a routine must be declared *final* to prevent a derived class from overriding it. In C++, routines are not overridable by default. A routine must be declared *virtual* in the base class to be overridable. In Visual Basic, a routine must be declared *overridable* in the base class and the derived class should use the *overrides* keyword.

Here are some of the class-related areas that vary significantly depending on the language:

- Behavior of overridden constructors and destructors in an inheritance tree

- Behavior of constructors and destructors under exception-handling conditions

- Importance of default constructors (constructors with no arguments)

- Time at which a destructor or finalizer is called

- Wisdom of overriding the language's built-in operators, including assignment and equality

- How memory is handled as objects are created and destroyed or as they are declared and go out of scope

Detailed discussions of these issues are beyond the scope of this book, but the "Additional Resources" section points to good language-specific resources.

6.6 Beyond Classes: Packages

Cross-Reference For more on the distinction between classes and packages, see "Levels of Design" in Section 5.2.

Classes are currently the best way for programmers to achieve modularity. But modularity is a big topic, and it extends beyond classes. Over the past several decades, software development has advanced in large part by increasing the granularity of the aggregations that we have to work with. The first aggregation we had was the statement, which at the time seemed like a big step up from machine instructions. Then came subroutines, and later came classes.

It's evident that we could better support the goals of abstraction and encapsulation if we had good tools for aggregating groups of objects. Ada supported the notion of . packages more than a decade ago, and Java supports packages today. If you're programming in a language that doesn't support packages directly, you can create your own poor-programmer's version of a package and enforce it through programming standards that include the following:

- Naming conventions that differentiate which classes are public and which are for the package's private use

- Naming conventions, code-organization conventions (project structure), or both that identify which package each class belongs to

- Rules that define which packages are allowed to use which other packages, including whether the usage can be inheritance, containment, or both

These workarounds are good examples of the distinction between programming *in* a language vs. programming *into* a language. For more on this distinction, see Section 34.4, "Program into Your Language, Not in It."

cc2e.com/0672

Cross-Reference This is a checklist of considerations about the quality of the class. For a list of the steps used to build a class, see the checklist "The Pseudocode Programming Process" in Chapter 9, page 233.

CHECKLIST: Class Quality
Abstract Data Types
- ❏ Have you thought of the classes in your program as abstract data types and evaluated their interfaces from that point of view?

Abstraction
- ❏ Does the class have a central purpose?

- ❏ Is the class well named, and does its name describe its central purpose?

- ❏ Does the class's interface present a consistent abstraction?

- ❏ Does the class's interface make obvious how you should use the class?

- ❏ Is the class's interface abstract enough that you don't have to think about how its services are implemented? Can you treat the class as a black box?

- ❏ Are the class's services complete enough that other classes don't have to meddle with its internal data?

- ❏ Has unrelated information been moved out of the class?

- ❏ Have you thought about subdividing the class into component classes, and have you subdivided it as much as you can?

- ❏ Are you preserving the integrity of the class's interface as you modify the class?

Encapsulation

- ❏ Does the class minimize accessibility to its members?
- ❏ Does the class avoid exposing member data?
- ❏ Does the class hide its implementation details from other classes as much as the programming language permits?
- ❏ Does the class avoid making assumptions about its users, including its derived classes?
- ❏ Is the class independent of other classes? Is it loosely coupled?

Inheritance

- ❏ Is inheritance used only to model "is a" relationships—that is, do derived classes adhere to the Liskov Substitution Principle?
- ❏ Does the class documentation describe the inheritance strategy?
- ❏ Do derived classes avoid "overriding" non-overridable routines?
- ❏ Are common interfaces, data, and behavior as high as possible in the inheritance tree?
- ❏ Are inheritance trees fairly shallow?
- ❏ Are all data members in the base class private rather than protected?

Other Implementation Issues

- ❏ Does the class contain about seven data members or fewer?
- ❏ Does the class minimize direct and indirect routine calls to other classes?
- ❏ Does the class collaborate with other classes only to the extent absolutely necessary?
- ❏ Is all member data initialized in the constructor?
- ❏ Is the class designed to be used as deep copies rather than shallow copies unless there's a measured reason to create shallow copies?

Language-Specific Issues

- ❏ Have you investigated the language-specific issues for classes in your specific programming language?

Additional Resources

Classes in General

cc2e.com/0679

Meyer, Bertrand. *Object-Oriented Software Construction*, 2d ed. New York, NY: Prentice Hall PTR, 1997. This book contains an in-depth discussion of abstract data types and explains how they form the basis for classes. Chapters 14–16 discuss inheritance in depth. Meyer provides an argument in favor of multiple inheritance in Chapter 15.

Riel, Arthur J. *Object-Oriented Design Heuristics*. Reading, MA: Addison-Wesley, 1996. This book contains numerous suggestions for improving program design, mostly at the class level. I avoided the book for several years because it appeared to be too big—talk about people in glass houses! However, the body of the book is only about 200 pages long. Riel's writing is accessible and enjoyable. The content is focused and practical.

C++

cc2e.com/0686

Meyers, Scott. *Effective C++: 50 Specific Ways to Improve Your Programs and Designs*, 2d ed. Reading, MA: Addison-Wesley, 1998.

Meyers, Scott, 1996, *More Effective C++: 35 New Ways to Improve Your Programs and Designs*. Reading, MA: Addison-Wesley, 1996. Both of Meyers' books are canonical references for C++ programmers. The books are entertaining and help to instill a language-lawyer's appreciation for the nuances of C++.

Java

cc2e.com/0693

Bloch, Joshua. *Effective Java Programming Language Guide*. Boston, MA: Addison-Wesley, 2001. Bloch's book provides much good Java-specific advice as well as introducing more general, good object-oriented practices.

Visual Basic

cc2e.com/0600

The following books are good references on classes in Visual Basic:

Foxall, James. *Practical Standards for Microsoft Visual Basic .NET*. Redmond, WA: Microsoft Press, 2003.

Cornell, Gary, and Jonathan Morrison. *Programming VB .NET: A Guide for Experienced Programmers*. Berkeley, CA: Apress, 2002.

Barwell, Fred, et al. *Professional VB.NET*, 2d ed. Wrox, 2002.

Key Points

- Class interfaces should provide a consistent abstraction. Many problems arise from violating this single principle.

- A class interface should hide something—a system interface, a design decision, or an implementation detail.

- Containment is usually preferable to inheritance unless you're modeling an "is a" relationship.

- Inheritance is a useful tool, but it adds complexity, which is counter to Software's Primary Technical Imperative of managing complexity.

- Classes are your primary tool for managing complexity. Give their design as much attention as needed to accomplish that objective.

Chapter 7
High-Quality Routines

cc2e.com/0778

Contents

Related Topics

Chapter 6 described the details of creating classes. This chapter zooms in on routines, on the characteristics that make the difference between a good routine and a bad one. If you'd rather read about issues that affect the design of routines before wading into the nitty-gritty details, be sure to read Chapter 5, "Design in Construction," first and come back to this chapter later. Some important attributes of high-quality routines are also discussed in Chapter 8, "Defensive Programming." If you're more interested in reading about steps to create routines and classes, Chapter 9, "The Pseudocode Programming Process," might be a better place to start.

Before jumping into the details of high-quality routines, it will be useful to nail down two basic terms. What is a "routine"? A routine is an individual method or procedure invocable for a single purpose. Examples include a function in C++, a method in Java, a function or sub procedure in Microsoft Visual Basic. For some uses, macros in C and C++ can also be thought of as routines. You can apply many of the techniques for creating a high-quality routine to these variants.

What is a *high-quality* routine? That's a harder question. Perhaps the easiest answer is to show what a high-quality routine is not. Here's an example of a low-quality routine:

CODING HORROR

C++ Example of a Low-Quality Routine

```cpp
void HandleStuff( CORP_DATA & inputRec, int crntQtr, EMP_DATA empRec,
    double & estimRevenue, double ytdRevenue, int screenX, int screenY,
    COLOR_TYPE & newColor, COLOR_TYPE & prevColor, StatusType & status,
    int expenseType )
{
int i;
for ( i = 0; i < 100; i++ ) {
    inputRec.revenue[i] = 0;
    inputRec.expense[i] = corpExpense[ crntQtr ][ i ];
    }
UpdateCorpDatabase( empRec );
estimRevenue = ytdRevenue * 4.0 / (double) crntQtr;
newColor = prevColor;
status = SUCCESS;
if ( expenseType == 1 ) {
    for ( i = 0; i < 12; i++ )
        profit[i] = revenue[i] - expense.type1[i];
    }
else if ( expenseType == 2 )  {
        profit[i] = revenue[i] - expense.type2[i];
        }
else if ( expenseType == 3 )
        profit[i] = revenue[i] - expense.type3[i];
        }
```

What's wrong with this routine? Here's a hint: you should be able to find at least 10 different problems with it. Once you've come up with your own list, look at the following list:

- The routine has a bad name. *HandleStuff()* tells you nothing about what the routine does.

- The routine isn't documented. (The subject of documentation extends beyond the boundaries of individual routines and is discussed in Chapter 32, "Self-Documenting Code.")

- The routine has a bad layout. The physical organization of the code on the page gives few hints about its logical organization. Layout strategies are used haphazardly, with different styles in different parts of the routine. Compare the styles where *expenseType == 2* and *expenseType == 3*. (Layout is discussed in Chapter 31, "Layout and Style.")

- The routine's input variable, *inputRec,* is changed. If it's an input variable, its value should not be modified (and in C++ it should be declared *const*). If the value of the variable is supposed to be modified, the variable should not be called *inputRec.*

- The routine reads and writes global variables—it reads from *corpExpense* and writes to *profit*. It should communicate with other routines more directly than by reading and writing global variables.

- The routine doesn't have a single purpose. It initializes some variables, writes to a database, does some calculations—none of which seem to be related to each other in any way. A routine should have a single, clearly defined purpose.

- The routine doesn't defend itself against bad data. If *crntQtr* equals *0*, the expression *ytdRevenue * 4.0 / (double) crntQtr* causes a divide-by-zero error.

- The routine uses several magic numbers: *100, 4.0, 12, 2,* and *3*. Magic numbers are discussed in Section 12.1, "Numbers in General."

- Some of the routine's parameters are unused: *screenX* and *screenY* are not referenced within the routine.

- One of the routine's parameters is passed incorrectly: *prevColor* is labeled as a reference parameter (**&**) even though it isn't assigned a value within the routine.

- The routine has too many parameters. The upper limit for an understandable number of parameters is about 7; this routine has 11. The parameters are laid out in such an unreadable way that most people wouldn't try to examine them closely or even count them.

- The routine's parameters are poorly ordered and are not documented. (Parameter ordering is discussed in this chapter. Documentation is discussed in Chapter 32.)

cc2e.com/0799

Cross-Reference The class is also a good contender for the single greatest invention in computer science. For details on how to use classes effectively, see Chapter 6, "Working Classes."

Aside from the computer itself, the routine is the single greatest invention in computer science. The routine makes programs easier to read and easier to understand than any other feature of any programming language, and it's a crime to abuse this senior statesman of computer science with code like that in the example just shown.

The routine is also the greatest technique ever invented for saving space and improving performance. Imagine how much larger your code would be if you had to repeat the code for every call to a routine instead of branching to the routine. Imagine how hard it would be to make performance improvements in the same code used in a dozen places instead of making them all in one routine. The routine makes modern programming possible.

"OK," you say, "I already know that routines are great, and I program with them all the time. This discussion seems kind of remedial, so what do you want me to do about it?"

I want you to understand that many valid reasons to create a routine exist and that there are right ways and wrong ways to go about it. As an undergraduate computer-science student, I thought that the main reason to create a routine was to avoid duplicate code. The introductory textbook I used said that routines were good because the avoidance of duplication made a program easier to develop, debug, document, and maintain. Period. Aside from syntactic details about how to use parameters and local variables, that was the extent of the textbook's coverage. It was not a good or complete explanation of the theory and practice of routines. The following sections contain a much better explanation.

7.1 Valid Reasons to Create a Routine

Here's a list of valid reasons to create a routine. The reasons overlap somewhat, and they're not intended to make an orthogonal set.

KEY POINT

Reduce complexity The single most important reason to create a routine is to reduce a program's complexity. Create a routine to hide information so that you won't need to think about it. Sure, you'll need to think about it when you write the routine. But after it's written, you should be able to forget the details and use the routine without any knowledge of its internal workings. Other reasons to create routines—minimizing code size, improving maintainability, and improving correctness—are also good reasons, but without the abstractive power of routines, complex programs would be impossible to manage intellectually.

One indication that a routine needs to be broken out of another routine is deep nesting of an inner loop or a conditional. Reduce the containing routine's complexity by pulling the nested part out and putting it into its own routine.

Introduce an intermediate, understandable abstraction Putting a section of code into a well-named routine is one of the best ways to document its purpose. Instead of reading a series of statements like

```
if ( node <> NULL ) then
    while ( node.next <> NULL ) do
        node = node.next
        leafName = node.name
    end while
else
    leafName = ""
end if
```

you can read a statement like this:

```
leafName = GetLeafName( node )
```

The new routine is so short that nearly all it needs for documentation is a good name. The name introduces a higher level of abstraction than the original eight lines of code, which makes the code more readable and easier to understand, and it reduces complexity within the routine that originally contained the code.

Avoid duplicate code Undoubtedly the most popular reason for creating a routine is to avoid duplicate code. Indeed, creation of similar code in two routines implies an error in decomposition. Pull the duplicate code from both routines, put a generic version of the common code into a base class, and then move the two specialized routines into subclasses. Alternatively, you could migrate the common code into its own routine, and then let both call the part that was put into the new routine. With code in one place, you save the space that would have been used by duplicated code. Modifications will be easier because you'll need to modify the code in only one location. The code will be more reliable because you'll have to check only one place to ensure that the code is right. Modifications will be more reliable because you'll avoid making successive and slightly different modifications under the mistaken assumption that you've made identical ones.

Support subclassing   You need less new code to override a short, well-factored routine than a long, poorly factored routine. You'll also reduce the chance of error in subclass implementations if you keep overrideable routines simple.

Hide sequences   It's a good idea to hide the order in which events happen to be processed. For example, if the program typically gets data from the user and then gets auxiliary data from a file, neither the routine that gets the user data nor the routine that gets the file data should depend on the other routine's being performed first. Another example of a sequence might be found when you have two lines of code that read the top of a stack and decrement a *stackTop* variable. Put those two lines of code into a *PopStack()* routine to hide the assumption about the order in which the two operations must be performed. Hiding that assumption will be better than baking it into code from one end of the system to the other.

Hide pointer operations   Pointer operations tend to be hard to read and error prone. By isolating them in routines, you can concentrate on the intent of the operation rather than on the mechanics of pointer manipulation. Also, if the operations are done in only one place, you can be more certain that the code is correct. If you find a better data type than pointers, you can change the program without traumatizing the code that would have used the pointers.

Improve portability   Use of routines isolates nonportable capabilities, explicitly identifying and isolating future portability work. Nonportable capabilities include nonstandard language features, hardware dependencies, operating-system dependencies, and so on.

Simplify complicated boolean tests   Understanding complicated boolean tests in detail is rarely necessary for understanding program flow. Putting such a test into a function makes the code more readable because (1) the details of the test are out of the way and (2) a descriptive function name summarizes the purpose of the test.

Giving the test a function of its own emphasizes its significance. It encourages extra effort to make the details of the test readable inside its function. The result is that both the main flow of the code and the test itself become clearer. Simplifying a boolean test is an example of reducing complexity, which was discussed earlier.

Improve performance   You can optimize the code in one place instead of in several places. Having code in one place will make it easier to profile to find inefficiencies. Centralizing code into a routine means that a single optimization benefits all the code that uses that routine, whether it uses it directly or indirectly. Having code in one place makes it practical to recode the routine with a more efficient algorithm or in a faster, more efficient language.

Cross-Reference For details on information hiding, see "Hide Secrets (Information Hiding)" in Section 5.3.

To ensure all routines are small?   No. With so many good reasons for putting code into a routine, this one is unnecessary. In fact, some jobs are performed better in a single large routine. (The best length for a routine is discussed in Section 7.4, "How Long Can a Routine Be?")

Operations That Seem Too Simple to Put Into Routines

KEY POINT

One of the strongest mental blocks to creating effective routines is a reluctance to create a simple routine for a simple purpose. Constructing a whole routine to contain two or three lines of code might seem like overkill, but experience shows how helpful a good small routine can be.

Small routines offer several advantages. One is that they improve readability. I once had the following single line of code in about a dozen places in a program:

> **Pseudocode Example of a Calculation**
> ```
> points = deviceUnits * ( POINTS_PER_INCH / DeviceUnitsPerInch() )
> ```

This is not the most complicated line of code you'll ever read. Most people would eventually figure out that it converts a measurement in device units to a measurement in points. They would see that each of the dozen lines did the same thing. It could have been clearer, however, so I created a well-named routine to do the conversion in one place:

> **Pseudocode Example of a Calculation Converted to a Function**
> ```
> Function DeviceUnitsToPoints ( deviceUnits Integer ): Integer
>    DeviceUnitsToPoints = deviceUnits *
>       ( POINTS_PER_INCH / DeviceUnitsPerInch() )
> End Function
> ```

When the routine was substituted for the inline code, the dozen lines of code all looked more or less like this one:

> **Pseudocode Example of a Function Call to a Calculation Function**
> ```
> points = DeviceUnitsToPoints( deviceUnits )
> ```

This line is more readable—even approaching self-documenting.

This example hints at another reason to put small operations into functions: small operations tend to turn into larger operations. I didn't know it when I wrote the routine, but under certain conditions and when certain devices were active, *DeviceUnitsPerInch()* returned 0. That meant I had to account for division by zero, which took three more lines of code:

Pseudocode Example of a Calculation That Expands Under Maintenance

```
Function DeviceUnitsToPoints( deviceUnits: Integer ) Integer;
    if ( DeviceUnitsPerInch() <> 0 )
        DeviceUnitsToPoints = deviceUnits *
            ( POINTS_PER_INCH / DeviceUnitsPerInch() )
    else
        DeviceUnitsToPoints = 0
    end if
End Function
```

If that original line of code had still been in a dozen places, the test would have been repeated a dozen times, for a total of 36 new lines of code. A simple routine reduced the 36 new lines to 3.

Summary of Reasons to Create a Routine

Here's a summary list of the valid reasons for creating a routine:

- Reduce complexity
- Introduce an intermediate, understandable abstraction
- Avoid duplicate code
- Support subclassing
- Hide sequences
- Hide pointer operations
- Improve portability
- Simplify complicated boolean tests
- Improve performance

In addition, many of the reasons to create a class are also good reasons to create a routine:

- Isolate complexity
- Hide implementation details
- Limit effects of changes
- Hide global data
- Make central points of control
- Facilitate reusable code
- Accomplish a specific refactoring

7.2 Design at the Routine Level

The idea of cohesion was introduced in a paper by Wayne Stevens, Glenford Myers, and Larry Constantine (1974). Other more modern concepts, including abstraction and encapsulation, tend to yield more insight at the class level (and have, in fact, largely superceded cohesion at the class level), but cohesion is still alive and well as the workhorse design heuristic at the individual-routine level.

Cross-Reference For a discussion of cohesion in general, see "Aim for Strong Cohesion" in Section 5.3.

For routines, cohesion refers to how closely the operations in a routine are related. Some programmers prefer the term "strength": how strongly related are the operations in a routine? A function like *Cosine()* is perfectly cohesive because the whole routine is dedicated to performing one function. A function like *CosineAndTan()* has lower cohesion because it tries to do more than one thing. The goal is to have each routine do one thing well and not do anything else.

HARD DATA

The payoff is higher reliability. One study of 450 routines found that 50 percent of the highly cohesive routines were fault free, whereas only 18 percent of routines with low cohesion were fault free (Card, Church, and Agresti 1986). Another study of a different 450 routines (which is just an unusual coincidence) found that routines with the highest coupling-to-cohesion ratios had 7 times as many errors as those with the lowest coupling-to-cohesion ratios and were 20 times as costly to fix (Selby and Basili 1991).

Discussions about cohesion typically refer to several levels of cohesion. Understanding the concepts is more important than remembering specific terms. Use the concepts as aids in thinking about how to make routines as cohesive as possible.

Functional cohesion is the strongest and best kind of cohesion, occurring when a routine performs one and only one operation. Examples of highly cohesive routines include *sin()*, *GetCustomerName()*, *EraseFile()*, *CalculateLoanPayment()*, and *AgeFromBirthdate()*. Of course, this evaluation of their cohesion assumes that the routines do what their names say they do—if they do anything else, they are less cohesive and poorly named.

Several other kinds of cohesion are normally considered to be less than ideal:

- *Sequential cohesion* exists when a routine contains operations that must be performed in a specific order, that share data from step to step, and that don't make up a complete function when done together.

  An example of sequential cohesion is a routine that, given a birth date, calculates an employee's age and time to retirement. If the routine calculates the age and then uses that result to calculate the employee's time to retirement, it has sequential cohesion. If the routine calculates the age and then calculates the time to retirement in a completely separate computation that happens to use the same birth-date data, it has only communicational cohesion.

How would you make the routine functionally cohesive? You'd create separate routines to compute an employee's age given a birth date and compute time to retirement given a birth date. The time-to-retirement routine could call the age routine. They'd both have functional cohesion. Other routines could call either routine or both routines.

■ *Communicational cohesion* occurs when operations in a routine make use of the same data and aren't related in any other way. If a routine prints a summary report and then reinitializes the summary data passed into it, the routine has communicational cohesion: the two operations are related only by the fact that they use the same data.

To give this routine better cohesion, the summary data should be reinitialized close to where it's created, which shouldn't be in the report-printing routine. Split the operations into individual routines. The first prints the report. The second reinitializes the data, close to the code that creates or modifies the data. Call both routines from the higher-level routine that originally called the communicationally cohesive routine.

■ *Temporal cohesion* occurs when operations are combined into a routine because they are all done at the same time. Typical examples would be *Startup()*, *CompleteNewEmployee()*, and *Shutdown()*. Some programmers consider temporal cohesion to be unacceptable because it's sometimes associated with bad programming practices such as having a hodgepodge of code in a *Startup()* routine.

To avoid this problem, think of temporal routines as organizers of other events. The *Startup()* routine, for example, might read a configuration file, initialize a scratch file, set up a memory manager, and show an initial screen. To make it most effective, have the temporally cohesive routine call other routines to perform specific activities rather than performing the operations directly itself. That way, it will be clear that the point of the routine is to orchestrate activities rather than to do them directly.

This example raises the issue of choosing a name that describes the routine at the right level of abstraction. You could decide to name the routine *ReadConfigFileInitScratchFileEtc()*, which would imply that the routine had only coincidental cohesion. If you name it *Startup()*, however, it would be clear that it had a single purpose and clear that it had functional cohesion.

The remaining kinds of cohesion are generally unacceptable. They result in code that's poorly organized, hard to debug, and hard to modify. If a routine has bad cohesion, it's better to put effort into a rewrite to have better cohesion than investing in a pinpoint diagnosis of the problem. Knowing what to avoid can be useful, however, so here are the unacceptable kinds of cohesion:

- *Procedural cohesion* occurs when operations in a routine are done in a specified order. An example is a routine that gets an employee name, then an address, and then a phone number. The order of these operations is important only because it matches the order in which the user is asked for the data on the input screen. Another routine gets the rest of the employee data. The routine has procedural cohesion because it puts a set of operations in a specified order and the operations don't need to be combined for any other reason.

  To achieve better cohesion, put the separate operations into their own routines. Make sure that the calling routine has a single, complete job: *GetEmployee()* rather than *GetFirstPartOfEmployeeData()*. You'll probably need to modify the routines that get the rest of the data too. It's common to modify two or more original routines before you achieve functional cohesion in any of them.

- *Logical cohesion* occurs when several operations are stuffed into the same routine and one of the operations is selected by a control flag that's passed in. It's called logical cohesion because the control flow or "logic" of the routine is the only thing that ties the operations together—they're all in a big *if* statement or *case* statement together. It isn't because the operations are logically related in any other sense. Considering that the defining attribute of logical cohesion is that the operations are unrelated, a better name might "illogical cohesion."

  One example would be an *InputAll()* routine that inputs customer names, employee timecard information, or inventory data depending on a flag passed to the routine. Other examples would be *ComputeAll()*, *EditAll()*, *PrintAll()*, and *SaveAll()*. The main problem with such routines is that you shouldn't need to pass in a flag to control another routine's processing. Instead of having a routine that does one of three distinct operations, depending on a flag passed to it, it's cleaner to have three routines, each of which does one distinct operation. If the operations use some of the same code or share data, the code should be moved into a lower-level routine and the routines should be packaged into a class.

  Cross-Reference Although the routine might have better cohesion, a higher-level design issue is whether the system should be using a *case* statement instead of polymorphism. For more on this issue, see "Replace conditionals with polymorphism (especially repeated *case* statements)" in Section 24.3

  It's usually all right, however, to create a logically cohesive routine if its code consists solely of a series of *if* or *case* statements and calls to other routines. In such a case, if the routine's only function is to dispatch commands and it doesn't do any of the processing itself, that's usually a good design. The technical term for this kind of routine is "event handler." An event handler is often used in interactive environments such as the Apple Macintosh, Microsoft Windows, and other GUI environments.

- *Coincidental cohesion* occurs when the operations in a routine have no discernible relationship to each other. Other good names are "no cohesion" or "chaotic cohesion." The low-quality C++ routine at the beginning of this chapter had coincidental cohesion. It's hard to convert coincidental cohesion to any better kind of cohesion—you usually need to do a deeper redesign and reimplementation.

KEY POINT

None of these terms are magical or sacred. Learn the ideas rather than the terminology. It's nearly always possible to write routines with functional cohesion, so focus your attention on functional cohesion for maximum benefit.

7.3 Good Routine Names

Cross-Reference For details on naming variables, see Chapter 11, "The Power of Variable Names."

A good name for a routine clearly describes everything the routine does. Here are guidelines for creating effective routine names:

Describe everything the routine does In the routine's name, describe all the outputs and side effects. If a routine computes report totals and opens an output file, *Compute-ReportTotals()* is not an adequate name for the routine. *ComputeReportTotalsAndOpen-OutputFile()* is an adequate name but is too long and silly. If you have routines with side effects, you'll have many long, silly names. The cure is not to use less-descriptive routine names; the cure is to program so that you cause things to happen directly rather than with side effects.

Avoid meaningless, vague, or wishy-washy verbs Some verbs are elastic, stretched to cover just about any meaning. Routine names like *HandleCalculation()*, *PerformServices()*, *OutputUser()*, *ProcessInput()*, and *DealWithOutput()* don't tell you what the routines do. At the most, these names tell you that the routines have something to do with calculations, services, users, input, and output. The exception would be when the verb "handle" was used in the specific technical sense of handling an event.

KEY POINT

Sometimes the only problem with a routine is that its name is wishy-washy; the routine itself might actually be well designed. If *HandleOutput()* is replaced with *FormatAndPrintOutput()*, you have a pretty good idea of what the routine does.

In other cases, the verb is vague because the operations performed by the routine are vague. The routine suffers from a weakness of purpose, and the weak name is a symptom. If that's the case, the best solution is to restructure the routine and any related routines so that they all have stronger purposes and stronger names that accurately describe them.

CODING HORROR

Don't differentiate routine names solely by number One developer wrote all his code in one big function. Then he took every 15 lines and created functions named *Part1*, *Part2*, and so on. After that, he created one high-level function that called each part. This method of creating and naming routines is especially egregious (and rare, I hope). But programmers sometimes use numbers to differentiate routines with names like *OutputUser*, *OutputUser1*, and *OutputUser2*. The numerals at the ends of these names provide no indication of the different abstractions the routines represent, and the routines are thus poorly named.

Make names of routines as long as necessary Research shows that the optimum average length for a variable name is 9 to 15 characters. Routines tend to be more complicated than variables, and good names for them tend to be longer. On the other hand, routine names are often attached to object names, which essentially provides part of the name for free. Overall, the emphasis when creating a routine name should be to make the name as clear as possible, which means you should make its name as long or short as needed to make it understandable.

Cross-Reference For the distinction between procedures and functions, see Section 7.6, "Special Considerations in the Use of Functions," later in this chapter.

To name a function, use a description of the return value   A function returns a value, and the function should be named for the value it returns. For example, *cos()*, *customerId.Next()*, *printer.IsReady()*, and *pen.CurrentColor()* are all good function names that indicate precisely what the functions return.

To name a procedure, use a strong verb followed by an object   A procedure with functional cohesion usually performs an operation on an object. The name should reflect what the procedure does, and an operation on an object implies a verb-plus-object name. *PrintDocument()*, *CalcMonthlyRevenues()*, *CheckOrderInfo()*, and *RepaginateDocument()* are samples of good procedure names.

In object-oriented languages, you don't need to include the name of the object in the procedure name because the object itself is included in the call. You invoke routines with statements like *document.Print()*, *orderInfo.Check()*, and *monthlyRevenues.Calc()*. Names like *document.PrintDocument()* are redundant and can become inaccurate when they're carried through to derived classes. If *Check* is a class derived from *Document*, *check.Print()* seems clearly to be printing a check, whereas *check.PrintDocument()* sounds like it might be printing a checkbook register or monthly statement, but it doesn't sound like it's printing a check.

Cross-Reference For a similar list of opposites in variable names, see "Common Opposites in Variable Names" in Section 11.1.

Use opposites precisely   Using naming conventions for opposites helps consistency, which helps readability. Opposite-pairs like *first/last* are commonly understood. Opposite-pairs like *FileOpen()* and *_lclose()* are not symmetrical and are confusing. Here are some common opposites:

add/remove	increment/decrement	open/close
begin/end	insert/delete	show/hide
create/destroy	lock/unlock	source/target
first/last	min/max	start/stop
get/put	next/previous	up/down
get/set	old/new	

Establish conventions for common operations   In some systems, it's important to distinguish among different kinds of operations. A naming convention is often the easiest and most reliable way of indicating these distinctions.

The code on one of my projects assigned each object a unique identifier. We neglected to establish a convention for naming the routines that would return the object identifier, so we had routine names like these:

```
employee.id.Get()
dependent.GetId()
supervisor()
candidate.id()
```

The *Employee* class exposed its *id* object, which in turn exposed its *Get()* routine. The *Dependent* class exposed a *GetId()* routine. The *Supervisor* class made the *id* its default return value. The *Candidate* class made use of the fact that the *id* object's default return value was the *id*, and exposed the *id* object. By the middle of the project, no one could remember which of these routines was supposed to be used on which object, but by that time too much code had been written to go back and make everything consistent. Consequently, every person on the team had to devote an unnecessary amount of gray matter to remembering the inconsequential detail of which syntax was used on which class to retrieve the *id*. A naming convention for retrieving *id*s would have eliminated this annoyance.

7.4 How Long Can a Routine Be?

On their way to America, the Pilgrims argued about the best maximum length for a routine. After arguing about it for the entire trip, they arrived at Plymouth Rock and started to draft the Mayflower Compact. They still hadn't settled the maximum-length question, and since they couldn't disembark until they'd signed the compact, they gave up and didn't include it. The result has been an interminable debate ever since about how long a routine can be.

The theoretical best maximum length is often described as one screen or one or two pages of program listing, approximately 50 to 150 lines. In this spirit, IBM once limited routines to 50 lines, and TRW limited them to two pages (McCabe 1976). Modern programs tend to have volumes of extremely short routines mixed in with a few longer routines. Long routines are far from extinct, however. Shortly before finishing this book, I visited two client sites within a month. Programmers at one site were wrestling with a routine that was about 4,000 lines of code long, and programmers at the other site were trying to tame a routine that was more than 12,000 lines long!

A mountain of research on routine length has accumulated over the years, some of which is applicable to modern programs, and some of which isn't:

HARD DATA

- A study by Basili and Perricone found that routine size was inversely correlated with errors: as the size of routines increased (up to 200 lines of code), the number of errors per line of code decreased (Basili and Perricone 1984).

- Another study found that routine size was not correlated with errors, even though structural complexity and amount of data were correlated with errors (Shen et al. 1985).

- A 1986 study found that small routines (32 lines of code or fewer) were not correlated with lower cost or fault rate (Card, Church, and Agresti 1986; Card and Glass 1990). The evidence suggested that larger routines (65 lines of code or more) were cheaper to develop per line of code.

- An empirical study of 450 routines found that small routines (those with fewer than 143 source statements, including comments) had 23 percent more errors per line of code than larger routines but were 2.4 times less expensive to fix than larger routines (Selby and Basili 1991).

- Another study found that code needed to be changed least when routines averaged 100 to 150 lines of code (Lind and Vairavan 1989).

- A study at IBM found that the most error-prone routines were those that were larger than 500 lines of code. Beyond 500 lines, the error rate tended to be proportional to the size of the routine (Jones 1986a).

Where does all this leave the question of routine length in object-oriented programs? A large percentage of routines in object-oriented programs will be accessor routines, which will be very short. From time to time, a complex algorithm will lead to a longer routine, and in those circumstances, the routine should be allowed to grow organically up to 100–200 lines. (A line is a noncomment, nonblank line of source code.) Decades of evidence say that routines of such length are no more error prone than shorter routines. Let issues such as the routine's cohesion, depth of nesting, number of variables, number of decision points, number of comments needed to explain the routine, and other complexity-related considerations dictate the length of the routine rather than imposing a length restriction per se.

That said, if you want to write routines longer than about 200 lines, be careful. None of the studies that reported decreased cost, decreased error rates, or both with larger routines distinguished among sizes larger than 200 lines, and you're bound to run into an upper limit of understandability as you pass 200 lines of code.

7.5 How to Use Routine Parameters

HARD DATA

Interfaces between routines are some of the most error-prone areas of a program. One often-cited study by Basili and Perricone (1984) found that 39 percent of all errors were internal interface errors—errors in communication between routines. Here are a few guidelines for minimizing interface problems:

Cross-Reference For details on documenting routine parameters, see "Commenting Routines" in Section 32.5. For details on formatting parameters, see Section 31.7, "Laying Out Routines."

Put parameters in input-modify-output order   Instead of ordering parameters randomly or alphabetically, list the parameters that are input-only first, input-and-output second, and output-only third. This ordering implies the sequence of operations happening within the routine-inputting data, changing it, and sending back a result. Here are examples of parameter lists in Ada:

Ada Example of Parameters in Input-Modify-Output Order

```
procedure InvertMatrix(
   originalMatrix: in Matrix;
   resultMatrix: out Matrix
);
...

procedure ChangeSentenceCase(
   desiredCase: in StringCase;
   sentence: in out Sentence
);
...

procedure PrintPageNumber(
   pageNumber: in Integer;
   status: out StatusType
);
```

Ada uses *in* and *out* keywords to make input and output parameters clear.

This ordering convention conflicts with the C-library convention of putting the modified parameter first. The input-modify-output convention makes more sense to me, but if you consistently order parameters in some way, you will still do the readers of your code a service.

Consider creating your own* in *and* out *keywords Other modern languages don't support the *in* and *out* keywords like Ada does. In those languages, you might still be able to use the preprocessor to create your own *in* and *out* keywords:

C++ Example of Defining Your Own *In* and *Out* Keywords

```
#define IN
#define OUT
void InvertMatrix(
   IN Matrix originalMatrix,
   OUT Matrix *resultMatrix
);
...

void ChangeSentenceCase(
   IN StringCase desiredCase,
   IN OUT Sentence *sentenceToEdit
);
...

void PrintPageNumber(
   IN int pageNumber,
   OUT StatusType &status
);
```

In this case, the *IN* and *OUT* macro-keywords are used for documentation purposes. To make the value of a parameter changeable by the called routine, the parameter still needs to be passed as a pointer or as a reference parameter.

Before adopting this technique, be sure to consider a pair of significant drawbacks. Defining your own *IN* and *OUT* keywords extends the C++ language in a way that will be unfamiliar to most people reading your code. If you extend the language this way, be sure to do it consistently, preferably projectwide. A second limitation is that the *IN* and *OUT* keywords won't be enforceable by the compiler, which means that you could potentially label a parameter as *IN* and then modify it inside the routine anyway. That could lull a reader of your code into assuming code is correct when it isn't. Using C++'s *const* keyword will normally be the preferable means of identifying input-only parameters.

If several routines use similar parameters, put the similar parameters in a consistent order   The order of routine parameters can be a mnemonic, and inconsistent order can make parameters hard to remember. For example, in C, the *fprintf()* routine is the same as the *printf()* routine except that it adds a file as the first argument. A similar routine, *fputs()*, is the same as *puts()* except that it adds a file as the last argument. This is an aggravating, pointless difference that makes the parameters of these routines harder to remember than they need to be.

On the other hand, the routine *strncpy()* in C takes the arguments target string, source string, and maximum number of bytes, in that order, and the routine *memcpy()* takes the same arguments in the same order. The similarity between the two routines helps in remembering the parameters in either routine.

HARD DATA

Use all the parameters   If you pass a parameter to a routine, use it. If you aren't using it, remove the parameter from the routine interface. Unused parameters are correlated with an increased error rate. In one study, 46 percent of routines with no unused variables had no errors, and only 17 to 29 percent of routines with more than one unreferenced variable had no errors (Card, Church, and Agresti 1986).

This rule to remove unused parameters has one exception. If you're compiling part of your program conditionally, you might compile out parts of a routine that use a certain parameter. Be nervous about this practice, but if you're convinced it works, that's OK too. In general, if you have a good reason not to use a parameter, go ahead and leave it in place. If you don't have a good reason, make the effort to clean up the code.

Put status or error variables last   By convention, status variables and variables that indicate an error has occurred go last in the parameter list. They are incidental to the main purpose of the routine, and they are output-only parameters, so it's a sensible convention.

Don't use routine parameters as working variables   It's dangerous to use the parameters passed to a routine as working variables. Use local variables instead. For example, in the following Java fragment, the variable *inputVal* is improperly used to store intermediate results of a computation:

Java Example of Improper Use of Input Parameters
```java
int Sample( int inputVal ) {
   inputVal = inputVal * CurrentMultiplier( inputVal );
   inputVal = inputVal + CurrentAdder( inputVal );
   ...
   return inputVal;
}
```

At this point, *inputVal* no longer contains the value that was input.

In this code fragment, *inputVal* is misleading because by the time execution reaches the last line, *inputVal* no longer contains the input value; it contains a computed value based in part on the input value, and it is therefore misnamed. If you later need to modify the routine to use the original input value in some other place, you'll probably use *inputVal* and assume that it contains the original input value when it actually doesn't.

How do you solve the problem? Can you solve it by renaming *inputVal*? Probably not. You could name it something like *workingVal*, but that's an incomplete solution because the name fails to indicate that the variable's original value comes from outside the routine. You could name it something ridiculous like *inputValThatBecomesWorkingVal* or give up completely and name it *x* or *val*, but all these approaches are weak.

A better approach is to avoid current and future problems by using working variables explicitly. The following code fragment demonstrates the technique:

Java Example of Good Use of Input Parameters
```java
int Sample( int inputVal ) {
   int workingVal = inputVal;
   workingVal = workingVal * CurrentMultiplier( workingVal );
   workingVal = workingVal + CurrentAdder( workingVal );
   ...

   ...
   return workingVal;
}
```

If you need to use the original value of *inputVal* here or somewhere else, it's still available.

Introducing the new variable *workingVal* clarifies the role of *inputVal* and eliminates the chance of erroneously using *inputVal* at the wrong time. (Don't take this reasoning as a justification for literally naming a variable *inputVal* or *workingVal*. In general, *inputVal* and *workingVal* are terrible names for variables, and these names are used in this example only to make the variables' roles clear.)

Assigning the input value to a working variable emphasizes where the value comes from. It eliminates the possibility that a variable from the parameter list will be modified accidentally. In C++, this practice can be enforced by the compiler using the keyword *const*. If you designate a parameter as *const*, you're not allowed to modify its value within a routine.

Cross-Reference For details on interface assumptions, see the introduction to Chapter 8, "Defensive Programming." For details on documentation, see Chapter 32, "Self-Documenting Code."

Document interface assumptions about parameters   If you assume the data being passed to your routine has certain characteristics, document the assumptions as you make them. It's not a waste of effort to document your assumptions both in the routine itself and in the place where the routine is called. Don't wait until you've written the routine to go back and write the comments—you won't remember all your assumptions. Even better than commenting your assumptions, use assertions to put them into code.

What kinds of interface assumptions about parameters should you document?

- Whether parameters are input-only, modified, or output-only
- Units of numeric parameters (inches, feet, meters, and so on)
- Meanings of status codes and error values if enumerated types aren't used
- Ranges of expected values
- Specific values that should never appear

HARD DATA

Limit the number of a routine's parameters to about seven   Seven is a magic number for people's comprehension. Psychological research has found that people generally cannot keep track of more than about seven chunks of information at once (Miller 1956). This discovery has been applied to an enormous number of disciplines, and it seems safe to conjecture that most people can't keep track of more than about seven routine parameters at once.

In practice, how much you can limit the number of parameters depends on how your language handles complex data types. If you program in a modern language that supports structured data, you can pass a composite data type containing 13 fields and think of it as one mental "chunk" of data. If you program in a more primitive language, you might need to pass all 13 fields individually.

Cross-Reference For details on how to think about interfaces, see "Good Abstraction" in Section 6.2.

If you find yourself consistently passing more than a few arguments, the coupling among your routines is too tight. Design the routine or group of routines to reduce the coupling. If you are passing the same data to many different routines, group the routines into a class and treat the frequently used data as class data.

Consider an input, modify, and output naming convention for parameters   If you find that it's important to distinguish among input, modify, and output parameters, establish a naming convention that identifies them. You could prefix them with *i_*, *m_*, and *o_*. If you're feeling verbose, you could prefix them with *Input_*, *Modify_*, and *Output_*.

***Pass the variables or objects that the routine needs to maintain its interface
abstraction*** There are two competing schools of thought about how to pass members
of an object to a routine. Suppose you have an object that exposes data through 10
access routines and the called routine needs three of those data elements to do its job.

Proponents of the first school of thought argue that only the three specific elements
needed by the routine should be passed. They argue that doing this will keep the connections between routines to a minimum; reduce coupling; and make them easier to
understand, reuse, and so on. They say that passing the whole object to a routine violates the principle of encapsulation by potentially exposing all 10 access routines to
the routine that's called.

Proponents of the second school argue that the whole object should be passed. They
argue that the interface can remain more stable if the called routine has the flexibility
to use additional members of the object without changing the routine's interface.
They argue that passing three specific elements violates encapsulation by exposing
which specific data elements the routine is using.

I think both these rules are simplistic and miss the most important consideration:
what abstraction is presented by the routine's interface? If the abstraction is that the routine expects you to have three specific data elements, and it is only a coincidence that
those three elements happen to be provided by the same object, then you should pass
the three specific data elements individually. However, if the abstraction is that you
will always have that particular object in hand and the routine will do something or
other with that object, then you truly do break the abstraction when you expose the
three specific data elements.

If you're passing the whole object and you find yourself creating the object, populat-
ing it with the three elements needed by the called routine, and then pulling those elements out of the object after the routine is called, that's an indication that you should
be passing the three specific elements rather than the whole object. (In general, code
that "sets up" for a call to a routine or "takes down" after a call to a routine is an indication that the routine is not well designed.)

If you find yourself frequently changing the parameter list to the routine, with the
parameters coming from the same object each time, that's an indication that you
should be passing the whole object rather than specific elements.

Use named parameters In some languages, you can explicitly associate formal parameters with actual parameters. This makes parameter usage more self-documenting and helps avoid errors from mismatching parameters. Here's an example in Visual Basic:

Visual Basic Example of Explicitly Identifying Parameters

```
Private Function Distance3d( _
    ByVal xDistance As Coordinate, _
    ByVal yDistance As Coordinate, _
    ByVal zDistance As Coordinate _
)
   ...
End Function
...
Private Function Velocity( _
    ByVal latitude as Coordinate, _
    ByVal longitude as Coordinate, _
    ByVal elevation as Coordinate _
)
   ...
    Distance = Distance3d( xDistance := latitude, yDistance := longitude, _
        zDistance := elevation )
   ...
End Function
```

Here's where the formal parameters are declared. →

Here's where the actual parameters are mapped to the formal parameters. →

This technique is especially useful when you have longer-than-average lists of identically typed arguments, which increases the chances that you can insert a parameter mismatch without the compiler detecting it. Explicitly associating parameters may be overkill in many environments, but in safety-critical or other high-reliability environments the extra assurance that parameters match up the way you expect can be worthwhile.

Make sure actual parameters match formal parameters Formal parameters, also known as "dummy parameters," are the variables declared in a routine definition. Actual parameters are the variables, constants, or expressions used in the actual routine calls.

A common mistake is to put the wrong type of variable in a routine call—for example, using an integer when a floating point is needed. (This is a problem only in weakly typed languages like C when you're not using full compiler warnings. Strongly typed languages such as C++ and Java don't have this problem.) When arguments are input only, this is seldom a problem; usually the compiler converts the actual type to the formal type before passing it to the routine. If it is a problem, usually your compiler gives you a warning. But in some cases, particularly when the argument is used for both input and output, you can get stung by passing the wrong type of argument.

Develop the habit of checking types of arguments in parameter lists and heeding compiler warnings about mismatched parameter types.

7.6 Special Considerations in the Use of Functions

Modern languages such as C++, Java, and Visual Basic support both functions and procedures. A function is a routine that returns a value; a procedure is a routine that does not. In C++, all routines are typically called "functions"; however, a function with a *void* return type is semantically a procedure. The distinction between functions and procedures is as much a semantic distinction as a syntactic one, and semantics should be your guide.

When to Use a Function and When to Use a Procedure

Purists argue that a function should return only one value, just as a mathematical function does. This means that a function would take only input parameters and return its only value through the function itself. The function would always be named for the value it returned, as *sin()*, *CustomerID()*, and *ScreenHeight()* are. A procedure, on the other hand, could take input, modify, and output parameters—as many of each as it wanted to.

A common programming practice is to have a function that operates as a procedure and returns a status value. Logically, it works as a procedure, but because it returns a value, it's officially a function. For example, you might have a routine called *FormatOutput()* used with a *report* object in statements like this one:

```
if ( report.FormatOutput( formattedReport ) = Success ) then ...
```

In this example, *report.FormatOutput()* operates as a procedure in that it has an output parameter, *formattedReport*, but it is technically a function because the routine itself returns a value. Is this a valid way to use a function? In defense of this approach, you could maintain that the function return value has nothing to do with the main purpose of the routine, formatting output, or with the routine name, *report.FormatOutput()*. In that sense it operates more as a procedure does even if it is technically a function. The use of the return value to indicate the success or failure of the procedure is not confusing if the technique is used consistently.

The alternative is to create a procedure that has a status variable as an explicit parameter, which promotes code like this fragment:

```
report.FormatOutput( formattedReport, outputStatus )
if ( outputStatus = Success ) then ...
```

I prefer the second style of coding, not because I'm hard-nosed about the difference between functions and procedures but because it makes a clear separation between the routine call and the test of the status value. To combine the call and the test into one line of code increases the density of the statement and, correspondingly, its complexity. The following use of a function is fine too:

```
outputStatus = report.FormatOutput( formattedReport )
if ( outputStatus = Success ) then ...
```

In short, use a function if the primary purpose of the routine is to return the value indicated by the function name. Otherwise, use a procedure.

Setting the Function's Return Value

Using a function creates the risk that the function will return an incorrect return value. This usually happens when the function has several possible paths and one of the paths doesn't set a return value. To reduce this risk, do the following:

Check all possible return paths   When creating a function, mentally execute each path to be sure that the function returns a value under all possible circumstances. It's good practice to initialize the return value at the beginning of the function to a default value—this provides a safety net in the event that the correct return value is not set.

Don't return references or pointers to local data   As soon as the routine ends and the local data goes out of scope, the reference or pointer to the local data will be invalid. If an object needs to return information about its internal data, it should save the information as class member data. It should then provide accessor functions that return the values of the member data items rather than references or pointers to local data.

7.7 Macro Routines and Inline Routines

Cross-Reference Even if your language doesn't have a macro preprocessor, you can build your own. For details, see Section 30.5, "Building Your Own Programming Tools."

Routines created with preprocessor macros call for a few unique considerations. The following rules and examples pertain to using the preprocessor in C++. If you're using a different language or preprocessor, adapt the rules to your situation.

Fully parenthesize macro expressions   Because macros and their arguments are expanded into code, be careful that they expand the way you want them to. One common problem lies in creating a macro like this one:

C++ Example of a Macro That Doesn't Expand Properly
```
#define Cube( a ) a*a*a
```

If you pass this macro nonatomic values for *a*, it won't do the multiplication properly. If you use the expression *Cube(x+1)*, it expands to *x+1 * x + 1 * x + 1*, which, because of the precedence of the multiplication and addition operators, is not what you want. A better, but still not perfect, version of the macro looks like this:

C++ Example of a Macro That Still Doesn't Expand Properly
```
#define Cube( a ) (a)*(a)*(a)
```

This is close, but still no cigar. If you use *Cube()* in an expression that has operators with higher precedence than multiplication, the *(a)*(a)*(a)* will be torn apart. To prevent that, enclose the whole expression in parentheses:

C++ Example of a Macro That Works

```
#define Cube( a ) ((a)*(a)*(a))
```

Surround multiple-statement macros with curly braces   A macro can have multiple statements, which is a problem if you treat it as if it were a single statement. Here's an example of a macro that's headed for trouble:

CODING
HORROR

C++ Example of a Nonworking Macro with Multiple Statements

```
#define LookupEntry( key, index ) \
    index = (key - 10) / 5; \
    index = min( index, MAX_INDEX ); \
    index = max( index, MIN_INDEX );
...

for ( entryCount = 0; entryCount < numEntries; entryCount++ )
    LookupEntry( entryCount, tableIndex[ entryCount ] );
```

This macro is headed for trouble because it doesn't work as a regular function would. As it's shown, the only part of the macro that's executed in the *for* loop is the first line of the macro:

```
index = (key - 10) / 5;
```

To avoid this problem, surround the macro with curly braces:

C++ Example of a Macro with Multiple Statements That Works

```
#define LookupEntry( key, index ) { \
    index = (key - 10) / 5; \
    index = min( index, MAX_INDEX ); \
    index = max( index, MIN_INDEX ); \
}
```

The practice of using macros as substitutes for function calls is generally considered risky and hard to understand—bad programming practice—so use this technique only if your specific circumstances require it.

Name macros that expand to code like routines so that they can be replaced by routines if necessary   The convention in C++ for naming macros is to use all capital letters. If the macro can be replaced by a routine, however, name it using the naming convention for routines instead. That way you can replace macros with routines and vice versa without changing anything but the routine involved.

Following this recommendation entails some risk. If you commonly use ++ and − as side effects (as part of other statements), you'll get burned when you use macros that you think are routines. Considering the other problems with side effects, this is yet another reason to avoid using side effects.

Limitations on the Use of Macro Routines

Modern languages like C++ provide numerous alternatives to the use of macros:

- *const* for declaring constant values
- *inline* for defining functions that will be compiled as inline code
- *template* for defining standard operations like *min*, *max*, and so on in a type-safe way
- *enum* for defining enumerated types
- *typedef* for defining simple type substitutions

KEY POINT

As Bjarne Stroustrup, designer of C++ points out, "Almost every macro demonstrates a flaw in the programming language, in the program, or in the programmer.... When you use macros, you should expect inferior service from tools such as debuggers, cross-reference tools, and profilers" (Stroustrup 1997). Macros are useful for supporting conditional compilation—see Section 8.6, "Debugging Aids"—but careful programmers generally use a macro as an alternative to a routine only as a last resort.

Inline Routines

C++ supports an *inline* keyword. An inline routine allows the programmer to treat the code as a routine at code-writing time, but the compiler will generally convert each instance of the routine into inline code at compile time. The theory is that *inline* can help produce highly efficient code that avoids routine-call overhead.

Use inline routines sparingly   Inline routines violate encapsulation because C++ requires the programmer to put the code for the implementation of the inline routine in the header file, which exposes it to every programmer who uses the header file.

Inline routines require a routine's full code to be generated every time the routine is invoked, which for an inline routine of any size will increase code size. That can create problems of its own.

The bottom line on inlining for performance reasons is the same as the bottom line on any other coding technique that's motivated by performance: profile the code and measure the improvement. If the anticipated performance gain doesn't justify the bother of profiling the code to verify the improvement, it doesn't justify the erosion in code quality either.

cc2e.com/0792

Cross-Reference This is a checklist of considerations about the quality of the routine. For a list of the steps used to build a routine, see the checklist "The Pseudocode Programming Process" in Chapter 9, page 215.

CHECKLIST: High-Quality Routines

Big-Picture Issues

- ❑ Is the reason for creating the routine sufficient?
- ❑ Have all parts of the routine that would benefit from being put into routines of their own been put into routines of their own?
- ❑ Is the routine's name a strong, clear verb-plus-object name for a procedure or a description of the return value for a function?
- ❑ Does the routine's name describe everything the routine does?
- ❑ Have you established naming conventions for common operations?
- ❑ Does the routine have strong, functional cohesion—doing one and only one thing and doing it well?
- ❑ Do the routines have loose coupling—are the routine's connections to other routines small, intimate, visible, and flexible?
- ❑ Is the length of the routine determined naturally by its function and logic, rather than by an artificial coding standard?

Parameter-Passing Issues

- ❑ Does the routine's parameter list, taken as a whole, present a consistent interface abstraction?
- ❑ Are the routine's parameters in a sensible order, including matching the order of parameters in similar routines?
- ❑ Are interface assumptions documented?
- ❑ Does the routine have seven or fewer parameters?
- ❑ Is each input parameter used?
- ❑ Is each output parameter used?
- ❑ Does the routine avoid using input parameters as working variables?
- ❑ If the routine is a function, does it return a valid value under all possible circumstances?

Key Points

- The most important reason for creating a routine is to improve the intellectual manageability of a program, and you can create a routine for many other good reasons. Saving space is a minor reason; improved readability, reliability, and modifiability are better reasons.

- Sometimes the operation that most benefits from being put into a routine of its own is a simple one.

- You can classify routines into various kinds of cohesion, but you can make most routines functionally cohesive, which is best.

- The name of a routine is an indication of its quality. If the name is bad and it's accurate, the routine might be poorly designed. If the name is bad and it's inaccurate, it's not telling you what the program does. Either way, a bad name means that the program needs to be changed.

- Functions should be used only when the primary purpose of the function is to return the specific value described by the function's name.

- Careful programmers use macro routines with care and only as a last resort.

Chapter 8

Defensive Programming

cc2e.com/0861

Contents

Related Topics

- Information hiding: "Hide Secrets (Information Hiding)" in Section 5.3

- Design for change: "Identify Areas Likely to Change" in Section 5.3

- Software architecture: Section 3.5

- Design in Construction: Chapter 5

- Debugging: Chapter 23

KEY POINT

Defensive programming doesn't mean being defensive about your programming—"It does so work!" The idea is based on defensive driving. In defensive driving, you adopt the mind-set that you're never sure what the other drivers are going to do. That way, you make sure that if they do something dangerous you won't be hurt. You take responsibility for protecting yourself even when it might be the other driver's fault. In defensive programming, the main idea is that if a routine is passed bad data, it won't be hurt, even if the bad data is another routine's fault. More generally, it's the recognition that programs will have problems and modifications, and that a smart programmer will develop code accordingly.

This chapter describes how to protect yourself from the cold, cruel world of invalid data, events that can "never" happen, and other programmers' mistakes. If you're an experienced programmer, you might skip the next section on handling input data and begin with Section 8.2, which reviews the use of assertions.

8.1 Protecting Your Program from Invalid Inputs

In school you might have heard the expression, "Garbage in, garbage out." That expression is essentially software development's version of caveat emptor: let the user beware.

KEY POINT

For production software, garbage in, garbage out isn't good enough. A good program never puts out garbage, regardless of what it takes in. A good program uses "garbage in, nothing out," "garbage in, error message out," or "no garbage allowed in" instead. By today's standards, "garbage in, garbage out" is the mark of a sloppy, nonsecure program.

There are three general ways to handle garbage in:

Check the values of all data from external sources   When getting data from a file, a user, the network, or some other external interface, check to be sure that the data falls within the allowable range. Make sure that numeric values are within tolerances and that strings are short enough to handle. If a string is intended to represent a restricted range of values (such as a financial transaction ID or something similar), be sure that the string is valid for its intended purpose; otherwise reject it. If you're working on a secure application, be especially leery of data that might attack your system: attempted buffer overflows, injected SQL commands, injected HTML or XML code, integer overflows, data passed to system calls, and so on.

Check the values of all routine input parameters   Checking the values of routine input parameters is essentially the same as checking data that comes from an external source, except that the data comes from another routine instead of from an external interface. The discussion in Section 8.5, "Barricade Your Program to Contain the Damage Caused by Errors," provides a practical way to determine which routines need to check their inputs.

Decide how to handle bad inputs   Once you've detected an invalid parameter, what do you do with it? Depending on the situation, you might choose any of a dozen different approaches, which are described in detail in Section 8.3, "Error-Handling Techniques," later in this chapter.

Defensive programming is useful as an adjunct to the other quality-improvement techniques described in this book. The best form of defensive coding is not inserting errors in the first place. Using iterative design, writing pseudocode before code, writing test cases before writing the code, and having low-level design inspections are all activities that help to prevent inserting defects. They should thus be given a higher priority than defensive programming. Fortunately, you can use defensive programming in combination with the other techniques.

As Figure 8-1 suggests, protecting yourself from seemingly small problems can make more of a difference than you might think. The rest of this chapter describes specific options for checking data from external sources, checking input parameters, and handling bad inputs.

Mike Siegel/The Seattle Times

Figure 8-1   Part of the Interstate-90 floating bridge in Seattle sank during a storm because the flotation tanks were left uncovered, they filled with water, and the bridge became too heavy to float. During construction, protecting yourself against the small stuff matters more than you might think.

8.2 Assertions

An assertion is code that's used during development—usually a routine or macro—that allows a program to check itself as it runs. When an assertion is true, that means everything is operating as expected. When it's false, that means it has detected an unexpected error in the code. For example, if the system assumes that a customer-information file will never have more than 50,000 records, the program might contain an assertion that the number of records is less than or equal to 50,000. As long as the number of records is less than or equal to 50,000, the assertion will be silent. If it encounters more than 50,000 records, however, it will loudly "assert" that an error is in the program.

KEY POINT

Assertions are especially useful in large, complicated programs and in high-reliability programs. They enable programmers to more quickly flush out mismatched interface assumptions, errors that creep in when code is modified, and so on.

An assertion usually takes two arguments: a boolean expression that describes the assumption that's supposed to be true, and a message to display if it isn't. Here's what a Java assertion would look like if the variable *denominator* were expected to be nonzero:

> **Java Example of an Assertion**
> ```
> assert denominator != 0 : "denominator is unexpectedly equal to 0.";
> ```

This assertion asserts that *denominator* is not equal to *0*. The first argument, *denominator != 0*, is a boolean expression that evaluates to *true* or *false*. The second argument is a message to print if the first argument is *false*—that is, if the assertion is false.

Use assertions to document assumptions made in the code and to flush out unexpected conditions. Assertions can be used to check assumptions like these:

- That an input parameter's value falls within its expected range (or an output parameter's value does)

- That a file or stream is open (or closed) when a routine begins executing (or when it ends executing)

- That a file or stream is at the beginning (or end) when a routine begins executing (or when it ends executing)

- That a file or stream is open for read-only, write-only, or both read and write

- That the value of an input-only variable is not changed by a routine

- That a pointer is non-null

- That an array or other container passed into a routine can contain at least *X* number of data elements

- That a table has been initialized to contain real values

- That a container is empty (or full) when a routine begins executing (or when it finishes)

- That the results from a highly optimized, complicated routine match the results from a slower but clearly written routine

Of course, these are just the basics, and your own routines will contain many more specific assumptions that you can document using assertions.

Normally, you don't want users to see assertion messages in production code; assertions are primarily for use during development and maintenance. Assertions are normally compiled into the code at development time and compiled out of the code for production. During development, assertions flush out contradictory assumptions, unexpected conditions, bad values passed to routines, and so on. During production, they can be compiled out of the code so that the assertions don't degrade system performance.

Building Your Own Assertion Mechanism

Cross-Reference Building your own assertion routine is a good example of programming "into" a language rather than just programming "in" a language. For more details on this distinction, see Section 34.4, "Program into Your Language, Not in It."

Many languages have built-in support for assertions, including C++, Java, and Microsoft Visual Basic. If your language doesn't directly support assertion routines, they are easy to write. The standard C++ *assert* macro doesn't provide for text messages. Here's an example of an improved *ASSERT* implemented as a C++ macro:

C++ Example of an Assertion Macro
```cpp
#define ASSERT( condition, message ) {        \
    if ( !(condition) ) {                      \
        LogError( "Assertion failed: ",        \
            #condition, message );             \
        exit( EXIT_FAILURE );                  \
    }                                          \
}
```

Guidelines for Using Assertions

Here are some guidelines for using assertions:

Use error-handling code for conditions you expect to occur; use assertions for conditions that should **never** *occur*   Assertions check for conditions that should *never* occur. Error-handling code checks for off-nominal circumstances that might not occur very often, but that have been anticipated by the programmer who wrote the code and that need to be handled by the production code. Error handling typically checks for bad input data; assertions check for bugs in the code.

If error-handling code is used to address an anomalous condition, the error handling will enable the program to respond to the error gracefully. If an assertion is fired for an anomalous condition, the corrective action is not merely to handle an error gracefully—the corrective action is to change the program's source code, recompile, and release a new version of the software.

A good way to think of assertions is as executable documentation—you can't rely on them to make the code work, but they can document assumptions more actively than program-language comments can.

Avoid putting executable code into assertions   Putting code into an assertion raises the possibility that the compiler will eliminate the code when you turn off the assertions. Suppose you have an assertion like this:

Cross-Reference You could view this as one of many problems associated with putting multiple statements on one line. For more examples, see "Using Only One Statement per Line" in Section 31.5.

Visual Basic Example of a Dangerous Use of an Assertion

```
Debug.Assert( PerformAction() ) ' Couldn't perform action
```

The problem with this code is that, if you don't compile the assertions, you don't compile the code that performs the action. Put executable statements on their own lines, assign the results to status variables, and test the status variables instead. Here's an example of a safe use of an assertion:

Visual Basic Example of a Safe Use of an Assertion

```
actionPerformed = PerformAction()
Debug.Assert( actionPerformed ) ' Couldn't perform action
```

Further Reading For much more on preconditions and postconditions, see *Object-Oriented Software Construction* (Meyer 1997).

Use assertions to document and verify preconditions and postconditions   Preconditions and postconditions are part of an approach to program design and development known as "design by contract" (Meyer 1997). When preconditions and postconditions are used, each routine or class forms a contract with the rest of the program.

Preconditions are the properties that the client code of a routine or class promises will be true before it calls the routine or instantiates the object. Preconditions are the client code's obligations to the code it calls.

Postconditions are the properties that the routine or class promises will be true when it concludes executing. Postconditions are the routine's or class's obligations to the code that uses it.

Assertions are a useful tool for documenting preconditions and postconditions. Comments could be used to document preconditions and postconditions, but, unlike comments, assertions can check dynamically whether the preconditions and postconditions are true.

In the following example, assertions are used to document the preconditions and postcondition of the *Velocity* routine.

Visual Basic Example of Using Assertions to Document Preconditions and Postconditions

```
Private Function Velocity ( _
   ByVal latitude As Single, _
   ByVal longitude As Single, _
   ByVal elevation As Single _
   ) As Single

   ' Preconditions
   Debug.Assert ( -90 <= latitude And latitude <= 90 )
   Debug.Assert ( 0 <= longitude And longitude < 360 )
   Debug.Assert ( -500 <= elevation And elevation <= 75000 )
```

```
    ...

    ' Postconditions
    Debug.Assert ( 0 <= returnVelocity And returnVelocity <= 600 )

    ' return value
    Velocity = returnVelocity
End Function
```

If the variables *latitude*, *longitude*, and *elevation* were coming from an external source, invalid values should be checked and handled by error-handling code rather than by assertions. If the variables are coming from a trusted, internal source, however, and the routine's design is based on the assumption that these values will be within their valid ranges, then assertions are appropriate.

Cross-Reference For more on robustness, see "Robustness vs. Correctness" in Section 8.3, later in this chapter.

For highly robust code, assert and then handle the error anyway   For any given error condition, a routine will generally use either an assertion or error-handling code, but not both. Some experts argue that only one kind is needed (Meyer 1997).

But real-world programs and projects tend to be too messy to rely solely on assertions. On a large, long-lasting system, different parts might be designed by different designers over a period of 5–10 years or more. The designers will be separated in time, across numerous versions. Their designs will focus on different technologies at different points in the system's development. The designers will be separated geographically, especially if parts of the system are acquired from external sources. Programmers will have worked to different coding standards at different points in the system's lifetime. On a large development team, some programmers will inevitably be more conscientious than others and some parts of the code will be reviewed more rigorously than other parts of the code. Some programmers will unit test their code more thoroughly than others. With test teams working across different geographic regions and subject to business pressures that result in test coverage that varies with each release, you can't count on comprehensive, system-level regression testing, either.

In such circumstances, both assertions and error-handling code might be used to address the same error. In the source code for Microsoft Word, for example, conditions that should always be true are asserted, but such errors are also handled by error-handling code in case the assertion fails. For extremely large, complex, long-lived applications like Word, assertions are valuable because they help to flush out as many development-time errors as possible. But the application is so complex (millions of lines of code) and has gone through so many generations of modification that it isn't realistic to assume that every conceivable error will be detected and corrected before the software ships, and so errors must be handled in the production version of the system as well.

Here's an example of how that might work in the *Velocity* example:

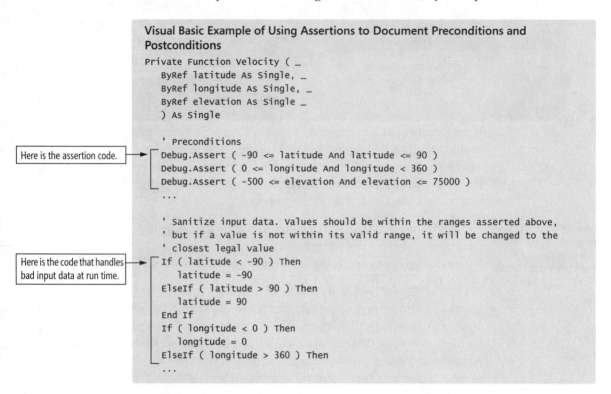

Visual Basic Example of Using Assertions to Document Preconditions and Postconditions

```vb
Private Function Velocity ( _
   ByRef latitude As Single, _
   ByRef longitude As Single, _
   ByRef elevation As Single _
   ) As Single

   ' Preconditions
   Debug.Assert ( -90 <= latitude And latitude <= 90 )
   Debug.Assert ( 0 <= longitude And longitude < 360 )
   Debug.Assert ( -500 <= elevation And elevation <= 75000 )
   ...

   ' Sanitize input data. Values should be within the ranges asserted above,
   ' but if a value is not within its valid range, it will be changed to the
   ' closest legal value
   If ( latitude < -90 ) Then
       latitude = -90
   ElseIf ( latitude > 90 ) Then
       latitude = 90
   End If
   If ( longitude < 0 ) Then
       longitude = 0
   ElseIf ( longitude > 360 ) Then
   ...
```

Here is the assertion code.

Here is the code that handles bad input data at run time.

8.3 Error-Handling Techniques

Assertions are used to handle errors that should never occur in the code. How do you handle errors that you do expect to occur? Depending on the specific circumstances, you might want to return a neutral value, substitute the next piece of valid data, return the same answer as the previous time, substitute the closest legal value, log a warning message to a file, return an error code, call an error-processing routine or object, display an error message, or shut down—or you might want to use a combination of these responses.

Here are some more details on these options:

Return a neutral value Sometimes the best response to bad data is to continue operating and simply return a value that's known to be harmless. A numeric computation might return 0. A string operation might return an empty string, or a pointer operation might return an empty pointer. A drawing routine that gets a bad input value for color in a video game might use the default background or foreground color. A drawing routine that displays x-ray data for cancer patients, however, would not want to display a "neutral value." In that case, you'd be better off shutting down the program than displaying incorrect patient data.

Substitute the next piece of valid data   When processing a stream of data, some circumstances call for simply returning the next valid data. If you're reading records from a database and encounter a corrupted record, you might simply continue reading until you find a valid record. If you're taking readings from a thermometer 100 times per second and you don't get a valid reading one time, you might simply wait another 1/100th of a second and take the next reading.

Return the same answer as the previous time   If the thermometer-reading software doesn't get a reading one time, it might simply return the same value as last time. Depending on the application, temperatures might not be very likely to change much in 1/100th of a second. In a video game, if you detect a request to paint part of the screen an invalid color, you might simply return the same color used previously. But if you're authorizing transactions at a cash machine, you probably wouldn't want to use the "same answer as last time"—that would be the previous user's bank account number!

Substitute the closest legal value   In some cases, you might choose to return the closest legal value, as in the *Velocity* example earlier. This is often a reasonable approach when taking readings from a calibrated instrument. The thermometer might be calibrated between 0 and 100 degrees Celsius, for example. If you detect a reading less than 0, you can substitute 0, which is the closest legal value. If you detect a value greater than 100, you can substitute 100. For a string operation, if a string length is reported to be less than 0, you could substitute 0. My car uses this approach to error handling whenever I back up. Since my speedometer doesn't show negative speeds, when I back up it simply shows a speed of 0—the closest legal value.

Log a warning message to a file   When bad data is detected, you might choose to log a warning message to a file and then continue on. This approach can be used in conjunction with other techniques like substituting the closest legal value or substituting the next piece of valid data. If you use a log, consider whether you can safely make it publicly available or whether you need to encrypt it or protect it some other way.

Return an error code   You could decide that only certain parts of a system will handle errors. Other parts will not handle errors locally; they will simply report that an error has been detected and trust that some other routine higher up in the calling hierarchy will handle the error. The specific mechanism for notifying the rest of the system that an error has occurred could be any of the following:

- Set the value of a status variable
- Return status as the function's return value
- Throw an exception by using the language's built-in exception mechanism

In this case, the specific error-reporting mechanism is less important than the decision about which parts of the system will handle errors directly and which will just report that they've occurred. If security is an issue, be sure that calling routines always check return codes.

Call an error-processing routine/object   Another approach is to centralize error handling in a global error-handling routine or error-handling object. The advantage of this approach is that error-processing responsibility can be centralized, which can make debugging easier. The tradeoff is that the whole program will know about this central capability and will be coupled to it. If you ever want to reuse any of the code from the system in another system, you'll have to drag the error-handling machinery along with the code you reuse.

This approach has an important security implication. If your code has encountered a buffer overrun, it's possible that an attacker has compromised the address of the handler routine or object. Thus, once a buffer overrun has occurred while an application is running, it is no longer safe to use this approach.

Display an error message wherever the error is encountered   This approach minimizes error-handling overhead; however, it does have the potential to spread user interface messages through the entire application, which can create challenges when you need to create a consistent user interface, when you try to clearly separate the UI from the rest of the system, or when you try to localize the software into a different language. Also, beware of telling a potential attacker of the system too much. Attackers sometimes use error messages to discover how to attack a system.

Handle the error in whatever way works best locally   Some designs call for handling all errors locally—the decision of which specific error-handling method to use is left up to the programmer designing and implementing the part of the system that encounters the error.

This approach provides individual developers with great flexibility, but it creates a significant risk that the overall performance of the system will not satisfy its requirements for correctness or robustness (more on this in a moment). Depending on how developers end up handling specific errors, this approach also has the potential to spread user interface code throughout the system, which exposes the program to all the problems associated with displaying error messages.

Shut down   Some systems shut down whenever they detect an error. This approach is useful in safety-critical applications. For example, if the software that controls radiation equipment for treating cancer patients receives bad input data for the radiation dosage, what is its best error-handling response? Should it use the same value as last time? Should it use the closest legal value? Should it use a neutral value? In this case, shutting down is the best option. We'd much prefer to reboot the machine than to run the risk of delivering the wrong dosage.

A similar approach can be used to improve the security of Microsoft Windows. By default, Windows continues to operate even when its security log is full. But you can configure Windows to halt the server if the security log becomes full, which can be appropriate in a security-critical environment.

Robustness vs. Correctness

As the video game and x-ray examples show us, the style of error processing that is most appropriate depends on the kind of software the error occurs in. These examples also illustrate that error processing generally favors more correctness or more robustness. Developers tend to use these terms informally, but, strictly speaking, these terms are at opposite ends of the scale from each other. *Correctness* means never returning an inaccurate result; returning no result is better than returning an inaccurate result. *Robustness* means always trying to do something that will allow the software to keep operating, even if that leads to results that are inaccurate sometimes.

Safety-critical applications tend to favor correctness to robustness. It is better to return no result than to return a wrong result. The radiation machine is a good example of this principle.

Consumer applications tend to favor robustness to correctness. Any result whatsoever is usually better than the software shutting down. The word processor I'm using occasionally displays a fraction of a line of text at the bottom of the screen. If it detects that condition, do I want the word processor to shut down? No. I know that the next time I hit Page Up or Page Down, the screen will refresh and the display will be back to normal.

High-Level Design Implications of Error Processing

KEY POINT

With so many options, you need to be careful to handle invalid parameters in consistent ways throughout the program. The way in which errors are handled affects the software's ability to meet requirements related to correctness, robustness, and other nonfunctional attributes. Deciding on a general approach to bad parameters is an architectural or high-level design decision and should be addressed at one of those levels.

Once you decide on the approach, make sure you follow it consistently. If you decide to have high-level code handle errors and low-level code merely report errors, make sure the high-level code actually handles the errors! Some languages give you the option of ignoring the fact that a function is returning an error code—in C++, you're not required to do anything with a function's return value—but don't ignore error information! Test the function return value. If you don't expect the function ever to produce an error, check it anyway. The whole point of defensive programming is guarding against errors you don't expect.

This guideline holds true for system functions as well as for your own functions. Unless you've set an architectural guideline of not checking system calls for errors, check for error codes after each call. If you detect an error, include the error number and the description of the error.

8.4 Exceptions

Exceptions are a specific means by which code can pass along errors or exceptional events to the code that called it. If code in one routine encounters an unexpected condition that it doesn't know how to handle, it throws an exception, essentially throwing up its hands and yelling, "I don't know what to do about this—I sure hope somebody else knows how to handle it!" Code that has no sense of the context of an error can return control to other parts of the system that might have a better ability to interpret the error and do something useful about it.

Exceptions can also be used to straighten out tangled logic within a single stretch of code, such as the "Rewrite with *try-finally*" example in Section 17.3. The basic structure of an exception is that a routine uses *throw* to throw an exception object. Code in some other routine up the calling hierarchy will *catch* the exception within a *try-catch* block.

Popular languages vary in how they implement exceptions. Table 8-1 summarizes the major differences in three of them:

Table 8-1   Popular-Language Support for Exceptions

Exception Attribute	C++	Java	Visual Basic
Try-catch support	yes	yes	yes
Try-catch-finally support	no	yes	yes
What can be thrown	*Exception* object or object derived from *Exception* class; object pointer; object reference; data type like string or int	*Exception* object or object derived from *Exception* class	*Exception* object or object derived from *Exception* class
Effect of uncaught exception	Invokes *std::unexpected()*, which by default invokes *std::terminate()*, which by default invokes *abort()*	Terminates thread of execution if exception is a "checked exception"; no effect if exception is a "runtime exception"	Terminates program
Exceptions thrown must be defined in class interface	No	Yes	No
Exceptions caught must be defined in class interface	No	Yes	No

Exceptions have an attribute in common with inheritance: used judiciously, they can reduce complexity. Used imprudently, they can make code almost impossible to follow. This section contains suggestions for realizing the benefits of exceptions and avoiding the difficulties often associated with them.

Programs that use exceptions as part of their normal processing suffer from all the readability and maintainability problems of classic spaghetti code.
—Andy Hunt and Dave Thomas

Use exceptions to notify other parts of the program about errors that should not be ignored   The overriding benefit of exceptions is their ability to signal error conditions in such a way that they cannot be ignored (Meyers 1996). Other approaches to handling errors create the possibility that an error condition can propagate through a code base undetected. Exceptions eliminate that possibility.

Throw an exception only for conditions that are truly exceptional   Exceptions should be reserved for conditions that are truly exceptional—in other words, for conditions that cannot be addressed by other coding practices. Exceptions are used in similar circumstances to assertions—for events that are not just infrequent but for events that should *never* occur.

Exceptions represent a tradeoff between a powerful way to handle unexpected conditions on the one hand and increased complexity on the other. Exceptions weaken encapsulation by requiring the code that calls a routine to know which exceptions might be thrown inside the code that's called. That increases code complexity, which works against what Chapter 5, "Design in Construction," refers to as Software's Primary Technical Imperative: Managing Complexity.

Don't use an exception to pass the buck   If an error condition can be handled locally, handle it locally. Don't throw an uncaught exception in a section of code if you can handle the error locally.

Avoid throwing exceptions in constructors and destructors unless you catch them in the same place   The rules for how exceptions are processed become very complicated very quickly when exceptions are thrown in constructors and destructors. In C++, for example, destructors aren't called unless an object is fully constructed, which means if code within a constructor throws an exception, the destructor won't be called, thereby setting up a possible resource leak (Meyers 1996, Stroustrup 1997). Similarly complicated rules apply to exceptions within destructors.

Language lawyers might say that remembering rules like these is "trivial," but programmers who are mere mortals will have trouble remembering them. It's better programming practice simply to avoid the extra complexity such code creates by not writing that kind of code in the first place.

Cross-Reference For more on maintaining consistent interface abstractions, see "Good Abstraction" in Section 6.2.

Throw exceptions at the right level of abstraction   A routine should present a consistent abstraction in its interface, and so should a class. The exceptions thrown are part of the routine interface, just like specific data types are.

When you choose to pass an exception to the caller, make sure the exception's level of abstraction is consistent with the routine interface's abstraction. Here's an example of what not to do:

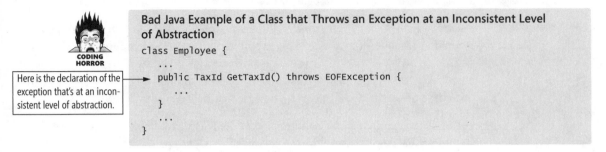

Here is the declaration of the exception that's at an inconsistent level of abstraction.

Bad Java Example of a Class that Throws an Exception at an Inconsistent Level of Abstraction

```java
class Employee {
   ...
   public TaxId GetTaxId() throws EOFException {
      ...
   }
   ...
}
```

The *GetTaxId()* code passes the lower-level *EOFException* exception back to its caller. It doesn't take ownership of the exception itself; it exposes some details about how it's implemented by passing the lower-level exception to its caller. This effectively couples the routine's client's code not to the *Employee* class's code but to the code below the *Employee* class that throws the *EOFException* exception. Encapsulation is broken, and intellectual manageability starts to decline.

Instead, the *GetTaxId()* code should pass back an exception that's consistent with the class interface of which it's a part, like this:

Good Java Example of a Class that Throws an Exception at a Consistent Level of Abstraction

Here is the declaration of the exception that contributes to a consistent level of abstraction.

```java
class Employee {
   ...
   public TaxId GetTaxId() throws EmployeeDataNotAvailable {
      ...
   }
   ...
}
```

The exception-handling code inside *GetTaxId()* will probably just map the *io_disk_not_ready* exception onto the *EmployeeDataNotAvailable* exception, which is fine because that's sufficient to preserve the interface abstraction.

Include in the exception message all information that led to the exception Every exception occurs in specific circumstances that are detected at the time the code throws the exception. This information is invaluable to the person who reads the exception message. Be sure the message contains the information needed to understand why the exception was thrown. If the exception was thrown because of an array index error, be sure the exception message includes the upper and lower array limits and the value of the illegal index.

Avoid empty* catch *blocks   Sometimes it's tempting to pass off an exception that you don't know what to do with, like this:

CODING HORROR

> **Bad Java Example of Ignoring an Exception**
> ```
> try {
>    ...
>    // lots of code
>    ...
> } catch ( AnException exception ) {
> }
> ```

Such an approach says that either the code within the *try* block is wrong because it raises an exception for no reason, or the code within the *catch* block is wrong because it doesn't handle a valid exception. Determine which is the root cause of the problem, and then fix either the *try* block or the *catch* block.

You might occasionally find rare circumstances in which an exception at a lower level really doesn't represent an exception at the level of abstraction of the calling routine. If that's the case, at least document why an empty *catch* block is appropriate. You could "document" that case with comments or by logging a message to a file, as follows:

> **Good Java Example of Ignoring an Exception**
> ```
> try {
>    ...
>    // lots of code
>    ...
> } catch ( AnException exception ) {
>    LogError( "Unexpected exception" );
> }
> ```

Know the exceptions your library code throws   If you're working in a language that doesn't require a routine or class to define the exceptions it throws, be sure you know what exceptions are thrown by any library code you use. Failing to catch an exception generated by library code will crash your program just as fast as failing to catch an exception you generated yourself. If the library code doesn't document the exceptions it throws, create prototyping code to exercise the libraries and flush out the exceptions.

Consider building a centralized exception reporter   One approach to ensuring consistency in exception handling is to use a centralized exception reporter. The centralized exception reporter provides a central repository for knowledge about what kinds of exceptions there are, how each exception should be handled, formatting of exception messages, and so on.

Here is an example of a simple exception handler that simply prints a diagnostic message:

Further Reading For a more detailed explanation of this technique, see *Practical Standards for Microsoft Visual Basic .NET* (Foxall 2003).

Visual Basic Example of a Centralized Exception Reporter, Part 1

```
Sub ReportException( _
    ByVal className, _
    ByVal thisException As Exception _
)
    Dim message As String
    Dim caption As String

    message = "Exception: " & thisException.Message & "." & ControlChars.CrLf & _
        "Class:   " & className & ControlChars.CrLf & _
        "Routine: " & thisException.TargetSite.Name & ControlChars.CrLf
    caption = "Exception"
    MessageBox.Show( message, caption, MessageBoxButtons.OK, _
        MessageBoxIcon.Exclamation )

End Sub
```

You would use this generic exception handler with code like this:

Visual Basic Example of a Centralized Exception Reporter, Part 2

```
Try
    ...
Catch exceptionObject As Exception
    ReportException( CLASS_NAME, exceptionObject )
End Try
```

The code in this version of *ReportException()* is simple. In a real application, you could make the code as simple or as elaborate as needed to meet your exception-handling needs.

If you do decide to build a centralized exception reporter, be sure to consider the general issues involved in centralized error handling, which are discussed in "Call an error-processing routine/object" in Section 8.3.

Standardize your project's use of exceptions   To keep exception handling as intellectually manageable as possible, you can standardize your use of exceptions in several ways:

- If you're working in a language like C++ that allows you to throw a variety of kinds of objects, data, and pointers, standardize on what specifically you will throw. For compatibility with other languages, consider throwing only objects derived from the *Exception* base class.

- Consider creating your own project-specific exception class, which can serve as the base class for all exceptions thrown on your project. This supports centralizing and standardizing logging, error reporting, and so on.

- Define the specific circumstances under which code is allowed to use *throw-catch* syntax to perform error processing locally.

- Define the specific circumstances under which code is allowed to throw an exception that won't be handled locally.

- Determine whether a centralized exception reporter will be used.

- Define whether exceptions are allowed in constructors and destructors.

Cross-Reference For numerous alternative error-handling approaches, see Section 8.3, "Error-Handling Techniques," earlier in this chapter.

Consider alternatives to exceptions   Several programming languages have supported exceptions for 5–10 years or more, but little conventional wisdom has emerged about how to use them safely.

Some programmers use exceptions to handle errors just because their language provides that particular error-handling mechanism. You should always consider the full set of error-handling alternatives: handling the error locally, propagating the error by using an error code, logging debug information to a file, shutting down the system, or using some other approach. Handling errors with exceptions just because your language provides exception handling is a classic example of programming *in* a language rather than programming *into* a language. (For details on that distinction, see Section 4.3, "Your Location on the Technology Wave," and Section 34.4, "Program into Your Language, Not in It."

Finally, consider whether your program really needs to handle exceptions, period. As Bjarne Stroustrup points out, sometimes the best response to a serious run-time error is to release all acquired resources and abort. Let the user rerun the program with proper input (Stroustrup 1997).

8.5 Barricade Your Program to Contain the Damage Caused by Errors

Barricades are a damage-containment strategy. The reason is similar to that for having isolated compartments in the hull of a ship. If the ship runs into an iceberg and pops open the hull, that compartment is shut off and the rest of the ship isn't affected. They are also similar to firewalls in a building. A building's firewalls prevent fire from spreading from one part of a building to another part. (Barricades used to be called "firewalls," but the term "firewall" now commonly refers to blocking hostile network traffic.)

One way to barricade for defensive programming purposes is to designate certain interfaces as boundaries to "safe" areas. Check data crossing the boundaries of a safe area for validity, and respond sensibly if the data isn't valid. Figure 8-2 illustrates this concept.

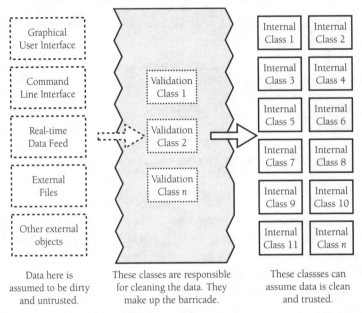

| Data here is assumed to be dirty and untrusted. | These classes are responsible for cleaning the data. They make up the barricade. | These classses can assume data is clean and trusted. |

Figure 8-2 Defining some parts of the software that work with dirty data and some that work with clean data can be an effective way to relieve the majority of the code of the responsibility for checking for bad data.

This same approach can be used at the class level. The class's public methods assume the data is unsafe, and they are responsible for checking the data and sanitizing it. Once the data has been accepted by the class's public methods, the class's private methods can assume the data is safe.

Another way of thinking about this approach is as an operating-room technique. Data is sterilized before it's allowed to enter the operating room. Anything that's in the operating room is assumed to be safe. The key design decision is deciding what to put in the operating room, what to keep out, and where to put the doors—which routines are considered to be inside the safety zone, which are outside, and which sanitize the data. The easiest way to do this is usually by sanitizing external data as it arrives, but data often needs to be sanitized at more than one level, so multiple levels of sterilization are sometimes required.

Convert input data to the proper type at input time Input typically arrives in the form of a string or number. Sometimes the value will map onto a boolean type like "yes" or "no." Sometimes the value will map onto an enumerated type like *Color_Red*, *Color_Green*, and *Color_Blue*. Carrying data of questionable type for any length of time in a program increases complexity and increases the chance that someone can crash your program by inputting a color like "Yes." Convert input data to the proper form as soon as possible after it's input.

Relationship Between Barricades and Assertions

The use of barricades makes the distinction between assertions and error handling clean-cut. Routines that are outside the barricade should use error handling because it isn't safe to make any assumptions about the data. Routines inside the barricade should use assertions, because the data passed to them is supposed to be sanitized before it's passed across the barricade. If one of the routines inside the barricade detects bad data, that's an error in the program rather than an error in the data.

The use of barricades also illustrates the value of deciding at the architectural level how to handle errors. Deciding which code is inside and which is outside the barricade is an architecture-level decision.

8.6 Debugging Aids

Another key aspect of defensive programming is the use of debugging aids, which can be a powerful ally in quickly detecting errors.

Don't Automatically Apply Production Constraints to the Development Version

Further Reading For more on using debug code to support defensive programming, see *Writing Solid Code* (Maguire 1993).

A common programmer blind spot is the assumption that limitations of the production software apply to the development version. The production version has to run fast. The development version might be able to run slow. The production version has to be stingy with resources. The development version might be allowed to use resources extravagantly. The production version shouldn't expose dangerous operations to the user. The development version can have extra operations that you can use without a safety net.

One program I worked on made extensive use of a quadruply linked list. The linked-list code was error prone, and the linked list tended to get corrupted. I added a menu option to check the integrity of the linked list.

In debug mode, Microsoft Word contains code in the idle loop that checks the integrity of the *Document* object every few seconds. This helps to detect data corruption quickly, and it makes for easier error diagnosis.

KEY POINT

Be willing to trade speed and resource usage during development in exchange for built-in tools that can make development go more smoothly.

Introduce Debugging Aids Early

The earlier you introduce debugging aids, the more they'll help. Typically, you won't go to the effort of writing a debugging aid until after you've been bitten by a problem several times. If you write the aid after the first time, however, or use one from a previous project, it will help throughout the project.

Use Offensive Programming

Cross-Reference For more details on handling unanticipated cases, see "Tips for Using *case* Statements" in Section 15.2.

Exceptional cases should be handled in a way that makes them obvious during development and recoverable when production code is running. Michael Howard and David LeBlanc refer to this approach as "offensive programming" (Howard and LeBlanc 2003).

Suppose you have a *case* statement that you expect to handle only five kinds of events. During development, the default case should be used to generate a warning that says "Hey! There's another case here! Fix the program!" During production, however, the default case should do something more graceful, like writing a message to an error-log file.

A dead program normally does a lot less damage than a crippled one.
—*Andy Hunt and Dave Thomas*

Here are some ways you can program offensively:

■ Make sure *assert*s abort the program. Don't allow programmers to get into the habit of just hitting the Enter key to bypass a known problem. Make the problem painful enough that it will be fixed.

■ Completely fill any memory allocated so that you can detect memory allocation errors.

■ Completely fill any files or streams allocated to flush out any file-format errors.

■ Be sure the code in each *case* statement's *default* or *else* clause fails hard (aborts the program) or is otherwise impossible to overlook.

■ Fill an object with junk data just before it's deleted.

■ Set up the program to e-mail error log files to yourself so that you can see the kinds of errors that are occurring in the released software, if that's appropriate for the kind of software you're developing.

Sometimes the best defense is a good offense. Fail hard during development so that you can fail softer during production.

Plan to Remove Debugging Aids

If you're writing code for your own use, it might be fine to leave all the debugging code in the program. If you're writing code for commercial use, the performance penalty in size and speed can be prohibitive. Plan to avoid shuffling debugging code in and out of a program. Here are several ways to do that:

Cross-Reference For details on version control, see Section 28.2, "Configuration Management."

Use version-control tools and build tools like ant and make Version-control tools can build different versions of a program from the same source files. In development mode, you can set the build tool to include all the debug code. In production mode, you can set it to exclude any debug code you don't want in the commercial version.

Use a built-in preprocessor If your programming environment has a preprocessor—as C++ does, for example—you can include or exclude debug code at the flick of a compiler switch. You can use the preprocessor directly or by writing a macro that works with preprocessor definitions. Here's an example of writing code using the preprocessor directly:

C++ Example of Using the Preprocessor Directly to Control Debug Code

To include the debugging code, use *#define* to define the symbol *DEBUG*. To exclude the debugging code, don't define *DEBUG*.

```
#define DEBUG
...

#if defined( DEBUG )
// debugging code
...

#endif
```

This theme has several variations. Rather than just defining *DEBUG*, you can assign it a value and then test for the value rather than testing whether it's defined. That way you can differentiate between different levels of debug code. You might have some debug code that you want in your program all the time, so you surround that by a statement like *#if DEBUG > 0*. Other debug code might be for specific purposes only, so you can surround it by a statement like *#if DEBUG == POINTER_ERROR*. In other places, you might want to set debug levels, so you could have statements like *#if DEBUG > LEVEL_A*.

If you don't like having *#if defined()*s spread throughout your code, you can write a preprocessor macro to accomplish the same task. Here's an example:

C++ Example of Using a Preprocessor Macro to Control Debug Code

This code is included or excluded, depending on whether *DEBUG* has been defined.

```
#define DEBUG
#if defined( DEBUG )
#define DebugCode( code_fragment )   { code_fragment }
#else
#define DebugCode( code_fragment )
#endif
...

DebugCode(
    statement 1;
    statement 2;
    ...
    statement n;
);
...
```

As in the first example of using the preprocessor, this technique can be altered in a variety of ways that make it more sophisticated than completely including all debug code or completely excluding all of it.

Cross-Reference For more information on preprocessors and for direction to sources of information on writing one of your own, see "Macro Preprocessors" in Section 30.3.

Write your own preprocessor If a language doesn't include a preprocessor, it's fairly easy to write one for including and excluding debug code. Establish a convention for designating debug code, and write your precompiler to follow that convention. For example, in Java you could write a precompiler to respond to the keywords //#BEGIN DEBUG and //#END DEBUG. Write a script to call the preprocessor, and then compile the processed code. You'll save time in the long run, and you won't mistakenly compile the unprocessed code.

Cross-Reference For details on stubs, see "Building Scaffolding to Test Individual Routines" in Section 22.5.

Use debugging stubs In many instances, you can call a routine to do debugging checks. During development, the routine might perform several operations before control returns to the caller. For production code, you can replace the complicated routine with a stub routine that merely returns control immediately to the caller or that performs a couple of quick operations before returning control. This approach incurs only a small performance penalty, and it's a quicker solution than writing your own preprocessor. Keep both the development and production versions of the routines so that you can switch back and forth during future development and production.

You might start with a routine designed to check pointers that are passed to it:

C++ Example of a Routine That Uses a Debugging Stub
```
void DoSomething(
   SOME_TYPE *pointer;
   ...
   ) {

   // check parameters passed in
   CheckPointer( pointer );
   ...

}
```
This line calls the routine to check the pointer.

During development, the *CheckPointer()* routine would perform full checking on the pointer. It would be slow but effective, and it could look like this:

C++ Example of a Routine for Checking Pointers During Development
```
void CheckPointer( void *pointer ) {
   // perform check 1--maybe check that it's not NULL
   // perform check 2--maybe check that its dogtag is legitimate
   // perform check 3--maybe check that what it points to isn't corrupted
   ...
   // perform check n--...
}
```
This routine checks any pointer that's passed to it. It can be used during development to perform as many checks as you can bear.

When the code is ready for production, you might not want all the overhead associated with this pointer checking. You could swap out the preceding routine and swap in this routine:

> This routine just returns immediately to the caller.

C++ Example of a Routine for Checking Pointers During Production

```cpp
void CheckPointer( void *pointer ) {
    // no code; just return to caller
}
```

This is not an exhaustive survey of all the ways you can plan to remove debugging aids, but it should be enough to give you an idea for some things that will work in your environment.

8.7 Determining How Much Defensive Programming to Leave in Production Code

One of the paradoxes of defensive programming is that during development, you'd like an error to be noticeable—you'd rather have it be obnoxious than risk overlooking it. But during production, you'd rather have the error be as unobtrusive as possible, to have the program recover or fail gracefully. Here are some guidelines for deciding which defensive programming tools to leave in your production code and which to leave out:

Leave in code that checks for important errors   Decide which areas of the program can afford to have undetected errors and which areas cannot. For example, if you were writing a spreadsheet program, you could afford to have undetected errors in the screen-update area of the program because the main penalty for an error is only a messy screen. You could not afford to have undetected errors in the calculation engine because such errors might result in subtly incorrect results in someone's spreadsheet. Most users would rather suffer a messy screen than incorrect tax calculations and an audit by the IRS.

Remove code that checks for trivial errors   If an error has truly trivial consequences, remove code that checks for it. In the previous example, you might remove the code that checks the spreadsheet screen update. "Remove" doesn't mean physically remove the code. It means use version control, precompiler switches, or some other technique to compile the program without that particular code. If space isn't a problem, you could leave in the error-checking code but have it log messages to an error-log file unobtrusively.

Remove code that results in hard crashes   As I mentioned, during development, when your program detects an error, you'd like the error to be as noticeable as possible so that you can fix it. Often, the best way to accomplish that goal is to have the program print a debugging message and crash when it detects an error. This is useful even for minor errors.

During production, your users need a chance to save their work before the program crashes and they are probably willing to tolerate a few anomalies in exchange for keeping the program going long enough for them to do that. Users don't appreciate anything that results in the loss of their work, regardless of how much it helps debugging and ultimately improves the quality of the program. If your program contains debugging code that could cause a loss of data, take it out of the production version.

Leave in code that helps the program crash gracefully   If your program contains debugging code that detects potentially fatal errors, leave the code in that allows the program to crash gracefully. In the Mars Pathfinder, for example, engineers left some of the debug code in by design. An error occurred after the Pathfinder had landed. By using the debug aids that had been left in, engineers at JPL were able to diagnose the problem and upload revised code to the Pathfinder, and the Pathfinder completed its mission perfectly (March 1999).

Log errors for your technical support personnel   Consider leaving debugging aids in the production code but changing their behavior so that it's appropriate for the production version. If you've loaded your code with assertions that halt the program during development, you might consider changing the assertion routine to log messages to a file during production rather than eliminating them altogether.

Make sure that the error messages you leave in are friendly   If you leave internal error messages in the program, verify that they're in language that's friendly to the user. In one of my early programs, I got a call from a user who reported that she'd gotten a message that read "You've got a bad pointer allocation, Dog Breath!" Fortunately for me, she had a sense of humor. A common and effective approach is to notify the user of an "internal error" and list an e-mail address or phone number the user can use to report it.

8.8 Being Defensive About Defensive Programming

Too much of anything is bad, but too much whiskey is just enough.
—*Mark Twain*

Too much defensive programming creates problems of its own. If you check data passed as parameters in every conceivable way in every conceivable place, your program will be fat and slow. What's worse, the additional code needed for defensive programming adds complexity to the software. Code installed for defensive programming is not immune to defects, and you're just as likely to find a defect in defensive-programming code as in any other code—more likely, if you write the code casually. Think about where you need to be defensive, and set your defensive-programming priorities accordingly.

cc2e.com/0868

CHECKLIST: Defensive Programming

General

- ❑ Does the routine protect itself from bad input data?

- ❑ Have you used assertions to document assumptions, including preconditions and postconditions?

- ❑ Have assertions been used only to document conditions that should never occur?

- ❑ Does the architecture or high-level design specify a specific set of error-handling techniques?

- ❑ Does the architecture or high-level design specify whether error handling should favor robustness or correctness?

- ❑ Have barricades been created to contain the damaging effect of errors and reduce the amount of code that has to be concerned about error processing?

- ❑ Have debugging aids been used in the code?

- ❑ Have debugging aids been installed in such a way that they can be activated or deactivated without a great deal of fuss?

- ❑ Is the amount of defensive programming code appropriate—neither too much nor too little?

- ❑ Have you used offensive-programming techniques to make errors difficult to overlook during development?

Exceptions

- ❑ Has your project defined a standardized approach to exception handling?

- ❑ Have you considered alternatives to using an exception?

- ❑ Is the error handled locally rather than throwing a nonlocal exception, if possible?

- ❑ Does the code avoid throwing exceptions in constructors and destructors?

- ❑ Are all exceptions at the appropriate levels of abstraction for the routines that throw them?

- ❑ Does each exception include all relevant exception background information?

- ❑ Is the code free of empty *catch* blocks? (Or if an empty *catch* block truly is appropriate, is it documented?)

> **Security Issues**
>
> ❑ Does the code that checks for bad input data check for attempted buffer overflows, SQL injection, HTML injection, integer overflows, and other malicious inputs?
>
> ❑ Are all error-return codes checked?
>
> ❑ Are all exceptions caught?
>
> ❑ Do error messages avoid providing information that would help an attacker break into the system?

Additional Resources

cc2e.com/0875

Take a look at the following defensive-programming resources:

Security

Howard, Michael, and David LeBlanc. *Writing Secure Code*, 2d ed. Redmond, WA: Microsoft Press, 2003. Howard and LeBlanc cover the security implications of trusting input. The book is eye-opening in that it illustrates just how many ways a program can be breached—some of which have to do with construction practices and many of which don't. The book spans a full range of requirements, design, code, and test issues.

Assertions

Maguire, Steve. *Writing Solid Code*. Redmond, WA: Microsoft Press, 1993. Chapter 2 contains an excellent discussion on the use of assertions, including several interesting examples of assertions in well-known Microsoft products.

Stroustrup, Bjarne. *The C++ Programming Language*, 3d ed. Reading, MA: Addison-Wesley, 1997. Section 24.3.7.2 describes several variations on the theme of implementing assertions in C++, including the relationship between assertions and preconditions and postconditions.

Meyer, Bertrand. *Object-Oriented Software Construction*, 2d ed. New York, NY: Prentice Hall PTR, 1997. This book contains the definitive discussion of preconditions and postconditions.

Exceptions

Meyer, Bertrand. *Object-Oriented Software Construction*, 2d ed. New York, NY: Prentice Hall PTR, 1997. Chapter 12 contains a detailed discussion of exception handling.

Stroustrup, Bjarne. *The C++ Programming Language*, 3d ed. Reading, MA: Addison-Wesley, 1997. Chapter 14 contains a detailed discussion of exception handling in C++. Section 14.11 contains an excellent summary of 21 tips for handling C++ exceptions.

Meyers, Scott. *More Effective C++: 35 New Ways to Improve Your Programs and Designs*. Reading, MA: Addison-Wesley, 1996. Items 9–15 describe numerous nuances of exception handling in C++.

Arnold, Ken, James Gosling, and David Holmes. *The Java Programming Language*, 3d ed. Boston, MA: Addison-Wesley, 2000. Chapter 8 contains a discussion of exception handling in Java.

Bloch, Joshua. *Effective Java Programming Language Guide*. Boston, MA: Addison-Wesley, 2001. Items 39–47 describe nuances of exception handling in Java.

Foxall, James. *Practical Standards for Microsoft Visual Basic .NET*. Redmond, WA: Microsoft Press, 2003. Chapter 10 describes exception handling in Visual Basic.

Key Points

- Production code should handle errors in a more sophisticated way than "garbage in, garbage out."

- Defensive-programming techniques make errors easier to find, easier to fix, and less damaging to production code.

- Assertions can help detect errors early, especially in large systems, high-reliability systems, and fast-changing code bases.

- The decision about how to handle bad inputs is a key error-handling decision and a key high-level design decision.

- Exceptions provide a means of handling errors that operates in a different dimension from the normal flow of the code. They are a valuable addition to the programmer's intellectual toolbox when used with care, and they should be weighed against other error-processing techniques.

- Constraints that apply to the production system do not necessarily apply to the development version. You can use that to your advantage, adding code to the development version that helps to flush out errors quickly.

Chapter 9

The Pseudocode Programming Process

Contents

- 9.1 Summary of Steps in Building Classes and Routines: page 216
- 9.2 Pseudocode for Pros: page 218
- 9.3 Constructing Routines by Using the PPP: page 220
- 9.4 Alternatives to the PPP: page 232

Related Topics

- Creating high-quality classes: Chapter 6
- Characteristics of high-quality routines: Chapter 7
- Design in Construction: Chapter 5
- Commenting style: Chapter 32

Although you could view this whole book as an extended description of the programming process for creating classes and routines, this chapter puts the steps in context. This chapter focuses on programming in the small—on the specific steps for building an individual class and its routines, the steps that are critical on projects of all sizes. The chapter also describes the Pseudocode Programming Process (PPP), which reduces the work required during design and documentation and improves the quality of both.

If you're an expert programmer, you might just skim this chapter, but look at the summary of steps and review the tips for constructing routines using the Pseudocode Programming Process in Section 9.3. Few programmers exploit the full power of the process, and it offers many benefits.

The PPP is not the only procedure for creating classes and routines. Section 9.4, at the end of this chapter, describes the most popular alternatives, including test-first development and design by contract.

9.1 Summary of Steps in Building Classes and Routines

Class construction can be approached from numerous directions, but usually it's an iterative process of creating a general design for the class, enumerating specific routines within the class, constructing specific routines, and checking class construction as a whole. As Figure 9-1 suggests, class creation can be a messy process for all the reasons that design is a messy process (reasons that are described in Section 5.1, "Design Challenges").

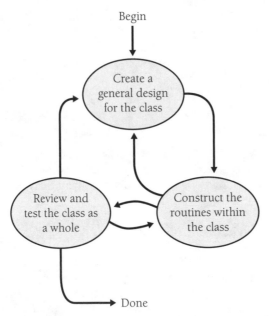

Figure 9-1 Details of class construction vary, but the activities generally occur in the order shown here.

Steps in Creating a Class

The key steps in constructing a class are:

Create a general design for the class Class design includes numerous specific issues. Define the class's specific responsibilities, define what "secrets" the class will hide, and define exactly what abstraction the class interface will capture. Determine whether the class will be derived from another class and whether other classes will be allowed to derive from it. Identify the class's key public methods, and identify and design any nontrivial data members used by the class. Iterate through these topics as many times as needed to create a straightforward design for the routine. These considerations and many others are discussed in more detail in Chapter 6, "Working Classes."

Construct each routine within the class   Once you've identified the class's major routines in the first step, you must construct each specific routine. Construction of each routine typically unearths the need for additional routines, both minor and major, and issues arising from creating those additional routines often ripple back to the overall class design.

Review and test the class as a whole   Normally, each routine is tested as it's created. After the class as a whole becomes operational, the class as a whole should be reviewed and tested for any issues that can't be tested at the individual-routine level.

Steps in Building a Routine

Many of a class's routines will be simple and straightforward to implement: accessor routines, pass-throughs to other objects' routines, and the like. Implementation of other routines will be more complicated, and creation of those routines benefits from a systematic approach. The major activities involved in creating a routine—designing the routine, checking the design, coding the routine, and checking the code—are typically performed in the order shown in Figure 9-2.

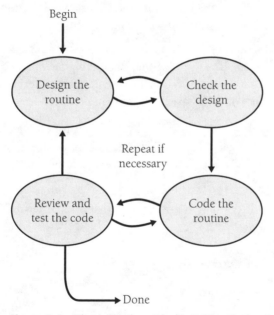

Figure 9-2   These are the major activities that go into constructing a routine. They're usually performed in the order shown.

Experts have developed numerous approaches to creating routines, and my favorite approach is the Pseudocode Programming Process, described in the next section.

9.2 Pseudocode for Pros

The term "pseudocode" refers to an informal, English-like notation for describing how an algorithm, a routine, a class, or a program will work. The Pseudocode Programming Process defines a specific approach to using pseudocode to streamline the creation of code within routines.

Because pseudocode resembles English, it's natural to assume that any English-like description that collects your thoughts will have roughly the same effect as any other. In practice, you'll find that some styles of pseudocode are more useful than others. Here are guidelines for using pseudocode effectively:

- Use English-like statements that precisely describe specific operations.

- Avoid syntactic elements from the target programming language. Pseudocode allows you to design at a slightly higher level than the code itself. When you use programming-language constructs, you sink to a lower level, eliminating the main benefit of design at a higher level, and you saddle yourself with unnecessary syntactic restrictions.

Cross-Reference For details on commenting at the level of intent, see "Kinds of Comments" in Section 32.4.

- Write pseudocode at the level of intent. Describe the meaning of the approach rather than how the approach will be implemented in the target language.

- Write pseudocode at a low enough level that generating code from it will be nearly automatic. If the pseudocode is at too high a level, it can gloss over problematic details in the code. Refine the pseudocode in more and more detail until it seems as if it would be easier to simply write the code.

Once the pseudocode is written, you build the code around it and the pseudocode turns into programming-language comments. This eliminates most commenting effort. If the pseudocode follows the guidelines, the comments will be complete and meaningful.

Here's an example of a design in pseudocode that violates virtually all the principles just described:

CODING HORROR

Example of Bad Pseudocode
```
increment resource number by 1
allocate a dlg struct using malloc
if malloc() returns NULL then return 1
invoke OSrsrc_init to initialize a resource for the operating system
*hRsrcPtr = resource number
return 0
```

What is the intent of this block of pseudocode? Because it's poorly written, it's hard to tell. This so-called pseudocode is bad because it includes target language coding details, such as *hRsrcPtr* (in specific C-language pointer notation) and *malloc()* (a specific C-language function). This pseudocode block focuses on how the code will be written rather than on the meaning of the design. It gets into coding details—whether the routine returns a *1* or a *0*. If you think about this pseudocode from the standpoint of whether it will turn into good comments, you'll begin to understand that it isn't much help.

Here's a design for the same operation in a much-improved pseudocode:

Example of Good Pseudocode

```
Keep track of current number of resources in use
If another resource is available
    Allocate a dialog box structure
    If a dialog box structure could be allocated
        Note that one more resource is in use
        Initialize the resource
        Store the resource number at the location provided by the caller
    Endif
Endif
Return true if a new resource was created; else return false
```

This pseudocode is better than the first because it's written entirely in English; it doesn't use any syntactic elements of the target language. In the first example, the pseudocode could have been implemented only in C. In the second example, the pseudocode doesn't restrict the choice of languages. The second block of pseudocode is also written at the level of intent. What does the second block of pseudocode mean? It is probably easier for you to understand than the first block.

Even though it's written in clear English, the second block of pseudocode is precise and detailed enough that it can easily be used as a basis for programming-language code. When the pseudocode statements are converted to comments, they'll be a good explanation of the code's intent.

Here are the benefits you can expect from using this style of pseudocode:

- Pseudocode makes reviews easier. You can review detailed designs without examining source code. Pseudocode makes low-level design reviews easier and reduces the need to review the code itself.

- Pseudocode supports the idea of iterative refinement. You start with a high-level design, refine the design to pseudocode, and then refine the pseudocode to source code. This successive refinement in small steps allows you to check your design as you drive it to lower levels of detail. The result is that you catch high-level errors at the highest level, mid-level errors at the middle level, and low-level errors at the lowest level—before any of them becomes a problem or contaminates work at more detailed levels.

Further Reading For more information on the advantages of making changes at the least-value stage, see Andy Grove's *High Output Management* (Grove 1983).

■ Pseudocode makes changes easier. A few lines of pseudocode are easier to change than a page of code. Would you rather change a line on a blueprint or rip out a wall and nail in the two-by-fours somewhere else? The effects aren't as physically dramatic in software, but the principle of changing the product when it's most malleable is the same. One of the keys to the success of a project is to catch errors at the "least-value stage," the stage at which the least effort has been invested. Much less has been invested at the pseudocode stage than after full coding, testing, and debugging, so it makes economic sense to catch the errors early.

■ Pseudocode minimizes commenting effort. In the typical coding scenario, you write the code and add comments afterward. In the PPP, the pseudocode statements become the comments, so it actually takes more work to remove the comments than to leave them in.

■ Pseudocode is easier to maintain than other forms of design documentation. With other approaches, design is separated from the code, and when one changes, the two fall out of agreement. With the PPP, the pseudocode statements become comments in the code. As long as the inline comments are maintained, the pseudocode's documentation of the design will be accurate.

KEY POINT

As a tool for detailed design, pseudocode is hard to beat. One survey found that programmers prefer pseudocode for the way it eases construction in a programming language, for its ability to help them detect insufficiently detailed designs, and for the ease of documentation and ease of modification it provides (Ramsey, Atwood, and Van Doren 1983). Pseudocode isn't the only tool for detailed design, but pseudocode and the PPP are useful tools to have in your programmer's toolbox. Try them. The next section shows you how.

9.3 Constructing Routines by Using the PPP

This section describes the activities involved in constructing a routine, namely these:

■ Design the routine.

■ Code the routine.

■ Check the code.

■ Clean up loose ends.

■ Repeat as needed.

Design the Routine

Cross-Reference For details on other aspects of design, see Chapters 5 through 8.

Once you've identified a class's routines, the first step in constructing any of the class's more complicated routines is to design it. Suppose that you want to write a routine to output an error message depending on an error code, and suppose that you call the routine *ReportErrorMessage()*. Here's an informal spec for *ReportErrorMessage()*:

> ReportErrorMessage() *takes an error code as an input argument and outputs an error message corresponding to the code. It's responsible for handling invalid codes. If the program is operating interactively,* ReportErrorMessage() *displays the message to the user. If it's operating in command-line mode,* ReportErrorMessage() *logs the message to a message file. After outputting the message,* ReportErrorMessage() *returns a status value, indicating whether it succeeded or failed.*

The rest of the chapter uses this routine as a running example. The rest of this section describes how to design the routine.

Cross-Reference For details on checking prerequisites, see Chapter 3, "Measure Twice, Cut Once: Upstream Prerequisites," and Chapter 4, "Key Construction Decisions."

Check the prerequisites   Before doing any work on the routine itself, check to see that the job of the routine is well defined and fits cleanly into the overall design. Check to be sure that the routine is actually called for, at the very least indirectly, by the project's requirements.

Define the problem the routine will solve   State the problem the routine will solve in enough detail to allow creation of the routine. If the high-level design is sufficiently detailed, the job might already be done. The high-level design should at least indicate the following:

- The information the routine will hide

- Inputs to the routine

- Outputs from the routine

Cross-Reference For details on preconditions and postconditions, see "Use assertions to document and verify preconditions and postconditions" in Section 8.2.

- Preconditions that are guaranteed to be true before the routine is called (input values within certain ranges, streams initialized, files opened or closed, buffers filled or flushed, etc.)

- Postconditions that the routine guarantees will be true before it passes control back to the caller (output values within specified ranges, streams initialized, files opened or closed, buffers filled or flushed, etc.)

Here's how these concerns are addressed in the *ReportErrorMessage()* example:

- The routine hides two facts: the error message text and the current processing method (interactive or command line).

- There are no preconditions guaranteed to the routine.

- The input to the routine is an error code.

- Two kinds of output are called for: the first is the error message, and the second is the status that *ReportErrorMessage()* returns to the calling routine.

- The routine guarantees that the status value will have a value of either *Success* or *Failure*.

Cross-Reference For details on naming routines, see Section 7.3, "Good Routine Names."

Name the routine   Naming the routine might seem trivial, but good routine names are one sign of a superior program and they're not easy to come up with. In general, a routine should have a clear, unambiguous name. If you have trouble creating a good name, that usually indicates that the purpose of the routine isn't clear. A vague, wishy-washy name is like a politician on the campaign trail. It sounds as if it's saying something, but when you take a hard look, you can't figure out what it means. If you can make the name clearer, do so. If the wishy-washy name results from a wishy-washy design, pay attention to the warning sign. Back up and improve the design.

In the example, *ReportErrorMessage()* is unambiguous. It is a good name.

Further Reading For a different approach to construction that focuses on writing test cases first, see *Test-Driven Development: By Example* (Beck 2003).

Decide how to test the routine   As you're writing the routine, think about how you can test it. This is useful for you when you do unit testing and for the tester who tests your routine independently.

In the example, the input is simple, so you might plan to test *ReportErrorMessage()* with all valid error codes and a variety of invalid codes.

Research functionality available in the standard libraries   The single biggest way to improve both the quality of your code and your productivity is to reuse good code. If you find yourself grappling to design a routine that seems overly complicated, ask whether some or all of the routine's functionality might already be available in the library code of the language, platform, or tools you're using. Ask whether the code might be available in library code maintained by your company. Many algorithms have already been invented, tested, discussed in the trade literature, reviewed, and improved. Rather than spending your time inventing something when someone has already written a Ph.D. dissertation on it, take a few minutes to look through the code that's already been written and make sure you're not doing more work than necessary.

Think about error handling   Think about all the things that could possibly go wrong in the routine. Think about bad input values, invalid values returned from other routines, and so on.

Routines can handle errors numerous ways, and you should choose consciously how to handle errors. If the program's architecture defines the program's error-handling strategy, you can simply plan to follow that strategy. In other cases, you have to decide what approach will work best for the specific routine.

Think about efficiency   Depending on your situation, you can address efficiency in one of two ways. In the first situation, in the vast majority of systems, efficiency isn't critical. In such a case, see that the routine's interface is well abstracted and its code is readable so that you can improve it later if you need to. If you have good encapsulation, you can replace a slow, resource-hogging, high-level language implementation with a better algorithm or a fast, lean, low-level language implementation, and you won't affect any other routines.

Cross-Reference For details on efficiency, see Chapter 25, "Code-Tuning Strategies," and Chapter 26, "Code-Tuning Techniques."

In the second situation—in the minority of systems—performance is critical. The performance issue might be related to scarce database connections, limited memory, few available handles, ambitious timing constraints, or some other scarce resource. The architecture should indicate how many resources each routine (or class) is allowed to use and how fast it should perform its operations.

Design your routine so that it will meet its resource and speed goals. If either resources or speed seems more critical, design so that you trade resources for speed or vice versa. It's acceptable during initial construction of the routine to tune it enough to meet its resource and speed budgets.

Aside from taking the approaches suggested for these two general situations, it's usually a waste of effort to work on efficiency at the level of individual routines. The big optimizations come from refining the high-level design, not the individual routines. You generally use micro-optimizations only when the high-level design turns out not to support the system's performance goals, and you won't know that until the whole program is done. Don't waste time scraping for incremental improvements until you know they're needed.

Research the algorithms and data types   If functionality isn't available in the available libraries, it might still be described in an algorithms book. Before you launch into writing complicated code from scratch, check an algorithms book to see what's already available. If you use a predefined algorithm, be sure to adapt it correctly to your programming language.

Write the pseudocode   You might not have much in writing after you finish the preceding steps. The main purpose of the steps is to establish a mental orientation that's useful when you actually write the routine.

Cross-Reference This discussion assumes that good design techniques are used to create the pseudocode version of the routine. For details on design, see Chapter 5, "Design in Construction."

With the preliminary steps completed, you can begin to write the routine as high-level pseudocode. Go ahead and use your programming editor or your integrated environment to write the pseudocode—the pseudocode will be used shortly as the basis for programming-language code.

Start with the general and work toward something more specific. The most general part of a routine is a header comment describing what the routine is supposed to do, so first write a concise statement of the purpose of the routine. Writing the statement will help you clarify your understanding of the routine. Trouble in writing the general comment is a warning that you need to understand the routine's role in the program better. In general, if it's hard to summarize the routine's role, you should probably assume that something is wrong. Here's an example of a concise header comment describing a routine:

> **Example of a Header Comment for a Routine**
>
> ```
> This routine outputs an error message based on an error code
> supplied by the calling routine. The way it outputs the message
> depends on the current processing state, which it retrieves
> on its own. It returns a value indicating success or failure.
> ```

After you've written the general comment, fill in high-level pseudocode for the routine. Here's the pseudocode for this example:

> **Example of Pseudocode for a Routine**
>
> ```
> This routine outputs an error message based on an error code
> supplied by the calling routine. The way it outputs the message
> depends on the current processing state, which it retrieves
> on its own. It returns a value indicating success or failure.
>
> set the default status to "fail"
> look up the message based on the error code
>
> if the error code is valid
>     if doing interactive processing, display the error message
>     interactively and declare success
>
>     if doing command line processing, log the error message to the
>     command line and declare success
>
> if the error code isn't valid, notify the user that an internal error
> has been detected
>
> return status information
> ```

Again, note that the pseudocode is written at a fairly high level. It certainly isn't written in a programming language. Instead, it expresses in precise English what the routine needs to do.

Cross-Reference For details on effective use of variables, see Chapters 10 through 13.

Think about the data You can design the routine's data at several different points in the process. In this example, the data is simple and data manipulation isn't a prominent part of the routine. If data manipulation is a prominent part of the routine, it's worthwhile to think about the major pieces of data before you think about the routine's logic. Definitions of key data types are useful to have when you design the logic of a routine.

Cross-Reference For details on review techniques, see Chapter 21, "Collaborative Construction."

Check the pseudocode Once you've written the pseudocode and designed the data, take a minute to review the pseudocode you've written. Back away from it, and think about how you would explain it to someone else.

Ask someone else to look at it or listen to you explain it. You might think that it's silly to have someone look at 11 lines of pseudocode, but you'll be surprised. Pseudocode can make your assumptions and high-level mistakes more obvious than programming-language code does. People are also more willing to review a few lines of pseudocode than they are to review 35 lines of C++ or Java.

Make sure you have an easy and comfortable understanding of what the routine does and how it does it. If you don't understand it conceptually, at the pseudocode level, what chance do you have of understanding it at the programming-language level? And if you don't understand it, who else will?

Cross-Reference For more on iteration, see Section 34.8, "Iterate, Repeatedly, Again and Again."

Try a few ideas in pseudocode, and keep the best (iterate)   Try as many ideas as you can in pseudocode before you start coding. Once you start coding, you get emotionally involved with your code and it becomes harder to throw away a bad design and start over.

The general idea is to iterate the routine in pseudocode until the pseudocode statements become simple enough that you can fill in code below each statement and leave the original pseudocode as documentation. Some of the pseudocode from your first attempt might be high-level enough that you need to decompose it further. Be sure you do decompose it further. If you're not sure how to code something, keep working with the pseudocode until you are sure. Keep refining and decomposing the pseudocode until it seems like a waste of time to write it instead of the actual code.

Code the Routine

Once you've designed the routine, construct it. You can perform construction steps in a nearly standard order, but feel free to vary them as you need to. Figure 9-3 shows the steps in constructing a routine.

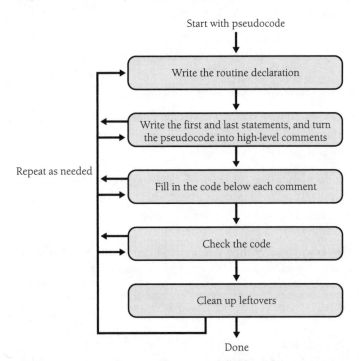

Figure 9-3   You'll perform all of these steps as you design a routine but not necessarily in any particular order.

Write the routine declaration Write the routine interface statement—the function declaration in C++, method declaration in Java, function or sub procedure declaration in Microsoft Visual Basic, or whatever your language calls for. Turn the original header comment into a programming-language comment. Leave it in position above the pseudocode you've already written. Here are the example routine's interface statement and header in C++:

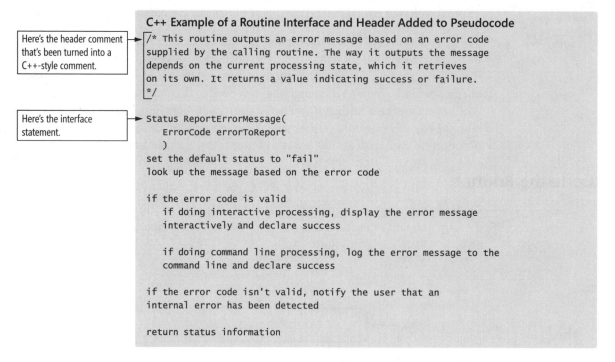

C++ Example of a Routine Interface and Header Added to Pseudocode

Here's the header comment that's been turned into a C++-style comment.

```
/* This routine outputs an error message based on an error code
supplied by the calling routine. The way it outputs the message
depends on the current processing state, which it retrieves
on its own. It returns a value indicating success or failure.
*/
```

Here's the interface statement.

```
Status ReportErrorMessage(
    ErrorCode errorToReport
    )
set the default status to "fail"
look up the message based on the error code

if the error code is valid
    if doing interactive processing, display the error message
    interactively and declare success

    if doing command line processing, log the error message to the
    command line and declare success

if the error code isn't valid, notify the user that an
internal error has been detected

return status information
```

This is a good time to make notes about any interface assumptions. In this case, the interface variable *errorToReport* is straightforward and typed for its specific purpose, so it doesn't need to be documented.

Turn the pseudocode into high-level comments Keep the ball rolling by writing the first and last statements: { and } in C++. Then turn the pseudocode into comments. Here's how it would look in the example:

C++ Example of Writing the First and Last Statements Around Pseudocode

```
/* This routine outputs an error message based on an error code
supplied by the calling routine. The way it outputs the message
depends on the current processing state, which it retrieves
on its own. It returns a value indicating success or failure.
*/

Status ReportErrorMessage(
    ErrorCode errorToReport
    ) {
```

The pseudocode statements from here down have been turned into C++ comments.

```
// set the default status to "fail"
// look up the message based on the error code
// if the error code is valid
   // if doing interactive processing, display the error message
   // interactively and declare success

   // if doing command line processing, log the error message to the
   // command line and declare success

// if the error code isn't valid, notify the user that an
// internal error has been detected

// return status information
}
```

At this point, the character of the routine is evident. The design work is complete, and you can sense how the routine works even without seeing any code. You should feel that converting the pseudocode to programming-language code will be mechanical, natural, and easy. If you don't, continue designing in pseudocode until the design feels solid.

Cross-Reference This is a case where the writing metaphor works well—in the small. For criticism of applying the writing metaphor in the large, see "Software Penmanship: Writing Code" in Section 2.3.

Fill in the code below each comment   Fill in the code below each line of pseudocode comment. The process is a lot like writing a term paper. First you write an outline, and then you write a paragraph for each point in the outline. Each pseudocode comment describes a block or paragraph of code. Like the lengths of literary paragraphs, the lengths of code paragraphs vary according to the thought being expressed, and the quality of the paragraphs depends on the vividness and focus of the thoughts in them.

In this example, the first two pseudocode comments give rise to two lines of code:

C++ Example of Expressing Pseudocode Comments as Code

```
/* This routine outputs an error message based on an error code
supplied by the calling routine. The way it outputs the message
depends on the current processing state, which it retrieves
on its own. It returns a value indicating success or failure.
*/

Status ReportErrorMessage(
   ErrorCode errorToReport
   ) {
   // set the default status to "fail"
   Status errorMessageStatus = Status_Failure;

   // look up the message based on the error code
   Message errorMessage = LookupErrorMessage( errorToReport );

   // if the error code is valid
      // if doing interactive processing, display the error message
      // interactively and declare success

      // if doing command line processing, log the error message to the
      // command line and declare success
```

Here's the code that's been filled in.

Here's the new variable *errorMessage*.

```
    // if the error code isn't valid, notify the user that an
    // internal error has been detected

    // return status information
}
```

This is a start on the code. The variable *errorMessage* is used, so it needs to be declared. If you were commenting after the fact, two lines of comments for two lines of code would nearly always be overkill. In this approach, however, it's the semantic content of the comments that's important, not how many lines of code they comment. The comments are already there, and they explain the intent of the code, so leave them in.

The code below each of the remaining comments needs to be filled in:

C++ Example of a Complete Routine Created with the Pseudocode Programming Process

```
/* This routine outputs an error message based on an error code
supplied by the calling routine. The way it outputs the message
depends on the current processing state, which it retrieves
on its own. It returns a value indicating success or failure.
*/

Status ReportErrorMessage(
    ErrorCode errorToReport
    ) {
    // set the default status to "fail"
    Status errorMessageStatus = Status_Failure;

    // look up the message based on the error code
    Message errorMessage = LookupErrorMessage( errorToReport );

    // if the error code is valid
    if ( errorMessage.ValidCode() ) {
        // determine the processing method
        ProcessingMethod errorProcessingMethod = CurrentProcessingMethod();

        // if doing interactive processing, display the error message
        // interactively and declare success
        if ( errorProcessingMethod == ProcessingMethod_Interactive ) {
            DisplayInteractiveMessage( errorMessage.Text() );
            errorMessageStatus = Status_Success;
        }

        // if doing command line processing, log the error message to the
        // command line and declare success
        else if ( errorProcessingMethod == ProcessingMethod_CommandLine ) {
            CommandLine messageLog;
            if ( messageLog.Status() == CommandLineStatus_Ok ) {
                messageLog.AddToMessageQueue( errorMessage.Text() );
                messageLog.FlushMessageQueue();
                errorMessageStatus = Status_Success;
            }
```

The code for each comment has been filled in from here down.

This code is a good candidate for being further decomposed into a new routine: *DisplayCommandLine-Message()*.

This code and comment are new and are the result of fleshing out the *if* test.

This code and comment are also new.

```
        else {
            // can't do anything because the routine is already error processing
        }
    else {
        // can't do anything because the routine is already error processing
    }
}

// if the error code isn't valid, notify the user that an
// internal error has been detected
else {
    DisplayInteractiveMessage(
        "Internal Error: Invalid error code in ReportErrorMessage()"
    );
}

// return status information
return errorMessageStatus;
}
```

Each comment has given rise to one or more lines of code. Each block of code forms a complete thought based on the comment. The comments have been retained to provide a higher-level explanation of the code. All variables have been declared and defined close to the point they're first used. Each comment should normally expand to about 2 to 10 lines of code. (Because this example is just for purposes of illustration, the code expansion is on the low side of what you should usually experience in practice.)

Now look again at the spec on page 221 and the initial pseudocode on page 224. The original five-sentence spec expanded to 15 lines of pseudocode (depending on how you count the lines), which in turn expanded into a page-long routine. Even though the spec was detailed, creation of the routine required substantial design work in pseudocode and code. That low-level design is one reason why "coding" is a nontrivial task and why the subject of this book is important.

Check whether code should be further factored   In some cases, you'll see an explosion of code below one of the initial lines of pseudocode. In this case, you should consider taking one of two courses of action:

Cross-Reference For more on refactoring, see Chapter 24, "Refactoring."

- Factor the code below the comment into a new routine. If you find one line of pseudocode expanding into more code that than you expected, factor the code into its own routine. Write the code to call the routine, including the routine name. If you've used the PPP well, the name of the new routine should drop out easily from the pseudocode. Once you've completed the routine you were originally creating, you can dive into the new routine and apply the PPP again to that routine.

- Apply the PPP recursively. Rather than writing a couple dozen lines of code below one line of pseudocode, take the time to decompose the original line of pseudocode into several more lines of pseudocode. Then continue filling in the code below each of the new lines of pseudocode.

Check the Code

After designing and implementing the routine, the third big step in constructing it is checking to be sure that what you've constructed is correct. Any errors you miss at this stage won't be found until later testing. They're more expensive to find and correct then, so you should find all that you can at this stage.

Cross-Reference For details on checking for errors in architecture and require-ments, see Chapter 3, "Measure Twice, Cut Once: Upstream Prerequisites."

A problem might not appear until the routine is fully coded for several reasons. An error in the pseudocode might become more apparent in the detailed implementation logic. A design that looks elegant in pseudocode might become clumsy in the imple-mentation language. Working with the detailed implementation might disclose an error in the architecture, high-level design, or requirements. Finally, the code might have an old-fashioned, mongrel coding error—nobody's perfect! For all these reasons, review the code before you move on.

Mentally check the routine for errors   The first formal check of a routine is mental. The cleanup and informal checking steps mentioned earlier are two kinds of mental checks. Another is executing each path mentally. Mentally executing a routine is diffi-cult, and that difficulty is one reason to keep your routines small. Make sure that you check nominal paths and endpoints and all exception conditions. Do this both by yourself, which is called "desk checking," and with one or more peers, which is called a "peer review," a "walk-through," or an "inspection," depending on how you do it.

HARD DATA

One of the biggest differences between hobbyists and professional programmers is the difference that grows out of moving from superstition into understanding. The word "superstition" in this context doesn't refer to a program that gives you the creeps or generates extra errors when the moon is full. It means substituting feelings about the code for understanding. If you often find yourself suspecting that the compiler or the hardware made an error, you're still in the realm of superstition. A study con-ducted many years ago found that only about five percent of all errors are hardware, compiler, or operating-system errors (Ostrand and Weyuker 1984). Today, that per-centage would probably be even lower. Programmers who have moved into the realm of understanding always suspect their own work first because they know that they cause 95 percent of errors. Understand the role of each line of code and why it's needed. Nothing is ever right just because it seems to work. If you don't know why it works, it probably doesn't—you just don't know it yet.

KEY POINT

Bottom line: A working routine isn't enough. If you don't know why it works, study it, discuss it, and experiment with alternative designs until you do.

Compile the routine   After reviewing the routine, compile it. It might seem inefficient to wait this long to compile since the code was completed several pages ago. Admit-tedly, you might have saved some work by compiling the routine earlier and letting the computer check for undeclared variables, naming conflicts, and so on.

You'll benefit in several ways, however, by not compiling until late in the process. The main reason is that when you compile new code, an internal stopwatch starts ticking. After the first compile, you step up the pressure: "I'll get it right with just one more compile." The "Just One More Compile" syndrome leads to hasty, error-prone changes that take more time in the long run. Avoid the rush to completion by not compiling until you've convinced yourself that the routine is right.

The point of this book is to show how to rise above the cycle of hacking something together and running it to see if it works. Compiling before you're sure your program works is often a symptom of the hacker mindset. If you're not caught in the hacking-and-compiling cycle, compile when you feel it's appropriate. But be conscious of the tug most people feel toward "hacking, compiling, and fixing" their way to a working program.

Here are some guidelines for getting the most out of compiling your routine:

- Set the compiler's warning level to the pickiest level possible. You can catch an amazing number of subtle errors simply by allowing the compiler to detect them.

- Use validators. The compiler checking performed by languages like C can be supplemented by use of tools like lint. Even code that isn't compiled, such as HTML and JavaScript, can be checked by validation tools.

- Eliminate the causes of all error messages and warnings. Pay attention to what the messages tell you about your code. A large number of warnings often indicates low-quality code, and you should try to understand each warning you get. In practice, warnings you've seen again and again have one of two possible effects: you ignore them and they camouflage other, more important, warnings, or they simply become annoying. It's usually safer and less painful to rewrite the code to solve the underlying problem and eliminate the warnings.

Step through the code in the debugger   Once the routine compiles, put it into the debugger and step through each line of code. Make sure each line executes as you expect it to. You can find many errors by following this simple practice.

Cross-Reference For details, see Chapter 22, "Developer Testing." Also see "Building Scaffolding to Test Individual Classes" in Section 22.5.

Test the code   Test the code using the test cases you planned or created while you were developing the routine. You might have to develop scaffolding to support your test cases—that is, code that's used to support routines while they're tested and that isn't included in the final product. Scaffolding can be a test-harness routine that calls your routine with test data, or it can be stubs called by your routine.

Cross-Reference For details, see Chapter 23, "Debugging."

Remove errors from the routine   Once an error has been detected, it has to be removed. If the routine you're developing is buggy at this point, chances are good that it will stay buggy. If you find that a routine is unusually buggy, start over. Don't hack around it—rewrite it. Hacks usually indicate incomplete understanding and guarantee errors both now and later. Creating an entirely new design for a buggy routine pays off. Few things are more satisfying than rewriting a problematic routine and never finding another error in it.

Clean Up Leftovers

When you've finished checking your code for problems, check it for the general characteristics described throughout this book. You can take several cleanup steps to make sure that the routine's quality is up to your standards:

- Check the routine's interface. Make sure that all input and output data is accounted for and that all parameters are used. For more details, see Section 7.5, "How to Use Routine Parameters."

- Check for general design quality. Make sure the routine does one thing and does it well, that it's loosely coupled to other routines, and that it's designed defensively. For details, see Chapter 7, "High-Quality Routines."

- Check the routine's variables. Check for inaccurate variable names, unused objects, undeclared variables, improperly initialized objects, and so on. For details, see the chapters on using variables, Chapters 10 through 13.

- Check the routine's statements and logic. Check for off-by-one errors, infinite loops, improper nesting, and resource leaks. For details, see the chapters on statements, Chapters 14 through 19.

- Check the routine's layout. Make sure you've used white space to clarify the logical structure of the routine, expressions, and parameter lists. For details, see Chapter 31, "Layout and Style."

- Check the routine's documentation. Make sure the pseudocode that was translated into comments is still accurate. Check for algorithm descriptions, for documentation on interface assumptions and nonobvious dependencies, for justification of unclear coding practices, and so on. For details, see Chapter 32, "Self-Documenting Code."

- Remove redundant comments. Sometimes a pseudocode comment turns out to be redundant with the code the comment describes, especially when the PPP has been applied recursively and the comment just precedes a call to a well-named routine.

Repeat Steps as Needed

If the quality of the routine is poor, back up to the pseudocode. High-quality programming is an iterative process, so don't hesitate to loop through the construction activities again.

9.4 Alternatives to the PPP

For my money, the PPP is the best method for creating classes and routines. Here are some different approaches recommended by other experts. You can use these approaches as alternatives or as supplements to the PPP.

Test-first development   Test-first is a popular development style in which test cases are written prior to writing any code. This approach is described in more detail in "Test First or Test Last?" in Section 22.2. A good book on test-first programming is Kent Beck's *Test-Driven Development: By Example* (Beck 2003).

Refactoring   Refactoring is a development approach in which you improve code through a series of semantic preserving transformations. Programmers use patterns of bad code or "smells" to identify sections of code that need to be improved. Chapter 24, "Refactoring," describes this approach in detail, and a good book on the topic is Martin Fowler's *Refactoring: Improving the Design of Existing Code* (Fowler 1999).

Design by contract   Design by contract is a development approach in which each routine is considered to have preconditions and postconditions. This approach is described in "Use assertions to document and verify preconditions and postconditions" in Section 8.2. The best source of information on design by contract is Bertrand Meyers's *Object-Oriented Software Construction* (Meyer 1997).

Hacking?   Some programmers try to hack their way toward working code rather than using a systematic approach like the PPP. If you've ever found that you've coded yourself into a corner in a routine and have to start over, that's an indication that the PPP might work better. If you find yourself losing your train of thought in the middle of coding a routine, that's another indication that the PPP would be beneficial. Have you ever simply forgotten to write part of a class or part of routine? That hardly ever happens if you're using the PPP. If you find yourself staring at the computer screen not knowing where to start, that's a surefire sign that the PPP would make your programming life easier.

cc2e.com/0943

Cross-Reference The point of this list is to check whether you followed a good set of steps to create a routine. For a checklist that focuses on the quality of the routine itself, see the "High-Quality Routines" checklist in Chapter 7, page 185.

CHECKLIST: The Pseudocode Programming Process

- ❏ Have you checked that the prerequisites have been satisfied?

- ❏ Have you defined the problem that the class will solve?

- ❏ Is the high-level design clear enough to give the class and each of its routines a good name?

- ❏ Have you thought about how to test the class and each of its routines?

- ❏ Have you thought about efficiency mainly in terms of stable interfaces and readable implementations or mainly in terms of meeting resource and speed budgets?

- ❏ Have you checked the standard libraries and other code libraries for applicable routines or components?

- ❏ Have you checked reference books for helpful algorithms?

> ❑ Have you designed each routine by using detailed pseudocode?
>
> ❑ Have you mentally checked the pseudocode? Is it easy to understand?
>
> ❑ Have you paid attention to warnings that would send you back to design (use of global data, operations that seem better suited to another class or another routine, and so on)?
>
> ❑ Did you translate the pseudocode to code accurately?
>
> ❑ Did you apply the PPP recursively, breaking routines into smaller routines when needed?
>
> ❑ Did you document assumptions as you made them?
>
> ❑ Did you remove comments that turned out to be redundant?
>
> ❑ Have you chosen the best of several iterations, rather than merely stopping after your first iteration?
>
> ❑ Do you thoroughly understand your code? Is it easy to understand?

Key Points

- Constructing classes and constructing routines tends to be an iterative process. Insights gained while constructing specific routines tend to ripple back through the class's design.

- Writing good pseudocode calls for using understandable English, avoiding features specific to a single programming language, and writing at the level of intent (describing what the design does rather than how it will do it).

- The Pseudocode Programming Process is a useful tool for detailed design and makes coding easy. Pseudocode translates directly into comments, ensuring that the comments are accurate and useful.

- Don't settle for the first design you think of. Iterate through multiple approaches in pseudocode and pick the best approach before you begin writing code.

- Check your work at each step, and encourage others to check it too. That way, you'll catch mistakes at the least expensive level, when you've invested the least amount of effort.

Part III
Variables

Chapter 10

General Issues in Using Variables

cc2e.com/1085

Contents

Related Topics

- Naming variables: Chapter 11
- Fundamental data types: Chapter 12
- Unusual data types: Chapter 13
- Formatting data declarations: "Laying Out Data Declarations" in Section 31.5
- Documenting variables: "Commenting Data Declarations" in Section 32.5

It's normal and desirable for construction to fill in small gaps in the requirements and architecture. It would be inefficient to draw blueprints to such a microscopic level that every detail was completely specified. This chapter describes a nuts-and-bolts construction issue: the ins and outs of using variables.

The information in this chapter should be particularly valuable to you if you're an experienced programmer. It's easy to start using hazardous practices before you're fully aware of your alternatives and then to continue to use them out of habit even after you've learned ways to avoid them. An experienced programmer might find the discussions on binding time in Section 10.6 and on using each variable for one purpose in Section 10.8 particularly interesting. If you're not sure whether you qualify as an "experienced programmer," take the "Data Literacy Test" in the next section and find out.

Throughout this chapter I use the word "variable" to refer to objects as well as to built-in data types like integers and arrays. The phrase "data type" generally refers to built-in data types, while the word "data" refers to either objects or built-in types.

10.1 Data Literacy

KEY POINT

The first step in creating effective data is knowing which kind of data to create. A good repertoire of data types is a key part of a programmer's toolbox. A tutorial in data types is beyond the scope of this book, but the "Data Literacy Test" will help you determine how much more you might need to learn about them.

The Data Literacy Test

Put a *1* next to each term that looks familiar. If you think you know what a term means but aren't sure, give yourself a *0.5*. Add the points when you're done, and interpret your score according to the scoring table below.

_____ abstract data type		_____ literal	
_____ array		_____ local variable	
_____ bitmap		_____ lookup table	
_____ boolean variable		_____ member data	
_____ B-tree		_____ pointer	
_____ character variable		_____ private	
_____ container class		_____ retroactive synapse	
_____ double precision		_____ referential integrity	
_____ elongated stream		_____ stack	
_____ enumerated type		_____ string	
_____ floating point		_____ structured variable	
_____ heap		_____ tree	
_____ index		_____ typedef	
_____ integer		_____ union	
_____ linked list		_____ value chain	
_____ named constant		_____ variant	
		_____ **Total Score**	

Here is how you can interpret the scores (loosely):

0–14	You are a beginning programmer, probably in your first year of computer science in school or teaching yourself your first programming language. You can learn a lot by reading one of the books listed in the next subsection. Many of the descriptions of techniques in this part of the book are addressed to advanced programmers, and you'll get more out of them after you've read one of these books.
15–19	You are an intermediate programmer or an experienced programmer who has forgotten a lot. Although many of the concepts will be familiar to you, you too can benefit from reading one of the books listed below.
20–24	You are an expert programmer. You probably already have the books listed below on your shelf.
25–29	You know more about data types than I do. Consider writing your own computer book. (Send me a copy!)
30–32	You are a pompous fraud. The terms "elongated stream," "retroactive synapse," and "value chain" don't refer to data types—I made them up. Please read the "Intellectual Honesty" section in Chapter 33, "Personal Character"!

Additional Resources on Data Types

These books are good sources of information about data types:

Cormen, H. Thomas, Charles E. Leiserson, Ronald L. Rivest. *Introduction to Algorithms*. New York, NY: McGraw Hill. 1990.

Sedgewick, Robert. *Algorithms in C++, Parts 1-4*, 3d ed. Boston, MA: Addison-Wesley, 1998.

Sedgewick, Robert. *Algorithms in C++, Part 5*, 3d ed. Boston, MA: Addison-Wesley, 2002.

10.2 Making Variable Declarations Easy

Cross-Reference For details on layout of variable declarations, see "Laying Out Data Declarations" in Section 31.5. For details on documenting them, see "Commenting Data Declarations" in Section 32.5.

This section describes what you can do to streamline the task of declaring variables. To be sure, this is a small task, and you might think it's too small to deserve its own section in this book. Nevertheless, you spend a lot of time creating variables, and developing the right habits can save time and frustration over the life of a project.

Implicit Declarations

Some languages have implicit variable declarations. For example, if you use a variable in Microsoft Visual Basic without declaring it, the compiler declares it for you automatically (depending on your compiler settings).

Implicit declaration is one of the most hazardous features available in any language. If you program in Visual Basic, you know how frustrating it is to try to figure out why *acctNo* doesn't have the right value and then notice that *acctNum* is the variable that's reinitialized to *0*. This kind of mistake is an easy one to make if your language doesn't require you to declare variables.

KEY POINT

If you're programming in a language that requires you to declare variables, you have to make two mistakes before your program will bite you. First you have to put both *acctNum* and *acctNo* into the body of the routine. Then you have to declare both variables in the routine. This is a harder mistake to make, and it virtually eliminates the synonymous-variables problem. Languages that require you to declare data explicitly are, in essence, requiring you to use data more carefully, which is one of their primary advantages. What do you do if you program in a language with implicit declarations? Here are some suggestions:

Turn off implicit declarations   Some compilers allow you to disable implicit declarations. For example, in Visual Basic you would use an *Option Explicit* statement, which forces you to declare all variables before you use them.

Declare all variables   As you type in a new variable, declare it, even though the compiler doesn't require you to. This won't catch all the errors, but it will catch some of them.

Cross-Reference For details on the standardization of abbreviations, see "General Abbreviation Guidelines" in Section 11.6.

Use naming conventions   Establish a naming convention for common suffixes such as *Num* and *No* so that you don't use two variables when you mean to use one.

Check variable names   Use the cross-reference list generated by your compiler or another utility program. Many compilers list all the variables in a routine, allowing you to spot both *acctNum* and *acctNo*. They also point out variables that you've declared and not used.

10.3 Guidelines for Initializing Variables

KEY POINT

Improper data initialization is one of the most fertile sources of error in computer programming. Developing effective techniques for avoiding initialization problems can save a lot of debugging time.

The problems with improper initialization stem from a variable's containing an initial value that you do not expect it to contain. This can happen for any of several reasons:

Cross-Reference For a testing approach based on data initialization and use patterns, see "Data-Flow Testing" in Section 22.3.

- The variable has never been assigned a value. Its value is whatever bits happened to be in its area of memory when the program started.

- The value in the variable is outdated. The variable was assigned a value at some point, but the value is no longer valid.

- Part of the variable has been assigned a value and part has not.

This last theme has several variations. You can initialize some of the members of an object but not all of them. You can forget to allocate memory and then initialize the "variable" the uninitialized pointer points to. This means that you are really selecting a random portion of computer memory and assigning it some value. It might be memory that contains data. It might be memory that contains code. It might be the operating system. The symptom of the pointer problem can manifest itself in completely surprising ways that are different each time—that's what makes debugging pointer errors harder than debugging other errors.

Following are guidelines for avoiding initialization problems:

Initialize each variable as it's declared   Initializing variables as they're declared is an inexpensive form of defensive programming. It's a good insurance policy against initialization errors. The example below ensures that *studentGrades* will be reinitialized each time you call the routine that contains it.

> **C++ Example of Initialization at Declaration Time**
> ```cpp
> float studentGrades[ MAX_STUDENTS ] = { 0.0 };
> ```

Cross-Reference Checking input parameters is a form of defensive programming. For details on defensive programming, see Chapter 8, "Defensive Programming."

Initialize each variable close to where it's first used   Some languages, including Visual Basic, don't support initializing variables as they're declared. That can lead to coding styles like the following one, in which declarations are grouped together and then initializations are grouped together—all far from the first actual use of the variables.

CODING HORROR

> **Visual Basic Example of Bad Initialization**
> ```vb
> ' declare all variables
> Dim accountIndex As Integer
> Dim total As Double
> Dim done As Boolean
>
> ' initialize all variables
> accountIndex = 0
> total = 0.0
> done = False
> ...
>
> ' code using accountIndex
> ...
>
> ' code using total
> ...
>
> ' code using done
> While Not done
>    ...
> ```

A better practice is to initialize variables as close as possible to where they're first used:

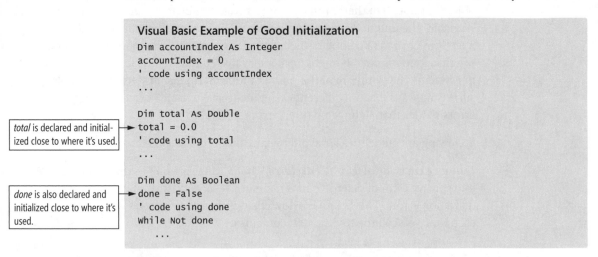

Visual Basic Example of Good Initialization
```
Dim accountIndex As Integer
accountIndex = 0
' code using accountIndex
...

Dim total As Double
total = 0.0
' code using total
...

Dim done As Boolean
done = False
' code using done
while Not done
    ...
```

total is declared and initialized close to where it's used.

done is also declared and initialized close to where it's used.

The second example is superior to the first for several reasons. By the time execution of the first example gets to the code that uses *done*, *done* could have been modified. If that's not the case when you first write the program, later modifications might make it so. Another problem with the first approach is that throwing all the initializations together creates the impression that all the variables are used throughout the whole routine—when in fact *done* is used only at the end. Finally, as the program is modified (as it will be, if only by debugging), loops might be built around the code that uses *done*, and *done* will need to be reinitialized. The code in the second example will require little modification in such a case. The code in the first example is more prone to producing an annoying initialization error.

Cross-Reference For more details on keeping related actions together, see Section 10.4, "Scope."

This is an example of the Principle of Proximity: keep related actions together. The same principle applies to keeping comments close to the code they describe, keeping loop setup code close to the loop, grouping statements in straight-line code, and to many other areas.

Ideally, declare and define each variable close to where it's first used A declaration establishes a variable's type. A definition assigns the variable a specific value. In languages that support it, such as C++ and Java, variables should be declared and defined close to where they are first used. Ideally, each variable should be defined at the same time it's declared, as shown next:

Java Example of Good Initialization
```
int accountIndex = 0;
// code using accountIndex
...
```

total is initialized close to where it's used.

```
double total = 0.0;
// code using total
...
```

done is also initialized close to where it's used.

```
boolean done = false;
// code using done
while ( ! done ) {
    ...
```

Cross-Reference For more details on keeping related actions together, see Section 14.2, "Statements Whose Order Doesn't Matter."

*Use **final** or **const** when possible*   By declaring a variable to be *final* in Java or *const* in C++, you can prevent the variable from being assigned a value after it's initialized. The *final* and *const* keywords are useful for defining class constants, input-only parameters, and any local variables whose values are intended to remain unchanged after initialization.

Pay special attention to counters and accumulators   The variables i, j, k, *sum*, and *total* are often counters or accumulators. A common error is forgetting to reset a counter or an accumulator before the next time it's used.

Initialize a class's member data in its constructor   Just as a routine's variables should be initialized within each routine, a class's data should be initialized within its constructor. If memory is allocated in the constructor, it should be freed in the destructor.

Check the need for reinitialization   Ask yourself whether the variable will ever need to be reinitialized, either because a loop in the routine uses the variable many times or because the variable retains its value between calls to the routine and needs to be reset between calls. If it needs to be reinitialized, make sure that the initialization statement is inside the part of the code that's repeated.

Initialize named constants once; initialize variables with executable code   If you're using variables to emulate named constants, it's OK to write code that initializes them once, at the beginning of the program. To do this, initialize them in a *Startup()* routine. Initialize true variables in executable code close to where they're used. One of the most common program modifications is to change a routine that was originally called once so that you call it multiple times. Variables that are initialized in a program-level *Startup()* routine aren't reinitialized the second time through the routine.

Use the compiler setting that automatically initializes all variables   If your compiler supports such an option, having the compiler set to automatically initialize all variables is an easy variation on the theme of relying on your compiler. Relying on specific compiler settings, however, can cause problems when you move the code to another machine and another compiler. Make sure you document your use of the compiler setting; assumptions that rely on specific compiler settings are hard to uncover otherwise.

Take advantage of your compiler's warning messages   Many compilers warn you that you're using an uninitialized variable.

Cross-Reference For more on checking input parameters, see Section 8.1, "Protecting Your Program from Invalid Inputs," and the rest of Chapter 8, "Defensive Programming."

Check input parameters for validity   Another valuable form of initialization is checking input parameters for validity. Before you assign input values to anything, make sure the values are reasonable.

Use a memory-access checker to check for bad pointers   In some operating systems, the operating-system code checks for invalid pointer references. In others, you're on your own. You don't have to stay on your own, however, because you can buy memory-access checkers that check your program's pointer operations.

Initialize working memory at the beginning of your program   Initializing working memory to a known value helps to expose initialization problems. You can take any of several approaches:

- You can use a preprogram memory filler to fill the memory with a predictable value. The value *0* is good for some purposes because it ensures that uninitialized pointers point to low memory, making it relatively easy to detect them when they're used. On the Intel processors, *0xCC* is a good value to use because it's the machine code for a breakpoint interrupt; if you are running code in a debugger and try to execute your data rather than your code, you'll be awash in breakpoints. Another virtue of the value *0xCC* is that it's easy to recognize in memory dumps—and it's rarely used for legitimate reasons. Alternatively, Brian Kernighan and Rob Pike suggest using the constant *0xDEADBEEF* as memory filler that's easy to recognize in a debugger (1999).

- If you're using a memory filler, you can change the value you use to fill the memory once in awhile. Shaking up the program sometimes uncovers problems that stay hidden if the environmental background never changes.

- You can have your program initialize its working memory at startup time. Whereas the purpose of using a preprogram memory filler is to expose defects, the purpose of this technique is to hide them. By filling working memory with the same value every time, you guarantee that your program won't be affected by random variations in the startup memory.

10.4 Scope

"Scope" is a way of thinking about a variable's celebrity status: how famous is it? Scope, or visibility, refers to the extent to which your variables are known and can be referenced throughout a program. A variable with limited or small scope is known in only a small area of a program—a loop index used in only one small loop, for instance. A variable with large scope is known in many places in a program—a table of employee information that's used throughout a program, for instance.

Different languages handle scope in different ways. In some primitive languages, all variables are global. You therefore don't have any control over the scope of a variable, and that can create a lot of problems. In C++ and similar languages, a variable can be visible to a block (a section of code enclosed in curly brackets), a routine, a class (and possibly its derived classes), or the whole program. In Java and C#, a variable can also be visible to a package or namespace (a collection of classes).

The following sections provide guidelines that apply to scope.

Localize References to Variables

The code between references to a variable is a "window of vulnerability." In the window, new code might be added, inadvertently altering the variable, or someone reading the code might forget the value the variable is supposed to contain. It's always a good idea to localize references to variables by keeping them close together.

The idea of localizing references to a variable is pretty self-evident, but it's an idea that lends itself to formal measurement. One method of measuring how close together the references to a variable are is to compute the "span" of a variable. Here's an example:

Java Example of Variable Span
```java
a = 0;
b = 0;
c = 0;
a = b + c;
```

In this case, two lines come between the first reference to a and the second, so a has a span of two. One line comes between the two references to b, so b has a span of one, and c has a span of zero. Here's another example:

Java Example of Spans of One and Zero
```java
a = 0;
b = 0;
c = 0;
b = a + 1;
b = b / c;
```

Further Reading For more information on variable span, see *Software Engineering Metrics and Models* (Conte, Dunsmore, and Shen 1986).

In this case, there is one line between the first reference to b and the second, for a span of one. There are no lines between the second reference to b and the third, for a span of zero.

The average span is computed by averaging the individual spans. In the second example, for b, $(1+0)/2$ equals an average span of 0.5. When you keep references to variables close together, you enable the person reading your code to focus on one section at a time. If the references are far apart, you force the reader to jump around in the program. Thus the main advantage of keeping references to variables together is that it improves program readability.

Keep Variables "Live" for as Short a Time as Possible

A concept that's related to variable span is variable "live time," the total number of statements over which a variable is live. A variable's life begins at the first statement in which it's referenced; its life ends at the last statement in which it's referenced.

Unlike span, live time isn't affected by how many times the variable is used between the first and last times it's referenced. If the variable is first referenced on line 1 and last referenced on line 25, it has a live time of 25 statements. If those are the only two lines in which it's used, it has an average span of 23 statements. If the variable were used on every line from line 1 through line 25, it would have an average span of 0 statements, but it would still have a live time of 25 statements. Figure 10-1 illustrates both span and live time.

Figure 10-1   "Long live time" means that a variable is live over the course of many statements. "Short live time" means it's live for only a few statements. "Span" refers to how close together the references to a variable are.

As with span, the goal with respect to live time is to keep the number low, to keep a variable live for as short a time as possible. And as with span, the basic advantage of maintaining a low number is that it reduces the window of vulnerability. You reduce the chance of incorrectly or inadvertently altering a variable between the places in which you intend to alter it.

A second advantage of keeping the live time short is that it gives you an accurate picture of your code. If a variable is assigned a value in line 10 and not used again until line 45, the very space between the two references implies that the variable is used between lines 10 and 45. If the variable is assigned a value in line 44 and used in line 45, no other uses of the variable are implied, and you can concentrate on a smaller section of code when you're thinking about that variable.

A short live time also reduces the chance of initialization errors. As you modify a program, straight-line code tends to turn into loops and you tend to forget initializations that were made far away from the loop. By keeping the initialization code and the loop code closer together, you reduce the chance that modifications will introduce initialization errors.

A short live time makes your code more readable. The fewer lines of code a reader has to keep in mind at once, the easier your code is to understand. Likewise, the shorter the live time, the less code you have to keep on your screen when you want to see all the references to a variable during editing and debugging.

Finally, short live times are useful when splitting a large routine into smaller routines. If references to variables are kept close together, it's easier to refactor related sections of code into routines of their own.

Measuring the Live Time of a Variable

You can formalize the concept of live time by counting the number of lines between the first and last references to a variable (including both the first and last lines). Here's an example with live times that are too long:

Java Example of Variables with Excessively Long Live Times

```
1    // initialize all variables
2    recordIndex = 0;
3    total = 0;
4    done = false;
     ...
26   while ( recordIndex < recordCount ) {
27   ...
28       recordIndex = recordIndex + 1;    ← Last reference to recordIndex.
         ...

64   while ( !done ) {
         ...
69       if ( total > projectedTotal ) {    ← Last reference to total.
70           done = true;                    ← Last reference to done.
```

Here are the live times for the variables in this example:

recordIndex	(line 28 - line 2 + 1) = 27
total	(line 69 - line 3 + 1) = 67
done	(line 70 - line 4 + 1) = 67
Average Live Time	(27 + 67 + 67) / 3 ≈ 54

The example has been rewritten below so that the variable references are closer together:

Java Example of Variables with Good, Short Live Times

Initialization of *recordIndex* is moved down from line 3. →

```
   ...
25 recordIndex = 0;
26 while ( recordIndex < recordCount ) {
27 ...
28    recordIndex = recordIndex + 1;
   ...
```

Initialization of *total* and *done* are moved down from lines 4 and 5. →

```
62 total = 0;
63 done = false;
64 while ( !done ) {
    ...
69    if ( total > projectedTotal ) {
70       done = true;
```

Here are the live times for the variables in this example:

recordIndex	(line 28 - line 25 + 1) = 4
total	(line 69 - line 62 + 1) = 8
done	(line 70 - line 63 + 1) = 8
Average Live Time	(4 + 8 + 8) / 3 ≈ 7

Further Reading For more information on "live" variables, see *Software Engineering Metrics and Models* (Conte, Dunsmore, and Shen 1986).

Intuitively, the second example seems better than the first because the initializations for the variables are performed closer to where the variables are used. The measured difference in average live time between the two examples is significant: An average of 54 vs. an average of 7 provides good quantitative support for the intuitive preference for the second piece of code.

Does a hard number separate a good live time from a bad one? A good span from a bad one? Researchers haven't yet produced that quantitative data, but it's safe to assume that minimizing both span and live time is a good idea.

If you try to apply the ideas of span and live time to global variables, you'll find that global variables have enormous spans and live times—one of many good reasons to avoid global variables.

General Guidelines for Minimizing Scope

Here are some specific guidelines you can use to minimize scope:

Cross-Reference For details on initializing variables close to where they're used, see Section 10.3, "Guidelines for Initializing Variables," earlier in this chapter.

Initialize variables used in a loop immediately before the loop rather than back at the beginning of the routine containing the loop   Doing this improves the chance that when you modify the loop, you'll remember to make corresponding modifications to the loop initialization. Later, when you modify the program and put another loop around the initial loop, the initialization will work on each pass through the new loop rather than on only the first pass.

Cross-Reference For more on this style of variable declaration and definition, see "Ideally, declare and define each variable close to where it's first used" in Section 10.3.

Don't assign a value to a variable until just before the value is used   You might have experienced the frustration of trying to figure out where a variable was assigned its value. The more you can do to clarify where a variable receives its value, the better. Languages like C++ and Java support variable initializations like these:

C++ Example of Good Variable Declarations and Initializations
```
int receiptIndex = 0;
float dailyReceipts = TodaysReceipts();
double totalReceipts = TotalReceipts( dailyReceipts );
```

Cross-Reference For more details on keeping related statements together, see Section 14.2, "Statements Whose Order Doesn't Matter."

Group related statements   The following examples show a routine for summarizing daily receipts and illustrate how to put references to variables together so that they're easier to locate. The first example illustrates the violation of this principle:

C++ Example of Using Two Sets of Variables in a Confusing Way
```
void SummarizeData(...) {
   ...
   GetOldData( oldData, &numOldData );
   GetNewData( newData, &numNewData );
   totalOldData = Sum( oldData, numOldData );
   totalNewData = Sum( newData, numNewData );
   PrintOldDataSummary( oldData, totalOldData, numOldData );
   PrintNewDataSummary( newData, totalNewData, numNewData );
   SaveOldDataSummary( totalOldData, numOldData );
   SaveNewDataSummary( totalNewData, numNewData );
   ...
}
```

Statements using two sets of variables.

Note that, in this example, you have to keep track of *oldData*, *newData*, *numOldData*, *numNewData*, *totalOldData*, and *totalNewData* all at once—six variables for just this short fragment. The next example shows how to reduce that number to only three elements within each block of code:

C++ Example of Using Two Sets of Variables More Understandably

```
void SummarizeData( ... ) {
   GetOldData( oldData, &numOldData );
   totalOldData = Sum( oldData, numOldData );
   PrintOldDataSummary( oldData, totalOldData, numOldData );
   SaveOldDataSummary( totalOldData, numOldData );
   ...
   GetNewData( newData, &numNewData );
   totalNewData = Sum( newData, numNewData );
   PrintNewDataSummary( newData, totalNewData, numNewData );
   SaveNewDataSummary( totalNewData, numNewData );
   ...
}
```

Statements using oldData.

Statements using newData.

When the code is broken up, the two blocks are each shorter than the original block and individually contain fewer variables. They're easier to understand, and if you need to break this code out into separate routines, the shorter blocks with fewer variables will promote better-defined routines.

Break groups of related statements into separate routines All other things being equal, a variable in a shorter routine will tend to have smaller span and live time than a variable in a longer routine. By breaking related statements into separate, smaller routines, you reduce the scope that the variable can have.

Cross-Reference For more on global variables, see Section 13.3, "Global Data."

Begin with most restricted visibility, and expand the variable's scope only if necessary Part of minimizing the scope of a variable is keeping it as local as possible. It is much more difficult to reduce the scope of a variable that has had a large scope than to expand the scope of a variable that has had a small scope—in other words, it's harder to turn a global variable into a class variable than it is to turn a class variable into a global variable. It's harder to turn a protected data member into a private data member than vice versa. For that reason, when in doubt, favor the smallest possible scope for a variable: local to a specific loop, local to an individual routine, then private to a class, then protected, then package (if your programming language supports that), and global only as a last resort.

Comments on Minimizing Scope

Many programmers' approach to minimizing variables' scope depends on their views of the issues of "convenience" and "intellectual manageability." Some programmers make many of their variables global because global scope makes variables convenient to access and the programmers don't have to fool around with parameter lists and class-scoping rules. In their minds, the convenience of being able to access variables at any time outweighs the risks involved.

Cross-Reference The idea of minimizing scope is related to the idea of information hiding. For details, see "Hide Secrets (Information Hiding)" in Section 5.3.

Other programmers prefer to keep their variables as local as possible because local scope helps intellectual manageability. The more information you can hide, the less you have to keep in mind at any one time. The less you have to keep in mind, the smaller the chance that you'll make an error because you forgot one of the many details you needed to remember.

KEY POINT

The difference between the "convenience" philosophy and the "intellectual manageability" philosophy boils down to a difference in emphasis between writing programs and reading them. Maximizing scope might indeed make programs easy to write, but a program in which any routine can use any variable at any time is harder to understand than a program that uses well-factored routines. In such a program, you can't understand only one routine; you have to understand all the other routines with which that routine shares global data. Such programs are hard to read, hard to debug, and hard to modify.

Cross-Reference For details on using access routines, see "Using Access Routines Instead of Global Data" in Section 13.3.

Consequently, you should declare each variable to be visible to the smallest segment of code that needs to see it. If you can confine the variable's scope to a single loop or to a single routine, great. If you can't confine the scope to one routine, restrict the visibility to the routines in a single class. If you can't restrict the variable's scope to the class that's most responsible for the variable, create access routines to share the variable's data with other classes. You'll find that you rarely, if ever, need to use naked global data.

10.5 Persistence

"Persistence" is another word for the life span of a piece of data. Persistence takes several forms. Some variables persist

- for the life of a particular block of code or routine. Variables declared inside a *for* loop in C++ or Java are examples of this kind of persistence.

- as long as you allow them to. In Java, variables created with *new* persist until they are garbage collected. In C++, variables created with *new* persist until you *delete* them.

- for the life of a program. Global variables in most languages fit this description, as do *static* variables in C++ and Java.

- forever. These variables might include values that you store in a database between executions of a program. For example, if you have an interactive program in which users can customize the color of the screen, you can store their colors in a file and then read them back each time the program is loaded.

The main problem with persistence arises when you assume that a variable has a longer persistence than it really does. The variable is like that jug of milk in your refrigerator. It's supposed to last a week. Sometimes it lasts a month, and sometimes it turns sour after five days. A variable can be just as unpredictable. If you try to use the value of a variable after its normal life span is over, will it have retained its value? Sometimes the value in the variable is sour, and you know that you've got an error. Other times, the computer leaves the old value in the variable, letting you imagine that you have used it correctly.

Here are a few steps you can take to avoid this kind of problem:

Cross-Reference Debug code is easy to include in access routines and is discussed more in "Advantages of Access Routines" in Section 13.3.

- Use debug code or assertions in your program to check critical variables for reasonable values. If the values aren't reasonable, display a warning that tells you to look for improper initialization.

- Set variables to "unreasonable values" when you're through with them. For example, you could set a pointer to null after you delete it.

- Write code that assumes data isn't persistent. For example, if a variable has a certain value when you exit a routine, don't assume it has the same value the next time you enter the routine. This doesn't apply if you're using language-specific features that guarantee the value will remain the same, such as *static* in C++ and Java.

- Develop the habit of declaring and initializing all data right before it's used. If you see data that's used without a nearby initialization, be suspicious!

10.6 Binding Time

An initialization topic with far-reaching implications for program maintenance and modifiability is "binding time": the time at which the variable and its value are bound together (Thimbleby 1988). Are they bound together when the code is written? When it is compiled? When it is loaded? When the program is run? Some other time?

It can be to your advantage to use the latest binding time possible. In general, the later you make the binding time, the more flexibility you build into your code. The next example shows binding at the earliest possible time, when the code is written:

> **Java Example of a Variable That's Bound at Code-Writing Time**
> ```
> titleBar.color = 0xFF; // 0xFF is hex value for color blue
> ```

The value *0xFF* is bound to the variable *titleBar.color* at the time the code is written because *0xFF* is a literal value hard-coded into the program. Hard-coding like this is nearly always a bad idea because if this *0xFF* changes, it can get out of synch with *0xFF*s used elsewhere in the code that must be the same value as this one.

Here's an example of binding at a slightly later time, when the code is compiled:

> **Java Example of a Variable That's Bound at Compile Time**
> ```
> private static final int COLOR_BLUE = 0xFF;
> private static final int TITLE_BAR_COLOR = COLOR_BLUE;
> ...
> titleBar.color = TITLE_BAR_COLOR;
> ```

TITLE_BAR_COLOR is a named constant, an expression for which the compiler substitutes a value at compile time. This is nearly always better than hard-coding, if your language supports it. It increases readability because TITLE_BAR_COLOR tells you more about what is being represented than 0xFF does. It makes changing the title bar color easier because one change accounts for all occurrences. And it doesn't incur a run-time performance penalty.

Here's an example of binding later, at run time:

> **Java Example of a Variable That's Bound at Run Time**
> ```
> titleBar.color = ReadTitleBarColor();
> ```

ReadTitleBarColor() is a routine that reads a value while a program is executing, perhaps from the Microsoft Windows registry file or a Java properties file.

The code is more readable and flexible than it would be if a value were hard-coded. You don't need to change the program to change titleBar.color; you simply change the contents of the source that's read by ReadTitleBarColor(). This approach is commonly used for interactive applications in which a user can customize the application environment.

There is still another variation in binding time, which has to do with when the ReadTitleBarColor() routine is called. That routine could be called once at program load time, each time the window is created, or each time the window is drawn—each alternative represents successively later binding times.

To summarize, following are the times a variable can be bound to a value in this example. (The details could vary somewhat in other cases.)

- Coding time (use of magic numbers)
- Compile time (use of a named constant)
- Load time (reading a value from an external source such as the Windows registry file or a Java properties file)
- Object instantiation time (such as reading the value each time a window is created)
- Just in time (such as reading the value each time the window is drawn)

In general, the earlier the binding time, the lower the flexibility and the lower the complexity. For the first two options, using named constants is preferable to using magic numbers for many reasons, so you can get the flexibility that named constants provide just by using good programming practices. Beyond that, the greater the flexibility desired, the higher the complexity of the code needed to support that flexibility and the more error-prone the code will be. Because successful programming depends on minimizing complexity, a skilled programmer will build in as much flexibility as needed to meet the software's requirements but will not add flexibility—and related complexity—beyond what's required.

10.7 Relationship Between Data Types and Control Structures

Data types and control structures relate to each other in well-defined ways that were originally described by the British computer scientist Michael Jackson (Jackson 1975). This section sketches the regular relationship between data and control flow.

Jackson draws connections between three types of data and corresponding control structures:

Cross-Reference For details on sequences, see Chapter 14, "Organizing Straight-Line Code."

Sequential data translates to sequential statements in a program   Sequences consist of clusters of data used together in a certain order, as suggested by Figure 10-2. If you have five statements in a row that handle five different values, they are sequential statements. If you read an employee's name, Social Security Number, address, phone number, and age from a file, you'd have sequential statements in your program to read sequential data from the file.

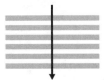

Figure 10-2   Sequential data is data that's handled in a defined order.

Cross-Reference For details on conditionals, see Chapter 15, "Using Conditionals."

Selective data translates to **if** ***and*** **case** ***statements in a program***   In general, selective data is a collection in which one of several pieces of data is used at any particular time, but only one, as shown in Figure 10-3. The corresponding program statements must do the actual selection, and they consist of *if-then-else* or *case* statements. If you had an employee payroll program, you might process employees differently depending on whether they were paid hourly or salaried. Again, patterns in the code match patterns in the data.

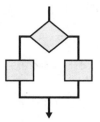

Figure 10-3   Selective data allows you to use one piece or the other, but not both.

Cross-Reference For details on loops, see Chapter 16, "Controlling Loops."

Iterative data translates to **for, repeat,** *and* **while** *looping structures in a program*
Iterative data is the same type of data repeated several times, as suggested by Figure 10-4. Typically, iterative data is stored as elements in a container, records in a file, or elements in an array. You might have a list of Social Security Numbers that you read from a file. The iterative data would match the iterative code loop used to read the data.

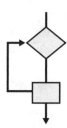

Figure 10-4   Iterative data is repeated.

Your real data can be combinations of the sequential, selective, and iterative types of data. You can combine the simple building blocks to describe more complicated data types.

10.8 Using Each Variable for Exactly One Purpose

It's possible to use variables for more than one purpose in several subtle ways. You're better off without this kind of subtlety.

KEY POINT

Use each variable for one purpose only   It's sometimes tempting to use one variable in two different places for two different activities. Usually, the variable is named inappropriately for one of its uses or a "temporary" variable is used in both cases (with the usual unhelpful name *x* or *temp*). Here's an example that shows a temporary variable that's used for two purposes:

CODING
HORROR

C++ Example of Using One Variable for Two Purposes—Bad Practice

```cpp
// Compute roots of a quadratic equation.
// This code assumes that (b*b-4*a*c) is positive.
temp = Sqrt( b*b - 4*a*c );
root[0] = ( -b + temp ) / ( 2 * a );
root[1] = ( -b - temp ) / ( 2 * a );
...

// swap the roots
temp = root[0];
root[0] = root[1];
root[1] = temp;
```

Cross-Reference Routine parameters should also be used for one purpose only. For details on using routine parameters, see Section 7.5, "How to Use Routine Parameters."

Question: What is the relationship between *temp* in the first few lines and *temp* in the last few? Answer: The two *temp*s have no relationship. Using the same variable in both instances makes it seem as though they're related when they're not. Creating unique variables for each purpose makes your code more readable. Here's an improvement:

C++ Example of Using Two Variables for Two Purposes—Good Practice

```cpp
// Compute roots of a quadratic equation.
// This code assumes that (b*b-4*a*c) is positive.
discriminant = Sqrt( b*b - 4*a*c );
root[0] = ( -b + discriminant ) / ( 2 * a );
root[1] = ( -b - discriminant ) / ( 2 * a );
...

// swap the roots
oldRoot = root[0];
root[0] = root[1];
root[1] = oldRoot;
```

Avoid variables with hidden meanings   Another way in which a variable can be used for more than one purpose is to have different values for the variable mean different things. For example:

CODING
HORROR

- The value in the variable *pageCount* might represent the number of pages printed, unless it equals *-1*, in which case it indicates that an error has occurred.

- The variable *customerId* might represent a customer number, unless its value is greater than *500,000*, in which case you subtract *500,000* to get the number of a delinquent account.

- The variable *bytesWritten* might be the number of bytes written to an output file, unless its value is negative, in which case it indicates the number of the disk drive used for the output.

Avoid variables with these kinds of hidden meanings. The technical name for this kind of abuse is "hybrid coupling" (Page-Jones 1988). The variable is stretched over two jobs, meaning that the variable is the wrong type for one of the jobs. In the *page-Count* example, *pageCount* normally indicates the number of pages; it's an integer. When *pageCount* is *-1*, however, it indicates that an error has occurred; the integer is moonlighting as a boolean!

Even if the double use is clear to you, it won't be to someone else. The extra clarity you'll achieve by using two variables to hold two kinds of information will amaze you. And no one will begrudge you the extra storage.

HARD DATA

Make sure that all declared variables are used   The opposite of using a variable for more than one purpose is not using it at all. A study by Card, Church, and Agresti found that unreferenced variables were correlated with higher fault rates (1986). Get in the habit of checking to be sure that all variables that are declared are used. Some compilers and utilities (such as lint) report unused variables as a warning.

cc2e.com/1092

Cross-Reference For a checklist that applies to specific types of data rather than general issues, see the checklist in Chapter 12, "Fundamental Data Types," on page 316. For issues in naming variables, see the checklist in Chapter 11, "The Power of Variable Names," on page 288.

CHECKLIST: General Considerations In Using Data

Initializing Variables

- ❏ Does each routine check input parameters for validity?

- ❏ Does the code declare variables close to where they're first used?

- ❏ Does the code initialize variables as they're declared, if possible?

- ❏ Does the code initialize variables close to where they're first used, if it isn't possible to declare and initialize them at the same time?

- ❏ Are counters and accumulators initialized properly and, if necessary, reinitialized each time they are used?

- ❏ Are variables reinitialized properly in code that's executed repeatedly?

- ❏ Does the code compile with no warnings from the compiler? (And have you turned on all the available warnings?)

- ❏ If your language uses implicit declarations, have you compensated for the problems they cause?

Other General Issues in Using Data

- ❏ Do all variables have the smallest scope possible?

- ❏ Are references to variables as close together as possible, both from each reference to a variable to the next reference and in total live time?

- ❏ Do control structures correspond to the data types?

❑ Are all the declared variables being used?

❑ Are all variables bound at appropriate times—that is, are you striking a conscious balance between the flexibility of late binding and the increased complexity associated with late binding?

❑ Does each variable have one and only one purpose?

❑ Is each variable's meaning explicit, with no hidden meanings?

Key Points

■ Data initialization is prone to errors, so use the initialization techniques described in this chapter to avoid the problems caused by unexpected initial values.

■ Minimize the scope of each variable. Keep references to a variable close together. Keep it local to a routine or class. Avoid global data.

■ Keep statements that work with the same variables as close together as possible.

■ Early binding tends to limit flexibility but minimize complexity. Late binding tends to increase flexibility but at the price of increased complexity.

■ Use each variable for one and only one purpose.

Chapter 11

The Power of Variable Names

cc2e.com/1184

Contents

Related Topics

As important as the topic of good names is to effective programming, I have never read a discussion that covered more than a handful of the dozens of considerations that go into creating good names. Many programming texts devote a few paragraphs to choosing abbreviations, spout a few platitudes, and expect you to fend for yourself. I intend to be guilty of the opposite: to inundate you with more information about good names than you will ever be able to use!

This chapter's guidelines apply primarily to naming variables—objects and primitive data. But they also apply to naming classes, packages, files, and other programming entities. For details on naming routines, see Section 7.3, "Good Routine Names."

11.1 Considerations in Choosing Good Names

You can't give a variable a name the way you give a dog a name—because it's cute or it has a good sound. Unlike the dog and its name, which are different entities, a variable and a variable's name are essentially the same thing. Consequently, the goodness or badness of a variable is largely determined by its name. Choose variable names with care.

Here's an example of code that uses bad variable names:

CODING HORROR

> **Java Example of Poor Variable Names**
> ```java
> x = x - xx;
> xxx = fido + SalesTax( fido );
> x = x + LateFee( x1, x ) + xxx;
> x = x + Interest( x1, x );
> ```

What's happening in this piece of code? What do *x1*, *xx*, and *xxx* mean? What does *fido* mean? Suppose someone told you that the code computed a total customer bill based on an outstanding balance and a new set of purchases. Which variable would you use to print the customer's bill for just the new set of purchases?

Here's a version of the same code that makes these questions easier to answer:

> **Java Example of Good Variable Names**
> ```java
> balance = balance - lastPayment;
> monthlyTotal = newPurchases + SalesTax( newPurchases );
> balance = balance + LateFee( customerID, balance ) + monthlyTotal;
> balance = balance + Interest( customerID, balance );
> ```

In view of the contrast between these two pieces of code, a good variable name is readable, memorable, and appropriate. You can use several general rules of thumb to achieve these goals.

The Most Important Naming Consideration

KEY POINT

The most important consideration in naming a variable is that the name fully and accurately describe the entity the variable represents. An effective technique for coming up with a good name is to state in words what the variable represents. Often that statement itself is the best variable name. It's easy to read because it doesn't contain cryptic abbreviations, and it's unambiguous. Because it's a full description of the entity, it won't be confused with something else. And it's easy to remember because the name is similar to the concept.

For a variable that represents the number of people on the U.S. Olympic team, you would create the name *numberOfPeopleOnTheUsOlympicTeam*. A variable that represents the number of seats in a stadium would be *numberOfSeatsInTheStadium*. A variable that represents the maximum number of points scored by a country's team in any modern Olympics would be *maximumNumberOfPointsInModernOlympics*. A variable that contains the current interest rate is better named *rate* or *interestRate* than *r* or *x*. You get the idea.

Note two characteristics of these names. First, they're easy to decipher. In fact, they don't need to be deciphered at all because you can simply read them. But second, some of the names are long—too long to be practical. I'll get to the question of variable-name length shortly.

Table 11-1 shows several examples of variable names, good and bad:

Table 11-1 Examples of Good and Bad Variable Names

Purpose of Variable	Good Names, Good Descriptors	Bad Names, Poor Descriptors
Running total of checks written to date	*runningTotal, checkTotal*	*written, ct, checks, CHKTTL, x, x1, x2*
Velocity of a bullet train	*velocity, trainVelocity, velocityInMph*	*velt, v, tv, x, x1, x2, train*
Current date	*currentDate, todaysDate*	*cd, current, c, x, x1, x2, date*
Lines per page	*linesPerPage*	*lpp, lines, l, x, x1, x2*

The names *currentDate* and *todaysDate* are good names because they fully and accurately describe the idea of "current date." In fact, they use the obvious words. Programmers sometimes overlook using the ordinary words, which is often the easiest solution. Because they're too short and not at all descriptive, *cd* and *c* are poor names. *current* is poor because it doesn't tell you what is current. *date* is almost a good name, but it's a poor name in the final analysis because the date involved isn't just any date, but the current date; *date* by itself gives no such indication. *x*, *x1*, and *x2* are poor names because they're always poor names—*x* traditionally represents an unknown quantity; if you don't want your variables to be unknown quantities, think of better names.

KEY POINT

Names should be as specific as possible. Names like *x*, *temp*, and *i* that are general enough to be used for more than one purpose are not as informative as they could be and are usually bad names.

Problem Orientation

A good mnemonic name generally speaks to the problem rather than the solution. A good name tends to express the *what* more than the *how*. In general, if a name refers to some aspect of computing rather than to the problem, it's a *how* rather than a *what*. Avoid such a name in favor of a name that refers to the problem itself.

A record of employee data could be called *inputRec* or *employeeData*. *inputRec* is a computer term that refers to computing ideas—input and record. *employeeData* refers to the problem domain rather than the computing universe. Similarly, for a bit field indicating printer status, *bitFlag* is a more computerish name than *printerReady*. In an accounting application, *calcVal* is more computerish than *sum*.

Optimum Name Length

The optimum length for a name seems to be somewhere between the lengths of *x* and *maximumNumberOfPointsInModernOlympics*. Names that are too short don't convey enough meaning. The problem with names like *x1* and *x2* is that even if you can discover what *x* is, you won't know anything about the relationship between *x1* and *x2*. Names that are too long are hard to type and can obscure the visual structure of a program.

HARD DATA

Gorla, Benander, and Benander found that the effort required to debug a program was minimized when variables had names that averaged 10 to 16 characters (1990). Programs with names averaging 8 to 20 characters were almost as easy to debug. The guideline doesn't mean that you should try to make all of your variable names 9 to 15 or 10 to 16 characters long. It does mean that if you look over your code and see many names that are shorter, you should check to be sure that the names are as clear as they need to be.

You'll probably come out ahead by taking the Goldilocks-and-the-Three-Bears approach to naming variables, as Table 11-2 illustrates.

Table 11-2 Variable Names That Are Too Long, Too Short, or Just Right

Too long:	*numberOfPeopleOnTheUsOlympicTeam*
	numberOfSeatsInTheStadium
	maximumNumberOfPointsInModernOlympics
Too short:	*n, np, ntm*
	n, ns, nsisd
	m, mp, max, points
Just right:	*numTeamMembers, teamMemberCount*
	numSeatsInStadium, seatCount
	teamPointsMax, pointsRecord

The Effect of Scope on Variable Names

Cross-Reference Scope is discussed in more detail in Section 10.4, "Scope."

Are short variable names always bad? No, not always. When you give a variable a short name like *i*, the length itself says something about the variable—namely, that the variable is a scratch value with a limited scope of operation.

A programmer reading such a variable should be able to assume that its value isn't used outside a few lines of code. When you name a variable *i*, you're saying, "This variable is a run-of-the-mill loop counter or array index and doesn't have any significance outside these few lines of code."

A study by W. J. Hansen found that longer names are better for rarely used variables or global variables and shorter names are better for local variables or loop variables

(Shneiderman 1980). Short names are subject to many problems, however, and some careful programmers avoid them altogether as a matter of defensive-programming policy.

Use qualifiers on names that are in the global namespace If you have variables that are in the global namespace (named constants, class names, and so on), consider whether you need to adopt a convention for partitioning the global namespace and avoiding naming conflicts. In C++ and C#, you can use the *namespace* keyword to partition the global namespace.

C++ Example of Using the *namespace* Keyword to Partition the Global Namespace

```
namespace UserInterfaceSubsystem {
   ...
   // lots of declarations
   ...
}

namespace DatabaseSubsystem {
   ...
   // lots of declarations
   ...
}
```

If you declare an *Employee* class in both the *UserInterfaceSubsystem* and the *Database-Subsystem*, you can identify which you wanted to refer to by writing *UserInterfaceSubsystem::Employee* or *DatabaseSubsystem::Employee*. In Java, you can accomplish the same thing by using packages.

In languages that don't support namespaces or packages, you can still use naming conventions to partition the global namespace. One convention is to require that globally visible classes be prefixed with subsystem mnemonic. The user interface employee class might become *uiEmployee*, and the database employee class might become *dbEmployee*. This minimizes the risk of global-namespace collisions.

Computed-Value Qualifiers in Variable Names

Many programs have variables that contain computed values: totals, averages, maximums, and so on. If you modify a name with a qualifier like *Total*, *Sum*, *Average*, *Max*, *Min*, *Record*, *String*, or *Pointer*, put the modifier at the end of the name.

This practice offers several advantages. First, the most significant part of the variable name, the part that gives the variable most of its meaning, is at the front, so it's most prominent and gets read first. Second, by establishing this convention, you avoid the confusion you might create if you were to use both *totalRevenue* and *revenueTotal* in the same program. The names are semantically equivalent, and the convention would prevent their being used as if they were different. Third, a set of names like *revenueTotal*, *expenseTotal*, *revenueAverage*, and *expenseAverage* has a pleasing symmetry. A set of names like *totalRevenue*, *expenseTotal*, *revenueAverage*, and *averageExpense* doesn't appeal to a sense of order. Finally, the consistency improves readability and eases maintenance.

An exception to the rule that computed values go at the end of the name is the customary position of the *Num* qualifier. Placed at the beginning of a variable name, *Num* refers to a total: *numCustomers* is the total number of customers. Placed at the end of the variable name, *Num* refers to an index: *customerNum* is the number of the current customer. The *s* at the end of *numCustomers* is another tip-off about the difference in meaning. But, because using *Num* so often creates confusion, it's probably best to sidestep the whole issue by using *Count* or *Total* to refer to a total number of customers and *Index* to refer to a specific customer. Thus, *customerCount* is the total number of customers and *customerIndex* refers to a specific customer.

Common Opposites in Variable Names

Cross-Reference For a similar list of opposites in routine names, see "Use opposites precisely" in Section 7.3.

Use opposites precisely. Using naming conventions for opposites helps consistency, which helps readability. Pairs like *begin/end* are easy to understand and remember. Pairs that depart from common-language opposites tend to be hard to remember and are therefore confusing. Here are some common opposites:

- begin/end
- first/last
- locked/unlocked
- min/max
- next/previous
- old/new
- opened/closed
- visible/invisible
- source/target
- source/destination
- up/down

11.2 Naming Specific Types of Data

In addition to the general considerations in naming data, special considerations come up in the naming of specific kinds of data. This section describes considerations specifically for loop variables, status variables, temporary variables, boolean variables, enumerated types, and named constants.

Naming Loop Indexes

Cross-Reference For details on loops, see Chapter 16, "Controlling Loops."

Guidelines for naming variables in loops have arisen because loops are such a common feature of computer programming. The names *i*, *j*, and *k* are customary:

Java Example of a Simple Loop Variable Name
```
for ( i = firstItem; i < lastItem; i++ ) {
   data[ i ] = 0;
}
```

If a variable is to be used outside the loop, it should be given a name more meaningful than *i*, *j*, or *k*. For example, if you are reading records from a file and need to remember how many records you've read, a name like *recordCount* would be appropriate:

Java Example of a Good Descriptive Loop Variable Name
```
recordCount = 0;
while ( moreScores() ) {
   score[ recordCount ] = GetNextScore();
   recordCount++;
}

// lines using recordCount
...
```

If the loop is longer than a few lines, it's easy to forget what *i* is supposed to stand for and you're better off giving the loop index a more meaningful name. Because code is so often changed, expanded, and copied into other programs, many experienced programmers avoid names like *i* altogether.

One common reason loops grow longer is that they're nested. If you have several nested loops, assign longer names to the loop variables to improve readability.

Java Example of Good Loop Names in a Nested Loop
```
for ( teamIndex = 0; teamIndex < teamCount; teamIndex++ ) {
   for ( eventIndex = 0; eventIndex < eventCount[ teamIndex ]; eventIndex++ ) {
      score[ teamIndex ][ eventIndex ] = 0;
   }
}
```

Carefully chosen names for loop-index variables avoid the common problem of index cross-talk: saying *i* when you mean *j* and *j* when you mean *i*. They also make array accesses clearer: *score[teamIndex][eventIndex]* is more informative than *score[i][j]*.

If you have to use *i*, *j*, and *k*, don't use them for anything other than loop indexes for simple loops—the convention is too well established, and breaking it to use them in other ways is confusing. The simplest way to avoid such problems is simply to think of more descriptive names than *i*, *j*, and *k*.

Naming Status Variables

Status variables describe the state of your program. Here's a naming guideline:

Think of a better name than flag for status variables It's better to think of flags as status variables. A flag should never have *flag* in its name because that doesn't give you any clue about what the flag does. For clarity, flags should be assigned values and their values should be tested with enumerated types, named constants, or global variables that act as named constants. Here are some examples of flags with bad names:

CODING HORROR

> **C++ Examples of Cryptic Flags**
> ```
> if ( flag ) ...
> if ( statusFlag & 0x0F ) ...
> if ( printFlag == 16 ) ...
> if ( computeFlag == 0 ) ...
>
> flag = 0x1;
> statusFlag = 0x80;
> printFlag = 16;
> computeFlag = 0;
> ```

Statements like *statusFlag = 0x80* give you no clue about what the code does unless you wrote the code or have documentation that tells you both what *statusFlag* is and what *0x80* represents. Here are equivalent code examples that are clearer:

> **C++ Examples of Better Use of Status Variables**
> ```
> if ( dataReady ) ...
> if ( characterType & PRINTABLE_CHAR ) ...
> if ( reportType == ReportType_Annual ) ...
> if ( recalcNeeded = false ) ...
>
> dataReady = true;
> characterType = CONTROL_CHARACTER;
> reportType = ReportType_Annual;
> recalcNeeded = false;
> ```

Clearly, *characterType = CONTROL_CHARACTER* is more meaningful than *statusFlag = 0x80*. Likewise, the conditional *if (reportType == ReportType_Annual)* is clearer than *if (printFlag == 16)*. The second example shows that you can use this approach with enumerated types as well as predefined named constants. Here's how you could use named constants and enumerated types to set up the values used in the example:

> **Declaring Status Variables in C++**
> ```
> // values for CharacterType
> const int LETTER = 0x01;
> const int DIGIT = 0x02;
> const int PUNCTUATION = 0x04;
> const int LINE_DRAW = 0x08;
> ```

```
const int PRINTABLE_CHAR = ( LETTER | DIGIT | PUNCTUATION | LINE_DRAW );

const int CONTROL_CHARACTER = 0x80;

// values for ReportType
enum ReportType {
   ReportType_Daily,
   ReportType_Monthly,
   ReportType_Quarterly,
   ReportType_Annual,
   ReportType_All
};
```

When you find yourself "figuring out" a section of code, consider renaming the variables. It's OK to figure out murder mysteries, but you shouldn't need to figure out code. You should be able to read it.

Naming Temporary Variables

Temporary variables are used to hold intermediate results of calculations, as temporary placeholders, and to hold housekeeping values. They're usually called *temp*, *x*, or some other vague and nondescriptive name. In general, temporary variables are a sign that the programmer does not yet fully understand the problem. Moreover, because the variables are officially given a "temporary" status, programmers tend to treat them more casually than other variables, increasing the chance of errors.

Be leery of "temporary" variables   It's often necessary to preserve values temporarily. But in one way or another, most of the variables in your program are temporary. Calling a few of them temporary may indicate that you aren't sure of their real purposes. Consider the following example:

C++ Example of an Uninformative "Temporary" Variable Name
```
// Compute solutions of a quadratic equation.
// This assumes that (b^2-4*a*c) is positive.
temp = sqrt( b^2 - 4*a*c );
solution[0] = ( -b + temp ) / ( 2 * a );
solution[1] = ( -b - temp ) / ( 2 * a );
```

It's fine to store the value of the expression *sqrt(b^2 - 4 * a * c)* in a variable, especially since it's used in two places later. But the name *temp* doesn't tell you anything about what the variable does. A better approach is shown in this example:

C++ Example with a "Temporary" Variable Name Replaced with a Real Variable
```
// Compute solutions of a quadratic equation.
// This assumes that (b^2-4*a*c) is positive.
discriminant = sqrt( b^2 - 4*a*c );
solution[0] = ( -b + discriminant ) / ( 2 * a );
solution[1] = ( -b - discriminant ) / ( 2 * a );
```

This is essentially the same code, but it's improved with the use of an accurate, descriptive variable name.

Naming Boolean Variables

Following are a few guidelines to use in naming boolean variables:

Keep typical boolean names in mind   Here are some particularly useful boolean variable names:

- **done**   Use *done* to indicate whether something is done. The variable can indicate whether a loop is done or some other operation is done. Set *done* to *false* before something is done, and set it to *true* when something is completed.

- **error**   Use *error* to indicate that an error has occurred. Set the variable to *false* when no error has occurred and to *true* when an error has occurred.

- **found**   Use *found* to indicate whether a value has been found. Set *found* to *false* when the value has not been found and to *true* once the value has been found. Use *found* when searching an array for a value, a file for an employee ID, a list of paychecks for a certain paycheck amount, and so on.

- **success or ok**   Use *success* or *ok* to indicate whether an operation has been successful. Set the variable to *false* when an operation has failed and to *true* when an operation has succeeded. If you can, replace *success* with a more specific name that describes precisely what it means to be successful. If the program is successful when processing is complete, you might use *processingComplete* instead. If the program is successful when a value is found, you might use *found* instead.

Give boolean variables names that imply true or false   Names like *done* and *success* are good boolean names because the state is either *true* or *false*; something is done or it isn't; it's a success or it isn't. Names like *status* and *sourceFile*, on the other hand, are poor boolean names because they're not obviously *true* or *false*. What does it mean if *status* is *true*? Does it mean that something has a status? Everything has a status. Does *true* mean that the status of something is OK? Or does *false* mean that nothing has gone wrong? With a name like *status*, you can't tell.

For better results, replace *status* with a name like *error* or *statusOK*, and replace *sourceFile* with *sourceFileAvailable* or *sourceFileFound*, or whatever the variable represents.

Some programmers like to put *Is* in front of their boolean names. Then the variable name becomes a question: *isDone? isError? isFound? isProcessingComplete?* Answering the question with *true* or *false* provides the value of the variable. A benefit of this approach is that it won't work with vague names: *isStatus?* makes no sense at all. A drawback is that it makes simple logical expressions less readable: *if (isFound)* is slightly less readable than *if (found)*.

Use positive boolean variable names   Negative names like *notFound*, *notdone*, and *notSuccessful* are difficult to read when they are negated—for example,

```
if not notFound
```

Such a name should be replaced by *found*, *done*, or *processingComplete* and then negated with an operator as appropriate. If what you're looking for is found, you have *found* instead of *not notFound*.

Naming Enumerated Types

Cross-Reference For details on using enumerated types, see Section 12.6, "Enumerated Types."

When you use an enumerated type, you can ensure that it's clear that members of the type all belong to the same group by using a group prefix, such as *Color_*, *Planet_*, or *Month_*. Here are some examples of identifying elements of enumerated types using prefixes:

Visual Basic Example of Using a Prefix Naming Convention for Enumerated Types
```
Public Enum Color
    Color_Red
    Color_Green
    Color_Blue
End Enum

Public Enum Planet
    Planet_Earth
    Planet_Mars
    Planet_Venus
End Enum

Public Enum Month
    Month_January
    Month_February
    ...
    Month_December
End Enum
```

In addition, the enum type itself (*Color*, *Planet*, or *Month*) can be identified in various ways, including all caps or prefixes (*e_Color*, *e_Planet*, or *e_Month*). A person could argue that an enum is essentially a user-defined type and so the name of the enum should be formatted the same as other user-defined types like classes. A different argument would be that enums are types, but they are also constants, so the enum type name should be formatted as constants. This book uses the convention of mixed case for enumerated type names.

In some languages, enumerated types are treated more like classes, and the members of the enumeration are always prefixed with the enum name, like *Color.Color_Red* or *Planet.Planet_Earth*. If you're working in that kind of language, it makes little sense to repeat the prefix, so you can treat the name of the enum type itself as the prefix and simplify the names to *Color.Red* and *Planet.Earth*.

Naming Constants

Cross-Reference For details on using named constants, see Section 12.7, "Named Constants."

When naming constants, name the abstract entity the constant represents rather than the number the constant refers to. *FIVE* is a bad name for a constant (regardless of whether the value it represents is 5.0). *CYCLES_NEEDED* is a good name. *CYCLES_NEEDED* can equal 5.0 or 6.0. *FIVE = 6.0* would be ridiculous. By the same token, *BAKERS_DOZEN* is a poor constant name; *DONUTS_MAX* is a good constant name.

11.3 The Power of Naming Conventions

Some programmers resist standards and conventions—and with good reason. Some standards and conventions are rigid and ineffective—destructive to creativity and program quality. This is unfortunate since effective standards are some of the most powerful tools at your disposal. This section discusses why, when, and how you should create your own standards for naming variables.

Why Have Conventions?

Conventions offer several specific benefits:

- They let you take more for granted. By making one global decision rather than many local ones, you can concentrate on the more important characteristics of the code.

- They help you transfer knowledge across projects. Similarities in names give you an easier and more confident understanding of what unfamiliar variables are supposed to do.

- They help you learn code more quickly on a new project. Rather than learning that Anita's code looks like this, Julia's like that, and Kristin's like something else, you can work with a more consistent set of code.

- They reduce name proliferation. Without naming conventions, you can easily call the same thing by two different names. For example, you might call total points both *pointTotal* and *totalPoints*. This might not be confusing to you when you write the code, but it can be enormously confusing to a new programmer who reads it later.

- They compensate for language weaknesses. You can use conventions to emulate named constants and enumerated types. The conventions can differentiate among local, class, and global data and can incorporate type information for types that aren't supported by the compiler.

- They emphasize relationships among related items. If you use object data, the compiler takes care of this automatically. If your language doesn't support objects, you can supplement it with a naming convention. Names like *address*, *phone*, and *name* don't indicate that the variables are related. But suppose you decide that all employee-data variables should begin with an *Employee* prefix. *employeeAddress*, *employeePhone*, and *employeeName* leave no doubt that the variables are related. Programming conventions can make up for the weakness of the language you're using.

KEY POINT

The key is that any convention at all is often better than no convention. The convention may be arbitrary. The power of naming conventions doesn't come from the specific convention chosen but from the fact that a convention exists, adding structure to the code and giving you fewer things to worry about.

When You Should Have a Naming Convention

There are no hard-and-fast rules for when you should establish a naming convention, but here are a few cases in which conventions are worthwhile:

- When multiple programmers are working on a project
- When you plan to turn a program over to another programmer for modifications and maintenance (which is nearly always)
- When your programs are reviewed by other programmers in your organization
- When your program is so large that you can't hold the whole thing in your brain at once and must think about it in pieces
- When the program will be long-lived enough that you might put it aside for a few weeks or months before working on it again
- When you have a lot of unusual terms that are common on a project and want to have standard terms or abbreviations to use in coding

You always benefit from having some kind of naming convention. The considerations above should help you determine the extent of the convention to use on a particular project.

Degrees of Formality

Cross-Reference For details on the differences in formality in small and large projects, see Chapter 27, "How Program Size Affects Construction."

Different conventions have different degrees of formality. An informal convention might be as simple as "Use meaningful names." Other informal conventions are described in the next section. In general, the degree of formality you need is dependent on the number of people working on a program, the size of the program, and the program's expected life span. On tiny, throwaway projects, a strict convention might be unnecessary overhead. On larger projects in which several people are involved, either initially or over the program's life span, formal conventions are an indispensable aid to readability.

11.4 Informal Naming Conventions

Most projects use relatively informal naming conventions such as the ones laid out in this section.

Guidelines for a Language-Independent Convention

Here are some guidelines for creating a language-independent convention:

Differentiate between variable names and routine names   The convention this book uses is to begin variable and object names with lower case and routine names with upper case: *variableName* vs. *RoutineName()*.

Differentiate between classes and objects   The correspondence between class names and object names—or between types and variables of those types—can get tricky. Several standard options exist, as shown in the following examples:

Option 1: Differentiating Types and Variables via Initial Capitalization
```
Widget widget;
LongerWidget longerWidget;
```

Option 2: Differentiating Types and Variables via All Caps
```
WIDGET widget;
LONGERWIDGET longerWidget
```

Option 3: Differentiating Types and Variables via the "t_" Prefix for Types
```
t_Widget Widget;
t_LongerWidget LongerWidget;
```

Option 4: Differentiating Types and Variables via the "a" Prefix for Variables
```
Widget aWidget;
LongerWidget aLongerWidget;
```

Option 5: Differentiating Types and Variables via Using More Specific Names for the Variables
```
Widget employeeWidget;
LongerWidget fullEmployeeWidget;
```

Each of these options has strengths and weaknesses. Option 1 is a common convention in case-sensitive languages including C++ and Java, but some programmers are uncomfortable differentiating names solely on the basis of capitalization. Indeed, creating names that differ only in the capitalization of the first letter in the name seems to provide too little "psychological distance" and too small a visual distinction between the two names.

The Option 1 approach can't be applied consistently in mixed-language environments if any of the languages are case-insensitive. In Microsoft Visual Basic, for example, *Dim widget as Widget* will generate a syntax error because *widget* and *Widget* are treated as the same token.

Option 2 creates a more obvious distinction between the type name and the variable name. For historical reasons, all caps are used to indicate constants in C++ and Java, however, and the approach is subject to the same problems in mixed-language environments that Option 1 is subject to.

Option 3 works adequately in all languages, but some programmers dislike the idea of prefixes for aesthetic reasons.

Option 4 is sometimes used as an alternative to Option 3, but it has the drawback of altering the name of every instance of a class instead of just the one class name.

Option 5 requires more thought on a variable-by-variable basis. In most instances, being forced to think of a specific name for a variable results in more readable code. But sometimes a *widget* truly is just a generic *widget*, and in those instances you'll find yourself coming up with less-than-obvious names, like *genericWidget*, which are arguably less readable.

In short, each of the available options involves tradeoffs. The code in this book uses Option 5 because it's the most understandable in situations in which the person reading the code isn't necessarily familiar with a less intuitive naming convention.

Identify global variables One common programming problem is misuse of global variables. If you give all global variable names a *g_* prefix, for example, a programmer seeing the variable *g_RunningTotal* will know it's a global variable and treat it as such.

Identify member variables Identify a class's member data. Make it clear that the variable isn't a local variable and that it isn't a global variable either. For example, you can identify class member variables with an *m_* prefix to indicate that it is member data.

Identify type definitions Naming conventions for types serve two purposes: they explicitly identify a name as a type name, and they avoid naming clashes with variables. To meet those considerations, a prefix or suffix is a good approach. In C++, the customary approach is to use all uppercase letters for a type name—for example, *COLOR* and *MENU*. (This convention applies to *typedefs* and *structs*, not class names.) But this creates the possibility of confusion with named preprocessor constants. To avoid confusion, you can prefix the type names with *t_*, such as *t_Color* and *t_Menu*.

Identify named constants Named constants need to be identified so that you can tell whether you're assigning a variable a value from another variable (whose value might change) or from a named constant. In Visual Basic, you have the additional possibility that the value might be from a function. Visual Basic doesn't require function names to use parentheses, whereas in C++ even a function with no parameters uses parentheses.

One approach to naming constants is to use a prefix like *c_* for constant names. That would give you names like *c_RecsMax* or *c_LinesPerPageMax*. In C++ and Java, the convention is to use all uppercase letters, possibly with underscores to separate words, *RECSMAX* or *RECS_ MAX* and *LINESPERPAGEMAX* or *LINES_PER_PAGE_ MAX*.

Identify elements of enumerated types   Elements of enumerated types need to be identified for the same reasons that named constants do—to make it easy to tell that the name is for an enumerated type as opposed to a variable, named constant, or function. The standard approach applies: you can use all caps or an *e_* or *E_* prefix for the name of the type itself and use a prefix based on the specific type like *Color_* or *Planet_* for the members of the type.

Identify input-only parameters in languages that don't enforce them   Sometimes input parameters are accidentally modified. In languages such as C++ and Visual Basic, you must indicate explicitly whether you want a value that's been modified to be returned to the calling routine. This is indicated with the ***, *&*, and *const* qualifiers in C++ or *ByRef* and *ByVal* in Visual Basic.

In other languages, if you modify an input variable, it is returned whether you like it or not. This is especially true when passing objects. In Java, for example, all objects are passed "by value," so when you pass an object to a routine, the contents of the object can be changed within the called routine (Arnold, Gosling, Holmes 2000).

Cross-Reference Augmenting a language with a naming convention to make up for limitations in the language itself is an example of programming *into* a language instead of just programming in it. For more details on programming *into* a language, see Section 34.4, "Program into Your Language, Not in It."

In those languages, if you establish a naming convention in which input-only parameters are given a *const* prefix (or *final*, *nonmodifiable*, or something comparable) , you'll know an error has occurred when you see anything with a *const* prefix on the left side of an equal sign. If you see *constMax.SetNewMax(...)*, you'll know it's a goof because the *const* prefix indicates that the variable isn't supposed to be modified.

Format names to enhance readability   Two common techniques for increasing readability are using capitalization and spacing characters to separate words. For example, *GYMNASTICSPOINTTOTAL* is less readable than *gymnasticsPointTotal* or *gymnastics_point_total*. C++, Java, Visual Basic, and other languages allow for mixed uppercase and lowercase characters. C++, Java, Visual Basic, and other languages also allow the use of the underscore (_) separator.

Try not to mix these techniques; that makes code hard to read. If you make an honest attempt to use any of these readability techniques consistently, however, it will improve your code. People have managed to have zealous, blistering debates over fine points such as whether the first character in a name should be capitalized (*PointsTotal* vs. *pointsTotal*), but as long as you and your team are consistent, it won't make much difference. This book uses initial lowercase because of the strength of the Java practice and to facilitate similarity in style across several languages.

Guidelines for Language-Specific Conventions

Follow the naming conventions of the language you're using. You can find books for most languages that describe style guidelines. Guidelines for C, C++, Java, and Visual Basic are provided in the following sections.

C Conventions

Further Reading The classic book on C programming style is *C Programming Guidelines* (Plum 1984).

Several naming conventions apply specifically to the C programming language:

- *c* and *ch* are character variables.
- *i* and *j* are integer indexes.
- *n* is a number of something.
- *p* is a pointer.
- *s* is a string.
- Preprocessor macros are in *ALL_CAPS*. This is usually extended to include type-defs as well.
- Variable and routine names are in *all_lowercase*.
- The underscore (_) character is used as a separator: *letters_in_lowercase* is more readable than *lettersinlowercase*.

These are the conventions for generic, UNIX-style and Linux-style C programming, but C conventions are different in different environments. In Microsoft Windows, C programmers tend to use a form of the Hungarian naming convention and mixed uppercase and lowercase letters for variable names. On the Macintosh, C programmers tend to use mixed-case names for routines because the Macintosh toolbox and operating-system routines were originally designed for a Pascal interface.

C++ Conventions

Further Reading For more on C++ programming style, see *The Elements of C++ Style* (Misfeldt, Bumgardner, and Gray 2004).

Here are the conventions that have grown up around C++ programming:

- *i* and *j* are integer indexes.
- *p* is a pointer.
- Constants, typedefs, and preprocessor macros are in *ALL_CAPS*.
- Class and other type names are in *MixedUpperAndLowerCase()*.
- Variable and function names use lowercase for the first word, with the first letter of each following word capitalized—for example, *variableOrRoutineName*.
- The underscore is not used as a separator within names, except for names in all caps and certain kinds of prefixes (such as those used to identify global variables).

As with C programming, this convention is far from standard and different environments have standardized on different convention details.

Java Conventions

Further Reading For more on Java programming style, see *The Elements of Java Style*, 2d ed. (Vermeulen et al. 2000).

In contrast with C and C++, Java style conventions have been well established since the language's beginning:

- *i* and *j* are integer indexes.

- Constants are in *ALL_CAPS* separated by underscores.

- Class and interface names capitalize the first letter of each word, including the first word—for example, *ClassOrInterfaceName*.

- Variable and method names use lowercase for the first word, with the first letter of each following word capitalized—for example, *variableOrRoutineName*.

- The underscore is not used as a separator within names except for names in all caps.

- The *get* and *set* prefixes are used for accessor methods.

Visual Basic Conventions

Visual Basic has not really established firm conventions. The next section recommends a convention for Visual Basic.

Mixed-Language Programming Considerations

When programming in a mixed-language environment, the naming conventions (as well as formatting conventions, documentation conventions, and other conventions) can be optimized for overall consistency and readability—even if that means going against convention for one of the languages that's part of the mix.

In this book, for example, variable names all begin with lowercase, which is consistent with conventional Java programming practice and some but not all C++ conventions. This book formats all routine names with an initial capital letter, which follows the C++ convention. The Java convention would be to begin method names with lowercase, but this book uses routine names that begin in uppercase across all languages for the sake of overall readability.

Sample Naming Conventions

The standard conventions above tend to ignore several important aspects of naming that were discussed over the past few pages—including variable scoping (private, class, or global), differentiating between class, object, routine, and variable names, and other issues.

The naming-convention guidelines can look complicated when they're strung across several pages. They don't need to be terribly complex, however, and you can adapt them to your needs. Variable names include three kinds of information:

- The contents of the variable (what it represents)
- The kind of data (named constant, primitive variable, user-defined type, or class)
- The scope of the variable (private, class, package, or global)

Tables 11-3, 11-4, and 11-5 provide naming conventions for C, C++, Java, and Visual Basic that have been adapted from the guidelines presented earlier. These specific conventions aren't necessarily recommended, but they give you an idea of what an informal naming convention includes.

Table 11-3   Sample Naming Conventions for C++ and Java

Entity	Description
ClassName	Class names are in mixed uppercase and lowercase with an initial capital letter.
TypeName	Type definitions, including enumerated types and type-defs, use mixed uppercase and lowercase with an initial capital letter.
EnumeratedTypes	In addition to the rule above, enumerated types are always stated in the plural form.
localVariable	Local variables are in mixed uppercase and lowercase with an initial lowercase letter. The name should be independent of the underlying data type and should refer to whatever the variable represents.
routineParameter	Routine parameters are formatted the same as local variables.
RoutineName()	Routines are in mixed uppercase and lowercase. (Good routine names are discussed in Section 7.3.)
m_ClassVariable	Member variables that are available to multiple routines within a class, but only within a class, are prefixed with an *m_*.
g_GlobalVariable	Global variables are prefixed with a *g_*.
CONSTANT	Named constants are in *ALL_CAPS*.
MACRO	Macros are in *ALL_CAPS*.
Base_EnumeratedType	Enumerated types are prefixed with a mnemonic for their base type stated in the singular—for example, *Color_Red*, *Color_Blue*.

Table 11-4   **Sample Naming Conventions for C**

Entity	Description
TypeName	Type definitions use mixed uppercase and lowercase with an initial capital letter.
GlobalRoutineName()	Public routines are in mixed uppercase and lowercase.
f_FileRoutineName()	Routines that are private to a single module (file) are prefixed with an *f_*.
LocalVariable	Local variables are in mixed uppercase and lowercase. The name should be independent of the underlying data type and should refer to whatever the variable represents.
RoutineParameter	Routine parameters are formatted the same as local variables.
f_FileStaticVariable	Module (file) variables are prefixed with an *f_*.
G_GLOBAL_GlobalVariable	Global variables are prefixed with a *G_* and a mnemonic of the module (file) that defines the variable in all uppercase—for example, *SCREEN_Dimensions*.
LOCAL_CONSTANT	Named constants that are private to a single routine or module (file) are in all uppercase—for example, *ROWS_MAX*.
G_GLOBALCONSTANT	Global named constants are in all uppercase and are prefixed with *G_* and a mnemonic of the module (file) that defines the named constant in all uppercase—for example, *G_SCREEN_ROWS_MAX*.
LOCALMACRO()	Macro definitions that are private to a single routine or module (file) are in all uppercase.
G_GLOBAL_MACRO()	Global macro definitions are in all uppercase and are prefixed with *G_* and a mnemonic of the module (file) that defines the macro in all uppercase—for example, *G_SCREEN_LOCATION()*.

Because Visual Basic is not case-sensitive, special rules apply for differentiating between type names and variable names. Take a look at Table 11-5.

Table 11-5   **Sample Naming Conventions for Visual Basic**

Entity	Description
C_ClassName	Class names are in mixed uppercase and lowercase with an initial capital letter and a *C_* prefix.
T_TypeName	Type definitions, including enumerated types and typedefs, use mixed uppercase and lowercase with an initial capital letter and a *T_* prefix.
T_EnumeratedTypes	In addition to the rule above, enumerated types are always stated in the plural form.

Table 11-5   Sample Naming Conventions for Visual Basic

Entity	Description
localVariable	Local variables are in mixed uppercase and lowercase with an initial lowercase letter. The name should be independent of the underlying data type and should refer to whatever the variable represents.
routineParameter	Routine parameters are formatted the same as local variables.
RoutineName()	Routines are in mixed uppercase and lowercase. (Good routine names are discussed in Section 7.3.)
m_ClassVariable	Member variables that are available to multiple routines within a class, but only within a class, are prefixed with an *m_*.
g_GlobalVariable	Global variables are prefixed with a *g_*.
CONSTANT	Named constants are in *ALL_CAPS*.
Base_EnumeratedType	Enumerated types are prefixed with a mnemonic for their base type stated in the singular—for example, *Color_Red*, *Color_Blue*.

11.5 Standardized Prefixes

Further Reading For further details on the Hungarian naming convention, see "The Hungarian Revolution" (Simonyi and Heller 1991).

Standardizing prefixes for common meanings provides a terse but consistent and readable approach to naming data. The best known scheme for standardizing prefixes is the Hungarian naming convention, which is a set of detailed guidelines for naming variables and routines (not Hungarians!) that was widely used at one time in Microsoft Windows programming. Although the Hungarian naming convention is no longer in widespread use, the basic idea of standardizing on terse, precise abbreviations continues to have value.

Standardized prefixes are composed of two parts: the user-defined type (UDT) abbreviation and the semantic prefix.

User-Defined Type Abbreviations

The UDT abbreviation identifies the data type of the object or variable being named. UDT abbreviations might refer to entities such as windows, screen regions, and fonts. A UDT abbreviation generally doesn't refer to any of the predefined data types offered by the programming language.

UDTs are described with short codes that you create for a specific program and then standardize on for use in that program. The codes are mnemonics such as *wn* for windows and *scr* for screen regions. Table 11-6 offers a sample list of UDTs that you might use in a program for a word processor.

Table 11-6   Sample of UDTs for a Word Processor

UDT Abbreviation	Meaning
ch	Character (a character not in the C++ sense, but in the sense of the data type a word-processing program would use to represent a character in a document)
doc	Document
pa	Paragraph
scr	Screen region
sel	Selection
wn	Window

When you use UDTs, you also define programming-language data types that use the same abbreviations as the UDTs. Thus, if you had the UDTs in Table 11-6, you'd see data declarations like these:

```
CH    chCursorPosition;
SCR   scrUserWorkspace;
DOC   docActive
PA    firstPaActiveDocument;
PA    lastPaActiveDocument;
WN    wnMain;
```

Again, these examples relate to a word processor. For use on your own projects, you'd create UDT abbreviations for the UDTs that are used most commonly within your environment.

Semantic Prefixes

Semantic prefixes go a step beyond the UDT and describe how the variable or object is used. Unlike UDTs, which vary from project to project, semantic prefixes are somewhat standard across projects. Table 11-7 shows a list of standard semantic prefixes.

Table 11-7   Semantic Prefixes

Semantic Prefix	Meaning
c	Count (as in the number of records, characters, and so on)
first	The first element that needs to be dealt with in an array. *first* is similar to *min* but relative to the current operation rather than to the array itself.
g	Global variable
i	Index into an array
last	The last element that needs to be dealt with in an array. *last* is the counterpart of *first*.

Table 11-7   **Semantic Prefixes**

Semantic Prefix	Meaning
lim	The upper limit of elements that need to be dealt with in an array. *lim* is not a valid index. Like *last*, *lim* is used as a counterpart of *first*. Unlike *last*, *lim* represents a noninclusive upper bound on the array; *last* represents a final, legal element. Generally, *lim* equals *last + 1*.
m	Class-level variable
max	The absolute last element in an array or other kind of list. *max* refers to the array itself rather than to operations on the array.
min	The absolute first element in an array or other kind of list.
p	Pointer

Semantic prefixes are formatted in lowercase or mixed uppercase and lowercase and are combined with the UDTs and with other semantic prefixes as needed. For example, the first paragraph in a document would be named *pa* to show that it's a paragraph and *first* to show that it's the first paragraph: *firstPa*. An index into the set of paragraphs would be named *iPa*; *cPa* is the count, or the number of paragraphs; and *firstPaActiveDocument* and *lastPaActiveDocument* are the first and last paragraphs in the current active document.

Advantages of Standardized Prefixes

KEY POINT

Standardized prefixes give you all the general advantages of having a naming convention as well as several other advantages. Because so many names are standard, you have fewer names to remember in any single program or class.

Standardized prefixes add precision to several areas of naming that tend to be imprecise. The precise distinctions between *min*, *first*, *last*, and *max* are particularly helpful.

Standardized prefixes make names more compact. For example, you can use *cpa* for the count of paragraphs rather than *totalParagraphs*. You can use *ipa* to identify an index into an array of paragraphs rather than *indexParagraphs* or *paragraphsIndex*.

Finally, standardized prefixes allow you to check types accurately when you're using abstract data types that your compiler can't necessarily check: *paReformat = docReformat* is probably wrong because *pa* and *doc* are different UDTs.

The main pitfall with standardized prefixes is a programmer neglecting to give the variable a meaningful name in addition to its prefix. If *ipa* unambiguously designates an index into an array of paragraphs, it's tempting not to make the name more meaningful like *ipaActiveDocument*. For readability, close the loop and come up with a descriptive name.

11.6 Creating Short Names That Are Readable

KEY POINT

The desire to use short variable names is in some ways a remnant of an earlier age of computing. Older languages like assembler, generic Basic, and Fortran limited variable names to 2–8 characters and forced programmers to create short names. Early computing was more closely linked to mathematics and its use of terms like i, j, and k as the variables in summations and other equations. In modern languages like C++, Java, and Visual Basic, you can create names of virtually any length; you have almost no reason to shorten meaningful names.

If circumstances do require you to create short names, note that some methods of shortening names are better than others. You can create good short variable names by eliminating needless words, using short synonyms, and using any of several abbreviation strategies. It's a good idea to be familiar with multiple techniques for abbreviating because no single technique works well in all cases.

General Abbreviation Guidelines

Here are several guidelines for creating abbreviations. Some of them contradict others, so don't try to use them all at the same time.

- Use standard abbreviations (the ones in common use, which are listed in a dictionary).
- Remove all nonleading vowels. (*computer* becomes *cmptr*, and *screen* becomes *scrn. apple* becomes *appl*, and *integer* becomes *intgr.*)
- Remove articles: *and, or, the,* and so on.
- Use the first letter or first few letters of each word.
- Truncate consistently after the first, second, or third (whichever is appropriate) letter of each word.
- Keep the first and last letters of each word.
- Use every significant word in the name, up to a maximum of three words.
- Remove useless suffixes—*ing, ed,* and so on.
- Keep the most noticeable sound in each syllable.
- Be sure not to change the meaning of the variable.
- Iterate through these techniques until you abbreviate each variable name to between 8 to 20 characters or the number of characters to which your language limits variable names.

Phonetic Abbreviations

Some people advocate creating abbreviations based on the sound of the words rather than their spelling. Thus *skating* becomes *sk8ing*, *highlight* becomes *hilite*, *before* becomes *b4*, *execute* becomes *xqt*, and so on. This seems too much like asking people to figure out personalized license plates to me, and I don't recommend it. As an exercise, figure out what these names mean:

ILV2SK8　　XMEQWK　　S2DTM8O　　NXTC　　TRMN8R

Comments on Abbreviations

You can fall into several traps when creating abbreviations. Here are some rules for avoiding pitfalls:

Don't abbreviate by removing one character from a word　Typing one character is little extra work, and the one-character savings hardly justifies the loss in readability. It's like the calendars that have "Jun" and "Jul." You have to be in a big hurry to spell June as "Jun." With most one-letter deletions, it's hard to remember whether you removed the character. Either remove more than one character or spell out the word.

Abbreviate consistently　Always use the same abbreviation. For example, use *Num* everywhere or *No* everywhere, but don't use both. Similarly, don't abbreviate a word in some names and not in others. For instance, don't use the full word *Number* in some places and the abbreviation *Num* in others.

Create names that you can pronounce　Use *xPos* rather than *xPstn* and *needsComp* rather than *ndsCmptg*. Apply the telephone test—if you can't read your code to someone over the phone, rename your variables to be more distinctive (Kernighan and Plauger 1978).

Avoid combinations that result in misreading or mispronunciation　To refer to the end of B, favor *ENDB* over *BEND*. If you use a good separation technique, you won't need this guideline since *B-END*, *BEnd*, or *b_end* won't be mispronounced.

Use a thesaurus to resolve naming collisions　One problem in creating short names is naming collisions—names that abbreviate to the same thing. For example, if you're limited to three characters and you need to use *fired* and *full revenue disbursal* in the same area of a program, you might inadvertently abbreviate both to *frd*.

One easy way to avoid naming collisions is to use a different word with the same meaning, so a thesaurus is handy. In this example, *dismissed* might be substituted for *fired* and *complete revenue disbursal* might be substituted for *full revenue disbursal*. The three-letter abbreviations become *dsm* and *crd*, eliminating the naming collision.

Document extremely short names with translation tables in the code In languages that allow only very short names, include a translation table to provide a reminder of the mnemonic content of the variables. Include the table as comments at the beginning of a block of code. Here's an example:

Fortran Example of a Good Translation Table

```
C ******************************************************************
C     Translation Table
C
C     Variable    Meaning
C     --------    -------
C     XPOS        x-Coordinate Position (in meters)
C     YPOS        Y-Coordinate Position (in meters)
C     NDSCMP      Needs Computing (=0 if no computation is needed;
C                                  =1 if computation is needed)
C     PTGTTL      Point Grand Total
C     PTVLMX      Point Value Maximum
C     PSCRMX      Possible Score Maximum
C ******************************************************************
```

You might think that this technique is outdated, but as recently as mid-2003 I worked with a client that had hundreds of thousands of lines of code written in RPG that was subject to a 6-character–variable-name limitation. These issues still come up from time to time.

Document all abbreviations in a project-level "Standard Abbreviations" document Abbreviations in code create two general risks:

- A reader of the code might not understand the abbreviation.

- Other programmers might use multiple abbreviations to refer to the same word, which creates needless confusion.

To address both these potential problems, you can create a "Standard Abbreviations" document that captures all the coding abbreviations used on your project. The document can be a word processor document or a spreadsheet. On a very large project, it could be a database. The document is checked into version control and checked out anytime anyone creates a new abbreviation in the code. Entries in the document should be sorted by the full word, not the abbreviation.

This might seem like a lot of overhead, but aside from a small amount of startup overhead, it really just sets up a mechanism that helps the project use abbreviations effectively. It addresses the first of the two general risks described above by documenting all abbreviations in use. The fact that a programmer can't create a new abbreviation without the overhead of checking the Standard Abbreviations document out of version control, entering the abbreviation, and checking it back in *is a good thing*. It means that an abbreviation won't be created unless it's so common that it's worth the hassle of documenting it.

This approach addresses the second risk by reducing the likelihood that a programmer will create a redundant abbreviation. A programmer who wants to abbreviate something will check out the abbreviations document and enter the new abbreviation. If there is already an abbreviation for the word the programmer wants to abbreviate, the programmer will notice that and will then use the existing abbreviation instead of creating a new one.

KEY POINT

The general issue illustrated by this guideline is the difference between write-time convenience and read-time convenience. This approach clearly creates a write-time *inconvenience*, but programmers over the lifetime of a system spend far more time reading code than writing code. This approach increases read-time convenience. By the time all the dust settles on a project, it might well also have improved write-time convenience.

Remember that names matter more to the reader of the code than to the writer   Read code of your own that you haven't seen for at least six months and notice where you have to work to understand what the names mean. Resolve to change the practices that cause such confusion.

11.7 Kinds of Names to Avoid

Here are some guidelines regarding variable names to avoid:

Avoid misleading names or abbreviations   Make sure that a name is unambiguous. For example, *FALSE* is usually the opposite of *TRUE* and would be a bad abbreviation for "Fig and Almond Season."

Avoid names with similar meanings   If you can switch the names of two variables without hurting the program, you need to rename both variables. For example, *input* and *inputValue*, *recordNum* and *numRecords*, and *fileNumber* and *fileIndex* are so semantically similar that if you use them in the same piece of code you'll easily confuse them and install some subtle, hard-to-find errors.

Cross-Reference The technical term for differences like this between similar variable names is "psychological distance." For details, see "How 'Psychological Distance' Can Help" in Section 23.4.

Avoid variables with different meanings but similar names   If you have two variables with similar names and different meanings, try to rename one of them or change your abbreviations. Avoid names like *clientRecs* and *clientReps*. They're only one letter different from each other, and the letter is hard to notice. Have at least two-letter differences between names, or put the differences at the beginning or at the end. *clientRecords* and *clientReports* are better than the original names.

***Avoid names that sound similar, such as* wrap *and* rap**   Homonyms get in the way when you try to discuss your code with others. One of my pet peeves about Extreme Programming (Beck 2000) is its overly clever use of the terms Goal Donor and Gold Owner, which are virtually indistinguishable when spoken. You end up having conversations like this:

> *I was just speaking with the Goal Donor–*
>
> *Did you say "Gold Owner" or "Goal Donor"?*
>
> *I said "Goal Donor."*
>
> *What?*
>
> *GOAL - - - DONOR!*
>
> *OK, Goal Donor. You don't have to yell, Goll' Darn it.*
>
> *Did you say "Gold Donut?"*

Remember that the telephone test applies to similar sounding names just as it does to oddly abbreviated names.

Avoid numerals in names   If the numerals in a name are really significant, use an array instead of separate variables. If an array is inappropriate, numerals are even more inappropriate. For example, avoid *file1* and *file2*, or *total1* and *total2*. You can almost always think of a better way to differentiate between two variables than by tacking a *1* or a *2* onto the end of the name. I can't say *never* use numerals. Some real-world entities (such as Route 66 or Interstate 405) have numerals embedded in them. But consider whether there are better alternatives before you create a name that includes numerals.

Avoid misspelled words in names   It's hard enough to remember how words are supposed to be spelled. To require people to remember "correct" misspellings is simply too much to ask. For example, misspelling *highlight* as *hilite* to save three characters makes it devilishly difficult for a reader to remember how *highlight* was misspelled. Was it *highlite*? *hilite*? *hilight*? *hilit*? *jai-a-lai-t*? Who knows?

Avoid words that are commonly misspelled in English   *Absense, acummulate, acsend, calender, concieve, defferred, definate, independance, occassionally, prefered, reciept, super-seed,* and many others are common misspellings in English. Most English handbooks contain a list of commonly misspelled words. Avoid using such words in your variable names.

Don't differentiate variable names solely by capitalization   If you're programming in a case-sensitive language such as C++, you may be tempted to use *frd* for *fired*, *FRD* for *final review duty*, and *Frd* for *full revenue disbursal*. Avoid this practice. Although the names are unique, the association of each with a particular meaning is arbitrary and confusing. *Frd* could just as easily be associated with *final review duty* and *FRD* with *full revenue disbursal*, and no logical rule will help you or anyone else to remember which is which.

Avoid multiple natural languages   In multinational projects, enforce use of a single natural language for all code, including class names, variable names, and so on. Reading another programmer's code can be a challenge; reading another programmer's code in Southeast Martian is impossible.

A more subtle problem occurs in variations of English. If a project is conducted in multiple English-speaking countries, standardize on one version of English so that you're not constantly wondering whether the code should say "color" or "colour," "check" or "cheque," and so on.

Avoid the names of standard types, variables, and routines   All programming-language guides contain lists of the language's reserved and predefined names. Read the list occasionally to make sure you're not stepping on the toes of the language you're using. For example, the following code fragment is legal in PL/I, but you would be a certifiable idiot to use it:

CODING HORROR

```
if if = then then
    then = else;
else else = if;
```

Don't use names that are totally unrelated to what the variables represent   Sprinkling names such as *margaret* and *pookie* throughout your program virtually guarantees that no one else will be able to understand it. Avoid your boyfriend's name, wife's name, favorite beer's name, or other clever (aka silly) names for variables, unless the program is really about your boyfriend, wife, or favorite beer. Even then, you would be wise to recognize that each of these might change, and that therefore the generic names *boyfriend*, *wife*, and *favoriteBeer* are superior!

Avoid names containing hard-to-read characters   Be aware that some characters look so similar that it's hard to tell them apart. If the only difference between two names is one of these characters, you might have a hard time telling the names apart. For example, try to circle the name that doesn't belong in each of the following sets:

```
eyeChart1      eyeChartI      eyeChart1
TTLCONFUSION   TTLCONFUSION   TTLCONFUSION
hard2Read      hardZRead      hard2Read
GRANDTOTAL     GRANDTOTAL     6RANDTOTAL
ttl5           ttlS           ttlS
```

Pairs that are hard to distinguish include (1 and l), (1 and I), (. and ,), (0 and O), (2 and Z), (; and :), (S and 5), and (G and 6).

Cross-Reference For considerations in using data, see the checklist on page 257 in Chapter 10, "General Issues in Using Variables."
Do details like these really matter? Indeed! Gerald Weinberg reports that in the 1970s, a comma was used in a Fortran *FORMAT* statement where a period should have been used. The result was that scientists miscalculated a spacecraft's trajectory and lost a space probe—to the tune of $1.6 billion (Weinberg 1983).

cc2e.com/1191

CHECKLIST: Naming Variables

General Naming Considerations

❑ Does the name fully and accurately describe what the variable represents?

❑ Does the name refer to the real-world problem rather than to the programming-language solution?

❑ Is the name long enough that you don't have to puzzle it out?

❑ Are computed-value qualifiers, if any, at the end of the name?

❑ Does the name use *Count* or *Index* instead of *Num*?

Naming Specific Kinds of Data

❑ Are loop index names meaningful (something other than *i*, *j*, or *k* if the loop is more than one or two lines long or is nested)?

❑ Have all "temporary" variables been renamed to something more meaningful?

❑ Are boolean variables named so that their meanings when they're *true* are clear?

❑ Do enumerated-type names include a prefix or suffix that indicates the category—for example, *Color_* for *Color_Red*, *Color_Green*, *Color_Blue*, and so on?

❑ Are named constants named for the abstract entities they represent rather than the numbers they refer to?

Naming Conventions

❑ Does the convention distinguish among local, class, and global data?

❑ Does the convention distinguish among type names, named constants, enumerated types, and variables?

❑ Does the convention identify input-only parameters to routines in languages that don't enforce them?

❑ Is the convention as compatible as possible with standard conventions for the language?

❑ Are names formatted for readability?

Short Names

❑ Does the code use long names (unless it's necessary to use short ones)?

❑ Does the code avoid abbreviations that save only one character?

❑ Are all words abbreviated consistently?

❑   Are the names pronounceable?

❑   Are names that could be misread or mispronounced avoided?

❑   Are short names documented in translation tables?

Common Naming Problems: Have You Avoided...

❑   ...names that are misleading?

❑   ...names with similar meanings?

❑   ...names that are different by only one or two characters?

❑   ...names that sound similar?

❑   ...names that use numerals?

❑   ...names intentionally misspelled to make them shorter?

❑   ...names that are commonly misspelled in English?

❑   ...names that conflict with standard library routine names or with pre-defined variable names?

❑   ...totally arbitrary names?

❑   ...hard-to-read characters?

Key Points

- Good variable names are a key element of program readability. Specific kinds of variables such as loop indexes and status variables require specific considerations.

- Names should be as specific as possible. Names that are vague enough or general enough to be used for more than one purpose are usually bad names.

- Naming conventions distinguish among local, class, and global data. They distinguish among type names, named constants, enumerated types, and variables.

- Regardless of the kind of project you're working on, you should adopt a variable naming convention. The kind of convention you adopt depends on the size of your program and the number of people working on it.

- Abbreviations are rarely needed with modern programming languages. If you do use abbreviations, keep track of abbreviations in a project dictionary or use the standardized prefixes approach.

- Code is read far more times than it is written. Be sure that the names you choose favor read-time convenience over write-time convenience.

Chapter 12
Fundamental Data Types

cc2e.com/1278

Contents

Related Topics

- Naming data: Chapter 11
- Unusual data types: Chapter 13
- General issues in using variables: Chapter 10
- Formatting data declarations: "Laying Out Data Declarations" in Section 31.5
- Documenting variables: "Commenting Data Declarations" in Section 32.5
- Creating classes: Chapter 6

The fundamental data types are the basic building blocks for all other data types. This chapter contains tips for using numbers (in general), integers, floating-point numbers, characters and strings, boolean variables, enumerated types, named constants, and arrays. The final section in this chapter describes how to create your own types.

This chapter covers basic troubleshooting for the fundamental types of data. If you've got your fundamental-data bases covered, skip to the end of the chapter, review the checklist of problems to avoid, and move on to the discussion of unusual data types in Chapter 13.

12.1 Numbers in General

Here are several guidelines for making your use of numbers less error-prone:

Cross-Reference For more details on using named constants instead of magic numbers, see Section 12.7, "Named Constants," later in this chapter.

Avoid "magic numbers" Magic numbers are literal numbers, such as *100* or *47524*, that appear in the middle of a program without explanation. If you program in a language that supports named constants, use them instead. If you can't use named constants, use global variables when it's feasible to do so.

Avoiding magic numbers yields three advantages:

- Changes can be made more reliably. If you use named constants, you won't overlook one of the *100*s or change a *100* that refers to something else.

- Changes can be made more easily. When the maximum number of entries changes from *100* to *200*, if you're using magic numbers you have to find all the *100*s and change them to *200*s. If you use *100+1* or *100-1*, you'll also have to find all the *101*s and *99*s and change them to *201*s and *199*s. If you're using a named constant, you simply change the definition of the constant from *100* to *200* in one place.

- Your code is more readable. Sure, in the expression

  ```
  for i = 0 to 99 do ...
  ```

  you can guess that *99* refers to the maximum number of entries. But the expression

  ```
  for i = 0 to MAX_ENTRIES-1 do ...
  ```

  leaves no doubt. Even if you're certain that a number will never change, you get a readability benefit if you use a named constant.

Use hard-coded 0s and 1s if you need to The values *0* and *1* are used to increment, decrement, and start loops at the first element of an array. The *0* in

```
for i = 0 to CONSTANT do ...
```

is OK, and the *1* in

```
total = total + 1
```

is OK. A good rule of thumb is that the only literals that should occur in the body of a program are *0* and *1*. Any other literals should be replaced with something more descriptive.

Anticipate divide-by-zero errors Each time you use the division symbol (/ in most languages), think about whether it's possible for the denominator of the expression to be *0*. If the possibility exists, write code to prevent a divide-by-zero error.

Make type conversions obvious   Make sure that someone reading your code will be aware of it when a conversion between different data types occurs. In C++ you could say

```
y = x + (float) i
```

and in Microsoft Visual Basic you could say

```
y = x + CSng( i )
```

This practice also helps to ensure that the conversion is the one you want to occur—different compilers do different conversions, so you're taking your chances otherwise.

Cross-Reference For a variation on this example, see "Avoid equality comparisons" in Section 12.3.

Avoid mixed-type comparisons   If *x* is a floating-point number and *i* is an integer, the test

```
if ( i = x ) then ...
```

is almost guaranteed not to work. By the time the compiler figures out which type it wants to use for the comparison, converts one of the types to the other, does a bunch of rounding, and determines the answer, you'll be lucky if your program runs at all. Do the conversion manually so that the compiler can compare two numbers of the same type and you know exactly what's being compared.

KEY POINT

Heed your compiler's warnings   Many modern compilers tell you when you have different numeric types in the same expression. Pay attention! Every programmer has been asked at one time or another to help someone track down a pesky error, only to find that the compiler had warned about the error all along. Top programmers fix their code to eliminate all compiler warnings. It's easier to let the compiler do the work than to do it yourself.

12.2 Integers

Bear these considerations in mind when using integers:

Check for integer division   When you're using integers, 7/10 does not equal 0.7. It usually equals 0, or minus infinity, or the nearest integer, or—you get the picture. What it equals varies from language to language. This applies equally to intermediate results. In the real world 10 * (7/10) = (10*7) / 10 = 7. Not so in the world of integer arithmetic. 10 * (7/10) equals 0 because the integer division (7/10) equals 0. The easiest way to remedy this problem is to reorder the expression so that the divisions are done last: (10*7) / 10.

Check for integer overflow   When doing integer multiplication or addition, you need to be aware of the largest possible integer. The largest possible unsigned integer is often 2^{32}-1 and is sometimes 2^{16}-1, or 65,535. The problem comes up when you multiply two numbers that produce a number bigger than the maximum integer. For example, if you multiply 250 * 300, the right answer is 75,000. But if the maximum integer is 65,535, the answer you'll get is probably 9464 because of integer overflow (75,000 - 65,536 = 9464). Table 12-1 shows the ranges of common integer types.

Table 12-1   Ranges for Different Types of Integers

Integer Type	Range
Signed 8-bit	-128 through 127
Unsigned 8-bit	0 through 255
Signed 16-bit	-32,768 through 32,767
Unsigned 16-bit	0 through 65,535
Signed 32-bit	-2,147,483,648 through 2,147,483,647
Unsigned 32-bit	0 through 4,294,967,295
Signed 64-bit	-9,223,372,036,854,775,808 through 9,223,372,036,854,775,807
Unsigned 64-bit	0 through 18,446,744,073,709,551,615

The easiest way to prevent integer overflow is to think through each of the terms in your arithmetic expression and try to imagine the largest value each can assume. For example, if in the integer expression $m = j * k$, the largest expected value for j is 200 and the largest expected value for k is 25, the largest value you can expect for m is *200 * 25 = 5,000*. This is OK on a 32-bit machine since the largest integer is 2,147,483,647. On the other hand, if the largest expected value for j is 200,000 and the largest expected value for k is 100,000, the largest value you can expect for m is *200,000 * 100,000 = 20,000,000,000*. This is not OK since 20,000,000,000 is larger than 2,147,483,647. In this case, you would have to use 64-bit integers or floating-point numbers to accommodate the largest expected value of m.

Also consider future extensions to the program. If m will never be bigger than 5,000, that's great. But if you expect m to grow steadily for several years, take that into account.

Check for overflow in intermediate results   The number at the end of the equation isn't the only number you have to worry about. Suppose you have the following code:

```
Java Example of Overflow of Intermediate Results
int termA = 1000000;
int termB = 1000000;
int product = termA * termB / 1000000;
System.out.println( "( " + termA + " * " + termB + " ) / 1000000 = " + product );
```

If you think the *Product* assignment is the same as *(1,00,000*1,000,000) / 1,000,000*, you might expect to get the answer *1,000,000*. But the code has to compute the intermediate result of *1,000,000*1,000,000* before it can divide by the final *1,000,000*, and that means it needs a number as big as *1,000,000,000,000*. Guess what? Here's the result:

```
( 1000000 * 1000000 ) / 1000000 = -727
```

If your integers go to only 2,147,483,647, the intermediate result is too large for the integer data type. In this case, the intermediate result that should be *1,000,000,000,000* is *-727,379,968*, so when you divide by *1,000,000*, you get *-727*, rather than *1,000,000*.

You can handle overflow in intermediate results the same way you handle integer overflow, by switching to a long-integer or floating-point type.

12.3 Floating-Point Numbers

KEY POINT

The main consideration in using floating-point numbers is that many fractional decimal numbers can't be represented accurately using the 1s and 0s available on a digital computer. Nonterminating decimals like 1/3 or 1/7 can usually be represented to only 7 or 15 digits of accuracy. In my version of Microsoft Visual Basic, a 32-bit floating-point representation of 1/3 equals 0.33333330. It's accurate to 7 digits. This is accurate enough for most purposes but inaccurate enough to trick you sometimes.

Following are a few specific guidelines for using floating-point numbers:

Cross-Reference For algorithms books that describe ways to solve these problems, see "Additional Resources on Data Types" in Section 10.1.

Avoid additions and subtractions on numbers that have greatly different magnitudes
With a 32-bit floating-point variable, 1,000,000.00 + 0.1 probably produces an answer of 1,000,000.00 because 32 bits don't give you enough significant digits to encompass the range between 1,000,000 and 0.1. Likewise, 5,000,000.02 - 5,000,000.01 is probably 0.0.

Solutions? If you have to add a sequence of numbers that contains huge differences like this, sort the numbers first, and then add them starting with the smallest values. Likewise, if you need to sum an infinite series, start with the smallest term—essentially, sum the terms backwards. This doesn't eliminate round-off problems, but it minimizes them. Many algorithms books have suggestions for dealing with cases like this.

1 is equal to 2 for sufficiently large values of 1.
—*Anonymous*

Avoid equality comparisons   Floating-point numbers that should be equal are not always equal. The main problem is that two different paths to the same number don't always lead to the same number. For example, 0.1 added 10 times rarely equals 1.0. The following example shows two variables, *nominal* and *sum*, that should be equal but aren't.

Java Example of a Bad Comparison of Floating-Point Numbers

> The variable *nominal* is a 64-bit real.

> *sum* is 10*0.1. It should be 1.0.

> Here's the bad comparison.

```java
double nominal = 1.0;
double sum = 0.0;

for ( int i = 0; i < 10; i++ ) {
    sum += 0.1;
}

if ( nominal == sum ) {
    System.out.println( "Numbers are the same." );
}
else {
    System.out.println( "Numbers are different." );
}
```

As you can probably guess, the output from this program is

```
Numbers are different.
```

The line-by-line values of *sum* in the *for* loop look like this:

```
0.1
0.2
0.30000000000000004
0.4
0.5
0.6
0.7
0.7999999999999999
0.8999999999999999
0.9999999999999999
```

Thus, it's a good idea to find an alternative to using an equality comparison for floating-point numbers. One effective approach is to determine a range of accuracy that is acceptable and then use a boolean function to determine whether the values are close enough. Typically, you'd write an *Equals()* function that returns *true* if the values are close enough and *false* otherwise. In Java, such a function would look like this:

Cross-Reference This example is proof of the maxim that there's an exception to every rule. Variables in this realistic example have digits in their names. For the rule *against* using digits in variable names, see Section 11.7, "Kinds of Names to Avoid."

Java Example of a Routine to Compare Floating-Point Numbers
```java
final double ACCEPTABLE_DELTA = 0.00001;
boolean Equals( double Term1, double Term2 ) {
   if ( Math.abs( Term1 - Term2 ) < ACCEPTABLE_DELTA ) {
      return true;
   }
   else {
      return false;
   }
}
```

If the code in the "bad comparison of floating-point numbers" example were converted so that this routine could be used for comparisons, the new comparison would look like this:

```
if ( Equals( Nominal, Sum ) ) ...
```

The output from the program when it uses this test is

```
Numbers are the same.
```

Depending on the demands of your application, it might be inappropriate to use a hard-coded value for *ACCEPTABLE_DELTA*. You might need to compute *ACCEPTABLE_DELTA* based on the size of the two numbers being compared.

Anticipate rounding errors   Rounding-error problems are no different from the problem of numbers with greatly different magnitudes. The same issue is involved, and many of the same techniques help to solve rounding problems. In addition, here are common specific solutions to rounding problems:

■ Change to a variable type that has greater precision. If you're using single-precision floating point, change to double-precision floating point, and so on.

Cross-Reference Usually the performance impact of converting to BCD will be minimal. If you're concerned about the performance impact, see Section 25.6, "Summary of the Approach to Code Tuning."

■ Change to binary coded decimal (BCD) variables. The BCD scheme is typically slower and takes up more storage space, but it prevents many rounding errors. This is particularly valuable if the variables you're using represent dollars and cents or other quantities that must balance precisely.

■ Change from floating-point to integer variables. This is a roll-your-own approach to BCD variables. You will probably have to use 64-bit integers to get the precision you want. This technique requires you to keep track of the fractional part of your numbers yourself. Suppose you were originally keeping track of dollars using floating point with cents expressed as fractional parts of dollars. This is a normal way to handle dollars and cents. When you switch to integers, you have to keep track of cents using integers and of dollars using multiples of 100 cents. In other words, you multiply dollars by 100 and keep the cents in the 0-to-99 range of the variable. This might seem absurd at first glance, but it's an effective solution in terms of both speed and accuracy. You can make these manipulations easier by creating a *DollarsAndCents* class that hides the integer representation and supports the necessary numeric operations.

Check language and library support for specific data types   Some languages, including Visual Basic, have data types such as *Currency* that specifically support data that is sensitive to rounding errors. If your language has a built-in data type that provides such functionality, use it!

12.4 Characters and Strings

This section provides some tips for using strings. The first applies to strings in all languages.

Cross-Reference Issues for using magic characters and strings are similar to those for magic numbers discussed in Section 12.1, "Numbers in General."

Avoid magic characters and strings   Magic characters are literal characters (such as 'A') and magic strings are literal strings (such as "*Gigamatic Accounting Program*") that appear throughout a program. If you program in a language that supports the use of named constants, use them instead. Otherwise, use global variables. Several reasons for avoiding literal strings exist:

■ For commonly occurring strings like the name of your program, command names, report titles, and so on, you might at some point need to change the string's contents. For example, "*Gigamatic Accounting Program*" might change to "*New and Improved! Gigamatic Accounting Program*" for a later version.

■ International markets are becoming increasingly important, and it's easier to translate strings that are grouped in a string resource file than it is to translate to them *in situ* throughout a program.

■ String literals tend to take up a lot of space. They're used for menus, messages, help screens, entry forms, and so on. If you have too many, they grow beyond control and cause memory problems. String space isn't a concern in many environments, but in embedded systems programming and other applications in which storage space is at a premium, solutions to string-space problems are easier to implement if the strings are relatively independent of the source code.

■ Character and string literals are cryptic. Comments or named constants clarify your intentions. In the next example, the meaning of *0x1B* isn't clear. The use of the *ESCAPE* constant makes the meaning more obvious.

C++ Examples of Comparisons Using Strings

Bad! →
```
if ( input_char == 0x1B ) ...
```
Better! →
```
if ( input_char == ESCAPE ) ...
```

Watch for off-by-one errors Because substrings can be indexed much as arrays are, watch for off-by-one errors that read or write past the end of a string.

cc2e.com/1285

Know how your language and environment support Unicode In some languages such as Java, all strings are Unicode. In others such as C and C++, handling Unicode strings requires its own set of functions. Conversion between Unicode and other character sets is often required for communication with standard and third-party libraries. If some strings won't be in Unicode (for example, in C or C++), decide early on whether to use the Unicode character set at all. If you decide to use Unicode strings, decide where and when to use them.

Decide on an internationalization/localization strategy early in the lifetime of a program Issues related to internationalization and localization are major issues. Key considerations are deciding whether to store all strings in an external resource and whether to create separate builds for each language or to determine the specific language at run time.

cc2e.com/1292

If you know you only need to support a single alphabetic language, consider using an ISO 8859 character set For applications that need to support only a single alphabetic language (such as English) and that don't need to support multiple languages or an ideographic language (such as written Chinese), the ISO 8859 extended-ASCII-type standard makes a good alternative to Unicode.

If you need to support multiple languages, use Unicode   Unicode provides more comprehensive support for international character sets than ISO 8859 or other standards.

Decide on a consistent conversion strategy among string types   If you use multiple string types, one common approach that helps keep the string types distinct is to keep all strings in a single format within the program and convert the strings to other formats as close as possible to input and output operations.

Strings in C

C++'s standard template library string class has eliminated most of the traditional problems with strings in C. For those programmers working directly with C strings, here are some ways to avoid common pitfalls:

Be aware of the difference between string pointers and character arrays   The problem with string pointers and character arrays arises because of the way C handles strings. Be alert to the difference between them in two ways:

- Be suspicious of any expression containing a string that involves an equal sign. String operations in C are nearly always done with *strcmp()*, *strcpy()*, *strlen()*, and related routines. Equal signs often imply some kind of pointer error. In C, assignments do not copy string literals to a string variable. Suppose you have a statement like

  ```
  StringPtr = "Some Text String";
  ```

  In this case, *"Some Text String"* is a pointer to a literal text string and the assignment merely sets the pointer *StringPtr* to point to the text string. The assignment does not copy the contents to *StringPtr*.

- Use a naming convention to indicate whether the variables are arrays of characters or pointers to strings. One common convention is to use *ps* as a prefix to indicate a *pointer* to a *string* and *ach* as a prefix for an *array* of *characters*. Although they're not always wrong, you should regard expressions involving both *ps* and *ach* prefixes with suspicion.

Declare C-style strings to have length CONSTANT+1   In C and C++, off-by-one errors with C-style strings are common because it's easy to forget that a string of length *n* requires *n + 1* bytes of storage and to forget to leave room for the null terminator (the byte set to 0 at the end of the string). An effective way to avoid such problems is to use named constants to declare all strings. A key in this approach is that you use the named constant the same way every time. Declare the string to be length *CONSTANT+1*, and then use *CONSTANT* to refer to the length of a string in the rest of the code. Here's an example:

C Example of Good String Declarations

```
/* Declare the string to have length of "constant+1".
   Every other place in the program, "constant" rather
   than "constant+1" is used. */
```

The string is declared to be of length *NAME_LENGTH +1*. → `char name[ NAME_LENGTH + 1 ] = { 0 }; /* string of length NAME_LENGTH */`

```
...
/* Example 1: Set the string to all 'A's using the constant,
   NAME_LENGTH, as the number of 'A's that can be copied.
   Note that NAME_LENGTH rather than NAME_LENGTH + 1 is used. */
```

Operations on the string using *NAME_LENGTH* here... →
```
for ( i = 0; i < NAME_LENGTH; i++ )
   name[ i ] = 'A';
...
```

```
/* Example 2: Copy another string into the first string using
   the constant as the maximum length that can be copied. */
```

...and here. → `strncpy( name, some_other_name, NAME_LENGTH );`

If you don't have a convention to handle this, you'll sometimes declare the string to be of length *NAME_LENGTH* and have operations on it with *NAME_LENGTH-1*; at other times you'll declare the string to be of length *NAME_LENGTH+1* and have operations on it work with length *NAME_LENGTH*. Every time you use a string, you'll have to remember which way you declared it.

When you use strings the same way every time, you don't have to remember how you dealt with each string individually and you eliminate mistakes caused by forgetting the specifics of an individual string. Having a convention minimizes mental overload and programming errors.

Cross-Reference For more details on initializing data, see Section 10.3, "Guidelines for Initializing Variables."

Initialize strings to null to avoid endless strings C determines the end of a string by finding a null terminator, a byte set to 0 at the end of the string. No matter how long you think the string is, C doesn't find the end of the string until it finds a 0 byte. If you forget to put a null at the end of the string, your string operations might not act the way you expect them to.

You can avoid endless strings in two ways. First, initialize arrays of characters to *0* when you declare them:

C Example of a Good Declaration of a Character Array

```
char EventName[ MAX_NAME_LENGTH + 1 ] = { 0 };
```

Second, when you allocate strings dynamically, initialize them to *0* by using *calloc()* instead of *malloc()*. *calloc()* allocates memory and initializes it to *0*. *malloc()* allocates memory without initializing it, so you take your chances when you use memory allocated by *malloc()*.

Cross-Reference For more discussion of arrays, read Section 12.8, "Arrays," later in this chapter.

Use arrays of characters instead of pointers in C If memory isn't a constraint—and often it isn't—declare all your string variables as arrays of characters. This helps to avoid pointer problems, and the compiler will give you more warnings when you do something wrong.

Use **strncpy()** *instead of* **strcpy()** *to avoid endless strings* String routines in C come in safe versions and dangerous versions. The more dangerous routines such as *strcpy()* and *strcmp()* keep going until they run into a null terminator. Their safer companions, *strncpy()* and *strncmp()*, take a parameter for maximum length so that even if the strings go on forever, your function calls won't.

12.5 Boolean Variables

It's hard to misuse logical or boolean variables, and using them thoughtfully makes your program cleaner.

Cross-Reference For details on using comments to document your program, see Chapter 32, "Self-Documenting Code."

Use boolean variables to document your program Instead of merely testing a boolean expression, you can assign the expression to a variable that makes the implication of the test unmistakable. For example, in the next fragment, it's not clear whether the purpose of the *if* test is to check for completion, for an error condition, or for something else:

Cross-Reference For an example of using a boolean function to document your program, see "Making Complicated Expressions Simple" in Section 19.1.

Java Example of Boolean Test in Which the Purpose Is Unclear
```
if ( ( elementIndex < 0 ) || ( MAX_ELEMENTS < elementIndex ) ||
   ( elementIndex == lastElementIndex )
   ) {
   ...
}
```

In the next fragment, the use of boolean variables makes the purpose of the *if* test clearer:

Java Example of Boolean Test in Which the Purpose Is Clear
```
finished = ( ( elementIndex < 0 ) || ( MAX_ELEMENTS < elementIndex ) );
repeatedEntry = ( elementIndex == lastElementIndex );
if ( finished || repeatedEntry ) {
   ...
}
```

Use boolean variables to simplify complicated tests Often, when you have to code a complicated test, it takes several tries to get it right. When you later try to modify the test, it can be hard to understand what the test was doing in the first place. Logical variables can simplify the test. In the previous example, the program is really testing for two conditions: whether the routine is finished and whether it's working on a repeated entry. By creating the boolean variables *finished* and *repeatedEntry*, you make the *if* test simpler: easier to read, less error prone, and easier to modify.

Here's another example of a complicated test:

CODING HORROR

> **Visual Basic Example of a Complicated Test**
> ```
> If ( ( document.AtEndOfStream() ) And ( Not inputError ) ) And _
>    ( ( MIN_LINES <= lineCount ) And ( lineCount <= MAX_LINES ) ) And _
>    ( Not ErrorProcessing() ) Then
>    ' do something or other
>    ...
> End If
> ```

The test in the example is fairly complicated but not uncommonly so. It places a heavy mental burden on the reader. My guess is that you won't even try to understand the *if* test but will look at it and say, "I'll figure it out later if I really need to." Pay attention to that thought because that's exactly the same thing other people do when they read your code and it contains tests like this.

Here's a rewrite of the code with boolean variables added to simplify the test:

> **Visual Basic Example of a Simplified Test**
> ```
> allDataRead = ( document.AtEndOfStream() ) And ( Not inputError )
> legalLineCount = ( MIN_LINES <= lineCount ) And ( lineCount <= MAX_LINES )
> If ( allDataRead ) And ( legalLineCount ) And ( Not ErrorProcessing() ) Then
>     ' do something or other
>     ...
> End If
> ```

Here's the simplified test.

This second version is simpler. My guess is that you'll read the boolean expression in the *if* test without any difficulty.

Create your own boolean type, if necessary   Some languages, such as C++, Java, and Visual Basic have a predefined boolean type. Others, such as C, do not. In languages such as C, you can define your own boolean type. In C, you'd do it this way:

> **C Example of Defining the *BOOLEAN* Type Using a Simple *typedef***
> ```
> typedef int BOOLEAN;
> ```

Or you could do it this way, which provides the added benefit of defining *true* and *false* at the same time:

> **C Example of Defining the *Boolean* Type Using an Enum**
> ```
> enum Boolean {
>    True=1,
>    False=(!True)
> };
> ```

Declaring variables to be *BOOLEAN* rather than *int* makes their intended use more obvious and makes your program a little more self-documenting.

12.6 Enumerated Types

An enumerated type is a type of data that allows each member of a class of objects to be described in English. Enumerated types are available in C++ and Visual Basic and are generally used when you know all the possible values of a variable and want to express them in words. Here are some examples of enumerated types in Visual Basic:

Visual Basic Examples of Enumerated Types
```
Public Enum Color
   Color_Red
   Color_Green
   Color_Blue
End Enum

Public Enum Country
   Country_China
   Country_England
   Country_France
   Country_Germany
   Country_India
   Country_Japan
   Country_Usa
End Enum

Public Enum Output
   Output_Screen
   Output_Printer
   Output_File
End Enum
```

Enumerated types are a powerful alternative to shopworn schemes in which you explicitly say, "1 stands for red, 2 stands for green, 3 stands for blue...." This ability suggests several guidelines for using enumerated types:

Use enumerated types for readability   Instead of writing statements like

```
if chosenColor = 1
```

you can write more readable expressions like

```
if chosenColor = Color_Red
```

Anytime you see a numeric literal, ask whether it makes sense to replace it with an enumerated type.

Enumerated types are especially useful for defining routine parameters. Who knows what the parameters to this function call are?

> **C++ Examples of a Routine Call That Would be Better with Enumerated Types**
> ```
> int result = RetrievePayrollData( data, true, false, false, true );
> ```

In contrast, the parameters to this function call are more understandable:

> **C++ Examples of a Routine Call That Uses Enumerated Types for Readability**
> ```
> int result = RetrievePayrollData(
>     data,
>     EmploymentStatus_CurrentEmployee,
>     PayrollType_Salaried,
>     SavingsPlan_NoDeduction,
>     MedicalCoverage_IncludeDependents
> );
> ```

Use enumerated types for reliability   With a few languages (Ada in particular), an enumerated type lets the compiler perform more thorough type checking than it can with integer values and constants. With named constants, the compiler has no way of knowing that the only legal values are *Color_Red*, *Color_Green*, and *Color_Blue*. The compiler won't object to statements like *color = Country_England* or *country = Output_Printer*. If you use an enumerated type, declaring a variable as *Color*, the compiler will allow the variable to be assigned only the values *Color_Red*, *Color_Green*, and *Color_Blue*.

Use enumerated types for modifiability   Enumerated types make your code easy to modify. If you discover a flaw in your "1 stands for red, 2 stands for green, 3 stands for blue" scheme, you have to go through your code and change all the *1s*, *2s*, *3s*, and so on. If you use an enumerated type, you can continue adding elements to the list just by putting them into the type definition and recompiling.

Use enumerated types as an alternative to boolean variables   Often, a boolean variable isn't rich enough to express the meanings it needs to. For example, suppose you have a routine return *true* if it has successfully performed its task and *False* otherwise. Later you might find that you really have two kinds of *False*. The first kind means that the task failed and the effects are limited to the routine itself; the second kind means that the task failed and caused a fatal error that will need to be propagated to the rest of the program. In this case, an enumerated type with the values *Status_Success*, *Status_Warning*, and *Status_FatalError* would be more useful than a boolean with the values *true* and *false*. This scheme can easily be expanded to handle additional distinctions in the kinds of success or failure.

Check for invalid values   When you test an enumerated type in an *if* or *case* statement, check for invalid values. Use the *else* clause in a *case* statement to trap invalid values:

> **Good Visual Basic Example of Checking for Invalid Values in an Enumerated Type**
> ```
> Select Case screenColor
>    Case Color_Red
>       ...
>    Case Color_Blue
>       ...
>    Case Color_Green
>       ...
>    Case Else
>       DisplayInternalError( False, "Internal Error 752: Invalid color." )
> End Select
> ```

Here's the test for the invalid value. → (points to `Case Else`)

Define the first and last entries of an enumeration for use as loop limits   Defining the first and last elements in an enumeration to be *Color_First*, *Color_Last*, *Country_First*, *Country_Last*, and so on allows you to write a loop that loops through the elements of an enumeration. You set up the enumerated type by using explicit values, as shown here:

> **Visual Basic Example of Setting *First* and *Last* Values in an Enumerated Type**
> ```
> Public Enum Country
>    Country_First = 0
>    Country_China = 0
>    Country_England = 1
>    Country_France = 2
>    Country_Germany = 3
>    Country_India = 4
>    Country_Japan = 5
>    Country_Usa = 6
>    Country_Last = 6
> End Enum
> ```

Now the *Country_First* and *Country_Last* values can be used as loop limits:

> **Good Visual Basic Example of Looping Through Elements in an Enumeration**
> ```
> ' compute currency conversions from US currency to target currency
> Dim usaCurrencyConversionRate( Country_Last ) As Single
> Dim iCountry As Country
> For iCountry = Country_First To Country_Last
>    usaCurrencyConversionRate( iCountry ) = ConversionRate( Country_Usa, iCountry )
> Next
> ```

Reserve the first entry in the enumerated type as invalid   When you declare an enumerated type, reserve the first value as an invalid value. Many compilers assign the first element in an enumerated type to the value *0*. Declaring the element that's mapped to *0* to be invalid helps to catch variables that were not properly initialized because they are more likely to be *0* than any other invalid value.

Here's how the *Country* declaration would look with that approach:

Visual Basic Example of Declaring the First Value in an Enumeration to Be Invalid

```
Public Enum Country
   Country_InvalidFirst = 0
   Country_First = 1
   Country_China = 1
   Country_England = 2
   Country_France = 3
   Country_Germany = 4
   Country_India = 5
   Country_Japan = 6
   Country_Usa = 7
   Country_Last = 7
End Enum
```

Define precisely how* First *and* Last *elements are to be used in the project coding standard, and use them consistently Using *InvalidFirst*, *First*, and *Last* elements in enumerations can make array declarations and loops more readable. But it has the potential to create confusion about whether the valid entries in the enumeration begin at *0* or *1* and whether the first and last elements of the enumeration are valid. If this technique is used, the project's coding standard should require that *InvalidFirst*, *First*, and *Last* elements be used consistently in all enumerations to reduce errors.

Beware of pitfalls of assigning explicit values to elements of an enumeration Some languages allow you to assign specific values to elements within an enumeration, as shown in this C++ example:

C++ Example of Explicitly Assigning Values to an Enumeration

```
enum Color {
   Color_InvalidFirst = 0,
   Color_First = 1,
   Color_Red = 1,
   Color_Green = 2,
   Color_Blue = 4,
   Color_Black = 8,
   Color_Last = 8
};
```

In this example, if you declared a loop index of type *Color* and attempted to loop through *Color*s, you would loop through the invalid values of 3, 5, 6, and 7 as well as the valid values of 1, 2, 4, and 8.

If Your Language Doesn't Have Enumerated Types

If your language doesn't have enumerated types, you can simulate them with global variables or classes. For example, you could use these declarations in Java:

Cross-Reference At the time I'm writing this, Java does not support enumerated types. By the time you read this, it probably will. This is a good example of the "rolling wave of technology" discussed in Section 4.3, "Your Location on the Technology Wave."

Java Example of Simulating Enumerated Types

```java
// set up Country enumerated type
class Country {
    private Country() {}
    public static final Country China = new Country();
    public static final Country England = new Country();
    public static final Country France = new Country();
    public static final Country Germany = new Country();
    public static final Country India = new Country();
    public static final Country Japan = new Country();
}

// set up Output enumerated type
class Output {
    private Output() {}
    public static final Output Screen = new Output();
    public static final Output Printer = new Output();
    public static final Output File = new Output();
}
```

These enumerated types make your program more readable because you can use the public class members such as *Country.England* and *Output.Screen* instead of named constants. This particular method of creating enumerated types is also typesafe; because each type is declared as a class, the compiler will check for invalid assignments such as *Output output = Country.England* (Bloch 2001).

In languages that don't support classes, you can achieve the same basic effect through disciplined use of global variables for each of the elements of the enumeration.

12.7 Named Constants

A named constant is like a variable except that you can't change the constant's value once you've assigned it. Named constants enable you to refer to fixed quantities, such as the maximum number of employees, by a name rather than a number—*MAXIMUM_EMPLOYEES* rather than *1000*, for instance.

Using a named constant is a way of "parameterizing" your program—putting an aspect of your program that might change into a parameter that you can change in one place rather than having to make changes throughout the program. If you have ever declared an array to be as big as you think it will ever need to be and then run out of space because it wasn't big enough, you can appreciate the value of named constants.

When an array size changes, you change only the definition of the constant you used to declare the array. This "single-point control" goes a long way toward making software truly "soft": easy to work with and change.

Use named constants in data declarations Using named constants helps program readability and maintainability in data declarations and in statements that need to know the size of the data they are working with. In the following example, you use *LOCAL_NUMBER_LENGTH* to describe the length of employee phone numbers rather than the literal 7.

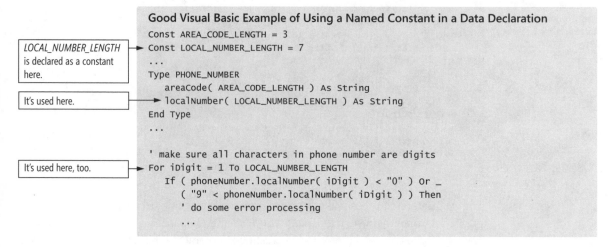

Good Visual Basic Example of Using a Named Constant in a Data Declaration

LOCAL_NUMBER_LENGTH is declared as a constant here.

It's used here.

It's used here, too.

```
Const AREA_CODE_LENGTH = 3
Const LOCAL_NUMBER_LENGTH = 7
...
Type PHONE_NUMBER
    areaCode( AREA_CODE_LENGTH ) As String
    localNumber( LOCAL_NUMBER_LENGTH ) As String
End Type
...

' make sure all characters in phone number are digits
For iDigit = 1 To LOCAL_NUMBER_LENGTH
    If ( phoneNumber.localNumber( iDigit ) < "0" ) Or _
        ( "9" < phoneNumber.localNumber( iDigit ) ) Then
        ' do some error processing
        ...
```

This is a simple example, but you can probably imagine a program in which the information about the phone-number length is needed in many places.

At the time you create the program, the employees all live in one country, so you need only seven digits for their phone numbers. As the company expands and branches are established in different countries, you'll need longer phone numbers. If you have parameterized, you can make the change in only one place: in the definition of the named constant *LOCAL_NUMBER_LENGTH*.

Further Reading For more details on the value of single-point control, see pages 57–60 of *Software Conflict* (Glass 1991).

As you might expect, the use of named constants has been shown to greatly aid program maintenance. As a general rule, any technique that centralizes control over things that might change is a good technique for reducing maintenance efforts (Glass 1991).

Avoid literals, even "safe" ones In the following loop, what do you think the *12* represents?

Visual Basic Example of Unclear Code

```
For i = 1 To 12
    profit( i ) = revenue( i ) - expense( i )
Next
```

Because of the specific nature of the code, it appears that the code is probably looping through the 12 months in a year. But are you *sure*? Would you bet your Monty Python collection on it?

In this case, you don't need to use a named constant to support future flexibility: it's not very likely that the number of months in a year will change anytime soon. But if the way the code is written leaves any shadow of a doubt about its purpose, clarify it with a well-named constant, like this:

Visual Basic Example of Clearer Code

```
For i = 1 To NUM_MONTHS_IN_YEAR
    profit( i ) = revenue( i ) - expense( i )
Next
```

This is better, but, to complete the example, the loop index should also be named something more informative:

Visual Basic Example of Even Clearer Code

```
For month = 1 To NUM_MONTHS_IN_YEAR
    profit( month ) = revenue( month ) - expense( month )
Next
```

This example seems quite good, but we can push it even one step further by using an enumerated type:

Visual Basic Example of Very Clear Code

```
For month = Month_January To Month_December
    profit( month ) = revenue( month ) - expense( month )
Next
```

With this final example, there can be no doubt about the purpose of the loop. Even if you think a literal is safe, use named constants instead. Be a fanatic about rooting out literals in your code. Use a text editor to search for 2, 3, 4, 5, 6, 7, 8, and 9 to make sure you haven't used them accidentally.

Cross-Reference For details on simulating enumerated types, see "If Your Language Doesn't Have Enumerated Types" in the previous section, Section 12.6.

Simulate named constants with appropriately scoped variables or classes   If your language doesn't support named constants, you can create your own. By using an approach similar to the approach suggested in the earlier Java example in which enumerated types were simulated, you can gain many of the advantages of named constants. Typical scoping rules apply: prefer local scope, class scope, and global scope in that order.

Use named constants consistently   It's dangerous to use a named constant in one place and a literal in another to represent the same entity. Some programming practices beg for errors; this one is like calling an 800 number and having errors delivered to your door. If the value of the named constant needs to be changed, you'll change it and think you've made all the necessary changes. You'll overlook the hard-coded literals, your program will develop mysterious defects, and fixing them will be a lot harder than picking up the phone and yelling for help.

12.8 Arrays

Arrays are the simplest and most common type of structured data. In some languages, arrays are the only type of structured data. An array contains a group of items that are all of the same type and that are directly accessed through the use of an array index. Here are some tips on using arrays.

KEY POINT

Make sure that all array indexes are within the bounds of the array   In one way or another, all problems with arrays are caused by the fact that array elements can be accessed randomly. The most common problem arises when a program tries to access an array element that's out of bounds. In some languages, this produces an error; in others, it simply produces bizarre and unexpected results.

Consider using containers instead of arrays, or think of arrays as sequential structures   Some of the brightest people in computer science have suggested that arrays never be accessed randomly, but only sequentially (Mills and Linger 1986). Their argument is that random accesses in arrays are similar to random *goto*s in a program: such accesses tend to be undisciplined, error prone, and hard to prove correct. They suggest using sets, stacks, and queues, whose elements are accessed sequentially, rather than using arrays.

HARD DATA

In a small experiment, Mills and Linger found that designs created this way resulted in fewer variables and fewer variable references. The designs were relatively efficient and led to highly reliable software.

Consider using container classes that you can access sequentially—sets, stacks, queues, and so on—as alternatives before you automatically choose an array.

Cross-Reference Issues in using arrays and loops are similar and related. For details on loops, see Chapter 16, "Controlling Loops."

Check the end points of arrays   Just as it's helpful to think through the end points in a loop structure, you can catch a lot of errors by checking the end points of arrays. Ask yourself whether the code correctly accesses the first element of the array or mistakenly accesses the element before or after the first element. What about the last element? Will the code make an off-by-one error? Finally, ask yourself whether the code correctly accesses the middle elements of the array.

If an array is multidimensional, make sure its subscripts are used in the correct order   It's easy to say *Array[i][j]* when you mean *Array[j][i]*, so take the time to double-check that the indexes are in the right order. Consider using more meaningful names than *i* and *j* in cases in which their roles aren't immediately clear.

Watch out for index cross-talk   If you're using nested loops, it's easy to write *Array[j]* when you mean *Array[i]*. Switching loop indexes is called "index cross-talk." Check for this problem. Better yet, use more meaningful index names than *i* and *j* to make it harder to commit cross-talk mistakes in the first place.

In C, use the* ARRAY_LENGTH() *macro to work with arrays   You can build extra flexibility into your work with arrays by defining an *ARRAY_LENGTH()* macro that looks like this:

C Example of Defining an *ARRAY_LENGTH()* Macro

```
#define ARRAY_LENGTH( x )   (sizeof(x)/sizeof(x[0]))
```

When you use operations on an array, instead of using a named constant for the upper bound of the array size, use the *ARRAY_LENGTH()* macro. Here's an example:

C Example of Using the *ARRAY_LENGTH()* Macro for Array Operations

```
ConsistencyRatios[] =
    { 0.0, 0.0, 0.58, 0.90, 1.12,
    1.24, 1.32, 1.41, 1.45, 1.49,
    1.51, 1.48, 1.56, 1.57, 1.59 };
    ...
```

Here's where the macro is used. → `for ( ratioIdx = 0; ratioIdx < ARRAY_LENGTH( ConsistencyRatios ); ratioIdx++ );`

```
    ...
```

This technique is particularly useful for dimensionless arrays such as the one in this example. If you add or subtract entries, you don't have to remember to change a named constant that describes the array's size. Of course, the technique works with dimensioned arrays too, but if you use this approach, you don't always need to set up an extra named constant for the array definition.

12.9 Creating Your Own Types (Type Aliasing)

KEY POINT

Programmer-defined data types are one of the most powerful capabilities a language can give you to clarify your understanding of a program. They protect your program against unforeseen changes and make it easier to read—all without requiring you to design, construct, or test new classes. If you're using C, C++, or another language that allows user-defined types, take advantage of them!

Cross-Reference In many cases, it's better to create a class than to create a simple data type. For details, see Chapter 6, "Working Classes."

To appreciate the power of type creation, suppose you're writing a program to convert coordinates in an *x*, *y*, *z* system to latitude, longitude, and elevation. You think that double-precision floating-point numbers might be needed but would prefer to write a program with single-precision floating-point numbers until you're absolutely sure. You can create a new type specifically for coordinates by using a *typedef* statement in

C or C++ or the equivalent in another language. Here's how you'd set up the type definition in C++:

C++ Example of Creating a Type

```
typedef float Coordinate;  // for coordinate variables
```

This type definition declares a new type, *Coordinate*, that's functionally the same as the type *float*. To use the new type, you declare variables with it just as you would with a predefined type such as *float*. Here's an example:

C++ Example of Using the Type You've Created

```
Routine1( ... ) {
   Coordinate latitude;     // latitude in degrees
   Coordinate longitude;    // longitude in degrees
   Coordinate elevation;    // elevation in meters from earth center
   ...
}
...

Routine2( ... ) {
   Coordinate x;    // x coordinate in meters
   Coordinate y;    // y coordinate in meters
   Coordinate z;    // z coordinate in meters
   ...
}
```

In this code, the variables *latitude*, *longitude*, *elevation*, *x*, *y*, and *z* are all declared to be of type *Coordinate*.

Now suppose that the program changes and you find that you need to use double-precision variables for coordinates after all. Because you defined a type specifically for coordinate data, all you have to change is the type definition. And you have to change it in only one place: in the *typedef* statement. Here's the changed type definition:

C++ Example of Changed Type Definition

> The original *float* has changed to *double*.

```
typedef double Coordinate;  // for coordinate variables
```

Here's a second example—this one in Pascal. Suppose you're creating a payroll system in which employee names are a maximum of 30 characters long. Your users have told you that no one *ever* has a name longer than 30 characters. Do you hard-code the number *30* throughout your program? If you do, you trust your users a lot more than I trust mine! A better approach is to define a type for employee names:

Pascal Example of Creating a Type for Employee Names

```
Type
   employeeName = array[ 1..30 ] of char;
```

When a string or an array is involved, it's usually wise to define a named constant that indicates the length of the string or array and then use the named constant in the type definition. You'll find many places in your program in which to use the constant—this is just the first place in which you'll use it. Here's how it looks:

Pascal Example of Better Type Creation

Here's the declaration of the named constant.

Here's where the named constant is used.

```
Const
   NAME_LENGTH = 30;
   ...
Type
   employeeName = array[ 1..NAME_LENGTH ] of char;
```

A more powerful example would combine the idea of creating your own types with the idea of information hiding. In some cases, the information you want to hide is information about the type of the data.

The coordinates example in C++ is about halfway to information hiding. If you always use *Coordinate* rather than *float* or *double*, you effectively hide the type of the data. In C++, this is about all the information hiding the language does for you. For the rest, you or subsequent users of your code have to have the discipline not to look up the definition of *Coordinate*. C++ gives you figurative, rather than literal, information-hiding ability.

Other languages, such as Ada, go a step further and support literal information hiding. Here's how the *Coordinate* code fragment would look in an Ada package that declares it:

Ada Example of Hiding Details of a Type Inside a Package

This statement declares *Coordinate* as private to the package.

```
package Transformation is
   type Coordinate is private;
   ...
```

Here's how *Coordinate* looks in another package, one that uses it:

Ada Example of Using a Type from Another Package

```
with Transformation;
...
procedure Routine1(...) ...
   latitude:  Coordinate;
   longitude: Coordinate;
begin
   -- statements using latitude and longitude
   ...
end Routine1;
```

Notice that the *Coordinate* type is declared as *private* in the package specification. That means that the only part of the program that knows the definition of the *Coordinate* type is the private part of the *Transformation* package. In a development environment with a group of programmers, you could distribute only the package specification, which would make it harder for a programmer working on another package to look up the underlying type of *Coordinate*. The information would be literally hidden. Languages like C++ that require you to distribute the definition of *Coordinate* in header files undermine true information hiding.

These examples have illustrated several reasons to create your own types:

- **To make modifications easier**   It's little work to create a new type, and it gives you a lot of flexibility.

- **To avoid excessive information distribution**   Hard typing spreads data-typing details around your program instead of centralizing them in one place. This is an example of the information-hiding principle of centralization discussed in Section 6.2.

- **To increase reliability**   In Ada, you can define types such as *type Age is range 0..99*. The compiler then generates run-time checks to verify that any variable of type *Age* is always within the range *0..99*.

- **To make up for language weaknesses**   If your language doesn't have the predefined type you want, you can create it yourself. For example, C doesn't have a boolean or logical type. This deficiency is easy to compensate for by creating the type yourself:

```
typedef int Boolean;
```

Why Are the Examples of Creating Your Own Types in Pascal and Ada?

Pascal and Ada have gone the way of the stegosaurus and, in general, the languages that have replaced them are more usable. In the area of simple type definitions, however, I think C++, Java, and Visual Basic represent a case of three steps forward and one step back. An Ada declaration like

```
currentTemperature: INTEGER range 0..212;
```

contains important semantic information that a statement like

```
int temperature;
```

does not. Going a step further, a type declaration like

```
type Temperature is range 0..212;
...
currentTemperature: Temperature;
```

allows the compiler to ensure that *currentTemperature* is assigned only to other variables with the *Temperature* type, and very little extra coding is required to provide that extra safety margin.

Of course, a programmer could create a *Temperature* class to enforce the same semantics that were enforced automatically by the Ada language, but the step from creating a simple data type in one line of code to creating a class is a big step. In many situations, a programmer would create the simple type but would not step up to the additional effort of creating a class.

Guidelines for Creating Your Own Types

Cross-Reference In each case, consider whether creating a class might work better than a simple data type. For details, see Chapter 6, "Working Classes."

Keep these guidelines in mind as you create your own "user-defined" types:

Create types with functionally oriented names   Avoid type names that refer to the kind of computer data underlying the type. Use type names that refer to the parts of the real-world problem that the new type represents. In the previous examples, the definitions created well-named types for coordinates and names—real-world entities. Similarly, you could create types for currency, payment codes, ages, and so on—aspects of real-world problems.

Be wary of creating type names that refer to predefined types. Type names like *BigInteger* or *LongString* refer to computer data rather than the real-world problem. The big advantage of creating your own type is that it provides a layer of insulation between your program and the implementation language. Type names that refer to the underlying programming-language types poke holes in that insulation. They don't give you much advantage over using a predefined type. Problem-oriented names, on the other hand, buy you easy modifiability and data declarations that are self-documenting.

Avoid predefined types   If there is any possibility that a type might change, avoid using predefined types anywhere but in *typedef* or *type* definitions. It's easy to create new types that are functionally oriented, and it's hard to change data in a program that uses hardwired types. Moreover, use of functionally oriented type declarations partially documents the variables declared with them. A declaration like *Coordinate x* tells you a lot more about *x* than a declaration like *float x*. Use your own types as much as you can.

Don't redefine a predefined type   Changing the definition of a standard type can create confusion. For example, if your language has a predefined type *Integer*, don't create your own type called *Integer*. Readers of your code might forget that you've redefined the type and assume that the *Integer* they see is the *Integer* they're used to seeing.

Define substitute types for portability   In contrast to the advice that you not change the definition of a standard type, you might want to define substitutes for the standard types so that on different hardware platforms you can make the variables represent exactly the same entities. For example, you can define a type *INT32* and use it instead of *int*, or a type *LONG64* instead of *long*. Originally, the only difference between the two types would be their capitalization. But when you moved the program to a new hardware platform, you could redefine the capitalized versions so that they could match the data types on the original hardware.

Be sure not to define types that are easily mistaken for predefined types. It would be possible to define *INT* rather than *INT32*, but you're better off creating a clean distinction between types you define and types provided by the language.

***Consider creating a class rather than using a* typedef**   Simple *typedefs* can go a long way toward hiding information about a variable's underlying type. In some cases, however, you might want the additional flexibility and control you'll achieve by creating a class. For details, see Chapter 6, "Working Classes."

cc2e.com/1206

Cross-Reference For a checklist that applies to general data issues rather than to issues with specific types of data, see the checklist on page 257 in Chapter 10, "General Issues in Using Variables." For a checklist of considerations in naming varieties, see the checklist on page 288 in Chapter 11, "The Power of Variable Names."

CHECKLIST: Fundamental Data

Numbers in General

❑ Does the code avoid magic numbers?

❑ Does the code anticipate divide-by-zero errors?

❑ Are type conversions obvious?

❑ If variables with two different types are used in the same expression, will the expression be evaluated as you intend it to be?

❑ Does the code avoid mixed-type comparisons?

❑ Does the program compile with no warnings?

Integers

❑ Do expressions that use integer division work the way they're meant to?

❑ Do integer expressions avoid integer-overflow problems?

Floating-Point Numbers

❑ Does the code avoid additions and subtractions on numbers with greatly different magnitudes?

❑ Does the code systematically prevent rounding errors?

❑ Does the code avoid comparing floating-point numbers for equality?

Characters and Strings

❑ Does the code avoid magic characters and strings?

❑ Are references to strings free of off-by-one errors?

❑ Does C code treat string pointers and character arrays differently?

❑ Does C code follow the convention of declaring strings to be length *CONSTANT+1*?

❑ Does C code use arrays of characters rather than pointers, when appropriate?

❑ Does C code initialize strings to *NULLs* to avoid endless strings?

❑ Does C code use *strncpy()* rather than *strcpy()*? And *strncat()* and *strncmp()*?

Boolean Variables

❑ Does the program use additional boolean variables to document conditional tests?

❑ Does the program use additional boolean variables to simplify conditional tests?

Enumerated Types

❑ Does the program use enumerated types instead of named constants for their improved readability, reliability, and modifiability?

❑ Does the program use enumerated types instead of boolean variables when a variable's use cannot be completely captured with *true* and *false*?

❑ Do tests using enumerated types test for invalid values?

❑ Is the first entry in an enumerated type reserved for "invalid"?

Named Constants

❑ Does the program use named constants for data declarations and loop limits rather than magic numbers?

❑ Have named constants been used consistently—not used as named constants in some places and as literals in others?

Arrays

❑ Are all array indexes within the bounds of the array?

❑ Are array references free of off-by-one errors?

❑ Are all subscripts on multidimensional arrays in the correct order?

❑ In nested loops, is the correct variable used as the array subscript, avoiding loop-index cross-talk?

> **Creating Types**
>
> ❑ Does the program use a different type for each kind of data that might change?
>
> ❑ Are type names oriented toward the real-world entities the types represent rather than toward programming-language types?
>
> ❑ Are the type names descriptive enough to help document data declarations?
>
> ❑ Have you avoided redefining predefined types?
>
> ❑ Have you considered creating a new class rather than simply redefining a type?

Key Points

- Working with specific data types means remembering many individual rules for each type. Use this chapter's checklist to make sure that you've considered the common problems.

- Creating your own types makes your programs easier to modify and more self-documenting, if your language supports that capability.

- When you create a simple type using *typedef* or its equivalent, consider whether you should be creating a new class instead.

Chapter 13
Unusual Data Types

cc2e.com/1378

Contents

- 13.1 Structures: page 319
- 13.2 Pointers: page 323
- 13.3 Global Data: page 335

Related Topics

- Fundamental data types: Chapter 12
- Defensive programming: Chapter 8
- Unusual control structures: Chapter 17
- Complexity in software development: Section 5.2

Some languages support exotic kinds of data in addition to the data types discussed in Chapter 12, "Fundamental Data Types." Section 13.1 describes when you might still use structures rather than classes in some circumstances. Section 13.2 describes the ins and outs of using pointers. If you've ever encountered problems associated with using global data, Section 13.3 explains how to avoid such difficulties. If you think the data types described in this chapter are not the types you normally read about in modern object-oriented programming books, you're right. That's why the chapter is called "*Unusual* Data Types."

13.1 Structures

The term "structure" refers to data that's built up from other types. Because arrays are a special case, they are treated separately in Chapter 12. This section deals with user-created structured data—*struct*s in C and C++ and *Structures* in Microsoft Visual Basic. In Java and C++, classes also sometimes perform as structures (when the class consists entirely of public data members with no public routines).

You'll generally want to create classes rather than structures so that you can take advantage of the privacy and functionality offered by classes in addition to the public data supported by structures. But sometimes directly manipulating blocks of data can be useful, so here are some reasons for using structures:

Use structures to clarify data relationships Structures bundle groups of related items together. Sometimes the hardest part of figuring out a program is figuring out which data goes with which other data. It's like going to a small town and asking who's related to whom. You come to find out that everybody's kind of related to everybody else, but not really, and you never get a good answer.

If the data has been carefully structured, figuring out what goes with what is much easier. Here's an example of data that hasn't been structured:

> **Visual Basic Example of Misleading, Unstructured Variables**
> ```
> name = inputName
> address = inputAddress
> phone = inputPhone
> title = inputTitle
> department = inputDepartment
> bonus = inputBonus
> ```

Because this data is unstructured, it looks as if all the assignment statements belong together. Actually, *name*, *address*, and *phone* are variables associated with individual employees, and *title*, *department*, and *bonus* are variables associated with a supervisor. The code fragment provides no hint that there are two kinds of data at work. In the code fragment below, the use of structures makes the relationships clearer:

> **Visual Basic Example of More Informative, Structured Variables**
> ```
> employee.name = inputName
> employee.address = inputAddress
> employee.phone = inputPhone
>
> supervisor.title = inputTitle
> supervisor.department = inputDepartment
> supervisor.bonus = inputBonus
> ```

In the code that uses structured variables, it's clear that some of the data is associated with an employee, other data with a supervisor.

Use structures to simplify operations on blocks of data You can combine related elements into a structure and perform operations on the structure. It's easier to operate on the structure than to perform the same operation on each of the elements. It's also more reliable, and it takes fewer lines of code.

Suppose you have a group of data items that belong together—for instance, data about an employee in a personnel database. If the data isn't combined into a structure, merely copying the group of data can involve a lot of statements. Here's an example in Visual Basic:

Visual Basic Example of Copying a Group of Data Items Clumsily

```
newName = oldName
newAddress = oldAddress
newPhone = oldPhone
newSsn = oldSsn
newGender = oldGender
newSalary = oldSalary
```

Every time you want to transfer information about an employee, you have to have this whole group of statements. If you ever add a new piece of employee information—for example, *numWithholdings*—you have to find every place at which you have a block of assignments and add an assignment for *newNumWithholdings = oldNumWithholdings*.

Imagine how horrible swapping data between two employees would be. You don't have to use your imagination—here it is:

CODING HORROR

Visual Basic Example of Swapping Two Groups of Data the Hard Way

```
' swap new and old employee data
previousOldName = oldName
previousOldAddress = oldAddress
previousOldPhone = oldPhone
previousOldSsn = oldSsn
previousOldGender = oldGender
previousOldSalary = oldSalary

oldName = newName
oldAddress = newAddress
oldPhone = newPhone
oldSsn = newSsn
oldGender = newGender
oldSalary = newSalary

newName = previousOldName
newAddress = previousOldAddress
newPhone = previousOldPhone
newSsn = previousOldSsn
newGender = previousOldGender
newSalary = previousOldSalary
```

An easier way to approach the problem is to declare a structured variable:

Visual Basic Example of Declaring Structures

```
Structure Employee
    name As String
    address As String
    phone As String
    ssn As String
    gender As String
    salary As long
```

```
End Structure
Dim newEmployee As Employee
Dim oldEmployee As Employee
Dim previousOldEmployee As Employee
```

Now you can switch all the elements in the old and new employee structures with three statements:

Visual Basic Example of an Easier Way to Swap Two Groups of Data

```
previousOldEmployee = oldEmployee
oldEmployee = newEmployee
newEmployee = previousOldEmployee
```

If you want to add a field such as *numWithholdings*, you simply add it to the *Structure* declaration. Neither the three statements above nor any similar statements throughout the program need to be modified. C++ and other languages have similar capabilities.

Cross-Reference For details on how much data to share between routines, see "Keep Coupling Loose" in Section 5.3.

Use structures to simplify parameter lists   You can simplify routine parameter lists by using structured variables. The technique is similar to the one just shown. Rather than passing each of the elements needed individually, you can group related elements into a structure and pass the whole enchilada as a group structure. Here's an example of the hard way to pass a group of related parameters:

Visual Basic Example of a Clumsy Routine Call Without a Structure

```
HardWayRoutine( name, address, phone, ssn, gender, salary )
```

And this is an example of the easy way to call a routine by using a structured variable that contains the elements of the first parameter list:

Visual Basic Example of an Elegant Routine Call with a Structure

```
EasyWayRoutine( employee )
```

If you want to add *numWithholdings* to the first kind of call, you have to wade through your code and change every call to *HardWayRoutine()*. If you add a *numWithholdings* element to *Employee*, you don't have to change the parameters to *EasyWayRoutine()* at all.

Cross-Reference For details on the hazards of passing too much data, see "Keep Coupling Loose" in Section 5.3.

You can carry this technique to extremes, putting all the variables in your program into one big, juicy variable and then passing it everywhere. Careful programmers avoid bundling data any more than is logically necessary. Furthermore, careful programmers avoid passing a structure as a parameter when only one or two fields from the structure are needed—they pass the specific fields needed instead. This is an aspect of information hiding: some information is hidden *in* routines, and some is hidden *from* routines. Information is passed around on a need-to-know basis.

Use structures to reduce maintenance   Because you group related data when you use structures, changing a structure requires fewer changes throughout a program. This is especially true in sections of code that aren't logically related to the change in the structure. Since changes tend to produce errors, fewer changes mean fewer errors. If your *Employee* structure has a *title* field and you decide to delete it, you don't need to change any of the parameter lists or assignment statements that use the whole structure. Of course, you have to change any code that deals specifically with employee titles, but that is conceptually related to deleting the *title* field and is hard to overlook.

The big advantage of structured data is found in sections of code that bear no logical relation to the *title* field. Sometimes programs have statements that refer conceptually to a collection of data rather than to individual components. In such cases, individual components, such as the *title* field, are referenced merely because they are part of the collection. Such sections of code don't have any logical reason to work with the *title* field specifically, and those sections are easy to overlook when you change *title*. If you use a structure, it's all right to overlook such sections because the code refers to the collection of related data rather than to each component individually.

13.2 Pointers

KEY POINT

Pointer usage is one of the most error-prone areas of modern programming, to such an extent that modern languages like Java, C#, and Visual Basic don't provide a pointer data type. Using pointers is inherently complicated, and using them correctly requires that you have an excellent understanding of your compiler's memory-management scheme. Many common security problems, especially buffer overruns, can be traced back to erroneous use of pointers (Howard and LeBlanc 2003).

Even if your language doesn't require you to use pointers, a good understanding of pointers will help your understanding of how your programming language works. A liberal dose of defensive programming practices will help even further.

Paradigm for Understanding Pointers

Conceptually, every pointer consists of two parts: a location in memory and a knowledge of how to interpret the contents of that location.

Location in Memory

The location in memory is an address, often expressed in hexadecimal notation. An address on a 32-bit processor would be a 32-bit value, such as *0x0001EA40*. The pointer itself contains only this address. To use the data the pointer points to, you have to go to that address and interpret the contents of memory at that location. If you were to look at the memory in that location, it would be just a collection of bits. It has to be interpreted to be meaningful.

Knowledge of How to Interpret the Contents

The knowledge of how to interpret the contents of a location in memory is provided by the base type of the pointer. If a pointer points to an integer, what that really means is that the compiler interprets the memory location given by the pointer as an integer. Of course, you can have an integer pointer, a string pointer, and a floating-point pointer all pointing at the same memory location. But only one of the pointers interprets the contents at that location correctly.

In thinking about pointers, it's helpful to remember that memory doesn't have any inherent interpretation associated with it. It is only through use of a specific type of pointer that the bits in a particular location are interpreted as meaningful data.

Figure 13-1 shows several views of the same location in memory, interpreted in several different ways.

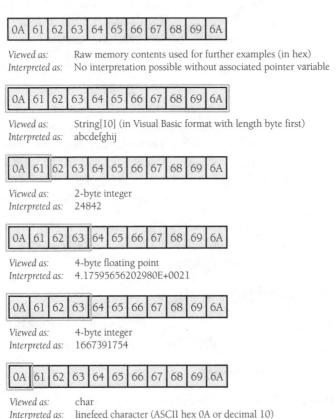

| 0A | 61 | 62 | 63 | 64 | 65 | 66 | 67 | 68 | 69 | 6A |

Viewed as: Raw memory contents used for further examples (in hex)
Interpreted as: No interpretation possible without associated pointer variable

| 0A | 61 | 62 | 63 | 64 | 65 | 66 | 67 | 68 | 69 | 6A |

Viewed as: String[10] (in Visual Basic format with length byte first)
Interpreted as: abcdefghij

| 0A | 61 | 62 | 63 | 64 | 65 | 66 | 67 | 68 | 69 | 6A |

Viewed as: 2-byte integer
Interpreted as: 24842

| 0A | 61 | 62 | 63 | 64 | 65 | 66 | 67 | 68 | 69 | 6A |

Viewed as: 4-byte floating point
Interpreted as: 4.17595656202980E+0021

| 0A | 61 | 62 | 63 | 64 | 65 | 66 | 67 | 68 | 69 | 6A |

Viewed as: 4-byte integer
Interpreted as: 1667391754

| 0A | 61 | 62 | 63 | 64 | 65 | 66 | 67 | 68 | 69 | 6A |

Viewed as: char
Interpreted as: linefeed character (ASCII hex 0A or decimal 10)

Figure 13-1   The amount of memory used by each data type is shown by double lines.

In each of the cases in Figure 13-1, the pointer points to the location containing the hex value *0x0A*. The number of bytes used beyond the *0A* depends on how the memory is interpreted. The way memory contents are used also depends on how the memory is interpreted. (It also depends on what processor you're using, so keep that in mind if you try to duplicate these results on your Desktop Cray.) The same raw memory contents can be interpreted as a string, an integer, a floating point, or anything else—it all depends on the base type of the pointer that points to the memory.

General Tips on Pointers

With many types of defects, locating the error is the easiest part of dealing with the error and correcting it is the hard part. Pointer errors are different. A pointer error is usually the result of a pointer's pointing somewhere it shouldn't. When you assign a value to a bad pointer variable, you write data into an area of memory you shouldn't. This is called "memory corruption." Sometimes memory corruption produces horrible, fiery system crashes; sometimes it alters the results of a calculation in another part of the program; sometimes it causes your program to skip routines unpredictably; and sometimes it doesn't do anything at all. In the last case, the pointer error is a ticking time bomb, waiting to ruin your program five minutes before you show it to your most important customer. Symptoms of pointer errors tend to be unrelated to causes of pointer errors. Thus, most of the work in correcting a pointer error is locating the cause.

KEY POINT

Working with pointers successfully requires a two-pronged strategy. First, avoid installing pointer errors in the first place. Pointer errors are so difficult to find that extra preventive measures are justified. Second, detect pointer errors as soon after they are coded as possible. Symptoms of pointer errors are so erratic that extra measures to make the symptoms more predictable are justified. Here's how to achieve these key goals:

Isolate pointer operations in routines or classes   Suppose you use a linked list in several places in a program. Rather than traversing the list manually each place it's used, write access routines such as *NextLink()*, *PreviousLink()*, *InsertLink()*, and *DeleteLink()*. By minimizing the number of places in which pointers are accessed, you minimize the possibility of making careless mistakes that spread throughout your program and take forever to find. Because the code is then relatively independent of data-implementation details, you also improve the chance that you can reuse it in other programs. Writing routines for pointer allocation is another way to centralize control over your data.

Declare and define pointers at the same time   Assigning a variable its initial value close to where it is declared is generally good programming practice, and it's all the more valuable when working with pointers. Here is an example of what not to do:

CODING HORROR

C++ Example of Bad Pointer Initialization

```
Employee *employeePtr;
// lots of code
...
employeePtr = new Employee;
```

If even this code works correctly initially, it's error-prone under modification because a chance exists that someone will try to use *employeePtr* between the point where the pointer is declared and the time it's initialized. Here's a safer approach:

> **C++ Example of Good Pointer Initialization**
> ```
> // lots of code
> ...
> Employee *employeePtr = new Employee;
> ```

Delete pointers at the same scoping level as they were allocated   Keep allocation and deallocation of pointers symmetric. If you use a pointer within a single scope, call *new* to allocate and *delete* to deallocate the pointer within the same scope. If you allocate a pointer inside a routine, deallocate it inside a sister routine. If you allocate a pointer inside an object's constructor, deallocate it inside the object's destructor. A routine that allocates memory and then expects its client code to deallocate the memory manually creates an inconsistency that is ripe for error.

Check pointers before using them   Before you use a pointer in a critical part of your program, make sure the memory location it points to is reasonable. For example, if you expect memory locations to be between *StartData* and *EndData*, you should take a suspicious view of a pointer that points before *StartData* or after *EndData*. You'll have to determine what the values of *StartData* and *EndData* are in your environment. You can set this up to work automatically if you use pointers through access routines rather than manipulate them directly.

Check the variable referenced by the pointer before using it   Sometimes you can perform reasonableness checks on the value the pointer points to. For example, if you're supposed to be pointing to an integer value between 0 and 1000, you should be suspicious of values over 1000. If you're pointing to a C++-style string, you might be suspicious of strings with lengths greater than 100. This can also be done automatically if you work with pointers through access routines.

Use dog-tag fields to check for corrupted memory   A "tag field" or "dog tag" is a field you add to a structure solely for the purpose of error checking. When you allocate a variable, put a value that should remain unchanged into its tag field. When you use the structure—especially when you delete the memory—check the tag field's value. If the tag field doesn't have the expected value, the data has been corrupted.

When you delete the pointer, corrupt the field so that if you accidentally try to free the same pointer again, you'll detect the corruption. For example, let's say that you need to allocate 100 bytes:

1. First, *new* 104 bytes, 4 bytes more than requested.

104 bytes

2. Set the first 4 bytes to a dog-tag value, and then return a pointer to the memory that starts after that.

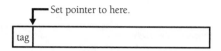

Set pointer to here.

tag

3. When the time comes to delete the pointer, check the tag.

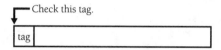

Check this tag.

tag

4. If the tag is OK, set it to *0* or some other value that you and your program recognize as an invalid tag value. You don't want the value to be mistaken for a valid tag after the memory has been freed. Set the data to *0*, *0xCC*, or some other non-random value for the same reason.

5. Finally, delete the pointer.

Free the whole 104 bytes

Putting a dog tag at the beginning of the memory block you've allocated allows you to check for redundant attempts to deallocate the memory block without needing to maintain a list of all the memory blocks you've allocated. Putting the dog tag at the end of the memory block allows you to check for overwriting memory beyond the location that was supposed to be used. You can use tags at the beginning and the end of the block to accomplish both objectives.

You can use this approach in concert with the reasonableness check suggested earlier—checking that the pointers are between *StartData* and *EndData*. To be sure that a pointer points to a reasonable location, rather than checking for a probable range of memory, check to see that the pointer is in the list of allocated pointers.

You could check the tag field just once before you delete the variable. A corrupted tag would then tell you that sometime during the life of that variable its contents were corrupted. The more often you check the tag field, however, the closer to the root of the problem you will detect the corruption.

Add explicit redundancies   An alternative to using a tag field is to use certain fields twice. If the data in the redundant fields doesn't match, you know memory has been corrupted. This can result in a lot of overhead if you manipulate pointers directly. If you isolate pointer operations in routines, however, it adds duplicate code in only a few places.

Use extra pointer variables for clarity   By all means, don't skimp on pointer variables. The point is made elsewhere that a variable shouldn't be used for more than one purpose. This is especially true for pointer variables. It's hard enough to figure out

what someone is doing with a linked list without having to figure out why one
genericLink variable is used over and over again or what *pointer->next->last->next* is
pointing at. Consider this code fragment:

C++ Example of Traditional Node Insertion Code

```cpp
void InsertLink(
    Node *currentNode,
    Node *insertNode
    ) {
    // insert "insertNode" after "currentNode"
    insertNode->next = currentNode->next;
    insertNode->previous = currentNode;
    if ( currentNode->next != NULL ) {
        currentNode->next->previous = insertNode;
    }
    currentNode->next = insertNode;
}
```

This line is needlessly
difficult.

This is traditional code for inserting a node in a linked list, and it's needlessly hard to
understand. Inserting a new node involves three objects: the current node, the node
currently following the current node, and the node to be inserted between them. The
code fragment explicitly acknowledges only two objects: *insertNode* and *currentNode*.
It forces you to figure out and remember that *currentNode->next* is also involved. If you
tried to diagram what is happening without the node originally following *currentNode*,
you would get something like this:

A better diagram would identify all three objects. It would look like this:

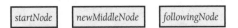

Here's code that explicitly references all three of the objects involved:

C++ Example of More Readable Node-Insertion Code

```cpp
void InsertLink(
    Node *startNode,
    Node *newMiddleNode
    ) {
    // insert "newMiddleNode" between "startNode" and "followingNode"
    Node *followingNode = startNode->next;
    newMiddleNode->next = followingNode;
    newMiddleNode->previous = startNode;
    if ( followingNode != NULL ) {
        followingNode->previous = newMiddleNode;
    }
    startNode->next = newMiddleNode;
}
```

This code fragment has an extra line of code, but without the first fragment's *current-Node->next->previous*, it's easier to follow.

Simplify complicated pointer expressions   Complicated pointer expressions are hard to read. If your code contains expressions like p->q->r->s.data, think about the person who has to read the expression. Here's a particularly egregious example:

CODING HORROR

C++ Example of a Pointer Expression That's Hard to Understand

```
for ( rateIndex = 0; rateIndex < numRates; rateIndex++ ) {
   netRate[ rateIndex ] = baseRate[ rateIndex ] * rates->discounts->factors->net;
}
```

Complicated expressions like the pointer expression in this example make for code that has to be figured out rather than read. If your code contains a complicated expression, assign it to a well-named variable to clarify the intent of the operation. Here's an improved version of the example:

C++ Example of Simplifying a Complicated Pointer Expression

```
quantityDiscount = rates->discounts->factors->net;
for ( rateIndex = 0; rateIndex < numRates; rateIndex++ ) {
   netRate[ rateIndex ] = baseRate[ rateIndex ] * quantityDiscount;
}
```

With this simplification, not only do you get a gain in readability, but you might also get a boost in performance from simplifying the pointer operation inside the loop. As usual, you'd have to measure the performance benefit before you bet any folding money on it.

Draw a picture   Code descriptions of pointers can get confusing. It usually helps to draw a picture. For example, a picture of the linked-list insertion problem might look like the one shown in Figure 13-2.

Cross-Reference Diagrams such as the one in Figure 13-2 can become part of the external documentation of your program. For details on good documentation practices, see Chapter 32, "Self-Documenting Code."

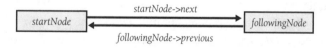

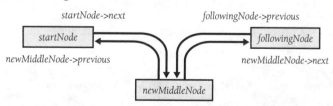

Figure 13-2   An example of a picture that helps us think through the steps involved in relinking pointers.

Delete pointers in linked lists in the right order A common problem in working with dynamically allocated linked lists is freeing the first pointer in the list first and then not being able to get to the next pointer in the list. To avoid this problem, make sure that you have a pointer to the next element in a list before you free the current one.

Allocate a reserve parachute of memory If your program uses dynamic memory, you need to avoid the problem of suddenly running out of memory, leaving your user and your user's data lost in RAM space. One way to give your program a margin of error is to preallocate a memory parachute. Determine how much memory your program needs to save work, clean up, and exit gracefully. Allocate that amount of memory at the beginning of the program as a reserve parachute, and leave it alone. When you run out of memory, free the reserve parachute, clean up, and shut down.

Further Reading For an excellent discussion of safe approaches to handling pointers in C, see *Writing Solid Code* (Maguire 1993).

Shred your garbage Pointer errors are hard to debug because the point at which the memory the pointer points to becomes invalid is not deterministic. Sometimes the memory contents will look valid long after the pointer is freed. Other times, the memory will change right away.

In C, you can force errors related to using deallocated pointers to be more consistent by overwriting memory blocks with junk data right before they're deallocated. As with many other operations, you can do this automatically if you use access routines. In C, each time you delete a pointer, you could use code like this:

C Example of Forcing a Deallocated Object to Contain Junk Data
```
pointer->SetContentsToGarbage();
delete pointer;
```

Of course, this technique will not work in C++ where the pointer points to an object, and it requires you to implement a Set Contents to Garbage routine for each object..

Set pointers to null after deleting or freeing them A common type of pointer error is the "dangling pointer," use of a pointer that has been *delete*'d or *free*'d. One reason pointer errors are hard to detect is that sometimes the error doesn't produce any symptoms. By setting pointers to null after freeing them, you don't change the fact that you can read data pointed to by a dangling pointer. But you do ensure that writing data to a dangling pointer produces an error. It will probably be an ugly, nasty, disaster of an error, but at least you'll find it instead of someone else finding it.

The code preceding the *delete* operation in the previous example could be augmented to handle this, too:

C++ Example of Setting a Pointer to Null After Deleting It
```
pointer->SetContentsToGarbage();
delete pointer;
pointer = NULL;
```

Check for bad pointers before deleting a variable   One of the best ways to ruin a program is to *delete()* or *free()* a pointer after it has already been *delete*'d or *free*'d. Unfortunately, few languages detect this kind of problem.

Setting freed pointers to null also allows you to check whether a pointer is set to null before you use it or attempt to delete it again; if you don't set freed pointers to null, you won't have that option. That suggests another addition to the pointer deletion code:

C++ Example of Asserting That a Pointer Is Not Null Before Deleting It
```
ASSERT( pointer != NULL, "Attempting to delete null pointer." );
pointer->SetContentsToGarbage();
delete pointer;
pointer = NULL;
```

Keep track of pointer allocations   Keep a list of the pointers you have allocated. This allows you to check whether a pointer is in the list before you dispose of it. Here's an example of how the standard pointer deletion code could be modified to include that:

C++ Example of Checking Whether a Pointer Has Been Allocated
```
ASSERT( pointer != NULL, "Attempting to delete null pointer." );
if ( IsPointerInList( pointer ) ) {
   pointer->SetContentsToGarbage();
   RemovePointerFromList( pointer );
   delete pointer;
   pointer = NULL;
}
else {
   ASSERT( FALSE, "Attempting to delete unallocated pointer." );
}
```

Write cover routines to centralize your strategy to avoiding pointer problems   As you can see from this example, you can end up with quite a lot of extra code each time a pointer is *new*'d or *delete*'d. Some of the techniques described in this section are mutually exclusive or redundant, and you wouldn't want to have multiple, conflicting strategies in use in the same code base. For example, you don't need to create and check dog-tag values if you're maintaining your own list of valid pointers.

You can minimize programming overhead and reduce chance of errors by creating cover routines for common pointer operations. In C++, you could use these two routines:

- *SAFE_NEW*   This routine calls new to allocate the pointer, adds the new pointer to a list of allocated pointers, and returns the newly allocated pointer to the calling routine. It can also be checked for an exception or a null return from new (aka an "out-of-memory" error) in this one place only, which simplifies error processing in other parts of your program.

- *SAFE_DELETE* This routine checks to see whether the pointer passed to it is in the list of allocated pointers. If it is in the list, it sets the variable the pointer pointed at to garbage values, removes the pointer from the list, calls C++'s delete operator to deallocate the pointer, and sets the pointer to null. If the pointer isn't in the list, *SAFE_DELETE* displays a diagnostic message and stops the program.

Implemented here as a macro, the *SAFE_DELETE* routine looks like this:

C++ Example of Putting a Wrapper Around Pointer Deletion Code

```
#define SAFE_DELETE( pointer ) { \
    ASSERT( pointer != NULL, "Attempting to delete null pointer."); \
    if ( IsPointerInList( pointer ) ) { \
        pointer->SetContentsToGarbage();
        RemovePointerFromList( pointer ); \
        delete pointer; \
        pointer = NULL; \
    } \
    else { \
        ASSERT( FALSE, "Attempting to delete unallocated pointer." ); \
    } \
}
```

Cross-Reference For details on planning to remove code used for debugging, see "Plan to Remove Debugging Aids" in Section 8.6.

In C++, this routine will delete individual pointers, but you would also need to implement a similar *SAFE_DELETE_ARRAY* routine to delete arrays.

By centralizing memory handling in these two routines, you can also make *SAFE_NEW* and *SAFE_DELETE* behave differently in debug mode vs. production mode. For example, when *SAFE_DELETE* detects an attempt to free a null pointer during development, it might stop the program, but during production it might simply log an error and continue processing.

You can easily adapt this scheme to *calloc* and *free* in C and to other languages that use pointers.

Use a nonpointer technique Pointers are harder than average to understand, they're error-prone, and they tend to require machine-dependent, unportable code. If you can think of an alternative to using a pointer that works reasonably, save yourself a few headaches and use it instead.

C++-Pointer Pointers

Further Reading For many more tips on using pointers in C++, see *Effective C++*, 2d ed. (Meyers 1998) and *More Effective C++* (Meyers 1996).

C++ introduces some specific wrinkles related to using pointers and references. The following subsections describe guidelines that apply to using pointers in C++:

Understand the difference between pointers and references In C++, both pointers (*) and the references (&) refer indirectly to an object. To the uninitiated the only difference appears to be a purely cosmetic distinction between referring to fields as *object->field* vs. *object.field*. The most significant differences are that a reference must always refer to an object, whereas a pointer can point to null, and what a reference refers to can't be changed after the reference is initialized.

Use pointers for "pass by reference" parameters and use* const *references for "pass by value" parameters   C++ defaults to passing arguments to routines by value rather than by reference. When you pass an object to a routine by value, C++ creates a copy of the object, and when the object is passed back to the calling routine, a copy is created again. For large objects, that copying can eat up time and other resources. Consequently, when passing objects to a routine, you usually want to avoid copying the object, which means you want to pass it by reference rather than by value.

Sometimes, however, you would like to have the *semantics* of a pass by value—that is, that the passed object should not be altered—with the *implementation* of a pass by reference—that is, passing the actual object rather than a copy.

In C++, the resolution to this issue is that you use pointers for pass by reference and—odd as the terminology might sound—"*const* references" for pass by value! Here's an example:

C++ Example of Passing Parameters by Reference and by Value

```
void SomeRoutine(
    const LARGE_OBJECT &nonmodifiableObject,
    LARGE_OBJECT *modifiableObject
);
```

This approach provides the additional benefit of providing a syntactic differentiation within the called routine between objects that are supposed to be treated as modifiable and those that aren't. In a modifiable object, the references to members will use the *object->member* notation, whereas for nonmodifiable objects references to members will use *object.member* notation.

The limitation of this approach is difficulties propagating *const* references. If you control your own code base, it's good discipline to use *const* whenever possible (Meyers 1998), and you should be able to declare pass-by-value parameters as *const* references. For library code or other code you don't control, you'll run into problems using *const* routine parameters. The fallback position is still to use references for read-only parameters but not declare them *const*. With that approach, you won't realize the full benefits of the compiler checking for attempts to modify nonmodifiable arguments to a routine, but you'll at least give yourself the visual distinction between *object->member* and *object.member*.

Use* auto_ptrs   If you haven't developed the habit of using *auto_ptrs*, get into the habit! By deleting memory automatically when the *auto_ptr* goes out of scope, *auto_ptrs* avoid many of the memory-leakage problems associated with regular pointers. In Scott Meyers's *More Effective C++*, Item #9 contains a good discussion of *auto_ptr* (Meyers 1996).

Get smart about smart pointers Smart pointers are a replacement for regular pointers or "dumb" pointers (Meyers 1996). They operate similarly to regular pointers, but they provide more control over resource management, copy operations, assignment operations, object construction, and object destruction. The issues involved are specific to C++. *More Effective C++*, Item #28, contains a complete discussion.

C-Pointer Pointers

Here are a few tips on using pointers that apply specifically to the C language:

Use explicit pointer types rather than the default type C lets you use *char* or *void* pointers for any type of variable. As long as the pointer points, the language doesn't really care what it points at. If you use explicit types for your pointers, however, the compiler can give you warnings about mismatched pointer types and inappropriate dereferences. If you don't, it can't. Use the specific pointer type whenever you can.

The corollary to this rule is to use explicit type casting when you have to make a type conversion. For example, in this fragment, it's clear that a variable of type *NODE_PTR* is being allocated:

C Example of Explicit Type Casting
```
NodePtr = (NODE_PTR) calloc( 1, sizeof( NODE ) );
```

Avoid type casting Avoiding type casting doesn't have anything to do with going to acting school or getting out of always playing "the heavy." It has to do with avoiding squeezing a variable of one type into the space for a variable of another type. Type casting turns off your complier's ability to check for type mismatches and therefore creates a hole in your defensive-programming armor. A program that requires many type casts probably has some architectural gaps that need to be revisited. Redesign if that's possible; otherwise, try to avoid type casts as much as you can.

Follow the asterisk rule for parameter passing You can pass an argument back from a routine in C only if you have an asterisk (*) in front of the argument in the assignment statement. Many C programmers have difficulty determining when C allows a value to be passed back to a calling routine. It's easy to remember that, as long as you have an asterisk in front of the parameter when you assign it a value, the value is passed back to the calling routine. Regardless of how many asterisks you stack up in the declaration, you must have at least one in the assignment statement if you want to pass back a value. For example, in the following fragment, the value assigned to *parameter* isn't passed back to the calling routine because the assignment statement doesn't use an asterisk:

> **C Example of Parameter Passing That Won't Work**
> ```c
> void TryToPassBackAValue( int *parameter ) {
>    parameter = SOME_VALUE;
> }
> ```

Here, the value assigned to *parameter* is passed back because *parameter* has an asterisk in front of it:

> **C Example of Parameter Passing That Will Work**
> ```c
> void TryToPassBackAValue( int *parameter ) {
>    *parameter = SOME_VALUE;
> }
> ```

Use sizeof() *to determine the size of a variable in a memory allocation*   It's easier to use *sizeof()* than to look up the size in a manual, and *sizeof()* works for structures you create yourself, which aren't in the manual. Because it's calculated at compile time, *sizeof()* doesn't carry a performance penalty. It's portable—recompiling in a different environment automatically changes the value calculated by *sizeof()*. And it requires little maintenance since you can change types you have defined and allocations will be adjusted automatically.

13.3 Global Data

Cross-Reference For details on the differences between global data and class data, see "Class data mistaken for global data" in Section 5.3.

Global variables are accessible anywhere in a program. The term is also sometimes used sloppily to refer to variables with a broader scope than local variables—such as class variables that are accessible anywhere within a class. But accessibility anywhere within a single class does not by itself mean that a variable is global.

Most experienced programmers have concluded that using global data is riskier than using local data. Most experienced programmers have also concluded that access to data from several routines is pretty useful.

KEY POINT

Even if global variables don't always produce errors, however, they're hardly ever the best way to program. The rest of this section fully explores the issues involved.

Common Problems with Global Data

If you use global variables indiscriminately or you feel that not being able to use them is restrictive, you probably haven't caught on to the full value of information hiding and modularity yet. Modularity, information hiding, and the associated use of well-designed classes might not be revealed truths, but they go a long way toward making large programs understandable and maintainable. Once you get the message, you'll want to write routines and classes with as little connection as possible to global variables and the outside world.

People cite numerous problems in using global data, but the problems boil down to a small number of major issues:

Inadvertent changes to global data   You might change the value of a global variable in one place and mistakenly think that it has remained unchanged somewhere else. Such a problem is known as a "side effect." For example, in this example, *theAnswer* is a global variable:

| theAnswer is a global variable. |
| GetOtherAnswer() changes theAnswer. |
| averageAnswer is wrong. |

Visual Basic Example of a Side-Effect Problem
```
theAnswer = GetTheAnswer()
otherAnswer = GetOtherAnswer()
averageAnswer = (theAnswer + otherAnswer) / 2
```

You might assume that the call to *GetOtherAnswer()* doesn't change the value of *theAnswer*; if it does, the average in the third line will be wrong. And, in fact, *GetOtherAnswer()* does change the value of *theAnswer*, so the program has an error to be fixed.

Bizarre and exciting aliasing problems with global data   "Aliasing" refers to calling the same variable by two or more different names. This happens when a global variable is passed to a routine and then used by the routine both as a global variable and as a parameter. Here's a routine that uses a global variable:

CODING HORROR

Visual Basic Example of a Routine That's Ripe for an Aliasing Problem
```
Sub WriteGlobal( ByRef inputVar As Integer )
    inputVar = 0
    globalVar = inputVar + 5
    MsgBox( "Input Variable:  " & Str( inputVar ) )
    MsgBox( "Global Variable: " & Str( globalVar ) )
End Sub
```

Here's the code that calls the routine with the global variable as an argument:

Visual Basic Example of Calling the Routine with an Argument, Which Exposes an Aliasing Problem
```
WriteGlobal( globalVar )
```

Since *inputVar* is initialized to *0* and *WriteGlobal()* adds 5 to *inputVar* to get *globalVar*, you'd expect *globalVar* to be 5 more than *inputVar*. But here's the surprising result:

The Result of the Aliasing Problem in Visual Basic
```
Input Variable:  5
Global Variable: 5
```

The subtlety here is that *globalVar* and *inputVar* are actually the same variable! Since *globalVar* is passed into *WriteGlobal()* by the calling routine, it's referenced or "aliased" by two different names. The effect of the *MsgBox()* lines is thus quite different from the one intended: they display the same variable twice, even though they refer to two different names.

KEY POINT

Re-entrant code problems with global data   Code that can be entered by more than one thread of control is becoming increasingly common. Multithreaded code creates the possibility that global data will be shared not only among routines, but among different copies of the same program. In such an environment, you have to make sure that global data keeps its meaning even when multiple copies of a program are running. This is a significant problem, and you can avoid it by using techniques suggested later in this section.

Code reuse hindered by global data   To use code from one program in another program, you have to be able to pull it out of the first program and plug it into the second. Ideally, you'd be able to lift out a single routine or class, plug it into another program, and continue merrily on your way.

Global data complicates the picture. If the class you want to reuse reads or writes global data, you can't just plug it into the new program. You have to modify the new program or the old class so that they're compatible. If you take the high road, you'll modify the old class so that it doesn't use global data. If you do that, the next time you need to reuse the class you'll be able to plug it in with no extra fuss. If you take the low road, you'll modify the new program to create the global data that the old class needs to use. This is like a virus; not only does the global data affect the original program, but it also spreads to new programs that use any of the old program's classes.

Uncertain initialization-order issues with global data   The order in which data is initialized among different "translation units" (files) is not defined in some languages, notably C++. If the initialization of a global variable in one file uses a global variable that was initialized in a different file, all bets are off on the second variable's value unless you take explicit steps to ensure the two variables are initialized in the right sequence.

This problem is solvable with a workaround that Scott Meyers describes in *Effective C++*, Item #47 (Meyers 1998). But the trickiness of the solution is representative of the extra complexity that using global data introduces.

Modularity and intellectual manageability damaged by global data   The essence of creating programs that are larger than a few hundred lines of code is managing complexity. The only way you can intellectually manage a large program is to break it into pieces so that you only have to think about one part at a time. Modularization is the most powerful tool at your disposal for breaking a program into pieces.

Global data pokes holes in your ability to modularize. If you use global data, can you concentrate on one routine at a time? No. You have to concentrate on one routine and every other routine that uses the same global data. Although global data doesn't completely destroy a program's modularity, it weakens it, and that's reason enough to try to find better solutions to your problems.

Reasons to Use Global Data

Data purists sometimes argue that programmers should never use global data, but most programs use "global data" when the term is broadly construed. Data in a database is global data, as is data in configuration files such as the Windows registry. Named constants are global data, just not global variables.

Used with discipline, global variables are useful in several situations:

Preservation of global values   Sometimes you have data that applies conceptually to your whole program. This might be a variable that reflects the state of a program—for example, interactive vs. command-line mode, or normal vs. error-recovery mode. Or it might be information that's needed throughout a program—for example, a data table that every routine in the program uses.

Cross-Reference For more details on named constants, see Section 12.7, "Named Constants."

Emulation of named constants   Although C++, Java, Visual Basic, and most modern languages support named constants, some languages such as Python, Perl, Awk, and UNIX shell script still don't. You can use global variables as substitutes for named constants when your language doesn't support them. For example, you can replace the literal values *1* and *0* with the global variables *TRUE* and *FALSE* set to *1* and *0*, or you can replace *66* as the number of lines per page with *LINES_PER_PAGE = 66*. It's easier to change code later when this approach is used, and the code tends to be easier to read. This disciplined use of global data is a prime example of the distinction between programming *in* vs. programming *into* a language, which is discussed more in Section 34.4, "Program into Your Language, Not in It."

Emulation of enumerated types   You can also use global variables to emulate enumerated types in languages such as Python that don't support enumerated types directly.

Streamlining use of extremely common data   Sometimes you have so many references to a variable that it appears in the parameter list of every routine you write. Rather than including it in every parameter list, you can make it a global variable. However, in cases in which a variable seems to be accessed everywhere, it rarely is. Usually it's accessed by a limited set of routines you can package into a class with the data they work on. More on this later.

Eliminating tramp data   Sometimes you pass data to a routine or class merely so that it can be passed to another routine or class. For example, you might have an error-processing object that's used in each routine. When the routine in the middle of the call chain doesn't use the object, the object is called "tramp data." Use of global variables can eliminate tramp data.

Use Global Data Only as a Last Resort

Before you resort to using global data, consider a few alternatives:

Begin by making each variable local and make variables global only as you need to
Make all variables local to individual routines initially. If you find they're needed elsewhere, make them private or protected class variables before you go so far as to make them global. If you finally find that you have to make them global, do it, but only when you're sure you have to. If you start by making a variable global, you'll never make it local, whereas if you start by making it local, you might never need to make it global.

Distinguish between global and class variables   Some variables are truly global in that they are accessed throughout a whole program. Others are really class variables, used heavily only within a certain set of routines. It's OK to access a class variable any way you want to within the set of routines that use it heavily. If routines outside the class need to use it, provide the variable's value by means of an access routine. Don't access class values directly—as if they were global variables—even if your programming language allows you to. This advice is tantamount to saying "Modularize! Modularize! Modularize!"

Use access routines   Creating access routines is the workhorse approach to getting around problems with global data. More on that in the next section.

Using Access Routines Instead of Global Data

KEY POINT

Anything you can do with global data, you can do better with access routines. The use of access routines is a core technique for implementing abstract data types and achieving information hiding. Even if you don't want to use a full-blown abstract data type, you can still use access routines to centralize control over your data and to protect yourself against changes.

Advantages of Access Routines

Using access routines has multiple advantages:

- You get centralized control over the data. If you discover a more appropriate implementation of the structure later, you don't have to change the code everywhere the data is referenced. Changes don't ripple through your whole program. They stay inside the access routines.

Cross-Reference For more details on barricading, see Section 8.5, "Barricade Your Program to Contain the Damage Caused by Errors."

- You can ensure that all references to the variable are barricaded. If you push elements onto the stack with statements like *stack.array[stack.top] = newElement*, you can easily forget to check for stack overflow and make a serious mistake. If you use access routines—for example, *PushStack(newElement)*—you can write the check for stack overflow into the *PushStack()* routine. The check will be done automatically every time the routine is called, and you can forget about it.

Cross-Reference For details on information hiding, see "Hide Secrets (Information Hiding)" in Section 5.3.

- You get the general benefits of information hiding automatically. Access routines are an example of information hiding, even if you don't design them for that reason. You can change the interior of an access routine without changing the rest of the program. Access routines allow you to redecorate the interior of your house and leave the exterior unchanged so that your friends still recognize it.

- Access routines are easy to convert to an abstract data type. One advantage of access routines is that you can create a level of abstraction that's harder to do when you're working with global data directly. For example, instead of writing code that says *if lineCount > MAX_LINES*, an access routine allows you to write code that says *if PageFull()*. This small change documents the intent of the *if lineCount test*, and it does so in the code. It's a small gain in readability, but consistent attention to such details makes the difference between beautifully crafted software and code that's just hacked together.

How to Use Access Routines

Here's the short version of the theory and practice of access routines: Hide data in a class. Declare that data by using the *static* keyword or its equivalent to ensure only a single instance of the data exists. Write routines that let you look at the data and change it. Require code outside the class to use the access routines rather than working directly with the data.

For example, if you have a global status variable *g_globalStatus* that describes your program's overall status, you can create two access routines: *globalStatus.Get()* and *globalStatus.Set()*, each of which does what it sounds like it does. Those routines access a variable hidden within the class that replaces *g_globalStatus*. The rest of the program can get all the benefit of the formerly global variable by accessing *globalStatus.Get()* and *globalStatus.Set()*.

Cross-Reference Restricting access to global variables even when your language doesn't directly support that is an example of programming *into* a language vs. programming *in* a language. For more details, see Section 34.4, "Program into Your Language, Not in It."

If your language doesn't support classes, you can still create access routines to manipulate the global data but you'll have to enforce restrictions on the use of the global data through coding standards in lieu of built-in programming language enforcement.

Here are a few detailed guidelines for using access routines to hide global variables when your language doesn't have built-in support:

Require all code to go through the access routines for the data   A good convention is to require all global data to begin with the *g_* prefix, and to further require that no code access a variable with the *g_* prefix except that variable's access routines. All other code reaches the data through the access routines.

Don't just throw all your global data into the same barrel   If you throw all your global data into a big pile and write access routines for it, you eliminate the problems of global data but you miss out on some of the advantages of information hiding and abstract data types. As long as you're writing access routines, take a moment to think about which class each global variable belongs in and then package the data and its access routines with the other data and routines in that class.

Use locking to control access to global variables Similar to concurrency control in a multiuser database environment, locking requires that before the value of a global variable can be used or updated, the variable must be "checked out." After the variable is used, it's checked back in. During the time it's in use (checked out), if some other part of the program tries to check it out, the lock/unlock routine displays an error message or fires an assertion.

Cross-Reference For details on planning for differences between developmental and production versions of a program, see "Plan to Remove Debugging Aids" in Section 8.6 and Section 8.7, "Determining How Much Defensive Programming to Leave in Production Code."

This description of locking ignores many of the subtleties of writing code to fully support concurrency. For that reason, simplified locking schemes like this one are most useful during the development stage. Unless the scheme is very well thought out, it probably won't be reliable enough to be put into production. When the program is put into production, the code is modified to do something safer and more graceful than displaying error messages. For example, it might log an error message to a file when it detects multiple parts of the program trying to lock the same global variable.

This sort of development-time safeguard is fairly easy to implement when you use access routines for global data, but it would be awkward to implement if you were using global data directly.

Build a level of abstraction into your access routines Build access routines at the level of the problem domain rather than at the level of the implementation details. That approach buys you improved readability as well as insurance against changes in the implementation details.

Compare the pairs of statements in Table 13-1:

Table 13-1 Accessing Global Data Directly and Through Access Routines

Direct Use of Global Data	Use of Global Data Through Access Routines
node = node.next	*account = NextAccount(account)*
node = node.next	*employee = NextEmployee(employee)*
node = node.next	*rateLevel = NextRateLevel(rateLevel)*
event = eventQueue[queueFront]	*event = HighestPriorityEvent()*
event = eventQueue[queueBack]	*event = LowestPriorityEvent()*

In the first three examples, the point is that an abstract access routine tells you a lot more than a generic structure. If you use the structure directly, you do too much at once: you show both what the structure itself is doing (moving to the next link in a linked list) and what's being done with respect to the entity it represents (getting an account, next employee, or rate level). This is a big burden to put on a simple data-structure assignment. Hiding the information behind abstract access routines lets the code speak for itself and makes the code read at the level of the problem domain, rather than at the level of implementation details.

Keep all accesses to the data at the same level of abstraction If you use an access routine to do one thing to a structure, you should use an access routine to do everything else to it too. If you read from the structure with an access routine, write to it with an access routine. If you call *InitStack()* to initialize a stack and *PushStack()* to push an item onto the stack, you've created a consistent view of the data. If you pop the stack by writing *value = array[stack.top]*, you've created an inconsistent view of the data. The inconsistency makes it harder for others to understand the code. Create a *PopStack()* routine instead of writing *value = array[stack top]*.

Cross-Reference Using access routines for an event queue suggests the need to create a class. For details, see Chapter 6, "Working Classes."

In the example pairs of statements in Table 13-1, the two event-queue operations occurred in parallel. Inserting an event into the queue would be trickier than either of the two operations in the table, requiring several lines of code to find the place to insert the event, adjust existing events to make room for the new event, and adjust the front or back of the queue. Removing an event from the queue would be just as complicated. During coding, the complex operations would be put into routines and the others would be left as direct data manipulations. This would create an ugly, nonparallel use of the structure. Now compare the pairs of statements in Table 13-2:

Table 13-2   Parallel and Nonparallel Uses of Complex Data

Nonparallel Use of Complex Data	Parallel Use of Complex Data
event = EventQueue[queueFront]	*event = HighestPriorityEvent()*
event = EventQueue[queueBack]	*event = LowestPriorityEvent()*
AddEvent(event)	*AddEvent(event)*
eventCount = eventCount - 1	*RemoveEvent(event)*

Although you might think that these guidelines apply only to large programs, access routines have shown themselves to be a productive way of avoiding the problems of global data. As a bonus, they make the code more readable and add flexibility.

How to Reduce the Risks of Using Global Data

In most instances, global data is really class data for a class that hasn't been designed or implemented very well. In a few instances, data really does need to be global, but accesses to it can be wrapped with access routines to minimize potential problems. In a tiny number of remaining instances, you really do need to use global data. In those cases, you might think of following the guidelines in this section as getting shots so that you can drink the water when you travel to a foreign country: they're kind of painful, but they improve the odds of staying healthy.

Cross-Reference For details on naming conventions for global variables, see "Identify global variables" in Section 11.4.

Develop a naming convention that makes global variables obvious You can avoid some mistakes just by making it obvious that you're working with global data. If you're using global variables for more than one purpose (for example, as variables and as substitutes for named constants), make sure your naming convention differentiates among the types of uses.

Create a well-annotated list of all your global variables   Once your naming convention indicates that a variable is global, it's helpful to indicate what the variable does. A list of global variables is one of the most useful tools that someone working with your program can have.

Don't use global variables to contain intermediate results   If you need to compute a new value for a global variable, assign the global variable the final value at the end of the computation rather than using it to hold the result of intermediate calculations.

Don't pretend you're not using global data by putting all your data into a monster object and passing it everywhere   Putting everything into one huge object might satisfy the letter of the law by avoiding global variables, but it's pure overhead, producing none of the benefits of true encapsulation. If you use global data, do it openly. Don't try to disguise it with obese objects.

Additional Resources

cc2e.com/1385

Following are more resources that cover unusual data types:

Maguire, Steve. *Writing Solid Code*. Redmond, WA: Microsoft Press, 1993. Chapter 3 contains an excellent discussion of the hazards of pointer use and numerous specific tips for avoiding problems with pointers.

Meyers, Scott. *Effective C++*, 2d ed. Reading, MA: Addison-Wesley, 1998; Meyers, Scott, *More Effective C++*. Reading, MA: Addison-Wesley, 1996. As the titles suggest, these books contain numerous specific tips for improving C++ programs, including guidelines for using pointers safely and effectively. *More Effective C++* in particular contains an excellent discussion of C++'s memory management issues.

cc2e.com/1392

CHECKLIST: Considerations in Using Unusual Data Types

Structures

❑ Have you used structures instead of naked variables to organize and manipulate groups of related data?

❑ Have you considered creating a class as an alternative to using a structure?

Global Data

❑ Are all variables local or of class scope unless they absolutely need to be global?

❑ Do variable naming conventions differentiate among local, class, and global data?

❑ Are all global variables documented?

❑ Is the code free of pseudoglobal data—mammoth objects containing a mishmash of data that's passed to every routine?

❑ Are access routines used instead of global data?

❑ Are access routines and data organized into classes?

❑ Do access routines provide a level of abstraction beyond the underlying data type implementations?

❑ Are all related access routines at the same level of abstraction?

Pointers

❑ Are pointer operations isolated in routines?

❑ Are pointer references valid, or could the pointer be dangling?

❑ Does the code check pointers for validity before using them?

❑ Is the variable that the pointer references checked for validity before it's used?

❑ Are pointers set to null after they're freed?

❑ Does the code use all the pointer variables needed for the sake of readability?

❑ Are pointers in linked lists freed in the right order?

❑ Does the program allocate a reserve parachute of memory so that it can shut down gracefully if it runs out of memory?

❑ Are pointers used only as a last resort, when no other method is available?

Key Points

■ Structures can help make programs less complicated, easier to understand, and easier to maintain.

■ Whenever you consider using a structure, consider whether a class would work better.

■ Pointers are error-prone. Protect yourself by using access routines or classes and defensive-programming practices.

■ Avoid global variables, not just because they're dangerous, but because you can replace them with something better.

■ If you can't avoid global variables, work with them through access routines. Access routines give you everything that global variables give you, and more.

Part IV
Statements

Chapter 14

Organizing Straight-Line Code

cc2e.com/1465

Contents

- 14.1 Statements That Must Be in a Specific Order: page 347
- 14.2 Statements Whose Order Doesn't Matter: page 351

Related Topics

- General control topics: Chapter 19
- Code with conditionals: Chapter 15
- Code with loops: Chapter 16
- Scope of variables and objects: Section 10.4, "Scope"

This chapter turns from a data-centered view of programming to a statement-centered view. It introduces the simplest kind of control flow: putting statements and blocks of statements in sequential order.

Although organizing straight-line code is a relatively simple task, some organizational subtleties influence code quality, correctness, readability, and maintainability.

14.1 Statements That Must Be in a Specific Order

The easiest sequential statements to order are those in which the order counts. Here's an example:

Java Example of Statements in Which Order Counts
```java
data = ReadData();
results = CalculateResultsFromData( data );
PrintResults( results );
```

Unless something mysterious is happening with this code fragment, the statement must be executed in the order shown. The data must be read before the results can be calculated, and the results must be calculated before they can be printed.

The underlying concept in this example is that of dependencies. The third statement depends on the second, the second on the first. In this example, the fact that one statement depends on another is obvious from the routine names. In the following code fragment, the dependencies are less obvious:

> **Java Example of Statements in Which Order Counts, but Not Obviously**
> ```
> revenue.ComputeMonthly();
> revenue.ComputeQuarterly();
> revenue.ComputeAnnual();
> ```

In this case, the quarterly revenue calculation assumes that the monthly revenues have already been calculated. A familiarity with accounting—or even common sense—might tell you that quarterly revenues have to be calculated before annual revenues. There is a dependency, but it's not obvious merely from reading the code. And here, the dependencies aren't obvious—they're literally hidden:

> **Visual Basic Example of Statements in Which Order Dependencies Are Hidden**
> ```
> ComputeMarketingExpense
> ComputeSalesExpense
> ComputeTravelExpense
> ComputePersonnelExpense
> DisplayExpenseSummary
> ```

Suppose that *ComputeMarketingExpense()* initializes the class member variables that all the other routines put their data into. In such a case, it needs to be called before the other routines. How could you know that from reading this code? Because the routine calls don't have any parameters, you might be able to guess that each of these routines accesses class data. But you can't know for sure from reading this code.

KEY POINT

When statements have dependencies that require you to put them in a certain order, take steps to make the dependencies clear. Here are some simple guidelines for ordering statements:

Organize code so that dependencies are obvious In the Microsoft Visual Basic example just presented, *ComputeMarketingExpense()* shouldn't initialize the class member variables. The routine names suggest that *ComputeMarketingExpense()* is similar to *ComputeSalesExpense()*, *ComputeTravelExpense()*, and the other routines except that it works with marketing data rather than with sales data or other data. Having *ComputeMarketingExpense()* initialize the member variable is an arbitrary practice you should avoid. Why should initialization be done in that routine instead of one of the other two? Unless you can think of a good reason, you should write another routine, *InitializeExpenseData()*, to initialize the member variable. The routine's name is a clear indication that it should be called before the other expense routines.

Name routines so that dependencies are obvious In the Visual Basic example, *ComputeMarketingExpense()* is misnamed because it does more than compute marketing expenses; it also initializes member data. If you're opposed to creating an additional routine to initialize the data, at least give *ComputeMarketingExpense()* a name that describes all the functions it performs. In this case, *ComputeMarketingExpenseAndInitializeMemberData()* would be an adequate name. You might say it's a terrible name because it's so long, but the name describes what the routine does and is not terrible. The routine itself is terrible!

Cross-Reference For details on using routines and their parameters, see Chapter 5, "Design in Construction."

Use routine parameters to make dependencies obvious   Again in the Visual Basic example, since no data is passed between routines, you don't know whether any of the routines use the same data. By rewriting the code so that data is passed between the routines, you set up a clue that the execution order is important. The new code would look like this:

Visual Basic Example of Data That Suggests an Order Dependency

```
InitializeExpenseData( expenseData )
ComputeMarketingExpense( expenseData )
ComputeSalesExpense( expenseData )
ComputeTravelExpense( expenseData )
ComputePersonnelExpense( expenseData )
DisplayExpenseSummary( expenseData )
```

Because all the routines use *expenseData*, you have a hint that they might be working on the same data and that the order of the statements might be important.

In this particular example, a better approach might be to convert the routines to functions that take *expenseData* as inputs and return updated *expenseData* as outputs, which makes it even clearer that the code includes order dependencies.

Visual Basic Example of Data and Routine Calls That Suggest an Order Dependency

```
expenseData = InitializeExpenseData( expenseData )
expenseData = ComputeMarketingExpense( expenseData )
expenseData = ComputeSalesExpense( expenseData )
expenseData = ComputeTravelExpense( expenseData )
expenseData = ComputePersonnelExpense( expenseData )
DisplayExpenseSummary( expenseData )
```

Data can also indicate that execution order isn't important, as in this case:

Visual Basic Example of Data That Doesn't Indicate an Order Dependency

```
ComputeMarketingExpense( marketingData )
ComputeSalesExpense( salesData )
ComputeTravelExpense( travelData )
ComputePersonnelExpense( personnelData )
DisplayExpenseSummary( marketingData, salesData, travelData, personnelData )
```

Since the routines in the first four lines don't have any data in common, the code implies that the order in which they're called doesn't matter. Because the routine in the fifth line uses data from each of the first four routines, you can assume that it needs to be executed after the first four routines.

Document unclear dependencies with comments   Try first to write code without order dependencies. Try second to write code that makes dependencies obvious. If you're still concerned that an order dependency isn't explicit enough, document it. Documenting unclear dependencies is one aspect of documenting coding assumptions, which is critical to writing maintainable, modifiable code. In the Visual Basic example, comments along these lines would be helpful:

Visual Basic Example of Statements in Which Order Dependencies Are Hidden but Clarified with Comments

```
' Compute expense data. Each of the routines accesses the
' member data expenseData. DisplayExpenseSummary
' should be called last because it depends on data calculated
' by the other routines.
InitializeExpenseData
ComputeMarketingExpense
ComputeSalesExpense
ComputeTravelExpense
ComputePersonnelExpense
DisplayExpenseSummary
```

This code doesn't use the techniques for making order dependencies obvious. It's better to rely on such techniques rather than on comments, but if you're maintaining tightly controlled code or you can't improve the code itself for some other reason, use documentation to compensate for code weaknesses.

Check for dependencies with assertions or error-handling code   If the code is critical enough, you might use status variables and error-handling code or assertions to document critical sequential dependencies. For example, in the class's constructor, you might initialize a class member variable *isExpenseDataInitialized* to *false*. Then in *InitializeExpenseData*(), you can set *isExpenseDataInitialized* to *true*. Each function that depends on *expenseData* being initialized can then check whether *isExpenseDataInitialized* has been set to *true* before performing additional operations on *expenseData*. Depending on how extensive the dependencies are, you might also need variables like *isMarketingExpenseComputed*, *isSalesExpenseComputed*, and so on.

This technique creates new variables, new initialization code, and new error-checking code, all of which create additional possibilities for error. The benefits of this technique should be weighed against the additional complexity and increased chance of secondary errors that this technique creates.

14.2 Statements Whose Order Doesn't Matter

You might encounter cases in which it seems as if the order of a few statements or a few blocks of code doesn't matter at all. One statement doesn't depend on, or logically follow, another statement. But ordering affects readability, performance, and maintainability, and in the absence of execution-order dependencies, you can use secondary criteria to determine the order of statements or blocks of code. The guiding principle is the Principle of Proximity: *Keep related actions together*.

Making Code Read from Top to Bottom

As a general principle, make the program read from top to bottom rather than jumping around. Experts agree that top-to-bottom order contributes most to readability. Simply making the control flow from top to bottom at run time isn't enough. If someone who is reading your code has to search the whole program to find needed information, you should reorganize the code. Here's an example:

```
C++ Example of Bad Code That Jumps Around
MarketingData marketingData;
SalesData salesData;
TravelData travelData;

travelData.ComputeQuarterly();
salesData.ComputeQuarterly();
marketingData.ComputeQuarterly();

salesData.ComputeAnnual();
marketingData.ComputeAnnual();
travelData.ComputeAnnual();

salesData.Print();
travelData.Print();
marketingData.Print();
```

Suppose that you want to determine how *marketingData* is calculated. You have to start at the last line and track all references to *marketingData* back to the first line. *marketingData* is used in only a few other places, but you have to keep in mind how *marketingData* is used everywhere between the first and last references to it. In other words, you have to look at and think about every line of code in this fragment to figure out how *marketingData* is calculated. And of course this example is simpler than code you see in life-size systems. Here's the same code with better organization:

```
C++ Example of Good, Sequential Code That Reads from Top to Bottom
MarketingData marketingData;
marketingData.ComputeQuarterly();
marketingData.ComputeAnnual();
marketingData.Print();
```

```
SalesData salesData;
salesData.ComputeQuarterly();
salesData.ComputeAnnual();
salesData.Print();

TravelData travelData;
travelData.ComputeQuarterly();
travelData.ComputeAnnual();
travelData.Print();
```

Cross-Reference A more technical definition of "live" variables is given in "Measuring the Live Time of a Variable" in Section 10.4.

This code is better in several ways. References to each object are kept close together; they're "localized." The number of lines of code in which the objects are "live" is small. And perhaps most important, the code now looks as if it could be broken into separate routines for marketing, sales, and travel data. The first code fragment gave no hint that such a decomposition was possible.

Grouping Related Statements

Cross-Reference If you follow the Pseudocode Programming Process, your code will automatically be grouped into related statements. For details on the process, see Chapter 9, "The Pseudocode Programming Process."

Put related statements together. They can be related because they operate on the same data, perform similar tasks, or depend on each other's being performed in order.

An easy way to test whether related statements are grouped well is to print out a listing of your routine and then draw boxes around the related statements. If the statements are ordered well, you'll get a picture like that shown in Figure 14-1, in which the boxes don't overlap.

Figure 14-1   If the code is well organized into groups, boxes drawn around related sections don't overlap. They might be nested.

Cross-Reference For more on keeping operations on variables together, see Section 10.4, "Scope."

If statements aren't ordered well, you'll get a picture something like that shown in Figure 14-2, in which the boxes do overlap. If you find that your boxes overlap, reorganize your code so that related statements are grouped better.

Figure 14-2   If the code is organized poorly, boxes drawn around related sections overlap.

Once you've grouped related statements, you might find that they're strongly related and have no meaningful relationship to the statements that precede or follow them. In such a case, you might want to refactor the strongly related statements into their own routine.

cc2e.com/1472

Checklist: Organizing Straight-Line Code

- ❏ Does the code make dependencies among statements obvious?
- ❏ Do the names of routines make dependencies obvious?
- ❏ Do parameters to routines make dependencies obvious?
- ❏ Do comments describe any dependencies that would otherwise be unclear?
- ❏ Have housekeeping variables been used to check for sequential dependencies in critical sections of code?
- ❏ Does the code read from top to bottom?
- ❏ Are related statements grouped together?
- ❏ Have relatively independent groups of statements been moved into their own routines?

Key Points

- The strongest principle for organizing straight-line code is ordering dependencies.

- Dependencies should be made obvious through the use of good routine names, parameter lists, comments, and–if the code is critical enough–housekeeping variables.

- If code doesn't have order dependencies, keep related statements as close together as possible.

Chapter 15

Using Conditionals

cc2e.com/1538

Contents

Related Topics

A conditional is a statement that controls the execution of other statements; execution of the other statements is "conditioned" on statements such as *if*, *else*, *case*, and *switch*. Although it makes sense logically to refer to loop controls such as *while* and *for* as conditionals too, by convention they've been treated separately. Chapter 16, "Controlling Loops," will examine *while* and *for* statements.

15.1 *if* Statements

Depending on the language you're using, you might be able to use any of several kinds of *if* statements. The simplest is the plain *if* or *if-then* statement. The *if-then-else* is a little more complex, and chains of *if-then-else-if* are the most complex.

Plain *if-then* Statements

Follow these guidelines when writing *if* statements:

KEY POINT

Write the nominal path through the code first; then write the unusual cases Write your code so that the normal path through the code is clear. Make sure that the rare cases don't obscure the normal path of execution. This is important for both readability and performance.

Make sure that you branch correctly on equality Using > instead of >= or < instead of <= is analogous to making an off-by-one error in accessing an array or computing a loop index. In a loop, think through the endpoints to avoid an off-by-one error. In a conditional statement, think through the equals case to avoid one.

Cross-Reference For other ways to handle error-processing code, see "Summary of Techniques for Reducing Deep Nesting" in Section 19.4.

Put the normal case *after the* if *rather than after the* else Put the case you normally expect to process first. This is in line with the general principle of putting code that results from a decision as close as possible to the decision. Here's a code example that does a lot of error processing, haphazardly checking for errors along the way:

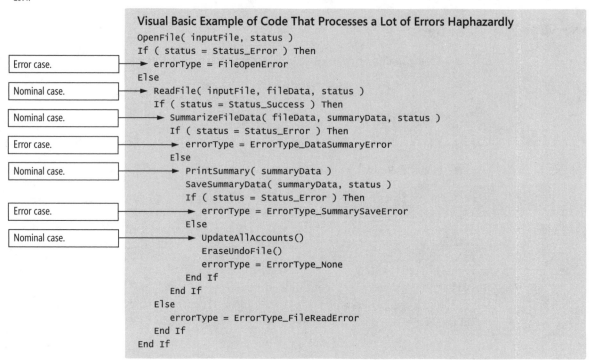

Visual Basic Example of Code That Processes a Lot of Errors Haphazardly

```
OpenFile( inputFile, status )
If ( status = Status_Error ) Then
    errorType = FileOpenError
Else
    ReadFile( inputFile, fileData, status )
    If ( status = Status_Success ) Then
        SummarizeFileData( fileData, summaryData, status )
        If ( status = Status_Error ) Then
            errorType = ErrorType_DataSummaryError
        Else
            PrintSummary( summaryData )
            SaveSummaryData( summaryData, status )
            If ( status = Status_Error ) Then
                errorType = ErrorType_SummarySaveError
            Else
                UpdateAllAccounts()
                EraseUndoFile()
                errorType = ErrorType_None
            End If
        End If
    Else
        errorType = ErrorType_FileReadError
    End If
End If
```

Labels pointing to lines:
- Error case. → `errorType = FileOpenError`
- Nominal case. → `ReadFile( inputFile, fileData, status )`
- Nominal case. → `SummarizeFileData( fileData, summaryData, status )`
- Error case. → `errorType = ErrorType_DataSummaryError`
- Nominal case. → `PrintSummary( summaryData )`
- Error case. → `errorType = ErrorType_SummarySaveError`
- Nominal case. → `UpdateAllAccounts()`

This code is hard to follow because the nominal cases and the error cases are all mixed together. It's hard to find the path that is normally taken through the code. In addition, because the error conditions are sometimes processed in the *if* clause rather than the *else* clause, it's hard to figure out which *if* test the normal case goes with. In the following rewritten code, the normal path is consistently coded first and all the error cases are coded last. This makes it easier to find and read the nominal case.

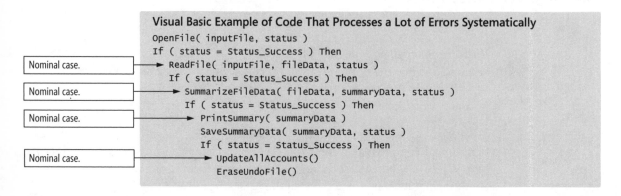

Visual Basic Example of Code That Processes a Lot of Errors Systematically

```
OpenFile( inputFile, status )
If ( status = Status_Success ) Then
    ReadFile( inputFile, fileData, status )
    If ( status = Status_Success ) Then
        SummarizeFileData( fileData, summaryData, status )
        If ( status = Status_Success ) Then
            PrintSummary( summaryData )
            SaveSummaryData( summaryData, status )
            If ( status = Status_Success ) Then
                UpdateAllAccounts()
                EraseUndoFile()
```

Labels pointing to lines:
- Nominal case. → `ReadFile( inputFile, fileData, status )`
- Nominal case. → `SummarizeFileData( fileData, summaryData, status )`
- Nominal case. → `PrintSummary( summaryData )`
- Nominal case. → `UpdateAllAccounts()`

```
                    errorType = ErrorType_None
              Else
                errorType = ErrorType_SummarySaveError
              End If
          Else
            errorType = ErrorType_DataSummaryError
          End If
      Else
        errorType = ErrorType_FileReadError
      End If
  Else
    errorType = ErrorType_FileOpenError
  End If
```

Error case.

Error case.

Error case.

Error case.

In the revised example, you can read the main flow of the *if* tests to find the normal case. The revision puts the focus on reading the main flow rather than on wading through the exceptional cases, so the code is easier to read overall. The stack of error conditions at the bottom of the nest is a sign of well-written error-processing code.

This example illustrates one systematic approach to handling normal cases and error cases. A variety of other solutions to this problem are discussed throughout this book, including using guard clauses, converting to polymorphic dispatch, and extracting the inner part of the test into a separate routine. For a complete list of available approaches, see "Summary of Techniques for Reducing Deep Nesting" in Section 19.4.

Follow the if *clause with a meaningful statement* Sometimes you see code like the next example, in which the *if* clause is null:

CODING HORROR

Java Example of a Null *if* Clause
```java
if ( SomeTest )
    ;
else {
    // do something
    ...
}
```

Cross-Reference One key to constructing an effective *if* statement is writing the right boolean expression to control it. For details on using boolean expressions effectively, see Section 19.1, "Boolean Expressions."

Most experienced programmers would avoid code like this if only to avoid the work of coding the extra null line and the *else* line. It looks silly and is easily improved by negating the predicate in the *if* statement, moving the code from the *else* clause to the *if* clause, and eliminating the *else* clause. Here's how the code would look after those changes:

Java Example of a Converted Null *if* Clause
```java
if ( ! someTest ) {
    // do something
    ...
}
```

Consider the* else *clause If you think you need a plain *if* statement, consider whether you don't actually need an *if-then-else* statement. A classic General Motors analysis found that 50 to 80 percent of *if* statements should have had an *else* clause (Elshoff 1976).

One option is to code the *else* clause—with a null statement if necessary—to show that the *else* case has been considered. Coding null *else*s just to show that that case has been considered might be overkill, but at the very least, take the *else* case into account. When you have an *if* test without an *else*, unless the reason is obvious, use comments to explain why the *else* clause isn't necessary, like so:

Java Example of a Helpful, Commented *else* Clause

```java
// if color is valid
if ( COLOR_MIN <= color && color <= COLOR_MAX ) {
   // do something
   ...
}
else {
   // else color is invalid
   // screen not written to -- safely ignore command
}
```

Test the* else *clause for correctness When testing your code, you might think that the main clause, the *if*, is all that needs to be tested. If it's possible to test the *else* clause, however, be sure to do that.

Check for reversal of the* if *and* else *clauses A common mistake in programming *if-then*s is to flip-flop the code that's supposed to follow the *if* clause and the code that's supposed to follow the *else* clause or to get the logic of the *if* test backward. Check your code for this common error.

Chains of *if-then-else* Statements

In languages that don't support *case* statements—or that support them only partially—you'll often find yourself writing chains of *if-then-else* tests. For example, the code to categorize a character might use a chain like this one:

Cross-Reference For more details on simplifying complicated expressions, see Section 19.1, "Boolean Expressions."

C++ Example of Using an *if-then-else* Chain to Categorize a Character

```cpp
if ( inputCharacter < SPACE ) {
   characterType = CharacterType_ControlCharacter;
}
else if (
   inputCharacter == ' ' ||
   inputCharacter == ',' ||
   inputCharacter == '.' ||
   inputCharacter == '!' ||
   inputCharacter == '(' ||
   inputCharacter == ')' ||
```

```cpp
      inputCharacter == ':' ||
      inputCharacter == ';' ||
      inputCharacter == '?' ||
      inputCharacter == '-'
      ) {
      characterType = CharacterType_Punctuation;
   }
   else if ( '0' <= inputCharacter && inputCharacter <= '9' ) {
      characterType = CharacterType_Digit;
   }
   else if (
      ( 'a' <= inputCharacter && inputCharacter <= 'z' ) ||
      ( 'A' <= inputCharacter && inputCharacter <= 'Z' )
      ) {
      characterType = CharacterType_Letter;
   }
```

Consider these guidelines when writing such *if-then-else* chains:

Simplify complicated tests with boolean function calls   One reason the code in the previous example is hard to read is that the tests that categorize the character are complicated. To improve readability, you can replace them with calls to boolean functions. Here's how the example's code looks when the tests are replaced with boolean functions:

C++ Example of an *if-then-else* Chain That Uses Boolean Function Calls

```cpp
if ( IsControl( inputCharacter ) ) {
   characterType = CharacterType_ControlCharacter;
}
else if ( IsPunctuation( inputCharacter ) ) {
   characterType = CharacterType_Punctuation;
}
else if ( IsDigit( inputCharacter ) ) {
   characterType = CharacterType_Digit;
}
else if ( IsLetter( inputCharacter ) ) {
   characterType = CharacterType_Letter;
}
```

Put the most common cases first   By putting the most common cases first, you minimize the amount of exception-case handling code someone has to read to find the usual cases. You improve efficiency because you minimize the number of tests the code does to find the most common cases. In the example just shown, letters would be more common than punctuation but the test for punctuation is made first. Here's the code revised so that it tests for letters first:

C++ Example of Testing the Most Common Case First

This test, the most common, is now done first. →
```cpp
if ( IsLetter( inputCharacter ) ) {
   characterType = CharacterType_Letter;
}
```

```
else if ( IsPunctuation( inputCharacter ) ) {
    characterType = CharacterType_Punctuation;
}
else if ( IsDigit( inputCharacter ) ) {
    characterType = CharacterType_Digit;
}
else if ( IsControl( inputCharacter ) ) {
    characterType = CharacterType_ControlCharacter;
}
```

> This test, the least common, is now done last.

Make sure that all cases are covered   Code a final *else* clause with an error message or assertion to catch cases you didn't plan for. This error message is intended for you rather than for the user, so word it appropriately. Here's how you can modify the character-classification example to perform an "other cases" test:

Cross-Reference This is also a good example of how you can use a chain of *if-then-else* tests instead of deeply nested code. For details on this technique, see Section 19.4, "Taming Dangerously Deep Nesting."

C++ Example of Using the Default Case to Trap Errors

```cpp
if ( IsLetter( inputCharacter ) ) {
    characterType = CharacterType_Letter;
}
else if ( IsPunctuation( inputCharacter ) ) {
    characterType = CharacterType_Punctuation;
}
else if ( IsDigit( inputCharacter ) ) {
    characterType = CharacterType_Digit;
}
else if ( IsControl( inputCharacter ) ) {
    characterType = CharacterType_ControlCharacter;
}
else {
    DisplayInternalError( "Unexpected type of character detected." );
}
```

Replace if-then-else *chains with other constructs if your language supports them*   A few languages—Microsoft Visual Basic and Ada, for example—provide *case* statements that support use of strings, enums, and logical functions. Use them—they are easier to code and easier to read than *if-then-else* chains. Code for classifying character types by using a *case* statement in Visual Basic would be written like this:

Visual Basic Example of Using a *case* Statement Instead of an *if-then-else* Chain

```vb
Select Case inputCharacter
    Case "a" To "z"
        characterType = CharacterType_Letter
    Case " ", ",", ".", "!", "(", ")", ":", ";", "?", "-"
        characterType = CharacterType_Punctuation
    Case "0" To "9"
        characterType = CharacterType_Digit
    Case FIRST_CONTROL_CHARACTER To LAST_CONTROL_CHARACTER
        characterType = CharacterType_Control
    Case Else
        DisplayInternalError( "Unexpected type of character detected." )
End Select
```

15.2 *case* Statements

The *case* or *switch* statement is a construct that varies a great deal from language to language. C++ and Java support *case* only for ordinal types taken one value at a time. Visual Basic supports *case* for ordinal types and has powerful shorthand notations for expressing ranges and combinations of values. Many scripting languages don't support *case* statements at all.

The following sections present guidelines for using *case* statements effectively:

Choosing the Most Effective Ordering of Cases

You can choose from among a variety of ways to organize the cases in a *case* statement. If you have a small *case* statement with three options and three corresponding lines of code, the order you use doesn't matter much. If you have a long *case* statement—for example, a *case* statement that handles dozens of events in an event-driven program—order is significant. Following are some ordering possibilities:

Order cases alphabetically or numerically   If cases are equally important, putting them in A-B-C order improves readability. That way a specific case is easy to pick out of the group.

Put the normal case first   If you have one normal case and several exceptions, put the normal case first. Indicate with comments that it's the normal case and that the others are unusual.

Order cases by frequency   Put the most frequently executed cases first and the least frequently executed last. This approach has two advantages. First, human readers can find the most common cases easily. Readers scanning the list for a specific case are likely to be interested in one of the most common cases, and putting the common ones at the top of the code makes the search quicker.

Tips for Using *case* Statements

Here are several tips for using *case* statements:

Cross-Reference For other tips on simplifying code, see Chapter 24, "Refactoring."

Keep the actions of each case simple   Keep the code associated with each case short. Short code following each case helps make the structure of the *case* statement clear. If the actions performed for a case are complicated, write a routine and call the routine from the case rather than putting the code into the case itself.

Don't make up phony variables to be able to use the case statement   A *case* statement should be used for simple data that's easily categorized. If your data isn't simple, use chains of *if-then-else*s instead. Phony variables are confusing, and you should avoid them. For example, don't do this:

Java Example of Creating a Phony *case* Variable—Bad Practice

```java
action = userCommand[ 0 ];
switch ( action ) {
   case 'c':
           Copy();
   break;
   case 'd':
           DeleteCharacter();
   break;
   case 'f':
           Format();
   break;
   case 'h':
           Help();
   break;
   ...
   default:
           HandleUserInputError( ErrorType.InvalidUserCommand );
}
```

The variable that controls the *case* statement is *action*. In this case, *action* is created by peeling off the first character of the *userCommand* string, a string that was entered by the user.

Cross-Reference In contrast to this advice, sometimes you can improve readability by assigning a complicated expression to a well-named boolean variable or function. For details, see "Making Complicated Expressions Simple" in Section 19.1.

This troublemaking code is from the wrong side of town and invites problems. In general, when you manufacture a variable to use in a *case* statement, the real data might not map onto the *case* statement the way you want it to. In this example, if the user types **copy**, the *case* statement peels off the first "c" and correctly calls the *Copy()* routine. On the other hand, if the user types **cement overshoes**, **clambake**, or **cellulite**, the *case* statement also peels off the "c" and calls *Copy()*. The test for an erroneous command in the *case* statement's *else* clause won't work very well because it will miss only erroneous first letters rather than erroneous commands.

Rather than making up a phony variable, this code should use a chain of *if-then-else-if* tests to check the whole string. A virtuous rewrite of the code looks like this:

Java Example of Using *if-then-else*s Instead of a Phony *case* Variable—Good Practice

```java
if ( UserCommand.equals( COMMAND_STRING_COPY ) ) {
   Copy();
}
else if ( UserCommand.equals( COMMAND_STRING_DELETE ) ) {
   DeleteCharacter();
}
else if ( UserCommand.equals( COMMAND_STRING_FORMAT ) ) {
   Format();
}
else if ( UserCommand.equals( COMMAND_STRING_HELP ) ) {
   Help();
}
...
else {
   HandleUserInputError( ErrorType_InvalidCommandInput );
}
```

Use the default clause only to detect legitimate defaults   You might sometimes have only one case remaining and decide to code that case as the default clause. Though sometimes tempting, that's dumb. You lose the automatic documentation provided by *case*-statement labels, and you lose the ability to detect errors with the default clause.

Such *case* statements break down under modification. If you use a legitimate default, adding a new case is trivial—you just add the case and the corresponding code. If you use a phony default, the modification is more difficult. You have to add the new case, possibly making it the new default, and then change the case previously used as the default so that it's a legitimate case. Use a legitimate default in the first place.

Use the default clause to detect errors   If the default clause in a *case* statement isn't being used for other processing and isn't supposed to occur, put a diagnostic message in it:

Java Example of Using the Default Case to Detect Errors—Good Practice

```java
switch ( commandShortcutLetter ) {
    case 'a':
            PrintAnnualReport();
    break;
    case 'p':
            // no action required, but case was considered
    break;
    case 'q':
            PrintQuarterlyReport();
    break;
    case 's':
            PrintSummaryReport();
    break;
    default:
            DisplayInternalError( "Internal Error 905: Call customer support." );
}
```

Messages like this are useful in both debugging and production code. Most users prefer a message like "Internal Error: Please call customer support" to a system crash or, worse, subtly incorrect results that look right until the user's boss checks them.

If the default clause is used for some purpose other than error detection, the implication is that every case selector is correct. Double-check to be sure that every value that could possibly enter the *case* statement would be legitimate. If you come up with some that wouldn't be legitimate, rewrite the statements so that the default clause will check for errors.

In C++ and Java, avoid dropping through the end of a case statement   C-like languages (C, C++, and Java) don't automatically break out of each case. Instead, you have to code the end of each case explicitly. If you don't code the end of a case, the program drops through the end and executes the code for the next case. This can lead to some particularly egregious coding practices, including the following horrible example:

CODING HORROR

Cross-Reference This code's formatting makes it look better than it is. For details on how to use formatting to make good code look good and bad code look bad, see "Endline Layout" in Section 31.3 and the rest of Chapter 31, "Layout and Style."

C++ Example of Abusing the *case* Statement
```cpp
switch ( InputVar ) {
   case 'A': if ( test ) {
                    // statement 1
                    // statement 2
      case 'B':     // statement 3
                    // statement 4
                    ...
                 }
             ...
             break;
   ...
}
```

This practice is bad because it intermingles control constructs. Nested control constructs are hard enough to understand; overlapping constructs are all but impossible. Modifications of case 'A' or case 'B' will be harder than brain surgery, and it's likely that the cases will need to be cleaned up before any modifications will work. You might as well do it right the first time. In general, it's a good idea to avoid dropping through the end of a *case* statement.

In C++, clearly and unmistakably identify flow-throughs at the end of a case *statement* If you intentionally write code to drop through the end of a case, clearly comment the place at which it happens and explain why it needs to be coded that way.

C++ Example of Documenting Falling Through the End of a *case* Statement
```cpp
switch ( errorDocumentationLevel ) {
   case DocumentationLevel_Full:
      DisplayErrorDetails( errorNumber );
      // FALLTHROUGH -- Full documentation also prints summary comments

   case DocumentationLevel_Summary:
      DisplayErrorSummary( errorNumber );
      // FALLTHROUGH -- Summary documentation also prints error number

   case DocumentationLevel_NumberOnly:
      DisplayErrorNumber( errorNumber );
      break;

   default:
      DisplayInternalError( "Internal Error 905: Call customer support." );
}
```

This technique is useful about as often as you find someone who would rather have a used Pontiac Aztek than a new Corvette. Generally, code that falls through from one case to another is an invitation to make mistakes as the code is modified, and it should be avoided.

cc2e.com/1545

CHECKLIST: Using Conditionals

if-then Statements

- ❑ Is the nominal path through the code clear?
- ❑ Do *if-then* tests branch correctly on equality?
- ❑ Is the *else* clause present and documented?
- ❑ Is the *else* clause correct?
- ❑ Are the *if* and *else* clauses used correctly—not reversed?
- ❑ Does the normal case follow the *if* rather than the *else*?

if-then-else-if Chains

- ❑ Are complicated tests encapsulated in boolean function calls?
- ❑ Are the most common cases tested first?
- ❑ Are all cases covered?
- ❑ Is the *if-then-else-if* chain the best implementation—better than a *case* statement?

case Statements

- ❑ Are cases ordered meaningfully?
- ❑ Are the actions for each case simple—calling other routines if necessary?
- ❑ Does the *case* statement test a real variable, not a phony one that's made up solely to use and abuse the *case* statement?
- ❑ Is the use of the default clause legitimate?
- ❑ Is the default clause used to detect and report unexpected cases?
- ❑ In C, C++, or Java, does the end of each case have a *break*?

Key Points

- For simple *if-else* statements, pay attention to the order of the *if* and *else* clauses, especially if they process a lot of errors. Make sure the nominal case is clear.

- For *if-then-else* chains and *case* statements, choose an order that maximizes readability.

- To trap errors, use the default clause in a *case* statement or the last *else* in a chain of *if-then-else* statements.

- All control constructs are not created equal. Choose the control construct that's most appropriate for each section of code.

Chapter 16

Controlling Loops

cc2e.com/1609

Contents

Related Topics

"Loop" is an informal term that refers to any kind of iterative control structure—any structure that causes a program to repeatedly execute a block of code. Common loop types are *for*, *while*, and *do-while* in C++ and Java, and *For-Next*, *While-Wend*, and *Do-Loop-While* in Microsoft Visual Basic. Using loops is one of the most complex aspects of programming; knowing how and when to use each kind of loop is a decisive factor in constructing high-quality software.

16.1 Selecting the Kind of Loop

In most languages, you'll use a few kinds of loops:

- The counted loop is performed a specific number of times, perhaps one time for each employee.

- The continuously evaluated loop doesn't know ahead of time how many times it will be executed and tests whether it has finished on each iteration. For example, it runs while money remains, until the user selects quit, or until it encounters an error.

- The endless loop executes forever once it has started. It's the kind you find in embedded systems such as pacemakers, microwave ovens, and cruise controls.

- The iterator loop performs its action once for each element in a container class.

The kinds of loops are differentiated first by flexibility—whether the loop executes a specified number of times or whether it tests for completion on each iteration.

The kinds of loops are also differentiated by the location of the test for completion. You can put the test at the beginning, the middle, or the end of the loop. This characteristic tells you whether the loop executes at least once. If the loop is tested at the beginning, its body isn't necessarily executed. If the loop is tested at the end, its body is executed at least once. If the loop is tested in the middle, the part of the loop that precedes the test is executed at least once, but the part of the loop that follows the test isn't necessarily executed at all.

Flexibility and the location of the test determine the kind of loop to choose as a control structure. Table 16-1 shows the kinds of loops in several languages and describes each loop's flexibility and test location.

Table 16-1   **The Kinds of Loops**

Language	Kind of Loop	Flexibility	Test Location
Visual Basic	*For-Next*	rigid	beginning
	While-Wend	flexible	beginning
	Do-Loop-While	flexible	beginning or end
	For-Each	rigid	beginning
C, C++, C#, Java	*for*	flexible	beginning
	while	flexible	beginning
	do-while	flexible	end
	foreach[*]	rigid	beginning

* Available only in C#. Planned for other languages, including Java, at the time of this writing.

When to Use a *while* Loop

Novice programmers sometimes think that a *while* loop is continuously evaluated and that it terminates the instant the *while* condition becomes false, regardless of which statement in the loop is being executed (Curtis et al. 1986). Although it's not quite that flexible, a *while* loop is a flexible loop choice. If you don't know ahead of time exactly how many times you'll want the loop to iterate, use a *while* loop. Contrary to what some novices think, the test for the loop exit is performed only once each time through the loop, and the main issue with respect to *while* loops is deciding whether to test at the beginning or the end of the loop.

Loop with Test at the Beginning

For a loop that tests at the beginning, you can use a *while* loop in C++, C#, Java, Visual Basic, and most other languages. You can emulate a *while* loop in other languages.

Loop with Test at the End

You might occasionally have a situation in which you want a flexible loop, but the loop needs to execute at least one time. In such a case, you can use a *while* loop that is tested at its end. You can use *do-while* in C++, C#, and Java, *Do-Loop-While* in Visual Basic, or you can emulate end-tested loops in other languages.

When to Use a Loop-With-Exit Loop

A loop-with-exit loop is a loop in which the exit condition appears in the middle of the loop rather than at the beginning or at the end. The loop-with-exit loop is available explicitly in Visual Basic, and you can emulate it with the structured constructs *while* and *break* in C++, C, and Java or with *goto*s in other languages.

Normal Loop-With-Exit Loops

A loop-with-exit loop usually consists of the loop beginning, the loop body (including an exit condition), and the loop end, as in this Visual Basic example:

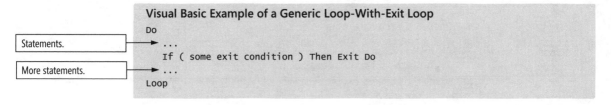

Visual Basic Example of a Generic Loop-With-Exit Loop

```
Do
    ...
    If ( some exit condition ) Then Exit Do
    ...
Loop
```

Statements.

More statements.

The typical use of a loop-with-exit loop is for the case in which testing at the beginning or at the end of the loop requires coding a loop-and-a-half. Here's a C++ example of a case that warrants a loop-with-exit loop but doesn't use one:

C++ Example of Duplicated Code That Will Break Down Under Maintenance

```
// Compute scores and ratings.
score  = 0;
GetNextRating( &ratingIncrement );
rating = rating + ratingIncrement;
while ( ( score < targetScore ) && ( ratingIncrement != 0 ) ) {
    GetNextScore( &scoreIncrement );
    score = score + scoreIncrement;
    GetNextRating( &ratingIncrement );
    rating = rating + ratingIncrement;
}
```

These lines appear here...

...and are repeated here.

The two lines of code at the top of the example are repeated in the last two lines of code of the *while* loop. During modification, you can easily forget to keep the two sets of lines parallel. Another programmer modifying the code probably won't even realize that the two sets of lines are supposed to be modified in parallel. Either way, the result will be errors arising from incomplete modifications. Here's how you can rewrite the code more clearly:

C++ Example of a Loop-With-Exit Loop That's Easier to Maintain

```cpp
// Compute scores and ratings. The code uses an infinite loop
// and a break statement to emulate a loop-with-exit loop.
score = 0;
while ( true ) {
   GetNextRating( &ratingIncrement );
   rating = rating + ratingIncrement;

   if ( !( ( score < targetScore ) && ( ratingIncrement != 0 ) ) ) {
      break;
   }

   GetNextScore( &scoreIncrement );
   score = score + scoreIncrement;
}
```

This is the loop-exit condition (and now it could be simplified using DeMorgan's Theorems, described in Section 19.1).

Here's how the same code is written in Visual Basic:

Visual Basic Example of a Loop-With-Exit Loop

```vb
' Compute scores and ratings
score = 0
Do
   GetNextRating( ratingIncrement )
   rating = rating + ratingIncrement

   If ( not ( score < targetScore and ratingIncrement <> 0 ) ) Then Exit Do

   GetNextScore( ScoreIncrement )
   score = score + scoreIncrement
Loop
```

Consider these finer points when you use this kind of loop:

Cross-Reference Details on exit conditions are presented later in this chapter. For details on using comments with loops, see "Commenting Control Structures" in Section 32.5.

Put all the exit conditions in one place. Spreading them around practically guarantees that one exit condition or another will be overlooked during debugging, modification, or testing.

Use comments for clarification. If you use the loop-with-exit loop technique in a language that doesn't support it directly, use comments to make what you're doing clear.

HARD DATA

The loop-with-exit loop is a one-entry, one-exit, structured control construct, and it is the preferred kind of loop control (Software Productivity Consortium 1989). It has been shown to be easier to understand than other kinds of loops. A study of student programmers compared this kind of loop with those that exited at either the top or the bottom (Soloway, Bonar, and Ehrlich 1983). Students scored 25 percent higher on a test of comprehension when loop-with-exit loops were used, and the authors of the study concluded that the loop-with-exit structure more closely models the way people think about iterative control than other loop structures do.

In common practice, the loop-with-exit loop isn't widely used yet. The jury is still locked in a smoky room arguing about whether it's a good practice for production code. Until the jury is in, the loop-with-exit loop is a good technique to have in your programmer's toolbox—as long as you use it carefully.

Abnormal Loop-With-Exit Loops

Another kind of loop-with-exit loop that's used to avoid a loop-and-a-half is shown here:

CODING HORROR

C++ Example of Entering the Middle of a Loop with a *goto*—Bad Practice
```cpp
goto Start;
while ( expression ) {
   // do something
   ...

   Start:

   // do something else
   ...
}
```

At first glance, this seems to be similar to the previous loop-with-exit examples. It's used in simulations in which // *do something* doesn't need to be executed at the first pass through the loop but // *do something* else does. It's a one-in, one-out control construct: the only way into the loop is through the *goto* at the top, and the only way out of the loop is through the *while* test. This approach has two problems: it uses a *goto*, and it's unusual enough to be confusing.

In C++, you can accomplish the same effect without using a *goto*, as demonstrated in the following example. If the language you're using doesn't support a *break* command, you can emulate one with a *goto*.

C++ Example of Code Rewritten Without a *goto*—Better Practice

The blocks before and after the *break* have been switched.
```cpp
while ( true ) {
   // do something else
   ...
```

```
    if ( !( expression ) ) {
       break;
    }

    // do something
    ...
}
```

When to Use a *for* Loop

Further Reading For more good guidelines on using *for* loops, see *Writing Solid Code* (Maguire 1993).

A *for* loop is a good choice when you need a loop that executes a specified number of times. You can use *for* in C++, C, Java, Visual Basic, and most other languages.

Use *for* loops for simple activities that don't require internal loop controls. Use them when the loop control involves simple increments or simple decrements, such as iterating through the elements in a container. The point of a *for* loop is that you set it up at the top of the loop and then forget about it. You don't have to do anything inside the loop to control it. If you have a condition under which execution has to jump out of a loop, use a *while* loop instead.

Likewise, don't explicitly change the index value of a *for* loop to force it to terminate. Use a *while* loop instead. The *for* loop is for simple uses. Most complicated looping tasks are better handled by a *while* loop.

When to Use a *foreach* Loop

The *foreach* loop or its equivalent (*foreach* in C#, *For-Each* in Visual Basic, *for-in* in Python) is useful for performing an operation on each member of an array or other container. It has the advantage of eliminating loop-housekeeping arithmetic and therefore eliminating any chance of errors in the loop-housekeeping arithmetic. Here's an example of this kind of loop:

C# Example of a *foreach* Loop
```csharp
int [] fibonacciSequence = new int [] { 0, 1, 1, 2, 3, 5, 8, 13, 21, 34 };
int oddFibonacciNumbers = 0;
int evenFibonacciNumbers = 0;

// count the number of odd and even numbers in a Fibonacci sequence
foreach ( int fibonacciNumber in fibonacciSequence ) {
    if ( fibonacciNumber % 2 ) == 0 ) {
        evenFibonacciNumbers++;
    }
    else {
        oddFibonacciNumbers++;
    }
}

Console.WriteLine( "Found {0} odd numbers and {1} even numbers.",
    oddFibonacciNumbers, evenFibonacciNumbers );
```

16.2 Controlling the Loop

What can go wrong with a loop? Any answer would have to include incorrect or omitted loop initialization, omitted initialization of accumulators or other variables related to the loop, improper nesting, incorrect termination of the loop, forgetting to increment a loop variable or incrementing the variable incorrectly, and indexing an array element from a loop index incorrectly.

KEY POINT

You can forestall these problems by observing two practices. First, minimize the number of factors that affect the loop. Simplify! Simplify! Simplify! Second, treat the inside of the loop as if it were a routine—keep as much of the control as possible outside the loop. Explicitly state the conditions under which the body of the loop is to be executed. Don't make the reader look inside the loop to understand the loop control. Think of a loop as a black box: the surrounding program knows the control conditions but not the contents.

Cross-Reference If you use the *while (true)-break* technique described earlier, the exit condition is inside the black box. Even if you use only one exit condition, you lose the benefit of treating the loop as a black box.

C++ Example of Treating a Loop as a Black Box
```cpp
while ( !inputFile.EndOfFile() && moreDataAvailable ) {



}
```

What are the conditions under which this loop terminates? Clearly, all you know is that either *inputFile.EndOfFile()* becomes true or *moreDataAvailable* becomes false.

Entering the Loop

Use these guidelines when entering a loop:

Enter the loop from one location only   A variety of loop-control structures allows you to test at the beginning, middle, or end of a loop. These structures are rich enough to allow you to enter the loop from the top every time. You don't need to enter at multiple locations.

Put initialization code directly before the loop   The Principle of Proximity advocates putting related statements together. If related statements are strewn across a routine, it's easy to overlook them during modification and to make the modifications incorrectly. If related statements are kept together, it's easier to avoid errors during modification.

Cross-Reference For more on limiting the scope of loop variables, see "Limit the scope of loop-index variables to the loop itself" later in this chapter.

Keep loop-initialization statements with the loop they're related to. If you don't, you're more likely to cause errors when you generalize the loop into a bigger loop and forget to modify the initialization code. The same kind of error can occur when you move or copy the loop code into a different routine without moving or copying its initialization code. Putting initializations away from the loop—in the data-declaration section or in a housekeeping section at the top of the routine that contains the loop—invites initialization troubles.

Use **while(true)** *for infinite loops*   You might have a loop that runs without terminating—for example, a loop in firmware such as a pacemaker or a microwave oven. Or you might have a loop that terminates only in response to an event—an "event loop." You could code such an infinite loop in several ways. Faking an infinite loop with a statement like *for i = 1 to 99999* is a poor choice because the specific loop limits muddy the intent of the loop—*99999* could be a legitimate value. Such a fake infinite loop can also break down under maintenance.

The *while(true)* idiom is considered a standard way of writing an infinite loop in C++, Java, Visual Basic, and other languages that support comparable structures. Some programmers prefer to use *for(;;)*, which is an accepted alternative.

Prefer **for** *loops when they're appropriate*   The *for* loop packages loop-control code in one place, which makes for easily readable loops. One mistake programmers commonly make when modifying software is changing the loop-initialization code at the top of a *while* loop but forgetting to change related code at the bottom. In a *for* loop, all the relevant code is together at the top of the loop, which makes correct modifications easier. If you can use the *for* loop appropriately instead of another kind of loop, do it.

Don't use a **for** *loop when a* **while** *loop is more appropriate*   A common abuse of the flexible *for* loop structure in C++, C#, and Java is haphazardly cramming the contents of a *while* loop into a *for* loop header. The following example shows a *while* loop crammed into a *for* loop header:

CODING
HORROR

C++ Example of a *while* Loop Abusively Crammed into a *for* Loop Header
```
// read all the records from a file
for ( inputFile.MoveToStart(), recordCount = 0; !inputFile.EndOfFile();
    recordCount++ ) {
    inputFile.GetRecord();
}
```

The advantage of C++'s *for* loop over *for* loops in other languages is that it's more flexible about the kinds of initialization and termination information it can use. The weakness inherent in such flexibility is that you can put statements into the loop header that have nothing to do with controlling the loop.

Reserve the *for* loop header for loop-control statements—statements that initialize the loop, terminate it, or move it toward termination. In the example just shown, the *inputFile.GetRecord()* statement in the body of the loop moves the loop toward termination, but the *recordCount* statements don't; they're housekeeping statements that don't control the loop's progress. Putting the *recordCount* statements in the loop header and leaving the *inputFile.GetRecord()* statement out is misleading; it creates the false impression that *recordCount* controls the loop.

If you want to use the *for* loop rather than the *while* loop in this case, put the loop-control statements in the loop header and leave everything else out. Here's the right way to use the loop header:

C++ Example of Logical if Unconventional Use of a *for* Loop Header

```
recordCount = 0;
for ( inputFile.MoveToStart(); !inputFile.EndOfFile(); inputFile.GetRecord() ) {
   recordCount++;
}
```

The contents of the loop header in this example are all related to control of the loop. The *inputFile.MoveToStart()* statement initializes the loop, the *!inputFile.EndOfFile()* statement tests whether the loop has finished, and the *inputFile.GetRecord()* statement moves the loop toward termination. The statements that affect *recordCount* don't directly move the loop toward termination and are appropriately not included in the loop header. The *while* loop is probably still more appropriate for this job, but at least this code uses the loop header logically. For the record, here's how the code looks when it uses a *while* loop:

C++ Example of Appropriate Use of a *while* Loop

```
// read all the records from a file
inputFile.MoveToStart();
recordCount = 0;
while ( !inputFile.EndOfFile() ) {
   inputFile.GetRecord();
   recordCount++;
}
```

Processing the Middle of the Loop

The following subsections describe handling the middle of a loop:

Use { and } to enclose the statements in a loop   Use code brackets every time. They don't cost anything in speed or space at run time, they help readability, and they help prevent errors as the code is modified. They're a good defensive-programming practice.

Avoid empty loops   In C++ and Java, it's possible to create an empty loop, one in which the work the loop is doing is coded on the same line as the test that checks whether the work is finished. Here's an example:

C++ Example of an Empty Loop

```
while ( ( inputChar = dataFile.GetChar() ) != CharType_Eof ) {
   ;
}
```

In this example, the loop is empty because the *while* expression includes two things: the work of the loop—*inputChar = dataFile.GetChar()*—and a test for whether the loop should terminate—*inputChar != CharType_Eof*. The loop would be clearer if it were recoded so that the work it does is evident to the reader:

C++ Example of an Empty Loop Converted to an Occupied Loop

```
do {
    inputChar = dataFile.GetChar();
} while ( inputChar != CharType_Eof );
```

The new code takes up three full lines rather than one line and a semicolon, which is appropriate since it does the work of three lines rather than that of one line and a semicolon.

Keep loop-housekeeping chores at either the beginning or the end of the loop Loop-housekeeping chores are expressions like *i = i + 1* or *j++*, expressions whose main purpose isn't to do the work of the loop but to control the loop. The housekeeping is done at the end of the loop in this example:

C++ Example of Housekeeping Statements at the End of a Loop

```
nameCount = 0;
totalLength = 0;
while ( !inputFile.EndOfFile() ) {
    // do the work of the loop
    inputFile >> inputString;
    names[ nameCount ] = inputString;
    ...

    // prepare for next pass through the loop--housekeeping
    nameCount++;
    totalLength = totalLength + inputString.length();
}
```

Here are the housekeeping statements.

As a general rule, the variables you initialize before the loop are the variables you'll manipulate in the housekeeping part of the loop.

Cross-Reference For more on optimization, see Chapter 25, "Code-Tuning Strategies," and Chapter 26, "Code-Tuning Techniques."

Make each loop perform only one function The mere fact that a loop can be used to do two things at once isn't sufficient justification for doing them together. Loops should be like routines in that each one should do only one thing and do it well. If it seems inefficient to use two loops where one would suffice, write the code as two loops, comment that they could be combined for efficiency, and then wait until benchmarks show that the section of the program poses a performance problem before changing the two loops into one.

Exiting the Loop

These subsections describe handling the end of a loop:

Assure yourself that the loop ends This is fundamental. Mentally simulate the execution of the loop until you are confident that, in all circumstances, it ends. Think through the nominal cases, the endpoints, and each of the exceptional cases.

Make loop-termination conditions obvious If you use a *for* loop and don't fool around with the loop index and don't use a *goto* or *break* to get out of the loop, the termination condition will be obvious. Likewise, if you use a *while* or *repeat-until* loop and put all the control in the *while* or *repeat-until* clause, the termination condition will be obvious. The key is putting the control in one place.

Don't monkey with the loop index of a for ***loop to make the loop terminate*** Some programmers jimmy the value of a *for* loop index to make the loop terminate early. Here's an example:

CODING HORROR

Here's the monkeying.

```Java
Java Example of Monkeying with a Loop Index
for ( int i = 0; i < 100; i++ ) {
   // some code
   ...
   if ( ... ) {
      i = 100;
   }

   // more code
   ...
}
```

The intent in this example is to terminate the loop under some condition by setting *i* to *100*, a value that's larger than the end of the *for* loop's range of *0* through *99*. Virtually all good programmers avoid this practice; it's the sign of an amateur. When you set up a *for* loop, the loop counter is off limits. Use a *while* loop to provide more control over the loop's exit conditions.

Avoid code that depends on the loop index's final value It's bad form to use the value of the loop index after the loop. The terminal value of the loop index varies from language to language and implementation to implementation. The value is different when the loop terminates normally and when it terminates abnormally. Even if you happen to know what the final value is without stopping to think about it, the next person to read the code will probably have to think about it. It's better form and more self-documenting if you assign the final value to a variable at the appropriate point inside the loop.

This code misuses the index's final value:

C++ Example of Code That Misuses a Loop Index's Terminal Value
```cpp
for ( recordCount = 0; recordCount < MAX_RECORDS; recordCount++ ) {
   if ( entry[ recordCount ] == testValue ) {
      break;
   }
}
// lots of code
...
if ( recordCount < MAX_RECORDS ) {
   return( true );
}
else {
   return( false );
}
```

Here's the misuse of the loop index's terminal value.

In this fragment, the second test for *recordCount < MaxRecords* makes it appear that the loop is supposed to loop though all the values in *entry[]* and return *true* if it finds the one equal to *testValue* and *false* otherwise. It's hard to remember whether the index gets incremented past the end of the loop, so it's easy to make an off-by-one error. You're better off writing code that doesn't depend on the index's final value. Here's how to rewrite the code:

C++ Example of Code That Doesn't Misuse a Loop Index's Terminal Value
```cpp
found = false;
for ( recordCount = 0; recordCount < MAX_RECORDS; recordCount++ ) {
   if ( entry[ recordCount ] == testValue ) {
      found = true;
      break;
   }
}
// lots of code
...
return( found );
```

This second code fragment uses an extra variable and keeps references to *recordCount* more localized. As is often the case when an extra boolean variable is used, the resulting code is clearer.

Consider using safety counters   A safety counter is a variable you increment each pass through a loop to determine whether a loop has been executed too many times. If you have a program in which an error would be catastrophic, you can use safety counters to ensure that all loops end. This C++ loop could profitably use a safety counter:

C++ Example of a Loop That Could Use a Safety Counter
```
do {
   node = node->Next;
   ...
} while ( node->Next != NULL );
```

Here's the same code with the safety counters added:

C++ Example of Using a Safety Counter
```
safetyCounter = 0;
do {
   node = node->Next;
   ...
   safetyCounter++;
   if ( safetyCounter >= SAFETY_LIMIT ) {
      Assert( false, "Internal Error: Safety-Counter Violation." );
   }
   ...
} while ( node->Next != NULL );
```

Here's the safety-counter code.

Safety counters are not a cure-all. Introduced into the code one at a time, safety counters increase complexity and can lead to additional errors. Because they aren't used in every loop, you might forget to maintain safety-counter code when you modify loops in parts of the program that do use them. If safety counters are instituted as a projectwide standard for critical loops, however, you learn to expect them and the safety-counter code is no more prone to produce errors later than any other code is.

Exiting Loops Early

Many languages provide a means of causing a loop to terminate in some way other than completing the *for* or *while* condition. In this discussion, *break* is a generic term for *break* in C++, C, and Java; for *Exit-Do* and *Exit-For* in Visual Basic; and for similar constructs, including those simulated with *goto*s in languages that don't support *break* directly. The *break* statement (or equivalent) causes a loop to terminate through the normal exit channel; the program resumes execution at the first statement following the loop.

The *continue* statement is similar to *break* in that it's an auxiliary loop-control statement. Rather than causing a loop exit, however, *continue* causes the program to skip the loop body and continue executing at the beginning of the next iteration of the loop. A *continue* statement is shorthand for an *if-then* clause that would prevent the rest of the loop from being executed.

Consider using break ***statements rather than boolean flags in a*** while ***loop*** In some cases, adding boolean flags to a *while* loop to emulate exits from the body of the loop makes the loop hard to read. Sometimes you can remove several levels of indentation inside a loop and simplify loop control just by using a *break* instead of a series of *if* tests.

Putting multiple *break* conditions into separate statements and placing them near the code that produces the *break* can reduce nesting and make the loop more readable.

Be wary of a loop with a lot of breaks scattered through it   A loop's containing a lot of *breaks* can indicate unclear thinking about the structure of the loop or its role in the surrounding code. A proliferation of *breaks* raises the possibility that the loop could be more clearly expressed as a series of loops rather than as one loop with many exits.

According to an article in *Software Engineering Notes*, the software error that brought down the New York City phone systems for 9 hours on January 15, 1990, was due to an extra *break* statement (SEN 1990):

C++ Example of Erroneous Use of a *break* Statement Within a *do-switch-if* Block
```
do {
   ...
   switch
      ...
      if () {
         ...
         break;
         ...
      }
      ...
} while ( ... );
```

This *break* was intended for the *if* but broke out of the *switch* instead.

Multiple *breaks* don't necessarily indicate an error, but their existence in a loop is a warning sign, a canary in a coal mine that's gasping for air instead of singing as loud as it should be.

Use continue *for tests at the top of a loop*   A good use of *continue* is for moving execution past the body of the loop after testing a condition at the top. For example, if the loop reads records, discards records of one kind, and processes records of another kind, you could put a test like this one at the top of the loop:

Pseudocode Example of a Relatively Safe Use of *continue*
```
while ( not eof( file ) ) do
   read( record, file )
   if ( record.Type <> targetType ) then
      continue

   -- process record of targetType
   ...
end while
```

Using *continue* in this way lets you avoid an *if* test that would effectively indent the entire body of the loop. If, on the other hand, the *continue* occurs toward the middle or end of the loop, use an *if* instead.

Use the labeled break ***structure if your language supports it*** Java supports use of labeled *break*s to prevent the kind of problem experienced with the New York City telephone outage. A labeled *break* can be used to exit a *for* loop, an *if* statement, or any block of code enclosed in braces (Arnold, Gosling, and Holmes 2000).

Here's a possible solution to the New York City telephone code problem, with the programming language changed from C++ to Java to show the labeled break:

Java Example of a Better Use of a Labeled *break* Statement Within a *do-switch-if* Block

```
do {
    ...
    switch
        ...
        CALL_CENTER_DOWN:
        if () {
            ...
            break CALL_CENTER_DOWN;
            ...
        }
    ...
} while ( ... );
```

The target of the labeled *break* is unambiguous.

Use break ***and*** continue ***only with caution*** Use of *break* eliminates the possibility of treating a loop as a black box. Limiting yourself to only one statement to control a loop's exit condition is a powerful way to simplify your loops. Using a *break* forces the person reading your code to look inside the loop for an understanding of the loop control. That makes the loop more difficult to understand.

Use *break* only after you have considered the alternatives. You don't know with certainty whether *continue* and *break* are virtuous or evil constructs. Some computer scientists argue that they are a legitimate technique in structured programming; some argue that they aren't. Because you don't know in general whether *continue* and *break* are right or wrong, use them, but only with a fear that you might be wrong. It really is a simple proposition: if you can't defend a *break* or a *continue*, don't use it.

Checking Endpoints

A single loop usually has three cases of interest: the first case, an arbitrarily selected middle case, and the last case. When you create a loop, mentally run through the first, middle, and last cases to make sure that the loop doesn't have any off-by-one errors. If you have any special cases that are different from the first or last case, check those too. If the loop contains complex computations, get out your calculator and manually check the calculations.

KEY POINT

Willingness to perform this kind of check is a key difference between efficient and inefficient programmers. Efficient programmers do the work of mental simulations and hand calculations because they know that such measures help them find errors.

Inefficient programmers tend to experiment randomly until they find a combination that seems to work. If a loop isn't working the way it's supposed to, the inefficient programmer changes the < sign to a <= sign. If that fails, the inefficient programmer changes the loop index by adding or subtracting 1. Eventually the programmer using this approach might stumble onto the right combination or simply replace the original error with a more subtle one. Even if this random process results in a correct program, it doesn't result in the programmer's knowing why the program is correct.

You can expect several benefits from mental simulations and hand calculations. The mental discipline results in fewer errors during initial coding, in more rapid detection of errors during debugging, and in a better overall understanding of the program. The mental exercise means that you understand how your code works rather than guessing about it.

Using Loop Variables

Here are some guidelines for using loop variables:

Cross-Reference For details on naming loop variables, see "Naming Loop Indexes" in Section 11.2.

Use ordinal or enumerated types for limits on both arrays and loops   Generally, loop counters should be integer values. Floating-point values don't increment well. For example, you could add 1.0 to 26,742,897.0 and get 26,742,897.0 instead of 26,742,898.0. If this incremented value were a loop counter, you'd have an infinite loop.

KEY POINT

Use meaningful variable names to make nested loops readable   Arrays are often indexed with the same variables that are used for loop indexes. If you have a one-dimensional array, you might be able to get away with using i, j, or k to index it. But if you have an array with two or more dimensions, you should use meaningful index names to clarify what you're doing. Meaningful array-index names clarify both the purpose of the loop and the part of the array you intend to access.

Here's code that doesn't put this principle to work; it uses the meaningless names i, j, and k instead:

CODING HORROR

Java Example of Bad Loop Variable Names
```java
for ( int i = 0; i < numPayCodes; i++ ) {
   for ( int j = 0; j < 12; j++ ) {
      for ( int k = 0; k < numDivisions; k++ ) {
         sum = sum + transaction[ j ][ i ][ k ];
      }
   }
}
```

What do you think the array indexes in *transaction* mean? Do *i*, *j*, and *k* tell you anything about the contents of *transaction*? If you had the declaration of *transaction*, could you easily determine whether the indexes were in the right order? Here's the same loop with more readable loop variable names:

Java Example of Good Loop Variable Names
```java
for ( int payCodeIdx = 0; payCodeIdx < numPayCodes; payCodeIdx++ ) {
    for (int month = 0; month < 12; month++ ) {
        for ( int divisionIdx = 0; divisionIdx < numDivisions; divisionIdx++ ) {
            sum = sum + transaction[ month ][ payCodeIdx ][ divisionIdx ];
        }
    }
}
```

What do you think the array indexes in *transaction* mean this time? In this case, the answer is easier to come by because the variable names *payCodeIdx*, *month*, and *divisionIdx* tell you a lot more than *i*, *j*, and *k* did. The computer can read the two versions of the loop equally easily. People can read the second version more easily than the first, however, and the second version is better since your primary audience is made up of humans, not computers.

Use meaningful names to avoid loop-index cross-talk   Habitual use of *i*, *j*, and *k* can give rise to index cross-talk—using the same index name for two different purposes. Take a look at this example:

C++ Example of Index Cross-Talk

i is used first here...

```cpp
for ( i = 0;  i < numPayCodes; i++ ) {
    // lots of code
    ...
    for ( j = 0; j < 12; j++ ) {
        // lots of code
        ...
```

...and again here.

```cpp
        for ( i = 0; i < numDivisions; i++ ) {
            sum = sum + transaction[ j ][ i ][ k ];
        }
    }
}
```

The use of *i* is so habitual that it's used twice in the same nesting structure. The second *for* loop controlled by *i* conflicts with the first, and that's index cross-talk. Using more meaningful names than *i*, *j*, and *k* would have prevented the problem. In general, if the body of a loop has more than a couple of lines, if it might grow, or if it's in a group of nested loops, avoid *i*, *j*, and *k*.

Limit the scope of loop-index variables to the loop itself   Loop-index cross-talk and other uses of loop indexes outside their loops is such a significant problem that the designers of Ada decided to make *for* loop indexes invalid outside their loops; trying to use one outside its *for* loop generates an error at compile time.

C++ and Java implement the same idea to some extent—they allow loop indexes to be declared within a loop, but they don't require it. In the example on page 378, the *recordCount* variable could be declared inside the *for* statement, which would limit its scope to the *for* loop, like this:

C++ Example of Declaring a Loop-Index Variable Within a *for* loop
```
for ( int recordCount = 0; recordCount < MAX_RECORDS; recordCount++ ) {
   // looping code that uses recordCount
}
```

In principle, this technique should allow creation of code that redeclares *recordCount* in multiple loops without any risk of misusing the two different *recordCounts*. That usage would give rise to code that looks like this:

C++ Example of Declaring Loop-Indexes Within *for* loops and Reusing Them Safely— Maybe!
```
for ( int recordCount = 0; recordCount < MAX_RECORDS; recordCount++ ) {
   // looping code that uses recordCount
}
// intervening code
for ( int recordCount = 0; recordCount < MAX_RECORDS; recordCount++ ) {
   // additional looping code that uses a different recordCount
}
```

This technique is helpful for documenting the purpose of the *recordCount* variable; however, don't rely on your compiler to enforce *recordCount*'s scope. Section 6.3.3.1 of *The C++ Programming Language* (Stroustrup 1997) says that *recordCount* should have a scope limited to its loop. When I checked this functionality with three different C++ compilers, however, I got three different results:

- The first compiler flagged *recordCount* in the second *for* loop for multiple variable declarations and generated an error.

- The second compiler accepted *recordCount* in the second *for* loop but allowed it to be used outside the first *for* loop.

- The third compiler allowed both usages of *recordCount* and did not allow either one to be used outside the *for* loop in which it was declared.

As is often the case with more esoteric language features, compiler implementations can vary.

How Long Should a Loop Be?

Loop length can be measured in lines of code or depth of nesting. Here are some guidelines:

Make your loops short enough to view all at once   If you usually look at loops on your monitor and your monitor displays 50 lines, that puts a 50-line restriction on you. Experts have suggested a loop-length limit of one page. When you begin to appreciate the principle of writing simple code, however, you'll rarely write loops longer than 15 or 20 lines.

Cross-Reference For details on simplifying nesting, see Section 19.4, "Taming Dangerously Deep Nesting."

Limit nesting to three levels   Studies have shown that the ability of programmers to comprehend a loop deteriorates significantly beyond three levels of nesting (Yourdon 1986a). If you're going beyond that number of levels, make the loop shorter (conceptually) by breaking part of it into a routine or simplifying the control structure.

Move loop innards of long loops into routines   If the loop is well designed, the code on the inside of a loop can often be moved into one or more routines that are called from within the loop.

Make long loops especially clear   Length adds complexity. If you write a short loop, you can use riskier control structures such as *break* and *continue*, multiple exits, complicated termination conditions, and so on. If you write a longer loop and feel any concern for your reader, you'll give the loop a single exit and make the exit condition unmistakably clear.

16.3 Creating Loops Easily—From the Inside Out

If you sometimes have trouble coding a complex loop—which most programmers do—you can use a simple technique to get it right the first time. Here's the general process. Start with one case. Code that case with literals. Then indent it, put a loop around it, and replace the literals with loop indexes or computed expressions. Put another loop around that, if necessary, and replace more literals. Continue the process as long as you have to. When you finish, add all the necessary initializations. Since you start at the simple case and work outward to generalize it, you might think of this as coding from the inside out.

Cross-Reference Coding a loop from the inside out is similar to the process described in Chapter 9, "The Pseudocode Programming Process."

Suppose you're writing a program for an insurance company. It has life-insurance rates that vary according to a person's age and sex. Your job is to write a routine that computes the total life-insurance premium for a group. You need a loop that takes the rate for each person in a list and adds it to a total. Here's how you'd do it.

First, in comments, write the steps the body of the loop needs to perform. It's easier to write down what needs to be done when you're not thinking about details of syntax, loop indexes, array indexes, and so on.

> **Step 1: Creating a Loop from the Inside Out (Pseudocode Example)**
> ```
> -- get rate from table
> -- add rate to total
> ```

Second, convert the comments in the body of the loop to code, as much as you can without actually writing the whole loop. In this case, get the rate for one person and add it to the overall total. Use concrete, specific data rather than abstractions.

table doesn't have any indexes yet.

> **Step 2: Creating a Loop from the Inside Out (Pseudocode Example)**
> ```
> rate = table[ ]
> totalRate = totalRate + rate
> ```

The example assumes that *table* is an array that holds the rate data. You don't have to worry about the array indexes at first. *rate* is the variable that holds the rate data selected from the rate table. Likewise, *totalRate* is a variable that holds the total of the rates.

Next, put in indexes for the *table* array:

> **Step 3: Creating a Loop from the Inside Out (Pseudocode Example)**
> ```
> rate = table[ census.Age ][ census.Gender ]
> totalRate = totalRate + rate
> ```

The array is accessed by age and sex, so *census.Age* and *census.Gender* are used to index the array. The example assumes that *census* is a structure that holds information about people in the group to be rated.

The next step is to build a loop around the existing statements. Since the loop is supposed to compute the rates for each person in a group, the loop should be indexed by person.

> **Step 4: Creating a Loop from the Inside Out (Pseudocode Example)**
> ```
> For person = firstPerson to lastPerson
>    rate = table[ census.Age, census.Gender ]
>    totalRate = totalRate + rate
> End For
> ```

All you have to do here is put the *for* loop around the existing code and then indent the existing code and put it inside a *begin-end* pair. Finally, check to make sure that the variables that depend on the *person* loop index have been generalized. In this case, the *census* variable varies with *person*, so it should be generalized appropriately.

> **Step 5: Creating a Loop from the Inside Out (Pseudocode Example)**
> ```
> For person = firstPerson to lastPerson
>    rate = table[ census[ person ].Age, census[ person ].Gender ]
>    totalRate = totalRate + rate
> End For
> ```

Finally, write any initializations that are needed. In this case, the *totalRate* variable needs to be initialized.

> **Final Step: Creating a Loop from the Inside Out (Pseudocode Example)**
> ```
> totalRate = 0
> For person = firstPerson to lastPerson
>    rate = table[ census[ person ].Age, census[ person ].Gender ]
>    totalRate = totalRate + rate
> End For
> ```

If you had to put another loop around the *person* loop, you would proceed in the same way. You don't need to follow the steps rigidly. The idea is to start with something concrete, worry about only one thing at a time, and build up the loop from simple components. Take small, understandable steps as you make the loop more general and complex. That way, you minimize the amount of code you have to concentrate on at any one time and therefore minimize the chance of error.

16.4 Correspondence Between Loops and Arrays

Cross-Reference For further discussion of the correspondence between loops and arrays, see Section 10.7, "Relationship Between Data Types and Control Structures."

Loops and arrays are often related. In many instances, a loop is created to perform an array manipulation, and loop counters correspond one-to-one with array indexes. For example, these Java *for* loop indexes correspond to the array indexes:

> **Java Example of an Array Multiplication**
> ```java
> for ( int row = 0; row < maxRows; row++ ) {
>    for ( int column = 0; column < maxCols; column++ ) {
>       product[ row ][ column ] = a[ row ][ column ] * b[ row ][ column ];
>    }
> }
> ```

In Java, a loop is necessary for this array operation. But it's worth noting that looping structures and arrays aren't inherently connected. Some languages, especially APL and Fortran 90 and later, provide powerful array operations that eliminate the need for loops like the one just shown. Here's an APL code fragment that performs the same operation:

> **APL Example of an Array Multiplication**
> ```
> product <- a x b
> ```

The APL is simpler and less error-prone. It uses only three operands, whereas the Java fragment uses 17. It doesn't have loop variables, array indexes, or control structures to code incorrectly.

One point of this example is that you do some programming to solve a problem and some to solve it in a particular language. The language you use to solve a problem substantially affects your solution.

cc2e.com/1616

CHECKLIST: Loops

Loop Selection and Creation

- ❑ Is a *while* loop used instead of a *for* loop, if appropriate?
- ❑ Was the loop created from the inside out?

Entering the Loop

- ❑ Is the loop entered from the top?
- ❑ Is initialization code directly before the loop?
- ❑ If the loop is an infinite loop or an event loop, is it constructed cleanly rather than using a kludge such as *for i = 1 to 9999*?
- ❑ If the loop is a C++, C, or Java *for* loop, is the loop header reserved for loop-control code?

Inside the Loop

- ❑ Does the loop use { and } or their equivalent to enclose the loop body and prevent problems arising from improper modifications?
- ❑ Does the loop body have something in it? Is it nonempty?
- ❑ Are housekeeping chores grouped, at either the beginning or the end of the loop?
- ❑ Does the loop perform one and only one function, as a well-defined routine does?
- ❑ Is the loop short enough to view all at once?
- ❑ Is the loop nested to three levels or less?
- ❑ Have long loop contents been moved into their own routine?
- ❑ If the loop is long, is it especially clear?

Loop Indexes

- ❑ If the loop is a *for* loop, does the code inside it avoid monkeying with the loop index?

- ❑ Is a variable used to save important loop-index values rather than using the loop index outside the loop?

- ❑ Is the loop index an ordinal type or an enumerated type—not floating-point?

- ❑ Does the loop index have a meaningful name?

- ❑ Does the loop avoid index cross-talk?

Exiting the Loop

- ❑ Does the loop end under all possible conditions?

- ❑ Does the loop use safety counters—if you've instituted a safety-counter standard?

- ❑ Is the loop's termination condition obvious?

- ❑ If *break* or *continue* are used, are they correct?

Key Points

- ■ Loops are complicated. Keeping them simple helps readers of your code.

- ■ Techniques for keeping loops simple include avoiding exotic kinds of loops, minimizing nesting, making entries and exits clear, and keeping housekeeping code in one place.

- ■ Loop indexes are subjected to a great deal of abuse. Name them clearly, and use them for only one purpose.

- ■ Think through the loop carefully to verify that it operates normally under each case and terminates under all possible conditions.

Chapter 17

Unusual Control Structures

cc2e.com/1778

Contents

Related Topics

- General control issues: Chapter 19

- Straight-line code: Chapter 14

- Code with conditionals: Chapter 15

- Code with loops: Chapter 16

- Exception handling: Section 8.4

Several control constructs exist in a hazy twilight zone somewhere between being leading-edge and being discredited and disproved—often in both places at the same time! These constructs aren't available in all languages but can be useful when used with care in those languages that do offer them.

17.1 Multiple Returns from a Routine

Most languages support some means of exiting from a routine partway through the routine. The *return* and *exit* statements are control constructs that enable a program to exit from a routine at will. They cause the routine to terminate through the normal exit channel, returning control to the calling routine. The word *return* is used here as a generic term for *return* in C++ and Java, *Exit Sub* and *Exit Function* in Microsoft Visual Basic, and similar constructs. Here are guidelines for using the *return* statement:

KEY POINT

Use a* return *when it enhances readability In certain routines, once you know the answer, you want to return it to the calling routine immediately. If the routine is defined in such a way that it doesn't require any further cleanup once it detects an error, not returning immediately means that you have to write more code.

The following is a good example of a case in which returning from multiple places in a routine makes sense:

C++ Example of a Good Multiple Return from a Routine

This routine returns a *Comparison* enumerated type.

```cpp
Comparison Compare( int value1, int value2 ) {
    if ( value1 < value2 ) {
        return Comparison_LessThan;
    }
    else if ( value1 > value2 ) {
        return Comparison_GreaterThan;
    }
    return Comparison_Equal;
}
```

Other examples are less clear-cut, as the next subsection illustrates.

Use guard clauses (early returns or exits) to simplify complex error processing
Code that has to check for numerous error conditions before performing its nominal actions can result in deeply indented code and can obscure the nominal case, as shown here:

Visual Basic Code That Obscures the Nominal Case

This is the code for the nominal case.

```vb
If file.validName() Then
    If file.Open() Then
        If encryptionKey.valid() Then
            If file.Decrypt( encryptionKey ) Then
                ' lots of code
                ...
            End If
        End If
    End If
End If
```

Indenting the main body of the routine inside four *if* statements is aesthetically ugly, especially if there's much code inside the innermost *if* statement. In such cases, the flow of the code is sometimes clearer if the erroneous cases are checked first, clearing the way for the nominal path through the code. Here's how that might look:

Simple Visual Basic Code That Uses Guard Clauses to Clarify the Nominal Case

```vb
' set up, bailing out if errors are found
If Not file.validName() Then Exit Sub
If Not file.Open() Then Exit Sub
If Not encryptionKey.valid() Then Exit Sub
If Not file.Decrypt( encryptionKey ) Then Exit Sub

' lots of code
...
```

This simple code makes this technique look like a tidy solution, but production code often requires more extensive housekeeping or cleanup when an error condition is detected. Here is a more realistic example:

More Realistic Visual Basic Code That Uses Guard Clauses to Clarify the Nominal Case

```
' set up, bailing out if errors are found
If Not file.validName() Then
    errorStatus = FileError_InvalidFileName
    Exit Sub
End If

If Not file.Open() Then
    errorStatus = FileError_CantOpenFile
    Exit Sub
End If

If Not encryptionKey.valid() Then
    errorStatus = FileError_InvalidEncryptionKey
    Exit Sub
End If

If Not file.Decrypt( encryptionKey ) Then
    errorStatus = FileError_CantDecryptFile
    Exit Sub
End If
```

> This is the code for the nominal case. ➔
```
' lots of code
...
```

With production-size code, the *Exit Sub* approach creates a noticeable amount of code before the nominal case is handled. The *Exit Sub* approach does avoid the deep nesting of the first example, however, and, if the code in the first example were expanded to show setting an *errorStatus* variable, the *Exit Sub* approach would do a better job of keeping related statements together. When all the dust settles, the *Exit Sub* approach does appear more readable and maintainable, just not by a very wide margin.

Minimize the number of returns in each routine   It's harder to understand a routine when, reading it at the bottom, you're unaware of the possibility that it returned somewhere above. For that reason, use returns judiciously—only when they improve readability.

17.2 Recursion

In recursion, a routine solves a small part of a problem itself, divides the problem into smaller pieces, and then calls itself to solve each of the smaller pieces. Recursion is usually called into play when a small part of the problem is easy to solve and a large part is easy to decompose into smaller pieces.

KEY POINT

Recursion isn't useful often, but when used judiciously it produces elegant solutions, as in this example in which a sorting algorithm makes excellent use of recursion:

Java Example of a Sorting Algorithm That Uses Recursion

```java
void QuickSort( int firstIndex, int lastIndex, String [] names ) {
    if ( lastIndex > firstIndex ) {
        int midPoint = Partition( firstIndex, lastIndex, names );
        QuickSort( firstIndex, midPoint-1, names );
        QuickSort( midPoint+1, lastIndex, names )
    }
}
```

Here are the recursive calls.

In this case, the sorting algorithm chops an array in two and then calls itself to sort each half of the array. When it calls itself with a subarray that's too small to sort—such as (*lastIndex* <= *firstIndex*)—it stops calling itself.

For a small group of problems, recursion can produce simple, elegant solutions. For a slightly larger group of problems, it can produce simple, elegant, hard-to-understand solutions. For most problems, it produces massively complicated solutions—in those cases, simple iteration is usually more understandable. Use recursion selectively.

Example of Recursion

Suppose you have a data type that represents a maze. A maze is basically a grid, and at each point on the grid you might be able to turn left, turn right, move up, or move down. You'll often be able to move in more than one direction.

How do you write a program to find its way through the maze, as shown in Figure 17-1? If you use recursion, the answer is fairly straightforward. You start at the beginning and then try all possible paths until you find your way out of the maze. The first time you visit a point, you try to move left. If you can't move left, you try to go up or down, and if you can't go up or down, you try to go right. You don't have to worry about getting lost because you drop a few bread crumbs on each spot as you visit it, and you don't visit the same spot twice.

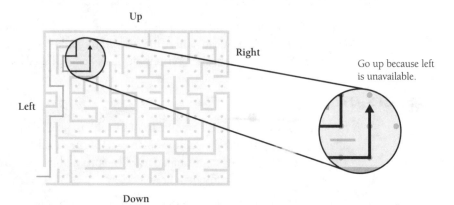

Figure 17-1   Recursion can be a valuable tool in the battle against complexity—when used to attack suitable problems.

The recursive code looks like this:

C++ Example of Moving Through a Maze Recursively

```cpp
bool FindPathThroughMaze( Maze maze, Point position ) {
   // if the position has already been tried, don't try it again
   if ( AlreadyTried( maze, position ) ) {
      return false;
   }

   // if this position is the exit, declare success
   if ( ThisIsTheExit( maze, position ) ) {
      return true;
   }

   // remember that this position has been tried
   RememberPosition( maze, position );

   // check the paths to the left, up, down, and to the right; if
   // any path is successful, stop looking
   if ( MoveLeft( maze, position, &newPosition ) ) {
      if ( FindPathThroughMaze( maze, newPosition ) ) {
         return true;
      }
   }

   if ( MoveUp( maze, position, &newPosition ) ) {
      if ( FindPathThroughMaze( maze, newPosition ) ) {
         return true;
      }
   }

   if ( MoveDown( maze, position, &newPosition ) ) {
      if ( FindPathThroughMaze( maze, newPosition ) ) {
         return true;
      }
   }

   if ( MoveRight( maze, position, &newPosition ) ) {
      if ( FindPathThroughMaze( maze, newPosition ) ) {
         return true;
      }
   }
   return false;
}
```

The first line of code checks to see whether the position has already been tried. One key aim in writing a recursive routine is the prevention of infinite recursion. In this case, if you don't check for having tried a point, you might keep trying it infinitely.

The second statement checks to see whether the position is the exit from the maze. If *ThisIsTheExit()* returns *true*, the routine itself returns *true*.

The third statement remembers that the position has been visited. This prevents the infinite recursion that would result from a circular path.

The remaining lines in the routine try to find a path to the left, up, down, and to the right. The code stops the recursion if the routine ever returns *true*—that is, when the routine finds a path through the maze.

The logic used in this routine is fairly straightforward. Most people experience some initial discomfort using recursion because it's self-referential. In this case, however, an alternative solution would be much more complicated and recursion works well.

Tips for Using Recursion

Keep these tips in mind when using recursion:

Make sure the recursion stops   Check the routine to make sure that it includes a non-recursive path. That usually means that the routine has a test that stops further recursion when it's not needed. In the maze example, the tests for *AlreadyTried()* and *ThisIsTheExit()* ensure that the recursion stops.

Use safety counters to prevent infinite recursion   If you're using recursion in a situation that doesn't allow a simple test such as the one just described, use a safety counter to prevent infinite recursion. The safety counter has to be a variable that's not re-created each time you call the routine. Use a class member variable or pass the safety counter as a parameter. Here's an example:

Visual Basic Example of Using a Safety Counter to Prevent Infinite Recursion

> The recursive routine must be able to change the value of *safetyCounter*, so in Visual Basic it's a *ByRef* parameter.

```
Public Sub RecursiveProc( ByRef safetyCounter As Integer )
    If ( safetyCounter > SAFETY_LIMIT ) Then
        Exit Sub
    End If
    safetyCounter = safetyCounter + 1
    ...
    RecursiveProc( safetyCounter )
End Sub
```

In this case, if the routine exceeds the safety limit, it stops recursing.

If you don't want to pass the safety counter as an explicit parameter, you could use a member variable in C++, Java, or Visual Basic, or the equivalent in other languages.

Limit recursion to one routine   Cyclic recursion (A calls B calls C calls A) is dangerous because it's hard to detect. Mentally managing recursion in one routine is tough enough; understanding recursion that spans routines is too much. If you have cyclic recursion, you can usually redesign the routines so that the recursion is restricted to a single routine. If you can't and you still think that recursion is the best approach, use safety counters as a recursive insurance policy.

Keep an eye on the stack   With recursion, you have no guarantees about how much stack space your program uses and it's hard to predict in advance how the program will behave at run time. You can take a couple of steps to control its run-time behavior, however.

First, if you use a safety counter, one of the considerations in setting a limit for it should be how much stack you're willing to allocate to the recursive routine. Set the safety limit low enough to prevent a stack overflow.

Second, watch for allocation of local variables in recursive functions, especially memory-intensive objects. In other words, use *new* to create objects on the heap rather than letting the compiler create *auto* objects on the stack.

Don't use recursion for factorials or Fibonacci numbers   One problem with computer-science textbooks is that they present silly examples of recursion. The typical examples are computing a factorial or computing a Fibonacci sequence. Recursion is a powerful tool, and it's really dumb to use it in either of those cases. If a programmer who worked for me used recursion to compute a factorial, I'd hire someone else. Here's the recursive version of the factorial routine:

**CODING
HORROR**

Java Example of an Inappropriate Solution: Using Recursion to Compute a Factorial
```java
int Factorial( int number ) {
   if ( number == 1 ) {
      return 1;
   }
   else {
      return number * Factorial( number - 1 );
   }
}
```

In addition to being slow and making the use of run-time memory unpredictable, the recursive version of this routine is harder to understand than the iterative version, which follows:

Java Example of an Appropriate Solution: Using Iteration to Compute a Factorial
```java
int Factorial( int number ) {
   int intermediateResult = 1;
   for ( int factor = 2; factor <= number; factor++ ) {
      intermediateResult = intermediateResult * factor;
   }
   return intermediateResult;
}
```

You can draw three lessons from this example. First, computer-science textbooks aren't doing the world any favors with their examples of recursion. Second, and more important, recursion is a much more powerful tool than its confusing use in computing factorials or Fibonacci numbers would suggest. Third, and most important, you should consider alternatives to recursion before using it. You can do anything with stacks and iteration that you can do with recursion. Sometimes one approach works better; sometimes the other does. Consider both before you choose either one.

17.3 *goto*

cc2e.com/1785

You might think the debate related to *goto*s is extinct, but a quick trip through modern source-code repositories like *SourceForge.net* shows that the *goto* is still alive and well and living deep in your company's server. Moreover, modern equivalents of the *goto* debate still crop up in various guises, including debates about multiple returns, multiple loop exits, named loop exits, error processing, and exception handling.

The Argument Against *goto*s

The general argument against *goto*s is that code without *goto*s is higher-quality code. The famous letter that sparked the original controversy was Edsger Dijkstra's "Go To Statement Considered Harmful" in the March 1968 *Communications of the ACM*. Dijkstra observed that the quality of code was inversely proportional to the number of *goto*s the programmer used. In subsequent work, Dijkstra has argued that code that doesn't contain *goto*s can more easily be proven correct.

Code containing *goto*s is hard to format. Indentation should be used to show logical structure, and *goto*s have an effect on logical structure. Using indentation to show the logical structure of a *goto* and its target, however, is difficult or impossible.

Use of *goto*s defeats compiler optimizations. Some optimizations depend on a program's flow of control residing within a few statements. An unconditional *goto* makes the flow harder to analyze and reduces the ability of the compiler to optimize the code. Thus, even if introducing a *goto* produces an efficiency at the source-language level, it may well reduce overall efficiency by thwarting compiler optimizations.

Proponents of *goto*s sometimes argue that they make code faster or smaller. But code containing *goto*s is rarely the fastest or smallest possible. Donald Knuth's marvelous, classic article "Structured Programming with go to Statements" gives several examples of cases in which using *goto*s makes for slower and larger code (Knuth 1974).

In practice, the use of *goto*s leads to the violation of the principle that code should flow strictly from top to bottom. Even if *goto*s aren't confusing when used carefully, once *goto*s are introduced, they spread through the code like termites through a rotting house. If any *goto*s are allowed, the bad creep in with the good, so it's better not to allow any of them.

Overall, experience in the two decades that followed the publication of Dijkstra's letter showed the folly of producing *goto*-laden code. In a survey of the literature, Ben Shneiderman concluded that the evidence supports Dijkstra's view that we're better off without the *goto* (1980), and many modern languages, including Java, don't even have *goto*s.

The Argument for *goto*s

The argument for the *goto* is characterized by an advocacy of its careful use in specific circumstances rather than its indiscriminate use. Most arguments against *goto*s speak against indiscriminate use. The *goto* controversy erupted when Fortran was the most popular language. Fortran had no presentable loop structures, and in the absence of good advice on programming loops with *goto*s, programmers wrote a lot of spaghetti code. Such code was undoubtedly correlated with the production of low-quality programs, but it has little to do with the careful use of a *goto* to make up for a gap in a modern language's capabilities.

A well-placed *goto* can eliminate the need for duplicate code. Duplicate code leads to problems if the two sets of code are modified differently. Duplicate code increases the size of source and executable files. The bad effects of the *goto* are outweighed in such a case by the risks of duplicate code.

Cross-Reference For details on using *goto*s in code that allocates resources, see "Error Processing and *goto*s" in this section. See also the discussion of exception handling in Section 8.4, "Exceptions."

The *goto* is useful in a routine that allocates resources, performs operations on those resources, and then deallocates the resources. With a *goto*, you can clean up in one section of code. The *goto* reduces the likelihood of your forgetting to deallocate the resources in each place you detect an error.

In some cases, the *goto* can result in faster and smaller code. Knuth's 1974 article cited a few cases in which the *goto* produced a legitimate gain.

Good programming doesn't mean eliminating *goto*s. Methodical decomposition, refinement, and selection of control structures automatically lead to *goto*-free programs in most cases. Achieving *goto*-less code is not the aim but the outcome, and putting the focus on avoiding *goto*s isn't helpful.

The evidence suggests only that deliberately chaotic control structure degrades [programmer] performance. These experiments provide virtually no evidence for the beneficial effect of any specific method of structuring control flow.
—*B. A. Sheil*

Decades' worth of research with *goto*s failed to demonstrate their harmfulness. In a survey of the literature, B. A. Sheil concluded that unrealistic test conditions, poor data analysis, and inconclusive results failed to support the claim of Shneiderman and others that the number of bugs in code was proportional to the number of *goto*s (1981). Sheil didn't go so far as to conclude that using *goto*s is a good idea—rather, that experimental evidence against them was not conclusive.

Finally, the *goto* has been incorporated into many modern languages, including Visual Basic, C++, and the Ada language, the most carefully engineered programming language in history. Ada was developed long after the arguments on both sides of the *goto* debate had been fully developed, and after considering all sides of the issue, Ada's engineers decided to include the *goto*.

The Phony *goto* Debate

A primary feature of most *goto* discussions is a shallow approach to the question. The arguer on the "*goto*s are evil" side presents a trivial code fragment that uses *goto*s and then shows how easy it is to rewrite the fragment without *goto*s. This proves mainly that it's easy to write trivial code without *goto*s.

The arguer on the "I can't live without *goto*s" side usually presents a case in which eliminating a *goto* results in an extra comparison or the duplication of a line of code. This proves mainly that there's a case in which using a *goto* results in one less comparison—not a significant gain on today's computers.

Most textbooks don't help. They provide a trivial example of rewriting some code without a *goto* as if that covers the subject. Here's a disguised example of a trivial piece of code from such a textbook:

C++ Example of Code That's Supposed to Be Easy to Rewrite Without *goto*s

```cpp
do {
   GetData( inputFile, data );
   if ( eof( inputFile ) ) {
      goto LOOP_EXIT;
   }
   DoSomething( data );
} while ( data != -1 );
LOOP_EXIT:
```

The book quickly replaces this code with *goto*-less code:

C++ Example of Supposedly Equivalent Code, Rewritten Without *goto*s

```cpp
GetData( inputFile, data );
while ( ( !eof( inputFile ) ) && ( ( data != -1 ) ) ) {
   DoSomething( data );
   GetData( inputFile, data )
}
```

This so-called "trivial" example contains an error. In the case in which *data* equals *-1* entering the loop, the translated code detects the *-1* and exits the loop before executing *DoSomething()*. The original code executes *DoSomething()* before the *-1* is detected. The programming book trying to show how easy it is to code without *goto*s translated its own example incorrectly. But the author of that book shouldn't feel too bad; other books make similar mistakes. Even the pros have difficulty translating code that uses *goto*s.

Here's a faithful translation of the code with no *goto*s:

```
C++ Example of Truly Equivalent Code, Rewritten Without gotos
do {
    GetData( inputFile, data );
    if ( !eof( inputFile )) {
        DoSomething( data );
    }
} while ( ( data != -1 ) && ( !eof( inputFile ) ) );
```

Even with a correct translation of the code, the example is still phony because it shows a trivial use of the *goto*. Such cases are not the ones for which thoughtful programmers choose a *goto* as their preferred form of control.

It would be hard at this late date to add anything worthwhile to the theoretical *goto* debate. What's not usually addressed, however, is the situation in which a programmer fully aware of the *goto*-less alternatives chooses to use a *goto* to enhance readability and maintainability.

The following sections present cases in which some experienced programmers have argued for using *goto*s. The discussions provide examples of code with *goto*s and code rewritten without *goto*s and evaluate the tradeoffs between the versions.

Error Processing and *goto*s

Writing highly interactive code calls for paying a lot of attention to error processing and cleaning up resources when errors occur. The following code example purges a group of files. The routine first gets a group of files to be purged, and then it finds each file, opens it, overwrites it, and erases it. The routine checks for errors at each step.

```
Visual Basic Code with gotos That Processes Errors and Cleans Up Resources
' This routine purges a group of files.
Sub PurgeFiles( ByRef errorState As Error_Code )
    Dim fileIndex As Integer
    Dim fileToPurge As Data_File
    Dim fileList As File_List
    Dim numFilesToPurge As Integer

    MakePurgeFileList( fileList, numFilesToPurge )

    errorState = FileStatus_Success
    fileIndex = 0
    While ( fileIndex < numFilesToPurge )
        fileIndex = fileIndex + 1
        If Not ( FindFile( fileList( fileIndex ), fileToPurge ) ) Then
            errorState = FileStatus_FileFindError
            GoTo END_PROC
        End If
```

Here's a *GoTo*.

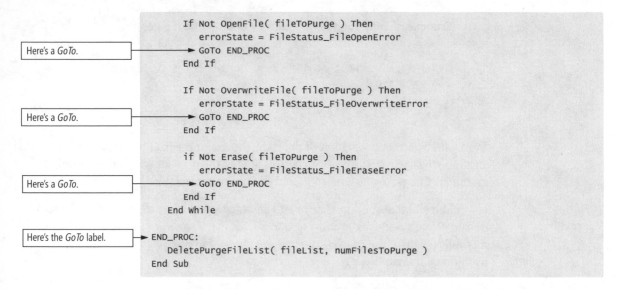

Here's a *GoTo*.

Here's a *GoTo*.

Here's a *GoTo*.

Here's the *GoTo* label.

```
        If Not OpenFile( fileToPurge ) Then
            errorState = FileStatus_FileOpenError
            GoTo END_PROC
        End If

        If Not OverwriteFile( fileToPurge ) Then
            errorState = FileStatus_FileOverwriteError
            GoTo END_PROC
        End If

        if Not Erase( fileToPurge ) Then
            errorState = FileStatus_FileEraseError
            GoTo END_PROC
        End If
    End While

END_PROC:
    DeletePurgeFileList( fileList, numFilesToPurge )
End Sub
```

This routine is typical of circumstances in which experienced programmers decide to use a *goto*. Similar cases come up when a routine needs to allocate and clean up resources like database connections, memory, or temporary files. The alternative to *goto*s in those cases is usually duplicating code to clean up the resources. In such cases, a programmer might balance the evil of the *goto* against the headache of duplicate-code maintenance and decide that the *goto* is the lesser evil.

You can rewrite the previous routine in a couple of ways to avoid *goto*s, and both ways involve tradeoffs. The possible rewrite strategies follow:

***Rewrite with nested** if statements*   To rewrite with nested *if* statements, nest the *if* statements so that each is executed only if the previous test succeeds. This is the standard, textbook programming approach to eliminating *goto*s. Here's a rewrite of the routine using the standard approach:

Cross-Reference This routine could also be rewritten with *break* and no *goto*s. For details on that approach, see "Exiting Loops Early" in Section 16.2.

Visual Basic Code That Avoids *goto*s by Using Nested *if*s
```
' This routine purges a group of files.
Sub PurgeFiles( ByRef errorState As Error_Code )
    Dim fileIndex As Integer
    Dim fileToPurge As Data_File
    Dim fileList As File_List
    Dim numFilesToPurge As Integer

    MakePurgeFileList( fileList, numFilesToPurge )

    errorState = FileStatus_Success
    fileIndex = 0
    While ( fileIndex < numFilesToPurge And errorState = FileStatus_Success )

        fileIndex = fileIndex + 1
```

The *While* test has been changed to add a test for *errorState*.

```
                If FindFile( fileList( fileIndex ), fileToPurge ) Then
                    If OpenFile( fileToPurge ) Then
                        If OverwriteFile( fileToPurge ) Then
                            If Not Erase( fileToPurge ) Then
                                errorState = FileStatus_FileEraseError
                            End If
                        Else ' couldn't overwrite file
                            errorState = FileStatus_FileOverwriteError
                        End If
                    Else ' couldn't open file
                        errorState = FileStatus_FileOpenError
                    End If
                Else ' couldn't find file
                    errorState = FileStatus_FileFindError
                End If
            End While
            DeletePurgeFileList( fileList, numFilesToPurge )
        End Sub
```

> This line is 13 lines away from the *If* statement that invokes it.

For people used to programming without *goto*s, this code might be easier to read than the *goto* version, and if you use it, you won't have to face an inquisition from the *goto* goon squad.

Cross-Reference For more details on indentation and other coding layout issues, see Chapter 31, "Layout and Style." For details on nesting levels, see Section 19.4, "Taming Dangerously Deep Nesting."

The main disadvantage of this nested-*if* approach is that the nesting level is deep, very deep. To understand the code, you have to keep the whole set of nested *if*s in your mind at once. Moreover, the distance between the error-processing code and the code that invokes it is too great: the code that sets *errorState* to *FileStatus_FileFindError*, for example, is 13 lines from the *if* statement that invokes it.

With the *goto* version, no statement is more than four lines from the condition that invokes it. And you don't have to keep the whole structure in your mind at once. You can essentially ignore any preceding conditions that were successful and focus on the next operation. In this case, the *goto* version is more readable and more maintainable than the nested-*if* version.

Rewrite with a status variable   To rewrite with a status variable (also called a state variable), create a variable that indicates whether the routine is in an error state. In this case, the routine already uses the *errorState* status variable, so you can use that.

Visual Basic Code That Avoids *goto*s by Using a Status Variable

```
' This routine purges a group of files.
Sub PurgeFiles( ByRef errorState As Error_Code )
    Dim fileIndex As Integer
    Dim fileToPurge As Data_File
    Dim fileList As File_List
    Dim numFilesToPurge As Integer

    MakePurgeFileList( fileList, numFilesToPurge )

    errorState = FileStatus_Success
    fileIndex = 0
```

The *While* test has been changed to add a test for *errorState*.	
The status variable is tested.	
The status variable is tested.	
The status variable is tested.	

```
        While ( fileIndex < numFilesToPurge ) And ( errorState = FileStatus_Success )

            fileIndex = fileIndex + 1

            If Not FindFile( fileList( fileIndex ), fileToPurge ) Then
                errorState = FileStatus_FileFindError
            End If
            If ( errorState = FileStatus_Success ) Then
                If Not OpenFile( fileToPurge ) Then
                    errorState = FileStatus_FileOpenError
                End If
            End If
            If ( errorState = FileStatus_Success ) Then
                If Not OverwriteFile( fileToPurge ) Then
                    errorState = FileStatus_FileOverwriteError
                End If
            End If
            If ( errorState = FileStatus_Success ) Then
                If Not Erase( fileToPurge ) Then
                    errorState = FileStatus_FileEraseError
                End If
            End If
        End While
        DeletePurgeFileList( fileList, numFilesToPurge )
    End Sub
```

The advantage of the status-variable approach is that it avoids the deeply nested *if-then-else* structures of the first rewrite and is thus easier to understand. It also places the action following the *if-then-else* test closer to the test than the nested-*if* approach did, and it completely avoids *else* clauses.

Understanding the nested-*if* version requires some mental gymnastics. The status-variable version is easier to understand because it closely models the way people think about the problem. You find the file. If everything is OK, you open the file. If everything is still OK, you overwrite the file. If everything is still OK...

The disadvantage of this approach is that using status variables isn't as common a practice as it should be. Document their use fully, or some programmers might not understand what you're up to. In this example, the use of well-named enumerated types helps significantly.

Rewrite with try-finally Some languages, including Visual Basic and Java, provide a *try-finally* statement that can be used to clean up resources under error conditions.

To rewrite using the *try-finally* approach, enclose the code that would otherwise need to check for errors inside a *try* block, and place the cleanup code inside a *finally* block. The *try* block specifies the scope of the exception handling, and the *finally* block performs any resource cleanup. The *finally* block will always be called regardless of whether an exception is thrown and regardless of whether the *PurgeFiles()* routine *Catches* any exception that's thrown.

Visual Basic Code That Avoids *gotos* by Using *try-finally*

```
' This routine purges a group of files. Exceptions are passed to the caller.
Sub PurgeFiles()
    Dim fileIndex As Integer
    Dim fileToPurge As Data_File
    Dim fileList As File_List
    Dim numFilesToPurge As Integer
    MakePurgeFileList( fileList, numFilesToPurge )
    Try
        fileIndex = 0
        While ( fileIndex < numFilesToPurge )
            fileIndex = fileIndex + 1
            FindFile( fileList( fileIndex ), fileToPurge )
            OpenFile( fileToPurge )
            OverwriteFile( fileToPurge )
            Erase( fileToPurge )
        End While
    Finally
        DeletePurgeFileList( fileList, numFilesToPurge )
    End Try
End Sub
```

This approach assumes that all function calls throw exceptions for failures rather than returning error codes.

The advantage of the *try-finally* approach is that it is simpler than the *goto* approach and doesn't use *gotos*. It also avoids the deeply nested *if-then-else* structures.

The limitation of the *try-finally* approach is that it must be implemented consistently throughout a code base. If the previous code were part of a code base that used error codes in addition to exceptions, the exception code would be required to set error codes for each possible error, and that requirement would make the code about as complicated as the other approaches.

Comparison of the Approaches

Cross-Reference For a complete list of techniques that can be applied to situations like this, see "Summary of Techniques for Reducing Deep Nesting" in Section 19.4.

Each of the four methods has something to be said for it. The *goto* approach avoids deep nesting and unnecessary tests but of course has *gotos*. The nested-*if* approach avoids *gotos* but is deeply nested and gives an exaggerated picture of the logical complexity of the routine. The status-variable approach avoids *gotos* and deep nesting but introduces extra tests. And the *try-finally* approach avoids both *gotos* and deep nesting but isn't available in all languages.

The *try-finally* approach is the most straightforward in languages that provide *try-finally* and in code bases that haven't already standardized on another approach. If *try-finally* isn't an option, the status-variable approach is slightly preferable to the *goto* and nested-*if* approaches because it's more readable and it models the problem better, but that doesn't make it the best approach in all circumstances.

Any of these techniques works well when applied consistently to all the code in a project. Consider all the tradeoffs, and then make a projectwide decision about which method to favor.

*goto*s and Sharing Code in an *else* Clause

One challenging situation in which some programmers would use a *goto* is the case in which you have two conditional tests and an *else* clause and you want to execute code in one of the conditions and in the *else* clause. Here's an example of a case that could drive someone to *goto*:

CODING
HORROR

C++ Example of Sharing Code in an *else* Clause with a *goto*

```cpp
if ( statusOk ) {
   if ( dataAvailable ) {
      importantVariable = x;
      goto MID_LOOP;
   }
}
else {
   importantVariable = GetValue();

   MID_LOOP:

   // lots of code
   ...
}
```

This is a good example because it's logically tortuous—it's nearly impossible to read it as it stands, and it's hard to rewrite it correctly without a *goto*. If you think you can easily rewrite it without *goto*s, ask someone to review your code! Several expert programmers have rewritten it incorrectly.

You can rewrite the code in several ways. You can duplicate code, put the common code into a routine and call it from two places, or retest the conditions. In most languages, the rewrite will be a tiny bit larger and slower than the original, but it will be extremely close. Unless the code is in a really hot loop, rewrite it without thinking about efficiency.

The best rewrite would be to put the *// lots of code* part into its own routine. Then you can call the routine from the places you would otherwise have used as origins or destinations of *goto*s and preserve the original structure of the conditional. Here's how it looks:

C++ Example of Sharing Code in an *else* Clause by Putting Common Code into a Routine

```cpp
if ( statusOk ) {
   if ( dataAvailable ) {
      importantVariable = x;
      DoLotsOfCode( importantVariable );
   }
}
else {
   importantVariable = GetValue();
   DoLotsOfCode( importantVariable );
}
```

Normally, writing a new routine is the best approach. Sometimes, however, it's not practical to put duplicated code into its own routine. In this case, you can work around the impractical solution by restructuring the conditional so that you keep the code in the same routine rather than putting it into a new routine:

C++ Example of Sharing Code in an *else* Clause Without a *goto*

```
if ( ( statusOk && dataAvailable ) || !statusOk ) {
   if ( statusOk && dataAvailable ) {
      importantVariable = x;
   }
   else {
      importantVariable = GetValue();
   }

   // lots of code
   ...
}
```

Cross-Reference Another approach to this problem is to use a decision table. For details, see Chapter 18, "Table-Driven Methods."

This is a faithful and mechanical translation of the logic in the *goto* version. It tests *statusOK* two extra times and *dataAvailable* once, but the code is equivalent. If retesting the conditionals bothers you, notice that the value of *statusOK* doesn't need to be tested twice in the first *if* test. You can also drop the test for *dataAvailable* in the second *if* test.

Summary of Guidelines for Using *goto*s

KEY POINT

Use of *goto*s is a matter of religion. My dogma is that in modern languages, you can easily replace nine out of ten *goto*s with equivalent sequential constructs. In these simple cases, you should replace *goto*s out of habit. In the hard cases, you can still exorcise the *goto* in nine out of ten cases: You can break the code into smaller routines, use *try-finally*, use nested *if*s, test and retest a status variable, or restructure a conditional. Eliminating the *goto* is harder in these cases, but it's good mental exercise and the techniques discussed in this section give you the tools to do it.

In the remaining one case out of 100 in which a *goto* is a legitimate solution to the problem, document it clearly and use it. If you have your rain boots on, it's not worth walking around the block to avoid a mud puddle. But keep your mind open to *goto*-less approaches suggested by other programmers. They might see something you don't.

Here's a summary of guidelines for using *goto*s:

- Use *goto*s to emulate structured control constructs in languages that don't support them directly. When you do, emulate them exactly. Don't abuse the extra flexibility the *goto* gives you.

- Don't use the *goto* when an equivalent built-in construct is available.

Cross-Reference For details on improving efficiency, see Chapter 25, "Code-Tuning Strategies," and Chapter 26, "Code-Tuning Techniques."

- Measure the performance of any *goto* used to improve efficiency. In most cases, you can recode without *goto*s for improved readability and no loss in efficiency. If your case is the exception, document the efficiency improvement so that *goto*-less evangelists won't remove the *goto* when they see it.

- Limit yourself to one *goto* label per routine unless you're emulating structured constructs.

- Limit yourself to *goto*s that go forward, not backward, unless you're emulating structured constructs.

- Make sure all *goto* labels are used. Unused labels might be an indication of missing code, namely the code that goes to the labels. If the labels aren't used, delete them.

- Make sure a *goto* doesn't create unreachable code.

- If you're a manager, adopt the perspective that a battle over a single *goto* isn't worth the loss of the war. If the programmer is aware of the alternatives and is willing to argue, the *goto* is probably OK.

17.4 Perspective on Unusual Control Structures

At one time or another, someone thought that each of the following control structures was a good idea:

- Unrestricted use of *goto*s

- Ability to compute a *goto* target dynamically and jump to the computed location

- Ability to use *goto* to jump from the middle of one routine into the middle of another routine

- Ability to call a routine with a line number or label that allowed execution to begin somewhere in the middle of the routine

- Ability to have the program generate code on the fly and then execute the code it just wrote

At one time, each of these ideas was regarded as acceptable or even desirable, even though now they all look hopelessly quaint, outdated, or dangerous. The field of software development has advanced largely through *restricting* what programmers can do with their code. Consequently, I view unconventional control structures with strong skepticism. I suspect that the majority of constructs in this chapter will eventually find their way onto the programmer's scrap heap along with computed *goto* labels, variable routine entry points, self-modifying code, and other structures that favored flexibility and convenience over structure and the ability to manage complexity.

Additional Resources

cc2e.com/1792

The following resources also address unusual control structures:

Returns

Fowler, Martin. *Refactoring: Improving the Design of Existing Code*. Reading, MA: Addison-Wesley, 1999. In the description of the refactoring called "Replace Nested Conditional with Guard Clauses," Fowler suggests using multiple *return* statements from a routine to reduce nesting in a set of *if* statements. Fowler argues that multiple *return*s are an appropriate means of achieving greater clarity, and that no harm arises from having multiple returns from a routine.

gotos

These articles contain the whole *goto* debate. It erupts from time to time in most workplaces, textbooks, and magazines, but you won't hear anything that wasn't fully explored 20 years ago.

cc2e.com/1799

Dijkstra, Edsger. "Go To Statement Considered Harmful." *Communications of the ACM* 11, no. 3 (March 1968): 147–48, also available from *www.cs.utexas.edu/users/EWD/*. This is the famous letter in which Dijkstra put the match to the paper and ignited one of the longest-running controversies in software development.

Wulf, W. A. "A Case Against the GOTO." *Proceedings of the 25th National ACM Conference*, August 1972: 791–97. This paper was another argument against the indiscriminate use of *goto*s. Wulf argued that if programming languages provided adequate control structures, *goto*s would become largely unnecessary. Since 1972, when the paper was written, languages such as C++, Java, and Visual Basic have proven Wulf correct.

Knuth, Donald. "Structured Programming with go to Statements," 1974. In *Classics in Software Engineering*, edited by Edward Yourdon. Englewood Cliffs, NJ: Yourdon Press, 1979. This long paper isn't entirely about *goto*s, but it includes a horde of code examples that are made more efficient by eliminating *goto*s and another horde of code examples that are made more efficient by adding *goto*s.

Rubin, Frank. "'GOTO Considered Harmful' Considered Harmful." *Communications of the ACM* 30, no. 3 (March 1987): 195–96. In this rather hotheaded letter to the editor, Rubin asserts that *goto*-less programming has cost businesses "hundreds of millions of dollars." He then offers a short code fragment that uses a *goto* and argues that it's superior to *goto*-less alternatives.

The response that Rubin's letter generated was more interesting than the letter itself. For five months, *Communications of the ACM (CACM)* published letters that offered different versions of Rubin's original seven-line program. The letters were evenly divided between those defending *goto*s and those castigating them. Readers suggested roughly 17 different rewrites, and the rewritten code fully covered the spectrum of approaches to avoiding *goto*s. The editor of *CACM* noted that the letter had generated more response by far than any other issue ever considered in the pages of *CACM*.

For the follow-up letters, see

- *Communications of the ACM* 30, no. 5 (May 1987): 351–55.
- *Communications of the ACM* 30, no. 6 (June 1987): 475–78.
- *Communications of the ACM* 30, no. 7 (July 1987): 632–34.

- *Communications of the ACM* 30, no. 8 (August 1987): 659–62.
- *Communications of the ACM* 30, no. 12 (December 1987): 997, 1085.

cc2e.com/1706

Clark, R. Lawrence, "A Linguistic Contribution of GOTO-less Programming," *Datamation*, December 1973. This classic paper humorously argues for replacing the "go to" statement with the "come from" statement. It was also reprinted in the April 1974 edition of *Communications of the ACM.*

cc2e.com/1713

CHECKLIST: Unusual Control Structures

return

- ❑ Does each routine use *return* only when necessary?
- ❑ Do *return*s enhance readability?

Recursion

- ❑ Does the recursive routine include code to stop the recursion?
- ❑ Does the routine use a safety counter to guarantee that the routine stops?
- ❑ Is recursion limited to one routine?
- ❑ Is the routine's depth of recursion within the limits imposed by the size of the program's stack?
- ❑ Is recursion the best way to implement the routine? Is it better than simple iteration?

goto

- ❑ Are *goto*s used only as a last resort, and then only to make code more readable and maintainable?
- ❑ If a *goto* is used for the sake of efficiency, has the gain in efficiency been measured and documented?
- ❑ Are *goto*s limited to one label per routine?
- ❑ Do all *goto*s go forward, not backward?
- ❑ Are all *goto* labels used?

Key Points

- Multiple *return*s can enhance a routine's readability and maintainability, and they help prevent deeply nested logic. They should, nevertheless, be used carefully.
- Recursion provides elegant solutions to a small set of problems. Use it carefully, too.
- In a few cases, *goto*s are the best way to write code that's readable and maintainable. Such cases are rare. Use *goto*s only as a last resort.

Chapter 18
Table-Driven Methods

cc2e.com/1865

Contents

Related Topics

- Information hiding: "Hide Secrets (Information Hiding)" in Section 5.3
- Class design: Chapter 6
- Using decision tables to replace complicated logic: in Section 19.1
- Substitute table lookups for complicated expressions: in Section 26.1

A table-driven method is a scheme that allows you to look up information in a table rather than using logic statements (*if* and *case*) to figure it out. Virtually anything you can select with logic statements, you can select with tables instead. In simple cases, logic statements are easier and more direct. As the logic chain becomes more complex, tables become increasingly attractive.

If you're already familiar with table-driven methods, this chapter might be just a review. In that case, you might examine "Flexible-Message-Format Example" in Section 18.2 for a good example of how an object-oriented design isn't necessarily better than any other kind of design just because it's object-oriented, and then you might move on to the discussion of general control issues in Chapter 19.

18.1 General Considerations in Using Table-Driven Methods

KEY POINT

Used in appropriate circumstances, table-driven code is simpler than complicated logic, easier to modify, and more efficient. Suppose you wanted to classify characters into letters, punctuation marks, and digits; you might use a complicated chain of logic like this one:

Java Example of Using Complicated Logic to Classify a Character

```java
if ( ( ( 'a' <= inputChar ) && ( inputChar <= 'z' ) ) ||
   ( ( 'A' <= inputChar ) && ( inputChar <= 'Z' ) ) ) {
   charType = CharacterType.Letter;
}
else if ( ( inputChar == ' ' ) || ( inputChar == ',' ) ||
   ( inputChar == '.' ) || ( inputChar == '!' ) || ( inputChar == '(' ) ||
   ( inputChar == ')' ) || ( inputChar == ':' ) || ( inputChar == ';' ) ||
   ( inputChar == '?' ) || ( inputChar == '-' ) ) {
   charType = CharacterType.Punctuation;
}
else if ( ( '0' <= inputChar ) && ( inputChar <= '9' ) ) {
   charType = CharacterType.Digit;
}
```

If you used a lookup table instead, you'd store the type of each character in an array that's accessed by character code. The complicated code fragment just shown would be replaced by this:

Java Example of Using a Lookup Table to Classify a Character

```java
charType = charTypeTable[ inputChar ];
```

This fragment assumes that the *charTypeTable* array has been set up earlier. You put your program's knowledge into its data rather than into its logic—in the table instead of in the *if* tests.

Two Issues in Using Table-Driven Methods

KEY POINT

When you use table-driven methods, you have to address two issues. First you have to address the question of how to look up entries in the table. You can use some data to access a table directly. If you need to classify data by month, for example, keying into a month table is straightforward. You can use an array with indexes 1 through 12.

Other data is too awkward to be used to look up a table entry directly. If you need to classify data by Social Security Number, for example, you can't use the Social Security Number to key into the table directly unless you can afford to store 999-99-9999 entries in your table. You're forced to use a more complicated approach. Here's a list of ways to look up an entry in a table:

- Direct access
- Indexed access
- Stair-step access

Each of these kinds of accesses is described in more detail in subsections later in this chapter.

KEY POINT

The second issue you have to address if you're using a table-driven method is what you should store in the table. In some cases, the result of a table lookup is data. If that's the case, you can store the data in the table. In other cases, the result of a table lookup is an action. In such a case, you can store a code that describes the action or, in some languages, you can store a reference to the routine that implements the action. In either of these cases, tables become more complicated.

18.2 Direct Access Tables

Like all lookup tables, direct-access tables replace more complicated logical control structures. They are "direct access" because you don't have to jump through any complicated hoops to find the information you want in the table. As Figure 18-1 suggests, you can pick out the entry you want directly.

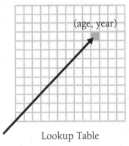

(age, year)

Lookup Table

Figure 18-1   As the name suggests, a direct-access table allows you to access the table element you're interested in directly.

Days-in-Month Example

Suppose you need to determine the number of days per month (forgetting about leap year, for the sake of argument). A clumsy way to do it, of course, is to write a large *if* statement:

Visual Basic Example of a Clumsy Way to Determine the Number of Days in a Month
```
If ( month = 1 ) Then
    days = 31
ElseIf ( month = 2 ) Then
    days = 28
ElseIf ( month = 3 ) Then
    days = 31
ElseIf ( month = 4 ) Then
    days = 30
ElseIf ( month = 5 ) Then
    days = 31
ElseIf ( month = 6 ) Then
    days = 30
ElseIf ( month = 7 ) Then
    days = 31
```

```
ElseIf ( month = 8 ) Then
   days = 31
ElseIf ( month = 9 ) Then
   days = 30
ElseIf ( month = 10 ) Then
   days = 31
ElseIf ( month = 11 ) Then
   days = 30
ElseIf ( month = 12 ) Then
   days = 31
End If
```

An easier and more modifiable way to perform the same function is to put the data in a table. In Microsoft Visual Basic, you'd first set up the table:

Visual Basic Example of an Elegant Way to Determine the Number of Days in a Month

```
' Initialize Table of "Days Per Month" Data
Dim daysPerMonth() As Integer = _
   { 31, 28, 31, 30, 31, 30, 31, 31, 30, 31, 30, 31 }
```

Now, instead of using the long *if* statement, you can just use a simple array access to find out the number of days in a month:

Visual Basic Example of an Elegant Way to Determine the Number of Days in a Month (continued)

```
days = daysPerMonth( month-1 )
```

If you wanted to account for leap year in the table-lookup version, the code would still be simple, assuming *LeapYearIndex()* has a value of either *0* or *1*:

Visual Basic Example of an Elegant Way to Determine the Number of Days in a Month (continued)

```
days = daysPerMonth( month-1, LeapYearIndex() )
```

In the *if*-statement version, the long string of *if*s would grow even more complicated if leap year were considered.

Determining the number of days per month is a convenient example because you can use the *month* variable to look up an entry in the table. You can often use the data that would have controlled a lot of *if* statements to access a table directly.

Insurance Rates Example

Suppose you're writing a program to compute medical insurance rates and you have rates that vary by age, gender, marital status, and whether a person smokes. If you had to write a logical control structure for the rates, you'd get something like this:

CODING HORROR

Java Example of a Clumsy Way to Determine an Insurance Rate

```java
if ( gender == Gender.Female ) {
   if ( maritalStatus == MaritalStatus.Single ) {
      if ( smokingStatus == SmokingStatus.NonSmoking ) {
         if ( age < 18 ) {
            rate = 200.00;
         }
         else if ( age == 18 ) {
            rate = 250.00;
         }
         else if ( age == 19 ) {
            rate = 300.00;
         }
         ...
         else if ( 65 < age ) {
            rate = 450.00;
         }
      }
      else {
         if ( age < 18 ) {
            rate = 250.00;
         }
         else if ( age == 18 ) {
            rate = 300.00;
         }
         else if ( age == 19 ) {
            rate = 350.00;
         }
         ...
         else if ( 65 < age ) {
            rate = 575.00;
         }
      }
   }
   else if ( maritalStatus == MaritalStatus.Married )
   ...
}
```

The abbreviated version of the logic structure should be enough to give you an idea of how complicated this kind of thing can get. It doesn't show married females, any males, or most of the ages between 18 and 65. You can imagine how complicated it would get when you programmed the whole rate table.

You might say, "Yeah, but why did you do a test for each age? Why don't you just put the rates in arrays for each age?" That's a good question, and one obvious improvement would be to put the rates into separate arrays for each age.

A better solution, however, is to put the rates into arrays for all the factors, not just age. Here's how you would declare the array in Visual Basic:

Visual Basic Example of Declaring Data to Set Up an Insurance Rates Table

```
Public Enum SmokingStatus
    SmokingStatus_First = 0
    SmokingStatus_Smoking = 0
    SmokingStatus_NonSmoking = 1
    SmokingStatus_Last = 1
End Enum

Public Enum Gender
    Gender_First = 0
    Gender_Male = 0
    Gender_Female = 1
    Gender_Last = 1
End Enum

Public Enum MaritalStatus
    MaritalStatus_First = 0
    MaritalStatus_Single = 0
    MaritalStatus_Married = 1
    MaritalStatus_Last = 1
End Enum

Const MAX_AGE As Integer = 125

Dim rateTable ( SmokingStatus_Last, Gender_Last, MaritalStatus_Last, _
    MAX_AGE ) As Double
```

Cross-Reference One advantage of a table-driven approach is that you can put the table's data in a file and read it at run time. That allows you to change something like an insurance rates table without changing the program itself. For more on the idea, see Section 10.6, "Binding Time."

Once you declare the array, you have to figure out some way of putting data into it. You can use assignment statements, read the data from a disk file, compute the data, or do whatever is appropriate. After you've set up the data, you've got it made when you need to calculate a rate. The complicated logic shown earlier is replaced with a simple statement like this one:

Visual Basic Example of an Elegant Way to Determine an Insurance Rate

```
rate = rateTable( smokingStatus, gender, maritalStatus, age )
```

This approach has the general advantages of replacing complicated logic with a table lookup. The table lookup is more readable and easier to change.

Flexible-Message-Format Example

You can use a table to describe logic that's too dynamic to represent in code. With the character-classification example, the days-in-the-month example, and the insurance rates example, you at least knew that you could write a long string of *if* statements if you needed to. In some cases, however, the data is too complicated to describe with hard-coded *if* statements.

If you think you've got the idea of how direct-access tables work, you might want to skip the next example. It's a little more complicated than the earlier examples, though, and it further demonstrates the power of table-driven approaches.

Suppose you're writing a routine to print messages that are stored in a file. The file usually has about 500 messages, and each file has about 20 kinds of messages. The messages originally come from a buoy and give water temperature, the buoy's location, and so on.

Each of the messages has several fields, and each message starts with a header that has an ID to let you know which of the 20 or so kinds of messages you're dealing with. Figure 18-2 illustrates how the messages are stored.

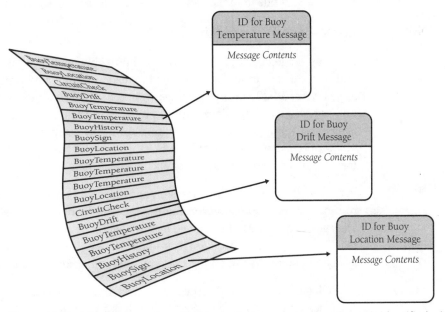

Figure 18-2   Messages are stored in no particular order, and each one is identified with a message ID.

The format of the messages is volatile, determined by your customer, and you don't have enough control over your customer to stabilize it. Figure 18-3 shows what a few of the messages look like in detail.

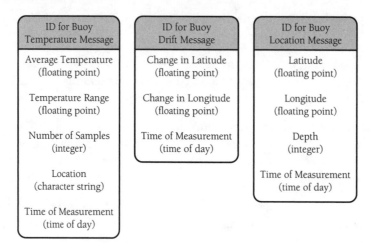

Figure 18-3 Aside from the Message ID, each kind of message has its own format.

Logic-Based Approach

If you used a logic-based approach, you'd probably read each message, check the ID, and then call a routine that's designed to read, interpret, and print each kind of message. If you had 20 kinds of messages, you'd have 20 routines. You'd also have who-knows-how-many lower-level routines to support them—for example, you'd have a *PrintBuoyTemperatureMessage()* routine to print the buoy temperature message. An object-oriented approach wouldn't be much better: you'd typically use an abstract message object with a subclass for each message type.

Each time the format of any message changed, you'd have to change the logic in the routine or class responsible for that message. In the detailed message earlier, if the average-temperature field changed from a floating point to something else, you'd have to change the logic of *PrintBuoyTemperatureMessage()*. (If the buoy itself changed from a "floating point" to something else, you'd have to get a new buoy!)

In the logic-based approach, the message-reading routine consists of a loop to read each message, decode the ID, and then call one of 20 routines based on the message ID. Here's the pseudocode for the logic-based approach:

Cross-Reference This low-level pseudocode is used for a different purpose than the pseudocode you use for routine design. For details on designing in pseudocode, see Chapter 9, "The Pseudocode Programming Process."

```
While more messages to read
   Read a message header
   Decode the message ID from the message header
   If the message header is type 1 then
      Print a type 1 message
   Else if the message header is type 2 then
      Print a type 2 message
   ...
   Else if the message header is type 19 then
      Print a type 19 message
   Else if the message header is type 20 then
      Print a type 20 message
```

The pseudocode is abbreviated because you can get the idea without seeing all 20 cases.

Object-Oriented Approach

If you were using a rote object-oriented approach, the logic would be hidden in the object inheritance structure but the basic structure would be just as complicated:

```
While more messages to read
   Read a message header
   Decode the message ID from the message header
   If the message header is type 1 then
      Instantiate a type 1 message object
   Else if the message header is type 2 then
      Instantiate a type 2 message object
   ...
   Else if the message header is type 19 then
      Instantiate a type 19 message object
   Else if the message header is type 20 then
      Instantiate a type 20 message object
   End if
End While
```

Regardless of whether the logic is written directly or contained within specialized classes, each of the 20 kinds of messages will have its own routine for printing its message. Each routine could also be expressed in pseudocode. This is the pseudocode for the routine to read and print the buoy temperature message:

```
Print "Buoy Temperature Message"

Read a floating-point value
Print "Average Temperature"
Print the floating-point value

Read a floating-point value
Print "Temperature Range"
Print the floating-point value

Read an integer value
Print "Number of Samples"
Print the integer value

Read a character string
Print "Location"
Print the character string

Read a time of day
Print "Time of Measurement"
Print the time of day
```

This is the code for just one kind of message. Each of the other 19 kinds of messages would require similar code. And if a 21st kind of message was added, either a 21st routine or a 21st subclass would need to be added—either way a new message type would require the code to be changed.

Table-Driven Approach

The table-driven approach is more economical than the previous approach. The message-reading routine consists of a loop that reads each message header, decodes the ID, looks up the message description in the *Message* array, and then calls the same routine every time to decode the message. With a table-driven approach, you can describe the format of each message in a table rather than hard-coding it in program logic. This makes it easier to code originally, generates less code, and makes it easier to maintain without changing code.

To use this approach, you start by listing the kinds of messages and the types of fields. In C++, you could define the types of all the possible fields this way:

> **C++ Example of Defining Message Data Types**
> ```
> enum FieldType {
>    FieldType_FloatingPoint,
>    FieldType_Integer,
>    FieldType_String,
>    FieldType_TimeOfDay,
>    FieldType_Boolean,
>    FieldType_BitField,
>    FieldType_Last = FieldType_BitField
> };
> ```

Rather than hard-coding printing routines for each of the 20 kinds of messages, you can create a handful of routines that print each of the primary data types—floating point, integer, character string, and so on. You can describe the contents of each kind of message in a table (including the name of each field) and then decode each message based on the description in the table. A table entry to describe one kind of message might look like this:

> **Example of Defining a Message Table Entry**
> ```
> Message Begin
>    NumFields 5
>    MessageName "Buoy Temperature Message"
>    Field 1, FloatingPoint, "Average Temperature"
>    Field 2, FloatingPoint, "Temperature Range"
>    Field 3, Integer, "Number of Samples"
>    Field 4, String, "Location"
>    Field 5, TimeOfDay, "Time of Measurement"
> Message End
> ```

This table could be hard-coded in the program (in which case, each of the elements shown would be assigned to variables), or it could be read from a file at program startup time or later.

Once message definitions are read into the program, instead of having all the information embedded in a program's logic, you have it embedded in data. Data tends to be more flexible than logic. Data is easy to change when a message format changes. If you have to add a new kind of message, you can just add another element to the data table.

Here's the pseudocode for the top-level loop in the table-driven approach:

> The first three lines here are the same as in the logic-based approach.

```
While more messages to read
    Read a message header
    Decode the message ID from the message header
    Look up the message description in the message-description table
    Read the message fields and print them based on the message description
End While
```

Unlike the pseudocode for the logic-based approach, the pseudocode in this case isn't abbreviated because the logic is so much less complicated. In the logic below this level, you'll find one routine that's capable of interpreting a message description from the message description table, reading message data, and printing a message. That routine is more general than any of the logic-based message-printing routines but not much more complicated, and it will be one routine instead of 20:

```
While more fields to print
    Get the field type from the message description
    case ( field type )
        of ( floating point )
            read a floating-point value
            print the field label
            print the floating-point value

        of ( integer )
            read an integer value
            print the field label
            print the integer value

        of ( character string )
            read a character string
            print the field label
            print the character string

        of ( time of day )
            read a time of day
            print the field label
            print the time of day

        of ( boolean )
            read a single flag
            print the field label
            print the single flag

        of ( bit field )
            read a bit field
            print the field label
            print the bit field
    End Case
End While
```

Admittedly, this routine with its six cases is longer than the single routine needed to print the buoy temperature message. But this is the only routine you need. You don't need 19 other routines for the 19 other kinds of messages. This routine handles the six field types and takes care of all the kinds of messages.

This routine also shows the most complicated way of implementing this kind of table lookup because it uses a *case* statement. Another approach would be to create an abstract class *AbstractField* and then create subclasses for each field type. You won't need a *case* statement; you can call the member routine of the appropriate type of object.

Here's how you would set up the object types in C++:

C++ Example of Setting Up Object Types
```cpp
class AbstractField {
   public:
   virtual void ReadAndPrint( string, FileStatus & ) = 0;
};

class FloatingPointField : public AbstractField {
   public:
   virtual void ReadAndPrint( string, FileStatus & ) {
   ...
   }
};

class IntegerField ...
class StringField ...
...
```

This code fragment declares a member routine for each class that has a string parameter and a *FileStatus* parameter.

The next step is to declare an array to hold the set of objects. The array is the lookup table, and here's how it looks:

C++ Example of Setting Up a Table to Hold an Object of Each Type
```cpp
AbstractField* field[ Field_Last+1];
```

The final step required to set up the table of objects is to assign the names of specific objects to the *Field* array:

C++ Example of Setting Up a List of Objects
```cpp
field[ Field_FloatingPoint ] = new FloatingPointField();
field[ Field_Integer ] = new IntegerField();
field[ Field_String ] = new StringField();
field[ Field_TimeOfDay ] = new TimeOfDayField();
field[ Field_Boolean ] = new BooleanField();
field[ Field_BitField ] = new BitFieldField();
```

This code fragment assumes that *FloatingPointField* and the other identifiers on the right side of the assignment statements are names of objects of type *AbstractField*. Assigning the objects to array elements in the array means that you can call the correct *ReadAndPrint()* routine by referencing an array element instead of by using a specific kind of object directly.

Once the table of routines is set up, you can handle a field in the message simply by accessing the table of objects and calling one of the member routines in the table. The code looks like this:

C++ Example of Looking Up Objects and Member Routines in a Table

This stuff is just house-keeping for each field in a message.

This is the table lookup that calls a routine depending on the type of the field— just by looking it up in a table of objects.

```cpp
fieldIdx = 1;
while ( ( fieldIdx <= numFieldsInMessage ) && ( fileStatus == OK ) ) {
   fieldType = fieldDescription[ fieldIdx ].FieldType;
   fieldName = fieldDescription[ fieldIdx ].FieldName;
   field[ fieldType ].ReadAndPrint( fieldName, fileStatus );
   fieldIdx++;
}
```

Remember the original 34 lines of table-lookup pseudocode containing the *case* statement? If you replace the *case* statement with a table of objects, this is all the code you'd need to provide the same functionality. Incredibly, it's also all the code needed to replace all 20 of the individual routines in the logic-based approach. Moreover, if the message descriptions are read from a file, new message types won't require code changes unless there's a new field type.

You can use this approach in any object-oriented language. It's less error-prone, more maintainable, and more efficient than lengthy *if* statements, *case* statements, or copious subclasses.

The fact that a design uses inheritance and polymorphism doesn't make it a good design. The rote object-oriented design described earlier in the "Object-Oriented Approach" section would require as much code as a rote functional design—or more. That approach made the solution space more complicated, rather than less. The key design insight in this case is neither object orientation nor functional orientation—it's the use of a well thought out lookup table.

Fudging Lookup Keys

In each of the three previous examples, you could use the data to key into the table directly. That is, you could use *messageID* as a key without alteration, as you could use *month* in the days-per-month example and *gender*, *maritalStatus*, and *smokingStatus* in the insurance rates example.

You'd always like to key into a table directly because it's simple and fast. Sometimes, however, the data isn't cooperative. In the insurance rates example, *age* wasn't well behaved. The original logic had one rate for people under 18, individual rates for ages

18 through 65, and one rate for people over 65. This meant that for ages 0 through 17 and 66 and over, you couldn't use the age to key directly into a table that stored only one set of rates for several ages.

This leads to the topic of fudging table-lookup keys. You can fudge keys in several ways:

Duplicate information to make the key work directly   One straightforward way to make *age* work as a key into the rates table is to duplicate the under-18 rates for each of the ages 0 through 17 and then use the age to key directly into the table. You can do the same thing for ages 66 and over. The benefits of this approach are that the table structure itself is straightforward and the table accesses are also straightforward. If you needed to add age-specific rates for ages 17 and below, you could just change the table. The drawbacks are that the duplication would waste space for redundant information and increase the possibility of errors in the table—if only because the table would contain redundant data.

Transform the key to make it work directly   A second way to make *Age* work as a direct key is to apply a function to *Age* so that it works well. In this case, the function would have to change all ages 0 through 17 to one key, say 17, and all ages above 66 to another key, say 66. This particular range is well behaved enough that you could use *min()* and *max()* functions to make the transformation. For example, you could use the expression

```
max( min( 66, Age ), 17 )
```

to create a table key that ranges from 17 to 66.

Creating the transformation function requires that you recognize a pattern in the data you want to use as a key, and that's not always as simple as using the *min()* and *max()* routines. Suppose that in this example the rates were for five-year age bands instead of one-year bands. Unless you wanted to duplicate all your data five times, you'd have to come up with a function that divided *Age* by 5 properly and used the *min()* and *max()* routines.

Isolate the key transformation in its own routine   If you have to fudge data to make it work as a table key, put the operation that changes the data to a key into its own routine. A routine eliminates the possibility of using different transformations in different places. It makes modifications easier when the transformation changes. A good name for the routine, like *KeyFromAge()*, also clarifies and documents the purpose of the mathematical machinations.

If your environment provides ready-made key transformations, use them. For example, Java provides *HashMap*, which can be used to associate key/value pairs.

18.3 Indexed Access Tables

Sometimes a simple mathematical transformation isn't powerful enough to make the jump from data like *Age* to a table key. Some such cases are suited to the use of an indexed access scheme.

When you use indexes, you use the primary data to look up a key in an index table and then you use the value from the index table to look up the main data you're interested in.

Suppose you run a warehouse and have an inventory of about 100 items. Suppose further that each item has a four-digit part number that ranges from 0000 through 9999. In this case, if you want to use the part number to key directly into a table that describes some aspect of each item, you set up an index array with 10,000 entries (from 0 through 9999). The array is empty except for the 100 entries that correspond to part numbers of the 100 items in your warehouse. As Figure 18-4 shows, those entries point to an item-description table that has far fewer than 10,000 entries.

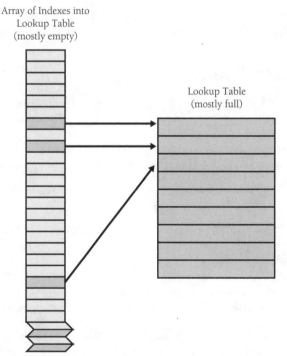

Figure 18-4   Rather than being accessed directly, an indexed access table is accessed via an intermediate index.

Indexed access schemes offer two main advantages. First, if each of the entries in the main lookup table is large, it takes a lot less space to create an index array with a lot of wasted space than it does to create a main lookup table with a lot of wasted space. For example, suppose that the main table takes 100 bytes per entry and that the index array takes 2 bytes per entry. Suppose that the main table has 100 entries and that the data used to access it has 10,000 possible values. In such a case, the choice is between having an index with 10,000 entries or a main data member with 10,000 entries. If you use an index, your total memory use is 30,000 bytes. If you forgo the index structure and waste space in the main table, your total memory use is 1,000,000 bytes.

The second advantage, even if you don't save space by using an index, is that it's sometimes cheaper to manipulate entries in an index than entries in a main table. For example, if you have a table with employee names, hiring dates, and salaries, you can create one index that accesses the table by employee name, another that accesses the table by hiring date, and a third that accesses the table by salary.

A final advantage of an index-access scheme is the general table-lookup advantage of maintainability. Data encoded in tables is easier to maintain than data embedded in code. To maximize the flexibility, put the index-access code in its own routine and call the routine when you need to get a table key from a part number. When it's time to change the table, you might decide to switch the index-accessing scheme or switch to another table-lookup scheme altogether. The access scheme will be easier to change if you don't spread index accesses throughout your program.

18.4 Stair-Step Access Tables

Yet another kind of table access is the stair-step method. This access method isn't as direct as an index structure, but it doesn't waste as much data space.

The general idea of stair-step structures, illustrated in Figure 18-5, is that entries in a table are valid for ranges of data rather than for distinct data points.

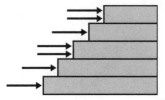

Figure 18-5 The stair-step approach categorizes each entry by determining the level at which it hits a "staircase." The "step" it hits determines its category.

For example, if you're writing a grading program, the "B" entry range might be from 75 percent to 90 percent. Here's a range of grades you might have to program someday:

≥ 90.0%	A
< 90.0%	B
< 75.0%	C
< 65.0%	D
< 50.0%	F

This is an ugly range for a table lookup because you can't use a simple data-transformation function to key into the letters *A* through *F*. An index scheme would be awkward because the numbers are floating point. You might consider converting the floating-point numbers to integers, and in this case that would be a valid design option, but for the sake of illustration, this example will stick with floating point.

To use the stair-step method, you put the upper end of each range into a table and then write a loop to check a score against the upper end of each range. When you find the point at which the score first exceeds the top of a range, you know what the grade is. With the stair-step technique, you have to be careful to handle the endpoints of the ranges properly. Here's the code in Visual Basic that assigns grades to a group of students based on this example:

Visual Basic Example of a Stair-Step Table Lookup

```
' set up data for grading table
Dim rangeLimit() As Double = { 50.0, 65.0, 75.0, 90.0, 100.0 }
Dim grade() As String =      { "F",  "D",  "C",  "B",   "A"  }
maxGradeLevel = grade.Length - 1
...

' assign a grade to a student based on the student's score
gradeLevel = 0
studentGrade = "A"
While ( ( studentGrade = "A" ) and ( gradeLevel < maxGradeLevel ) )
   If ( studentScore < rangeLimit( gradeLevel ) ) Then
      studentGrade = grade( gradeLevel )
   End If
   gradeLevel = gradeLevel + 1
Wend
```

Although this is a simple example, you can easily generalize it to handle multiple students, multiple grading schemes (for example, different grades for different point levels on different assignments), and changes in the grading scheme.

The advantage of this approach over other table-driven methods is that it works well with irregular data. The grading example is simple in that, although grades are assigned at irregular intervals, the numbers are "round," ending with 5s and 0s. The stair-step approach is equally well suited to data that doesn't end neatly with 5s and 0s. You can use the stair-step approach in statistics work for probability distributions with numbers like this:

Probability	Insurance Claim Amount
0.458747	$0.00
0.547651	$254.32
0.627764	$514.77
0.776883	$747.82
0.893211	$1,042.65

Probability	Insurance Claim Amount
0.957665	$5,887.55
0.976544	$12,836.98
0.987889	$27,234.12
...	

Ugly numbers like these defy any attempt to come up with a function to neatly transform them into table keys. The stair-step approach is the answer.

This approach also enjoys the general advantages of table-driven approaches: it's flexible and modifiable. If the grading ranges in the grading example were to change, the program could easily be adapted by modifying the entries in the *RangeLimit* array. You could easily generalize the grade-assignment part of the program so that it would accept a table of grades and corresponding cut-off scores. The grade-assignment part of the program wouldn't have to use scores expressed as percentages; it could use raw points rather than percentages, and the program wouldn't have to change much.

Here are a few subtleties to consider as you use the stair-step technique:

Watch the endpoints Make sure you've covered the case at the top end of each stair-step range. Run the stair-step search so that it finds items that map to any range other than the uppermost range, and then have the rest fall into the uppermost range. Sometimes this requires creating an artificial value for the top of the uppermost range.

Be careful about mistaking < for <=. Make sure that the loop terminates properly with values that fall into the top ranges and that the range boundaries are handled correctly.

Consider using a binary search rather then a sequential search In the grading example, the loop that assigns the grade searches sequentially through the list of grading limits. If you had a larger list, the cost of the sequential search might become prohibitive. If it does, you can replace it with a quasi-binary search. It's a "quasi" binary search because the point of most binary searches is to find a value. In this case, you don't expect to find the value; you expect to find the right category for the value. The binary-search algorithm must correctly determine where the value should go. Remember also to treat the endpoint as a special case.

Consider using indexed access instead of the stair-step technique An index-access scheme such as the ones described in Section 18.3 might be a good alternative to a stair-step technique. The searching required in the stair-step method can add up, and if execution speed is a concern, you might be willing to trade the space an extra index structure takes up for the time advantage you get with a more direct access method.

Obviously, this alternative isn't a good choice in all cases. In the grading example, you could probably use it; if you had only 100 discrete percentage points, the memory cost of setting up an index array wouldn't be prohibitive. If, on the other hand, you had the probability data listed earlier, you couldn't set up an indexing scheme because you can't key into entries with numbers like 0.458747 and 0.547651.

Cross-Reference For more on good approaches to choosing design alternatives, see Chapter 5, "Design in Construction."

In some cases, any of the several options might work. The point of design is choosing one of the several good options for your case. Don't worry too much about choosing the best one. As Butler Lampson, a distinguished engineer at Microsoft, says, it's better to strive for a good solution and avoid disaster rather than trying to find the best solution (Lampson 1984).

Put the stair-step table lookup into its own routine   When you create a transformation function that changes a value like *StudentGrade* into a table key, put it into its own routine.

18.5 Other Examples of Table Lookups

A few other examples of table lookups appear in other sections of the book. They're used in the course of discussing other techniques, and the contexts don't emphasize the table lookups per se. Here's where you'll find them:

- Looking up rates in an insurance table: Section 16.3, "Creating Loops Easily— From the Inside Out"

- Using decision tables to replace complicated logic: "Use decision tables to replace complicated conditions" in Section 19.1.

- Cost of memory paging during a table lookup: Section 25.3, "Kinds of Fat and Molasses"

- Combinations of boolean values (A or B or C): "Substitute Table Lookups for Complicated Expressions" in Section 26.1

- Precomputing values in a loan repayment table: Section 26.4, "Expressions."

cc2e.com/1872

CHECKLIST: Table-Driven Methods

- ❑ Have you considered table-driven methods as an alternative to complicated logic?

- ❑ Have you considered table-driven methods as an alternative to complicated inheritance structures?

- ❑ Have you considered storing the table's data externally and reading it at run time so that the data can be modified without changing code?

- ❑ If the table cannot be accessed directly via a straightforward array index (as in the *age* example), have you put the access-key calculation into a routine rather than duplicating the index calculation in the code?

Key Points

- Tables provide an alternative to complicated logic and inheritance structures. If you find that you're confused by a program's logic or inheritance tree, ask yourself whether you could simplify by using a lookup table.

- One key consideration in using a table is deciding how to access the table. You can access tables by using direct access, indexed access, or stair-step access.

- Another key consideration in using a table is deciding what exactly to put into the table.

Chapter 19

General Control Issues

cc2e.com/1978

Contents

Related Topics

No discussion of control would be complete unless it went into several general issues that crop up when you think about control constructs. Most of the information in this chapter is detailed and pragmatic. If you're reading for the theory of control structures rather than for the gritty details, concentrate on the historical perspective on structured programming in Section 19.5 and on the relationships between control structures in Section 19.6.

19.1 Boolean Expressions

Except for the simplest control structure, the one that calls for the execution of statements in sequence, all control structures depend on the evaluation of boolean expressions.

Using *true* and *false* for Boolean Tests

Use the identifiers *true* and *false* in boolean expressions rather than using values like 0 and 1. Most modern languages have a boolean data type and provide predefined identifiers for true and false. They make it easy—they don't even allow you to assign

431

values other than *true* or *false* to boolean variables. Languages that don't have a boolean data type require you to have more discipline to make boolean expressions readable. Here's an example of the problem:

**CODING
HORROR**

Visual Basic Examples of Using Ambiguous Flags for Boolean Values

```
Dim printerError As Integer
Dim reportSelected As Integer
Dim summarySelected As Integer
...
If printerError = 0 Then InitializePrinter()
If printerError = 1 Then NotifyUserOfError()

If reportSelected = 1 Then PrintReport()
If summarySelected = 1 Then PrintSummary()

If printerError = 0 Then CleanupPrinter()
```

If using flags like *0* and *1* is common practice, what's wrong with it? It's not clear from reading the code whether the function calls are executed when the tests are true or when they're false. Nothing in the code fragment itself tells you whether *1* represents true and *0* false or whether the opposite is true. It's not even clear that the values *1* and *0* are being used to represent true and false. For example, in the *If reportSelected = 1* line, the *1* could easily represent the first report, a *2* the second, a *3* the third; nothing in the code tells you that *1* represents either true or false. It's also easy to write *0* when you mean *1* and vice versa.

Use terms named *true* and *false* for tests with boolean expressions. If your language doesn't support such terms directly, create them using preprocessor macros or global variables. The previous code example is rewritten here using Microsoft Visual Basic's built-in *True* and *False*:

Cross-Reference For an even better approach to making these same tests, see the next code example.

Good, but Not Great Visual Basic Examples of Using *True* and *False* for Tests Instead of Numeric Values

```
Dim printerError As Boolean
Dim reportSelected As ReportType
Dim summarySelected As Boolean
...
If ( printerError = False ) Then InitializePrinter()
If ( printerError = True ) Then NotifyUserOfError()

If ( reportSelected = ReportType_First ) Then PrintReport()
If ( summarySelected = True ) Then PrintSummary()

If ( printerError = False ) Then CleanupPrinter()
```

Use of the *True* and *False* constants makes the intent clearer. You don't have to remember what *1* and *0* represent, and you won't accidentally reverse them. Moreover, in the rewritten code, it's now clear that some of the *1*s and *0*s in the original Visual Basic example weren't being used as boolean flags. The *If reportSelected = 1* line was not a boolean test at all; it tested whether the first report had been selected.

This approach tells the reader that you're making a boolean test. It's also harder to write *true* when you mean *false* than it is to write *1* when you mean *0*, and you avoid spreading the magic numbers *0* and *1* throughout your code. Here are some tips on defining *true* and *false* in boolean tests:

Compare boolean values to true *and* false *implicitly* You can write clearer tests by treating the expressions as boolean expressions. For example, write

```
while ( not done ) ...
while ( a > b ) ...
```

rather than

```
while ( done = false ) ...
while ( (a > b) = true ) ...
```

Using implicit comparisons reduces the number of terms that someone reading your code has to keep in mind, and the resulting expressions read more like conversational English. The previous example could be rewritten with even better style like this:

Better Visual Basic Examples of Testing for *True* and *False* Implicitly
```
Dim printerError As Boolean
Dim reportSelected As ReportType
Dim summarySelected As Boolean
...
If ( Not printerError ) Then InitializePrinter()
If ( printerError ) Then NotifyUserOfError()

If ( reportSelected = ReportType_First ) Then PrintReport()
If ( summarySelected ) Then PrintSummary()

If ( Not printerError ) Then CleanupPrinter()
```

Cross-Reference For details, see Section 12.5, "Boolean Variables."

If your language doesn't support boolean variables and you have to emulate them, you might not be able to use this technique because emulations of *true* and *false* can't always be tested with statements like *while (not done)*.

Making Complicated Expressions Simple

You can take several steps to simplify complicated expressions:

Break complicated tests into partial tests with new boolean variables Rather than creating a monstrous test with half a dozen terms, assign intermediate values to terms that allow you to perform a simpler test.

Move complicated expressions into boolean functions   If a test is repeated often or distracts from the main flow of the program, move the code for the test into a function and test the value of the function. For example, here's a complicated test:

Visual Basic Example of a Complicated Test

```
If ( ( document.AtEndOfStream ) And ( Not inputError ) ) And _
   ( ( MIN_LINES <= lineCount ) And ( lineCount <= MAX_LINES ) ) And _
   ( Not ErrorProcessing( ) ) Then
   ' do something or other
   ...
End If
```

This is an ugly test to have to read through if you're not interested in the test itself. By putting it into a boolean function, you can isolate the test and allow the reader to forget about it unless it's important. Here's how you could put the *if* test into a function:

Cross-Reference For details on the technique of using intermediate variables to clarify a boolean test, see "Use boolean variables to document your program" in Section 12.5.

Visual Basic Example of a Complicated Test Moved into a Boolean Function, with New Intermediate Variables to Make the Test Clearer

```
Function DocumentIsValid( _
   ByRef documentToCheck As Document, _
   lineCount As Integer, _
   inputError As Boolean _
   ) As Boolean

   Dim allDataRead As Boolean
   Dim legalLineCount As Boolean

   allDataRead = ( documentToCheck.AtEndOfStream ) And ( Not inputError )
   legalLineCount = ( MIN_LINES <= lineCount ) And ( lineCount <= MAX_LINES )
   DocumentIsValid = allDataRead And legalLineCount And ( Not ErrorProcessing() )

End Function
```

Intermediate variables are introduced here to clarify the test on the final line, below.

This example assumes that *ErrorProcessing()* is a boolean function that indicates the current processing status. Now, when you read through the main flow of the code, you don't have to read the complicated test:

Visual Basic Example of the Main Flow of the Code Without the Complicated Test

```
If ( DocumentIsValid( document, lineCount, inputError ) ) Then
   ' do something or other
   ...
End If
```

KEY POINT

If you use the test only once, you might not think it's worthwhile to put it into a routine. But putting the test into a well-named function improves readability and makes it easier for you to see what your code is doing, and that's a sufficient reason to do it.

The new function name introduces an abstraction into the program that documents the purpose of the test *in code*. That's even better than documenting the test with comments because the code is more likely to be read than the comments and it's more likely to be kept up to date, too.

Cross-Reference For details on using tables as substitutes for complicated logic, see Chapter 18, "Table-Driven Methods."

Use decision tables to replace complicated conditions Sometimes you have a complicated test involving several variables. It can be helpful to use a decision table to perform the test rather than using *ifs* or *cases*. A decision-table lookup is easier to code initially, having only a couple of lines of code and no tricky control structures. This minimization of complexity minimizes the opportunity for mistakes. If your data changes, you can change a decision table without changing the code; you only need to update the contents of the data structure.

Forming Boolean Expressions Positively

I ain't not no undummy.
—*Homer Simpson*

Not a few people don't have not any trouble understanding a nonshort string of nonpositives—that is, most people have trouble understanding a lot of negatives. You can do several things to avoid complicated negative boolean expressions in your programs:

In if statements, convert negatives to positives and flip-flop the code in the if and else clauses Here's an example of a negatively expressed test:

Java Example of a Confusing Negative Boolean Test

Here's the negative *not*. →
```java
if ( !statusOK ) {
    // do something
    ...
}
else {
    // do something else
    ...
}
```

You can change this to the following positively expressed test:

Java Example of a Clearer Positive Boolean Test

The test in this line has been reversed. →
The code in this block has been switched... →
...with the code in this block. →
```java
if ( statusOK ) {
    // do something else
    ...
}
else {
    // do something
    ...
}
```

Cross-Reference The recommendation to frame boolean expressions positively sometimes contradicts the recommendation to code the nominal case after the *if* rather than the *else*. (See Section 15.1, "*if* Statements.") In such a case, you have to think about the benefits of each approach and decide which is better for your situation.

The second code fragment is logically the same as the first but is easier to read because the negative expression has been changed to a positive.

Alternatively, you could choose a different variable name, one that would reverse the truth value of the test. In the example, you could replace *statusOK* with *ErrorDetected*, which would be true when *statusOK* was false.

Apply DeMorgan's Theorems to simplify boolean tests with negatives   DeMorgan's Theorems let you exploit the logical relationship between an expression and a version of the expression that means the same thing because it's doubly negated. For example, you might have a code fragment that contains the following test:

Java Example of a Negative Test
```
if ( !displayOK || !printerOK ) ...
```

This is logically equivalent to the following:

Java Example After Applying DeMorgan's Theorems
```
if ( !( displayOK && printerOK ) ) ...
```

Here you don't have to flip-flop *if* and *else* clauses; the expressions in the last two code fragments are logically equivalent. To apply DeMorgan's Theorems to the logical operator *and* or the logical operator *or* and a pair of operands, you negate each of the operands, switch the *and*s and *or*s, and negate the entire expression. Table 19-1 summarizes the possible transformations under DeMorgan's Theorems.

Table 19-1   Transformations of Logical Expressions Under DeMorgan's Theorems

Initial Expression	Equivalent Expression
not A and not B	not (A or B)
not A and B	not (A or not B)
A and not B	not (not A or B)
A and B	not (not A or not B)
not A or not B[*]	not (A and B)
not A or B	not (A and not B)
A or not B	not (not A and B)
A or B	not (not A and not B)

* This is the expression used in the example.

Using Parentheses to Clarify Boolean Expressions

Cross-Reference For an example of using parentheses to clarify other kinds of expressions, see "Parentheses" in Section 31.2.

If you have a complicated boolean expression, rather than relying on the language's evaluation order, parenthesize to make your meaning clear. Using parentheses makes less of a demand on your reader, who might not understand the subtleties of how your language evaluates boolean expressions. If you're smart, you won't depend on your own or your reader's in-depth memorization of evaluation precedence—especially when you have to switch among two or more languages. Using parentheses isn't like sending a telegram: you're not charged for each character—the extra characters are free.

Here's an expression with too few parentheses:

> **Java Example of an Expression Containing Too Few Parentheses**
> ```
> if ( a < b == c == d ) ...
> ```

This is a confusing expression to begin with, and it's even more confusing because it's not clear whether the coder means to test $(a < b) == (c == d)$ or $((a < b) == c) == d$. The following version of the expression is still a little confusing, but the parentheses help:

> **Java Example of an Expression Better Parenthesized**
> ```
> if ( ( a < b ) == ( c == d ) ) ...
> ```

In this case, the parentheses help readability and the program's correctness—the compiler wouldn't have interpreted the first code fragment this way. When in doubt, parenthesize.

Cross-Reference Many programmer-oriented text editors have commands that match parentheses, brackets, and braces. For details on programming editors, see "Editing" in Section 30.2.

Use a simple counting technique to balance parentheses   If you have trouble telling whether parentheses balance, here's a simple counting trick that helps. Start by saying "zero." Move along the expression, left to right. When you encounter an opening parenthesis, say "one." Each time you encounter another opening parenthesis, increase the number you say. Each time you encounter a closing parenthesis, decrease the number you say. If, at the end of the expression, you're back to 0, your parentheses are balanced.

> **Java Example of Balanced Parentheses**
> ```
> Read this.   →  if ( ( ( a < b ) == ( c == d ) ) && !done ) ...
>                    | | |       |     |       | |           |
> Say this.    →   0 1 2 3       2     3       2 1           0
> ```

In this example, you ended with a 0, so the parentheses are balanced. In the next example, the parentheses aren't balanced:

Java Example of Unbalanced Parentheses

```
if ( ( a < b ) == ( c == d ) ) && !done ) ...
   | |       |   |       | |           |
 0  1 2      1   2       1 0          -1
```

Read this. →
Say this. →

The 0 before you get to the last closing parenthesis is a tip-off that a parenthesis is missing before that point. You shouldn't get a 0 until the last parenthesis of the expression.

Fully parenthesize logical expressions   Parentheses are cheap, and they aid readability. Fully parenthesizing logical expressions as a matter of habit is good practice.

Knowing How Boolean Expressions Are Evaluated

Many languages have an implied form of control that comes into play in the evaluation of boolean expressions. Compilers for some languages evaluate each term in a boolean expression before combining the terms and evaluating the whole expression. Compilers for other languages have "short-circuit" or "lazy" evaluation, evaluating only the pieces necessary. This is particularly significant when, depending on the results of the first test, you might not want the second test to be executed. For example, suppose you're checking the elements of an array and you have the following test:

Pseudocode Example of an Erroneous Test

```
while ( i < MAX_ELEMENTS and item[ i ] <> 0 ) ...
```

If this whole expression is evaluated, you'll get an error on the last pass through the loop. The variable i equals *maxElements*, so the expression *item[i]* is equivalent to *item[maxElements]*, which is an array-index error. You might argue that it doesn't matter since you're only looking at the value, not changing it. But it's sloppy programming practice and could confuse someone reading the code. In many environments it will also generate either a run-time error or a protection violation.

In pseudocode, you could restructure the test so that the error doesn't occur:

Pseudocode Example of a Correctly Restructured Test

```
while ( i < MAX_ELEMENTS )
   if ( item[ i ] <> 0 ) then
      ...
```

This is correct because *item[i]* isn't evaluated unless i is less than *maxElements*.

Many modern languages provide facilities that prevent this kind of error from happening in the first place. For example, C++ uses short-circuit evaluation: if the first operand of the *and* is false, the second isn't evaluated because the whole expression would be false anyway. In other words, in C++ the only part of

```
if ( SomethingFalse && SomeCondition ) ...
```

that's evaluated is *SomethingFalse*. Evaluation stops as soon as *SomethingFalse* is identified as false.

Evaluation is similarly short-circuited with the *or* operator. In C++ and Java, the only part of

```
if ( somethingTrue || someCondition ) ...
```

that is evaluated is *somethingTrue*. The evaluation stops as soon as *somethingTrue* is identified as true because the expression is always true if any part of it is true. As a result of this method of evaluation, the following statement is a fine, legal statement.

Java Example of a Test That Works Because of Short-Circuit Evaluation
```
if ( ( denominator != 0 ) && ( ( item / denominator ) > MIN_VALUE ) ) ...
```

If this full expression were evaluated when *denominator* equaled *0*, the division in the second operand would produce a divide-by-zero error. But since the second part isn't evaluated unless the first part is true, it is never evaluated when *denominator* equals *0*, so no divide-by-zero error occurs.

On the other hand, because the *&& (and)* is evaluated left to right, the following logically equivalent statement doesn't work:

Java Example of a Test That Short-Circuit Evaluation Doesn't Rescue
```
if ( ( ( item / denominator ) > MIN_VALUE ) && ( denominator != 0 ) ) ...
```

In this case, *item / denominator* is evaluated before *denominator != 0*. Consequently, this code commits the divide-by-zero error.

Java further complicates this picture by providing "logical" operators. Java's logical *&* and *|* operators guarantee that all terms will be fully evaluated regardless of whether the truth or falsity of the expression could be determined without a full evaluation. In other words, in Java, this is safe:

Java Example of a Test That Works Because of Short-Circuit (Conditional) Evaluation
```
if ( ( denominator != 0 ) && ( ( item / denominator ) > MIN_VALUE ) ) ...
```

But this is not safe:

> **Java Example of a Test That Doesn't Work Because Short-Circuit Evaluation Isn't Guaranteed**
> ```
> if ( ( denominator != 0 ) & ( ( item / denominator ) > MIN_VALUE ) ) ...
> ```

KEY POINT

Different languages use different kinds of evaluation, and language implementers tend to take liberties with expression evaluation, so check the manual for the specific version of the language you're using to find out what kind of evaluation your language uses. Better yet, since a reader of your code might not be as sharp as you are, use nested tests to clarify your intentions instead of depending on evaluation order and short-circuit evaluation.

Writing Numeric Expressions in Number-Line Order

Organize numeric tests so that they follow the points on a number line. In general, structure your numeric tests so that you have comparisons like these:

```
MIN_ELEMENTS <= i and i <= MAX_ELEMENTS
i < MIN_ELEMENTS or MAX_ELEMENTS < i
```

The idea is to order the elements left to right, from smallest to largest. In the first line, *MIN_ELEMENTS* and *MAX_ELEMENTS* are the two endpoints, so they go at the ends. The variable *i* is supposed to be between them, so it goes in the middle. In the second example, you're testing whether *i* is outside the range, so *i* goes on the outside of the test at either end and *MIN_ELEMENTS* and *MAX_ELEMENTS* go on the inside. This approach maps easily to a visual image of the comparison in Figure 19-1:

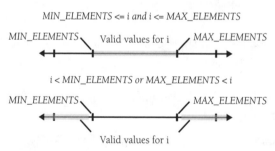

Figure 19-1 Examples of using number-line ordering for boolean tests.

If you're testing *i* against *MIN_ELEMENTS* only, the position of *i* varies depending on where *i* is when the test is successful. If *i* is supposed to be smaller, you'll have a test like this:

```
while ( i < MIN_ELEMENTS ) ...
```

But if *i* is supposed to be larger, you'll have a test like this:

```
while ( MIN_ELEMENTS < i ) ...
```

This approach is clearer than tests like

```
( i > MIN_ELEMENTS ) and ( i < MAX_ELEMENTS )
```

which give the reader no help in visualizing what is being tested.

Guidelines for Comparisons to *0*

Programming languages use *0* for several purposes. It's a numeric value. It's a null terminator in a string. It's the value of a null pointer. It's the value of the first item in an enumeration. It's *false* in logical expressions. Because it's used for so many purposes, you should write code that highlights the specific way *0* is used.

Compare logical variables implicitly   As mentioned earlier, it's appropriate to write logical expressions such as

```
while ( !done ) ...
```

This implicit comparison to *0* is appropriate because the comparison is in a logical expression.

Compare numbers to 0   Although it's appropriate to compare logical expressions implicitly, you should compare numeric expressions explicitly. For numbers, write

```
while ( balance != 0 ) ...
```

rather than

```
while ( balance ) ...
```

Compare characters to the null terminator ('\0') explicitly in C   Characters, like numbers, aren't logical expressions. Thus, for characters, write

```
while ( *charPtr != '\0' ) ...
```

rather than

```
while ( *charPtr ) ...
```

This recommendation goes against the common C convention for handling character data (as in the second example here), but it reinforces the idea that the expression is working with character data rather than logical data. Some C conventions aren't based on maximizing readability or maintainability, and this is an example of one. Fortunately, this whole issue is fading into the sunset as more code is written using C++ and STL strings.

Compare pointers to NULL   For pointers, write

```
while ( bufferPtr != NULL ) ...
```

rather than

```
while ( bufferPtr ) ...
```

Like the recommendation for characters, this one goes against the established C convention, but the gain in readability justifies it.

Common Problems with Boolean Expressions

Boolean expressions are subject to a few additional pitfalls that pertain to specific languages:

In C-derived languages, put constants on the left side of comparisons   C-derived languages pose some special problems with boolean expressions. If you have problems mistyping = instead of ==, consider the programming convention of putting constants and literals on the left sides of expressions, like this:

> **C++ Example of Putting a Constant on the Left Side of an Expression—An Error the Compiler Will Catch**
> ```
> if ( MIN_ELEMENTS = i ) ...
> ```

In this expression, the compiler should flag the single = as an error since assigning anything to a constant is invalid. In contrast, in the following expression, the compiler will flag this only as a warning, and only if you have compiler warnings fully turned on:

> **C++ Example of Putting a Constant on the Right Side of an Expression—An Error the Compiler Might Not Catch**
> ```
> if ( i = MIN_ELEMENTS ) ...
> ```

This recommendation conflicts with the recommendation to use number-line ordering. My personal preference is to use number-line ordering and let the compiler warn me about unintended assignments.

In C++, consider creating preprocessor macro substitutions for &&, ||, and == (but only as a last resort)   If you have such a problem, it's possible to create #*define* macros for boolean *and* and *or*, and use *AND* and *OR* instead of *&&* and ||. Similarly, using = when you mean == is an easy mistake to make. If you get stung often by this one, you might create a macro like *EQUALS* for logical equals (==).

Many experienced programmers view this approach as aiding readability for the programmer who can't keep details of the programming language straight but as degrading readability for the programmer who is more fluent in the language. In addition, most compilers will provide error warnings for usages of assignment and bitwise operators that seem like errors. Turning on full compiler warnings is usually a better option than creating nonstandard macros.

In Java, know the difference between a==b *and* a.equals(b)   In Java, *a==b* tests for whether *a* and *b* refer to the same object, whereas *a.equals(b)* tests for whether the objects have the same logical value. In general, Java programs should use expressions like *a.equals(b)* rather than *a==b*.

19.2 Compound Statements (Blocks)

A "compound statement" or "block" is a collection of statements that are treated as a single statement for purposes of controlling the flow of a program. Compound statements are created by writing { and } around a group of statements in C++, C#, C, and Java. Sometimes they are implied by the keywords of a command, such as *For* and *Next* in Visual Basic. Guidelines for using compound statements effectively follow:

Cross-Reference Many programmer-oriented text editors have commands that match braces, brackets, and parentheses. For details, see "Editing" in Section 30.2.

Write pairs of braces together   Fill in the middle after you write both the opening and closing parts of a block. People often complain about how hard it is to match pairs of braces or *begin*-and-*end* pairs, and that's a completely unnecessary problem. If you follow this guideline, you will never have trouble matching such pairs again.

Write this first:

```
for ( i = 0; i < maxLines; i++ )
```

Write this next:

```
for ( i = 0; i < maxLines; i++ ) {   }
```

Write this last:

```
for ( i = 0; i < maxLines; i++ ) {
   // whatever goes in here   ...
}
```

This applies to all blocking structures, including *if, for*, and *while* in C++ and Java and the *If-Then-Else, For-Next*, and *While-Wend* combinations in Visual Basic.

Use braces to clarify conditionals   Conditionals are hard enough to read without having to determine which statements go with the *if* test. Putting a single statement after an *if* test is sometimes appealing aesthetically, but under maintenance such statements tend to become more complicated blocks, and single statements are error-prone when that happens.

Use blocks to clarify your intentions regardless of whether the code inside the block is 1 line or 20.

19.3 Null Statements

In C++, it's possible to have a null statement, a statement consisting entirely of a semi-colon, as shown here:

> **C++ Example of a Traditional Null Statement**
> ```
> while ( recordArray.Read( index++ ) != recordArray.EmptyRecord() )
>    ;
> ```

The *while* in C++ requires that a statement follow, but it can be a null statement. The semicolon on a line by itself is a null statement. Here are guidelines for handling null statements in C++:

Cross-Reference The best way to handle null statements is probably to avoid them. For details, see "Avoid empty loops" in Section 16.2.

Call attention to null statements Null statements are uncommon, so make them obvious. One way is to give the semicolon of a null statement a line of its own. Indent it, just as you would any other statement. This is the approach shown in the previous example. Alternatively, you can use a set of empty braces to emphasize the null statement. Here are two examples:

> **C++ Examples of a Null Statement That's Emphasized**

This is one way to show the null statement.
```
while ( recordArray.Read( index++ ) ) != recordArray.EmptyRecord() ) {}

while ( recordArray.Read( index++ ) != recordArray.EmptyRecord() ) {
   ;
```
This is another way to show it.
```
}
```

Create a preprocessor* DoNothing() *macro or inline function for null statements
The statement doesn't do anything but make indisputably clear the fact that nothing is supposed to be done. This is similar to marking blank document pages with the statement "This page intentionally left blank." The page isn't really blank, but you know nothing else is supposed to be on it.

Here's how you can make your own null statement in C++ by using *#define*. (You could also create it as an *inline* function, which would have the same effect.)

> **C++ Example of a Null Statement That's Emphasized with *DoNothing()***
> ```
> #define DoNothing()
> ...
> while ( recordArray.Read( index++ ) != recordArray.EmptyRecord() ) {
>    DoNothing();
> }
> ```

In addition to using *DoNothing()* in empty *while* and *for* loops, you can use it for unimportant choices of a *switch* statement; including *DoNothing()* makes it clear that the case was considered and nothing is supposed to be done.

If your language doesn't support preprocessor macros or inline functions, you could create a *DoNothing()* routine that simply immediately returns control back to the calling routine.

Consider whether the code would be clearer with a non-null loop body   Most of the code that results in loops with empty bodies relies on side effects in the loop-control code. In most cases, the code is more readable when the side effects are made explicit, as shown here:

> **C++ Examples of Rewriting Code More Clearly with a Non-Null Loop Body**
>
> ```cpp
> RecordType record = recordArray.Read( index );
> index++;
> while ( record != recordArray.EmptyRecord() ) {
>    record = recordArray.Read( index );
>    index++;
> }
> ```

This approach introduces an additional loop-control variable and requires more lines of code, but it emphasizes straightforward programming practice rather than clever use of side effects. Such emphasis is preferable in production code.

19.4 Taming Dangerously Deep Nesting

HARD DATA

Excessive indentation, or "nesting," has been pilloried in computing literature for 25 years and is still one of the chief culprits in confusing code. Studies by Noam Chomsky and Gerald Weinberg suggest that few people can understand more than three levels of nested *ifs* (Yourdon 1986a), and many researchers recommend avoiding nesting to more than three or four levels (Myers 1976, Marca 1981, and Ledgard and Tauer 1987a). Deep nesting works against what Chapter 5, "Design in Construction," describes as Software's Primary Technical Imperative: Managing Complexity. That is reason enough to avoid deep nesting.

KEY POINT

It's not hard to avoid deep nesting. If you have deep nesting, you can redesign the tests performed in the *if* and *else* clauses or you can refactor code into simpler routines. The following subsections present several ways to reduce the nesting depth:

Simplify a nested if ***by retesting part of the condition***   If the nesting gets too deep, you can decrease the number of nesting levels by retesting some of the conditions. This code example has nesting that's deep enough to warrant restructuring:

CODING HORROR

> **C++ Example of Bad, Deeply Nested Code**
>
> ```cpp
> if ( inputStatus == InputStatus_Success ) {
>    // lots of code
>    ...
>    if ( printerRoutine != NULL ) {
> ```

Cross-Reference Retesting part of the condition to reduce complexity is similar to retesting a status variable. That technique is demonstrated in "Error Processing and *gotos*" in Section 17.3.

```
        // lots of code
        ...
        if ( SetupPage() ) {
            // lots of code
            ...
            if ( AllocMem( &printData ) ) {
                // lots of code
                ...
            }
        }
    }
}
```

This example is contrived to show nesting levels. The // *lots of code* parts are intended to suggest that the routine has enough code to stretch across several screens or across the page boundary of a printed code listing. Here's the code revised to use retesting rather than nesting:

C++ Example of Code Mercifully Unnested by Retesting

```
if ( inputStatus == InputStatus_Success ) {
    // lots of code
    ...
    if ( printerRoutine != NULL ) {
        // lots of code
        ...
    }
}

if ( ( ( inputStatus == InputStatus_Success ) &&
       ( printerRoutine != NULL ) && SetupPage() ) {
    // lots of code
    ...
    if ( AllocMem( &printData ) ) {
        // lots of code
        ...
    }
}
```

This is a particularly realistic example because it shows that you can't reduce the nesting level for free; you have to put up with a more complicated test in return for the reduced level of nesting. A reduction from four levels to two is a big improvement in readability, however, and is worth considering.

Simplify a nested* if *by using a* break *block An alternative to the approach just described is to define a section of code that will be executed as a block. If some condition in the middle of the block fails, execution skips to the end of the block.

C++ Example of Using a *break* Block

```
do {
    // begin break block
    if ( inputStatus != InputStatus_Success ) {
        break; // break out of block
    }
```

```
    // lots of code
    ...
    if ( printerRoutine == NULL ) {
        break; // break out of block
    }

    // lots of code
    ...
    if ( !SetupPage() ) {
        break; // break out of block
    }

    // lots of code
    ...
    if ( !AllocMem( &printData ) ) {
        break; // break out of block
    }

    // lots of code
    ...
} while (FALSE); // end break block
```

This technique is uncommon enough that it should be used only when your entire team is familiar with it and when it has been adopted by the team as an accepted coding practice.

Convert a nested if ***to a set of*** **if-then-elses**   If you think about a nested *if* test critically, you might discover that you can reorganize it so that it uses *if-then-elses* rather than nested *ifs*. Suppose you have a bushy decision tree like this:

Java Example of an Overgrown Decision Tree
```
if ( 10 < quantity ) {
    if ( 100 < quantity ) {
        if ( 1000 < quantity ) {
            discount = 0.10;
        }
        else {
            discount = 0.05;
        }
    }
    else {
        discount = 0.025;
    }
}
else {
    discount = 0.0;
}
```

This test is poorly organized in several ways, one of which is that the tests are redundant. When you test whether *quantity* is greater than *1000*, you don't also need to test whether it's greater than *100* and greater than *10*. Consequently, you can reorganize the code:

Java Example of a Nested *if* Converted to a Set of *if-then-elses*

```java
if ( 1000 < quantity ) {
   discount = 0.10;
}
else if ( 100 < quantity ) {
   discount = 0.05;
}
else if ( 10 < quantity ) {
   discount = 0.025;
}
else {
   discount = 0;
}
```

This solution is easier than some because the numbers increase neatly. Here's how you could rework the nested *if* if the numbers weren't so tidy:

Java Example of a Nested *if* Converted to a Set of *if-then-elses* When the Numbers Are "Messy"

```java
if ( 1000 < quantity ) {
   discount = 0.10;
}
else if ( ( 100 < quantity ) && ( quantity <= 1000 ) ) {
   discount = 0.05;
}
else if ( ( 10 < quantity ) && ( quantity <= 100 ) ) {
   discount = 0.025;
}
else if ( quantity <= 10 ) {
   discount = 0;
}
```

The main difference between this code and the previous code is that the expressions in the *else-if* clauses don't rely on previous tests. This code doesn't need the *else* clauses to work, and the tests actually could be performed in any order. The code could consist of four *ifs* and no *elses*. The only reason the *else* version is preferable is that it avoids repeating tests unnecessarily.

Convert a nested* if *to a* case *statement   You can recode some kinds of tests, particularly those with integers, to use a *case* statement rather than chains of *ifs* and *elses*. You can't use this technique in some languages, but it's a powerful technique for those in which you can. Here's how to recode the example in Visual Basic:

Visual Basic Example of Converting a Nested *if* to a *case* Statement

```vb
Select Case quantity
   Case 0 To 10
      discount = 0.0
   Case 11 To 100
      discount = 0.025
```

```
      Case 101 To 1000
         discount = 0.05
      Case Else
         discount = 0.10
End Select
```

This example reads like a book. When you compare it to the two examples of multiple indentations a few pages earlier, it seems like a particularly clean solution.

Factor deeply nested code into its own routine If deep nesting occurs inside a loop, you can often improve the situation by putting the inside of the loop into its own routine. This is especially effective if the nesting is a result of both conditionals and iterations. Leave the *if-then-else* branches in the main loop to show the decision branching, and then move the statements within the branches to their own routines. This code needs to be improved by such a modification:

C++ Example of Nested Code That Needs to Be Broken into Routines

```cpp
while ( !TransactionsComplete() ) {
   // read transaction record
   transaction = ReadTransaction();

   // process transaction depending on type of transaction
   if ( transaction.Type == TransactionType_Deposit ) {
      // process a deposit
      if ( transaction.AccountType == AccountType_Checking ) {
         if ( transaction.AccountSubType == AccountSubType_Business )
            MakeBusinessCheckDep( transaction.AccountNum, transaction.Amount );
         else if ( transaction.AccountSubType == AccountSubType_Personal )
            MakePersonalCheckDep( transaction.AccountNum, transaction.Amount );
         else if ( transaction.AccountSubType == AccountSubType_School )
            MakeSchoolCheckDep( transaction.AccountNum, transaction.Amount );
      }
      else if ( transaction.AccountType == AccountType_Savings )
         MakeSavingsDep( transaction.AccountNum, transaction.Amount );
      else if ( transaction.AccountType == AccountType_DebitCard )
         MakeDebitCardDep( transaction.AccountNum, transaction.Amount );
      else if ( transaction.AccountType == AccountType_MoneyMarket )
         MakeMoneyMarketDep( transaction.AccountNum, transaction.Amount );
      else if ( transaction.AccountType == AccountType_Cd )
         MakeCDDep( transaction.AccountNum, transaction.Amount );
   }
   else if ( transaction.Type == TransactionType_Withdrawal ) {
      // process a withdrawal
      if ( transaction.AccountType == AccountType_Checking )
         MakeCheckingWithdrawal( transaction.AccountNum, transaction.Amount );
      else if ( transaction.AccountType == AccountType_Savings )
         MakeSavingsWithdrawal( transaction.AccountNum, transaction.Amount );
      else if ( transaction.AccountType == AccountType_DebitCard )
         MakeDebitCardWithdrawal( transaction.AccountNum, transaction.Amount );
   }
```

Here's the *TransactionType_Transfer* transaction type.

```
else if ( transaction.Type == TransactionType_Transfer ) {
   MakeFundsTransfer(
      transaction.SourceAccountType,
      transaction.TargetAccountType,
      transaction.AccountNum,
      transaction.Amount
   );
}
else {
   // process unknown kind of transaction
   LogTransactionError( "Unknown Transaction Type", transaction );
}
}
```

Although it's complicated, this isn't the worst code you'll ever see. It's nested to only four levels, it's commented, it's logically indented, and the functional decomposition is adequate, especially for the *TransactionType_Transfer* transaction type. In spite of its adequacy, however, you can improve it by breaking the contents of the inner *if* tests into their own routines.

Cross-Reference This kind of functional decomposition is especially easy if you initially built the routine using the steps described in Chapter 9, "The Pseudocode Programming Process." Guidelines for functional decomposition are given in "Divide and Conquer" in Section 5.4.

C++ Example of Good, Nested Code After Decomposition into Routines

```cpp
while ( !TransactionsComplete() ) {
   // read transaction record
   transaction = ReadTransaction();

   // process transaction depending on type of transaction
   if ( transaction.Type == TransactionType_Deposit ) {
      ProcessDeposit(
         transaction.AccountType,
         transaction.AccountSubType,
         transaction.AccountNum,
         transaction.Amount
      );
   }
   else if ( transaction.Type == TransactionType_Withdrawal ) {
      ProcessWithdrawal(
         transaction.AccountType,
         transaction.AccountNum,
         transaction.Amount
      );
   }
   else if ( transaction.Type == TransactionType_Transfer ) {
      MakeFundsTransfer(
         transaction.SourceAccountType,
         transaction.TargetAccountType,
         transaction.AccountNum,
         transaction.Amount
      );
   }
   else {
      // process unknown transaction type
      LogTransactionError("Unknown Transaction Type", transaction );
   }
}
```

The code in the new routines has simply been lifted out of the original routine and formed into new routines. (The new routines aren't shown here.) The new code has several advantages. First, two-level nesting makes the structure simpler and easier to understand. Second, you can read, modify, and debug the shorter *while* loop on one screen—it doesn't need to be broken across screen or printed-page boundaries. Third, putting the functionality of *ProcessDeposit()* and *ProcessWithdrawal()* into routines accrues all the other general advantages of modularization. Fourth, it's now easy to see that the code could be broken into a *case* statement, which would make it even easier to read, as shown below:

C++ Example of Good, Nested Code After Decomposition and Use of a
***case* Statement**

```
while ( !TransactionsComplete() ) {
   // read transaction record
   transaction = ReadTransaction();

   // process transaction depending on type of transaction
   switch ( transaction.Type ) {
      case ( TransactionType_Deposit ):
         ProcessDeposit(
            transaction.AccountType,
            transaction.AccountSubType,
            transaction.AccountNum,
            transaction.Amount
            );
         break;

      case ( TransactionType_Withdrawal ):
         ProcessWithdrawal(
            transaction.AccountType,
            transaction.AccountNum,
            transaction.Amount
            );
         break;

      case ( TransactionType_Transfer ):
         MakeFundsTransfer(
            transaction.SourceAccountType,
            transaction.TargetAccountType,
            transaction.AccountNum,
            transaction.Amount
            );
         break;

      default:
         // process unknown transaction type
         LogTransactionError("Unknown Transaction Type", transaction );
         break;
   }
}
```

Use a more object-oriented approach   A straightforward way to simplify this particular code in an object-oriented environment is to create an abstract *Transaction* base class and subclasses for *Deposit*, *Withdrawal*, and *Transfer*.

C++ Example of Good Code That Uses Polymorphism

```cpp
TransactionData transactionData;
Transaction *transaction;

while ( !TransactionsComplete() ) {
   // read transaction record
   transactionData = ReadTransaction();

   // create transaction object, depending on type of transaction
   switch ( transactionData.Type ) {
      case ( TransactionType_Deposit ):
         transaction = new Deposit( transactionData );
         break;

      case ( TransactionType_Withdrawal ):
         transaction = new Withdrawal( transactionData );
         break;

      case ( TransactionType_Transfer ):
         transaction = new Transfer( transactionData );
         break;

      default:
         // process unknown transaction type
         LogTransactionError("Unknown Transaction Type", transactionData );
         return;
   }
   transaction->Complete();
   delete transaction;
}
```

In a system of any size, the *switch* statement would be converted to use a factory method that could be reused anywhere an object of *Transaction* type needed to be created. If this code were in such a system, this part of it would become even simpler:

Cross-Reference For more beneficial code improvements like this, see Chapter 24, "Refactoring."

C++ Example of Good Code That Uses Polymorphism and an Object Factory

```cpp
TransactionData transactionData;
Transaction *transaction;

while ( !TransactionsComplete() ) {
   // read transaction record and complete transaction
   transactionData = ReadTransaction();
   transaction = TransactionFactory.Create( transactionData );
   transaction->Complete();
   delete transaction;
}
```

For the record, the code in the *TransactionFactory.Create()* routine is a simple adaptation of the code from the prior example's *switch* statement:

C++ Example of Good Code for an Object Factory

```cpp
Transaction *TransactionFactory::Create(
   TransactionData transactionData
   ) {

   // create transaction object, depending on type of transaction
   switch ( transactionData.Type ) {
      case ( TransactionType_Deposit ):
         return new Deposit( transactionData );
         break;

      case ( TransactionType_Withdrawal ):
         return new Withdrawal( transactionData );
         break;

      case ( TransactionType_Transfer ):
         return new Transfer( transactionData );
         break;

      default:
         // process unknown transaction type
         LogTransactionError( "Unknown Transaction Type", transactionData );
         return NULL;
   }
}
```

Redesign deeply nested code   Some experts argue that *case* statements virtually always indicate poorly factored code in object-oriented programming and are rarely, if ever, needed (Meyer 1997). This transformation from *case* statements that invoke routines to an object factory with polymorphic method calls is one such example.

More generally, complicated code is a sign that you don't understand your program well enough to make it simple. Deep nesting is a warning sign that indicates a need to break out a routine or redesign the part of the code that's complicated. It doesn't mean you have to modify the routine, but you should have a good reason for not doing so if you don't.

Summary of Techniques for Reducing Deep Nesting

The following is a list of the techniques you can use to reduce deep nesting, along with references to the sections in this book that discuss the techniques:

- Retest part of the condition (this section)
- Convert to *if-then-else*s (this section)
- Convert to a *case* statement (this section)
- Factor deeply nested code into its own routine (this section)
- Use objects and polymorphic dispatch (this section)

- Rewrite the code to use a status variable (in Section 17.3)

- Use guard clauses to exit a routine and make the nominal path through the code clearer (in Section 17.1)

- Use exceptions (Section 8.4)

- Redesign deeply nested code entirely (this section)

19.5 A Programming Foundation: Structured Programming

The term "structured programming" originated in a landmark paper, "Structured Programming," presented by Edsger Dijkstra at the 1969 NATO conference on software engineering (Dijkstra 1969). By the time structured programming came and went, the term "structured" had been applied to every software-development activity, including structured analysis, structured design, and structured goofing off. The various structured methodologies weren't joined by any common thread except that they were all created at a time when the word "structured" gave them extra cachet.

The core of structured programming is the simple idea that a program should use only one-in, one-out control constructs (also called single-entry, single-exit control constructs). A one-in, one-out control construct is a block of code that has only one place it can start and only one place it can end. It has no other entries or exits. Structured programming isn't the same as structured, top-down design. It applies only at the detailed coding level.

A structured program progresses in an orderly, disciplined way, rather than jumping around unpredictably. You can read it from top to bottom, and it executes in much the same way. Less disciplined approaches result in source code that provides a less meaningful, less readable picture of how a program executes in the machine. Less readability means less understanding and, ultimately, lower program quality.

The central concepts of structured programming are still useful today and apply to considerations in using *break*, *continue*, *throw*, *catch*, *return*, and other topics.

The Three Components of Structured Programming

The next few sections describe the three constructs that constitute the core of structured programming.

Sequence

Cross-Reference For details on using sequences, see Chapter 14, "Organizing Straight-Line Code."

A sequence is a set of statements executed in order. Typical sequential statements include assignments and calls to routines. Here are two examples:

Java Examples of Sequential Code

```java
// a sequence of assignment statements
a = "1";
b = "2";
c = "3";

// a sequence of calls to routines
System.out.println( a );
System.out.println( b );
System.out.println( c );
```

Selection

Cross-Reference For details on using selections, see Chapter 15, "Using Conditionals."

A selection is a control structure that causes statements to be executed selectively. The *if-then-else* statement is a common example. Either the *if-then* clause or the *else* clause is executed, but not both. One of the clauses is "selected" for execution.

A *case* statement is another example of selection control. The *switch* statement in C++ and Java and the *select* statement in Visual Basic are all examples of *case*. In each instance, one of several cases is selected for execution. Conceptually, *if* statements and *case* statements are similar. If your language doesn't support *case* statements, you can emulate them with *if* statements. Here are two examples of selection:

Java Examples of Selection

```java
// selection in an if statement
if ( totalAmount > 0.0 ) {
   // do something
   ...
}
else {
   // do something else
   ...
}

// selection in a case statement
switch ( commandShortcutLetter ) {
   case 'a':
      PrintAnnualReport();
      break;
   case 'q':
      PrintQuarterlyReport();
      break;
   case 's':
      PrintSummaryReport();
      break;
   default:
      DisplayInternalError( "Internal Error 905: Call customer support." );
}
```

Iteration

Cross-Reference For details on using iterations, see Chapter 16, "Controlling Loops."

An iteration is a control structure that causes a group of statements to be executed multiple times. An iteration is commonly referred to as a "loop." Kinds of iterations include *For-Next* in Visual Basic and *while* and *for* in C++ and Java. This code fragment shows examples of iteration in Visual Basic:

```
Visual Basic Examples of Iteration
' example of iteration using a For loop
For index = first To last
   DoSomething( index )
Next

' example of iteration using a while loop
index = first
While ( index <= last )
   DoSomething ( index )
   index = index + 1
Wend

' example of iteration using a loop-with-exit loop
index = first
Do
   If ( index > last ) Then Exit Do
   DoSomething ( index )
   index = index + 1
Loop
```

The core thesis of structured programming is that any control flow whatsoever can be created from these three constructs of sequence, selection, and iteration (Böhm Jacopini 1966). Programmers sometimes favor language structures that increase convenience, but programming seems to have advanced largely by restricting what we are allowed to do with our programming languages. Prior to structured programming, use of *goto*s provided the ultimate in control-flow convenience, but code written that way turned out to be incomprehensible and unmaintainable. My belief is that use of any control structure other than the three standard structured programming constructs—that is, the use of *break*, *continue*, *return*, *throw-catch*, and so on—should be viewed with a critical eye.

19.6 Control Structures and Complexity

One reason so much attention has been paid to control structures is that they are a big contributor to overall program complexity. Poor use of control structures increases complexity; good use decreases it.

Make things as simple as possible—but no simpler.
—Albert Einstein

One measure of "programming complexity" is the number of mental objects you have to keep in mind simultaneously in order to understand a program. This mental juggling act is one of the most difficult aspects of programming and is the reason programming requires more concentration than other activities. It's the reason programmers get upset about "quick interruptions"—such interruptions are tantamount to asking a juggler to keep three balls in the air and hold your groceries at the same time.

KEY POINT

Intuitively, the complexity of a program would seem to largely determine the amount of effort required to understand it. Tom McCabe published an influential paper arguing that a program's complexity is defined by its control flow (1976). Other researchers have identified factors other than McCabe's cyclomatic complexity metric (such as the number of variables used in a routine), but they agree that control flow is at least one of the largest contributors to complexity, if not the largest.

How Important Is Complexity?

Cross-Reference For more on complexity, see "Software's Primary Technical Imperative: Managing Complexity" in Section 5.2.

Computer-science researchers have been aware of the importance of complexity for at least two decades. Many years ago, Edsger Dijkstra cautioned against the hazards of complexity: "The competent programmer is fully aware of the strictly limited size of his own skull; therefore, he approaches the programming task in full humility" (Dijkstra 1972). This does not imply that you should increase the capacity of your skull to deal with enormous complexity. It implies that you can never deal with enormous complexity and must take steps to reduce it wherever possible.

HARD DATA

Control-flow complexity is important because it has been correlated with low reliability and frequent errors (McCabe 1976, Shen et al. 1985). William T. Ward reported a significant gain in software reliability resulting from using McCabe's complexity metric at Hewlett-Packard (1989b). McCabe's metric was used on one 77,000-line program to identify problem areas. The program had a post-release defect rate of 0.31 defects per thousand lines of code. A 125,000-line program had a post-release defect rate of 0.02 defects per thousand lines of code. Ward reported that because of their lower complexity, both programs had substantially fewer defects than other programs at Hewlett-Packard. My own company, Construx Software, has experienced similar results using complexity measures to identify problematic routines in the 2000s.

General Guidelines for Reducing Complexity

You can better deal with complexity in one of two ways. First, you can improve your own mental juggling abilities by doing mental exercises. But programming itself is usually enough exercise, and people seem to have trouble juggling more than about five to nine mental entities (Miller 1956). The potential for improvement is small. Second, you can decrease the complexity of your programs and the amount of concentration required to understand them.

How to Measure Complexity

Further Reading The approach described here is based on Tom McCabe's influential paper "A Complexity Measure" (1976).

You probably have an intuitive feel for what makes a routine more or less complex. Researchers have tried to formalize their intuitive feelings and have come up with several ways of measuring complexity. Perhaps the most influential of the numeric techniques is Tom McCabe's, in which complexity is measured by counting the number of "decision points" in a routine. Table 19-2 describes a method for counting decision points.

Table 19-2   Techniques for Counting the Decision Points in a Routine

1. Start with 1 for the straight path through the routine.
2. Add 1 for each of the following keywords, or their equivalents: *if while repeat for and or*
3. Add 1 for each case in a *case* statement.

Here's an example:

```
if ( ( (status = Success) and done ) or
    ( not done and ( numLines >= maxLines ) ) ) then ...
```

In this fragment, you count 1 to start, 2 for the *if*, 3 for the *and*, 4 for the *or*, and 5 for the *and*. Thus, this fragment contains a total of five decision points.

What to Do with Your Complexity Measurement

After you have counted the decision points, you can use the number to analyze your routine's complexity:

0–5	The routine is probably fine.
6–10	Start to think about ways to simplify the routine.
10+	Break part of the routine into a second routine and call it from the first routine.

Moving part of a routine into another routine doesn't reduce the overall complexity of the program; it just moves the decision points around. But it reduces the amount of complexity you have to deal with at any one time. Since the important goal is to minimize the number of items you have to juggle mentally, reducing the complexity of a given routine is worthwhile.

The maximum of 10 decision points isn't an absolute limit. Use the number of decision points as a warning flag that indicates a routine might need to be redesigned. Don't use it as an inflexible rule. A *case* statement with many cases could be more than 10 elements long, and, depending on the purpose of the *case* statement, it might be foolish to break it up.

Other Kinds of Complexity

Further Reading For an excellent discussion of complexity metrics, see *Software Engineering Metrics and Models* (Conte, Dunsmore, and Shen 1986).

The McCabe measure of complexity isn't the only sound measure, but it's the measure most discussed in computing literature and it's especially helpful when you're thinking about control flow. Other measures include the amount of data used, the number of nesting levels in control constructs, the number of lines of code, the number of lines between successive references to variables ("span"), the number of lines that a variable is in use ("live time"), and the amount of input and output. Some researchers have developed composite metrics based on combinations of these simpler ones.

cc2e.com/1985

CHECKLIST: Control-Structure Issues

❑ Do expressions use *true* and *false* rather than *1* and *0*?

❑ Are boolean values compared to *true* and *false* implicitly?

❑ Are numeric values compared to their test values explicitly?

❑ Have expressions been simplified by the addition of new boolean variables and the use of boolean functions and decision tables?

❑ Are boolean expressions stated positively?

❑ Do pairs of braces balance?

❑ Are braces used everywhere they're needed for clarity?

❑ Are logical expressions fully parenthesized?

❑ Have tests been written in number-line order?

❑ Do Java tests uses *a.equals(b)* style instead of *a == b* when appropriate?

❑ Are null statements obvious?

❑ Have nested statements been simplified by retesting part of the conditional, converting to *if-then-else* or *case* statements, moving nested code into its own routine, converting to a more object-oriented design, or have they been improved in some other way?

❑ If a routine has a decision count of more than 10, is there a good reason for not redesigning it?

Key Points

- Making boolean expressions simple and readable contributes substantially to the quality of your code.

- Deep nesting makes a routine hard to understand. Fortunately, you can avoid it relatively easily.

- Structured programming is a simple idea that is still relevant: you can build any program out of a combination of sequences, selections, and iterations.

- Minimizing complexity is a key to writing high-quality code.

Part V
Code Improvements

Chapter 20
The Software-Quality Landscape

cc2e.com/2036

Contents

Related Topics

This chapter surveys software-quality techniques from a construction point of view. The entire book is about improving software quality, of course, but this chapter focuses on quality and quality assurance per se. It focuses more on big-picture issues than it does on hands-on techniques. If you're looking for practical advice about collaborative development, testing, and debugging, move on to the next three chapters.

20.1 Characteristics of Software Quality

Software has both external and internal quality characteristics. External characteristics are characteristics that a user of the software product is aware of, including the following:

- **Correctness** The degree to which a system is free from faults in its specification, design, and implementation.
- **Usability** The ease with which users can learn and use a system.

- **Efficiency**   Minimal use of system resources, including memory and execution time.

- **Reliability**   The ability of a system to perform its required functions under stated conditions whenever required—having a long mean time between failures.

- **Integrity**   The degree to which a system prevents unauthorized or improper access to its programs and its data. The idea of integrity includes restricting unauthorized user accesses as well as ensuring that data is accessed properly—that is, that tables with parallel data are modified in parallel, that date fields contain only valid dates, and so on.

- **Adaptability**   The extent to which a system can be used, without modification, in applications or environments other than those for which it was specifically designed.

- **Accuracy**   The degree to which a system, as built, is free from error, especially with respect to quantitative outputs. Accuracy differs from correctness; it is a determination of how well a system does the job it's built for rather than whether it was built correctly.

- **Robustness**   The degree to which a system continues to function in the presence of invalid inputs or stressful environmental conditions.

Some of these characteristics overlap, but all have different shades of meaning that are applicable more in some cases, less in others.

External characteristics of quality are the only kind of software characteristics that users care about. Users care about whether the software is easy to use, not about whether it's easy for you to modify. They care about whether the software works correctly, not about whether the code is readable or well structured.

Programmers care about the internal characteristics of the software as well as the external ones. This book is code-centered, so it focuses on the internal quality characteristics, including

- **Maintainability**   The ease with which you can modify a software system to change or add capabilities, improve performance, or correct defects.

- **Flexibility**   The extent to which you can modify a system for uses or environments other than those for which it was specifically designed.

- **Portability**   The ease with which you can modify a system to operate in an environment different from that for which it was specifically designed.

- **Reusability**   The extent to which and the ease with which you can use parts of a system in other systems.

- **Readability**   The ease with which you can read and understand the source code of a system, especially at the detailed-statement level.

- **Testability**   The degree to which you can unit-test and system-test a system; the degree to which you can verify that the system meets its requirements.

- **Understandability**   The ease with which you can comprehend a system at both the system-organizational and detailed-statement levels. Understandability has to do with the coherence of the system at a more general level than readability does.

As in the list of external quality characteristics, some of these internal characteristics overlap, but they too each have different shades of meaning that are valuable.

The internal aspects of system quality are the main subject of this book and aren't discussed further in this chapter.

The difference between internal and external characteristics isn't completely clear-cut because at some level internal characteristics affect external ones. Software that isn't internally understandable or maintainable impairs your ability to correct defects, which in turn affects the external characteristics of correctness and reliability. Software that isn't flexible can't be enhanced in response to user requests, which in turn affects the external characteristic of usability. The point is that some quality characteristics are emphasized to make life easier for the user and some are emphasized to make life easier for the programmer. Try to know which is which and when and how these characteristics interact.

The attempt to maximize certain characteristics inevitably conflicts with the attempt to maximize others. Finding an optimal solution from a set of competing objectives is one activity that makes software development a true engineering discipline. Figure 20-1 shows the way in which focusing on some external quality characteristics affects others. The same kinds of relationships can be found among the internal characteristics of software quality.

The most interesting aspect of this chart is that focusing on a specific characteristic doesn't always mean a tradeoff with another characteristic. Sometimes one hurts another, sometimes one helps another, and sometimes one neither hurts nor helps another. For example, correctness is the characteristic of functioning exactly to specification. Robustness is the ability to continue functioning even under unanticipated conditions. Focusing on correctness hurts robustness and vice versa. In contrast, focusing on adaptability helps robustness and vice versa.

The chart shows only typical relationships among the quality characteristics. On any given project, two characteristics might have a relationship that's different from their typical relationship. It's useful to think about your specific quality goals and whether each pair of goals is mutually beneficial or antagonistic.

How focusing on the factor below affects the factor to the right	Correctness	Usability	Efficiency	Reliability	Integrity	Adaptability	Accuracy	Robustness
Correctness	↑		↑	↑			↑	↓
Usability		↑				↑	↑	
Efficiency	↓		↑	↓	↓	↓	↓	
Reliability	↑			↑	↑		↑	↓
Integrity			↓	↑	↑			
Adaptability					↓	↑		↑
Accuracy	↑		↓	↑		↓	↑	↓
Robustness	↓	↑	↓	↓	↓	↑	↓	↑

Helps it ↑
Hurts it ↓

Figure 20-1 Focusing on one external characteristic of software quality can affect other characteristics positively, adversely, or not at all.

20.2 Techniques for Improving Software Quality

Software quality assurance is a planned and systematic program of activities designed to ensure that a system has the desired characteristics. Although it might seem that the best way to develop a high-quality product would be to focus on the product itself, in software quality assurance you also need to focus on the software-development process. Some of the elements of a software-quality program are described in the following subsections:

Software-quality objectives   One powerful technique for improving software quality is setting explicit quality objectives from among the external and internal characteristics described in the previous section. Without explicit goals, programmers might work to maximize characteristics different from the ones you expect them to maximize. The power of setting explicit goals is discussed in more detail later in this section.

Explicit quality-assurance activity   One common problem in assuring quality is that quality is perceived as a secondary goal. Indeed, in some organizations, quick and dirty programming is the rule rather than the exception. Programmers like Global Gary, who litter their code with defects and "complete" their programs quickly, are rewarded more than programmers like High-Quality Henry, who write excellent programs and make sure that they are usable before releasing them. In such organizations, it shouldn't be surprising that programmers don't make quality their first priority. The organization must show programmers that quality is a priority. Making the quality-assurance activity explicit makes the priority clear, and programmers will respond accordingly.

Cross-Reference For details on testing, see Chapter 22, "Developer Testing."

Testing strategy   Execution testing can provide a detailed assessment of a product's reliability. Part of quality assurance is developing a test strategy in conjunction with the product requirements, architecture, and design. Developers on many projects rely on testing as the primary method of both quality assessment and quality improvement. The rest of this chapter demonstrates in more detail that this is too heavy a burden for testing to bear by itself.

Cross-Reference For a discussion of one class of software-engineering guidelines appropriate for construction, see Section 4.2, "Programming Conventions."

Software-engineering guidelines   Guidelines should control the technical character of the software as it's developed. Such guidelines apply to all software development activities, including problem definition, requirements development, architecture, construction, and system testing. The guidelines in this book are, in one sense, a set of software-engineering guidelines for construction.

Informal technical reviews   Many software developers review their work before turning it over for formal review. Informal reviews include desk-checking the design or the code or walking through the code with a few peers.

Cross-Reference Reviews and inspections are discussed in Chapter 21, "Collaborative Construction."

Formal technical reviews   One part of managing a software-engineering process is catching problems at the "lowest-value" stage—that is, at the time at which the least investment has been made and at which problems cost the least to correct. To achieve such a goal, developers use "quality gates," periodic tests or reviews that determine whether the quality of the product at one stage is sufficient to support moving on to the next. Quality gates are usually used to transition between requirements development and architecture, architecture and construction, and construction and system testing. The "gate" can be an inspection, a peer review, a customer review, or an audit.

Cross-Reference For more details on how development approaches vary depending on the kind of project, see Section 3.2, "Determine the Kind of Software You're Working On."

A "gate" does not mean that architecture or requirements need to be 100 percent complete or frozen; it does mean that you will use the gate to determine whether the requirements or architecture are good enough to support downstream development. "Good enough" might mean that you've sketched out the most critical 20 percent of the requirements or architecture, or it might mean you've specified 95 percent in excruciating detail—which end of the scale you should aim for depends on the nature of your specific project.

External audits   An external audit is a specific kind of technical review used to determine the status of a project or the quality of a product being developed. An audit team is brought in from outside the organization and reports its findings to whoever commissioned the audit, usually management.

Development Process

Further Reading For a discussion of software development as a process, see *Professional Software Development* (McConnell 1994).

Each of the elements mentioned so far has something to do explicitly with assuring software quality and implicitly with the process of software development. Development efforts that include quality-assurance activities produce better software than those that do not. Other processes that aren't explicitly quality-assurance activities also affect software quality.

Cross-Reference For details
on change control, see
Section 28.2, "Configuration
Management."

Change-control procedures   One big obstacle to achieving software quality is uncontrolled changes. Uncontrolled requirements changes can result in disruption to design and coding. Uncontrolled changes in design can result in code that doesn't agree with its requirements, inconsistencies in the code, or more time spent modifying code to meet the changing design than spent moving the project forward. Uncontrolled changes in the code itself can result in internal inconsistencies and uncertainties about which code has been fully reviewed and tested and which hasn't. The natural effect of change is to destabilize and degrade quality, so handling changes effectively is a key to achieving high quality levels.

Measurement of results   Unless results of a quality-assurance plan are measured, you'll have no way to know whether the plan is working. Measurement tells you whether your plan is a success or a failure and also allows you to vary your process in a controlled way to see how it can be improved. You can also measure quality attributes themselves—correctness, usability, efficiency, and so on—and it's useful to do so. For details on measuring quality attributes, see Chapter 9 of *Principles of Software Engineering* (Gilb 1988).

HARD DATA

Prototyping   Prototyping is the development of realistic models of a system's key functions. A developer can prototype parts of a user interface to determine usability, critical calculations to determine execution time, or typical data sets to determine memory requirements. A survey of 16 published and 8 unpublished case studies compared prototyping to traditional, specification-development methods. The comparison revealed that prototyping can lead to better designs, better matches with user needs, and improved maintainability (Gordon and Bieman 1991).

Setting Objectives

Explicitly setting quality objectives is a simple, obvious step in achieving quality software, but it's easy to overlook. You might wonder whether, if you set explicit quality objectives, programmers will actually work to achieve them? The answer is, yes, they will, if they know what the objectives are and that the objectives are reasonable. Programmers can't respond to a set of objectives that change daily or that are impossible to meet.

Gerald Weinberg and Edward Schulman conducted a fascinating experiment to investigate the effect on programmer performance of setting quality objectives (1974). They had five teams of programmers work on five versions of the same program. The same five quality objectives were given to each of the five teams, and each team was told to optimize a different objective. One team was told to minimize the memory required, another was told to produce the clearest possible output, another was told to build the most readable code, another was told to use the minimum number of statements, and the last group was told to complete the program in the least amount of time possible. Table 20-1 shows how each team was ranked according to each objective.

Table 20-1 Team Ranking on Each Objective

Objective Team Was Told to Optimize	Minimum memory use	Most readable output	Most readable code	Least code	Minimum programming time
Minimum memory	1	4	4	2	5
Output readability	5	1	1	5	3
Program readability	3	2	2	3	4
Least code	2	5	3	1	3
Minimum programming time	4	3	5	4	1

Source: Adapted from "Goals and Performance in Computer Programming" (Weinberg and Schulman 1974).

HARD DATA

The results of this study were remarkable. Four of the five teams finished first in the objective they were told to optimize. The other team finished second in its objective. None of the teams did consistently well in all objectives.

The surprising implication is that people actually do what you ask them to do. Programmers have high achievement motivation: They will work to the objectives specified, but they must be told what the objectives are. The second implication is that, as expected, objectives conflict and it's generally not possible to do well on all of them.

20.3 Relative Effectiveness of Quality Techniques

The various quality-assurance practices don't all have the same effectiveness. Many techniques have been studied, and their effectiveness at detecting and removing defects is known. This and several other aspects of the "effectiveness" of the quality-assurance practices are discussed in this section.

Percentage of Defects Detected

If builders built buildings the way programmers wrote programs, then the first woodpecker that came along would destroy civilization.
—*Gerald Weinberg*

Some practices are better at detecting defects than others, and different methods find different kinds of defects. One way to evaluate defect-detection methods is to determine the percentage of defects they detect out of the total defects that exist at that point in the project. Table 20-2 shows the percentages of defects detected by several common defect-detection techniques.

Table 20-2 Defect-Detection Rates

Removal Step	Lowest Rate	Modal Rate	Highest Rate
Informal design reviews	25%	35%	40%
Formal design inspections	45%	55%	65%
Informal code reviews	20%	25%	35%
Formal code inspections	45%	60%	70%
Modeling or prototyping	35%	65%	80%
Personal desk-checking of code	20%	40%	60%
Unit test	15%	30%	50%
New function (component) test	20%	30%	35%
Integration test	25%	35%	40%
Regression test	15%	25%	30%
System test	25%	40%	55%
Low-volume beta test (<10 sites)	25%	35%	40%
High-volume beta test (>1,000 sites)	60%	75%	85%

Source: Adapted from *Programming Productivity* (Jones 1986a), "Software Defect-Removal Efficiency" (Jones 1996), and "What We Have Learned About Fighting Defects" (Shull et al. 2002).

HARD DATA

The most interesting facts that this data reveals is that the modal rates don't rise above 75 percent for any single technique and that the techniques average about 40 percent. Moreover, for the most common kinds of defect detection—unit testing and integration testing—the modal rates are only 30–35 percent. The typical organization uses a test-heavy defect-removal approach and achieves only about 85 percent defect-removal efficiency. Leading organizations use a wider variety of techniques and achieve defect-removal efficiencies of 95 percent or higher (Jones 2000).

The strong implication is that if project developers are striving for a higher defect-detection rate, they need to use a combination of techniques. A classic study by Glenford Myers confirmed this implication (1978b). Myers studied a group of programmers with a minimum of 7 and an average of 11 years of professional experience. Using a program with 15 known errors, he had each programmer look for errors by using one of these techniques:

- Execution testing against the specification
- Execution testing against the specification with the source code
- Walk-through/inspection using the specification and the source code

Myers found a huge variation in the number of defects detected in the program, ranging from 1.0 to 9.0 defects found. The average number found was 5.1, or about a third of those known.

When used individually, no method had a statistically significant advantage over any of the others. The variety of errors people found was so great, however, that any combination of two methods—including having two independent groups using the same method—increased the total number of defects found by a factor of almost 2. Studies at NASA's Software Engineering Laboratory, Boeing, and other companies have reported that different people tend to find different defects. Only about 20 percent of the errors found by inspections were found by more than one inspector (Kouchakdjian, Green, and Basili 1989; Tripp, Struck, and Pflug 1991; Schneider, Martin, and Tsai 1992).

Glenford Myers points out that human processes (inspections and walk-throughs, for instance) tend to be better than computer-based testing at finding certain kinds of errors and that the opposite is true for other kinds of errors (1979). This result was confirmed in a later study, which found that code reading detected more interface defects and functional testing detected more control defects (Basili, Selby, and Hutchens 1986). Test guru Boris Beizer reports that informal test approaches typically achieve only 50–60 percent test coverage unless you're using a coverage analyzer (Johnson 1994).

The upshot is that defect-detection methods work better in combination than they do singly. Jones made the same point when he observed that cumulative defect-detection efficiency is significantly higher than that of any individual technique. The outlook for the effectiveness of testing used by itself is bleak. Jones points out that a combination of unit testing, functional testing, and system testing often results in a cumulative defect detection of less than 60 percent, which is usually inadequate for production software.

This data can also be used to understand why programmers who begin working with a disciplined defect-removal technique such as Extreme Programming experience higher defect-removal levels than they have experienced previously. As Table 20-3 illustrates, the set of defect-removal practices used in Extreme Programming would be expected to achieve about 90 percent defect-removal efficiency in the average case and 97 percent in the best case, which is far better than the industry average of 85 percent defect removal. Although some people have linked this effectiveness to synergy among Extreme Programming's practices, it is really just a predictable outcome of using these specific defect-removal practices. Other combinations of practices can work equally well or better, and the determination of which specific defect-removal practices to use to achieve a desired quality level is one part of effective project planning.

Table 20-3   **Extreme Programming's Estimated Defect-Detection Rate**

Removal Step	Lowest Rate	Modal Rate	Highest Rate
Informal design reviews (pair programming)	25%	35%	40%
Informal code reviews (pair programming)	20%	25%	35%
Personal desk-checking of code	20%	40%	60%
Unit test	15%	30%	50%
Integration test	25%	35%	40%
Regression test	15%	25%	30%
Expected cumulative defect-removal efficiency	~74%	~90%	~97%

Cost of Finding Defects

Some defect-detection practices cost more than others. The most economical practices result in the least cost per defect found, all other things being equal. The qualification that all other things must be equal is important because per-defect cost is influenced by the total number of defects found, the stage at which each defect is found, and other factors besides the economics of a specific defect-detection technique.

HARD DATA

Most studies have found that inspections are cheaper than testing. A study at the Software Engineering Laboratory found that code reading detected about 80 percent more faults per hour than testing (Basili and Selby 1987). Another organization found that it cost six times as much to detect design defects by using testing as by using inspections (Ackerman, Buchwald, and Lewski 1989). A later study at IBM found that only 3.5 staff hours were needed to find each error when using code inspections, whereas 15–25 hours were needed to find each error through testing (Kaplan 1995).

Cost of Fixing Defects

The cost of finding defects is only one part of the cost equation. The other is the cost of fixing defects. It might seem at first glance that how the defect is found wouldn't matter—it would always cost the same amount to fix.

Cross-Reference For details on the fact that defects become more expensive the longer they stay in a system, see "Appeal to Data" in Section 3.1. For an up-close look at errors themselves, see Section 22.4, "Typical Errors."

That isn't true because the longer a defect remains in the system, the more expensive it becomes to remove. A detection technique that finds the error earlier therefore results in a lower cost of fixing it. Even more important, some techniques, such as inspections, detect the symptoms and causes of defects in one step; others, such as testing, find symptoms but require additional work to diagnose and fix the root cause. The result is that one-step techniques are substantially cheaper overall than two-step ones.

HARD DATA

Microsoft's applications division has found that it takes three hours to find and fix a defect by using code inspection, a one-step technique, and 12 hours to find and fix a defect by using testing, a two-step technique (Moore 1992). Collofello and Woodfield reported on a 700,000-line program built by over 400 developers (1989). They found that code reviews were several times as cost-effective as testing—a 1.38 return on investment vs. 0.17.

The bottom line is that an effective software-quality program must include a combination of techniques that apply to all stages of development. Here's a recommended combination for achieving higher-than-average quality:

- Formal inspections of all requirements, all architecture, and designs for critical parts of a system

- Modeling or prototyping

- Code reading or inspections

- Execution testing

20.4 When to Do Quality Assurance

Cross-Reference Quality assurance of upstream activities—requirements and architecture, for instance— is outside the scope of this book. The "Additional Resources" section at the end of the chapter describes books you can turn to for more information about them.

As Chapter 3 ("Measure Twice, Cut Once: Upstream Prerequisites") noted, the earlier an error is inserted into software, the more entangled it becomes in other parts of the software and the more expensive it becomes to remove. A fault in requirements can produce one or more corresponding faults in design, which can produce many corresponding faults in code. A requirements error can result in extra architecture or in bad architectural decisions. The extra architecture results in extra code, test cases, and documentation. Or a requirements error can result in architecture, code, and test cases that are thrown away. Just as it's a good idea to work out the defects in the blueprints for a house before pouring the foundation in concrete, it's a good idea to catch requirements and architecture errors before they affect later activities.

In addition, errors in requirements or architecture tend to be more sweeping than construction errors. A single architectural error can affect several classes and dozens of routines, whereas a single construction error is unlikely to affect more than one routine or class. For this reason, too, it's cost-effective to catch errors as early as you can.

KEY POINT

Defects creep into software at all stages. Consequently, you should emphasize quality-assurance work in the early stages and throughout the rest of the project. It should be planned into the project as work begins; it should be part of the technical fiber of the project as work continues; and it should punctuate the end of the project, verifying the quality of the product as work ends.

20.5 The General Principle of Software Quality

KEY POINT

There's no such thing as a free lunch, and even if there were, there's no guarantee that it would be any good. Software development is a far cry from *haute cuisine*, however, and software quality is unusual in a significant way. The General Principle of Software Quality is that improving quality reduces development costs.

Understanding this principle depends on understanding a key observation: the best way to improve productivity and quality is to reduce the time spent reworking code, whether the rework arises from changes in requirements, changes in design, or debugging. The industry-average productivity for a software product is about 10 to 50 of lines of delivered code per person per day (including all noncoding overhead). It takes only a matter of minutes to type in 10 to 50 lines of code, so how is the rest of the day spent?

Cross-Reference For details on the difference between writing an individual program and writing a software product, see "Programs, Products, Systems, and System Products" in Section 27.5.

Part of the reason for these seemingly low productivity figures is that industry average numbers like these factor nonprogrammer time into the lines-of-code-per-day figure. Tester time, project manager time, and administrative support time are all included. Noncoding activities, such as requirements development and architecture work, are also typically factored into those lines-of-code-per-day figures. But none of that is what takes up so much time.

The single biggest activity on most projects is debugging and correcting code that doesn't work properly. Debugging and associated refactoring and other rework consume about 50 percent of the time on a traditional, naive software-development cycle. (See Section 3.1, "Importance of Prerequisites," for more details.) Reducing debugging by preventing errors improves productivity. Therefore, the most obvious method of shortening a development schedule is to improve the quality of the product and decrease the amount of time spent debugging and reworking the software.

HARD DATA

This analysis is confirmed by field data. In a review of 50 development projects involving over 400 work-years of effort and almost 3 million lines of code, a study at NASA's Software Engineering Laboratory found that increased quality assurance was associated with decreased error rate but did not increase overall development cost (Card 1987).

A study at IBM produced similar findings:

> *Software projects with the lowest levels of defects had the shortest development schedules and the highest development productivity.... software defect removal is actually the most expensive and time-consuming form of work for software (Jones 2000).*

HARD DATA

The same effect holds true at the small end of the scale. In a 1985 study, 166 professional programmers wrote programs from the same specification. The resulting programs averaged 220 lines of code and a little under five hours to write. The fascinating result was that programmers who took the median time to complete their programs produced programs with the greatest number of errors. The programmers who took more or less than the median time produced programs with significantly fewer errors (DeMarco and Lister 1985). Figure 20-2 graphs the results.

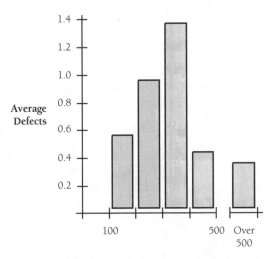

Time to Complete the Program in Minutes

Figure 20-2 Neither the fastest nor the slowest development approach produces the software with the most defects.

The two slowest groups took about five times as long to achieve roughly the same defect rate as the fastest group. It's not necessarily the case that writing software without defects takes more time than writing software with defects. As the graph shows, it can take less.

Admittedly, on certain kinds of projects, quality assurance costs money. If you're writing code for the space shuttle or for a medical life-support system, the degree of reliability required makes the project more expensive.

Compared to the traditional code-test-debug cycle, an enlightened software-quality program saves money. It redistributes resources away from debugging and refactoring into upstream quality-assurance activities. Upstream activities have more leverage on product quality than downstream activities, so the time you invest upstream saves more time downstream. The net effect is fewer defects, shorter development time, and lower costs. You'll see several more examples of the General Principle of Software Quality in the next three chapters.

cc2e.com/2043

> ### CHECKLIST: A Quality-Assurance Plan
>
> ❑ Have you identified specific quality characteristics that are important to your project?
>
> ❑ Have you made others aware of the project's quality objectives?
>
> ❑ Have you differentiated between external and internal quality characteristics?
>
> ❑ Have you thought about the ways in which some characteristics might compete with or complement others?
>
> ❑ Does your project call for the use of several different error-detection techniques suited to finding several different kinds of errors?
>
> ❑ Does your project include a plan to take steps to assure software quality during each stage of software development?
>
> ❑ Is the quality measured in some way so that you can tell whether it's improving or degrading?
>
> ❑ Does management understand that quality assurance incurs additional costs up front in order to save costs later?

Additional Resources

cc2e.com/2050

It's not hard to list books in this section because virtually any book on effective software methodologies describes techniques that result in improved quality and productivity. The difficulty is finding books that deal with software quality per se. Here are two:

Ginac, Frank P. *Customer Oriented Software Quality Assurance*. Englewood Cliffs, NJ: Prentice Hall, 1998. This is a very short book that describes quality attributes, quality metrics, QA programs, and the role of testing in quality, as well as well-known quality improvement programs, including the Software Engineering Institute's CMM and ISO 9000.

Lewis, William E. *Software Testing and Continuous Quality Improvement*, 2d ed. Auerbach Publishing, 2000. This book provides a comprehensive discussion of a quality life cycle, as well as extensive discussion of testing techniques. It also provides numerous forms and checklists.

Relevant Standards

cc2e.com/2057 *IEEE Std 730-2002, IEEE Standard for Software Quality Assurance Plans.*

IEEE Std 1061-1998, IEEE Standard for a Software Quality Metrics Methodology.

IEEE Std 1028-1997, Standard for Software Reviews.

IEEE Std 1008-1987 (R1993), Standard for Software Unit Testing.

IEEE Std 829-1998, Standard for Software Test Documentation.

Key Points

- Quality is free, in the end, but it requires a reallocation of resources so that defects are prevented cheaply instead of fixed expensively.

- Not all quality-assurance goals are simultaneously achievable. Explicitly decide which goals you want to achieve, and communicate the goals to other people on your team.

- No single defect-detection technique is completely effective by itself. Testing by itself is not optimally effective at removing errors. Successful quality-assurance programs use several different techniques to detect different kinds of errors.

- You can apply effective techniques during construction and many equally powerful techniques before construction. The earlier you find a defect, the less intertwined it will become with the rest of your code and the less damage it will cause.

- Quality assurance in the software arena is process-oriented. Software development doesn't have a repetitive phase that affects the final product like manufacturing does, so the quality of the result is controlled by the process used to develop the software.

Chapter 21

Collaborative Construction

cc2e.com/2185

Contents

Related Topics

You might have had an experience common to many programmers. You walk into another programmer's cubicle and say, "Would you mind looking at this code? I'm having some trouble with it." You start to explain the problem: "It can't be a result of this thing, because I did that. And it can't be the result of this other thing, because I did this. And it can't be the result of—wait a minute. It *could* be the result of that. Thanks!" You've solved your problem before your "helper" has had a chance to say a word.

In one way or another, all collaborative construction techniques are attempts to formalize the process of showing your work to someone else for the purpose of flushing out errors.

If you've read about inspections and pair programming before, you won't find much new information in this chapter. The extent of the hard data about the effectiveness of inspections in Section 21.3 might surprise you, and you might not have considered the code-reading alternative described in Section 21.4. You might also take a look at Table 21-1, "Comparison of Collaborative Construction Techniques," at the end of the chapter. If your knowledge is all from your own experience, read on! Other people have had different experiences, and you'll find some new ideas.

21.1 Overview of Collaborative Development Practices

"Collaborative construction" refers to pair programming, formal inspections, informal technical reviews, and document reading, as well as other techniques in which developers share responsibility for creating code and other work products. At my company, the term "collaborative construction" was coined by Matt Peloquin in about 2000. The term appears to have been coined independently by others in the same time frame.

HARD DATA

All collaborative construction techniques, despite their differences, are based on the ideas that developers are blind to some of the trouble spots in their work, that other people don't have the same blind spots, and that it's beneficial for developers to have someone else look at their work. Studies at the Software Engineering Institute have found that developers insert an average of 1 to 3 defects per hour into their designs and 5 to 8 defects per hour into code (Humphrey 1997), so attacking these blind spots is a key to effective construction.

Collaborative Construction Complements Other Quality-Assurance Techniques

HARD DATA

The primary purpose of collaborative construction is to improve software quality. As noted in Chapter 20, "The Software-Quality Landscape," software testing has limited effectiveness when used alone—the average defect-detection rate is only about 30 percent for unit testing, 35 percent for integration testing, and 35 percent for low-volume beta testing. In contrast, the average effectivenesses of design and code inspections are 55 and 60 percent (Jones 1996). The secondary benefit of collaborative construction is that it decreases development time, which in turn lowers development costs.

KEY POINT

Early reports on pair programming suggest that it can achieve a code-quality level similar to formal inspections (Shull et al 2002). The cost of full-up pair programming is probably higher than the cost of solo development—on the order of 10–25 percent higher—but the reduction in development time appears to be on the order of 45 percent, which in some cases may be a decisive advantage over solo development (Boehm and Turner 2004), although not over inspections which have produced similar results.

Technical reviews have been studied much longer than pair programming, and their results, as described in case studies and elsewhere, have been impressive:

HARD DATA

- IBM found that each hour of inspection prevented about 100 hours of related work (testing and defect correction) (Holland 1999).

- Raytheon reduced its cost of defect correction (rework) from about 40 percent of total project cost to about 20 percent through an initiative that focused on inspections (Haley 1996).

- Hewlett-Packard reported that its inspection program saved an estimated $21.5 million per year (Grady and Van Slack 1994).

- Imperial Chemical Industries found that the cost of maintaining a portfolio of about 400 programs was only about 10 percent as high as the cost of maintaining a similar set of programs that had not been inspected (Gilb and Graham 1993).

- A study of large programs found that each hour spent on inspections avoided an average of 33 hours of maintenance work and that inspections were up to 20 times more efficient than testing (Russell 1991).

- In a software-maintenance organization, 55 percent of one-line maintenance changes were in error before code reviews were introduced. After reviews were introduced, only 2 percent of the changes were in error (Freedman and Weinberg 1990). When all changes were considered, 95 percent were correct the first time after reviews were introduced. Before reviews were introduced, under 20 percent were correct the first time.

- A group of 11 programs were developed by the same group of people, and all were released to production. The first five were developed without reviews and averaged 4.5 errors per 100 lines of code. The other six were inspected and averaged only 0.82 errors per 100 lines of code. Reviews cut the errors by over 80 percent (Freedman and Weinberg 1990).

- Capers Jones reports that of all the software projects he has studied that have achieved 99 percent defect-removal rates or better, all have used formal inspections. Also, none of the projects that achieved less than 75 percent defect-removal efficiency used formal inspections (Jones 2000).

A number of these cases illustrate the General Principle of Software Quality, which holds that reducing the number of defects in the software also improves development time.

KEY POINT

Various studies have shown that in addition to being more effective at catching errors than testing, collaborative practices find different kinds of errors than testing does (Myers 1978; Basili, Selby, and Hutchens 1986). As Karl Wiegers points out, "A human reviewer can spot unclear error messages, inadequate comments, hard-coded variable values, and repeated code patterns that should be consolidated. Testing won't" (Wiegers 2002). A secondary effect is that when people know their work will be reviewed, they scrutinize it more carefully. Thus, even when testing is done effectively, reviews or other kinds of collaboration are needed as part of a comprehensive quality program.

Collaborative Construction Provides Mentoring in Corporate Culture and Programming Expertise

Informal review procedures were passed on from person to person in the general culture of computing for many years before they were acknowledged in print. The need for reviewing was so obvious to the best programmers that they rarely mentioned it in print, while the worst programmers believed they were so good that their work did not need reviewing.
—Daniel Freedman and Gerald Weinberg

Software standards can be written down and distributed, but if no one talks about them or encourages others to use them, they won't be followed. Reviews are an important mechanism for giving programmers feedback about their code. The code, the standards, and the reasons for making the code meet the standards are good topics for review discussions.

In addition to feedback about how well they follow standards, programmers need feedback about more subjective aspects of programming: formatting, comments, variable names, local and global variable use, design approaches, the-way-we-do-things-around-here, and so on. Programmers who are still wet behind the ears need guidance from those who are more knowledgeable, and more knowledgeable programmers who tend to be busy need to be encouraged to spend time sharing what they know. Reviews create a venue for more experienced and less experienced programmers to communicate about technical issues. As such, reviews are an opportunity for cultivating quality improvements in the future as much as in the present.

One team that used formal inspections reported that inspections quickly brought all the developers up to the level of the best developers (Tackett and Van Doren 1999).

Collective Ownership Applies to All Forms of Collaborative Construction

Cross-Reference A concept that spans all collaborative construction techniques is the idea of collective ownership. In some development models, programmers own the code they write and official or unofficial restrictions on modifying someone else's code exist. Collective ownership increases the need for work coordination, especially configuration management. For details, see Section 28.2, "Configuration Management."

With collective ownership, all code is owned by the group rather than by individuals and can be accessed and modified by various members of the group. This produces several valuable benefits:

■ Better code quality arises from multiple sets of eyes seeing the code and multiple programmers working on the code.

■ The impact of someone leaving the project is lessened because multiple people are familiar with each section of code.

■ Defect-correction cycles are shorter overall because any of several programmers can potentially be assigned to fix bugs on an as-available basis.

Some methodologies, such as Extreme Programming, recommend formally pairing programmers and rotating their work assignments over time. At my company, we've found that programmers don't need to pair up formally to achieve good code coverage. Over time we achieve cross-coverage through a combination of formal and informal technical reviews, pair programming when needed, and rotation of defect-correction assignments.

Collaboration Applies As Much Before Construction As After

This book is about construction, so collaboration on detailed design and code are the focus of this chapter. However, most of the comments about collaborative construction in this chapter also apply to estimates, plans, requirements, architecture, testing, and maintenance work. By studying the references at the end of the chapter, you can apply collaborative techniques to most software development activities.

21.2 Pair Programming

When pair programming, one programmer types in code at the keyboard and the other programmer watches for mistakes and thinks strategically about whether the code is being written correctly and whether the right code is being written. Pair programming was originally popularized by Extreme Programming (Beck 2000), but it is now being used more widely (Williams and Kessler 2002).

Keys to Success with Pair Programming

The basic concept of pair programming is simple, but its use nonetheless benefits from a few guidelines:

Support pair programming with coding standards   Pair programming will not be effective if the two people in the pair spend their time arguing about coding style. Try to standardize what Chapter 5, "Design in Construction," refers to as the "accidental attributes" of programming so that the programmers can focus on the "essential" task at hand.

Don't let pair programming turn into watching   The person without the keyboard should be an active participant in the programming. That person is analyzing the code, thinking ahead to what will be coded next, evaluating the design, and planning how to test the code.

Don't force pair programming of the easy stuff   One group that used pair programming for the most complicated code found it more expedient to do detailed design at the whiteboard for 15 minutes and then to program solo (Manzo 2002). Most organizations that have tried pair programming eventually settle into using pairs for part of their work but not all of it (Boehm and Turner 2004).

Rotate pairs and work assignments regularly   In pair programming, as with other collaborative development practices, benefit arises from different programmers learning different parts of the system. Rotate pair assignments regularly to encourage cross-pollination—some experts recommend changing pairs as often as daily (Reifer 2002).

Encourage pairs to match each other's pace   One partner going too fast limits the benefit of having the other partner. The faster partner needs to slow down, or the pair should be broken up and reconfigured with different partners.

Make sure both partners can see the monitor   Even seemingly mundane issues like being able to see the monitor and using fonts that are too small can cause problems.

Don't force people who don't like each other to pair   Sometimes personality conflicts prevent people from pairing effectively. It's pointless to force people who don't get along to pair, so be sensitive to personality matches (Beck 2000, Reifer 2002).

Avoid pairing all newbies   Pair programming works best when at least one of the partners has paired before (Larman 2004).

Assign a team leader   If your whole team wants to do 100 percent of its programming in pairs, you'll still need to assign one person to coordinate work assignments, be held accountable for results, and act as the point of contact for people outside the project.

Benefits of Pair Programming

Pair programming produces numerous benefits:

- It holds up better under stress than solo development. Pairs encourage each other to keep code quality high even when there's pressure to write quick and dirty code.

- It improves code quality. The readability and understandability of the code tends to rise to the level of the best programmer on the team.

- It shortens schedules. Pairs tend to write code faster and with fewer errors. The project team spends less time at the end of the project correcting defects.

- It produces all the other general benefits of collaborative construction, including disseminating corporate culture, mentoring junior programmers, and fostering collective ownership.

cc2e.com/2192

CHECKLIST: Effective Pair Programming

- ❑ Do you have a coding standard so that pair programmers stay focused on programming rather than on philosophical coding-style discussions?

- ❑ Are both partners participating actively?

- ❑ Are you avoiding pair programming everything and, instead, selecting the assignments that will really benefit from pair programming?

- ❑ Are you rotating pair assignments and work assignments regularly?

- ❑ Are the pairs well matched in terms of pace and personality?

- ❑ Is there a team leader to act as the focal point for management and other people outside the project?

21.3 Formal Inspections

Further Reading If you want to read the original article on inspections, see "Design and Code Inspections to Reduce Errors in Program Development" (Fagan 1976).

An inspection is a specific kind of review that has been shown to be extremely effective in detecting defects and to be relatively economical compared to testing. Inspections were developed by Michael Fagan and used at IBM for several years before Fagan published the paper that made them public. Although any review involves reading designs or code, an inspection differs from a run-of-the-mill review in several key ways:

- Checklists focus the reviewers' attention on areas that have been problems in the past.

- The inspection focuses on defect detection, not correction.

- Reviewers prepare for the inspection meeting beforehand and arrive with a list of the problems they've discovered.

- Distinct roles are assigned to all participants.

- The moderator of the inspection isn't the author of the work product under inspection.

- The moderator has received specific training in moderating inspections.

- The inspection meeting is held only if all participants have adequately prepared.

- Data is collected at each inspection and is fed into future inspections to improve them.

- General management doesn't attend the inspection meeting unless you're inspecting a project plan or other management materials. Technical leaders might attend.

What Results Can You Expect from Inspections?

HARD DATA

Individual inspections typically catch about 60 percent of defects, which is higher than other techniques except prototyping and high-volume beta testing. These results have been confirmed numerous times at various organizations, including Harris BCSD, National Software Quality Experiment, Software Engineering Institute, Hewlett Packard, and so on (Shull et al 2002).

The combination of design and code inspections usually removes 70–85 percent or more of the defects in a product (Jones 1996). Inspections identify error-prone classes early, and Capers Jones reports that they result in 20–30 percent fewer defects per 1000 lines of code than less formal review practices. Designers and coders learn to improve their work through participating in inspections, and inspections increase productivity by about 20 percent (Fagan 1976, Humphrey 1989, Gilb and Graham 1993, Wiegers 2002). On a project that uses inspections for design and code, the inspections will take up about 10–15 percent of project budget and will typically reduce overall project cost.

Inspections can also be used for assessing progress, but it's the technical progress that is assessed. That usually means answering two questions: Is the technical work being done? And is the technical work being done *well*? The answers to both questions are byproducts of formal inspections.

Roles During an Inspection

One key characteristic of an inspection is that each person involved has a distinct role to play. Here are the roles:

Moderator   The moderator is responsible for keeping the inspection moving at a rate that's fast enough to be productive but slow enough to find the most errors possible. The moderator must be technically competent—not necessarily an expert in the particular design or code under inspection, but capable of understanding relevant details. This person manages other aspects of the inspection, such as distributing the design or code to be reviewed, distributing the inspection checklist, setting up a meeting room, reporting inspection results, and following up on the action items assigned at the inspection meeting.

Author   The person who wrote the design or code plays a relatively minor role in the inspection. Part of the goal of an inspection is to be sure that the design or code speaks for itself. If the design or code under inspection turns out to be unclear, the author will be assigned the job of making it clearer. Otherwise, the author's duties are to explain parts of the design or code that are unclear and, occasionally, to explain why things that seem like errors are actually acceptable. If the project is unfamiliar to the reviewers, the author might also present an overview of the project in preparation for the inspection meeting.

Reviewer   A reviewer is anyone who has a direct interest in the design or code but who is not the author. A reviewer of a design might be the programmer who will implement the design. A tester or higher-level architect might also be involved. The role of the reviewers is to find defects. They usually find defects during preparation, and, as the design or code is discussed at the inspection meeting, the group should find considerably more defects.

Scribe   The scribe records errors that are detected and the assignments of action items during the inspection meeting. Neither the author nor the moderator should be the scribe.

Management   Including management in inspections is not usually a good idea. The point of a software inspection is that it is a purely technical review. Management's presence changes the interactions: people feel that they, instead of the review materials, are under evaluation, which changes the focus from technical to political. However, management has a right to know the results of an inspection, and an inspection report is prepared to keep management informed.

Similarly, under no circumstances should inspection results be used for performance appraisals. Don't kill the goose that lays the golden eggs. Code examined in an inspection is still under development. Evaluation of performance should be based on final products, not on work that isn't finished.

Overall, an inspection should have no fewer than three participants. It's not possible to have a separate moderator, author, and reviewer with fewer than three people, and those roles shouldn't be combined. Traditional advice is to limit an inspection to about six people because, with any more, the group becomes too large to manage. Researchers have generally found that having more than two to three reviewers doesn't appear to increase the number of defects found (Bush and Kelly 1989, Porter and Votta 1997). However, these general findings are not unanimous, and results appear to vary depending on the kind of material being inspected (Wiegers 2002). Pay attention to your experience, and adjust your approach accordingly.

General Procedure for an Inspection

An inspection consists of several distinct stages:

Planning   The author gives the design or code to the moderator. The moderator decides who will review the material and when and where the inspection meeting will occur; the moderator then distributes the design or code and a checklist that focuses the attention of the inspectors. Materials should be printed with line numbers to speed up error identification during the meeting.

Overview   When the reviewers aren't familiar with the project they are reviewing, the author can spend up to an hour or so describing the technical environment within which the design or code has been created. Having an overview tends to be a dangerous practice because it can lead to a glossing over of unclear points in the design or code under inspection. The design or code should speak for itself; the overview shouldn't speak for it.

Cross-Reference For a list of checklists you can use to improve code quality, see page xxix.

Preparation   Each reviewer works alone to scrutinize the design or code for errors. The reviewers use the checklist to stimulate and direct their examination of the review materials.

For a review of application code written in a high-level language, reviewers can prepare at about 500 lines of code per hour. For a review of system code written in a high-level language, reviewers can prepare at only about 125 lines of code per hour (Humphrey 1989). The most effective rate of review varies a great deal, so keep records of preparation rates in your organization to determine the rate that's most effective in your environment.

Some organizations have found that inspections are more effective when each reviewer is assigned a specific perspective. A reviewer might be asked to prepare for the inspection from the point of view of the maintenance programmer, the customer, or the designer, for example. Research on perspective-based reviews has not been comprehensive, but it suggests that perspective-based reviews might uncover more errors than general reviews.

An additional variation in inspection preparation is to assign each reviewer one or more scenarios to check. Scenarios can involve specific questions that a reviewer is assigned to answer, such as "Are there any requirements that are not satisfied by this design?" A scenario might also involve a specific task that a reviewer is assigned to perform, such as listing the specific requirements that a particular design element satisfies. You can also assign some reviewers to read the material front to back, back to front, or inside out.

Inspection Meeting   The moderator chooses someone other than the author to paraphrase the design or read the code (Wiegers 2003). All logic is explained, including each branch of each logical structure. During this presentation, the scribe records errors as they are detected, but discussion of an error stops as soon as it's recognized as an error. The scribe notes the type and the severity of the error, and the inspection moves on. If you have problems keeping the discussions focused, the moderator might ring a bell to get the group's attention and put the discussion back on track.

The rate at which the design or the code is considered should be neither too slow nor too fast. If it's too slow, attention can lag and the meeting won't be productive. If it's too fast, the group can overlook errors it would otherwise catch. Optimal inspection rates vary from environment to environment, just as preparation rates do. Keep records so that over time you can determine the optimal rate for your environment. Other organizations have found that for system code, an inspection rate of 90 lines of code per hour is optimal. For applications code, the inspection rate can be as rapid as 500 lines of code per hour (Humphrey 1989). An average of about 150–200 nonblank, noncomment source statements per hour is a good place to start (Wiegers 2002).

Don't discuss solutions during the meeting. The group should stay focused on identifying defects. Some inspection groups don't even allow discussion about whether a defect is really a defect. They assume that if someone is confused enough to think it's a defect, the design, code, or documentation needs to be clarified.

The meeting generally should not last more than two hours. This doesn't mean that you have to fake a fire alarm to get everyone out at the two-hour mark, but experience at IBM and other companies has been that reviewers can't concentrate for much more than about two hours at a time. For the same reason, it's unwise to schedule more than one inspection on the same day.

Inspection Report   Within a day of the inspection meeting, the moderator produces an inspection report (e-mail or equivalent) that lists each defect, including its type and severity. The inspection report helps to ensure that all defects will be corrected, and it's used to develop a checklist that emphasizes problems specific to the organization. If you collect data on the time spent and the number of errors found over time, you can respond to challenges about inspection's efficacy with hard data. Otherwise, you'll be limited to saying that inspections seem better. That won't be as convincing to someone who thinks testing seems better. You'll also be able to tell if inspections aren't working in your environment and modify or abandon them, as appropriate. Data collection is also important because any new methodology needs to justify its existence.

Rework   The moderator assigns defects to someone, usually the author, for repair. The assignee resolves each defect on the list.

Follow-Up   The moderator is responsible for seeing that all rework assigned during the inspection is carried out. Depending on the number of errors found and the severity of those errors, you might follow up by having the reviewers reinspect the entire work product, having the reviewers reinspect only the fixes, or allowing the author to complete the fixes without any follow-up.

Third-Hour Meeting   Even though during the inspection participants aren't allowed to discuss solutions to the problems raised, some might still want to. You can hold an informal, third-hour meeting to allow interested parties to discuss solutions after the official inspection is over.

Fine-Tuning the Inspection

Once you become skilled at performing inspections "by the book," you can usually find several ways to improve them. Don't introduce changes willy-nilly, though. "Instrument" the inspection process so that you know whether your changes are beneficial.

Companies have often found that removing or combining any of the stages costs more than is saved (Fagan 1986). If you're tempted to change the inspection process without measuring the effect of the change, don't. If you have measured the process and you know that your changed process works better than the one described here, go right ahead.

As you do inspections, you'll notice that certain kinds of errors occur more frequently than other kinds. Create a checklist that calls attention to those kinds of errors so that reviewers will focus on them. Over time, you'll find kinds of errors that aren't on the checklist; add those to it. You might find that some errors on the initial checklist cease to occur; remove those. After a few inspections, your organization will have a checklist for inspections customized to its needs, and it might also have some clues about trouble areas in which its programmers need more training or support. Limit your checklist to one page or less. Longer ones are hard to use at the level of detail needed in an inspection.

Egos in Inspections

Further Reading For a discussion of egoless programming, see *The Psychology of Computer Programming*, 2d ed. (Weinberg 1998).

The point of the inspection itself is to discover defects in the design or code. It is not to explore alternatives or to debate about who is right and who is wrong. The point is most certainly *not* to criticize the author of the design or code. The experience should be a positive one for the author in which it's obvious that group participation improves the program and is a learning experience for all involved. It should not convince the author that some people in the group are jerks or that it's time to look for a new job. Comments like "Anyone who knows Java knows that it's more efficient to loop from *0* to *num-1*, not *1* to *num*" are totally inappropriate, and if they occur, the moderator should make their inappropriateness unmistakably clear.

Because the design or code is being criticized and the author probably feels somewhat attached to it, the author will naturally feel some of the heat directed at the code. The author should anticipate hearing criticisms of several defects that aren't really defects and several more that seem debatable. In spite of that, the author should acknowledge each alleged defect and move on. Acknowledging a criticism doesn't imply that the author agrees with the content of the criticism. The author should not try to defend the work under review. After the review, the author can think about each point in private and decide whether it's valid.

Reviewers must remember that the author has the ultimate responsibility for deciding what to do about a defect. It's fine to enjoy finding defects (and outside the review, to enjoy proposing solutions), but each reviewer must respect the author's ultimate right to decide how to resolve an error.

Inspections and *Code Complete*

I had a personal experience using inspections on the second edition of *Code Complete*. For the first edition of this book I initially wrote a rough draft. After letting the rough draft of each chapter sit in a drawer for a week or two, I reread the chapter cold and corrected the errors I found. I then circulated the revised chapter to about a dozen peers for review, several of whom reviewed it quite thoroughly. I corrected the errors they found. After a few more weeks, I reviewed it again myself and corrected more errors. Finally, I submitted the manuscript to the publisher, where it was reviewed by a copy editor, technical editor, and proofreader. The book was in print for more than 10 years, and readers sent in about 200 corrections during that time.

You might think there wouldn't be many errors left in the book that had gone through all that review activity. But that wasn't the case. To create the second edition, I used formal inspections of the first edition to identify issues that needed to be addressed in the second edition. Teams of three to four reviewers prepared according to the guidelines described in this chapter. Somewhat to my surprise, our formal inspections found several hundred errors in the first edition text that had not previously been detected through any of the numerous review activities.

If I had any doubts about the value of formal inspections, my experience in creating the second edition of *Code Complete* eliminated them.

Inspection Summary

Inspection checklists encourage focused concentration. The inspection process is systematic because of its standard checklists and standard roles. It is also self-optimizing because it uses a formal feedback loop to improve the checklists and to monitor preparation and inspection rates. With this control over the process and continuing optimization, inspection quickly becomes a powerful technique almost no matter how it begins.

Further Reading For more details on the SEI's concept of developmental maturity, see *Managing the Software Process* (Humphrey 1989).

The Software Engineering Institute (SEI) has defined a Capability Maturity Model (CMM) that measures the effectiveness of an organization's software-development process (SEI 1995). The inspection process demonstrates what the highest level is like. The process is systematic and repeatable and uses measured feedback to improve itself. You can apply the same ideas to many of the techniques described in this book. When generalized to an entire development organization, these ideas are, in a nutshell, what it takes to move the organization to the highest possible level of quality and productivity.

cc2e.com/2199

CHECKLIST: Effective Inspections

❑ Do you have checklists that focus reviewer attention on areas that have been problems in the past?

❑ Have you focused the inspection on defect detection rather than correction?

❑ Have you considered assigning perspectives or scenarios to help reviewers focus their preparation work?

❑ Are reviewers given enough time to prepare before the inspection meeting, and is each one prepared?

❑ Does each participant have a distinct role to play—moderator, reviewer, scribe, and so on?

❑ Does the meeting move at a productive rate?

❑ Is the meeting limited to two hours?

❑ Have all inspection participants received specific training in conducting inspections, and has the moderator received special training in moderation skills?

❑ Is data about error types collected at each inspection so that you can tailor future checklists to your organization?

> ❑ Is data about preparation and inspection rates collected so that you can optimize future preparation and inspections?
>
> ❑ Are the action items assigned at each inspection followed up, either personally by the moderator or with a reinspection?
>
> ❑ Does management understand that it should not attend inspection meetings?
>
> ❑ Is there a follow-up plan to assure that fixes are made correctly?

21.4 Other Kinds of Collaborative Development Practices

Other kinds of collaboration haven't accumulated the body of empirical support that inspections or pair programming have, so they're covered in less depth here. The collaborations covered in this section includes walk-throughs, code reading, and dog-and-pony shows.

Walk-Throughs

A walk-through is a popular kind of review. The term is loosely defined, and at least some of its popularity can be attributed to the fact that people can call virtually any kind of review a "walk-through."

Because the term is so loosely defined, it's hard to say exactly what a walk-through is. Certainly, a walk-through involves two or more people discussing a design or code. It might be as informal as an impromptu bull session around a whiteboard; it might be as formal as a scheduled meeting with an overhead presentation prepared by the art department and a formal summary sent to management. In one sense, "where two or three are gathered together," there is a walk-through. Proponents of walk-throughs like the looseness of such a definition, so I'll just point out a few things that all walk-throughs have in common and leave the rest of the details to you:

- The walk-through is usually hosted and moderated by the author of the design or code under review.

- The walk-through focuses on technical issues—it's a working meeting.

- All participants prepare for the walk-through by reading the design or code and looking for errors.

- The walk-through is a chance for senior programmers to pass on experience and corporate culture to junior programmers. It's also a chance for junior programmers to present new methodologies and to challenge timeworn, possibly obsolete, assumptions.

- A walk-through usually lasts 30 to 60 minutes.

- The emphasis is on error detection, not correction.

- Management doesn't attend.

- The walk-through concept is flexible and can be adapted to the specific needs of the organization using it.

What Results Can You Expect from a Walk-Through?

Used intelligently and with discipline, a walk-through can produce results similar to those of an inspection—that is, it can typically find between 20 and 40 percent of the errors in a program (Myers 1979, Boehm 1987b, Yourdon 1989b, Jones 1996). But in general, walk-throughs have been found to be significantly less effective than inspections (Jones 1996).

HARD DATA

Used unintelligently, walk-throughs are more trouble than they're worth. The low end of their effectiveness, 20 percent, isn't worth much, and at least one organization (Boeing Computer Services) found peer reviews of code to be "extremely expensive." Boeing found it was difficult to motivate project personnel to apply walk-through techniques consistently, and when project pressures increased, walk-throughs became nearly impossible (Glass 1982).

I've become more critical of walk-throughs during the past 10 years as a result of what I've seen in my company's consulting business. I've found that when people have bad experiences with technical reviews, it is nearly always with informal practices such as walk-throughs rather than with formal inspections. A review is basically a meeting, and meetings are expensive. If you're going to incur the overhead of holding a meeting, it's worthwhile to structure the meeting as a formal inspection. If the work product you're reviewing doesn't justify the overhead of a formal inspection, it doesn't justify the overhead of a meeting at all. In such a case you're better off using document reading or another less interactive approach.

Inspections seem to be more effective than walk-throughs at removing errors. So why would anyone choose to use walk-throughs?

If you have a large review group, a walk-through is a good review choice because it brings many diverse viewpoints to bear on the item under review. If everyone involved in the walk-through can be convinced that the solution is all right, it probably doesn't have any major flaws.

If reviewers from other organizations are involved, a walk-through might also be preferable. Roles in an inspection are more formalized and require some practice before people perform them effectively. Reviewers who haven't participated in inspections before are at a disadvantage. If you want to solicit their contributions, a walk-through might be the best choice.

KEY POINT

Inspections are more focused than walk-throughs and generally pay off better. Consequently, if you're choosing a review standard for your organization, choose inspections first unless you have good reason not to.

Code Reading

Code reading is an alternative to inspections and walk-throughs. In code reading, you read source code and look for errors. You also comment on qualitative aspects of the code, such as its design, style, readability, maintainability, and efficiency.

HARD DATA

A study at NASA's Software Engineering Laboratory found that code reading detected about 3.3 defects per hour of effort. Testing detected about 1.8 errors per hour (Card 1987). Code reading also found 20 to 60 percent more errors over the life of the project than the various kinds of testing did.

Like the idea of a walk-through, the concept of code reading is loosely defined. A code reading usually involves two or more people reading code independently and then meeting with the author of the code to discuss it. Here's how code reading goes:

- In preparation for the meeting, the author of the code hands out source listings to the code readers. The listings are from 1000 to 10,000 lines of code; 4000 lines is typical.

- Two or more people read the code. Use at least two people to encourage competition between the reviewers. If you use more than two, measure everyone's contribution so that you know how much the extra people contribute.

- Reviewers read the code independently. Estimate a rate of about 1000 lines a day.

- When the reviewers have finished reading the code, the code-reading meeting is hosted by the author of the code. The meeting lasts one or two hours and focuses on problems discovered by the code readers. No one makes any attempt to walk through the code line by line. The meeting is not even strictly necessary.

- The author of the code fixes the problems identified by the reviewers.

KEY POINT

The difference between code reading on the one hand and inspections and walk-throughs on the other is that code reading focuses more on individual review of the code than on the meeting. The result is that each reviewer's time is focused on finding problems in the code. Less time is spent in meetings in which each person contributes only part of the time and in which a substantial amount of the effort goes into moderating group dynamics. Less time is spent delaying meetings until each person in the group can meet for two hours. Code readings are especially valuable in situations in which reviewers are geographically dispersed.

HARD DATA

A study of 13 reviews at AT&T found that the importance of the review meeting itself was overrated; 90 percent of the defects were found in preparation for the review meeting, and only about 10 percent were found during the review itself (Votta 1991, Glass 1999).

Dog-and-Pony Shows

Dog-and-pony shows are reviews in which a software product is demonstrated to a customer. Customer reviews are common in software developed for government contracts, which often stipulate that reviews will be held for requirements, design, and code. The purpose of a dog-and-pony show is to demonstrate to the customer that the project is OK, so it's a management review rather than a technical review.

Don't rely on dog-and-pony shows to improve the technical quality of your products. Preparing for them might have an indirect effect on technical quality, but usually more time is spent in making good-looking presentation slides than in improving the quality of the software. Rely on inspections, walk-throughs, or code reading for technical quality improvements.

Comparison of Collaborative Construction Techniques

What are the differences among the various kinds of collaborative construction? Table 21-1 provides a summary of each technique's major characteristics.

Table 21-1   Comparison of Collaborative Construction Techniques

Property	Pair Programming	Formal Inspection	Informal Review (Walk-Throughs)
Defined participant roles	Yes	Yes	No
Formal training in how to perform the roles	Maybe, through coaching	Yes	No
Who "drives" the collaboration	Person with the keyboard	Moderator	Author, usually
Focus of collaboration	Design, coding, testing, and defect correction	Defect detection only	Varies
Focused review effort—looks for the most frequently found kinds of errors	Informal, if at all	Yes	No
Follow-up to reduce bad fixes	Yes	Yes	No
Fewer future errors because of detailed error feedback to individual programmers	Incidental	Yes	Incidental
Improved process efficiency from analysis of results	No	Yes	No
Useful for nonconstruction activities	Possibly	Yes	Yes
Typical percentage of defects found	40–60%	45–70%	20–40%

Pair programming doesn't have decades of data supporting its effectiveness like formal inspection does, but the initial data suggests it's on roughly equal footing with inspections, and anecdotal reports have also been positive.

If pair programming and formal inspections produce similar results for quality, cost, and schedule, the choice between them becomes a matter of personal style rather than one of technical substance. Some people prefer to work solo, only occasionally breaking out of solo mode for inspection meetings. Others prefer to spend more of their time directly working with others. The choice between the two techniques can be driven by the work-style preference of a team's specific developers, and subgroups within the team might be allowed to choose which way they would like to do most of their work. You should also use different techniques with a project, as appropriate.

Additional Resources

cc2e.com/2106

Here are more resources concerning collaborative contruction:

Pair Programming

Williams, Laurie and Robert Kessler. *Pair Programming Illuminated*. Boston, MA: Addison Wesley, 2002. This book explains the detailed ins and outs of pair programming, including how to handle various personality matches (for example, expert and inexpert, introvert and extrovert) and other implementation issues.

Beck, Kent. *Extreme Programming Explained: Embrace Change*. Reading, MA: Addison Wesley, 2000. This book touches on pair programming briefly and shows how it can be used in conjunction with other mutually supportive techniques, including coding standards, frequent integration, and regression testing.

Reifer, Donald. "How to Get the Most Out of Extreme Programming/Agile Methods," *Proceedings, XP/Agile Universe 2002*. New York, NY: Springer; pp. 185–196. This paper summarizes industrial experience with Extreme Programming and agile methods and presents keys to success for pair programming.

Inspections

Wiegers, Karl. *Peer Reviews in Software: A Practical Guide*. Boston, MA: Addison Wesley, 2002. This well-written book describes the ins and outs of various kinds of reviews, including formal inspections and other, less formal practices. It's well researched, has a practical focus, and is easy to read.

Gilb, Tom and Dorothy Graham. *Software Inspection*. Wokingham, England: Addison-Wesley, 1993. This contains a thorough discussion of inspections circa the early 1990s. It has a practical focus and includes case studies that describe experiences several organizations have had in setting up inspection programs.

Fagan, Michael E. "Design and Code Inspections to Reduce Errors in Program Development." *IBM Systems Journal* 15, no. 3 (1976): 182–211.

Fagan, Michael E. "Advances in Software Inspections." *IEEE Transactions on Software Engineering*, SE-12, no. 7 (July 1986): 744–51. These two articles were written by the developer of inspections. They contain the meat of what you need to know to run an inspection, including all the standard inspection forms.

Relevant Standards

IEEE Std 1028-1997, Standard for Software Reviews

IEEE Std 730-2002, Standard for Software Quality Assurance Plans

Key Points

- Collaborative development practices tend to find a higher percentage of defects than testing and to find them more efficiently.

- Collaborative development practices tend to find different kinds of errors than testing does, implying that you need to use both reviews and testing to ensure the quality of your software.

- Formal inspections use checklists, preparation, well-defined roles, and continual process improvement to maximize error-detection efficiency. They tend to find more defects than walk-throughs.

- Pair programming typically costs about the same as inspections and produces similar quality code. Pair programming is especially valuable when schedule reduction is desired. Some developers prefer working in pairs to working solo.

- Formal inspections can be used on work products such as requirements, designs, and test cases, as well as on code.

- Walk-throughs and code reading are alternatives to inspections. Code reading offers more flexibility in using each person's time effectively.

Chapter 22
Developer Testing

cc2e.com/2261

Contents

Related Topics

Testing is the most popular quality-improvement activity—a practice supported by a wealth of industrial and academic research and by commercial experience. Software is tested in numerous ways, some of which are typically performed by developers and some of which are more commonly performed by specialized test personnel:

- *Unit testing* is the execution of a complete class, routine, or small program that has been written by a single programmer or team of programmers, which is tested in isolation from the more complete system.

- *Component testing* is the execution of a class, package, small program, or other program element that involves the work of multiple programmers or programming teams, which is tested in isolation from the more complete system.

- *Integration testing* is the combined execution of two or more classes, packages, components, or subsystems that have been created by multiple programmers or programming teams. This kind of testing typically starts as soon as there are two classes to test and continues until the entire system is complete.

■ *Regression testing* is the repetition of previously executed test cases for the purpose of finding defects in software that previously passed the same set of tests.

■ *System testing* is the execution of the software in its final configuration, including integration with other software and hardware systems. It tests for security, performance, resource loss, timing problems, and other issues that can't be tested at lower levels of integration.

In this chapter, "testing" refers to testing by the developer, which typically consists of unit tests, component tests, and integration tests but can sometimes include regression tests and system tests. Numerous additional kinds of testing are performed by specialized test personnel and are rarely performed by developers, including beta tests, customer-acceptance tests, performance tests, configuration tests, platform tests, stress tests, usability tests, and so on. These kinds of testing are not discussed further in this chapter.

KEY POINT

Testing is usually broken into two broad categories: black-box testing and white-box (or glass-box) testing. "Black-box testing" refers to tests in which the tester cannot see the inner workings of the item being tested. This obviously does not apply when you test code that you have written! "White-box testing" refers to tests in which the tester is aware of the inner workings of the item being tested. This is the kind of testing that you as a developer use to test your own code. Both black-box and white-box testing have strengths and weaknesses; this chapter focuses on white-box testing because that's the kind of testing that developers perform.

Some programmers use the terms "testing" and "debugging" interchangeably, but careful programmers distinguish between the two activities. Testing is a means of detecting errors. Debugging is a means of diagnosing and correcting the root causes of errors that have already been detected. This chapter deals exclusively with error detection. Error correction is discussed in detail in Chapter 23, "Debugging."

The whole topic of testing is much larger than the subject of testing during construction. System testing, stress testing, black-box testing, and other topics for test specialists are discussed in the "Additional Resources" section at the end of the chapter.

22.1 Role of Developer Testing in Software Quality

Cross-Reference For details on reviews, see Chapter 21, "Collaborative Construction."

Testing is an important part of any software-quality program, and in many cases it's the only part. This is unfortunate, because collaborative development practices in their various forms have been shown to find a higher percentage of errors than testing does, and they cost less than half as much per error found as testing does (Card 1987, Russell 1991, Kaplan 1995). Individual testing steps (unit test, component test, and integration test) typically find less than 50 percent of the errors present each. The combination of testing steps often finds less than 60 percent of the errors present (Jones 1998).

Programs do not acquire bugs as people acquire germs, by hanging around other buggy programs. Programmers must insert them.
—Harlan Mills

If you were to list a set of software-development activities on "Sesame Street" and ask, "Which of these things is not like the others?" the answer would be "Testing." Testing is a hard activity for most developers to swallow for several reasons:

■ Testing's goal runs counter to the goals of other development activities. The goal is to find errors. A successful test is one that breaks the software. The goal of every other development activity is to prevent errors and keep the software from breaking.

■ Testing can never completely prove the absence of errors. If you have tested extensively and found thousands of errors, does it mean that you've found all the errors or that you have thousands more to find? An absence of errors could mean ineffective or incomplete test cases as easily as it could mean perfect software.

■ Testing by itself does not improve software quality. Test results are an indicator of quality, but in and of themselves they don't improve it. Trying to improve software quality by increasing the amount of testing is like trying to lose weight by weighing yourself more often. What you eat before you step onto the scale determines how much you will weigh, and the software-development techniques you use determine how many errors testing will find. If you want to lose weight, don't buy a new scale; change your diet. If you want to improve your software, don't just test more; develop better.

HARD DATA

■ Testing requires you to assume that you'll find errors in your code. If you assume you won't, you probably won't, but only because you'll have set up a self-fulfilling prophecy. If you execute the program hoping that it won't have any errors, it will be too easy to overlook the errors you find. In a study that has become a classic, Glenford Myers had a group of experienced programmers test a program with 15 known defects. The average programmer found only 5 of the 15 errors. The best found only 9. The main source of undetected errors was that erroneous output was not examined carefully enough. The errors were visible, but the programmers didn't notice them (Myers 1978).

You must hope to find errors in your code. Such a hope might seem like an unnatural act, but you should hope that it's you who finds the errors and not someone else.

A key question is, How much time should be spent in developer testing on a typical project? A commonly cited figure for all testing is 50 percent of the time spent on the project, but that's misleading. First, that particular figure combines testing and debugging; testing alone takes less time. Second, that figure represents the amount of time that's typically spent rather than the time that should be spent. Third, the figure includes independent testing as well as developer testing.

As Figure 22-1 shows, depending on the project's size and complexity, developer testing should probably take 8 to 25 percent of the total project time. This is consistent with much of the data that has been reported.

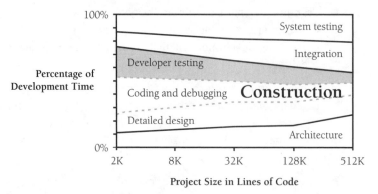

Figure 22-1 As the size of the project increases, developer testing consumes a smaller percentage of the total development time. The effects of program size are described in more detail in Chapter 27, "How Program Size Affects Construction."

A second question is, What do you do with the results of developer testing? Most immediately, you can use the results to assess the reliability of the product under development. Even if you never correct the defects that testing finds, testing describes how reliable the software is. Another use for the results is that they can and usually do guide corrections to the software. Finally, over time, the record of defects found through testing helps reveal the kinds of errors that are most common. You can use this information to select appropriate training classes, direct future technical review activities, and design future test cases.

Testing During Construction

The big, wide world of testing sometimes ignores the subject of this chapter: "white-box" or "glass-box" testing. You generally want to design a class to be a black box—a user of the class won't have to look past the interface to know what the class does. In testing the class, however, it's advantageous to treat it as a glass box, to look at the internal source code of the class as well as its inputs and outputs. If you know what's inside the box, you can test the class more thoroughly. Of course, you also have the same blind spots in testing the class that you had in writing it, and so black-box testing has advantages too.

During construction, you generally write a routine or class, check it mentally, and then review it or test it. Regardless of your integration or system-testing strategy, you should test each unit thoroughly before you combine it with any others. If you're writing several routines, you should test them one at a time. Routines aren't really any easier to test individually, but they're much easier to debug. If you throw several untested routines together at once and find an error, any of the several routines might be guilty. If you add one routine at a time to a collection of previously tested routines, you know that any new errors are the result of the new routine or of interactions with the new routine. The debugging job is easier.

Collaborative construction practices have many strengths to offer that testing can't match. But part of the problem with testing is that testing often isn't performed as well as it could be. A developer can perform hundreds of tests and still achieve only partial code coverage. A *feeling* of good test coverage doesn't mean that actual test coverage is adequate. An understanding of basic test concepts can support better testing and raise testing's effectiveness.

22.2 Recommended Approach to Developer Testing

A systematic approach to developer testing maximizes your ability to detect errors of all kinds with a minimum of effort. Be sure to cover this ground:

- Test for each relevant requirement to make sure that the requirements have been implemented. Plan the test cases for this step at the requirements stage or as early as possible—preferably before you begin writing the unit to be tested. Consider testing for common omissions in requirements. The level of security, storage, the installation procedure, and system reliability are all fair game for testing and are often overlooked at requirements time.

- Test for each relevant design concern to make sure that the design has been implemented. Plan the test cases for this step at the design stage or as early as possible—before you begin the detailed coding of the routine or class to be tested.

- Use "basis testing" to add detailed test cases to those that test the requirements and the design. Add data-flow tests, and then add the remaining test cases needed to thoroughly exercise the code. At a minimum, you should test every line of code. Basis testing and data-flow testing are described later in this chapter.

- Use a checklist of the kinds of errors you've made on the project to date or have made on previous projects.

Design the test cases along with the product. This can help avoid errors in requirements and design, which tend to be more expensive than coding errors. Plan to test and find defects as early as possible because it's cheaper to fix defects early.

Test First or Test Last?

Developers sometimes wonder whether it's better to write test cases after the code has been written or beforehand (Beck 2003). The defect-cost increase graph—see Figure 3-1 on page 30—suggests that writing test cases first will minimize the amount of time between when a defect is inserted into the code and when the defect is detected and removed. This turns out to be one of many reasons to write test cases first:

- Writing test cases before writing the code doesn't take any more effort than writing test cases after the code; it simply resequences the test-case-writing activity.

- When you write test cases first, you detect defects earlier and you can correct them more easily.

- Writing test cases first forces you to think at least a little bit about the requirements and design before writing code, which tends to produce better code.

- Writing test cases first exposes requirements problems sooner, before the code is written, because it's hard to write a test case for a poor requirement.

- If you save your test cases, which you should do, you can still test last, in addition to testing first.

All in all, I think test-first programming is one of the most beneficial software practices to emerge during the past decade and is a good general approach. But it isn't a testing panacea, because it's subject to the general limitations of developer testing, which are described next.

Limitations of Developer Testing

Watch for the following limitations with developer testing:

Developer tests tend to be "clean tests"   Developers tend to test for whether the code works (clean tests) rather than test for all the ways the code breaks (dirty tests). Immature testing organizations tend to have about five clean tests for every dirty test. Mature testing organizations tend to have five dirty tests for every clean test. This ratio is not reversed by reducing the clean tests; it's done by creating 25 times as many dirty tests (Boris Beizer in Johnson 1994).

HARD DATA

Developer testing tends to have an optimistic view of test coverage   Average programmers believe they are achieving 95 percent test coverage, but they're typically achieving more like 80 percent test coverage in the best case, 30 percent in the worst case, and more like 50-60 percent in the average case (Boris Beizer in Johnson 1994).

Developer testing tends to skip more sophisticated kinds of test coverage   Most developers view the kind of test coverage known as "100% statement coverage" as adequate. This is a good start, but it's hardly sufficient. A better coverage standard is to meet what's called "100% branch coverage," with every predicate term being tested for at least one true and one false value. Section 22.3, "Bag of Testing Tricks," provides more details about how to accomplish this.

None of these points reduce the value of developer testing, but they do help put developer testing into proper perspective. As valuable as developer testing is, it isn't sufficient to provide adequate quality assurance on its own and should be supplemented with other practices, including independent testing and collaborative construction techniques.

22.3 Bag of Testing Tricks

Why isn't it possible to prove that a program is correct by testing it? To use testing to prove that a program works, you'd have to test every conceivable input value to the program and every conceivable combination of input values. Even for simple programs, such an undertaking would become massively prohibitive. Suppose, for example, that you have a program that takes a name, an address, and a phone number and stores them in a file. This is certainly a simple program, much simpler than any whose correctness you'd really be worried about. Suppose further that each of the possible names and addresses is 20 characters long and that there are 26 possible characters to be used in them. This would be the number of possible inputs:

Name	26^{20} (20 characters, each with 26 possible choices)
Address	26^{20} (20 characters, each with 26 possible choices)
Phone Number	10^{10} (10 digits, each with 10 possible choices)
Total Possibilities	$= 26^{20} * 26^{20} * 10^{10} \approx 10^{66}$

Even with this relatively small amount of input, you have one-with-66-zeros possible test cases. To put this in perspective, if Noah had gotten off the ark and started testing this program at the rate of a trillion test cases per second, he would be far less than 1 percent of the way done today. Obviously, if you added a more realistic amount of data, the task of exhaustively testing all possibilities would become even more impossible.

Incomplete Testing

Cross-Reference One way of telling whether you've covered all the code is to use a coverage monitor. For details, see "Coverage Monitors" in Section 22.5, "Test-Support Tools," later in this chapter.

Since exhaustive testing is impossible, practically speaking, the art of testing is that of picking the test cases most likely to find errors. Of the 10^{66} possible test cases, only a few are likely to disclose errors that the others don't. You need to concentrate on picking a few that tell you different things rather than a set that tells you the same thing over and over.

When you're planning tests, eliminate those that don't tell you anything new—that is, tests on new data that probably won't produce an error if other, similar data didn't produce an error. Various people have proposed various methods of covering the bases efficiently, and several of these methods are discussed in the following sections.

Structured Basis Testing

In spite of the hairy name, structured basis testing is a fairly simple concept. The idea is that you need to test each statement in a program at least once. If the statement is a logical statement—an *if* or a *while*, for example—you need to vary the testing according to how complicated the expression inside the *if* or *while* is to make sure that the statement is fully tested. The easiest way to make sure that you've gotten all the bases covered is to calculate the number of paths through the program and then develop the minimum number of test cases that will exercise every path through the program.

You might have heard of "code coverage" testing or "logic coverage" testing. They are approaches in which you test all the paths through a program. Since they cover all paths, they're similar to structured basis testing, but they don't include the idea of covering all paths with a *minimal* set of test cases. If you use code coverage or logic coverage testing, you might create many more test cases than you would need to cover the same logic with structured basis testing.

Cross-Reference This procedure is similar to the one for measuring complexity in "How to Measure Complexity" in Section 19.6.

You can compute the minimum number of cases needed for basis testing in this straightforward way:

1. Start with 1 for the straight path through the routine.

2. Add 1 for each of the following keywords, or their equivalents: *if*, *while*, *repeat*, *for*, *and*, and *or*.

3. Add 1 for each case in a *case* statement. If the *case* statement doesn't have a default case, add 1 more.

Here's an example:

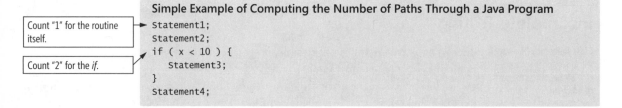

Simple Example of Computing the Number of Paths Through a Java Program

Count "1" for the routine itself.

Count "2" for the *if*.

```java
Statement1;
Statement2;
if ( x < 10 ) {
    Statement3;
}
Statement4;
```

In this instance, you start with one and count the *if* once to make a total of two. That means that you need to have at least two test cases to cover all the paths through the program. In this example, you'd need to have the following test cases:

- Statements controlled by *if* are executed (x < 10).

- Statements controlled by *if* aren't executed (x >= 10).

The sample code needs to be a little more realistic to give you an accurate idea of how this kind of testing works. Realism in this case includes code containing defects.

The following listing is a slightly more complicated example. This piece of code is used throughout the chapter and contains a few possible errors.

Example of Computing the Number of Cases Needed for Basis Testing of a Java Program

| Count "1" for the routine itself. |

```
1  // Compute Net Pay
2  totalWithholdings = 0;
3
4  for ( id = 0; id < numEmployees; id++ ) {
5
6     // compute social security withholding, if below the maximum
7     if ( m_employee[ id ].governmentRetirementWithheld < MAX_GOVT_RETIREMENT ) {
8        governmentRetirement = ComputeGovernmentRetirement( m_employee[ id ] );
9     }
10
11    // set default to no retirement contribution
12    companyRetirement = 0;
13
14    // determine discretionary employee retirement contribution
15    if ( m_employee[ id ].WantsRetirement &&
16       EligibleForRetirement( m_employee[ id ] ) ) {
17       companyRetirement = GetRetirement( m_employee[ id ] );
18    }
19
20    grossPay = ComputeGrossPay ( m_employee[ id ] );
21
22    // determine IRA contribution
23    personalRetirement = 0;
24    if ( EligibleForPersonalRetirement( m_employee[ id ] ) ) {
25       personalRetirement = PersonalRetirementContribution( m_employee[ id ],
26          companyRetirement, grossPay );
27    }
28
29    // make weekly paycheck
30    withholding = ComputeWithholding( m_employee[ id ] );
31    netPay = grossPay - withholding - companyRetirement - governmentRetirement -
32       personalRetirement;
33    PayEmployee( m_employee[ id ], netPay );
```

Annotations pointing to the code:
- Count "1" for the routine itself. → line 1
- Count "2" for the *for*. → line 4
- Count "3" for the *if*. → line 7
- Count "4" for the *if* and "5" for the *&&*. → line 15
- Count "6" for the *if*. → line 24

```
34
35    // add this employee's paycheck to total for accounting
36    totalWithholdings = totalWithholdings + withholding;
37    totalGovernmentRetirement = totalGovernmentRetirement + governmentRetirement;
38    totalRetirement = totalRetirement + companyRetirement;
39 }
40
41 SavePayRecords( totalWithholdings, totalGovernmentRetirement, totalRetirement );
```

In this example, you'll need one initial test case plus one for each of the five keywords, for a total of six. That doesn't mean that any six test cases will cover all the bases. It means that, at a minimum, six cases are required. Unless the cases are constructed carefully, they almost surely won't cover all the bases. The trick is to pay attention to the same keywords you used when counting the number of cases needed. Each keyword in the code represents something that can be either true or false; make sure you have at least one test case for each true and at least one for each false.

Here is a set of test cases that covers all the bases in this example:

Case	Test Description	Test Data
1	Nominal case	All boolean conditions are true
2	The initial *for* condition is false	*numEmployees < 1*
3	The first *if* is false	*m_employee[id].governmentRetirementWithheld >=MAX_GOVT_RETIREMENT*
4	The second *if* is false because the first part of the *and* is false	*not m_employee[id].WantsRetirement*
5	The second *if* is false because the second part of the *and* is false	*not EligibleForRetirement(m_employee[id])*
6	The third *if* is false	*not EligibleForPersonalRetirement(m_employee[id])*

Note: This table will be extended with additional test cases throughout the chapter.

If the routine were much more complicated than this, the number of test cases you'd have to use just to cover all the paths would increase pretty quickly. Shorter routines tend to have fewer paths to test. Boolean expressions without a lot of *and*s and *or*s have fewer variations to test. Ease of testing is another good reason to keep your routines short and your boolean expressions simple.

Now that you've created six test cases for the routine and satisfied the demands of structured basis testing, can you consider the routine to be fully tested? Probably not.

This kind of testing assures you only that all of the code will be executed. It does not account for variations in data.

Data-Flow Testing

Considering the last section and this one together gives you another example illustrating that control flow and data flow are equally important in computer programming.

Data-flow testing is based on the idea that data usage is at least as error-prone as control flow. Boris Beizer claims that at least half of all code consists of data declarations and initializations (Beizer 1990).

Data can exist in one of three states:

- **Defined**   The data has been initialized, but it hasn't been used yet.
- **Used** · The data has been used for computation, as an argument to a routine, or for something else.
- **Killed**   The data was once defined, but it has been undefined in some way. For example, if the data is a pointer, perhaps the pointer has been freed. If it's a for-loop index, perhaps the program is out of the loop and the programming language doesn't define the value of a for-loop index once it's outside the loop. If it's a pointer to a record in a file, maybe the file has been closed and the record pointer is no longer valid.

In addition to having the terms "defined," "used," and "killed," it's convenient to have terms that describe entering or exiting a routine immediately before or after doing something to a variable:

- **Entered**   The control flow enters the routine immediately before the variable is acted upon. A working variable is initialized at the top of a routine, for example.
- **Exited**   The control flow leaves the routine immediately after the variable is acted upon. A return value is assigned to a status variable at the end of a routine, for example.

Combinations of Data States

The normal combination of data states is that a variable is defined, used one or more times, and perhaps killed. View the following patterns suspiciously:

- **Defined-Defined**   If you have to define a variable twice before the value sticks, you don't need a better program, you need a better computer! It's wasteful and error-prone, even if not actually wrong.

- **Defined-Exited** If the variable is a local variable, it doesn't make sense to define it and exit without using it. If it's a routine parameter or a global variable, it might be all right.

- **Defined-Killed** Defining a variable and then killing it suggests that either the variable is extraneous or the code that was supposed to use the variable is missing.

- **Entered-Killed** This is a problem if the variable is a local variable. It wouldn't need to be killed if it hasn't been defined or used. If, on the other hand, it's a routine parameter or a global variable, this pattern is all right as long as the variable is defined somewhere else before it's killed.

- **Entered-Used** Again, this is a problem if the variable is a local variable. The variable needs to be defined before it's used. If, on the other hand, it's a routine parameter or a global variable, the pattern is all right if the variable is defined somewhere else before it's used.

- **Killed-Killed** A variable shouldn't need to be killed twice. Variables don't come back to life. A resurrected variable indicates sloppy programming. Double kills are also fatal for pointers—one of the best ways to hang your machine is to kill (free) a pointer twice.

- **Killed-Used** Using a variable after it has been killed is a logical error. If the code seems to work anyway (for example, a pointer that still points to memory that's been freed), that's an accident, and Murphy's Law says that the code will stop working at the time when it will cause the most mayhem.

- **Used-Defined** Using and then defining a variable might or might not be a problem, depending on whether the variable was also defined before it was used. Certainly if you see a used-defined pattern, it's worthwhile to check for a previous definition.

Check for these anomalous sequences of data states before testing begins. After you've checked for the anomalous sequences, the key to writing data-flow test cases is to exercise all possible defined-used paths. You can do this to various degrees of thoroughness, including

- All definitions. Test every definition of every variable—that is, every place at which any variable receives a value. This is a weak strategy because if you try to exercise every line of code, you'll do this by default.

- All defined-used combinations. Test every combination of defining a variable in one place and using it in another. This is a stronger strategy than testing all definitions because merely executing every line of code does not guarantee that every defined-used combination will be tested.

Here's an example:

Java Example of a Program Whose Data Flow Is to Be Tested

```java
if ( Condition 1 ) {
    x = a;
}
else {
    x = b;
}
if ( Condition 2 ) {
    y = x + 1;
}
else {
    y = x - 1;
}
```

To cover every path in the program, you need one test case in which *Condition 1* is true and one in which it's false. You also need a test case in which *Condition 2* is true and one in which it's false. This can be handled by two test cases: Case 1 (*Condition 1=True, Condition 2=True*) and Case 2 (*Condition 1=False, Condition 2=False*). Those two cases are all you need for structured basis testing. They're also all you need to exercise every line of code that defines a variable; they give you the weak form of data-flow testing automatically.

To cover every defined-used combination, however, you need to add a few more cases. Right now you have the cases created by having *Condition 1* and *Condition 2* true at the same time and *Condition 1* and *Condition 2* false at the same time:

```
x = a
...
y = x + 1
```

and

```
x = b
...
y = x - 1
```

But you need two more cases to test every defined-used combination: (1) *x = a* and then *y = x - 1* and (2) *x = b* and then *y = x + 1*. In this example, you can get these combinations by adding two more cases: Case 3 (*Condition 1=True, Condition 2=False*) and Case 4 (*Condition 1=False, Condition 2=True*).

A good way to develop test cases is to start with structured basis testing, which gives you some if not all of the defined-used data flows. Then add the cases you still need to have a complete set of defined-used data-flow test cases.

As discussed in the previous section, structured basis testing provided six test cases for the routine beginning on page 507. Data-flow testing of each defined-used pair requires several more test cases, some of which are covered by existing test cases and some of which aren't. Here are all the data-flow combinations that add test cases beyond the ones generated by structured basis testing:

Case	Test Description
7	Define *companyRetirement* in line 12, and use it first in line 26.
	This isn't necessarily covered by any of the previous test cases.
8	Define *companyRetirement* in line 12, and use it first in line 31.
	This isn't necessarily covered by any of the previous test cases.
9	Define *companyRetirement* in line 17, and use it first in line 31.
	This isn't necessarily covered by any of the previous test cases.

Once you run through the process of listing data-flow test cases a few times, you'll get a sense of which cases are fruitful and which are already covered. When you get stuck, list all the defined-used combinations. That might seem like a lot of work, but it's guaranteed to show you any cases that you didn't test for free in the basis-testing approach.

Equivalence Partitioning

Cross-Reference Equivalence partitioning is discussed in far more depth in the books listed in the "Additional Resources" section at the end of this chapter.

A good test case covers a large part of the possible input data. If two test cases flush out exactly the same errors, you need only one of them. The concept of "equivalence partitioning" is a formalization of this idea and helps reduce the number of test cases required.

In the listing beginning on page 507, line 7 is a good place to use equivalence partitioning. The condition to be tested is *m_employee[ID].governmentRetirementWithheld < MAX_GOVT_RETIREMENT*. This case has two equivalence classes: the class in which *m_employee[ID].governmentRetirementWithheld* is less than *MAX_GOVT_RETIREMENT* and the class in which it's greater than or equal to *MAX_GOVT_RETIREMENT*. Other parts of the program might have other related equivalence classes that imply that you need to test more than two possible values of *m_employee[ID].government-RetirementWithheld*, but as far as this part of the program is concerned, only two are needed.

Thinking about equivalence partitioning won't give you a lot of new insight into a program when you have already covered the program with basis and data-flow testing. It's especially helpful, however, when you're looking at a program from the outside (from a specification rather than the source code) or when the data is complicated and the complications aren't all reflected in the program's logic.

Error Guessing

Cross-Reference For details on heuristics, see Section 2.2, "How to Use Software Metaphors."

In addition to the formal test techniques, good programmers use a variety of less formal, heuristic techniques to expose errors in their code. One heuristic is the technique of error guessing. The term "error guessing" is a lowbrow name for a sensible concept. It means creating test cases based upon guesses about where the program might have errors, although it implies a certain amount of sophistication in the guessing.

You can base guesses on intuition or on past experience. Chapter 21, "Collaborative Construction," points out that one virtue of inspections is that they produce and maintain a list of common errors. The list is used to check new code. When you keep records of the kinds of errors you've made before, you improve the likelihood that your "error guess" will discover an error.

The next few sections describe specific kinds of errors that lend themselves to error guessing.

Boundary Analysis

One of the most fruitful areas for testing is boundary conditions—off-by-one errors. Saying *num – 1* when you mean *num* and saying >= when you mean > are common mistakes.

The idea of boundary analysis is to write test cases that exercise the boundary conditions. Pictorially, if you're testing for a range of values that are less than *max*, you have three possible conditions:

As shown, there are three boundary cases: just less than *max*, *max* itself, and just greater than *max*. It takes three cases to ensure that none of the common mistakes has been made.

The code sample on page 507 contains a check for *m_employee[ID]*.governmentRetirementWithheld < *MAX_GOVT_RETIREMENT*. According to the principles of boundary analysis, three cases should be examined:

Case	Test Description
1	Case 1 is defined so that the true condition for *m_employee[ID].governmentRetirementWithheld < MAX_GOVT_RETIREMENT* is the first case on the true side of the boundary. Thus, the Case 1 test case sets *m_employee[ID].governmentRetirementWithheld* to *MAX_GOVT_RETIREMENT – 1*. This test case was already generated.

3	Case 3 is defined so that the false condition for *m_employee[ID]. governmentRetirementWithheld < MAX_GOVT_RETIREMENT* is on the false side of the boundary. Thus, the Case 3 test case sets *m_employee[ID].governmentRetirementWithheld* to *MAX_GOVT_RETIREMENT + 1*. This test case was also already generated.
10	An additional test case is added for the case directly on the boundary in which *m_employee [ID].governmentRetirementWithheld = MAX_GOVT_RETIREMENT*.

Compound Boundaries

Boundary analysis also applies to minimum and maximum allowable values. In this example, it might be minimum or maximum *grossPay*, *companyRetirement*, or *PersonalRetirementContribution*, but because calculations of those values are outside the scope of the routine, test cases for them aren't discussed further here.

A more subtle kind of boundary condition occurs when the boundary involves a combination of variables. For example, if two variables are multiplied together, what happens when both are large positive numbers? Large negative numbers? *0*? What if all the strings passed to a routine are uncommonly long?

In the running example, you might want to see what happens to the variables *totalWithholdings*, *totalGovernmentRetirement*, and *totalRetirement* when every member of a large group of employees has a large salary—say, a group of programmers at $250,000 each. (We can always hope!) This calls for another test case:

Case	Test Description
11	A large group of employees, each of whom has a large salary (what constitutes "large" depends on the specific system being developed)—for the sake of example, we'll say 1000 employees, each with a salary of $250,000, none of whom have had any social security tax withheld and all of whom want retirement withholding.

A test case in the same vein but on the opposite side of the looking glass would be a small group of employees, each of whom has a salary of $0.00:

Case	Test Description
12	A group of 10 employees, each of whom has a salary of $0.00.

Classes of Bad Data

Aside from guessing that errors show up around boundary conditions, you can guess about and test for several other classes of bad data. Typical bad-data test cases include

- Too little data (or no data)
- Too much data

- The wrong kind of data (invalid data)
- The wrong size of data
- Uninitialized data

Some of the test cases you would think of if you followed these suggestions have already been covered. For example, "too little data" is covered by Cases 2 and 12, and it's hard to come up with anything for "wrong size of data." Classes of bad data nonetheless gives rise to a few more cases:

Case	Test Description
13	An array of 100,000,000 employees. Tests for too much data. Of course, how much is too much would vary from system to system, but for the sake of the example, assume that this is far too much.
14	A negative salary. Wrong kind of data.
15	A negative number of employees. Wrong kind of data.

Classes of Good Data

When you try to find errors in a program, it's easy to overlook the fact that the nominal case might contain an error. Usually the nominal cases described in the basis-testing section represent one kind of good data. Following are other kinds of good data that are worth checking. Checking each of these kinds of data can reveal errors, depending on the item being tested.

- Nominal cases—middle-of-the-road, expected values
- Minimum normal configuration
- Maximum normal configuration
- Compatibility with old data

The minimum normal configuration is useful for testing not just one item, but a group of items. It's similar in spirit to the boundary condition of many minimal values, but it's different in that it creates the set of minimum values out of the set of what is normally expected. One example would be to save an empty spreadsheet when testing a spreadsheet. For testing a word processor, it would be saving an empty document. In the case of the running example, testing the minimum normal configuration would add the following test case:

Case	Test Description
16	A group of one employee. To test the minimum normal configuration.

The maximum normal configuration is the opposite of the minimum. It's similar in spirit to boundary testing, but again, it creates a set of maximum values out of the set of expected values. An example of this would be saving a spreadsheet that's as large as the "maximum spreadsheet size" advertised on the product's packaging. Or printing the maximum-size spreadsheet. For a word processor, it would be saving a document of the largest recommended size. In the case of the running example, testing the maximum normal configuration depends on the maximum normal number of employees. Assuming it's 500, you would add the following test case:

Case	Test Description
17	A group of 500 employees. To test the maximum normal configuration.

The last kind of normal data testing—testing for compatibility with old data—comes into play when the program or routine is a replacement for an older program or routine. The new routine should produce the same results with old data that the old routine did, except in cases in which the old routine was defective. This kind of continuity between versions is the basis for regression testing, the purpose of which is to ensure that corrections and enhancements maintain previous levels of quality without backsliding. In the case of the running example, the compatibility criterion wouldn't add any test cases.

Use Test Cases That Make Hand-Checks Convenient

Let's suppose you're writing a test case for a nominal salary; you need a nominal salary, and the way you get one is to type in whatever numbers your hands land on. I'll try it:

1239078382346

OK. That's a pretty high salary, a little over a trillion dollars, in fact, but if I trim it so that it's somewhat realistic, I get *$90,783.82*.

Now, further suppose that the test case succeeds—that is, it finds an error. How do you know that it's found an error? Well, presumably, you know what the answer is and what it should be because you calculated the correct answer by hand. When you try to do hand-calculations with an ugly number like *$90,783.82*, however, you're as likely to make an error in the hand-calc as you are to discover one in your program. On the other hand, a nice, even number like *$20,000* makes number crunching a snap. The *0*s are easy to punch into the calculator, and multiplying by 2 is something most programmers can do without using their fingers and toes.

You might think that an ugly number like *$90,783.82* would be more likely to reveal errors, but it's no more likely to than any other number in its equivalence class.

22.4 Typical Errors

This section is dedicated to the proposition that you can test best when you know as much as possible about your enemy: errors.

Which Classes Contain the Most Errors?

KEY POINT

It's natural to assume that defects are distributed evenly throughout your source code. If you have an average of 10 defects per 1000 lines of code, you might assume that you'll have one defect in a class that contains 100 lines of code. This is a natural assumption, but it's wrong.

Capers Jones reported that a focused quality-improvement program at IBM identified 31 of 425 classes in the IMS system as error-prone. The 31 classes were repaired or completely redeveloped, and, in less than a year, customer-reported defects against IMS were reduced ten to one. Total maintenance costs were reduced by about 45 percent. Customer satisfaction improved from "unacceptable" to "good" (Jones 2000).

Most errors tend to be concentrated in a few highly defective routines. Here is the general relationship between errors and code:

HARD DATA

- Eighty percent of the errors are found in 20 percent of a project's classes or routines (Endres 1975, Gremillion 1984, Boehm 1987b, Shull et al 2002).

- Fifty percent of the errors are found in 5 percent of a project's classes (Jones 2000).

These relationships might not seem so important until you recognize a few corollaries. First, 20% of a project's routines contribute 80% of the cost of development (Boehm 1987b). That doesn't necessarily mean that the 20% that cost the most are the same as the 20% with the most defects, but it's pretty suggestive.

HARD DATA

Second, regardless of the exact proportion of the cost contributed by highly defective routines, highly defective routines are extremely expensive. In a classic study in the 1960s, IBM performed an analysis of its OS/360 operating system and found that errors were not distributed evenly across all routines but were concentrated into a few. Those error-prone routines were found to be "the most expensive entities in programming" (Jones 1986a). They contained as many as 50 defects per 1000 lines of code, and fixing them often cost 10 times what it took to develop the whole system. (The costs included customer support and in-the-field maintenance.)

Cross-Reference Another class of routines that tend to contain a lot of errors is the class of overly complex routines. For details on identifying and simplifying routines, see "General Guidelines for Reducing Complexity" in Section 19.6.

Third, the implication of expensive routines for development is clear. As the old expression goes, "time is money." The corollary is that "money is time," and if you can cut close to 80 percent of the cost by avoiding troublesome routines, you can cut a substantial amount of the schedule as well. This is a clear illustration of the General Principle of Software Quality: improving quality improves the development schedule and reduces development costs.

Fourth, the implication of avoiding troublesome routines for maintenance is equally clear. Maintenance activities should be focused on identifying, redesigning, and rewriting from the ground up those routines that have been identified as error-prone. In the IMS project mentioned earlier, productivity of IMS releases improved about 15 percent after replacement of the error-prone classes (Jones 2000).

Errors by Classification

Cross-Reference For a list of all the checklists in the book, see the list following the book's table of contents.

Several researchers have tried to classify errors by type and determine the extent to which each kind of error occurs. Every programmer has a list of errors that have been particularly troublesome: off-by-one errors, forgetting to reinitialize a loop variable, and so on. The checklists presented throughout the book provide more details.

Boris Beizer combined data from several studies, arriving at an exceptionally detailed error taxonomy (Beizer 1990). Following is a summary of his results:

25.18%	Structural
22.44%	Data
16.19%	Functionality as implemented
9.88%	Construction
8.98%	Integration
8.12%	Functional requirements
2.76%	Test definition or execution
1.74%	System, software architecture
4.71%	Unspecified

Beizer reported his results to a precise two decimal places, but the research into error types has generally been inconclusive. Different studies report wildly different kinds of errors, and studies that report on similar kinds of errors arrive at wildly different results, results that differ by 50% rather than by hundredths of a percentage point.

Given the wide variations in reports, combining results from multiple studies as Beizer has done probably doesn't produce meaningful data. But even if the data isn't conclusive, some of it is suggestive. Following are some of the suggestions that can be derived from the data:

HARD DATA

The scope of most errors is fairly limited   One study found that 85 percent of errors could be corrected without modifying more than one routine (Endres 1975).

Many errors are outside the domain of construction   Researchers conducting a series of 97 interviews found that the three most common sources of errors were thin application-domain knowledge, fluctuating and conflicting requirements, and communication and coordination breakdown (Curtis, Krasner, and Iscoe 1988).

If you see hoof prints, think horses—not zebras. The OS is probably not broken. And the database is probably just fine.
—*Andy Hunt and Dave Thomas*

Most construction errors are the programmers' fault   A pair of studies performed many years ago found that, of total errors reported, roughly 95% are caused by programmers, 2% by systems software (the compiler and the operating system), 2% by some other software, and 1% by the hardware (Brown and Sampson 1973, Ostrand and Weyuker 1984). Systems software and development tools are used by many more people today than they were in the 1970s and 1980s, and so my best guess is that, today, an even higher percentage of errors are the programmers' fault.

HARD DATA

Clerical errors (typos) are a surprisingly common source of problems   One study found that 36% of all construction errors were clerical mistakes (Weiss 1975). A 1987 study of almost 3 million lines of flight-dynamics software found that 18% of all errors were clerical (Card 1987). Another study found that 4% of all errors were spelling errors in messages (Endres 1975). In one of my programs, a colleague found several spelling errors simply by running all the strings from the executable file through a spelling checker. Attention to detail counts. If you doubt that, consider that three of the most expensive software errors of all time—costing $1.6 billion, $900 million, and $245 million—involved the change of a *single character* in a previously correct program (Weinberg 1983).

Misunderstanding the design is a recurring theme in studies of programmer errors
Beizer's compilation study, for what it's worth, found that 16% of the errors grew out of misinterpretations of the design (Beizer 1990). Another study found that 19% of the errors resulted from misunderstood design (Weiss 1975). It's worthwhile to take the time you need to understand the design thoroughly. Such time doesn't produce immediate dividends—you don't necessarily look like you're working—but it pays off over the life of the project.

Most errors are easy to fix   About 85% of errors can be fixed in less than a few hours. About 15% can be fixed in a few hours to a few days. And about 1% take longer (Weiss 1975, Ostrand and Weyuker 1984, Grady 1992). This result is supported by Barry Boehm's observation that about 20% of the errors take about 80% of the resources to fix (Boehm 1987b). Avoid as many of the hard errors as you can by doing requirements and design reviews upstream. Handle the numerous small errors as efficiently as you can.

It's a good idea to measure your own organization's experiences with errors   The diversity of results cited in this section indicates that people in different organizations have tremendously different experiences. That makes it hard to apply other organizations' experiences to yours. Some results go against common intuition; you might need to supplement your intuition with other tools. A good first step is to start measuring your development process so that you know where the problems are.

Proportion of Errors Resulting from Faulty Construction

If the data that classifies errors is inconclusive, so is much of the data that attributes errors to the various development activities. One certainty is that construction always results in a significant number of errors. Sometimes people argue that the errors caused by construction are cheaper to fix than the errors caused by requirements or design. Fixing individual construction errors might be cheaper, but the evidence doesn't support such a claim about the total cost.

Here are my conclusions:

HARD DATA

- On small projects, construction defects make up the vast bulk of all errors. In one study of coding errors on a small project (1000 lines of code), 75% of defects resulted from coding, compared to 10% from requirements and 15% from design (Jones 1986a). This error breakdown appears to be representative of many small projects.

- Construction defects account for at least 35% of all defects regardless of project size. Although the proportion of construction defects is smaller on large projects, they still account for at least 35% of all defects (Beizer 1990, Jones 2000). Some researchers have reported proportions in the 75% range even on very large projects (Grady 1987). In general, the better the application area is understood, the better the overall architecture is. Errors then tend to be concentrated in detailed design and coding (Basili and Perricone 1984).

- Construction errors, although cheaper to fix than requirements and design errors, are still expensive. A study of two very large projects at Hewlett-Packard found that the average construction defect cost 25–50% as much to fix as the average design error (Grady 1987). When the greater number of construction defects was figured into the overall equation, the total cost to fix construction defects was one to two times as much as the cost attributed to design defects.

Figure 22-2 provides a rough idea of the relationship between project size and the source of errors.

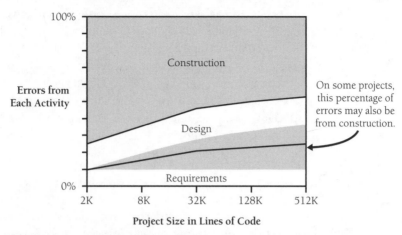

Project Size in Lines of Code

Figure 22-2 As the size of the project increases, the proportion of errors committed during construction decreases. Nevertheless, construction errors account for 45–75% of all errors on even the largest projects.

How Many Errors Should You Expect to Find?

The number of errors you should expect to find varies according to the quality of the development process you use. Here's the range of possibilities:

HARD DATA

- Industry average experience is about 1–25 errors per 1000 lines of code for delivered software. The software has usually been developed using a hodge-podge of techniques (Boehm 1981, Gremillion 1984, Yourdon 1989a, Jones 1998, Jones 2000, Weber 2003). Cases that have one-tenth as many errors as this are rare; cases that have 10 times more tend not to be reported. (They probably aren't ever completed!)

- The Applications Division at Microsoft experiences about 10–20 defects per 1000 lines of code during in-house testing and 0.5 defects per 1000 lines of code in released product (Moore 1992). The technique used to achieve this level is a combination of the code-reading techniques described in Section 21.4, "Other Kinds of Collaborative Development Practices," and independent testing.

- Harlan Mills pioneered "cleanroom development," a technique that has been able to achieve rates as low as 3 defects per 1000 lines of code during in-house testing and 0.1 defects per 1000 lines of code in released product (Cobb and Mills 1990). A few projects—for example, the space-shuttle software—have achieved a level of 0 defects in 500,000 lines of code by using a system of formal development methods, peer reviews, and statistical testing (Fishman 1996).

HARD DATA

- Watts Humphrey reports that teams using the Team Software Process (TSP) have achieved defect levels of about 0.06 defects per 1000 lines of code. TSP focuses on training developers not to create defects in the first place (Weber 2003).

The results of the TSP and cleanroom projects confirm another version of the General Principle of Software Quality: it's cheaper to build high-quality software than it is to build and fix low-quality software. Productivity for a fully checked-out, 80,000-line cleanroom project was 740 lines of code per work-month. The industry average rate for fully checked-out code is closer to 250–300 lines per work-month, including all noncoding overhead (Cusumano et al 2003). The cost savings and productivity come from the fact that virtually no time is devoted to debugging on TSP or cleanroom projects. No time spent on debugging? That is truly a worthy goal!

Errors in Testing Itself

KEY POINT

You may have had an experience like this: The software is found to be in error. You have a few immediate hunches about which part of the code might be wrong, but all that code seems to be correct. You run several more test cases to try to refine the error, but all the new test cases produce correct results. You spend several hours reading and rereading the code and hand-calculating the results. They all check out. After a few more hours, something causes you to reexamine the test data. Eureka! The error's in the test data! How idiotic it feels to waste hours tracking down an error in the test data rather than in the code!

HARD DATA

This is a common experience. Test cases are often as likely or more likely to contain errors than the code being tested (Weiland 1983, Jones 1986a, Johnson 1994). The reasons are easy to find—especially when the developer writes the test cases. Test cases tend to be created on the fly rather than through a careful design and construction process. They are often viewed as one-time tests and are developed with the care commensurate with something to be thrown away.

You can do several things to reduce the number of errors in your test cases:

Check your work   Develop test cases as carefully as you develop code. Such care certainly includes double-checking your own testing. Step through test code in a debugger, line by line, just as you would production code. Walk-throughs and inspections of test data are appropriate.

Plan test cases as you develop your software   Effective planning for testing should start at the requirements stage or as soon as you get the assignment for the program. This helps to avoid test cases based on mistaken assumptions.

Keep your test cases   Spend a little quality time with your test cases. Save them for regression testing and for work on version 2. It's easy to justify the trouble if you know you're going to keep them rather than throw them away.

Plug unit tests into a test framework   Write code for unit tests first, but integrate them into a systemwide test framework (like JUnit) as you complete each test. Having an integrated test framework prevents the tendency, just mentioned, to throw away test cases.

22.5 Test-Support Tools

This section surveys the kinds of testing tools you can buy commercially or build yourself. It won't name specific products because they could easily be out of date by the time you read this. Refer to your favorite programmer's magazine for the most recent specifics.

Building Scaffolding to Test Individual Classes

The term "scaffolding" comes from building construction. Scaffolding is built so that workers can reach parts of a building they couldn't reach otherwise. Software scaffolding is built for the sole purpose of making it easy to exercise code.

Further Reading For several good examples of scaffolding, see Jon Bentley's essay "A Small Matter of Programming" in *Programming Pearls*, 2d ed. (2000).

One kind of scaffolding is a class that's dummied up so that it can be used by another class that's being tested. Such a class is called a "mock object" or "stub object" (Mackinnon, Freemand, and Craig 2000; Thomas and Hunt 2002). A similar approach can be used with low-level routines, which are called "stub routines." You can make a mock object or stub routines more or less realistic, depending on how much veracity you need. In these cases, the scaffolding can

- Return control immediately, having taken no action.

- Test the data fed to it.

- Print a diagnostic message, perhaps an echo of the input parameters, or log a message to a file.

- Get return values from interactive input.

- Return a standard answer regardless of the input.

- Burn up the number of clock cycles allocated to the real object or routine.

- Function as a slow, fat, simple, or less accurate version of the real object or routine.

Another kind of scaffolding is a fake routine that calls the real routine being tested. This is called a "driver" or, sometimes, a "test harness." This scaffolding can

- Call the object with a fixed set of inputs.

- Prompt for input interactively and call the object with it.

- Take arguments from the command line (in operating systems that support it) and call the object.

- Read arguments from a file and call the object.

- Run through predefined sets of input data in multiple calls to the object.

Cross-Reference The line between testing tools and debugging tools is fuzzy. For details on debugging tools, see Section 23.5, "Debugging Tools—Obvious and Not-So-Obvious."

A final kind of scaffolding is the dummy file, a small version of the real thing that has the same types of components that a full-size file has. A small dummy file offers a couple of advantages. Because it's small, you can know its exact contents and can be reasonably sure that the file itself is error-free. And because you create it specifically for testing, you can design its contents so that any error in using it is conspicuous.

cc2e.com/2268

Obviously, building scaffolding requires some work, but if an error is ever detected in a class, you can reuse the scaffolding. And numerous tools exist to streamline creation of mock objects and other scaffolding. If you use scaffolding, the class can also be tested without the risk of its being affected by interactions with other classes. Scaffolding is particularly useful when subtle algorithms are involved. It's easy to get stuck in a rut in which it takes several minutes to execute each test case because the code being exercised is embedded in other code. Scaffolding allows you to exercise the code directly. The few minutes that you spend building scaffolding to exercise the deeply buried code can save hours of debugging time.

You can use any of the numerous test frameworks available to provide scaffolding for your programs (JUnit, CppUnit, NUnit, and so on). If your environment isn't supported by one of the existing test frameworks, you can write a few routines in a class and include a *main()* scaffolding routine in the file to test the class, even though the routines being tested aren't intended to stand by themselves. The *main()* routine can read arguments from the command line and pass them to the routine being tested so that you can exercise the routine on its own before integrating it with the rest of the program. When you integrate the code, leave the routines and the scaffolding code that exercises them in the file and use preprocessor commands or comments to deactivate the scaffolding code. Since it's preprocessed out, it doesn't affect the executable code, and since it's at the bottom of the file, it's not in the way visually. No harm is done by leaving it in. It's there if you need it again, and it doesn't burn up the time it would take to remove and archive it.

Diff Tools

Cross-Reference For details on regression testing, see "Retesting (Regression Testing)" in Section 22.6.

Regression testing, or retesting, is a lot easier if you have automated tools to check the actual output against the expected output. One easy way to check printed output is to redirect the output to a file and use a file-comparison tool such as diff to compare the new output against the expected output that was sent to a file previously. If the outputs aren't the same, you have detected a regression error.

Test-Data Generators

cc2e.com/2275

You can also write code to exercise selected pieces of a program systematically. A few years ago, I developed a proprietary encryption algorithm and wrote a file-encryption program to use it. The intent of the program was to encode a file so that it could be decoded only with the right password. The encryption didn't just change the file superficially; it altered the entire contents. It was critical that the program be able to decode a file properly, because the file would be ruined otherwise.

I set up a test-data generator that fully exercised the encryption and decryption parts of the program. It generated files of random characters in random sizes, from 0K through 500K. It generated passwords of random characters in random lengths from 1 through 255. For each random case, it generated two copies of the random file, encrypted one copy, reinitialized itself, decrypted the copy, and then compared each byte in the decrypted copy to the unaltered copy. If any bytes were different, the generator printed all the information I needed to reproduce the error.

I weighted the test cases toward the average length of my files, 30K, which was considerably shorter than the maximum length of 500K. If I had not weighted the test cases toward a shorter length, file lengths would have been uniformly distributed between 0K and 500K. The average tested file length would have been 250K. The shorter average length meant that I could test more files, passwords, end-of-file conditions, odd file lengths, and other circumstances that might produce errors than I could have with uniformly random lengths.

The results were gratifying. After running only about 100 test cases, I found two errors in the program. Both arose from special cases that might never have shown up in practice, but they were errors nonetheless and I was glad to find them. After fixing them, I ran the program for weeks, encrypting and decrypting over 100,000 files without an error. Given the range in file contents, lengths, and passwords I tested, I could confidently assert that the program was correct.

Here are some lessons from this story:

- Properly designed random-data generators can generate unusual combinations of test data that you wouldn't think of.

- Random-data generators can exercise your program more thoroughly than you can.

- You can refine randomly generated test cases over time so that they emphasize a realistic range of input. This concentrates testing in the areas most likely to be exercised by users, maximizing reliability in those areas.

- Modular design pays off during testing. I was able to pull out the encryption and decryption code and use it independently of the user-interface code, making the job of writing a test driver straightforward.

- You can reuse a test driver if the code it tests ever has to be changed. Once I had corrected the two early errors, I was able to start retesting immediately.

Coverage Monitors

cc2e.com/2282

HARD DATA

Karl Wiegers reports that testing done without measuring code coverage typically exercises only about 50–60% of the code (Wiegers 2002). A coverage monitor is a tool that keeps track of the code that's exercised and the code that isn't. A coverage monitor is especially useful for systematic testing because it tells you whether a set of test cases fully exercises the code. If you run your full set of test cases and the coverage monitor indicates that some code still hasn't been executed, you know that you need more tests.

Data Recorder/Logging

Some tools can monitor your program and collect information on the program's state in the event of a failure—similar to the "black box" that airplanes use to diagnose crash results. Strong logging aids error diagnosis and supports effective service after the software has been released.

You can build your own data recorder by logging significant events to a file. Record the system state prior to an error and details of the exact error conditions. This functionality can be compiled into the development version of the code and compiled out of the released version. Alternatively, if you implement logging with self-pruning storage and thoughtful placement and content of error messages, you can include logging functions in release versions.

Symbolic Debuggers

Cross-Reference The availability of debuggers varies according to the maturity of the technology environment. For more on this phenomenon, see Section 4.3, "Your Location on the Technology Wave."

A symbolic debugger is a technological supplement to code walk-throughs and inspections. A debugger has the capacity to step through code line by line, keep track of variables' values, and always interpret the code the same way the computer does. The process of stepping through a piece of code in a debugger and watching it work is enormously valuable.

Walking through code in a debugger is in many respects the same process as having other programmers step through your code in a review. Neither your peers nor the debugger has the same blind spots that you do. The additional benefit with a debugger is that it's less labor-intensive than a team review. Watching your code execute under a variety of input-data sets is good assurance that you've implemented the code you intended to.

A good debugger is even a good tool for learning about your language because you can see exactly how the code executes. You can toggle back and forth between a view of your high-level language code and a view of the assembler code to see how the high-level code is translated into assembler. You can watch registers and the stack to see how arguments are passed. You can look at code your compiler has optimized to see the kinds of optimizations that are performed. None of these benefits has much to do with the debugger's intended use—diagnosing errors that have already been detected—but imaginative use of a debugger produces benefits far beyond its initial charter.

System Perturbers

cc2e.com/2289

Another class of test-support tools are designed to perturb a system. Many people have stories of programs that work 99 times out of 100 but fail on the hundredth run-through with the same data. The problem is nearly always a failure to initialize a variable somewhere, and it's usually hard to reproduce because 99 times out of 100 the uninitialized variable happens to be 0.

Test-support tools in this class have a variety of capabilities:

- **Memory filling**   You want to be sure you don't have any uninitialized variables. Some tools fill memory with arbitrary values before you run your program so that uninitialized variables aren't set to 0 accidentally. In some cases, the memory might be set to a specific value. For example, on the x86 processor, the value 0xCC is the machine-language code for a breakpoint interrupt. If you fill memory with 0xCC and have an error that causes you to execute something you shouldn't, you'll hit a breakpoint in the debugger and detect the error.

- **Memory shaking**   In multitasking systems, some tools can rearrange memory as your program operates so that you can be sure you haven't written any code that depends on data being in absolute rather than relative locations.

- **Selective memory failing**   A memory driver can simulate low-memory conditions in which a program might be running out of memory, fail on a memory request, grant an arbitrary number of memory requests before failing, or fail on an arbitrary number of requests before granting one. This is especially useful for testing complicated programs that work with dynamically allocated memory.

- **Memory-access checking (bounds checking)**   Bounds checkers watch pointer operations to make sure your pointers behave themselves. Such a tool is useful for detecting uninitialized or dangling pointers.

Error Databases

cc2e.com/2296

One powerful test tool is a database of errors that have been reported. Such a database is both a management and a technical tool. It allows you to check for recurring errors, track the rate at which new errors are being detected and corrected, and track the status of open and closed errors and their severity. For details on what information you should keep in an error database, see Section 22.7, "Keeping Test Records."

22.6 Improving Your Testing

The steps for improving your testing are similar to the steps for improving any other process. You have to know exactly what the process does so that you can vary it slightly and observe the effects of the variation. When you observe a change that has a positive effect, you modify the process so that it becomes a little better. The following sections describe how to do this with testing.

Planning to Test

Cross-Reference Part of planning to test is formalizing your plans in writing. To find further information on test documentation, refer to the "Additional Resources" section at the end of Chapter 32.

One key to effective testing is planning from the beginning of the project to test. Putting testing on the same level of importance as design or coding means that time will be allocated to it, it will be viewed as important, and it will be a high-quality process. Test planning is also an element of making the testing process *repeatable*. If you can't repeat it, you can't improve it.

Retesting (Regression Testing)

Suppose that you've tested a product thoroughly and found no errors. Suppose that the product is then changed in one area and you want to be sure that it still passes all the tests it did before the change—that the change didn't introduce any new defects. Testing designed to make sure the software hasn't taken a step backward, or "regressed," is called "regression testing."

It's nearly impossible to produce a high-quality software product unless you can systematically retest it after changes have been made. If you run different tests after each change, you have no way of knowing for sure that no new defects have been introduced. Consequently, regression testing must run the same tests each time. Sometimes new tests are added as the product matures, but the old tests are kept too.

Automated Testing

KEY POINT

The only practical way to manage regression testing is to automate it. People become numbed from running the same tests many times and seeing the same test results many times. It becomes too easy to overlook errors, which defeats the purpose of regression testing. Test guru Boriz Beizer reports that the error rate in manual testing is comparable to the bug rate in the code being tested. He estimates that in manual testing, only about half of all the tests are executed properly (Johnson 1994).

Benefits of test automation include the following:

- An automated test has a lower chance of being wrong than a manual test.

- Once you automate a test, it's readily available for the rest of the project with little incremental effort on your part.

- If tests are automated, they can be run frequently to see whether any code check-ins have broken the code. Test automation is part of the foundation of test-intensive practices, such as the daily build and smoke test and Extreme Programming.

- Automated tests improve your chances of detecting any given problem at the earliest possible moment, which tends to minimize the work needed to diagnose and correct the problem.

- Automated tests provide a safety net for large-scale code changes because they increase your chance of quickly detecting defects inserted during the modifications.

Cross-Reference For more on the relationship between technology maturity and development practices, see Section 4.3, "Your Location on the Technology Wave."

- Automated tests are especially useful in new, volatile technology environments because they flush out changes in the environments sooner rather than later.

The main tools used to support automated testing provide test scaffolding, generate input, capture output, and compare actual output with expected output. The variety of tools discussed in the preceding section will perform some or all of these functions.

22.7 Keeping Test Records

KEY POINT

Aside from making the testing process repeatable, you need to measure the project so that you can tell for sure whether changes improve or degrade it. Here are a few kinds of data you can collect to measure your project:

- Administrative description of the defect (the date reported, the person who reported it, a title or description, the build number, the date fixed)

- Full description of the problem

- Steps to take to repeat the problem

- Suggested workaround for the problem

- Related defects

- Severity of the problem—for example, fatal, bothersome, or cosmetic

- Origin of the defect: requirements, design, coding, or testing

- Subclassification of a coding defect: off-by-one, bad assignment, bad array index, bad routine call, and so on

- Classes and routines changed by the fix

- Number of lines of code affected by the defect

- Hours to find the defect

- Hours to fix the defect

Once you collect the data, you can crunch a few numbers to determine whether your project is getting sicker or healthier:

- Number of defects in each class, sorted from worst class to best, possibly normalized by class size

- Number of defects in each routine, sorted from worst routine to best, possibly normalized by routine size

- Average number of testing hours per defect found

- Average number of defects found per test case

- Average number of programming hours per defect fixed

- Percentage of code covered by test cases

- Number of outstanding defects in each severity classification

Personal Test Records

In addition to project-level test records, you might find it useful to keep track of your personal test records. These records can include both a checklist of the errors you most commonly make as well as a record of the amount of time you spend writing code, testing code, and correcting errors.

Additional Resources

cc2e.com/2203   Federal truth-in-advising statutes compel me to disclose that several other books cover testing in more depth than this chapter does. Books that are devoted to testing discuss system and black-box testing, which haven't been discussed in this chapter. They also go into more depth on developer topics. They discuss formal approaches such as cause-effect graphing and the ins and outs of establishing an independent test organization.

Testing

Kaner, Cem, Jack Falk, and Hung Q. Nguyen. *Testing Computer Software*, 2d ed. New York, NY: John Wiley & Sons, 1999. This is probably the best current book on software testing. It is most applicable to testing applications that will be distributed to a widespread customer base, such as high-volume websites and shrink-wrap applications, but it is also generally useful.

Kaner, Cem, James Bach, and Bret Pettichord. *Lessons Learned in Software Testing*. New York, NY: John Wiley & Sons, 2002. This book is a good supplement to *Testing Computer Software*, 2d ed. It's organized into 11 chapters that enumerate 250 lessons learned by the authors.

Tamre, Louise. *Introducing Software Testing*. Boston, MA: Addison-Wesley, 2002. This is an accessible testing book targeted at developers who need to understand testing. Belying the title, the book goes into some depth on testing details that are useful even to experienced testers.

Whittaker, James A. *How to Break Software: A Practical Guide to Testing*. Boston, MA: Addison-Wesley, 2002. This book lists 23 attacks testers can use to make software fail and presents examples for each attack using popular software packages. You can use this book as a primary source of information about testing or, because its approach is distinctive, you can use it to supplement other testing books.

Whittaker, James A. "What Is Software Testing? And Why Is It So Hard?" *IEEE Software*, January 2000, pp. 70–79. This article is a good introduction to software testing issues and explains some of the challenges associated with effectively testing software.

Myers, Glenford J. *The Art of Software Testing*. New York, NY: John Wiley, 1979. This is the classic book on software testing and is still in print (though quite expensive). The contents of the book are straightforward: A Self-Assessment Test; The Psychology and Economics of Program Testing; Program Inspections, Walkthroughs, and Reviews; Test-Case Design; Class Testing; Higher-Order Testing; Debugging; Test Tools and Other Techniques. It's short (177 pages) and readable. The quiz at the beginning gets you started thinking like a tester and demonstrates how many ways a piece of code can be broken.

Test Scaffolding

Bentley, Jon. "A Small Matter of Programming" in *Programming Pearls*, 2d ed. Boston, MA: Addison-Wesley, 2000. This essay includes several good examples of test scaffolding.

Mackinnon, Tim, Steve Freeman, and Philip Craig. "Endo-Testing: Unit Testing with Mock Objects," *eXtreme Programming and Flexible Processes Software Engineering - XP2000" Conference*, 2000. This is the original paper to discuss the use of mock objects to support developer testing.

Thomas, Dave and Andy Hunt. "Mock Objects," *IEEE Software*, May/June 2002. This is a highly readable introduction to using mock objects to support developer testing.

cc2e.com/2217   *www.junit.org*. This site provides support for developers using JUnit. Similar resources are provided at *cppunit.sourceforge.net* and *nunit.sourceforge.net*.

Test First Development

Beck, Kent. *Test-Driven Development: By Example*. Boston, MA: Addison-Wesley, 2003. Beck describes the ins and outs of "test-driven development," a development approach that's characterized by writing test cases first and then writing the code to satisfy the test cases. Despite Beck's sometimes-evangelical tone, the advice is sound, and the book is short and to the point. The book has an extensive running example with real code.

Relevant Standards

IEEE Std 1008-1987 (R1993), Standard for Software Unit Testing

IEEE Std 829-1998, Standard for Software Test Documentation

IEEE Std 730-2002, Standard for Software Quality Assurance Plans

cc2e.com/2210

CHECKLIST: Test Cases

❑ Does each requirement that applies to the class or routine have its own test case?

❑ Does each element from the design that applies to the class or routine have its own test case?

❑ Has each line of code been tested with at least one test case? Has this been verified by computing the minimum number of tests necessary to exercise each line of code?

❑ Have all defined-used data-flow paths been tested with at least one test case?

❑ Has the code been checked for data-flow patterns that are unlikely to be correct, such as defined-defined, defined-exited, and defined-killed?

❑ Has a list of common errors been used to write test cases to detect errors that have occurred frequently in the past?

❑ Have all simple boundaries been tested: maximum, minimum, and off-by-one boundaries?

❑ Have compound boundaries been tested—that is, combinations of input data that might result in a computed variable that's too small or too large?

❑ Do test cases check for the wrong kind of data—for example, a negative number of employees in a payroll program?

❑ Are representative, middle-of-the-road values tested?

❑ Is the minimum normal configuration tested?

❑ Is the maximum normal configuration tested?

❑ Is compatibility with old data tested? And are old hardware, old versions of the operating system, and interfaces with old versions of other software tested?

❑ Do the test cases make hand-checks easy?

Key Points

- Testing by the developer is a key part of a full testing strategy. Independent testing is also important but is outside the scope of this book.

- Writing test cases before the code takes the same amount of time and effort as writing the test cases after the code, but it shortens defect-detection-debug-correction cycles.

- Even considering the numerous kinds of testing available, testing is only one part of a good software-quality program. High-quality development methods, including minimizing defects in requirements and design, are at least as important. Collaborative development practices are also at least as effective at detecting errors as testing, and these practices detect different kinds of errors.

- You can generate many test cases deterministically by using basis testing, data-flow analysis, boundary analysis, classes of bad data, and classes of good data. You can generate additional test cases with error guessing.

- Errors tend to cluster in a few error-prone classes and routines. Find that error-prone code, redesign it, and rewrite it.

- Test data tends to have a higher error density than the code being tested. Because hunting for such errors wastes time without improving the code, test-data errors are more aggravating than programming errors. Avoid them by developing your tests as carefully as your code.

- Automated testing is useful in general and is essential for regression testing.

- In the long run, the best way to improve your testing process is to make it regular, measure it, and use what you learn to improve it.

Chapter 23
Debugging

cc2e.com/2361

Contents

- 23.1 Overview of Debugging Issues: page 535
- 23.2 Finding a Defect: page 540
- 23.3 Fixing a Defect: page 550
- 23.4 Psychological Considerations in Debugging: page 554
- 23.5 Debugging Tools—Obvious and Not-So-Obvious: page 556

Related Topics

- The software-quality landscape: Chapter 20
- Developer testing: Chapter 22
- Refactoring: Chapter 24

> Debugging is twice as hard as writing the code in the first place. Therefore, if you write the code as cleverly as possible, you are, by definition, not smart enough to debug it.
> —Brian W. Kernighan

Debugging is the process of identifying the root cause of an error and correcting it. It contrasts with testing, which is the process of detecting the error initially. On some projects, debugging occupies as much as 50 percent of the total development time. For many programmers, debugging is the hardest part of programming.

Debugging doesn't have to be the hardest part. If you follow the advice in this book, you'll have fewer errors to debug. Most of the defects you'll have will be minor oversights and typos, easily found by looking at a source-code listing or stepping through the code in a debugger. For the remaining harder bugs, this chapter describes how to make debugging much easier than it usually is.

23.1 Overview of Debugging Issues

The late Rear Admiral Grace Hopper, co-inventor of COBOL, always said that the word "bug" in software dated back to the first large-scale digital computer, the Mark I (IEEE 1992). Programmers traced a circuit malfunction to the presence of a large moth that had found its way into the computer, and from that time on, computer problems were blamed on "bugs." Outside software, the word "bug" dates back at least to Thomas Edison, who is quoted as using it as early as 1878 (Tenner 1997).

The word "bug" is a cute word and conjures up images like this one:

The reality of software defects, however, is that bugs aren't organisms that sneak into your code when you forget to spray it with pesticide. They are errors. A bug in software means that a programmer made a mistake. The result of the mistake isn't like the cute picture shown above. It's more likely a note like this one:

In the context of this book, technical accuracy requires that mistakes in the code be called "errors," "defects," or "faults."

Role of Debugging in Software Quality

Like testing, debugging isn't a way to improve the quality of your software per se; it's a way to diagnose defects. Software quality must be built in from the start. The best way to build a quality product is to develop requirements carefully, design well, and use high-quality coding practices. Debugging is a last resort.

Variations in Debugging Performance

Why talk about debugging? Doesn't everyone know how to debug?

KEY POINT

No, not everyone knows how to debug. Studies of experienced programmers have found roughly a 20-to-1 difference in the time it takes experienced programmers to find the same set of defects found by by inexperienced programmers. Moreover, some programmers find more defects and make corrections more accurately. Here are the results of a classic study that examined how effectively professional programmers with at least four years of experience debugged a program with 12 defects:

	Fastest Three Programmers	Slowest Three Programmers
Average debug time (minutes)	5.0	14.1
Average number of defects not found	0.7	1.7
Average number of defects made correcting defects	3.0	7.7

Source: "Some Psychological Evidence on How People Debug Computer Programs" (Gould 1975)

HARD DATA

The three programmers who were best at debugging were able to find the defects in about one-third the time and inserted only about two-fifths as many new defects as the three who were the worst. The best programmer found all the defects and didn't insert any new defects in correcting them. The worst missed 4 of the 12 defects and inserted 11 new defects in correcting the 8 defects he found.

But this study doesn't really tell the whole story. After the first round of debugging, the fastest three programmers still have 3.7 defects left in their code and the slowest still have 9.4 defects. Neither group is done debugging yet. I wondered what would happen if I applied the same find-and-bad-fix ratios to additional debugging cycles. My results aren't statistically valid, but they're still interesting. When I applied the same find-and-bad-fix ratios to successive debugging cycles until each group had less than half a defect remaining, the fastest group required a total of three debugging cycles, whereas the slowest group required 14 debugging cycles. Bearing in mind that each cycle of the slower group takes almost three times as long as each cycle of the fastest group, the slowest group would take about 13 times as long to fully debug its programs as the fastest group, according to my nonscientific extrapolation of this study. This wide variation has been confirmed by other studies (Gilb 1977, Curtis 1981).

Cross-Reference For details on the relationship between quality and cost, see Section 20.5, "The General Principle of Software Quality."
In addition to providing insight into debugging, the evidence supports the General Principle of Software Quality: improving quality reduces development costs. The best programmers found the most defects, found the defects most quickly, and made correct modifications most often. You don't have to choose between quality, cost, and time—they all go hand in hand.

Defects as Opportunities

What does having a defect mean? Assuming that you don't want the program to have a defect, it means that you don't fully understand what the program does. The idea of not understanding what the program does is unsettling. After all, if you created the program, it should do your bidding. If you don't know exactly what you're telling the computer to do, you're only a small step away from merely trying different things until something seems to work—that is, programming by trial and error. And if you're programming by trial and error, defects are guaranteed. You don't need to learn how to fix defects; you need to learn how to avoid them in the first place.

Most people are somewhat fallible, however, and you might be an excellent programmer who has simply made a modest oversight. If this is the case, an error in your program provides a powerful opportunity for you to learn many things. You can:

Learn about the program you're working on You have something to learn about the program because if you already knew it perfectly, it wouldn't have a defect. You would have corrected it already.

Further Reading For details on practices that will help you learn about the kinds of errors you are personally prone to, see *A Discipline for Software Engineering* (Humphrey 1995).

Learn about the kinds of mistakes you make If you wrote the program, you inserted the defect. It's not every day that a spotlight exposes a weakness with glaring clarity, but such a day is an opportunity, so take advantage of it. Once you find the mistake, ask yourself how and why you made it. How could you have found it more quickly? How could you have prevented it? Does the code have other mistakes just like it? Can you correct them before they cause problems of their own?

Learn about the quality of your code from the point of view of someone who has to read it You'll have to read your code to find the defect. This is an opportunity to look critically at the quality of your code. Is it easy to read? How could it be better? Use your discoveries to refactor your current code or to improve the code you write next.

Learn about how you solve problems Does your approach to solving debugging problems give you confidence? Does your approach work? Do you find defects quickly? Or is your approach to debugging weak? Do you feel anguish and frustration? Do you guess randomly? Do you need to improve? Considering the amount of time many projects spend on debugging, you definitely won't waste time if you observe how you debug. Taking time to analyze and change the way you debug might be the quickest way to decrease the total amount of time it takes you to develop a program.

Learn about how you fix defects In addition to learning how you find defects, you can learn about how you fix them. Do you make the easiest possible correction by applying *goto* bandages and special-case makeup that changes the symptom but not the problem? Or do you make systemic corrections, demanding an accurate diagnosis and prescribing treatment for the heart of the problem?

All things considered, debugging is an extraordinarily rich soil in which to plant the seeds of your own improvement. It's where all construction roads cross: readability, design, code quality—you name it. This is where building good code pays off, especially if you do it well enough that you don't have to debug very often.

An Ineffective Approach

Unfortunately, programming classes in colleges and universities hardly ever offer instruction in debugging. If you studied programming in college, you might have had a lecture devoted to debugging. Although my computer-science education was excellent, the extent of the debugging advice I received was to "put print statements in the program to find the defect." This is not adequate. If other programmers' educational experiences are like mine, a great many programmers are being forced to reinvent debugging concepts on their own. What a waste!

The Devil's Guide to Debugging

Programmers do not always use available data to constrain their reasoning. They carry out minor and irrational repairs, and they often don't undo the *incorrect* repairs.
—*Iris Vessey*

In Dante's vision of hell, the lowest circle is reserved for Satan himself. In modern times, Old Scratch has agreed to share the lowest circle with programmers who don't learn to debug effectively. He tortures programmers by making them use these common debugging approaches:

Find the defect by guessing   To find the defect, scatter print statements randomly throughout a program. Examine the output to see where the defect is. If you can't find the defect with print statements, try changing things in the program until something seems to work. Don't back up the original version of the program, and don't keep a record of the changes you've made. Programming is more exciting when you're not quite sure what the program is doing. Stock up on cola and candy because you're in for a long night in front of the terminal.

Don't waste time trying to understand the problem   It's likely that the problem is trivial, and you don't need to understand it completely to fix it. Simply finding it is enough.

Fix the error with the most obvious fix   It's usually good just to fix the specific problem you see, rather than wasting a lot of time making some big, ambitious correction that's going to affect the whole program. This is a perfect example:

```
x = Compute( y )
if ( y = 17 )
   x = $25.15        -- Compute() doesn't work for y = 17, so fix it
```

Who needs to dig all the way into *Compute()* for an obscure problem with the value of *17* when you can just write a special case for it in the obvious place?

Debugging by Superstition

Satan has leased part of hell to programmers who debug by superstition. Every group has one programmer who has endless problems with demon machines, mysterious compiler defects, hidden language defects that appear when the moon is full, bad data, losing important changes, a possessed editor that saves programs incorrectly—you name it. This is "programming by superstition."

If you have a problem with a program you've written, it's your fault. It's not the computer's fault, and it's not the compiler's fault. The program doesn't do something different every time. It didn't write itself; you wrote it, so take responsibility for it.

KEY POINT

Even if an error at first appears not to be your fault, it's strongly in your interest to assume that it is. That assumption helps you debug. It's hard enough to find a defect in your code when you're looking for it; it's even harder when you assume your code is error-free. Assuming the error is your fault also improves your credibility. If you claim that an error arose from someone else's code, other programmers will believe that you have checked out the problem carefully. If you assume the error is yours, you avoid the embarrassment of having to recant publicly later when you find out that it was your defect after all.

23.2 Finding a Defect

Debugging consists of finding the defect and fixing it. Finding the defect—and understanding it—is usually 90 percent of the work.

Fortunately, you don't have to make a pact with Satan to find an approach to debugging that's better than random guessing. Debugging by thinking about the problem is much more effective and interesting than debugging with an eye of a newt and the dust of a frog's ear.

Suppose you were asked to solve a murder mystery. Which would be more interesting: going door to door throughout the county, checking every person's alibi for the night of October 17, or finding a few clues and deducing the murderer's identity? Most people would rather deduce the person's identity, and most programmers find the intellectual approach to debugging more satisfying. Even better, the effective programmers who debug in one-twentieth the time used by the ineffective programmers aren't randomly guessing about how to fix the program. They're using the scientific method—that is, the process of discovery and demonstration necessary for scientific investigation.

The Scientific Method of Debugging

Here are the steps you go through when you use the classic scientific method:

1. Gather data through repeatable experiments.

2. Form a hypothesis that accounts for the relevant data.

3. Design an experiment to prove or disprove the hypothesis.

4. Prove or disprove the hypothesis.

5. Repeat as needed.

KEY POINT

The scientific method has many parallels in debugging. Here's an effective approach for finding a defect:

1. Stabilize the error.

2. Locate the source of the error (the "fault").

    a. Gather the data that produces the defect.

    b. Analyze the data that has been gathered, and form a hypothesis about the defect.

    c. Determine how to prove or disprove the hypothesis, either by testing the program or by examining the code.

    d. Prove or disprove the hypothesis by using the procedure identified in 2(c).

3. Fix the defect.

4. Test the fix.

5. Look for similar errors.

The first step is similar to the scientific method's first step in that it relies on repeatability. The defect is easier to diagnose if you can stabilize it—that is, make it occur reliably. The second step uses the steps of the scientific method. You gather the test data that divulged the defect, analyze the data that has been produced, and form a hypothesis about the source of the error. You then design a test case or an inspection to evaluate the hypothesis, and you either declare success (regarding proving your hypothesis) or renew your efforts, as appropriate. When you have proven your hypothesis, you fix the defect, test the fix, and search your code for similar errors.

Let's look at each of the steps in conjunction with an example. Assume that you have an employee database program that has an intermittent error. The program is supposed to print a list of employees and their income-tax withholdings in alphabetical order. Here's part of the output:

```
Formatting, Fred Freeform      $5,877
Global, Gary                   $1,666
Modula, Mildred               $10,788
Many-Loop, Mavis               $8,889
Statement, Sue Switch          $4,000
Whileloop, Wendy               $7,860
```

The error is that *Many-Loop, Mavis* and *Modula, Mildred* are out of order.

Stabilize the Error

If a defect doesn't occur reliably, it's almost impossible to diagnose. Making an intermittent defect occur predictably is one of the most challenging tasks in debugging.

Cross-Reference For details on using pointers safely, see Section 13.2, "Pointers."

An error that doesn't occur predictably is usually an initialization error, a timing issue, or a dangling-pointer problem. If the calculation of a sum is right sometimes and wrong sometimes, a variable involved in the calculation probably isn't being initialized properly—most of the time it just happens to start at *0*. If the problem is a strange and unpredictable phenomenon and you're using pointers, you almost certainly have an uninitialized pointer or are using a pointer after the memory that it points to has been deallocated.

Stabilizing an error usually requires more than finding a test case that produces the error. It includes narrowing the test case to the simplest one that still produces the error. The goal of simplifying the test case is to make it so simple that changing any aspect of it changes the behavior of the error. Then, by changing the test case carefully and watching the program's behavior under controlled conditions, you can diagnose the problem. If you work in an organization that has an independent test team, sometimes it's the team's job to make the test cases simple. Most of the time, it's your job.

To simplify the test case, you bring the scientific method into play again. Suppose you have 10 factors that, used in combination, produce the error. Form a hypothesis about which factors were irrelevant to producing the error. Change the supposedly irrelevant factors, and rerun the test case. If you still get the error, you can eliminate those factors and you've simplified the test. Then you can try to simplify the test further. If you don't get the error, you've disproved that specific hypothesis and you know more than you did before. It might be that some subtly different change would still produce the error, but you know at least one specific change that does not.

In the employee withholdings example, when the program is run initially, *Many-Loop, Mavis* is listed after *Modula, Mildred*. When the program is run a second time, however, the list is fine:

```
Formatting, Fred Freeform    $5,877
Global, Gary                 $1,666
Many-Loop, Mavis             $8,889
Modula, Mildred             $10,788
Statement, Sue Switch        $4,000
Whileloop, Wendy             $7,860
```

It isn't until *Fruit-Loop, Frita* is entered and shows up in an incorrect position that you remember that *Modula, Mildred* had been entered just prior to showing up in the wrong spot too. What's odd about both cases is that they were entered singly. Usually, employees are entered in groups.

You hypothesize: the problem has something to do with entering a single new employee. If this is true, running the program again should put *Fruit-Loop, Frita* in the right position. Here's the result of a second run:

```
Formatting, Fred Freeform    $5,877
Fruit-Loop, Frita            $5,771
Global, Gary                 $1,666
Many-Loop, Mavis             $8,889
Modula, Mildred             $10,788
Statement, Sue Switch        $4,000
whileloop, Wendy             $7,860
```

This successful run supports the hypothesis. To confirm it, you want to try adding a few new employees, one at a time, to see whether they show up in the wrong order and whether the order changes on the second run.

Locate the Source of the Error

Locating the source of the error also calls for using the scientific method. You might suspect that the defect is a result of a specific problem, say an off-by-one error. You could then vary the parameter you suspect is causing the problem—one below the boundary, on the boundary, and one above the boundary—and determine whether your hypothesis is correct.

In the running example, the source of the problem could be an off-by-one defect that occurs when you add one new employee but not when you add two or more. Examining the code, you don't find an obvious off-by-one defect. Resorting to Plan B, you run a test case with a single new employee to see whether that's the problem. You add *Hardcase, Henry* as a single employee and hypothesize that his record will be out of order. Here's what you find:

```
Formatting, Fred Freeform    $5,877
Fruit-Loop, Frita            $5,771
Global, Gary                 $1,666
Hardcase, Henry                $493
Many-Loop, Mavis             $8,889
Modula, Mildred             $10,788
Statement, Sue Switch        $4,000
whileloop, Wendy             $7,860
```

The line for *Hardcase, Henry* is exactly where it should be, which means that your first hypothesis is false. The problem isn't caused simply by adding one employee at a time. It's either a more complicated problem or something completely different.

Examining the test-run output again, you notice that *Fruit-Loop, Frita* and *Many-Loop, Mavis* are the only names containing hyphens. *Fruit-Loop* was out of order when she was first entered, but *Many-Loop* wasn't, was she? Although you don't have a printout from the original entry, in the original error *Modula, Mildred* appeared to be out of order, but she was next to *Many-Loop*. Maybe *Many-Loop* was out of order and *Modula* was all right.

You hypothesize again: the problem arises from names with hyphens, not names that are entered singly.

But how does that account for the fact that the problem shows up only the first time an employee is entered? You look at the code and find that two different sorting routines are used. One is used when an employee is entered, and another is used when the data is saved. A closer look at the routine used when an employee is first entered shows that it isn't supposed to sort the data completely. It only puts the data in approximate order to speed up the save routine's sorting. Thus, the problem is that the data is printed before it's sorted. The problem with hyphenated names arises because the rough-sort routine doesn't handle niceties such as punctuation characters. Now, you can refine the hypothesis even further.

You hypothesize one last time: names with punctuation characters aren't sorted correctly until they're saved.

You later confirm this hypothesis with additional test cases.

Tips for Finding Defects

Once you've stabilized an error and refined the test case that produces it, finding its source can be either trivial or challenging, depending on how well you've written your code. If you're having a hard time finding a defect, it could be because the code isn't well written. You might not want to hear that, but it's true. If you're having trouble, consider these tips:

Use all the data available to make your hypothesis   When creating a hypothesis about the source of a defect, account for as much of the data as you can in your hypothesis. In the example, you might have noticed that *Fruit-Loop, Frita* was out of order and created a hypothesis that names beginning with an "F" are sorted incorrectly. That's a poor hypothesis because it doesn't account for the fact that *Modula, Mildred* was out of order or that names are sorted correctly the second time around. If the data doesn't fit the hypothesis, don't discard the data—ask why it doesn't fit, and create a new hypothesis.

The second hypothesis in the example—that the problem arises from names with hyphens, not names that are entered singly—didn't seem initially to account for the fact that names were sorted correctly the second time around either. In this case, however, the second hypothesis led to a more refined hypothesis that proved to be correct. It's all right that the hypothesis doesn't account for all of the data at first as long as you keep refining the hypothesis so that it does eventually.

Refine the test cases that produce the error   If you can't find the source of an error, try to refine the test cases further than you already have. You might be able to vary one parameter more than you had assumed, and focusing on one of the parameters might provide the crucial breakthrough.

Cross-Reference For more on unit test frameworks, see "Plug unit tests into a test framework" in Section 22.4.

Exercise the code in your unit test suite   Defects tend to be easier to find in small fragments of code than in large integrated programs. Use your unit tests to test the code in isolation.

Use available tools   Numerous tools are available to support debugging sessions: interactive debuggers, picky compilers, memory checkers, syntax-directed editors, and so on. The right tool can make a difficult job easy. With one tough-to-find error, for example, one part of the program was overwriting another part's memory. This error was difficult to diagnose using conventional debugging practices because the programmer couldn't determine the specific point at which the program was incorrectly overwriting memory. The programmer used a memory breakpoint to set a watch on a specific memory address. When the program wrote to that memory location, the debugger stopped the code and the guilty code was exposed.

This is an example of a problem that's difficult to diagnose analytically but that becomes quite simple when the right tool is applied.

Reproduce the error several different ways   Sometimes trying cases that are similar to the error-producing case but not exactly the same is instructive. Think of this approach as triangulating the defect. If you can get a fix on it from one point and a fix on it from another, you can better determine exactly where it is.

As illustrated by Figure 23-1, reproducing an error several different ways helps diagnose the cause of the error. Once you think you've identified the defect, run a case that's close to the cases that produce errors but that should not produce an error itself. If it does produce an error, you don't completely understand the problem yet. Errors often arise from combinations of factors, and trying to diagnose the problem with only one test case often doesn't diagnose the root problem.

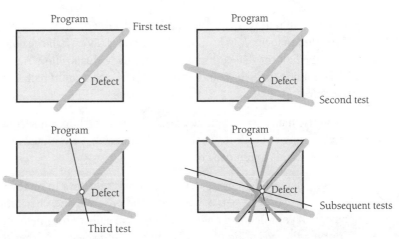

Figure 23-1   Try to reproduce an error several different ways to determine its exact cause.

Generate more data to generate more hypotheses   Choose test cases that are different from the test cases you already know to be erroneous or correct. Run them to generate more data, and use the new data to add to your list of possible hypotheses.

Use the results of negative tests   Suppose you create a hypothesis and run a test case to prove it. Suppose further that the test case disproves the hypothesis, so you still don't know the source of the error. You do know something you didn't before—namely, that the defect is not in the area you thought it was. That narrows your search field and the set of remaining possible hypotheses.

Brainstorm for possible hypotheses   Rather than limiting yourself to the first hypothesis you think of, try to come up with several. Don't analyze them at first—just come up with as many as you can in a few minutes. Then look at each hypothesis and think about test cases that would prove or disprove it. This mental exercise is helpful in breaking the debugging logjam that results from concentrating too hard on a single line of reasoning.

Keep a notepad by your desk, and make a list of things to try   One reason programmers get stuck during debugging sessions is that they go too far down dead-end paths. Make a list of things to try, and if one approach isn't working, move on to the next approach.

Narrow the suspicious region of the code   If you've been testing the whole program or a whole class or routine, test a smaller part instead. Use print statements, logging, or tracing to identify which section of code is producing the error.

If you need a more powerful technique to narrow the suspicious region of the code, systematically remove parts of the program and see whether the error still occurs. If it doesn't, you know it's in the part you took away. If it does, you know it's in the part you've kept.

Rather than removing regions haphazardly, divide and conquer. Use a binary search algorithm to focus your search. Try to remove about half the code the first time. Determine the half the defect is in, and then divide that section. Again, determine which half contains the defect, and again, chop that section in half. Continue until you find the defect.

If you use many small routines, you'll be able to chop out sections of code simply by commenting out calls to the routines. Otherwise, you can use comments or preprocessor commands to remove code.

If you're using a debugger, you don't necessarily have to remove pieces of code. You can set a breakpoint partway through the program and check for the defect that way instead. If your debugger allows you to skip calls to routines, eliminate suspects by skipping the execution of certain routines and seeing whether the error still occurs. The process with a debugger is otherwise similar to the one in which pieces of a program are physically removed.

Cross-Reference For more details on error-prone code, see "Target error-prone modules" in Section 24.5.

Be suspicious of classes and routines that have had defects before Classes that have had defects before are likely to continue to have defects. A class that has been troublesome in the past is more likely to contain a new defect than a class that has been defect-free. Reexamine error-prone classes and routines.

Check code that's changed recently If you have a new error that's hard to diagnose, it's usually related to code that's changed recently. It could be in completely new code or in changes to old code. If you can't find a defect, run an old version of the program to see whether the error occurs. If it doesn't, you know the error's in the new version or is caused by an interaction with the new version. Scrutinize the differences between the old and new versions. Check the version control log to see what code has changed recently. If that's not possible, use a diff tool to compare changes in the old, working source code to the new, broken source code.

Expand the suspicious region of the code It's easy to focus on a small section of code, sure that "the defect *must* be in this section." If you don't find it in the section, consider the possibility that the defect isn't in the section. Expand the area of code you suspect, and then focus on pieces of it by using the binary search technique described earlier.

Cross-Reference For a full discussion of integration, see Chapter 29, "Integration."

Integrate incrementally Debugging is easy if you add pieces to a system one at a time. If you add a piece to a system and encounter a new error, remove the piece and test it separately.

Check for common defects Use code-quality checklists to stimulate your thinking about possible defects. If you're following the inspection practices described in Section 21.3, "Formal Inspections," you'll have your own fine-tuned checklist of the common problems in your environment. You can also use the checklists that appear throughout this book. See the "List of Checklists" following the book's table of contents.

Cross-Reference For details on how involving other developers can put a beneficial distance between you and the problem, see Section 21.1, "Overview of Collaborative Development Practices."

Talk to someone else about the problem Some people call this "confessional debugging." You often discover your own defect in the act of explaining it to another person. For example, if you were explaining the problem in the salary example, you might sound like this:

> *Hey, Jennifer, have you got a minute? I'm having a problem. I've got this list of employee salaries that's supposed to be sorted, but some names are out of order. They're sorted all right the second time I print them out but not the first. I checked to see if it was new names, but I tried some that worked. I know they should be sorted the first time I print them because the program sorts all the names as they're entered and again when they're saved—wait a minute—no, it doesn't sort them when they're entered. That's right. It only orders them roughly. Thanks, Jennifer. You've been a big help.*

Jennifer didn't say a word, and you solved your problem. This result is typical, and this approach is a potent tool for solving difficult defects.

Take a break from the problem   Sometimes you concentrate so hard you can't think. How many times have you paused for a cup of coffee and figured out the problem on your way to the coffee machine? Or in the middle of lunch? Or on the way home? Or in the shower the next morning? If you're debugging and making no progress, once you've tried all the options, let it rest. Go for a walk. Work on something else. Go home for the day. Let your subconscious mind tease a solution out of the problem.

The auxiliary benefit of giving up temporarily is that it reduces the anxiety associated with debugging. The onset of anxiety is a clear sign that it's time to take a break.

Brute-Force Debugging

Brute force is an often-overlooked approach to debugging software problems. By "brute force," I'm referring to a technique that might be tedious, arduous, and time-consuming but that is *guaranteed* to solve the problem. Which specific techniques are guaranteed to solve a problem are context-dependent, but here are some general candidates:

- Perform a full design and/or code review on the broken code.
- Throw away the section of code and redesign/recode it from scratch.
- Throw away the whole program and redesign/recode it from scratch.
- Compile code with full debugging information.
- Compile code at pickiest warning level and fix all the picky compiler warnings.
- Strap on a unit test harness and test the new code in isolation.
- Create an automated test suite and run it all night.
- Step through a big loop in the debugger manually until you get to the error condition.
- Instrument the code with print, display, or other logging statements.
- Compile the code with a different compiler.
- Compile and run the program in a different environment.
- Link or run the code against special libraries or execution environments that produce warnings when code is used incorrectly.
- Replicate the end-user's full machine configuration.
- Integrate new code in small pieces, fully testing each piece as it's integrated.

Set a maximum time for quick and dirty debugging   For each brute-force technique, your reaction might well be, "I can't do that—it's too much work!" The point is that it's only too much work if it takes more time than what I call "quick and dirty debugging." It's always tempting to try for a quick guess rather than systematically instrumenting the code and giving the defect no place to hide. The gambler in each of us would rather use a risky approach that might find the defect in five minutes than the sure-fire approach that will find the defect in half an hour. The risk is that if the five-minute approach doesn't work, you get stubborn. Finding the defect the "easy" way becomes a matter of principle, and hours pass unproductively, as do days, weeks, months.... How often have you spent two hours debugging code that took only 30 minutes to write? That's a bad distribution of labor, and you would have been better off to rewrite the code than to debug bad code.

When you decide to go for the quick victory, set a maximum time limit for trying the quick way. If you go past the time limit, resign yourself to the idea that the defect is going to be harder to diagnose than you originally thought, and flush it out the hard way. This approach allows you to get the easy defects right away and the hard defects after a bit longer.

Make a list of brute-force techniques   Before you begin debugging a difficult error, ask yourself, "If I get stuck debugging this problem, is there some way that I am *guaranteed* to be able to fix the problem?" If you can identify at least one brute-force technique that will fix the problem—including rewriting the code in question—it's less likely that you'll waste hours or days when there's a quicker alternative.

Syntax Errors

Syntax-error problems are going the way of the woolly mammoth and the saber-toothed tiger. Compilers are getting better at diagnostic messages, and the days when you had to spend two hours finding a misplaced semicolon in a Pascal listing are almost gone. Here's a list of guidelines you can use to hasten the extinction of this endangered species:

Don't trust line numbers in compiler messages   When your compiler reports a mysterious syntax error, look immediately before and immediately after the error—the compiler could have misunderstood the problem or could simply have poor diagnostics. Once you find the real defect, try to determine the reason the compiler put the message on the wrong statement. Understanding your compiler better can help you find future defects.

Don't trust compiler messages   Compilers try to tell you exactly what's wrong, but compilers are dissembling little rascals, and you often have to read between the lines to know what one really means. For example, in UNIX C, you can get a message that says "floating exception" for an integer divide-by-0. With C++'s Standard Template

Library, you can get a pair of error messages: the first message is the real error in the use of the STL; the second message is a message from the compiler saying, "Error message too long for printer to print; message truncated." You can probably come up with many examples of your own.

Don't trust the compiler's second message Some compilers are better than others at detecting multiple errors. Some compilers get so excited after detecting the first error that they become giddy and overconfident; they prattle on with dozens of error messages that don't mean anything. Other compilers are more levelheaded, and although they must feel a sense of accomplishment when they detect an error, they refrain from spewing out inaccurate messages. When your compiler generates a series of cascading error messages, don't worry if you can't quickly find the source of the second or third error message. Fix the first one and recompile.

Divide and conquer The idea of dividing the program into sections to help detect defects works especially well for syntax errors. If you have a troublesome syntax error, remove part of the code and compile again. You'll either get no error (because the error's in the part you removed), get the same error (meaning you need to remove a different part), or get a different error (because you'll have tricked the compiler into producing a message that makes more sense).

Cross-Reference The availability of syntax-directed editors is one characteristic of early-wave vs. mature-wave programming environments. For details, see Section 4.3, "Your Location on the Technology Wave."

Find misplaced comments and quotation marks Many programming text editors automatically format comments, string literals, and other syntactical elements. In more primitive environments, a misplaced comment or quotation mark can trip up the compiler. To find the extra comment or quotation mark, insert the following sequence into your code in C, C++, and Java:

```
/*"/**/
```

This code phrase will terminate either a comment or string, which is useful in narrowing the space in which the unterminated comment or string is hiding.

23.3 Fixing a Defect

The hard part of debugging is finding the defect. Fixing the defect is the easy part. But as with many easy tasks, the fact that it's easy makes it especially error-prone. At least one study found that defect corrections have more than a 50 percent chance of being wrong the first time (Yourdon 1986b). Here are a few guidelines for reducing the chance of error:

KEY POINT

Understand the problem before you fix it "The Devil's Guide to Debugging" is right: the best way to make your life difficult and corrode the quality of your program is to fix problems without really understanding them. Before you fix a problem, make sure you understand it to the core. Triangulate the defect both with cases that should reproduce the error and with cases that shouldn't reproduce the error. Keep at it until you understand the problem well enough to predict its occurrence correctly every time.

Understand the program, not just the problem   If you understand the context in which a problem occurs, you're more likely to solve the problem completely rather than only one aspect of it. A study done with short programs found that programmers who achieve a global understanding of program behavior have a better chance of modifying it successfully than programmers who focus on local behavior, learning about the program only as they need to (Littman et al. 1986). Because the program in this study was small (280 lines), it doesn't prove that you should try to understand a 50,000-line program completely before you fix a defect. It does suggest that you should understand at least the code in the vicinity of the defect correction—the "vicinity" being not a few lines but a few hundred.

Confirm the defect diagnosis   Before you rush to fix a defect, make sure that you've diagnosed the problem correctly. Take the time to run test cases that prove your hypothesis and disprove competing hypotheses. If you've proven only that the error could be the result of one of several causes, you don't yet have enough evidence to work on the one cause; rule out the others first.

Never debug standing up.
—*Gerald Weinberg*

Relax   A programmer was ready for a ski trip. His product was ready to ship, he was already late, and he had only one more defect to correct. He changed the source file and checked it into version control. He didn't recompile the program and didn't verify that the change was correct.

In fact, the change was not correct, and his manager was outraged. How could he change code in a product that was ready to ship without checking it? What could be worse? Isn't this the pinnacle of professional recklessness?

If this isn't the height of recklessness, it's close and it's common. Hurrying to solve a problem is one of the most time-ineffective things you can do. It leads to rushed judgments, incomplete defect diagnosis, and incomplete corrections. Wishful thinking can lead you to see solutions where there are none. The pressure—often self-imposed—encourages haphazard trial-and-error solutions and the assumption that a solution works without verification that it does.

In striking contrast, during the final days of Microsoft Windows 2000 development, a developer needed to fix a defect that was the last remaining defect before a Release Candidate could be created. The developer changed the code, checked his fix, and tested his fix on his local build. But he didn't check the fix into version control at that point. Instead, he went to play basketball. He said, "I'm feeling too stressed right now to be sure that I've considered everything I should consider. I'm going to clear my mind for an hour, and then I'll come back and check in the code—once I've convinced myself that the fix is really correct."

Relax long enough to make sure your solution is right. Don't be tempted to take shortcuts. It might take more time, but it'll probably take less. If nothing else, you'll fix the problem correctly and your manager won't call you back from your ski trip.

Cross-Reference General issues involved in changing code are discussed in depth in Chapter 24, "Refactoring."

Save the original source code   Before you begin fixing the defect, be sure to archive a version of the code that you can return to later. It's easy to forget which change in a group of changes is the significant one. If you have the original source code, at least you can compare the old and the new files and see where the changes are.

Fix the problem, not the symptom   You should fix the symptom too, but the focus should be on fixing the underlying problem rather than wrapping it in programming duct tape. If you don't thoroughly understand the problem, you're not fixing the code. You're fixing the symptom and making the code worse. Suppose you have this code:

Java Example of Code That Needs to Be Fixed
```java
for ( claimNumber = 0; claimNumber < numClaims[ client ]; claimNumber++ ) {
   sum[ client ] = sum[ client ] + claimAmount[ claimNumber ];
}
```

Further suppose that when *client* equals *45*, *sum* turns out to be wrong by $3.45. Here's the wrong way to fix the problem:

CODING
HORROR

Java Example of Making the Code Worse by "Fixing" It
```java
for ( claimNumber = 0; claimNumber < numClaims[ client ]; claimNumber++ ) {
   sum[ client ] = sum[ client ] + claimAmount[ claimNumber ];
}

if ( client == 45 ) {
   sum[ 45 ] = sum[ 45 ] + 3.45;
}
```

Here's the "fix." →

Now suppose that when *client* equals 37 and the number of claims for the client is *0*, you're not getting *0*. Here's the wrong way to fix the problem:

CODING
HORROR

Java Example of Making the Code Worse by "Fixing" It (continued)
```java
for ( claimNumber = 0; claimNumber < numClaims[ client ]; claimNumber++ ) {
   sum[ client ] = sum[ client ] + claimAmount[ claimNumber ];
}

if ( client == 45 ) {
   sum[ 45 ] = sum[ 45 ] + 3.45;
}
else if ( ( client == 37 ) && ( numClaims[ client ] == 0 ) ) {
   sum[ 37 ] = 0.0;
}
```

Here's the second "fix." →

If this doesn't send a cold chill down your spine, you won't be affected by anything else in this book either. It's impossible to list all the problems with this approach in a book that's only around 1000 pages long, but here are the top three:

- The fixes won't work most of the time. The problems look as though they're the result of initialization defects. Initialization defects are, by definition, unpredictable, so the fact that the sum for client 45 is off by $3.45 today doesn't tell you anything about tomorrow. It could be off by $10,000.02, or it could be correct. That's the nature of initialization defects.

- It's unmaintainable. When code is special-cased to work around errors, the special cases become the code's most prominent feature. The $3.45 won't always be $3.45, and another error will show up later. The code will be modified again to handle the new special case, and the special case for $3.45 won't be removed. The code will become increasingly barnacled with special cases. Eventually the barnacles will be too heavy for the code to support, and the code will sink to the bottom of the ocean—a fitting place for it.

- It uses the computer for something that's better done by hand. Computers are good at predictable, systematic calculations, but humans are better at fudging data creatively. You'd be wiser to treat the output with whiteout and a typewriter than to monkey with the code.

Change the code only for good reason Related to fixing symptoms is the technique of changing code at random until it seems to work. The typical line of reasoning goes like this: "This loop seems to contain a defect. It's probably an off-by-one error, so I'll just put a *-1* here and try it. OK. That didn't work, so I'll just put a *+1* in instead. OK. That seems to work. I'll say it's fixed."

As popular as this practice is, it isn't effective. Making changes to code randomly is like rotating a Pontiac Aztek's tires to fix an engine problem. You're not learning anything; you're just goofing around. By changing the program randomly, you say in effect, "I don't know what's happening here, but I'll try this change and hope it works." Don't change code randomly. That's voodoo programming. The more different you make it without understanding it, the less confidence you'll have that it works correctly.

Before you make a change, be confident that it will work. Being wrong about a change should leave you astonished. It should cause self-doubt, personal reevaluation, and deep soul-searching. It should happen rarely.

Make one change at a time Changes are tricky enough when they're done one at a time. When done two at a time, they can introduce subtle errors that look like the original errors. Then you're in the awkward position of not knowing whether you didn't correct the error, whether you corrected the error but introduced a new one that looks similar, or whether you didn't correct the error and you introduced a similar new error. Keep it simple: make just one change at a time.

Cross-Reference For details on automated regression testing, see "Retesting (Regression Testing)" in Section 22.6.

Check your fix Check the program yourself, have someone else check it for you, or walk through it with someone else. Run the same triangulation test cases you used to diagnose the problem to make sure that all aspects of the problem have been resolved. If you've solved only part of the problem, you'll find out that you still have work to do.

Rerun the whole program to check for side effects of your changes. The easiest and most effective way to check for side effects is to run the program through an automated suite of regression tests in JUnit, CppUnit, or equivalent.

Add a unit test that exposes the defect   When you encounter an error that wasn't exposed by your test suite, add a test case to expose the error so that it won't be reintroduced later.

Look for similar defects   When you find one defect, look for others that are similar. Defects tend to occur in groups, and one of the values of paying attention to the kinds of defects you make is that you can correct all the defects of that kind. Looking for similar defects requires you to have a thorough understanding of the problem. Watch for the warning sign: if you can't figure out how to look for similar defects, that's a sign that you don't yet completely understand the problem.

23.4 Psychological Considerations in Debugging

Further Reading For an excellent discussion of psychological issues in debugging, as well as many other areas of software development, see *The Psychology of Computer Programming* (Weinberg 1998).

Debugging is as intellectually demanding as any other software-development activity. Your ego tells you that your code is good and doesn't have a defect even when you've seen that it has one. You have to think precisely—forming hypotheses, collecting data, analyzing hypotheses, and methodically rejecting them—with a formality that's unnatural to many people. If you're both building code and debugging it, you have to switch quickly between the fluid, creative thinking that goes with design and the rigidly critical thinking that goes with debugging. As you read your code, you have to battle the code's familiarity and guard against seeing what you expect to see.

How "Psychological Set" Contributes to Debugging Blindness

When you see a token in a program that says *Num*, what do you see? Do you see a misspelling of the word "Numb"? Or do you see the abbreviation for "Number"? Most likely, you see the abbreviation for "Number." This is the phenomenon of "psychological set"—seeing what you expect to see. What does this sign say?

In this classic puzzle, people often see only one "the." People see what they expect to see. Consider the following:

- Students learning *while* loops often expect a loop to be continuously evaluated; that is, they expect the loop to terminate as soon as the *while* condition becomes false, rather than only at the top or bottom (Curtis et al. 1986). They expect a *while* loop to act as "while" does in natural language.

HARD DATA

■ A programmer who unintentionally used both the variable *SYSTSTS* and the variable *SYSSTSTS* thought he was using a single variable. He didn't discover the problem until the program had been run hundreds of times and a book was written containing the erroneous results (Weinberg 1998).

■ A programmer looking at code like this code:

```
if ( x < y )
    swap = x;
    x = y;
    y = swap;
```

sometimes sees code like this code:

```
if ( x < y ) {
    swap = x;
    x = y;
    y = swap;
}
```

People expect a new phenomenon to resemble similar phenomena they've seen before. They expect a new control construct to work the same as old constructs; programming-langauge *while* statements to work the same as real-life "while" statements; and variable names to be the same as they've been before. You see what you expect to see and thus overlook differences, like the misspelling of the word "language" in the previous sentence.

What does psychological set have to do with debugging? First, it speaks to the importance of good programming practices. Good formatting, commenting, variable names, routine names, and other elements of programming style help structure the programming background so that likely defects appear as variations and stand out.

The second impact of psychological set is in selecting parts of the program to examine when an error is found. Research has shown that the programmers who debug most effectively mentally slice away parts of the program that aren't relevant during debugging (Basili, Selby, and Hutchens 1986). In general, the practice allows excellent programmers to narrow their search fields and find defects more quickly. Sometimes, however, the part of the program that contains the defect is mistakenly sliced away. You spend time scouring a section of code for a defect, and you ignore the section that contains the defect. You took a wrong turn at the fork in the road and need to back up before you can go forward again. Some of the suggestions in Section 23.2's discussion of tips for finding defects are designed to overcome this "debugging blindness."

How "Psychological Distance" Can Help

Cross-Reference For details on creating variable names that won't be confusing, see Section 11.7, "Kinds of Names to Avoid."

Psychological distance can be defined as the ease with which two items can be differentiated. If you are looking at a long list of words and have been told that they're all about ducks, you could easily mistake "Queck" for "Quack" because the two words look similar. The psychological distance between the words is small. You would be much less likely to mistake "Tuack" for "Quack" even though the difference is only one letter again. "Tuack" is less like "Quack" than "Queck" is because the first letter in a word is more prominent than the one in the middle.

Table 23-1 lists examples of psychological distances between variable names:

Table 23-1   Examples of Psychological Distance Between Variable Names

First Variable	Second Variable	Psychological Distance
stoppt	stcppt	Almost invisible
shiftrn	shiftrm	Almost none
dcount	bcount	Small
claims1	claims2	Small
product	sum	Large

As you debug, be ready for the problems caused by insufficient psychological distance between similar variable names and between similar routine names. As you construct code, choose names with large differences so that you avoid the problem.

23.5 Debugging Tools—Obvious and Not-So-Obvious

Cross-Reference The line between testing and debugging tools is fuzzy. See Section 22.5 for more on testing tools and Chapter 30 for more on software-development tools.

You can do much of the detailed, brain-busting work of debugging with debugging tools that are readily available. The tool that will drive the final stake through the heart of the defect vampire isn't yet available, but each year brings an incremental improvement in available capabilities.

Source-Code Comparators

A source-code comparator such as Diff is useful when you're modifying a program in response to errors. If you make several changes and need to remove some that you can't quite remember, a comparator can pinpoint the differences and jog your memory. If you discover a defect in a new version that you don't remember in an older version, you can compare the files to determine what changed.

Compiler Warning Messages

KEY POINT

One of the simplest and most effective debugging tools is your own compiler.

Set your compiler's warning level to the highest, pickiest level possible, and fix the errors it reports   It's sloppy to ignore compiler errors. It's even sloppier to turn off the warnings so that you can't even see them. Children sometimes think that if they close their eyes and can't see you, they've made you go away. Setting a switch on the compiler to turn off warnings just means you can't see the errors. It doesn't make them go away any more than closing your eyes makes an adult go away.

Assume that the people who wrote the compiler know a great deal more about your language than you do. If they're warning you about something, it usually means you have an opportunity to learn something new about your language. Make the effort to understand what the warning really means.

Treat warnings as errors   Some compilers let you treat warnings as errors. One reason to use the feature is that it elevates the apparent importance of a warning. Just as setting your watch five minutes fast tricks you into thinking it's five minutes later than it is, setting your compiler to treat warnings as errors tricks you into taking them more seriously. Another reason to treat warnings as errors is that they often affect how your program compiles. When you compile and link a program, warnings typically won't stop the program from linking, but errors typically will. If you want to check warnings before you link, set the compiler switch that treats warnings as errors.

Initiate projectwide standards for compile-time settings   Set a standard that requires everyone on your team to compile code using the same compiler settings. Otherwise, when you try to integrate code compiled by different people with different settings, you'll get a flood of error messages and an integration nightmare. This is easy to enforce if you use a project-standard make file or build script.

Extended Syntax and Logic Checking

You can use additional tools to check your code more thoroughly than your compiler does. For example, for C programmers, the lint utility painstakingly checks for use of uninitialized variables (writing = when you mean = =) and similarly subtle problems.

Execution Profilers

You might not think of an execution profiler as a debugging tool, but a few minutes spent studying a program profile can uncover some surprising (and hidden) defects.

For example, I had suspected that a memory-management routine in one of my programs was a performance bottleneck. Memory management had originally been a small component using a linearly ordered array of pointers to memory. I replaced the linearly ordered array with a hash table in the expectation that execution time would drop by at least half. But after profiling the code, I found no change in performance at all. I examined the code more closely and found a defect that was wasting a huge amount of time in the allocation algorithm. The bottleneck hadn't been the linear-search technique; it was the defect. I hadn't needed to optimize the search after all. Examine the output of an execution profiler to satisfy yourself that your program spends a reasonable amount of time in each area.

Test Frameworks/Scaffolding

Cross-Reference For details on scaffolding, see "Building Scaffolding to Test Individual Classes" in Section 22.5.

As mentioned in Section 23.2 on finding defects, pulling out a troublesome piece of code, writing code to test it, and executing it by itself is often the most effective way to exorcise the demons from an error-prone program.

Debuggers

Commercially available debuggers have advanced steadily over the years, and the capabilities available today can change the way you program. Good debuggers allow you to set breakpoints to break when execution reaches a specific line, or the nth time it reaches a specific line, or when a global variable changes, or when a variable is assigned a specific value. They allow you to step through code line by line, stepping through or over routines. They allow the program to be executed backwards, stepping back to the point where a defect originated. They allow you to log the execution of specific statements—similar to scattering "I'm here!" print statements throughout a program.

Good debuggers allow full examination of data, including structured and dynamically allocated data. They make it easy to view the contents of a linked list of pointers or a dynamically allocated array. They're intelligent about user-defined data types. They allow you to make ad hoc queries about data, assign new values, and continue program execution.

You can look at the high-level language or the assembly language generated by your compiler. If you're using several languages, the debugger automatically displays the correct language for each section of code. You can look at a chain of calls to routines and quickly view the source code of any routine. You can change parameters to a program within the debugger environment.

The best of today's debuggers also remember debugging parameters (breakpoints, variables being watched, and so on) for each individual program so that you don't have to re-create them for each program you debug.

System debuggers operate at the systems level rather than the applications level so that they don't interfere with the execution of the program being debugged. They're essential when you are debugging programs that are sensitive to timing or the amount of memory available.

An interactive debugger is an outstanding example of what is not needed—it encourages trial-and-error hacking rather than systematic design, and also hides marginal people barely qualified for precision programming.
—Harlan Mills

Given the enormous power offered by modern debuggers, you might be surprised that anyone would criticize them. But some of the most respected people in computer science recommend not using them. They recommend using your brain and avoiding debugging tools altogether. Their argument is that debugging tools are a crutch and that you find problems faster and more accurately by thinking about them than by relying on tools. They argue that you, rather than the debugger, should mentally execute the program to flush out defects.

Regardless of the empirical evidence, the basic argument against debuggers isn't valid. The fact that a tool can be misused doesn't imply that it should be rejected. You wouldn't avoid taking aspirin merely because it's possible to overdose. You wouldn't avoid mowing your lawn with a power mower just because it's possible to cut yourself. Any other powerful tool can be used or abused, and so can a debugger.

KEY POINT

The debugger isn't a substitute for good thinking. But, in some cases, thinking isn't a substitute for a good debugger either. The most effective combination is good thinking and a good debugger.

cc2e.com/2368

CHECKLISTS: Debugging Reminders

Techniques for Finding Defects

- ❏ Use all the data available to make your hypothesis.
- ❏ Refine the test cases that produce the error.
- ❏ Exercise the code in your unit test suite.
- ❏ Use available tools.
- ❏ Reproduce the error several different ways.
- ❏ Generate more data to generate more hypotheses.
- ❏ Use the results of negative tests.
- ❏ Brainstorm for possible hypotheses.
- ❏ Keep a notepad by your desk, and make a list of things to try.
- ❏ Narrow the suspicious region of the code.
- ❏ Be suspicious of classes and routines that have had defects before.
- ❏ Check code that's changed recently.
- ❏ Expand the suspicious region of the code.

❑ Integrate incrementally.

❑ Check for common defects.

❑ Talk to someone else about the problem.

❑ Take a break from the problem.

❑ Set a maximum time for quick and dirty debugging.

❑ Make a list of brute-force techniques, and use them.

Techniques for Syntax Errors

❑ Don't trust line numbers in compiler messages.

❑ Don't trust compiler messages.

❑ Don't trust the compiler's second message.

❑ Divide and conquer.

❑ Use a syntax-directed editor to find misplaced comments and quotation marks.

Techniques for Fixing Defects

❑ Understand the problem before you fix it.

❑ Understand the program, not just the problem.

❑ Confirm the defect diagnosis.

❑ Relax.

❑ Save the original source code.

❑ Fix the problem, not the symptom.

❑ Change the code only for good reason.

❑ Make one change at a time.

❑ Check your fix.

❑ Add a unit test that exposes the defect.

❑ Look for similar defects.

General Approach to Debugging

❑ Do you use debugging as an opportunity to learn more about your program, mistakes, code quality, and problem-solving approach?

❑ Do you avoid the trial-and-error, superstitious approach to debugging?

> ❑ Do you assume that errors are your fault?
>
> ❑ Do you use the scientific method to stabilize intermittent errors?
>
> ❑ Do you use the scientific method to find defects?
>
> ❑ Rather than using the same approach every time, do you use several different techniques to find defects?
>
> ❑ Do you verify that the fix is correct?
>
> ❑ Do you use compiler warning messages, execution profiling, a test framework, scaffolding, and interactive debugging?

Additional Resources

cc2e.com/2375

The following resources also address debugging:

Agans, David J. *Debugging: The Nine Indispensable Rules for Finding Even the Most Elusive Software and Hardware Problems.* Amacom, 2003. This book provides general debugging principles that can be applied in any language or environment.

Myers, Glenford J. *The Art of Software Testing.* New York, NY: John Wiley & Sons, 1979. Chapter 7 of this classic book is devoted to debugging.

Allen, Eric. *Bug Patterns In Java.* Berkeley, CA: Apress, 2002. This book lays out an approach to debugging Java programs that is conceptually very similar to what is described in this chapter, including "The Scientific Method of Debugging," distinguishing between debugging and testing, and identifying common bug patterns.

The following two books are similar in that their titles suggest they are applicable only to Microsoft Windows and .NET programs, but they both contain discussions of debugging in general, use of assertions, and coding practices that help to avoid bugs in the first place:

Robbins, John. *Debugging Applications for Microsoft .NET and Microsoft Windows.* Redmond, WA: Microsoft Press, 2003.

McKay, Everett N. and Mike Woodring. *Debugging Windows Programs: Strategies, Tools, and Techniques for Visual C++ Programmers.* Boston, MA: Addison-Wesley, 2000.

Key Points

- Debugging is a make-or-break aspect of software development. The best approach is to use other techniques described in this book to avoid defects in the first place. It's still worth your time to improve your debugging skills, however, because the difference between good and poor debugging performance is at least 10 to 1.

- A systematic approach to finding and fixing errors is critical to success. Focus your debugging so that each test moves you a step forward. Use the Scientific Method of Debugging.

- Understand the root problem before you fix the program. Random guesses about the sources of errors and random corrections will leave the program in worse condition than when you started.

- Set your compiler warning to the pickiest level possible, and fix the errors it reports. It's hard to fix subtle errors if you ignore the obvious ones.

- Debugging tools are powerful aids to software development. Find them and use them, and remember to use your brain at the same time.

Chapter 24

Refactoring

cc2e.com/2436

Contents

Related Topics

All successful software gets changed.
—Fred Brooks

Myth: a well-managed software project conducts methodical requirements development and defines a stable list of the program's responsibilities. Design follows requirements, and it is done carefully so that coding can proceed linearly, from start to finish, implying that most of the code can be written once, tested, and forgotten. According to the myth, the only time that the code is significantly modified is during the software-maintenance phase, something that happens only after the initial version of a system has been delivered.

HARD DATA

Reality: code evolves substantially during its initial development. Many of the changes seen during initial coding are at least as dramatic as changes seen during maintenance. Coding, debugging, and unit testing consume between 30 to 65 percent of the effort on a typical project, depending on the project's size. (See Chapter 27, "How Program Size Affects Construction," for details.) If coding and unit testing were straightforward processes, they would consume no more than 20–30 percent of the total effort on a project. Even on well-managed projects, however, requirements change by about one to four percent per month (Jones 2000). Requirements changes invariably cause corresponding code changes—sometimes substantial code changes.

KEY POINT

Another reality: modern development practices increase the potential for code changes during construction. In older life cycles, the focus—successful or not—was on avoiding code changes. More modern approaches move away from coding predictability. Current approaches are more code-centered, and over the life of a project, you can expect code to evolve more than ever.

24.1 Kinds of Software Evolution

Software evolution is like biological evolution in that some mutations are beneficial and many mutations are not. Good software evolution produces code whose development mimics the ascent from monkeys to Neanderthals to our current exalted state as software developers. Evolutionary forces sometimes beat on a program the other way, however, knocking the program into a deevolutionary spiral.

KEY POINT

The key distinction between kinds of software evolution is whether the program's quality improves or degrades under modification. If you fix errors with logical duct tape and superstition, quality degrades. If you treat modifications as opportunities to tighten up the original design of the program, quality improves. If you see that program quality is degrading, that's like that silent canary in a mine shaft I've mentioned before. It's a warning that the program is evolving in the wrong direction.

A second distinction in the kinds of software evolution is the one between changes made during construction and those made during maintenance. These two kinds of evolution differ in several ways. Construction changes are usually made by the original developers, usually before the program has been completely forgotten. The system isn't yet on line, so the pressure to finish changes is only schedule pressure—it's not 500 angry users wondering why their system is down. For the same reason, changes during construction can be more freewheeling—the system is in a more dynamic state, and the penalty for making mistakes is low. These circumstances imply a style of software evolution that's different from what you'd find during software maintenance.

Philosophy of Software Evolution

There is no code so big, twisted, or complex that maintenance can't make it worse.
—*Gerald Weinberg*

A common weakness in programmers' approaches to software evolution is that it goes on as an unselfconscious process. If you recognize that evolution during development is an inevitable and important phenomenon and plan for it, you can use it to your advantage.

Evolution is at once hazardous and an opportunity to approach perfection. When you have to make a change, strive to improve the code so that future changes are easier. You never know as much when you begin writing a program as you do afterward. When you have a chance to revise a program, use what you've learned to improve it. Make both your initial code and your changes with further change in mind.

The Cardinal Rule of Software Evolution is that evolution should improve the internal quality of the program. The following sections describe how to accomplish this.

24.2 Introduction to Refactoring

The key strategy in achieving The Cardinal Rule of Software Evolution is refactoring, which Martin Fowler defines as "a change made to the internal structure of the software to make it easier to understand and cheaper to modify without changing its observable behavior" (Fowler 1999). The word "refactoring" in modern programming grew out of Larry Constantine's original use of the word "factoring" in structured programming, which referred to decomposing a program into its constituent parts as much as possible (Yourdon and Constantine 1979).

Reasons to Refactor

Sometimes code degenerates under maintenance, and sometimes the code just wasn't very good in the first place. In either case, here are some warning signs —sometimes called "smells" (Fowler 1999)—that indicate where refactorings are needed:

Code is duplicated   Duplicated code almost always represents a failure to fully factor the design in the first place. Duplicate code sets you up to make parallel modifications—whenever you make changes in one place, you have to make parallel changes in another place. It also violates what Andrew Hunt and Dave Thomas refer to as the "DRY principle": Don't Repeat Yourself (2000). I think David Parnas says it best: "Copy and paste is a design error" (McConnell 1998b).

A routine is too long   In object-oriented programming, routines longer than a screen are rarely needed and usually represent the attempt to force-fit a structured programming foot into an object-oriented shoe.

One of my clients was assigned the task of breaking up a legacy system's longest routine, which was more than 12,000 lines long. With effort, he was able to reduce the size of the largest routine to only about 4,000 lines.

One way to improve a system is to increase its modularity—increase the number of well-defined, well-named routines that do one thing and do it well. When changes lead you to revisit a section of code, take the opportunity to check the modularity of the routines in that section. If a routine would be cleaner if part of it were made into a separate routine, create a separate routine.

A loop is too long or too deeply nested   Loop innards tend to be good candidates for being converted into routines, which helps to better factor the code and to reduce the loop's complexity.

A class has poor cohesion   If you find a class that takes ownership for a hodgepodge of unrelated responsibilities, that class should be broken up into multiple classes, each of which has responsibility for a cohesive set of responsibilities.

A class interface does not provide a consistent level of abstraction   Even classes that begin life with a cohesive interface can lose their original consistency. Class interfaces tend to morph over time as a result of modifications that are made in the heat of the moment and that favor expediency to interface integrity. Eventually the class interface becomes a Frankensteinian maintenance monster that does little to improve the intellectual manageability of the program.

A parameter list has too many parameters   Well-factored programs tend to have many small, well-defined routines that don't need large parameter lists. A long parameter list is a warning that the abstraction of the routine interface has not been well thought out.

Changes within a class tend to be compartmentalized   Sometimes a class has two or more distinct responsibilities. When that happens you find yourself changing either one part of the class or another part of the class—but few changes affect both parts of the class. That's a sign that the class should be cleaved into multiple classes along the lines of the separate responsibilities.

Changes require parallel modifications to multiple classes   I saw one project that had a checklist of about 15 classes that had to be modified whenever a new kind of output was added. When you find yourself routinely making changes to the same set of classes, that suggests the code in those classes could be rearranged so that changes affect only one class. In my experience, this is a hard ideal to accomplish, but it's nonetheless a good goal.

Inheritance hierarchies have to be modified in parallel   Finding yourself making a subclass of one class every time you make a subclass of another class is a special kind of parallel modification and should be addressed.

case *statements have to be modified in parallel*   Although *case* statements are not inherently bad, if you find yourself making parallel modifications to similar *case* statements in multiple parts of the program, you should ask whether inheritance might be a better approach.

Related data items that are used together are not organized into classes   If you find yourself repeatedly manipulating the same set of data items, you should ask whether those manipulations should be combined into a class of their own.

A routine uses more features of another class than of its own class   This suggests that the routine should be moved into the other class and then invoked by its old class.

A primitive data type is overloaded   Primitive data types can be used to represent an infinite number of real-world entities. If your program uses a primitive data type like an integer to represent a common entity such as money, consider creating a simple *Money* class so that the compiler can perform type checking on *Money* variables, so that you can add safety checks on the values assigned to money, and so on. If both *Money* and *Temperature* are integers, the compiler won't warn you about erroneous assignments like *bankBalance = recordLowTemperature*.

A class doesn't do very much   Sometimes the result of refactoring code is that an old class doesn't have much to do. If a class doesn't seem to be carrying its weight, ask if you should assign all of that class's responsibilities to other classes and eliminate the class altogether.

A chain of routines passes tramp data   Finding yourself passing data to one routine just so that routine can pass it to another routine is called "tramp data" (Page-Jones 1988). This might be OK, but ask yourself whether passing the specific data in question is consistent with the abstraction presented by each of the routine interfaces. If the abstraction for each routine is OK, passing the data is OK. If not, find some way to make each routine's interface more consistent.

A middleman object isn't doing anything   If you find that most of the code in a class is just passing off calls to routines in other classes, consider whether you should eliminate the middleman and call those other classes directly.

One class is overly intimate with another   Encapsulation (information hiding) is probably the strongest tool you have to make your program intellectually manageable and to minimize ripple effects of code changes. Anytime you see one class that knows more about another class than it should—including derived classes knowing too much about their parents—err on the side of stronger encapsulation rather than weaker.

A routine has a poor name   If a routine has a poor name, change the name of the routine where it's defined, change the name in all places it's called, and then recompile. As hard as it might be to do this now, it will be even harder later, so do it as soon as you notice it's a problem.

Data members are public   Public data members are, in my view, always a bad idea. They blur the line between interface and implementation, and they inherently violate encapsulation and limit future flexibility. Strongly consider hiding public data members behind access routines.

A subclass uses only a small percentage of its parents' routines   Typically this indicates that that subclass has been created because a parent class happened to contain the routines it needed, not because the subclass is logically a descendent of the superclass. Consider achieving better encapsulation by switching the subclass's relationship to its superclass from an is-a relationship to a has-a relationship; convert the superclass to member data of the former subclass, and expose only the routines in the former subclass that are really needed.

Comments are used to explain difficult code   Comments have an important role to play, but they should not be used as a crutch to explain bad code. The age-old wisdom is dead-on: "Don't document bad code—rewrite it" (Kernighan and Plauger 1978).

Cross-Reference For guidelines on the use of global variables, see Section 13.3, "Global Data." For an explanation of the differences between global data and class data, see "Class data mistaken for global data" in Section 5.3.

Global variables are used   When you revisit a section of code that uses global variables, take time to reexamine them. You might have thought of a way to avoid using global variables since the last time you visited that part of the code. Because you're less familiar with the code than when you first wrote it, you might now find the global variables sufficiently confusing that you're willing to develop a cleaner approach. You might also have a better sense of how to isolate global variables in access routines and a keener sense of the pain caused by not doing so. Bite the bullet and make the beneficial modifications. The initial coding will be far enough in the past that you can be objective about your work yet close enough that you will remember most of what you need to make the revisions correctly. The time during early revisions is the perfect time to improve the code.

A routine uses setup code before a routine call or takedown code after a routine call
Code like this should be a warning to you:

Bad C++ Example of Setup and Takedown Code for a Routine Call

This setup code is a warning.

```cpp
WithdrawalTransaction withdrawal;
withdrawal.SetCustomerId( customerId );
withdrawal.SetBalance( balance );
withdrawal.SetWithdrawalAmount( withdrawalAmount );
withdrawal.SetWithdrawalDate( withdrawalDate );

ProcessWithdrawal( withdrawal );
```

This takedown code is another warning.

```cpp
customerId = withdrawal.GetCustomerId();
balance = withdrawal.GetBalance();
withdrawalAmount = withdrawal.GetWithdrawalAmount();
withdrawalDate = withdrawal.GetWithdrawalDate();
```

A similar warning sign is when you find yourself creating a special constructor for the *WithdrawalTransaction* class that takes a subset of its normal initialization data so that you can write code like this:

Bad C++ Example of Setup and Takedown Code for a Method Call

```cpp
withdrawal = new WithdrawalTransaction( customerId, balance,
   withdrawalAmount, withdrawalDate );
withdrawal.ProcessWithdrawal();
delete withdrawal;
```

Anytime you see code that sets up for a call to a routine or takes down after a call to a routine, ask whether the routine interface is presenting the right abstraction. In this case, perhaps the parameter list of *ProcessWithdrawal* should be modified to support code like this:

> **Good C++ Example of a Routine That Doesn't Require Setup or Takedown Code**
> ```
> ProcessWithdrawal( customerId, balance, withdrawalAmount, withdrawalDate );
> ```

Note that the converse of this example presents a similar problem. If you find yourself usually having a *WithdrawalTransaction* object in hand but needing to pass several of its values to a routine like the one shown here, you should also consider refactoring the *ProcessWithdrawal* interface so that it requires the *WithdrawalTransaction* object rather than its individual fields:

> **C++ Example of Code That Requires Several Method Calls**
> ```
> ProcessWithdrawal( withdrawal.GetCustomerId(), withdrawal.GetBalance(),
>     withdrawal.GetWithdrawalAmount(), withdrawal.GetWithdrawalDate() );
> ```

Any of these approaches can be right, and any can be wrong—it depends on whether the *ProcessWithdrawal()* interface's abstraction is that it expects to have four distinct pieces of data or expects to have a *WithdrawalTransaction* object.

A program contains code that seems like it might be needed someday Programmers are notoriously bad at guessing what functionality might be needed someday. "Designing ahead" is subject to numerous predictable problems:

- Requirements for the "design ahead" code haven't been fully developed, which means the programmer will likely guess wrong about those future requirements. The "code ahead" work will ultimately be thrown away.

- If the programmer's guess about the future requirement is pretty close, the programmer still will not generally anticipate all the intricacies of the future requirement. These intricacies undermine the programmer's basic design assumptions, which means the "design ahead" work will have to be thrown away.

- Future programmers who use the "design ahead" code don't know that it was "design ahead" code, or they assume the code works better than it does. They assume that the code has been coded, tested, and reviewed to the same level as the other code. They waste a lot of time building code that uses the "design ahead" code, only to discover ultimately that the "design ahead" code doesn't actually work.

- The additional "design ahead" code creates additional complexity, which calls for additional testing, additional defect correction, and so on. The overall effect is to slow down the project.

Experts agree that the best way to prepare for future requirements is not to write speculative code; it's to make the *currently required* code as clear and straightforward as possible so that future programmers will know what it does and does not do and will make their changes accordingly (Fowler 1999, Beck 2000).

cc2e.com/2443

CHECKLIST: Reasons to Refactor

- ❑ Code is duplicated.
- ❑ A routine is too long.
- ❑ A loop is too long or too deeply nested.
- ❑ A class has poor cohesion.
- ❑ A class interface does not provide a consistent level of abstraction.
- ❑ A parameter list has too many parameters.
- ❑ Changes within a class tend to be compartmentalized.
- ❑ Changes require parallel modifications to multiple classes.
- ❑ Inheritance hierarchies have to be modified in parallel.
- ❑ *case* statements have to be modified in parallel.
- ❑ Related data items that are used together are not organized into classes.
- ❑ A routine uses more features of another class than of its own class.
- ❑ A primitive data type is overloaded.
- ❑ A class doesn't do very much.
- ❑ A chain of routines passes tramp data.
- ❑ A middleman object isn't doing anything.
- ❑ One class is overly intimate with another.
- ❑ A routine has a poor name.
- ❑ Data members are public.
- ❑ A subclass uses only a small percentage of its parents' routines.
- ❑ Comments are used to explain difficult code.
- ❑ Global variables are used.
- ❑ A routine uses setup code before a routine call or takedown code after a routine call.
- ❑ A program contains code that seems like it might be needed someday.

Reasons Not to Refactor

In common parlance, "refactoring" is used loosely to refer to fixing defects, adding functionality, modifying the design—essentially as a synonym for making any change to the code whatsoever. This common dilution of the term's meaning is unfortunate. Change in itself is not a virtue, but purposeful change, applied with a teaspoonful of discipline, can be the key strategy that supports steady improvement in a program's quality under maintenance and prevents the all-too-familiar software-entropy death spiral.

24.3 Specific Refactorings

In this section, I present a catalog of refactorings, many of which I describe by summarizing the more detailed descriptions presented in *Refactoring* (Fowler 1999). I have not, however, attempted to make this catalog exhaustive. In a sense, every case in this book that shows a "bad code" example and a "good code" example is a candidate for becoming a refactoring. In the interest of space, I've focused on the refactorings I personally have found most useful.

Data-Level Refactorings

Here are refactorings that improve the use of variables and other kinds of data.

Replace a magic number with a named constant   If you're using a numeric or string literal like *3.14*, replace that literal with a named constant like *PI*.

Rename a variable with a clearer or more informative name   If a variable's name isn't clear, change it to a better name. The same advice applies to renaming constants, classes, and routines, of course.

Move an expression inline   Replace an intermediate variable that was assigned the result of an expression with the expression itself.

Replace an expression with a routine   Replace an expression with a routine (usually so that the expression isn't duplicated in the code).

Introduce an intermediate variable   Assign an expression to an intermediate variable whose name summarizes the purpose of the expression.

Convert a multiuse variable to multiple single-use variables   If a variable is used for more than one purpose—common culprits are *i*, *j*, *temp*, and *x*—create separate variables for each usage, each of which has a more specific name.

Use a local variable for local purposes rather than a parameter   If an input-only routine parameter is being used as a local variable, create a local variable and use that instead.

Convert a data primitive to a class   If a data primitive needs additional behavior (including stricter type checking) or additional data, convert the data to an object and add the behavior you need. This can apply to simple numeric types like *Money* and *Temperature*. It can also apply to enumerated types like *Color*, *Shape*, *Country*, or *OutputType*.

Convert a set of type codes to a class or an enumeration   In older programs, it's common to see associations like

```
const int SCREEN = 0;
const int PRINTER = 1;
const int FILE = 2;
```

Rather than defining standalone constants, create a class so that you can receive the benefits of stricter type checking and set yourself up to provide richer semantics for *OutputType* if you ever need to. Creating an enumeration is sometimes a good alternative to creating a class.

Convert a set of type codes to a class with subclasses   If the different elements associated with different types might have different behavior, consider creating a base class for the type with subclasses for each type code. For the *OutputType* base class, you might create subclasses like *Screen*, *Printer*, and *File*.

Change an array to an object   If you're using an array in which different elements are different types, create an object that has a field for each former element of the array.

Encapsulate a collection   If a class returns a collection, having multiple instances of the collection floating around can create synchronization difficulties. Consider having the class return a read-only collection, and provide routines to add and remove elements from the collection.

Replace a traditional record with a data class   Create a class that contains the members of the record. Creating a class allows you to centralize error checking, persistence, and other operations that concern the record.

Statement-Level Refactorings

Here are refactorings that improve the use of individual statements.

Decompose a boolean expression   Simplify a boolean expression by introducing well-named intermediate variables that help document the meaning of the expression.

Move a complex boolean expression into a well-named boolean function   If the expression is complicated enough, this refactoring can improve readability. If the expression is used more than once, it eliminates the need for parallel modifications and reduces the chance of error in using the expression.

Consolidate fragments that are duplicated within different parts of a conditional   If you have the same lines of code repeated at the end of an *else* block that you have at the end of the *if* block, move those lines of code so that they occur after the entire *if-then-else* block.

Use **break** *or* **return** *instead of a loop control variable*   If you have a variable within a loop like *done* that's used to control the loop, use *break* or *return* to exit the loop instead.

Return as soon as you know the answer instead of assigning a return value within nested **if-then-else** *statements*   Code is often easiest to read and least error-prone if you exit a routine as soon as you know the return value. The alternative of setting a return value and then unwinding your way through a lot of logic can be harder to follow.

Replace conditionals (especially repeated **case** *statements) with polymorphism*
Much of the logic that used to be contained in *case* statements in structured programs can instead be baked into the inheritance hierarchy and accomplished through polymorphic routine calls.

Create and use null objects instead of testing for null values   Sometimes a null object will have generic behavior or data associated with it, such as referring to a resident whose name is not known as "occupant." In this case, consider moving the responsibility for handling null values out of the client code and into the class—that is, have the *Customer* class define the unknown resident as "occupant" instead of having *Customer*'s client code repeatedly test for whether the customer's name is known and substitute "occupant" if not.

Routine-Level Refactorings

Here are refactorings that improve code at the individual-routine level.

Extract routine/extract method   Remove inline code from one routine, and turn it into its own routine.

Move a routine's code inline   Take code from a routine whose body is simple and self-explanatory, and move that routine's code inline where it is used.

Convert a long routine to a class   If a routine is too long, sometimes turning it into a class and then further factoring the former routine into multiple routines will improve readability.

Substitute a simple algorithm for a complex algorithm   Replace a complicated algorithm with a simpler algorithm.

Add a parameter   If a routine needs more information from its caller, add a parameter so that that information can be provided.

Remove a parameter   If a routine no longer uses a parameter, remove it.

Separate query operations from modification operations   Normally, query operations don't change an object's state. If an operation like *GetTotals()* changes an object's state, separate the query functionality from the state-changing functionality and provide two separate routines.

Combine similar routines by parameterizing them   Two similar routines might differ only with respect to a constant value that's used within the routine. Combine the routines into one routine, and pass in the value to be used as a parameter.

Separate routines whose behavior depends on parameters passed in   If a routine executes different code depending on the value of an input parameter, consider breaking the routine into separate routines that can be called separately, without passing in that particular input parameter.

Pass a whole object rather than specific fields   If you find yourself passing several values from the same object into a routine, consider changing the routine's interface so that it takes the whole object instead.

Pass specific fields rather than a whole object   If you find yourself creating an object just so that you can pass it to a routine, consider modifying the routine so that it takes specific fields rather than a whole object.

Encapsulate downcasting   If a routine returns an object, it normally should return the most specific type of object it knows about. This is particularly applicable to routines that return iterators, collections, elements of collections, and so on.

Class Implementation Refactorings

Here are refactorings that improve code at the class level.

Change value objects to reference objects   If you find yourself creating and maintaining numerous copies of large or complex objects, change your usage of those objects so that only one master copy exists (the value object) and the rest of the code uses references to that object (reference objects).

Change reference objects to value objects   If you find yourself performing a lot of reference housekeeping for small or simple objects, change your usage of those objects so that all objects are value objects.

Replace virtual routines with data initialization   If you have a set of subclasses that vary only according to constant values they return, rather than overriding member routines in the derived classes, have the derived classes initialize the class with appropriate constant values, and then have generic code in the base class that works with those values.

Change member routine or data placement   Consider making several general changes in an inheritance hierarchy. These changes are normally performed to eliminate duplication in derived classes:

- Pull a routine up into its superclass.

- Pull a field up into its superclass.

- Pull a constructor body up into its superclass.

  Several other changes are normally made to support specialization in derived classes:

- Push a routine down into its derived classes.

- Push a field down into its derived classes.

- Push a constructor body down into its derived classes.

Extract specialized code into a subclass   If a class has code that's used by only a subset of its instances, move that specialized code into its own subclass.

Combine similar code into a superclass   If two subclasses have similar code, combine that code and move it into the superclass.

Class Interface Refactorings

Here are refactorings that make for better class interfaces.

Move a routine to another class   Create a new routine in the target class, and move the body of the routine from the source class into the target class. You can then call the new routine from the old routine.

Convert one class to two   If a class has two or more distinct areas of responsibility, break the class into multiple classes, each of which has a clearly defined responsibility.

Eliminate a class   If a class isn't doing much, move its code into other classes that are more cohesive and eliminate the class.

Hide a delegate   Sometimes Class A calls Class B and Class C, when really Class A should call only Class B and Class B should call Class C. Ask yourself what the right abstraction is for A's interaction with B. If B should be responsible for calling C, have B call C.

Remove a middleman   If Class A calls Class B and Class B calls Class C, sometimes it works better to have Class A call Class C directly. The question of whether you should delegate to Class B depends on what will best maintain the integrity of Class B's interface.

Replace inheritance with delegation   If a class needs to use another class but wants more control over its interface, make the superclass a field of the former subclass and then expose a set of routines that will provide a cohesive abstraction.

Replace delegation with inheritance   If a class exposes every public routine of a delegate class (member class), inherit from the delegate class instead of just using the class.

Introduce a foreign routine   If a class needs an additional routine and you can't modify the class to provide it, you can create a new routine within the client class that provides that functionality.

Introduce an extension class   If a class needs several additional routines and you can't modify the class, you can create a new class that combines the unmodifiable class's functionality with the additional functionality. You can do that either by subclassing the original class and adding new routines or by wrapping the class and exposing the routines you need.

Encapsulate an exposed member variable   If member data is public, change the member data to private and expose the member data's value through a routine instead.

Remove Set() routines for fields that cannot be changed   If a field is supposed to be set at object creation time and not changed afterward, initialize that field in the object's constructor rather than providing a misleading *Set()* routine.

Hide routines that are not intended to be used outside the class   If the class interface would be more coherent without a routine, hide the routine.

Encapsulate unused routines   If you find yourself routinely using only a portion of a class's interface, create a new interface to the class that exposes only those necessary routines. Be sure that the new interface provides a coherent abstraction.

Collapse a superclass and subclass if their implementations are very similar   If the subclass doesn't provide much specialization, combine it into its superclass.

System-Level Refactorings

Here are refactorings that improve code at the whole-system level.

Create a definitive reference source for data you can't control   Sometimes you have data maintained by the system that you can't conveniently or consistently access from other objects that need to know about that data. A common example is data maintained in a GUI control. In such a case, you can create a class that mirrors the data in the GUI control, and then have both the GUI control and the other code treat that class as the definitive source of that data.

Change unidirectional class association to bidirectional class association   If you have two classes that need to use each other's features but only one class can know about the other class, change the classes so that they both know about each other.

Change bidirectional class association to unidirectional class association   If you have two classes that know about each other's features but only one class that really needs to know about the other, change the classes so that one knows about the other but not vice versa.

Provide a factory method rather than a simple constructor   Use a factory method (routine) when you need to create objects based on a type code or when you want to work with reference objects rather than value objects.

Replace error codes with exceptions or vice versa   Depending on your error-handling strategy, make sure the code is using the standard approach.

cc2e.com/2450

CHECKLIST: Summary of Refactorings

Data-Level Refactorings

- ❏ Replace a magic number with a named constant.
- ❏ Rename a variable with a clearer or more informative name.
- ❏ Move an expression inline.
- ❏ Replace an expression with a routine.
- ❏ Introduce an intermediate variable.
- ❏ Convert a multiuse variable to a multiple single-use variables.
- ❏ Use a local variable for local purposes rather than a parameter.
- ❏ Convert a data primitive to a class.
- ❏ Convert a set of type codes to a class or an enumeration.
- ❏ Convert a set of type codes to a class with subclasses.
- ❏ Change an array to an object.
- ❏ Encapsulate a collection.
- ❏ Replace a traditional record with a data class.

Statement-Level Refactorings

- ❏ Decompose a boolean expression.
- ❏ Move a complex boolean expression into a well-named boolean function.

- ❑ Consolidate fragments that are duplicated within different parts of a conditional.
- ❑ Use *break* or *return* instead of a loop control variable.
- ❑ Return as soon as you know the answer instead of assigning a return value within nested *if-then-else* statements.
- ❑ Replace conditionals (especially repeated *case* statements) with polymorphism.
- ❑ Create and use null objects instead of testing for null values.

Routine-Level Refactorings

- ❑ Extract a routine.
- ❑ Move a routine's code inline.
- ❑ Convert a long routine to a class.
- ❑ Substitute a simple algorithm for a complex algorithm.
- ❑ Add a parameter.
- ❑ Remove a parameter.
- ❑ Separate query operations from modification operations.
- ❑ Combine similar routines by parameterizing them.
- ❑ Separate routines whose behavior depends on parameters passed in.
- ❑ Pass a whole object rather than specific fields.
- ❑ Pass specific fields rather than a whole object.
- ❑ Encapsulate downcasting.

Class Implementation Refactorings

- ❑ Change value objects to reference objects.
- ❑ Change reference objects to value objects.
- ❑ Replace virtual routines with data initialization.
- ❑ Change member routine or data placement.
- ❑ Extract specialized code into a subclass.
- ❑ Combine similar code into a superclass.

Class Interface Refactorings

- ❏ Move a routine to another class.
- ❏ Convert one class to two.
- ❏ Eliminate a class.
- ❏ Hide a delegate.
- ❏ Remove a middleman.
- ❏ Replace inheritance with delegation.
- ❏ Replace delegation with inheritance.
- ❏ Introduce a foreign routine.
- ❏ Introduce an extension class.
- ❏ Encapsulate an exposed member variable.
- ❏ Remove *Set()* routines for fields that cannot be changed.
- ❏ Hide routines that are not intended to be used outside the class.
- ❏ Encapsulate unused routines.
- ❏ Collapse a superclass and subclass if their implementations are very similar.

System-Level Refactorings

- ❏ Create a definitive reference source for data you can't control.
- ❏ Change unidirectional class association to bidirectional class association.
- ❏ Change bidirectional class association to unidirectional class association.
- ❏ Provide a factory routine rather than a simple constructor.
- ❏ Replace error codes with exceptions or vice versa.

24.4 Refactoring Safely

Opening up a working system is more like opening up a human brain and replacing a nerve than opening up a sink and replacing a washer. Would maintenance be easier if it was called "Software Brain Surgery?"
—Gerald Weinberg

Refactoring is a powerful technique for improving code quality. Like all powerful tools, refactoring can cause more harm than good if misused. A few simple guidelines can prevent refactoring missteps.

Save the code you start with   Before you begin refactoring, make sure you can get back to the code you started with. Save a version in your revision control system, or copy the correct files to a backup directory.

Keep refactorings small   Some refactorings are larger than others, and exactly what constitutes "one refactoring" can be a little fuzzy. Keep the refactorings small so that you fully understand all the impacts of the changes you make. The detailed refactorings described in *Refactoring* (Fowler 1999) provide many good examples of how to do this.

Do refactorings one at a time   Some refactorings are more complicated than others. For all but the simplest refactorings, do the refactorings one at a time, recompiling and retesting after a refactoring before doing the next one.

Make a list of steps you intend to take   A natural extension of the Pseudocode Programming Process is to make a list of the refactorings that will get you from Point A to Point B. Making a list helps you keep each change in context.

Make a parking lot   When you're midway through one refactoring, you'll sometimes find that you need another refactoring. Midway through that refactoring, you find a third refactoring that would be beneficial. For changes that aren't needed immediately, make a "parking lot," a list of the changes that you'd like to make at some point but that don't need to be made right now.

Make frequent checkpoints   It's easy to find the code suddenly going sideways while you're refactoring. In addition to saving the code you started with, save checkpoints at various steps in a refactoring session so that you can get back to a working program if you code yourself into a dead end.

Use your compiler warnings   It's easy to make small errors that slip past the compiler. Setting your compiler to the pickiest warning level possible will help catch many errors almost as soon as you type them.

Retest   Reviews of changed code should be complemented by retests. Of course, this is dependent on having a good set of test cases in the first place. Regression testing and other test topics are described in more detail in Chapter 22, "Developer Testing."

Add test cases   In addition to retesting with your old tests, add new unit tests to exercise the new code. Remove any test cases that have been made obsolete by the refactorings.

Cross-Reference For details on reviews, see Chapter 21, "Collaborative Construction."   *Review the changes*   If reviews are important the first time through, they are even more important during subsequent modifications. Ed Yourdon reports that programmers typically have more than a 50 percent chance of making an error on their first attempt to make a change (Yourdon 1986b). Interestingly, if programmers work with a substantial portion of the code, rather than just a few lines, the chance of making a correct modification improves, as shown in Figure 24-1. Specifically, as the number of lines changed increases from one to five lines, the chance of making a bad change increases. After that, the chance of making a bad change decreases.

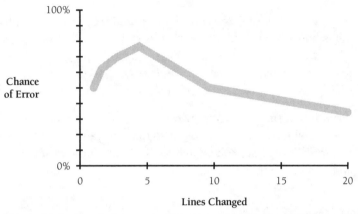

Figure 24-1   Small changes tend to be more error-prone than larger changes (Weinberg 1983).

Programmers treat small changes casually. They don't desk-check them, they don't have others review them, and they sometimes don't even run the code to verify that the fix works properly.

The moral is simple: treat simple changes as if they were complicated. One organization that introduced reviews for one-line changes found that its error rate went from 55 percent before reviews to 2 percent afterward (Freedman and Weinberg 1982). A telecommunications organization went from 86 percent correct before reviewing code changes to 99.6 percent afterward (Perrott 2004).

Adjust your approach depending on the risk level of the refactoring   Some refactorings are riskier than others. A refactoring like "Replace a magic number with a named constant" is relatively risk-free. Refactorings that involve class or routine interface changes, database schema changes, or changes to boolean tests, among others, tend to be more risky. For easier refactorings, you might streamline your refactoring process to do more than one refactoring at a time and to simply retest, without going through an official review.

For riskier refactorings, err on the side of caution. Do the refactorings one at a time. Have someone else review the refactoring or use pair programming for that refactoring, in addition to the normal compiler checking and unit tests.

Bad Times to Refactor

Refactoring is a powerful technique, but it isn't a panacea and it's subject to a few specific kinds of abuse.

> Do not partially write a feature with the intent of refactoring to get it complete later.
> —*John Manzo*

Don't use refactoring as a cover for code and fix The worst problem with refactoring is how it's misused. Programmers will sometimes say they're refactoring, when all they're really doing is tweaking the code, hoping to find a way to make it work. Refactoring refers to *changes in working code* that do not affect the program's behavior. Programmers who are tweaking broken code aren't refactoring; they're hacking.

> A big refactoring is a recipe for disaster.
> —*Kent Beck*

Avoid refactoring instead of rewriting Sometimes code doesn't need small changes—it needs to be tossed out so that you can start over. If you find yourself in a major refactoring session, ask yourself whether instead you should be redesigning and reimplementing that section of code from the ground up.

24.5 Refactoring Strategies

The number of refactorings that would be beneficial to any specific program is essentially infinite. Refactoring is subject to the same law of diminishing returns as other programming activities, and the 80/20 rule applies. Spend your time on the 20 percent of the refactorings that provide 80 percent of the benefit. Consider the following guidelines when deciding which refactorings are most important:

Refactor when you add a routine When you add a routine, check whether related routines are well organized. If not, refactor them.

Refactor when you add a class Adding a class often brings issues with existing code to the fore. Use this time as an opportunity to refactor other classes that are closely related to the class you're adding.

Refactor when you fix a defect Use the understanding you gain from fixing a bug to improve other code that might be prone to similar defects.

> **Cross-Reference** For more on error-prone code, see "Which Classes Contain the Most Errors?" in Section 22.4.

Target error-prone modules Some modules are more error-prone and brittle than others. Is there a section of code that you and everyone else on your team is afraid of? That's probably an error-prone module. Although most people's natural tendency is to avoid these challenging sections of code, targeting these sections for refactoring can be one of the more effective strategies (Jones 2000).

Target high-complexity modules   Another approach is to focus on modules that have the highest complexity ratings. (See "How to Measure Complexity" in Section 19.6 for details on these metrics.) One classic study found that program quality improved dramatically when maintenance programmers focused their improvement efforts on the modules that had the highest complexity (Henry and Kafura 1984).

In a maintenance environment, improve the parts you touch   Code that is never modified doesn't need to be refactored. But when you do touch a section of code, be sure you leave it better than you found it.

Define an interface between clean code and ugly code, and then move code across the interface   The "real world" is often messier than you'd like. The messiness might come from complicated business rules, hardware interfaces, or software interfaces. A common problem with geriatric systems is poorly written production code that must remain operational at all times.

An effective strategy for rejuvenating geriatric production systems is to designate some code as being in the messy real world, some code as being in an idealized new world, and some code as being the interface between the two. Figure 24-2 illustrates this idea.

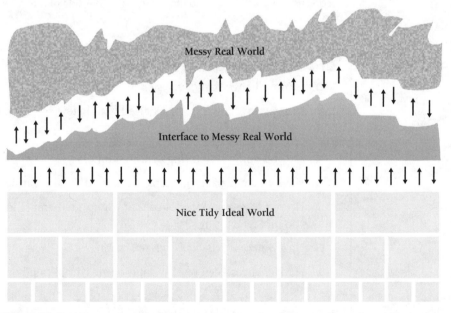

Figure 24-2   Your code doesn't have to be messy just because the real world is messy. Conceive your system as a combination of ideal code, interfaces from the ideal code to the messy real world, and the messy real world.

As you work with the system, you can begin moving code across the "real world interface" into a more organized ideal world. When you begin working with a legacy system, the poorly written legacy code might make up nearly all the system. One policy that works well is that anytime you touch a section of messy code, you are required to bring it up to current coding standards, give it clear variable names, and so on—effectively moving it into the ideal world. Over time this can provide for a rapid improvement in a code base, as shown in Figure 24-3.

Initial State
Mostly Poorly-Written Legacy Code

Target State
Mostly Well-Written Refactored Code

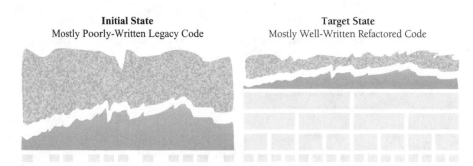

Figure 24-3 One strategy for improving production code is to refactor poorly written legacy code as you touch it, so as to move it to the other side of the "interface to the messy real world."

cc2e.com/2457

CHECKLIST: Refactoring Safely

- ❏ Is each change part of a systematic change strategy?

- ❏ Did you save the code you started with before beginning refactoring?

- ❏ Are you keeping each refactoring small?

- ❏ Are you doing refactorings one at a time?

- ❏ Have you made a list of steps you intend to take during your refactoring?

- ❏ Do you have a parking lot so that you can remember ideas that occur to you mid-refactoring?

- ❏ Have you retested after each refactoring?

- ❏ Have changes been reviewed if they are complicated or if they affect mission-critical code?

- ❏ Have you considered the riskiness of the specific refactoring and adjusted your approach accordingly?

- ❏ Does the change enhance the program's internal quality rather than degrade it?

- ❏ Have you avoided using refactoring as a cover for code and fix or as an excuse for not rewriting bad code?

Additional Resources

cc2e.com/2464

The process of refactoring has a lot in common with the process of fixing defects. For more on fixing defects, see Section 23.3, "Fixing a Defect." The risks associated with refactoring are similar to the risks associated with code tuning. For more on managing code-tuning risks, see Section 25.6, "Summary of the Approach to Code Tuning."

Fowler, Martin. *Refactoring: Improving the Design of Existing Code*. Reading, MA: Addison Wesley, 1999. This is the definitive guide to refactoring. It contains detailed discussions of many of the specific refactorings summarized in this chapter, as well as a handful of other refactorings not summarized here. Fowler provides numerous code samples to illustrate how each refactoring is performed step by step.

Key Points

- Program changes are a fact of life both during initial development and after initial release.

- Software can either improve or degrade as it's changed. The Cardinal Rule of Software Evolution is that internal quality should improve with code evolution.

- One key to success in refactoring is learning to pay attention to the numerous warning signs or smells that indicate a need to refactor.

- Another key to refactoring success is learning numerous specific refactorings.

- A final key to success is having a strategy for refactoring safely. Some refactoring approaches are better than others.

- Refactoring during development is the best chance you'll get to improve your program, to make all the changes you'll wish you'd made the first time. Take advantage of these opportunities during development!

Chapter 25
Code-Tuning Strategies

cc2e.com/2578

Contents

- 25.1 Performance Overview: page 588
- 25.2 Introduction to Code Tuning: page 591
- 25.3 Kinds of Fat and Molasses: page 597
- 25.4 Measurement: page 603
- 25.5 Iteration: page 605
- 25.6 Summary of the Approach to Code Tuning: page 606

Related Topics

- Code-tuning techniques: Chapter 26
- Software architecture: Section 3.5

This chapter discusses the question of performance tuning—historically, a controversial issue. Computer resources were severely limited in the 1960s, and efficiency was a paramount concern. As computers became more powerful in the 1970s, programmers realized how much their focus on performance had hurt readability and maintainability and code tuning received less attention. The return of performance limitations with the microcomputer revolution of the 1980s again brought efficiency to the fore, which then waned throughout the 1990s. In the 2000s, memory limitations in embedded software for devices such as telephones and PDAs and the execution time of interpreted code have once again made efficiency a key topic.

You can address performance concerns at two levels: strategic and tactical. This chapter addresses strategic performance issues: what performance is, how important it is, and the general approach to achieving it. If you already have a good grip on performance strategies and are looking for specific code-level techniques that improve performance, move on to Chapter 26, "Code-Tuning Techniques." Before you begin any major performance work, however, at least skim the information in this chapter so that you don't waste time optimizing when you should be doing other kinds of work.

25.1 Performance Overview

Code tuning is one way of improving a program's performance. You can often find other ways to improve performance more—and in less time and with less harm to the code—than by code tuning. This section describes the options.

Quality Characteristics and Performance

More computing sins are committed in the name of efficiency (without necessarily achieving it) than for any other single reason— including blind stupidity.
—W. A. Wulf

Some people look at the world through rose-colored glasses. Programmers like you and me tend to look at the world through code-colored glasses. We assume that the better we make the code, the more our clients and customers will like our software.

This point of view might have a mailing address somewhere in reality, but it doesn't have a street number and it certainly doesn't own any real estate. Users are more interested in tangible program characteristics than they are in code quality. Sometimes users are interested in raw performance, but only when it affects their work. Users tend to be more interested in program throughput than raw performance. Delivering software on time, providing a clean user interface, and avoiding downtime are often more significant.

Here's an illustration. I take at least 50 pictures a week on my digital camera. To upload the pictures to my computer, the software that came with the camera requires me to select each picture one by one, viewing them in a window that shows only six pictures at a time. Uploading 50 pictures is a tedious process that requires dozens of mouse clicks and lots of navigation through the six-picture window. After putting up with this for a few months, I bought a memory-card reader that plugs directly into my computer and that my computer thinks is a disk drive. Now I can use Windows Explorer to copy the pictures to my computer. What used to take dozens of mouse clicks and lots of waiting now requires about two mouse clicks, a Ctrl+A, and a drag and drop. I really don't care whether the memory card reader transfers each file in half the time or twice the time as the other software, because my throughput is faster. Regardless of whether the memory card reader's code is faster or slower, its performance is better.

KEY POINT

Performance is only loosely related to code speed. To the extent that you work on your code's speed, you're not working on other quality characteristics. Be wary of sacrificing other characteristics to make your code faster. Your work on speed might hurt overall performance rather than help it.

Performance and Code Tuning

Once you've chosen efficiency as a priority, whether its emphasis is on speed or on size, you should consider several options before choosing to improve either speed or size at the code level. Think about efficiency from each of these viewpoints:

- Program requirements
- Program design
- Class and routine design
- Operating-system interactions
- Code compilation
- Hardware
- Code tuning

Program Requirements

Performance is stated as a requirement far more often than it actually is a requirement. Barry Boehm tells the story of a system at TRW that initially required subsecond response time. This requirement led to a highly complex design and an estimated cost of $100 million. Further analysis determined that users would be satisfied with four-second responses 90 percent of the time. Modifying the response-time requirement reduced overall system cost by about $70 million. (Boehm 2000b).

Before you invest time solving a performance problem, make sure that you're solving a problem that needs to be solved.

Program Design

Cross-Reference For details on designing performance into a program, see the "Additional Resources" section at the end of this chapter.

Program design includes the major strokes of the design for a single program, mainly the way in which a program is divided into classes. Some program designs make it difficult to write a high-performance system. Others make it hard not to.

Consider the example of a real-world data-acquisition program for which the high-level design had identified measurement throughput as a key product attribute. Each measurement included time to make an electrical measurement, calibrate the value, scale the value, and convert it from sensor data units (such as millivolts) into engineering data units (such as degrees Celsius).

In this case, without addressing the risk in the high-level design, the programmers would have found themselves trying to optimize the math to evaluate a 13th-order polynomial in software—that is, a polynomial with 14 terms, including variables raised to the 13th power. Instead, they addressed the problem with different hardware and a high-level design that used dozens of 3rd-order polynomials. This change could not have been effected through code tuning, and it's unlikely that any amount of code tuning would have solved the problem. This is an example of a problem that had to be addressed at the program-design level.

Cross-Reference For details on the way programmers work toward objectives, see "Setting Objectives" in Section 20.2.

If you know that a program's size and speed are important, design the program's architecture so that you can reasonably meet your size and speed goals. Design a performance-oriented architecture, and then set resource goals for individual subsystems, features, and classes. This will help in several ways:

- Setting individual resource goals makes the system's ultimate performance predictable. If each feature meets its resource goals, the whole system will meet its goals. You can identify subsystems that have trouble meeting their goals early and target them for redesign or code tuning.

- The mere act of making goals explicit improves the likelihood that they'll be achieved. Programmers work to objectives when they know what they are; the more explicit the objectives, the easier they are to work to.

KEY POINT

- You can set goals that don't achieve efficiency directly but promote efficiency in the long run. Efficiency is often best treated in the context of other issues. For example, achieving a high degree of modifiability can provide a better basis for meeting efficiency goals than explicitly setting an efficiency target. With a highly modular, modifiable design, you can easily swap less-efficient components for more-efficient ones.

Class and Routine Design

Cross-Reference For more information about data types and algorithms, see the "Additional Resources" section at the end of the chapter.

Designing the internals of classes and routines presents another opportunity to design for performance. One performance key that comes into play at this level is the choice of data types and algorithms, which usually affect both the program's memory use and execution speed. This is the level at which you can choose quicksort rather than bubblesort or a binary search instead of a linear search.

Operating-System Interactions

Cross-Reference For code-level strategies that address slow or fat operating-system routines, see Chapter 26, "Code-Tuning Techniques."

If your program works with external files, dynamic memory, or output devices, it's probably interacting with the operating system. If performance isn't good, it might be because the operating-system routines are slow or fat. You might not be aware that the program is interacting with the operating system; sometimes your compiler generates system calls or your libraries invoke system calls you would never dream of. More on this later.

Code Compilation

Good compilers turn clear, high-level language code into optimized machine code. If you choose the right compiler, you might not need to think about optimizing speed any further.

The optimization results reported in Chapter 26 provide numerous examples of compiler optimizations that produce more efficient code than manual code tuning does.

Hardware

Sometimes the cheapest and best way to improve a program's performance is to buy new hardware. If you're distributing a program for nationwide use by hundreds of thousands of customers, buying new hardware isn't a realistic option. But if you're developing custom software for a few in-house users, a hardware upgrade might be the cheapest option. It saves the cost of initial performance work. It saves the cost of future maintenance problems caused by performance work. It improves the performance of every other program that runs on that hardware, too.

Code Tuning

Code tuning is the practice of modifying correct code in ways that make it run more efficiently, and it's the subject of the rest of this chapter. "Tuning" refers to small-scale changes that affect a single class, a single routine, or, more commonly, a few lines of code. "Tuning" does not refer to large-scale design changes or other higher-level means of improving performance.

You can make dramatic improvements at each level from system design through code tuning. Jon Bentley cites an argument that in some systems the improvements at each level can be multiplied (1982). Because you can achieve a 10-fold improvement in each of six levels, that implies a potential performance improvement of a million fold. Although such a multiplication of improvements requires a program in which gains at one level are independent of gains at other levels, which is rare, the potential is inspiring.

25.2 Introduction to Code Tuning

What is code tuning's appeal? It's not the most effective way to improve performance—program architecture, class design, and algorithm selection usually produce more dramatic improvements. Nor is it the easiest way to improve performance—buying new hardware or a compiler with a better optimizer is easier. And it's not the cheapest way to improve performance either—it takes more time to hand-tune code initially, and hand-tuned code is harder to maintain later.

Code tuning is appealing for several reasons. One attraction is that it seems to defy the laws of nature. It's incredibly satisfying to take a routine that executes in 20 microseconds, tweak a few lines, and reduce the execution speed to 2 microseconds.

It's also appealing because mastering the art of writing efficient code is a rite of passage to becoming a serious programmer. In tennis, you don't get any game points for the way you pick up a tennis ball, but you still need to learn the right way to do it. You can't just lean over and pick it up with your hand. If you're good, you whack it with the head of your racket until it bounces waist high and then you catch it. Whacking it more than three times, even not bouncing it the first time, is a serious failing. Despite its seeming unimportance, the way you pick up the ball carries a certain cachet within tennis culture. Similarly, no one but you and other programmers usually cares how tight your code is. Nonetheless, within the programming culture, writing microefficient code proves you're cool.

The problem with code tuning is that efficient code isn't necessarily "better" code. That's the subject of the next few sections.

The Pareto Principle

The Pareto Principle, also known as the 80/20 rule, states that you can get 80 percent of the result with 20 percent of the effort. The principle applies to a lot of areas other than programming, but it definitely applies to program optimization.

KEY POINT

Barry Boehm reports that 20 percent of a program's routines consume 80 percent of its execution time (1987b). In his classic paper "An Empirical Study of Fortran Programs," Donald Knuth found that less than four percent of a program usually accounts for more than 50 percent of its run time (1971).

Knuth used a line-count profiler to discover this surprising relationship, and the implications for optimization are clear. You should measure the code to find the hot spots and then put your resources into optimizing the few percent that are used the most. Knuth profiled his line-count program and found that it was spending half its execution time in two loops. He changed a few lines of code and doubled the speed of the profiler in less than an hour.

Jon Bentley describes a case in which a 1000-line program spent 80 percent of its time in a five-line square-root routine. By tripling the speed of the square-root routine, he doubled the speed of the program (1988). The Pareto Principle is also the source of the advice to write most of the code in an interpreted language like Python and then rewrite the hot spots in a faster compiled language like C.

Bentley also reports the case of a team that discovered half an operating system's time being spent in a small loop. They rewrote the loop in microcode and made the loop 10 times faster, but it didn't change the system's performance—they had rewritten the system's idle loop!

The team who designed the ALGOL language—the granddaddy of most modern languages and one of the most influential languages ever—received the following advice: "The best is the enemy of the good." Working toward perfection might prevent completion. Complete it first, and then perfect it. The part that needs to be perfect is usually small.

Old Wives' Tales

Much of what you've heard about code tuning is false, including the following common misapprehensions:

Reducing the lines of code in a high-level language improves the speed or size of the resulting machine code–false!   Many programmers cling tenaciously to the belief that if they can write code in one or two lines, it will be the most efficient possible. Consider the following code that initializes a 10-element array:

```
for i = 1 to 10
   a[ i ] = i
end for
```

Would you guess that these lines are faster or slower than the following 10 lines that do the same job?

```
a[ 1 ] = 1
a[ 2 ] = 2
a[ 3 ] = 3
a[ 4 ] = 4
a[ 5 ] = 5
a[ 6 ] = 6
a[ 7 ] = 7
a[ 8 ] = 8
a[ 9 ] = 9
a[ 10 ] = 10
```

If you follow the old "fewer lines are faster" dogma, you'll guess that the first code is faster. But tests in Microsoft Visual Basic and Java have shown that the second fragment is at least 60 percent faster than the first. Here are the numbers:

Language	*for*-Loop Time	Straight-Code Time	Time Savings	Performance Ratio
Visual Basic	8.47	3.16	63%	2.5:1
Java	12.6	3.23	74%	4:1

> **Note**   (1) Times in this and the following tables in this chapter are given in seconds and are meaningful only for comparisons across rows in each table. Actual times will vary according to the compiler, compiler options used, and the environment in which each test is run. (2) Benchmark results are typically made up of several thousand to many million executions of the code fragments to smooth out sample-to-sample fluctuations in the results. (3) Specific brands and versions of compilers aren't indicated. Performance characteristics vary significantly from brand to brand and from version to version. (4) Comparisons among results from different languages aren't always meaningful because compilers for different languages don't always offer comparable code-generation options. (5) The results shown for interpreted languages (PHP and Python) are typically based on less than 1% of the test runs used for the other languages. (6) Some of the "time savings" percentages might not be exactly reproducible from the data in these tables due to rounding of the "straight time" and "code-tuned time" entries.

This certainly doesn't imply that increasing the number of lines of high-level language code always improves speed or reduces size. It does imply that regardless of the aesthetic appeal of writing something with the fewest lines of code, no predictable relationship exists between the number of lines of code in a high-level language and a program's ultimate size and speed.

Certain operations are probably faster or smaller than others—false!   There's no room for "probably" when you're talking about performance. You must always measure performance to know whether your changes helped or hurt your program. The rules of the game change every time you change languages, compilers, versions of compilers, libraries, versions of libraries, processor, amount of memory on the machine, color of shirt you're wearing (OK, not this one), and so on. What was true on one machine with one set of tools can easily be false on another machine with a different set of tools.

This phenomenon suggests several reasons not to improve performance by code tuning. If you want your program to be portable, techniques that improve performance in one environment can degrade it in others. If you change compilers or upgrade, the new compiler might automatically optimize code the way you were hand-tuning it and your work will have been wasted. Even worse, your code tuning might defeat more powerful compiler optimizations that have been designed to work with straightforward code.

When you tune code, you're implicitly signing up to reprofile each optimization every time you change your compiler brand, compiler version, library version, and so on. If you don't reprofile, an optimization that improves performance under one version of a compiler or library might well degrade performance when you change the build environment.

> We should forget about small efficiencies, say about 97% of the time: premature optimization is the root of all evil.
> —*Donald Knuth*

You should optimize as you go—false!   One theory is that if you strive to write the fastest and smallest possible code as you write each routine, your program will be fast and small. This approach creates a forest-for-the-trees situation in which programmers ignore significant global optimizations because they're too busy with micro-optimizations. Here are the main problems with optimizing as you go along:

■ It's almost impossible to identify performance bottlenecks before a program is working completely. Programmers are very bad at guessing which four percent of the code accounts for 50 percent of the execution time, and so programmers who optimize as they go will, on average, spend 96 percent of their time optimizing code that doesn't need to be optimized. That leaves little time to optimize the four percent that really counts.

■ In the rare case in which developers identify the bottlenecks correctly, they overkill the bottlenecks they've identified and allow others to become critical. Again, the ultimate effect is a reduction in performance. Optimizations done after a system is complete can identify each problem area and its relative importance so that optimization time is allocated effectively.

■ Focusing on optimization during initial development detracts from achieving other program objectives. Developers immerse themselves in algorithm analysis and arcane debates that in the end don't contribute much value to the user. Concerns such as correctness, information hiding, and readability become secondary goals, even though performance is easier to improve later than these other concerns are. Post hoc performance work typically affects less than five percent of a program's code. Would you rather go back and do performance work on five percent of the code or readability work on 100 percent?

In short, premature optimization's primary drawback is its lack of perspective. Its victims include final code speed, performance attributes that are more important than code speed, program quality, and ultimately the software's users. If the development time saved by implementing the simplest program is devoted to optimizing the running program, the result will always be a program that runs faster than one developed with indiscriminate optimization efforts (Stevens 1981).

Occasionally, post hoc optimization won't be sufficient to meet performance goals and you'll have to make major changes in the completed code. In those cases, small, localized optimizations wouldn't have provided the gains needed anyway. The problem in such cases isn't inadequate code quality—it's inadequate software architecture.

If you need to optimize before a program is complete, minimize the risks by building perspective into your process. One way is to specify size and speed goals for features and then optimize to meet the goals as you go along. Setting such goals in a specification is a way to keep one eye on the forest while you figure out how big your particular tree is.

Further Reading For many other entertaining and enlightening anecdotes, see Gerald Weinberg's *Psychology of Computer Programming* (1998).

A fast program is just as important as a correct one—false! It's hardly ever true that programs need to be fast or small before they need to be correct. Gerald Weinberg tells the story of a programmer who was flown to Detroit to help debug a troubled program. The programmer worked with the team who had developed the program and concluded after several days that the situation was hopeless.

On the flight home, he mulled over the situation and realized what the problem was. By the end of the flight, he had an outline for the new code. He tested the code for several days and was about to return to Detroit when he got a telegram saying that the project had been cancelled because the program was impossible to write. He headed back to Detroit anyway and convinced the executives that the project could be completed.

Then he had to convince the project's original programmers. They listened to his presentation, and when he'd finished, the creator of the old system asked, "And how long does your program take?"

"That varies, but about ten seconds per input."

"Aha! But my program takes only one second per input." The veteran leaned back, satisfied that he'd stumped the upstart. The other programmers seemed to agree, but the new programmer wasn't intimidated.

"Yes, but your program *doesn't work*. If mine doesn't have to work, I can make it run instantly."

For a certain class of projects, speed or size is a major concern. This class is the minority, is much smaller than most people think, and is getting smaller all the time. For these projects, the performance risks must be addressed by up-front design. For other projects, early optimization poses a significant threat to overall software quality, *including performance.*

When to Tune

Jackson's Rules of Optimization: Rule 1. Don't do it. Rule 2 (for experts only). Don't do it yet—that is, not until you have a perfectly clear and unoptimized solution.
—*M. A. Jackson*

Use a high-quality design. Make the program right. Make it modular and easily modifiable so that it's easy to work on later. When it's complete and correct, check the performance. If the program lumbers, make it fast and small. Don't optimize until you know you need to.

A few years ago I worked on a C++ project that produced graphical outputs to analyze investment data. After my team got the first graph working, testing reported that the program took about 45 minutes to draw the graph, which was clearly not acceptable. We held a team meeting to decide what to do about it. One of the developers became irate and shouted, "If we want to have any chance of releasing an acceptable product, we've got to start rewriting the whole code base in assembler *right now*." I responded that I didn't think so—that four percent of the code probably accounted for 50 percent or more of the performance bottleneck. It would be best to address that four percent toward the end of the project. After a bit more shouting, our manager assigned me to do some initial performance work (which was really a case of "Oh no! Please don't throw me into that briar patch!").

As is often the case, a day's work identified a couple of glaring bottlenecks in the code. A small number of code-tuning changes reduced the drawing time from 45 minutes to less than 30 seconds. Far less than one percent of the code accounted for 90 percent of the run time. By the time we released the software months later, several additional code-tuning changes reduced that drawing time to a little more than 1 second.

Compiler Optimizations

Modern compiler optimizations might be more powerful than you expect. In the case I described earlier, my compiler did as good a job of optimizing a nested loop as I was able to do by rewriting the code in a supposedly more efficient style. When shopping for a compiler, compare the performance of each compiler on your program. Each compiler has different strengths and weaknesses, and some will be better suited to your program than others.

Optimizing compilers are better at optimizing straightforward code than they are at optimizing tricky code. If you do "clever" things like fooling around with loop indexes, your compiler has a harder time doing its job and your program suffers. See "Using Only One Statement Per Line" in Section 31.5 for an example in which a straightforward approach resulted in compiler-optimized code that was 11 percent faster than comparable "tricky" code.

With a good optimizing compiler, your code speed can improve 40 percent or more across the board. Many of the techniques described in the next chapter produce gains of only 15–30 percent. Why not just write clear code and let the compiler do the work? Here are the results of a few tests to check how much an optimizer speeded up an insertion-sort routine:

Language	Time Without Compiler Optimizations	Time with Compiler Optimizations	Time Savings	Performance Ratio
C++ compiler 1	2.21	1.05	52%	2:1
C++ compiler 2	2.78	1.15	59%	2.5:1
C++ compiler 3	2.43	1.25	49%	2:1
C# compiler	1.55	1.55	0%	1:1
Visual Basic	1.78	1.78	0%	1:1
Java VM 1	2.77	2.77	0%	1:1
Java VM 2	1.39	1.38	<1%	1:1
Java VM 3	2.63	2.63	0%	1:1

The only difference between versions of the routine was that compiler optimizations were turned off for the first compile and turned on for the second. Clearly, some compilers optimize better than others, and some are better without optimizations in the first place. Some Java Virtual Machines (JVMs) are also clearly better than others. You'll have to check your own compiler, JVM, or both to measure the effect.

25.3 Kinds of Fat and Molasses

In code tuning you find the parts of a program that are as slow as molasses in winter and as big as Godzilla and change them so that they are as fast as greased lightning and so skinny they can hide in the cracks between the other bytes in RAM. You always have to profile the program to know with any confidence which parts are slow and fat, but some operations have a long history of laziness and obesity, and you can start by investigating them.

Common Sources of Inefficiency

Here are several common sources of inefficiency:

Input/output operations   One of the most significant sources of inefficiency is unnecessary input/output (I/O). If you have a choice of working with a file in memory vs. on disk, in a database, or across a network, use an in-memory data structure unless space is critical.

Here's a performance comparison between code that accesses random elements in a 100-element in-memory array and code that accesses random elements of the same size in a 100-record disk file:

Language	External File Time	In-Memory Data Time	Time Savings	Performance Ratio
C++	6.04	0.000	100%	n/a
C#	12.8	0.010	100%	1000:1

According to this data, in-memory access is on the order of 1000 times faster than accessing data in an external file. Indeed with the C++ compiler I used, the time required for in-memory access wasn't measurable.

The performance comparison for a similar test of sequential access times is similar:

Language	External File Time	In-Memory Data Time	Time Savings	Performance Ratio
C++	3.29	0.021	99%	150:1
C#	2.60	0.030	99%	85:1

Note: The tests for sequential access were run with 13 times the data volume of the tests for random access, so the results are not comparable across the two types of tests.

If the test had used a slower medium for external access—for example, a hard disk across a network connection—the difference would have been even greater. The performance looks like this when a similar random-access test is performed on a network location instead of on the local machine:

Language	Local File Time	Network File Time	Time Savings
C++	6.04	6.64	-10%
C#	12.8	14.1	-10%

Of course, these results can vary dramatically depending on the speed of your network, network loading, distance of the local machine from the networked disk drive, speed of the networked disk drive compared to the speed of the local drive, current phase of the moon, and other factors.

Overall, the effect of in-memory access is significant enough to make you think twice about having I/O in a speed-critical part of a program.

Paging   An operation that causes the operating system to swap pages of memory is much slower than an operation that works on only one page of memory. Sometimes a simple change makes a huge difference. In the next example, one programmer wrote an initialization loop that produced many page faults on a system that used 4K pages.

Java Example of an Initialization Loop That Causes Many Page Faults

```java
for ( column = 0; column < MAX_COLUMNS; column++ ) {
   for ( row = 0; row < MAX_ROWS; row++ ) {
      table[ row ][ column ] = BlankTableElement();
   }
}
```

This is a nicely formatted loop with good variable names, so what's the problem? The problem is that each element of *table* is about 4000 bytes long. If *table* has too many rows, every time the program accesses a different row, the operating system will have to switch memory pages. The way the loop is structured, every single array access switches rows, which means that every single array access causes paging to disk.

The programmer restructured the loop this way:

Java Example of an Initialization Loop That Causes Few Page Faults

```java
for ( row = 0; row < MAX_ROWS; row++ ) {
   for ( column = 0; column < MAX_COLUMNS; column++ ) {
      table[ row ][ column ] = BlankTableElement();
   }
}
```

This code still causes a page fault every time it switches rows, but it switches rows only *MAX_ROWS* times instead of *MAX_ROWS * MAX_COLUMNS* times.

The specific performance penalty varies significantly. On a machine with limited memory, I measured the second code sample to be about 1000 times faster than the first code sample. On machines with more memory, I've measured the difference to be as small as a factor of 2, and it doesn't show up at all except for very large values of *MAX_ROWS* and *MAX_COLUMNS*.

System calls   Calls to system routines are often expensive. They often involve a context switch—saving the program's state, recovering the kernel's state, and the reverse. System routines include input/output operations to disk, keyboard, screen, printer, or other device; memory-management routines; and certain utility routines. If performance is an issue, find out how expensive your system calls are. If they're expensive, consider these options:

■ Write your own services. Sometimes you need only a small part of the functionality offered by a system routine and can build your own from lower-level system routines. Writing your own replacement gives you something that's faster, smaller, and better suited to your needs.

■ Avoid going to the system.

■ Work with the system vendor to make the call faster. Most vendors want to improve their products and are glad to learn about parts of their systems with weak performance. (They might seem a little grouchy about it at first, but they really are interested.)

In the code-tuning effort I described in "When to Tune" in Section 25.2, the program used an *AppTime* class that was derived from a commercially available *BaseTime* class. (These names have been changed to protect the guilty.) The *AppTime* object was the most common object in this application, and we instantiated tens of thousands of *AppTime* objects. After several months, we discovered that *BaseTime* was initializing itself to the system time in its constructor. For our purposes, the system time was irrelevant, which meant we were needlessly generating thousands of system-level calls. Simply overriding *BaseTime*'s constructor and initializing the *time* field to 0 instead of to the system time gave us about as much performance improvement as all the other changes we made put together.

Interpreted languages   Interpreted languages tend to exact significant performance penalties because they must process each programming-language instruction before creating and executing machine code. In the performance benchmarking I performed for this chapter and Chapter 26, I observed the approximate relationships in performance among different languages that are described in Table 25-1.

Table 25-1   Relative Execution Time of Programming Languages

Language	Type of Language	Execution Time Relative to C++
C++	Compiled	1:1
Visual Basic	Compiled	1:1
C#	Compiled	1:1
Java	Byte code	1.5:1
PHP	Interpreted	>100:1
Python	Interpreted	>100:1

As you can see, C++, Visual Basic, and C# are all comparable. Java is close but tends to be slower than the other languages. PHP and Python are interpreted languages, and code in those languages tended to run a factor of 100 or more slower than code in C++, Visual Basic, C#, and Java. The general numbers presented in this table must be viewed cautiously. For any particular piece of code, C++, Visual Basic, C#, or Java might be twice as fast or half as fast as the other languages. (You can see this for yourself in the detailed examples in Chapter 26.)

Errors A final source of performance problems is errors in the code. Errors can include leaving debugging code turned on (such as logging trace information to a file), forgetting to deallocate memory, improperly designing database tables, polling nonexistent devices until they time out, and so on.

A version 1.0 application I worked on had a particular operation that was much slower than other similar operations. A great deal of project mythology grew up to explain the slowness of this operation. We released version 1.0 without ever fully understanding why this particular operation was so slow. While working on the version 1.1 release, however, I discovered that the database table used by the operation wasn't indexed! Simply indexing the table improved performance by a factor of 30 for some operations. Defining an index on a commonly used table is not optimization; it's just good programming practice.

Relative Performance Costs of Common Operations

Although you can't count on some operations being more expensive than others without measuring them, certain operations tend to be more expensive. When you look for the molasses in your program, use Table 25-2 to help make some initial guesses about the sticky parts of your program.

Table 25-2   Costs of Common Operations

		Relative Time Consumed	
Operation	Example	C++	Java
Baseline (integer assignment)	*i = j*	*1*	*1*
Routine Calls			
Call routine with no parameters	*foo()*	1	n/a
Call private routine with no parameters	*this.foo()*	1	0.5
Call private routine with 1 parameter	*this.foo(i)*	1.5	0.5
Call private routine with 2 parameters	*this.foo(i, j)*	2	0.5
Object routine call	*bar.foo()*	2	1
Derived routine call	*derivedBar.foo()*	2	1
Polymorphic routine call	*abstractBar.foo()*	2.5	2
Object References			
Level 1 object dereference	*i = obj.num*	1	1
Level 2 object dereference	*i = obj1.obj2. num*	1	1
Each additional dereference	*i = obj1.obj2.obj3...*	not measurable	not measurable

Table 25-2   **Costs of Common Operations**

Operation	Example	Relative Time Consumed	
		C++	Java
Integer Operations			
Integer assignment (local)	$i = j$	1	1
Integer assignment (inherited)	$i = j$	1	1
Integer addition	$i = j + k$	1	1
Integer subtraction	$i = j - k$	1	1
Integer multiplication	$i = j * k$	1	1
Integer division	$i = j \backslash k$	5	1.5
Floating-Point Operations			
Floating-point assignment	$x = y$	1	1
Floating-point addition	$x = y + z$	1	1
Floating-point subtraction	$x = y - z$	1	1
Floating-point multiplication	$x = y * z$	1	1
Floating-point division	$x = y / z$	4	1
Transcendental Functions			
Floating-point square root	$x = sqrt(y)$	15	4
Floating-point sine	$x = sin(y)$	25	20
Floating-point logarithm	$x = log(y)$	25	20
Floating-point e^y	$x = exp(y)$	50	20
Arrays			
Access integer array with constant subscript	$i = a[5]$	1	1
Access integer array with variable subscript	$i = a[j]$	1	1
Access two-dimensional integer array with constant subscripts	$i = a[3, 5]$	1	1
Access two-dimensional integer array with variable subscripts	$i = a[j, k]$	1	1
Access floating-point array with constant subscript	$x = z[5]$	1	1
Access floating-point array with integer-variable subscript	$x = z[j]$	1	1
Access two-dimensional, floating-point array with constant subscripts	$x = z[3, 5]$	1	1
Access two-dimensional, floating-point array with integer-variable subscripts	$x = z[j, k]$	1	1

Note: Measurements in this table are highly sensitive to local machine environment, compiler optimizations, and code generated by specific compilers. Measurements between C++ and Java are not directly comparable.

The relative performance of these operations has changed significantly since the first edition of *Code Complete*, so if you're approaching code tuning with 10-year-old ideas about performance, you might need to update your thinking.

Most of the common operations are about the same price—routine calls, assignments, integer arithmetic, and floating-point arithmetic are all roughly equal. Transcendental math functions are extremely expensive. Polymorphic routine calls are a bit more expensive than other kinds of routine calls.

Table 25-2, or a similar one that you make, is the key that unlocks all the speed improvements described in Chapter 26. In every case, improving speed comes from replacing an expensive operation with a cheaper one. Chapter 26 provides examples of how to do so.

25.4 Measurement

Because small parts of a program usually consume a disproportionate share of the run time, measure your code to find the hot spots. Once you've found the hot spots and optimized them, measure the code again to assess how much you've improved it. Many aspects of performance are counterintuitive. The earlier case in this chapter, in which 10 lines of code were significantly faster and smaller than one line, is one example of the ways that code can surprise you.

KEY POINT

Experience doesn't help much with optimization either. A person's experience might have come from an old machine, language, or compiler—when any of those things changes, all bets are off. You can never be sure about the effect of an optimization until you measure the effect.

Many years ago now I wrote a program that summed the elements in a matrix. The original code looked like this:

C++ Example of Straightforward Code to Sum the Elements in a Matrix
```cpp
sum = 0;
for ( row = 0; row < rowCount; row++ ) {
   for ( column = 0; column < columnCount; column++ ) {
      sum = sum + matrix[ row ][ column ];
   }
}
```

This code was straightforward, but performance of the matrix-summation routine was critical, and I knew that all the array accesses and loop tests had to be expensive. I knew from computer-science classes that every time the code accessed a two-dimensional array, it performed expensive multiplications and additions. For a 100-by-100 matrix, that totaled 10,000 multiplications and additions, plus the loop overhead. By converting to pointer notation, I reasoned, I could increment a pointer and replace 10,000 expensive multiplications with 10,000 relatively cheap increment operations. I carefully converted the code to pointer notation and got this:

Further Reading Jon Bentley reported a similar experience in which converting to pointers hurt performance by about 10 percent. The same conversion had—in another setting—improved performance more than 50 percent. See "Software Exploratorium: Writing Efficient C Programs" (Bentley 1991).

C++ Example of an Attempt to Tune Code to Sum the Elements in a Matrix

```cpp
sum = 0;
elementPointer = matrix;
lastElementPointer = matrix[ rowCount - 1 ][ columnCount - 1 ] + 1;
while ( elementPointer < lastElementPointer ) {
    sum = sum + *elementPointer++;
}
```

Even though the code wasn't as readable as the first code, especially to programmers who aren't C++ experts, I was magnificently pleased with myself. For a 100-by-100 matrix, I calculated that I had saved 10,000 multiplications and a lot of loop overhead. I was so pleased that I decided to measure the speed improvement, something I didn't always do back then, so that I could pat myself on the back more quantitatively.

No programmer has *ever* been able to predict or analyze where performance bottlenecks are *without data*. No matter where you think it's going, you will be surprised to discover that it is going somewhere else.
—*Joseph M. Newcomer*

Do you know what I found? No improvement whatsoever. Not with a 100-by-100 matrix. Not with a 10-by-10 matrix. Not with any size matrix. I was so disappointed that I dug into the assembly code generated by the compiler to see why my optimization hadn't worked. To my surprise, it turned out that I was not the first programmer who ever needed to iterate through the elements of an array—the compiler's optimizer was already converting the array accesses to pointers. I learned that the only result of optimization you can usually be sure of without measuring performance is that you've made your code harder to read. If it's not worth measuring to know that it's more efficient, it's not worth sacrificing clarity for a performance gamble.

Measurements Need to Be Precise

Cross-Reference For a discussion of profiling tools, see "Code Tuning" in Section 30.3.

Performance measurements need to be precise. Timing your program with a stopwatch or by counting "one elephant, two elephant, three elephant" isn't precise. Profiling tools are useful, or you can use your system's clock and routines that record the elapsed times for computing operations.

Whether you use someone else's tool or write your own code to make the measurements, make sure that you're measuring only the execution time of the code you're tuning. Use the number of CPU clock ticks allocated to your program rather than the time of day. Otherwise, when the system switches from your program to another program, one of your routines will be penalized for the time spent executing another program. Likewise, try to factor out measurement overhead and program-startup overhead so that neither the original code nor the tuning attempt is unfairly penalized.

25.5 Iteration

Once you've identified a performance bottleneck, you'll be amazed at how much you can improve performance by code tuning. You'll rarely get a 10-fold improvement from one technique, but you can effectively combine techniques; so keep trying, even after you find one that works.

I once wrote a software implementation of the Data Encryption Standard (DES). Actually, I didn't write it once—I wrote it about 30 times. Encryption according to DES encodes digital data so that it can't be unscrambled without a password. The encryption algorithm is so convoluted that it seems like it's been used on itself. The performance goal for my DES implementation was to encrypt an 18K file in 37 seconds on an original IBM PC. My first implementation executed in 21 minutes and 40 seconds, so I had a long row to hoe.

Even though most individual optimizations were small, cumulatively they were significant. To judge from the percentage improvements, no three or even four optimizations would have met my performance goal. But the final combination was effective. The moral of the story is that if you dig deep enough, you can make some surprising gains.

The code tuning I did in this case is the most aggressive code tuning I've ever done. At the same time, the final code is the most unreadable, unmaintainable code I've ever written. The initial algorithm is complicated. The code resulting from the high-level language transformation was barely readable. The translation to assembler produced a single 500-line routine that I'm afraid to look at. In general, this relationship between code tuning and code quality holds true. Here's a table that shows a history of the optimizations:

Cross-Reference The techniques listed in this table are described in Chapter 26, "Code-Tuning Techniques."

Optimization	Benchmark Time	Improvement
Implement initially—straightforward	21:40	—
Convert from bit fields to arrays	7:30	65%
Unroll innermost *for* loop	6:00	20%
Remove final permutation	5:24	10%
Combine two variables	5:06	5%
Use a logical identity to combine the first two steps of the DES algorithm	4:30	12%
Make two variables share the same memory to reduce data shuttling in inner loop	3:36	20%
Make two variables share the same memory to reduce data shuttling in outer loop	3:09	13%
Unfold all loops and use literal array subscripts	1:36	49%

Remove routine calls and put all the code in line	0:45	53%
Rewrite the whole routine in assembler	0:22	51%
Final	**0:22**	**98%**

Note: The steady progress of optimizations in this table doesn't imply that all optimizations work. I haven't shown all the things I tried that doubled the run time. At least two-thirds of the optimizations I tried didn't work.

25.6 Summary of the Approach to Code Tuning

You should take the following steps as you consider whether code tuning can help you improve the performance of a program:

1. Develop the software by using well-designed code that's easy to understand and modify.

2. If performance is poor,

   a. Save a working version of the code so that you can get back to the "last known good state."

   b. Measure the system to find hot spots.

   c. Determine whether the weak performance comes from inadequate design, data types, or algorithms and whether code tuning is appropriate. If code tuning isn't appropriate, go back to step 1.

   d. Tune the bottleneck identified in step (c).

   e. Measure each improvement one at a time.

   f. If an improvement doesn't improve the code, revert to the code saved in step (a). (Typically, more than half the attempted tunings will produce only a negligible improvement in performance or degrade performance.)

3. Repeat from step 2.

Additional Resources

cc2e.com/2585

This section contains resources related to performance improvement in general. For additional resources that discuss specific code-tuning techniques, see the "Additional Resources" section at the end of Chapter 26.

Performance

Smith, Connie U. and Lloyd G. Williams. *Performance Solutions: A Practical Guide to Creating Responsive, Scalable Software*. Boston, MA: Addison-Wesley, 2002. This book covers software performance engineering, an approach for building performance into software systems at all stages of development. It makes extensive use of examples and case studies for several kinds of programs. It includes specific recommendations for Web applications and pays special attention to scalability.

cc2e.com/2592 Newcomer, Joseph M. "Optimization: Your Worst Enemy." May 2000, *www.flounder.com/optimization.htm*. Newcomer is an experienced systems programmer who describes the various pitfalls of ineffective optimization strategies in graphic detail.

Algorithms and Data Types

cc2e.com/2599 Knuth, Donald. *The Art of Computer Programming*, vol. 1, *Fundamental Algorithms*, 3d ed. Reading, MA: Addison-Wesley, 1997.

Knuth, Donald. *The Art of Computer Programming*, vol. 2, *Seminumerical Algorithms*, 3d ed. Reading, MA: Addison-Wesley, 1997.

Knuth, Donald. *The Art of Computer Programming*, vol. 3, *Sorting and Searching*, 2d ed. Reading, MA: Addison-Wesley, 1998.

These are the first three volumes of a series that was originally intended to grow to seven volumes. They can be somewhat intimidating. In addition to the English description of the algorithms, they're described in mathematical notation or MIX, an assembly language for the imaginary MIX computer. The books contain exhaustive details on a huge number of topics, and if you have an intense interest in a particular algorithm, you won't find a better reference.

Sedgewick, Robert. *Algorithms in Java, Parts 1-4*, 3d ed. Boston, MA: Addison-Wesley, 2002. This book's four parts contain a survey of the best methods of solving a wide variety of problems. Its subject areas include fundamentals, sorting, searching, abstract data type implementation, and advanced topics. Sedgewick's *Algorithms in Java, Part 5*, 3d ed. (2003) covers graph algorithms. Sedgewick's *Algorithms in C++, Parts 1-4*, 3d ed. (1998), *Algorithms in C++, Part 5*, 3d ed. (2002), *Algorithms in C, Parts 1-4*, 3d ed. (1997), and *Algorithms in C, Part 5*, 3d ed. (2001) are similarly organized. Sedgewick was a Ph.D. student of Knuth's.

cc2e.com/2506

> ## CHECKLIST: Code-Tuning Strategies
> ### Overall Program Performance
> ❑ Have you considered improving performance by changing the program requirements?
>
> ❑ Have you considered improving performance by modifying the program's design?
>
> ❑ Have you considered improving performance by modifying the class design?

❑   Have you considered improving performance by avoiding operating system interactions?

❑   Have you considered improving performance by avoiding I/O?

❑   Have you considered improving performance by using a compiled language instead of an interpreted language?

❑   Have you considered improving performance by using compiler optimizations?

❑   Have you considered improving performance by switching to different hardware?

❑   Have you considered code tuning only as a last resort?

Code-Tuning Approach

❑   Is your program fully correct before you begin code tuning?

❑   Have you measured performance bottlenecks before beginning code tuning?

❑   Have you measured the effect of each code-tuning change?

❑   Have you backed out the code-tuning changes that didn't produce the intended improvement?

❑   Have you tried more than one change to improve performance of each bottleneck—that is, *iterated*?

Key Points

■   Performance is only one aspect of overall software quality, and it's usually not the most important. Finely tuned code is only one aspect of overall performance, and it's usually not the most significant. Program architecture, detailed design, and data-structure and algorithm selection usually have more influence on a program's execution speed and size than the efficiency of its code does.

■   Quantitative measurement is a key to maximizing performance. It's needed to find the areas in which performance improvements will really count, and it's needed again to verify that optimizations improve rather than degrade the software.

■   Most programs spend most of their time in a small fraction of their code. You won't know which code that is until you measure it.

■   Multiple iterations are usually needed to achieve desired performance improvements through code tuning.

■   The best way to prepare for performance work during initial coding is to write clean code that's easy to understand and modify.

Chapter 26
Code-Tuning Techniques

cc2e.com/2665

Contents

- 26.1 Logic: page 610
- 26.2 Loops: page 616
- 26.3 Data Transformations: page 624
- 26.4 Expressions: page 630
- 26.5 Routines: page 639
- 26.6 Recoding in a Low-Level Language: page 640
- 26.7 The More Things Change, the More They Stay the Same: page 643

Related Topics

- Code-tuning strategies: Chapter 25
- Refactoring: Chapter 24

Code tuning has been a popular topic during most of the history of computer programming. Consequently, once you've decided that you need to improve performance and that you want to do it at the code level (bearing in mind the warnings from Chapter 25, "Code-Tuning Strategies"), you have a rich set of techniques at your disposal.

This chapter focuses on improving speed and includes a few tips for making code smaller. Performance usually refers to both speed and size, but size reductions tend to come more from redesigning classes and data than from tuning code. Code tuning refers to small-scale changes rather than changes in larger-scale designs.

Few of the techniques in this chapter are so generally applicable that you'll be able to copy the example code directly into your programs. The main purpose of the discussion here is to illustrate a handful of code tunings that you can adapt to your situation.

The code-tuning changes described in this chapter might seem cosmetically similar to the refactorings described in Chapter 24, but refactorings are changes that improve a program's internal structure (Fowler 1999). The changes in this chapter might better be called "anti-refactorings." Far from "improving the internal structure," these changes degrade the internal structure in exchange for gains in performance. This is true by definition. If the changes didn't degrade the internal structure, we wouldn't consider them to be optimizations; we would use them by default and consider them to be standard coding practice.

Cross-Reference Code tunings are heuristics. For more on heuristics, see Section 5.3, "Design Building Blocks: Heuristics."

Some books present code-tuning techniques as "rules of thumb" or cite research that suggests that a specific tuning will produce the desired effect. As you'll soon see, the "rules of thumb" concept applies poorly to code tuning. The only reliable rule of thumb is to measure the effect of each tuning in your environment. Thus, this chapter presents a catalog of "things to try," many of which won't work in your environment but some of which will work very well indeed.

26.1 Logic

Cross-Reference For other details on using statement logic, see Chapters 14–19.

Much of programming consists of manipulating logic. This section describes how to manipulate logical expressions to your advantage.

Stop Testing When You Know the Answer

Suppose you have a statement like

```
if ( 5 < x ) and ( x < 10 ) then ...
```

Once you've determined that *x* is not greater than 5, you don't need to perform the second half of the test.

Cross-Reference For more on short-circuit evaluation, see "Knowing How Boolean Expressions Are Evaluated" in Section 19.1.

Some languages provide a form of expression evaluation known as "short-circuit evaluation," which means that the compiler generates code that automatically stops testing as soon as it knows the answer. Short-circuit evaluation is part of C++'s standard operators and Java's "conditional" operators.

If your language doesn't support short-circuit evaluation natively, you have to avoid using *and* and *or*, adding logic instead. With short-circuit evaluation, the code above changes to this:

```
if ( 5 < x ) then
   if ( x < 10 ) then ...
```

The principle of not testing after you know the answer is a good one for many other kinds of cases as well. A search loop is a common case. If you're scanning an array of input numbers for a negative value and you simply need to know whether a negative value is present, one approach is to check every value, setting a *negativeFound* variable when you find one. Here's how the search loop would look:

C++ Example of Not Stopping After You Know the Answer
```
negativeInputFound = false;
for ( i = 0; i < count; i++ ) {
   if ( input[ i ] < 0 ) {
      negativeInputFound = true;
   }
}
```

A better approach would be to stop scanning as soon as you find a negative value. Any of these approaches would solve the problem:

- Add a *break* statement after the *negativeInputFound = true* line.

- If your language doesn't have *break*, emulate a *break* with a *goto* that goes to the first statement after the loop.

- Change the *for* loop to a *while* loop, and check for *negativeInputFound* as well as for incrementing the loop counter past *count*.

- Change the *for* loop to a *while* loop, put a sentinel value in the first array element after the last value entry, and simply check for a negative value in the *while* test. After the loop terminates, see whether the position of the first found value is in the array or one past the end. Sentinels are discussed in more detail later in the chapter.

Here are the results of using the *break* keyword in C++ and Java:

Language	Straight Time	Code-Tuned Time	Time Savings
C++	4.27	3.68	14%
Java	4.85	3.46	29%

> **Note** (1) Times in this and the following tables in this chapter are given in seconds and are meaningful only for comparisons across rows of each table. Actual times will vary according to the compiler, compiler options used, and the environment in which each test is run. (2) Benchmark results are typically made up of several thousand to many million executions of the code fragments to smooth out the sample-to-sample fluctuations in the results. (3) Specific brands and versions of compilers aren't indicated. Performance characteristics vary significantly from brand to brand and version to version. (4) Comparisons among results from different languages aren't always meaningful because compilers for different languages don't always offer comparable code-generation options. (5) The results shown for interpreted languages (PHP and Python) are typically based on less than 1% of the test runs used for the other languages. (6) Some of the "time savings" percentages might not be exactly reproducible from the data in these tables due to rounding of the "straight time" and "code-tuned time" entries.

The impact of this change varies a great deal depending on how many values you have and how often you expect to find a negative value. This test assumed an average of 100 values and assumed that a negative value would be found 50 percent of the time.

Order Tests by Frequency

Arrange tests so that the one that's fastest and most likely to be true is performed first. It should be easy to drop through the normal case, and if there are inefficiencies, they should be in processing the uncommon cases. This principle applies to *case* statements and to chains of *if-then-elses*.

Here's a *Select-Case* statement that responds to keyboard input in a word processor:

Visual Basic Example of a Poorly Ordered Logical Test

```
Select inputCharacter
   Case "+", "="
      ProcessMathSymbol( inputCharacter )
   Case "0" To "9"
      ProcessDigit( inputCharacter )
   Case ",", ".", ":", ";", "!", "?"
      ProcessPunctuation( inputCharacter )
   Case " "
      ProcessSpace( inputCharacter )
   Case "A" To "Z", "a" To "z"
      ProcessAlpha( inputCharacter )
   Case Else
      ProcessError( inputCharacter )
End Select
```

The cases in this *case* statement are ordered in something close to the ASCII sort order. In a *case* statement, however, the effect is often the same as if you had written a big set of *if-then-elses*, so if you get an "*a*" as an input character, the program tests whether it's a math symbol, a punctuation mark, a digit, or a space before determining that it's an alphabetic character. If you know the likely frequency of your input characters, you can put the most common cases first. Here's the reordered *case* statement:

Visual Basic Example of a Well-Ordered Logical Test

```
Select inputCharacter
   Case "A" To "Z", "a" To "z"
      ProcessAlpha( inputCharacter )
   Case " "
      ProcessSpace( inputCharacter )
   Case ",", ".", ":", ";", "!", "?"
      ProcessPunctuation( inputCharacter )
   Case "0" To "9"
      ProcessDigit( inputCharacter )
   Case "+", "="
      ProcessMathSymbol( inputCharacter )
   Case Else
      ProcessError( inputCharacter )
End Select
```

Because the most common case is usually found sooner in the optimized code, the net effect will be the performance of fewer tests. Following are the results of this optimization with a typical mix of characters:

Language	Straight Time	Code-Tuned Time	Time Savings
C#	0.220	0.260	-18%
Java	2.56	2.56	0%
Visual Basic	**0.280**	**0.260**	**7%**

Note: Benchmarked with an input mix of 78 percent alphabetic characters, 17 percent spaces, and 5 percent punctuation symbols.

The Microsoft Visual Basic results are as expected, but the Java and C# results are not as expected. Apparently that's because of the way *switch-case* statements are structured in C# and Java—because each value must be enumerated individually rather than in ranges, the C# and Java code doesn't benefit from the optimization as the Visual Basic code does. This result underscores the importance of not following any optimization advice blindly—specific compiler implementations will significantly affect the results.

You might assume that the code generated by the Visual Basic compiler for a set of *if-then-else*s that perform the same test as the *case* statement would be similar. Take a look at those results:

Language	Straight Time	Code-Tuned Time	Time Savings
C#	0.630	0.330	48%
Java	0.922	0.460	50%
Visual Basic	**1.36**	**1.00**	**26%**

The results are quite different. For the same number of tests, the Visual Basic compiler takes about five times as long in the unoptimized case, four times in the optimized case. This suggests that the compiler is generating different code for the *case* approach than for the *if-then-else* approach.

The improvement with *if-then-else*s is more consistent than it was with the *case* statements, but that's a mixed blessing. In C# and Visual Basic, both versions of the *case* statement approach are faster than both versions of the *if-then-else* approach, whereas in Java both versions are slower. This variation in results suggests a third possible optimization, described in the next section.

Compare Performance of Similar Logic Structures

The test described above could be performed using either a *case* if-then-elses. Depending on the environment, either approach might work better. Here is the data from the preceding two tables reformatted to present the "code-tuned" times comparing *if-then-else* and *case* performance:

Language	*case*	*if-then-else*	Time Savings	Performance Ratio
C#	0.260	0.330	-27%	1:1
Java	2.56	0.460	82%	6:1
Visual Basic	0.260	1.00	-258%	1:4

These results defy any logical explanation. In one of the languages, *case* is dramatically superior to *if-then-else*, and in another, *if-then-else* is dramatically superior to *case*. In the third language, the difference is relatively small. You might think that because C# and Java share similar syntax for *case* statements, their results would be similar, but in fact their results are opposite each other.

This example clearly illustrates the difficulty of performing any sort of "rule of thumb" or "logic" to code tuning—there is simply no reliable substitute for *measuring* results.

Substitute Table Lookups for Complicated Expressions

Cross-Reference For details on using table lookups to replace complicated logic, see Chapter 18, "Table-Driven Methods."

In some circumstances, a table lookup might be quicker than traversing a complicated chain of logic. The point of a complicated chain is usually to categorize something and then to take an action based on its category. As an abstract example, suppose you want to assign a category number to something based on which of three groups— Groups *A B* *C*—

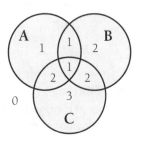

This complicated logic chain assigns the category numbers:

C++ Example of a Complicated Chain of Logic

```cpp
if ( ( a && !c ) || ( a && b && c ) ) {
    category = 1;
}
else if ( ( b && !a ) || ( a && c && !b ) ) {
    category = 2;
}
else if ( c && !a && !b ) {
    category = 3;
}
else {
    category = 0;
}
```

You can replace this test with a more modifiable and higher-performance lookup table:

C++ Example of Using a Table Lookup to Replace Complicated Logic

This table definition is somewhat difficult to understand. Any commenting you can do to make table definitions readable helps.

```cpp
// define categoryTable
static int categoryTable[ 2 ][ 2 ][ 2 ] = {
    // !b!c  !bc  b!c  bc
        0,    3,   2,   2,   //   !a
        1,    2,   1,   1,   //    a
};
...
category = categoryTable[ a ][ b ][ c ];
```

Although the definition of the table is hard to read, if it's well documented it won't be any harder to read than the code for the complicated chain of logic was. If the definition changes, the table will be much easier to maintain than the earlier logic would have been. Here are the performance results:

Language	Straight Time	Code-Tuned Time	Time Savings	Performance Ratio
C++	5.04	3.39	33%	1.5:1
Visual Basic	5.21	2.60	50%	2:1

Use Lazy Evaluation

One of my former roommates was a great procrastinator. He justified his laziness by saying that many of the things people feel rushed to do simply don't need to be done. If he waited long enough, he claimed, the things that weren't important would be procrastinated into oblivion and he wouldn't waste his time doing them.

Lazy evaluation is based on the principle my roommate used. If a program uses lazy evaluation, it avoids doing any work until the work is needed. Lazy evaluation is similar to just-in-time strategies that do the work closest to when it's needed.

Suppose, for example, that your program contains a table of 5000 values, generates the whole table at startup time, and then uses it as the program executes. If the program uses only a small percentage of the entries in the table, it might make more sense to compute them as they're needed rather than all at once. Once an entry is computed, it can still be stored for future reference (otherwise known as "cached").

26.2 Loops

Cross-Reference For other details on loops, see Chapter 16, "Controlling Loops."

Because loops are executed many times, the hot spots in a program are often inside loops. The techniques in this section make the loop itself faster.

Unswitching

Switching refers to making a decision inside a loop every time it's executed. If the decision doesn't change while the loop is executing, you can unswitch the loop by making the decision outside the loop. Usually this requires turning the loop inside out, putting loops inside the conditional rather than putting the conditional inside the loop. Here's an example of a loop before unswitching:

C++ Example of a Switched Loop

```cpp
for ( i = 0; i < count; i++ ) {
   if ( sumType == SUMTYPE_NET ) {
      netSum = netSum + amount[ i ];
   }
   else {
      grossSum = grossSum + amount[ i ];
   }
}
```

In this code, the test *if (sumType == SUMTYPE_NET)* is repeated through each iteration, even though it'll be the same each time through the loop. You can rewrite the code for a speed gain this way:

CODING
HORROR

C++ Example of an Unswitched Loop

```cpp
if ( sumType == SUMTYPE_NET ) {
   for ( i = 0; i < count; i++ ) {
      netSum = netSum + amount[ i ];
   }
}
else {
   for ( i = 0; i < count; i++ ) {
      grossSum = grossSum + amount[ i ];
   }
}
```

> **Note**   This code fragment violates several rules of good programming. Readability and maintenance are usually more important than execution speed or size, but in this chapter the topic is performance, and that implies a tradeoff with the other objectives. As in the last chapter, you'll see examples of coding practices here that aren't recommended in other parts of this book.

This is good for about a 20 percent time savings:

Language	Straight Time	Code-Tuned Time	Time Savings
C++	2.81	2.27	19%
Java	3.97	3.12	21%
Visual Basic	2.78	2.77	<1%
Python	8.14	5.87	28%

A hazard distinct to this case is that the two loops have to be maintained in parallel. If *count* changes to *clientCount*, you have to remember to change it in both places, which is an annoyance for you and a maintenance headache for anyone else who has to work with the code.

This example also illustrates a key challenge in code tuning: the effect of any specific code tuning is not predictable. The code tuning produced significant improvements in three of the four languages but not in Visual Basic. To perform this specific optimization in this specific version of Visual Basic would produce less maintainable code without any offsetting gain in performance. The general lesson is that you must measure the effect of each specific optimization to be sure of its effect—no exceptions.

Jamming

Jamming, or "fusion," is the result of combining two loops that operate on the same set of elements. The gain lies in cutting the loop overhead from two loops to one. Here's a candidate for loop jamming:

Visual Basic Example of Separate Loops That Could Be Jammed
```
For i = 0 to employeeCount - 1
    employeeName( i ) = ""
Next
...
For i = 0 to employeeCount - 1
    employeeEarnings( i ) = 0
Next
```

When you jam loops, you find code in two loops that you can combine into one. Usually, that means the loop counters have to be the same. In this example, both loops run from *0* to *employeeCount - 1*, so you can jam them:

Visual Basic Example of a Jammed Loop

```
For i = 0 to employeeCount - 1
    employeeName( i ) = ""
    employeeEarnings( i ) = 0
Next
```

Here are the savings:

Language	Straight Time	Code-Tuned Time	Time Savings
C++	3.68	2.65	28%
PHP	3.97	2.42	32%
Visual Basic	**3.75**	**3.56**	**4%**

Note: Benchmarked for the case in which *employeeCount* equals 100.

As before, the results vary significantly among languages.

Loop jamming has two main hazards. First, the indexes for the two parts that have been jammed might change so that they're no longer compatible. Second, you might not be able to combine the loops easily. Before you combine the loops, make sure they'll still be in the right order with respect to the rest of the code.

Unrolling

The goal of loop unrolling is to reduce the amount of loop housekeeping. In Chapter 25, a loop was completely unrolled and 10 lines of code were shown to be faster than 3. In that case, the loop that went from 3 to 10 lines was unrolled so that all 10 array accesses were done individually.

Although completely unrolling a loop is a fast solution and works well when you're dealing with a small number of elements, it's not practical when you have a large number of elements or when you don't know in advance how many elements you'll have. Here's an example of a general loop:

Java Example of a Loop That Can Be Unrolled

Normally, you'd probably use a *for* loop for a job like this, but to optimize, you'd have to convert to a *while* loop. For clarity, a *while* loop is shown here.

```
i = 0;
while ( i < count ) {
    a[ i ] = i;
    i = i + 1;
}
```

To unroll the loop partially, you handle two or more cases in each pass through the loop instead of one. This unrolling hurts readability but doesn't hurt the generality of the loop. Here's the loop unrolled once:

Java Example of a Loop That's Been Unrolled Once
```java
i = 0;
while ( i < count - 1 ) {
    a[ i ] = i;
    a[ i + 1 ] = i + 1;
    i = i + 2;
}
if ( i == count - 1 ) {
    a[ count - 1 ] = count - 1;
}
```

These lines pick up the case that might fall through the cracks if the loop went by twos instead of by ones.

The technique replaced the original *a[i] = i* line with two lines, and *i* is incremented by 2 rather than by *1*. The extra code after the *while* loop is needed when *count* is odd and the loop has one iteration left after the loop terminates.

When five lines of straightforward code expand to nine lines of tricky code, the code becomes harder to read and maintain. Except for the gain in speed, its quality is poor. Part of any design discipline, however, is making necessary tradeoffs. So, even though a particular technique generally represents poor coding practice, specific circumstances might make it the best one to use.

Here are the results of unrolling the loop:

Language	Straight Time	Code-Tuned Time	Time Savings
C++	1.75	1.15	34%
Java	**1.01**	**0.581**	**43%**
PHP	5.33	4.49	16%
Python	2.51	3.21	-27%

Note: Benchmarked for the case in which *count* equals 100.

A gain of 16 to 43 percent is respectable, although again you have to watch out for hurting performance, as the Python benchmark shows. The main hazard of loop unrolling is an off-by-one error in the code after the loop that picks up the last case.

What if you unroll the loop even further, going for two or more unrollings? Do you get more benefit if you unroll a loop twice?

Java Example of a Loop That's Been Unrolled Twice
```java
i = 0;
while ( i < count - 2 ) {
    a[ i ] = i;
    a[ i + 1 ] = i+1;
    a[ i + 2 ] = i+2;
    i = i + 3;
}
```

```
if ( i <= count - 1 ) {
    a[ count - 1 ] = count - 1;
}
if ( i == count - 2 ) {
    a[ count -2 ] = count - 2;
}
```

Here are the results of unrolling the loop the second time:

Language	Straight Time	Double Unrolled Time	Time Savings
C++	1.75	1.01	42%
Java	1.01	0.581	43%
PHP	5.33	3.70	31%
Python	2.51	2.79	-12%

Note: Benchmarked for the case in which count equals 100.

The results indicate that further loop unrolling can result in further time savings, but not necessarily so, as the Java measurement shows. The main concern is how Byzantine your code becomes. When you look at the previous code, you might not think it looks incredibly complicated, but when you realize that it started life a couple of pages ago as a five-line loop, you can appreciate the tradeoff between performance and readability.

Minimizing the Work Inside Loops

One key to writing effective loops is to minimize the work done inside a loop. If you can evaluate a statement or part of a statement outside a loop so that only the result is used inside the loop, do so. It's good programming practice, and in some cases it improves readability.

Suppose you have a complicated pointer expression inside a hot loop that looks like this:

C++ Example of a Complicated Pointer Expression Inside a Loop
```
for ( i = 0; i < rateCount; i++ ) {
    netRate[ i ] = baseRate[ i ] * rates->discounts->factors->net;
}
```

In this case, assigning the complicated pointer expression to a well-named variable improves readability and often improves performance.

C++ Example of Simplifying a Complicated Pointer Expression
```
quantityDiscount = rates->discounts->factors->net;
for ( i = 0; i < rateCount; i++ ) {
    netRate[ i ] = baseRate[ i ] * quantityDiscount;
}
```

The extra variable, *quantityDiscount*, makes it clear that the *baseRate* array is being multiplied by a quantity-discount factor to compute the net rate. That wasn't at all clear from the original expression in the loop. Putting the complicated pointer expression into a variable outside the loop also saves the pointer from being dereferenced three times for each pass through the loop, resulting in the following savings:

Language	Straight Time	Code-Tuned Time	Time Savings
C++	3.69	2.97	19%
C#	2.27	1.97	13%
Java	4.13	2.35	43%

Note: Benchmarked for the case in which *rateCount* equals 100.

Except for the Java compiler, the savings aren't anything to crow about, implying that during initial coding you can use whichever technique is more readable without worrying about the speed of the code until later.

Sentinel Values

When you have a loop with a compound test, you can often save time by simplifying the test. If the loop is a search loop, one way to simplify the test is to use a sentinel value, a value that you put just past the end of the search range and that's guaranteed to terminate the search.

The classic example of a compound test that can be improved by use of a sentinel is the search loop that checks both whether it has found the value it's seeking and whether it has run out of values. Here's the code:

C# Example of Compound Tests in a Search Loop

Here's the compound test. →

```
found = FALSE;
i = 0;
while ( ( !found ) && ( i < count ) ) {
    if ( item[ i ] == testValue ) {
        found = TRUE;
    }
    else {
        i++;
    }
}

if ( found ) {
    ...
```

In this code, each iteration of the loop tests for *!found* and for *i < count*. The purpose of the *!found* test is to determine when the desired element has been found. The purpose of the *i < count* test is to avoid running past the end of the array. Inside the loop, each value of *item[]* is tested individually, so the loop really has three tests for each iteration.

In this kind of search loop, you can combine the three tests so that you test only once per iteration by putting a "sentinel" at the end of the search range to stop the loop. In this case, you can simply assign the value you're looking for to the element just beyond the end of the search range. (Remember to leave space for that element when you declare the array.) You then check each element, and if you don't find the element until you find the one you stuck at the end, you know that the value you're looking for isn't really there. Here's the code:

C# Example of Using a Sentinel Value to Speed Up a Loop

```
// set sentinel value, preserving the original value
initialValue = item[ count ];
item[ count ] = testValue;

i = 0;
while ( item[ i ] != testValue ) {
   i++;
}

// check if value was found
if ( i < count ) {
   ...
```

Remember to allow space for the sentinel value at the end of the array.

When *item* is an array of integers, the savings can be dramatic:

Language	Straight Time	Code-Tuned Time	Time Savings	Performance Ratio
C#	0.771	0.590	23%	1.3:1
Java	1.63	0.912	44%	2:1
Visual Basic	1.34	0.470	65%	3:1

Note: Search is of a 100-element array of integers.

The Visual Basic results are particularly dramatic, but all the results are good. When the kind of array changes, however, the results also change. When *item* is an array of single-precision floating-point numbers, the results are as follows:

Language	Straight Time	Code-Tuned Time	Time Savings
C#	1.351	1.021	24%
Java	1.923	1.282	33%
Visual Basic	1.752	1.011	42%

Note: Search is of a 100-element array of 4-byte floating-point numbers.

As usual, the results vary significantly.

The sentinel technique can be applied to virtually any situation in which you use a linear search—to linked lists as well as arrays. The only caveats are that you must choose the sentinel value carefully and that you must be careful about how you put the sentinel value into the data structure.

Putting the Busiest Loop on the Inside

When you have nested loops, think about which loop you want on the outside and which you want on the inside. Following is an example of a nested loop that can be improved:

```
Java Example of a Nested Loop That Can Be Improved
for ( column = 0; column < 100; column++ ) {
   for ( row = 0; row < 5; row++ ) {
      sum = sum + table[ row ][ column ];
   }
}
```

The key to improving the loop is that the outer loop executes much more often than the inner loop. Each time the loop executes, it has to initialize the loop index, increment it on each pass through the loop, and check it after each pass. The total number of loop executions is 100 for the outer loop and 100 * 5 = 500 for the inner loop, for a total of 600 iterations. By merely switching the inner and outer loops, you can change the total number of iterations to 5 for the outer loop and 5 * 100 = 500 for the inner loop, for a total of 505 iterations. Analytically, you'd expect to save about (600 − 505) / 600 = 16 percent by switching the loops. Here's the measured difference in performance:

Language	Straight Time	Code-Tuned Time	Time Savings
C++	4.75	3.19	33%
Java	5.39	3.56	34%
PHP	4.16	3.65	12%
Python	3.48	3.33	4%

The results vary significantly, which shows once again that you have to measure the effect in your particular environment before you can be sure your optimization will help.

Strength Reduction

Reducing strength means replacing an expensive operation such as multiplication with a cheaper operation such as addition. Sometimes you'll have an expression inside a loop that depends on multiplying the loop index by a factor. Addition is usually faster than multiplication, and if you can compute the same number by adding the amount on each iteration of the loop rather than by multiplying, the code will typically run faster. Here's an example of code that uses multiplication:

Visual Basic Example of Multiplying a Loop Index

```
For i = 0 to saleCount - 1
    commission( i ) = (i + 1) * revenue * baseCommission * discount
Next
```

This code is straightforward but expensive. You can rewrite the loop so that you accumulate multiples rather than computing them each time. This reduces the strength of the operations from multiplication to addition.

Visual Basic Example of Adding Rather Than Multiplying

```
incrementalCommission = revenue * baseCommission * discount
cumulativeCommission = incrementalCommission
For i = 0 to saleCount - 1
    commission( i ) = cumulativeCommission
    cumulativeCommission = cumulativeCommission + incrementalCommission
Next
```

Multiplication is expensive, and this kind of change is like a manufacturer's coupon that gives you a discount on the cost of the loop. The original code incremented *i* each time and multiplied it by *revenue * baseCommission * discount*—first by 1, then by 2, then by 3, and so on. The optimized code sets *incrementalCommission* equal to *revenue * baseCommission * discount*. It then adds *incrementalCommission* to *cumulativeCommission* on each pass through the loop. On the first pass, it's been added once; on the second pass, it's been added twice; on the third pass, it's been added three times; and so on. The effect is the same as multiplying *incrementalCommission* by 1, then by 2, then by 3, and so on, but it's cheaper.

The key is that the original multiplication has to depend on the loop index. In this case, the loop index was the only part of the expression that varied, so the expression could be recoded more economically. Here's how much the rewrite helped in some test cases:

Language	Straight Time	Code-Tuned Time	Time Savings
C++	4.33	3.80	12%
Visual Basic	3.54	1.80	49%

Note: Benchmark performed with *saleCount* equals 20. All computed variables are floating point.

26.3 Data Transformations

Changes in data types can be a powerful aid in reducing program size and improving execution speed. Data-structure design is outside the scope of this book, but modest changes in the implementation of a specific data type can also improve performance. Here are a few ways to tune your data types.

Use Integers Rather Than Floating-Point Numbers

Cross-Reference For details on using integers and floating point, see Chapter 12, "Fundamental Data Types."

CODING HORROR

Integer addition and multiplication tend to be faster than floating point. Changing a loop index from a floating point to an integer, for example, can save time:

> **Visual Basic Example of a Loop That Uses a Time-Consuming Floating-Point Loop Index**
> ```
> Dim x As Single
> For x = 0 to 99
>    a( x ) = 0
> Next
> ```

Contrast this with a similar Visual Basic loop that explicitly uses the integer type:

> **Visual Basic Example of a Loop That Uses a Timesaving Integer Loop Index**
> ```
> Dim i As Integer
> For i = 0 to 99
>    a( i ) = 0
> Next
> ```

How much difference does it make? Here are the results for this Visual Basic code and for similar code in C++ and PHP:

Language	Straight Time	Code-Tuned Time	Time Savings	Performance Ratio
C++	2.80	0.801	71%	3.5:1
PHP	5.01	4.65	7%	1:1
Visual Basic	6.84	0.280	96%	25:1

Use the Fewest Array Dimensions Possible

Cross-Reference For details on arrays, see Section 12.8, "Arrays."

Conventional wisdom maintains that multiple dimensions on arrays are expensive. If you can structure your data so that it's in a one-dimensional array rather than a two-dimensional or three-dimensional array, you might be able to save some time. Suppose you have initialization code like this:

> **Java Example of a Standard, Two-Dimensional Array Initialization**
> ```java
> for ( row = 0; row < numRows; row++ ) {
>    for ( column = 0; column < numColumns; column++ ) {
>       matrix[ row ][ column ] = 0;
>    }
> }
> ```

When this code is run with 50 rows and 20 columns, it takes twice as long with my current Java compiler as when the array is restructured so that it's one-dimensional. Here's how the revised code would look:

> **Java Example of a One-Dimensional Representation of an Array**
> ```java
> for ( entry = 0; entry < numRows * numColumns; entry++ ) {
>    matrix[ entry ] = 0;
> }
> ```

And here's a summary of the results, with the addition of comparable results in several other languages:

Language	Straight Time	Code-Tuned Time	Time Savings	Performance Ratio
C++	8.75	7.82	11%	1:1
C#	3.28	2.99	9%	1:1
Java	**7.78**	**4.14**	**47%**	**2:1**
PHP	6.24	4.10	34%	1.5:1
Python	3.31	2.23	32%	1.5:1
Visual Basic	9.43	3.22	66%	3:1

Note: Times for Python and PHP aren't directly comparable to times for the other languages because they were run <1% as many iterations as the other languages.

The results of this optimization are excellent in Visual Basic and Java, good in PHP and Python, but mediocre in C++ and C#. Of course, the C# compiler's unoptimized time was easily the best of the group, so you can't be too hard on it.

This wide range of results again shows the hazard of following any code-tuning advice blindly. You can never be sure until you try the advice in your specific circumstances.

Minimize Array References

In addition to minimizing accesses to doubly or triply dimensioned arrays, it's often advantageous to minimize array accesses, period. A loop that repeatedly uses one element of an array is a good candidate for the application of this technique. Here's an example of an unnecessary array access:

> **C++ Example of Unnecessarily Referencing an Array Inside a Loop**
> ```cpp
> for ( discountType = 0; discountType < typeCount; discountType++ ) {
>    for ( discountLevel = 0; discountLevel < levelCount; discountLevel++ ) {
>       rate[ discountLevel ] = rate[ discountLevel ] * discount[ discountType ];
>    }
> }
> ```

The reference to *discount[discountType]* doesn't change when *discountLevel* changes in the inner loop. Consequently, you can move it out of the inner loop so that you'll have only one array access per execution of the outer loop rather than one for each execution of the inner loop. The next example shows the revised code.

C++ Example of Moving an Array Reference Outside a Loop

```cpp
for ( discountType = 0; discountType < typeCount; discountType++ ) {
   thisDiscount = discount[ discountType ];
   for ( discountLevel = 0; discountLevel < levelCount; discountLevel++ ) {
      rate[ discountLevel ] = rate[ discountLevel ] * thisDiscount;
   }
}
```

Here are the results:

Language	Straight Time	Code-Tuned Time	Time Savings
C++	32.1	34.5	-7%
C#	18.3	17.0	7%
Visual Basic	23.2	18.4	20%

Note: Benchmark times were computed for the case in which *typeCount* equals 10 and *levelCount* equals 100.

As usual, the results vary significantly from compiler to compiler.

Use Supplementary Indexes

Using a supplementary index means adding related data that makes accessing a data type more efficient. You can add the related data to the main data type, or you can store it in a parallel structure.

String-Length Index

One example of using a supplementary index can be found in the different string-storage strategies. In C, strings are terminated by a byte that's set to 0. In Visual Basic string format, a length byte hidden at the beginning of each string indicates how long the string is. To determine the length of a string in C, a program has to start at the beginning of the string and count each byte until it finds the byte that's set to 0. To determine the length of a Visual Basic string, the program just looks at the length byte. Visual Basic length byte is an example of augmenting a data type with an index to make certain operations—like computing the length of a string—faster.

You can apply the idea of indexing for length to any variable-length data type. It's often more efficient to keep track of the length of the structure rather than computing the length each time you need it.

Independent, Parallel Index Structure

Sometimes it's more efficient to manipulate an index to a data type than it is to manipulate the data type itself. If the items in the data type are big or hard to move (on disk, perhaps), sorting and searching index references is faster than working with the data directly. If each data item is large, you can create an auxiliary structure that consists of key values and pointers to the detailed information. If the difference in size between the data-structure item and the auxiliary-structure item is great enough, sometimes you can store the key item in memory even when the data item has to be stored externally. All searching and sorting is done in memory, and you have to access the disk only once, when you know the exact location of the item you want.

Use Caching

Caching means saving a few values in such a way that you can retrieve the most commonly used values more easily than the less commonly used values. If a program randomly reads records from a disk, for example, a routine might use a cache to save the records read most frequently. When the routine receives a request for a record, it checks the cache to see whether it has the record. If it does, the record is returned directly from memory rather than from disk.

In addition to caching records on disk, you can apply caching in other areas. In a Microsoft Windows font-proofing program, the performance bottleneck was in retrieving the width of each character as it was displayed. Caching the most recently used character width roughly doubled the display speed.

You can cache the results of time-consuming computations too—especially if the parameters to the calculation are simple. Suppose, for example, that you need to compute the length of the hypotenuse of a right triangle, given the lengths of the other two sides. The straightforward implementation of the routine would look like this:

Java Example of a Routine That's Conducive to Caching

```java
double Hypotenuse(
    double sideA,
    double sideB
    ) {
    return Math.sqrt( ( sideA * sideA ) + ( sideB * sideB ) );
}
```

If you know that the same values tend to be requested repeatedly, you can cache values this way:

Java Example of Caching to Avoid an Expensive Computation

```java
private double cachedHypotenuse = 0;
private double cachedSideA = 0;
private double cachedSideB = 0;

public double Hypotenuse(
   double sideA,
   double sideB
   ) {

   // check to see if the triangle is already in the cache
   if ( ( sideA == cachedSideA ) && ( sideB == cachedSideB ) ) {
      return cachedHypotenuse;
   }

   // compute new hypotenuse and cache it
   cachedHypotenuse = Math.sqrt( ( sideA * sideA ) + ( sideB * sideB ) );
   cachedSideA = sideA;
   cachedSideB = sideB;

   return cachedHypotenuse;
}
```

The second version of the routine is more complicated than the first and takes up more space, so speed has to be at a premium to justify it. Many caching schemes cache more than one element, so they have even more overhead. Here's the speed difference between these two versions:

Language	Straight Time	Code-Tuned Time	Time Savings	Performance Ratio
C++	4.06	1.05	74%	4:1
Java	2.54	1.40	45%	2:1
Python	8.16	4.17	49%	2:1
Visual Basic	24.0	12.9	47%	2:1

Note: The results shown assume that the cache is hit twice for each time it's set.

The success of the cache depends on the relative costs of accessing a cached element, creating an uncached element, and saving a new element in the cache. Success also depends on how often the cached information is requested. In some cases, success might also depend on caching done by the hardware. Generally, the more it costs to generate a new element and the more times the same information is requested, the more valuable a cache is. The cheaper it is to access a cached element and save new elements in the cache, the more valuable a cache is. As with other optimization techniques, caching adds complexity and tends to be error-prone.

26.4 Expressions

Cross-Reference For more information on expressions, see Section 19.1, "Boolean Expressions."

Much of the work in a program is done inside mathematical or logical expressions. Complicated expressions tend to be expensive, so this section looks at ways to make them cheaper.

Exploit Algebraic Identities

You can use algebraic identities to replace costly operations with cheaper ones. For example, the following expressions are logically equivalent:

```
not a and not b
not (a or b)
```

If you choose the second expression instead of the first, you can save a *not* operation.

Although the savings from avoiding a single *not* operation are probably inconsequential, the general principle is powerful. Jon Bentley describes a program that tested whether *sqrt(x) < sqrt(y)* (1982). Since *sqrt(x)* is less than *sqrt(y)* only when *x* is less than *y*, you can replace the first test with *x < y*. Given the cost of the *sqrt()* routine, you'd expect the savings to be dramatic, and they are. Here are the results:

Language	Straight Time	Code-Tuned Time	Time Savings	Performance Ratio
C++	7.43	0.010	99.9%	750:1
Visual Basic	4.59	0.220	95%	20:1
Python	4.21	0.401	90%	10:1

Use Strength Reduction

As mentioned earlier, strength reduction means replacing an expensive operation with a cheaper one. Here are some possible substitutions:

- Replace multiplication with addition.
- Replace exponentiation with multiplication.
- Replace trigonometric routines with their trigonometric identities.
- Replace *longlong* integers with *long*s or *int*s (but watch for performance issues associated with using native-length vs. non-native-length integers)
- Replace floating-point numbers with fixed-point numbers or integers.
- Replace double-precision floating points with single-precision numbers.
- Replace integer multiplication-by-two and division-by-two with shift operations.

Suppose you have to evaluate a polynomial. If you're rusty on polynomials, they're the things that look like $Ax^2 + Bx + C$. The letters A, B, and C are coefficients, and x is a variable. General code to evaluate an nth-order polynomial looks like this:

Visual Basic Example of Evaluating a Polynomial
```
value = coefficient( 0 )
For power = 1 To order
   value = value + coefficient( power ) * x^power
Next
```

If you're thinking about strength reduction, you'll look at the exponentiation operator with a jaundiced eye. One solution would be to replace the exponentiation with a multiplication on each pass through the loop, which is analogous to the strength-reduction case a few sections ago in which a multiplication was replaced with an addition. Here's how the reduced-strength polynomial evaluation would look:

Visual Basic Example of a Reduced-Strength Method of Evaluating a Polynomial
```
value = coefficient( 0 )
powerOfX = x
For power = 1 to order
   value = value + coefficient( power ) * powerOfX
   powerOfX = powerOfX * x
Next
```

This produces a noticeable advantage if you're working with second-order polynomials—that is, polynomials in which the highest-power term is squared—or higher-order polynomials:

Language	Straight Time	Code-Tuned Time	Time Savings	Performance Ratio
Python	3.24	2.60	20%	1:1
Visual Basic	**6.26**	**0.160**	**97%**	**40:1**

If you're serious about strength reduction, you still won't care for those two floating-point multiplications. The strength-reduction principle suggests that you can further reduce the strength of the operations in the loop by accumulating powers rather than multiplying them each time:

Visual Basic Example of Further Reducing the Strength Required to Evaluate a Polynomial
```
value = 0
For power = order to 1 Step -1
   value = ( value + coefficient( power ) ) * x
Next
value = value + coefficient( 0 )
```

This method eliminates the extra *powerOfX* variable and replaces the two multiplications in each pass through the loop with one. The results:

Language	Straight Time	First Optimization	Second Optimization	Savings over First Optimization
Python	3.24	2.60	2.53	3%
Visual Basic	**6.26**	**0.16**	**0.31**	**-94%**

This is a good example of theory not holding up very well to practice. The code with reduced strength seems like it should be faster, but it isn't. One possibility is that decrementing a loop by *1* instead of incrementing it by *1* in Visual Basic hurts performance, but you'd have to measure that hypothesis to be sure.

Initialize at Compile Time

If you're using a named constant or a magic number in a routine call and it's the only argument, that's a clue that you could precompute the number, put it into a constant, and avoid the routine call. The same principle applies to multiplications, divisions, additions, and other operations.

I once needed to compute the base-two logarithm of an integer, truncated to the nearest integer. The system didn't have a log-base-two routine, so I wrote my own. The quick and easy approach was to use this fact:

```
log(x)base = log(x) / log(base)
```

Given this identity, I could write a routine like this one:

Cross-Reference For details on binding variables to their values, see Section 10.6, "Binding Time."

C++ Example of a Log-Base-Two Routine Based on System Routines
```cpp
unsigned int Log2( unsigned int x ) {
    return (unsigned int) ( log( x ) / log( 2 ) );
}
```

This routine was really slow, and because the value of *log(2)* never changed, I replaced *log(2)* with its computed value, *0.69314718*, like this:

C++ Example of a Log-Base-Two Routine Based on a System Routine and a Constant
```cpp
const double LOG2 = 0.69314718;
...
unsigned int Log2( unsigned int x ) {
    return (unsigned int) ( log( x ) / LOG2 );
}
```

Since *log()* tends to be an expensive routine—much more expensive than type conversions or division—you'd expect that cutting the calls to the *log()* function by half would cut the time required for the routine by about half. Here are the measured results:

Language	Straight Time	Code-Tuned Time	Time Savings
C++	9.66	5.97	38%
Java	17.0	12.3	28%
PHP	2.45	1.50	39%

In this case, the educated guess about the relative importance of the division and type conversions and the estimate of 50 percent were pretty close. Considering the predictability of the results described in this chapter, the accuracy of my prediction in this case proves only that even a blind squirrel finds a nut occasionally.

Be Wary of System Routines

System routines are expensive and provide accuracy that's often wasted. Typical system math routines, for example, are designed to put an astronaut on the moon within ±2 feet of the target. If you don't need that degree of accuracy, you don't need to spend the time to compute it either.

In the previous example, the *Log2()* routine returned an integer value but used a floating-point *log()* routine to compute it. That was overkill for an integer result, so after my first attempt, I wrote a series of integer tests that were perfectly accurate for calculating an integer log2. Here's the code:

C++ Example of a Log-Base-Two Routine Based on Integers
```cpp
unsigned int Log2( unsigned int x ) {
   if ( x < 2 ) return 0 ;
   if ( x < 4 ) return 1 ;
   if ( x < 8 ) return 2 ;
   if ( x < 16 ) return 3 ;
   if ( x < 32 ) return 4 ;
   if ( x < 64 ) return 5 ;
   if ( x < 128 ) return 6 ;
   if ( x < 256 ) return 7 ;
   if ( x < 512 ) return 8 ;
   if ( x < 1024 ) return 9 ;
   ...
   if ( x < 2147483648 ) return 30;
   return 31 ;
}
```

This routine uses integer operations, never converts to floating point, and blows the doors off both floating-point versions:

Language	Straight Time	Code-Tuned Time	Time Savings	Performance Ratio
C++	9.66	0.662	93%	15:1
Java	17.0	0.882	95%	20:1
PHP	2.45	3.45	-41%	2:3

Most of the so-called "transcendental" functions are designed for the worst case—that is, they convert to double-precision floating point internally even if you give them an integer argument. If you find one in a tight section of code and don't need that much accuracy, give it your immediate attention.

Another option is to take advantage of the fact that a right-shift operation is the same as dividing by two. The number of times you can divide a number by two and still have a nonzero value is the same as the $\log_2$ of that number. Here's how code based on that observation looks:

CODING HORROR

C++ Example of an Alternative Log-Base-Two Routine Based on the Right-Shift Operator
```cpp
unsigned int Log2( unsigned int x ) {
    unsigned int i = 0;
    while ( ( x = ( x >> 1 ) ) != 0 ) {
        i++;
    }
    return i ;
}
```

To non-C++ programmers, this code is particularly hard to read. The complicated expression in the *while* condition is an example of a coding practice you should avoid unless you have a good reason to use it.

This routine takes about 350 percent longer than the longer version above, executing in 2.4 seconds rather than 0.66 seconds. But it's faster than the first approach, and it adapts easily to 32-bit, 64-bit, and other environments.

KEY POINT

This example highlights the value of not stopping after one successful optimization. The first optimization earned a respectable 30–40 percent savings but had nowhere near the impact of the second or third optimizations.

Use the Correct Type of Constants

Use named constants and literals that are the same type as the variables they're assigned to. When a constant and its related variable are different types, the compiler has to do a type conversion to assign the constant to the variable. A good compiler does the type conversion at compile time so that it doesn't affect run-time performance.

A less advanced compiler or an interpreter generates code for a run-time conversion, so you might be stuck. Here are some differences in performance between the initializations of a floating-point variable x and an integer variable i in two cases. In the first case, the initializations look like this:

```
x = 5
i = 3.14
```

and require type conversions, assuming x is a floating point variable and i is an integer. In the second case, they look like this:

```
x = 3.14
i = 5
```

and don't require type conversions. Here are the results, and the variation among compilers is once again notable:

Language	Straight Time	Code-Tuned Time	Time Savings	Performance Ratio
C++	1.11	0.000	100%	not measurable
C#	1.49	1.48	<1%	1:1
Java	1.66	1.11	33%	1.5:1
Visual Basic	0.721	0.000	100%	not measurable
PHP	0.872	0.847	3%	1:1

Precompute Results

A common low-level design decision is the choice of whether to compute results on the fly or compute them once, save them, and look them up as needed. If the results are used many times, it's often cheaper to compute them once and look them up the rest of the time.

This choice manifests itself in several ways. At the simplest level, you might compute part of an expression outside a loop rather than inside. An example of this appeared earlier in the chapter. At a more complicated level, you might compute a lookup table once when program execution begins, using it every time thereafter, or you might store results in a data file or embed them in a program.

Cross-Reference For more on using data in tables instead of complex logic, see Chapter 18, "Table-Driven Methods."

In a space-wars video game, for example, the programmers initially computed gravity coefficients for different distances from the sun. The computation for the gravity coefficients was expensive and affected performance. The program recognized relatively few distinct distances from the sun, however, so the programmers were able to precompute the gravity coefficients and store them in a 10-element array. The array lookup was much faster than the expensive computation.

Suppose you have a routine that computes payment amounts on automobile loans. The code for such a routine would look like this:

Java Example of a Complex Computation That Could Be Precomputed

```java
double ComputePayment(
    long loanAmount,
    int months,
    double interestRate
    ) {
    return loanAmount /
        (
        ( 1.0 - Math.pow( ( 1.0 + ( interestRate / 12.0 ) ), -months ) ) /
        ( interestRate / 12.0 )
        );
}
```

The formula for computing loan payments is complicated and fairly expensive. Putting the information into a table instead of computing it each time would probably be cheaper.

How big would the table be? The widest-ranging variable is *loanAmount*. The variable *interestRate* might range from 5 percent through 20 percent by quarter points, but that's only 61 distinct rates. *months* might range from 12 through 72, but that's only 61 distinct periods. *loanAmount* could conceivably range from $1000 through $100,000, which is more entries than you'd generally want to handle in a lookup table.

Most of the computation doesn't depend on *loanAmount*, however, so you can put the really ugly part of the computation (the denominator of the larger expression) into a table that's indexed by *interestRate* and *months*. You recompute the *loanAmount* part each time:

Java Example of Precomputing a Complex Computation

```java
double ComputePayment(
    long loanAmount,
    int months,
    double interestRate
    ) {
    int interestIndex =
        Math.round( ( interestRate - LOWEST_RATE ) * GRANULARITY * 100.00 );
    return loanAmount / loanDivisor[ interestIndex ][ months ];
}
```

The new variable *interestIndex* is created to provide a subscript into the *loanDivisor* array.

In this code, the hairy calculation has been replaced with the computation of an array index and a single array access. Here are the results of that change:

Language	Straight Time	Code-Tuned Time	Time Savings	Performance Ratio
Java	2.97	0.251	92%	10:1
Python	3.86	4.63	-20%	1:1

Depending on your circumstances, you would need to precompute the *loanDivisor* array at program initialization time or read it from a disk file. Alternatively, you could initialize it to *0*, compute each element the first time it's requested, store it, and look it up each time it's requested subsequently. That would be a form of caching, discussed earlier.

You don't have to create a table to take advantage of the performance gains you can achieve by precomputing an expression. Code similar to the code in the previous examples raises the possibility of a different kind of precomputation. Suppose you have code that computes payments for many loan amounts, as shown here:

Java Example of a Second Complex Computation That Could Be Precomputed

```java
double ComputePayments(
    int months,
    double interestRate
    ) {
    for ( long loanAmount = MIN_LOAN_AMOUNT; loanAmount < MAX_LOAN_AMOUNT;
        loanAmount++ ) {
        payment = loanAmount / (
            ( 1.0 - Math.pow( 1.0+(interestRate/12.0), - months ) ) /
            ( interestRate/12.0 )
            );
```

The following code would do something with *payment* here; for this example's point, it doesn't matter what.

```java
        ...
    }
}
```

Even without precomputing a table, you can precompute the complicated part of the expression outside the loop and use it inside the loop. Here's how it would look:

Java Example of Precomputing the Second Complex Computation

```java
double ComputePayments(
    int months,
    double interestRate
    ) {
    long loanAmount;
```

Here's the part that's precomputed.

```java
    double divisor = ( 1.0 - Math.pow( 1.0+(interestRate/12.0). - months ) ) /
        ( interestRate/12.0 );
    for ( long loanAmount = MIN_LOAN_AMOUNT; loanAmount <= MAX_LOAN_AMOUNT;
        loanAmount++ ) {
        payment = loanAmount / divisor;
        ...
    }
}
```

This is similar to the techniques suggested earlier of putting array references and pointer dereferences outside a loop. The results for Java in this case are comparable to the results of using the precomputed table in the first optimization:

Language	Straight Time	Code-Tuned Time	Time Savings	Performance Ratio
Java	7.43	0.24	97%	30:1
Python	5.00	1.69	66%	3:1

Python improved here, but not in the first optimization attempt. Many times when one optimization does not produce the desired results, a seemingly similar optimization will work as expected.

Optimizing a program by precomputation can take several forms:

- Computing results before the program executes, and wiring them into constants that are assigned at compile time

- Computing results before the program executes, and hard-coding them into variables used at run time

- Computing results before the program executes, and putting them into a file that's loaded at run time

- Computing results once, at program startup, and then referencing them each time they're needed

- Computing as much as possible before a loop begins, minimizing the work done inside the loop

- Computing results the first time they're needed, and storing them so that you can retrieve them when they're needed again

Eliminate Common Subexpressions

If you find an expression that's repeated several times, assign it to a variable and refer to the variable rather than recomputing the expression in several places. The loan-calculation example has a common subexpression that you could eliminate. This is the original code:

Java Example of a Common Subexpression

```java
payment = loanAmount / (
    ( 1.0 - Math.pow( 1.0 + ( interestRate / 12.0 ), -months ) ) /
    ( interestRate / 12.0 )
);
```

In this sample, you can assign *interestRate/12.0* to a variable that is then referenced twice rather than computing the expression twice. If you have chosen the variable name well, this optimization can improve the code's readability at the same time that it improves performance. This is the revised code:

Java Example of Eliminating a Common Subexpression
```java
monthlyInterest = interestRate / 12.0;
payment = loanAmount / (
     ( 1.0 - Math.pow( 1.0 + monthlyInterest, -months ) ) /
     monthlyInterest
  );
```

The savings in this case don't seem impressive:

Language	Straight Time	Code-Tuned Time	Time Savings
Java	2.94	2.83	4%
Python	3.91	3.94	-1%

It appears that the *Math.pow()* routine is so costly that it overshadows the savings from subexpression elimination. Or possibly the subexpression is already being eliminated by the compiler. If the subexpression were a bigger part of the cost of the whole expression or if the compiler optimizer were less effective, the optimization might have more impact.

26.5 Routines

Cross-Reference For details on working with routines, see Chapter 7, "High-Quality Routines."

One of the most powerful tools in code tuning is a good routine decomposition. Small, well-defined routines save space because they take the place of doing jobs separately in multiple places. They make a program easy to optimize because you can refactor code in one routine and thus improve every routine that calls it. Small routines are relatively easy to rewrite in a low-level language. Long, tortuous routines are hard enough to understand on their own; in a low-level language like assembler, they're impossible.

Rewrite Routines Inline

In the early days of computer programming, some machines imposed prohibitive performance penalties for calling a routine. A call to a routine meant that the operating system had to swap out the program, swap in a directory of routines, swap in the particular routine, execute the routine, swap out the routine, and swap the calling routine back in. All this swapping chewed up resources and made the program slow.

Modern computers collect a far smaller toll for calling a routine. Here are the results of putting a string-copy routine inline:

Language	Routine Time	Inline-Code Time	Time Savings
C++	0.471	0.431	8%
Java	13.1	14.4	-10%

In some cases, you might be able to save a few nanoseconds by putting the code from a routine into the program directly where it's needed via a language feature like C++'s *inline* keyword. If you're working in a language that doesn't support *inline* directly but that does have a macro preprocessor, you can use a macro to put the code in, switching it in and out as needed. But modern machines—and "modern" means any machine you're ever likely to work on—impose virtually no penalty for calling a routine. As the example shows, you're as likely to degrade performance by keeping code inline as to optimize it.

26.6 Recoding in a Low-Level Language

One long-standing piece of conventional wisdom that shouldn't be left unmentioned is the advice that when you run into a performance bottleneck, you should recode in a low-level language. If you're coding in C++, the low-level language might be assembler. If you're coding in Python, the low-level language might be C. Recoding in a low-level language tends to improve both speed and code size. Here is a typical approach to optimizing with a low-level language:

1. Write 100 percent of an application in a high-level language.

2. Fully test the application, and verify that it's correct.

Cross-Reference For details on the phenomenon of a small percentage of a program accounting for most of its run time, see "The Pareto Principle" in Section 25.2.

3. If performance improvements are needed after that, profile the application to identify hot spots. Since about 5 percent of a program usually accounts for about 50 percent of the running time, you can usually identify small pieces of the program as hot spots.

4. Recode a few small pieces in a low-level language to improve overall performance.

Whether you follow this well-beaten path depends on how comfortable you are with low-level languages, how well-suited the problem is to low-level languages, and on your level of desperation. I got my first exposure to this technique on the Data Encryption Standard program I mentioned in the previous chapter. I had tried every optimization I'd ever heard of, and the program was still twice as slow as the speed goal. Recoding part of the program in assembler was the only remaining option. As an assembler novice, about all I could do was make a straight translation from a high-level language to assembler, but I got a 50 percent improvement even at that rudimentary level.

Suppose you have a routine that converts binary data to uppercase ASCII characters. The next example shows the Delphi code to do it:

Delphi Example of Code That's Better Suited to Assembler
```
procedure HexExpand(
   var source: ByteArray;
   var target: WordArray;
   byteCount: word
);
var
   index: integer;
   targetIndex: integer;
begin
   targetIndex := 1;
   for index := 1 to byteCount do begin
      target[ targetIndex ] := ( (source[ index ] and $F0) shr 4 ) + $41;
      target[ targetIndex+1 ] := (source[ index ] and $0f) + $41;
      targetIndex := targetIndex + 2;
   end;
end;
```

Although it's hard to see where the fat is in this code, it contains a lot of bit manipulation, which isn't exactly Delphi's forte. Bit manipulation is assembler's forte, however, so this code is a good candidate for recoding. Here's the assembler code:

Example of a Routine Recoded in Assembler
```
procedure HexExpand(
   var source;
   var target;
   byteCount : Integer
);
   label
   EXPAND;

   asm
         MOV    ECX,byteCount      // load number of bytes to expand
         MOV    ESI,source         // source offset
         MOV    EDI,target         // target offset
         XOR    EAX,EAX            // zero out array offset

   EXPAND:
         MOV    EBX,EAX            // array offset
         MOV    DL,[ESI+EBX]       // get source byte
         MOV    DH,DL              // copy source byte

         AND    DH,$F              // get msbs
         ADD    DH,$41             // add 65 to make upper case

         SHR    DL,4               // move lsbs into position
         AND    DL,$F              // get lsbs
         ADD    DL,$41             // add 65 to make upper case
```

```
        SHL   BX,1              // double offset for target array offset
        MOV   [EDI+EBX],DX      // put target word

        INC   EAX               // increment array offset
        LOOP  EXPAND            // repeat until finished
   end;
```

Rewriting in assembler in this case was profitable, resulting in a time savings of 41 percent. It's logical to assume that code in a language that's more suited to bit manipulation—C++, for instance—would have less to gain than Delphi code would. Here are the results:

Language	High-Level Time	Assembler Time	Time Savings
C++	4.25	3.02	29%
Delphi	5.18	3.04	41%

The "before" picture in these measurements reflects the two languages' strengths at bit manipulation. The "after" picture looks virtually identical, and it appears that the assembler code has minimized the initial performance differences between Delphi and C++.

The assembler routine shows that rewriting in assembler doesn't have to produce a huge, ugly routine. Such routines are often quite modest, as this one is. Sometimes assembler code is almost as compact as its high-level-language equivalent.

A relatively easy and effective strategy for recoding in assembler is to start with a compiler that generates assembler listings as a byproduct of compilation. Extract the assembler code for the routine you need to tune, and save it in a separate source file. Using the compiler's assembler code as a base, hand-optimize the code, checking for correctness and measuring improvements at each step. Some compilers intersperse the high-level-language statements as comments in the assembler code. If yours does, you might keep them in the assembler code as documentation.

cc2e.com/2672

CHECKLIST: Code-Tuning Techniques
Improve Both Speed and Size

❑ Substitute table lookups for complicated logic.

❑ Jam loops.

❑ Use integer instead of floating-point variables.

❑ Initialize data at compile time.

❑ Use constants of the correct type.

❑ Precompute results.

❑ Eliminate common subexpressions.

❑ Translate key routines to a low-level language.

Improve Speed Only

- ❑ Stop testing when you know the answer.
- ❑ Order tests in *case* statements and *if-then-else* chains by frequency.
- ❑ Compare performance of similar logic structures.
- ❑ Use lazy evaluation.
- ❑ Unswitch loops that contain *if* tests.
- ❑ Unroll loops.
- ❑ Minimize work performed inside loops.
- ❑ Use sentinels in search loops.
- ❑ Put the busiest loop on the inside of nested loops.
- ❑ Reduce the strength of operations performed inside loops.
- ❑ Change multiple-dimension arrays to a single dimension.
- ❑ Minimize array references.
- ❑ Augment data types with indexes.
- ❑ Cache frequently used values.
- ❑ Exploit algebraic identities.
- ❑ Reduce strength in logical and mathematical expressions.
- ❑ Be wary of system routines.
- ❑ Rewrite routines inline.

26.7 The More Things Change, the More They Stay the Same

You might expect that performance attributes of systems would have changed somewhat in the 10 years since I wrote the first edition of *Code Complete*, and in some ways they have. Computers are dramatically faster and memory is more plentiful. In the first edition, I ran most of the tests in this chapter 10,000 to 50,000 times to get meaningful, measurable results. For this edition I had to run most tests 1 million to 100 million times. When you have to run a test 100 million times to get measurable results, you have to ask whether anyone will ever notice the impact in a real program. Computers have become so powerful that for many common kinds of programs, the level of performance optimization discussed in this chapter has become irrelevant.

In other ways, performance issues have hardly changed at all. People writing desktop applications may not need this information, but people writing software for embedded systems, real-time systems, and other systems with strict speed or space restrictions can still benefit from it.

The need to measure the impact of each and every attempt at code tuning has been a constant since Donald Knuth published his study of Fortran programs in 1971. According to the measurements in this chapter, the effect of any specific optimization is actually *less predictable* than it was 10 years ago. The effect of each code tuning is affected by the programming language, compiler, compiler version, code libraries, library versions, and compiler settings, among other things.

Code tuning invariably involves tradeoffs among complexity, readability, simplicity, and maintainability on the one hand and a desire to improve performance on the other. It introduces a high degree of maintenance overhead because of all the reprofiling that's required.

I have found that insisting on *measurable improvement* is a good way to resist the temptation to optimize prematurely and a good way to enforce a bias toward clear, straightforward code. If an optimization is important enough to haul out the profiler and measure the optimization's effect, then it's probably important enough to allow—as long as it works. But if an optimization isn't important enough to haul out the profiling machinery, it isn't important enough to degrade readability, maintainability, and other code characteristics. The impact of unmeasured code tuning on performance is speculative at best, whereas the impact on readability is as certain as it is detrimental.

Additional Resources

cc2e.com/2679

My favorite reference on code tuning is *Writing Efficient Programs* (Bentley, Englewood Cliffs, NJ: Prentice Hall, 1982). The book is out of print but worth reading if you can find it. It's an expert treatment of code tuning, broadly considered. Bentley describes techniques that trade time for space and space for time. He provides several examples of redesigning data types to reduce both space and time. His approach is a little more anecdotal than the one taken here, and his anecdotes are interesting. He takes a few routines through several optimization steps so that you can see the effects of first, second, and third attempts on a single problem. Bentley strolls through the primary contents of the book in 135 pages. The book has an unusually high signal-to-noise ratio—it's one of the rare gems that every practicing programmer should own.

Appendix 4 of Bentley's *Programming Pearls*, 2d ed. (Boston, MA: Addison-Wesley, 2000) contains a summary of the code-tuning rules from his earlier book.

cc2e.com/2686 You can also find a full array of technology-specific optimization books. Several are listed below, and the Web link to the left contains an up-to-date list.

Booth, Rick. *Inner Loops: A Sourcebook for Fast 32-bit Software Development.* Boston, MA: Addison-Wesley, 1997.

Gerber, Richard. *Software Optimization Cookbook: High-Performance Recipes for the Intel Architecture.* Intel Press, 2002.

Hasan, Jeffrey and Kenneth Tu. *Performance Tuning and Optimizing ASP.NET Applications.* Berkeley, CA: Apress, 2003.

Killelea, Patrick. *Web Performance Tuning*, 2d ed. Sebastopol, CA: O'Reilly & Associates, 2002.

Larman, Craig and Rhett Guthrie. *Java 2 Performance and Idiom Guide.* Englewood Cliffs, NJ: Prentice Hall, 2000.

Shirazi, Jack. *Java Performance Tuning.* Sebastopol, CA: O'Reilly & Associates, 2000.

Wilson, Steve and Jeff Kesselman. *Java Platform Performance: Strategies and Tactics.* Boston, MA: Addison-Wesley, 2000.

Key Points

- Results of optimizations vary widely with different languages, compilers, and environments. Without measuring each specific optimization, you'll have no idea whether it will help or hurt your program.

- The first optimization is often not the best. Even after you find a good one, keep looking for one that's better.

- Code tuning is a little like nuclear energy. It's a controversial, emotional topic. Some people think it's so detrimental to reliability and maintainability that they won't do it at all. Others think that with proper safeguards, it's beneficial. If you decide to use the techniques in this chapter, apply them with care.

Part VI
System Considerations

Chapter 27

How Program Size Affects Construction

cc2e.com/2761

Contents

Related Topics

- Prerequisites to construction: Chapter 3

- Determining the kind of software you're working on: Section 3.2

- Managing construction: Chapter 28

Scaling up in software development isn't a simple matter of taking a small project and making each part of it bigger. Suppose you wrote the 25,000-line Gigatron software package in 20 staff-months and found 500 errors in field testing. Suppose Gigatron 1.0 is successful, as is Gigatron 2.0, and you start work on the Gigatron Deluxe, a greatly enhanced version of the program that's expected to be 250,000 lines of code.

Even though it's 10 times as large as the original Gigatron, the Gigatron Deluxe won't take 10 times the effort to develop; it'll take 30 times the effort. Moreover, 30 times the total effort doesn't imply 30 times as much construction. It probably implies 25 times as much construction and 40 times as much architecture and system testing. You won't have 10 times as many errors either; you'll have 15 times as many—or more.

If you've been accustomed to working on small projects, your first medium-to-large project can rage riotously out of control, becoming an uncontrollable beast instead of the pleasant success you had envisioned. This chapter tells you what kind of beast to expect and where to find the whip and chair to tame it. In contrast, if you're accustomed to working on large projects, you might use approaches that are too formal on a small project. This chapter describes how you can economize to keep a small project from toppling under the weight of its own overhead.

27.1 Communication and Size

If you're the only person on a project, the only communication path is between you and the customer, unless you count the path across your corpus callosum, the path that connects the left side of your brain to the right. As the number of people on a project increases, the number of communication paths increases, too. The number doesn't increase additively as the number of people increases. It increases multiplicatively, proportionally to the square of the number of people, as illustrated in Figure 27-1.

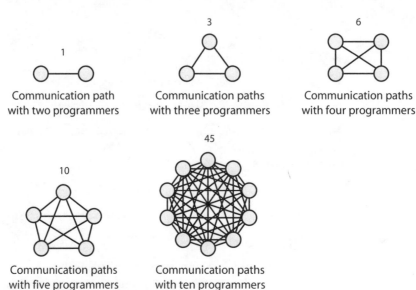

Figure 27-1   The number of communication paths increases proportionate to the square of the number of people on the team.

KEY POINT

As you can see, a two-person project has only one path of communication. A five-person project has 10 paths. A ten-person project has 45 paths, assuming that every person talks to every other person. The 10 percent of projects that have 50 or more programmers have at least 1,200 potential paths. The more communication paths you have, the more time you spend communicating and the more opportunities are created for communication mistakes. Larger-size projects demand organizational techniques that streamline communication or limit it in a sensible way.

The typical approach taken to streamlining communication is to formalize it in documents. Instead of having 50 people talk to each other in every conceivable combination, 50 people read and write documents. Some are text documents; some are graphic. Some are printed on paper; others are kept in electronic form.

27.2 Range of Project Sizes

Is the size of the project you're working on typical? The wide range of project sizes means that you can't consider any single size to be typical. One way of thinking about project size is to think about the size of a project team. Here's a crude estimate of the percentages of all projects that are done by teams of various sizes:

Team Size	Approximate Percentage of Projects
1–3	25%
4–10	30%
11–25	20%
26–50	15%
50+	10%

Source: Adapted from "A Survey of Software Engineering Practice: Tools, Methods, and Results" (Beck and Perkins 1983), *Agile Software Development Ecosystems* (Highsmith 2002), and *Balancing Agility and Discipline* (Boehm and Turner 2003).

One aspect of project size data that might not be immediately apparent is the difference between the percentages of projects of various sizes and the number of programmers who work on projects of each size. Because larger projects use more programmers on each project than do small ones, they employ a large percentage of all programmers. Here's a rough estimate of the percentage of all programmers who work on projects of various sizes:

Team Size	Approximate Percentage of Programmers
1–3	5%
4–10	10%
11–25	15%
26–50	20%
50+	50%

Source: Derived from data in "A Survey of Software Engineering Practice: Tools, Methods, and Results" (Beck and Perkins 1983), *Agile Software Development Ecosystems* (Highsmith 2002), and *Balancing Agility and Discipline* (Boehm and Turner 2003).

27.3 Effect of Project Size on Errors

Cross-Reference For more details on errors, see Section 22.4, "Typical Errors."

Both quantity and type of errors are affected by project size. You might not think that error type would be affected, but as project size increases, a larger percentage of errors can usually be attributed to mistakes in requirements and design, as shown in Figure 27-2.

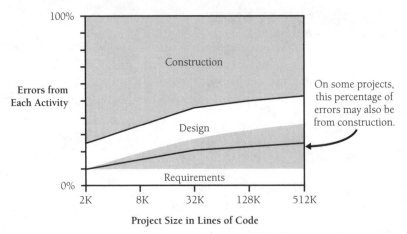

Figure 27-2 As project size increases, errors usually come more from requirements and design. Sometimes they still come primarily from construction (Boehm 1981, Grady 1987, Jones 1998).

HARD DATA

On small projects, construction errors make up about 75 percent of all the errors found. Methodology has less influence on code quality, and the biggest influence on program quality is often the skill of the individual writing the program (Jones 1998).

On larger projects, construction errors can taper off to about 50 percent of the total errors; requirements and architecture errors make up the difference. Presumably this is related to the fact that more requirements development and architectural design are required on large projects, so the opportunity for errors arising out of those activities is proportionally larger. In some very large projects, however, the proportion of construction errors remains high; sometimes even with 500,000 lines of code, up to 75 percent of the errors can be attributed to construction (Grady 1987).

KEY POINT

As the kinds of defects change with size, so do the numbers of defects. You would naturally expect a project that's twice as large as another to have twice as many errors. But the density of defects—the number of defects per 1000 lines of code—increases. The product that's twice as large is likely to have more than twice as many errors. Table 27-1 shows the range of defect densities you can expect on projects of various sizes.

Table 27-1   Project Size and Typical Error Density

Project Size (in Lines of Code)	Typical Error Density
Smaller than 2K	0–25 errors per thousand lines of code (KLOC)
2K–16K	0–40 errors per KLOC
16K–64K	0.5–50 errors per KLOC
64K–512K	2–70 errors per KLOC
512K or more	4–100 errors per KLOC
Sources: "Program Quality and Programmer Productivity" (Jones 1977), *Estimating Software Costs* (Jones 1998).	

Cross-Reference The data in this table represents average performance. A handful of organizations have reported better error rates than the minimums shown here. For examples, see "How Many Errors Should You Expect to Find?" in Section 22.4.

The data in this table was derived from specific projects, and the numbers might bear little resemblance to those for the projects you've worked on. As a snapshot of the industry, however, the data is illuminating. It indicates that the number of errors increases dramatically as project size increases, with very large projects having up to four times as many errors per thousand lines of code as small projects. A large project will need to work harder than a small project to achieve the same error rate.

27.4 Effect of Project Size on Productivity

Productivity has a lot in common with software quality when it comes to project size. At small sizes (2000 lines of code or smaller), the single biggest influence on productivity is the skill of the individual programmer (Jones 1998). As project size increases, team size and organization become greater influences on productivity.

HARD DATA

How big does a project need to be before team size begins to affect productivity? In "Prototyping Versus Specifying: a Multiproject Experiment," Boehm, Gray, and Seewaldt reported that smaller teams completed their projects with 39 percent higher productivity than larger teams. The size of the teams? Two people for the small projects and three for the large (1984). Table 27-2 gives the inside scoop on the general relationship between project size and productivity.

Table 27-2   Project Size and Productivity

Project Size (in Lines of Code)	Lines of Code per Staff-Year (Cocomo II Nominal in Parentheses)
1K	2,500–25,000 (4,000)
10K	2,000–25,000 (3,200)
100K	1,000–20,000 (2,600)
1,000K	700–10,000 (2,000)
10,000K	300–5,000 (1,600)

Source: Derived from data in *Measures for Excellence* (Putnam and Meyers 1992), *Industrial Strength Software* (Putnam and Meyers 1997), *Software Cost Estimation with Cocomo II* (Boehm et al. 2000), and "Software Development Worldwide: The State of the Practice" (Cusumano et al. 2003).

Productivity is substantially determined by the kind of software you're working on, personnel quality, programming language, methodology, product complexity, programming environment, tool support, how "lines of code" are counted, how nonprogrammer support effort is factored into the "lines of code per staff-year" figure, and many other factors, so the specific figures in Table 27-2 vary dramatically.

Realize, however, that the general trend the numbers show is significant. Productivity on small projects can be 2–3 times as high as productivity on large projects, and productivity can vary by a factor of 5–10 from the smallest projects to the largest.

27.5 Effect of Project Size on Development Activities

If you are working on a one-person project, the biggest influence on the project's success or failure is you. If you're working on a 25-person project, it's conceivable that you're still the biggest influence, but it's more likely that no one person will wear the medal for that distinction; your organization will be a stronger influence on the project's success or failure.

Activity Proportions and Size

As project size increases and the need for formal communications increases, the kinds of activities a project needs change dramatically. Figure 27-3 shows the proportions of development activities for projects of different sizes.

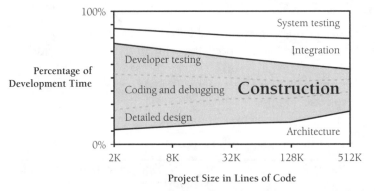

Figure 27-3   Construction activities dominate small projects. Larger projects require more architecture, integration work, and system testing to succeed. Requirements work is not shown on this diagram because requirements effort is not as directly a function of program size as other activities are (Albrecht 1979; Glass 1982; Boehm, Gray, and Seewaldt 1984; Boddie 1987; Card 1987; McGarry, Waligora, and McDermott 1989; Brooks 1995; Jones 1998; Jones 2000; Boehm et al. 2000).

KEY POINT

On a small project, construction is the most prominent activity by far, taking up as much as 65 percent of the total development time. On a medium-size project, construction is still the dominant activity but its share of the total effort falls to about 50 percent. On very large projects, architecture, integration, and system testing take up more time and construction becomes less dominant. In short, as project size increases, construction becomes a smaller part of the total effort. The chart looks as though you could extend it to the right and make construction disappear altogether, so in the interest of protecting my job, I've cut it off at 512K.

Construction becomes less predominant because as project size increases, the construction activities—detailed design, coding, debugging, and unit testing—scale up proportionately but many other activities scale up faster. Figure 27-4 provides an illustration.

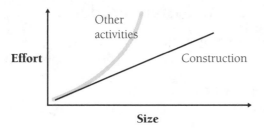

Figure 27-4 The amount of software construction work is a near-linear function of project size. Other kinds of work increase nonlinearly as project size increases.

Projects that are close in size will perform similar activities, but as sizes diverge, the kinds of activities will diverge, too. As the introduction to this chapter described, when the Gigatron Deluxe comes out at 10 times the size of the original Gigatron, it will need 25 times more construction effort, 25–50 times the planning effort, 30 times the integration effort, and 40 times the architecture and system testing.

HARD DATA

Proportions of activities vary because different activities become critical at different project sizes. Barry Boehm and Richard Turner found that spending about five percent of total project costs on architecture and requirements produced the lowest cost for projects in the 10,000-lines-of-code range. But for projects in the 100,000-lines-of-code range, spending 15–20 percent of project effort on architecture and requirements produced the best results (Boehm and Turner 2004).

Here's a list of activities that grow at a more-than-linear rate as project size increases:

- Communication
- Planning
- Management
- Requirements development
- System functional design
- Interface design and specification
- Architecture
- Integration
- Defect removal
- System testing
- Document production

Regardless of the size of a project, a few techniques are always valuable: disciplined coding practices, design and code inspections by other developers, good tool support, and use of high-level languages. These techniques are valuable on small projects and invaluable on large projects.

Programs, Products, Systems, and System Products

Further Reading For another explanation of this point, see Chapter 1 in *The Mythical Man-Month* (Brooks 1995).

Lines of code and team size aren't the only influences on a project's size. A more subtle influence is the quality and the complexity of the final software. The original Gigatron, the Gigatron Jr., might have taken only a month to write and debug. It was a single program written, tested, and documented by a single person. If the 2,500-line Gigatron Jr. took one month, why did the full-fledged 25,000-line Gigatron take 20 months?

The simplest kind of software is a single "program" that's used by itself by the person who developed it or, informally, by a few others.

A more sophisticated kind of program is a software "product," a program that's intended for use by people other than the original developer. A software product is used in environments that differ from the environment in which the product was created. It's extensively tested before it's released, it's documented, and it's capable of being maintained by others. A software product costs about three times as much to develop as a software program.

Another level of sophistication is required to develop a group of programs that work together. Such a group is called a software "system." Development of a system is more complicated than development of a simple program because of the complexity of developing interfaces among the pieces and the care needed to integrate the pieces. On the whole, a system also costs about three times as much as a simple program.

HARD DATA

When a "system product" is developed, it has the polish of a product and the multiple parts of a system. System products cost about nine times as much as simple programs (Brooks 1995, Shull et al. 2002).

A failure to appreciate the differences in polish and complexity among programs, products, systems, and system products is a common cause of estimation errors. Programmers who use their experience in building a program to estimate the schedule for building a system product can underestimate by a factor of almost 10. As you consider the following example, refer to the chart in Figure 27-3 (on page 654). If you used your experience in writing 2K lines of code to estimate the time it would take you to develop a 2K program, your estimate would be only 65 percent of the total time you'd actually need to perform all the activities that go into developing a program. Writing 2K lines of code doesn't take as long as creating a whole program that contains 2K lines of code. If you don't consider the time it takes to do nonconstruction activities, development will take 50 percent more time than you estimate.

As you scale up, construction becomes a smaller part of the total effort in a project. If you base your estimates solely on construction experience, the estimation error increases. If you used your own 2K construction experience to estimate the time it would take to develop a 32K program, your estimate would be only 50 percent of the total time required; development would take 100 percent more time than you would estimate.

The estimation error here would be completely attributable to your not understanding the effect of size on developing larger programs. If in addition you failed to consider the extra degree of polish required for a product rather than a mere program, the error could easily increase by a factor of three or more.

Methodology and Size

Methodologies are used on projects of all sizes. On small projects, methodologies tend to be casual and instinctive. On large projects, they tend to be rigorous and carefully planned.

Some methodologies can be so loose that programmers aren't even aware that they're using them. A few programmers argue that methodologies are too rigid and say that they won't touch them. While it may be true that a programmer hasn't selected a methodology consciously, any approach to programming constitutes a methodology, no matter how unconscious or primitive the approach is. Merely getting out of bed and going to work in the morning is a rudimentary methodology although not a very creative one. The programmer who insists on avoiding methodologies is really only avoiding choosing one explicitly—no one can avoid using them altogether.

KEY POINT

Formal approaches aren't always fun, and if they are misapplied, their overhead gobbles up their other savings. The greater complexity of larger projects, however, requires a greater conscious attention to methodology. Building a skyscraper requires a different approach than building a doghouse. Different sizes of software projects work the same way. On large projects, unconscious choices are inadequate to the task. Successful project planners choose their strategies for large projects explicitly.

In social settings, the more formal the event, the more uncomfortable your clothes have to be (high heels, neckties, and so on). In software development, the more formal the project, the more paper you have to generate to make sure you've done your homework. Capers Jones points out that a project of 1,000 lines of code will average about 7 percent of its effort on paperwork, whereas a 100,000-lines-of-code project will average about 26 percent of its effort on paperwork (Jones 1998).

This paperwork isn't created for the sheer joy of writing documents. It's created as a direct result of the phenomenon illustrated in Figure 27-1: the more people's brains you have to coordinate, the more formal documentation you need to coordinate them.

You don't create any of this documentation for its own sake. The point of writing a configuration-management plan, for example, isn't to exercise your writing muscles. The point of your writing the plan is to force you to think carefully about configuration management and to explain your plan to everyone else. The documentation is a tangible side effect of the real work you do as you plan and construct a software system. If you feel as though you're going through the motions and writing generic documents, something is wrong.

"More" is not better, as far as methodologies are concerned. In their review of agile vs. plan-driven methodologies, Barry Boehm and Richard Turner caution that you'll usually do better if you start your methods small and scale up for a large project than if you start with an all-inclusive method and pare it down for a small project (Boehm and Turner 2004). Some software pundits talk about "lightweight" and "heavyweight" methodologies, but in practice the key is to consider your project's specific size and type and then find the methodology that's "right-weight."

Additional Resources

cc2e.com/2768

Use the following resources to investigate this chapter's subject further:

Boehm, Barry and Richard Turner. *Balancing Agility and Discipline: A Guide for the Perplexed*. Boston, MA: Addison-Wesley, 2004. Boehm and Turner describe how project size affects the use of agile and plan-driven methods, along with other agile and plan-driven issues.

Cockburn, Alistair. *Agile Software Development*. Boston, MA: Addison-Wesley, 2002. Chapter 4 discusses issues involved in selecting appropriate project methodologies, including project size. Chapter 6 introduces Cockburn's Crystal Methodologies, which are defined approaches for developing projects of various sizes and degrees of criticality.

Boehm, Barry W. *Software Engineering Economics*. Englewood Cliffs, NJ: Prentice Hall, 1981. Boehm's book is an extensive treatment of the cost, productivity, and quality ramifications of project size and other variables in the software-development process. It includes discussions of the effect of size on construction and other activities. Chapter 11 is an excellent explanation of software's diseconomies of scale. Other information on project size is spread throughout the book. Boehm's 2000 book *Software Cost Estimation with Cocomo II* contains much more up-to-date information on Boehm's Cocomo estimating model, but the earlier book provides more in-depth background discussions that are still relevant.

Jones, Capers. *Estimating Software Costs*. New York, NY: McGraw-Hill, 1998. This book is packed with tables and graphs that dissect the sources of software development productivity. For the impact of project size specifically, Jones's 1986 book, *Programming Productivity*, contains an excellent discussion in the section titled "The Impact of Program Size" in Chapter 3.

Brooks, Frederick P., Jr. *The Mythical Man-Month: Essays on Software Engineering, Anniversary Edition* (2d ed.). Reading, MA: Addison-Wesley, 1995. Brooks was the manager of IBM's OS/360 development, a mammoth project that took 5000 staff-years. He discusses management issues pertaining to small and large teams and presents a particularly vivid account of chief-programmer teams in this engaging collection of essays.

DeGrace, Peter, and Leslie Stahl. *Wicked Problems, Righteous Solutions: A Catalogue of Modern Software Engineering Paradigms*. Englewood Cliffs, NJ: Yourdon Press, 1990. As the title suggests, this book catalogs approaches to developing software. As noted throughout this chapter, your approach needs to vary as the size of the project varies, and DeGrace and Stahl make that point clearly. The section titled "Attenuating and Truncating" in Chapter 5 discusses customizing software-development processes based on project size and formality. The book includes descriptions of models from NASA and the Department of Defense and a remarkable number of edifying illustrations.

Jones, T. Capers. "Program Quality and Programmer Productivity." *IBM Technical Report TR 02.764* (January 1977): 42–78. Also available in Jones's *Tutorial: Programming Productivity: Issues for the Eighties*, 2d ed. Los Angeles, CA: IEEE Computer Society Press, 1986. This paper contains the first in-depth analysis of the reasons large projects have different spending patterns than small ones. It's a thorough discussion of the differences between large and small projects, including requirements and quality-assurance measures. It's dated but still interesting.

Key Points

- As project size increases, communication needs to be supported. The point of most methodologies is to reduce communications problems, and a methodology should live or die on its merits as a communication facilitator.

- All other things being equal, productivity will be lower on a large project than on a small one.

- All other things being equal, a large project will have more errors per thousand lines of code than a small one.

- Activities that are taken for granted on small projects must be carefully planned on larger ones. Construction becomes less predominant as project size increases.

- Scaling up a lightweight methodology tends to work better than scaling down a heavyweight methodology. The most effective approach of all is using a "right-weight" methodology.

Chapter 28
Managing Construction

cc2e.com/2836

Contents

Related Topics

Managing software development has been a formidable challenge for the past several decades. As Figure 28-1 suggests, the general topic of software-project management extends beyond the scope of this book, but this chapter discusses a few specific management topics that apply directly to construction. If you're a developer, this chapter will help you understand the issues that managers need to consider. If you're a manager, this chapter will help you understand how management looks to developers as well as how to manage construction effectively. Because the chapter covers a broad collection of topics, several of its sections also describe where you can go for more information.

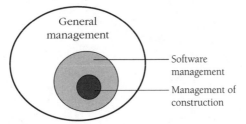

Figure 28-1   This chapter covers the software-management topics related to construction.

If you're interested in software management, be sure to read Section 3.2, "Determine the Kind of Software You're Working On," to understand the difference between traditional sequential approaches to development and modern iterative approaches. Be sure also to read Chapter 20, "The Software-Quality Landscape," and Chapter 27, "How Program Size Affects Construction." Quality goals and the size of the project both significantly affect how a specific software project should be managed.

28.1 Encouraging Good Coding

Because code is the primary output of construction, a key question in managing construction is "How do you encourage good coding practices?" In general, mandating a strict set of technical standards from the management position isn't a good idea. Programmers tend to view managers as being at a lower level of technical evolution, somewhere between single-celled organisms and the woolly mammoths that died out during the Ice Age, and if there are going to be programming standards, programmers need to buy into them.

If someone on a project is going to define standards, have a respected architect define the standards rather than the manager. Software projects operate as much on an "expertise hierarchy" as on an "authority hierarchy." If the architect is regarded as the project's thought leader, the project team will generally follow standards set by that person.

If you choose this approach, be sure the architect really is respected. Sometimes a project architect is just a senior person who has been around too long and is out of touch with production coding issues. Programmers will resent that kind of "architect" defining standards that are out of touch with the work they're doing.

Considerations in Setting Standards

Standards are more useful in some organizations than in others. Some developers welcome standards because they reduce arbitrary variance in the project. If your group resists adopting strict standards, consider a few alternatives: flexible guidelines, a collection of suggestions rather than guidelines, or a set of examples that embody the best practices.

Techniques for Encouraging Good Coding

This section describes several techniques for achieving good coding practices that are less heavy-handed than laying down rigid coding standards:

Cross-Reference For more details on pair programming, see Section 21.2, "Pair Programming."

Assign two people to every part of the project If two people have to work on each line of code, you'll guarantee that at least two people think it works and is readable. The mechanisms for teaming two people can range from pair programming to mentor-trainee pairs to buddy-system reviews.

Cross-Reference For details on reviews, see Section 21.3, "Formal Inspections," and Section 21.4, "Other Kinds of Collaborative Development Practices."

Review every line of code   A code review typically involves the programmer and at least two reviewers. That means that at least three people read every line of code. Another name for peer review is "peer pressure." In addition to providing a safety net in case the original programmer leaves the project, reviews improve code quality because the programmer knows that the code will be read by others. Even if your shop hasn't created explicit coding standards, reviews provide a subtle way of moving toward a group coding standard—decisions are made by the group during reviews, and over time the group derives its own standards.

Require code sign-offs   In other fields, technical drawings are approved and signed by the managing engineer. The signature means that to the best of the engineer's knowledge, the drawings are technically competent and error-free. Some companies treat code the same way. Before code is considered to be complete, senior technical personnel must sign the code listing.

Route good code examples for review   A big part of good management is communicating your objectives clearly. One way to communicate your objectives is to circulate good code to your programmers or post it for public display. In doing so, you provide a clear example of the quality you're aiming for. Similarly, a coding-standards manual can consist mainly of a set of "best code listings." Identifying certain listings as "best" sets an example for others to follow. Such a manual is easier to update than an English-language standards manual, and it effortlessly presents subtleties in coding style that are hard to capture point by point in prose descriptions.

Cross-Reference A large part of programming is communicating your work to other people. For details, see Section 33.5 and Section 34.3.

Emphasize that code listings are public assets   Programmers sometimes feel that the code they've written is "their code," as if it were private property. Although it is the result of their work, code is part of the project and should be freely available to anyone else on the project who needs it. It should be seen by others during reviews and maintenance, even if at no other time.

HARD DATA

One of the most successful projects ever reported developed 83,000 lines of code in 11 work-years of effort. Only one error that resulted in system failure was detected in the first 13 months of operation. This accomplishment is even more dramatic when you realize that the project was completed in the late 1960s, without online compilation or interactive debugging. Productivity on the project—7500 lines of code per work-year in the late 1960s—is still impressive by today's standards. The chief programmer on the project reported that one key to the project's success was the identification of all computer runs (erroneous and otherwise) as public rather than private assets (Baker and Mills 1973). This idea has extended into modern contexts, including Open Source Software (Raymond 2000) and Extreme Programming's idea of collective ownership (Beck 2000), as well as in other contexts.

Reward good code   Use your organization's reward system to reinforce good coding practices. Keep these considerations in mind as you develop your reinforcement system:

- The reward should be something that the programmer wants. (Many programmers find "attaboy" rewards distasteful, especially when they come from nontechnical managers.)

- Code that receives an award should be exceptionally good. If you give an award to a programmer everyone else knows does bad work, you look like Homer Simpson trying to run a nuclear reactor. It doesn't matter that the programmer has a cooperative attitude or always comes to work on time. You lose credibility if your reward doesn't match the technical merits of the situation. If you're not technically skilled enough to make the good-code judgment, don't! Don't make the award at all, or let your team choose the recipient.

One easy standard   If you're managing a programming project and you have a programming background, an easy and effective technique for eliciting good work is to say "I must be able to read and understand any code written for the project." That the manager isn't the hottest technical hotshot can be an advantage in that it might discourage "clever" or tricky code.

The Role of This Book

Most of this book is a discussion of good programming practices. It isn't intended to be used to justify rigid standards, and it's intended even less to be used as a set of rigid standards. Use this book as a basis for discussion, as a sourcebook of good programming practices, and for identifying practices that could be beneficial in your environment.

28.2 Configuration Management

A software project is dynamic. The code changes, the design changes, and the requirements change. What's more, changes in the requirements lead to more changes in the design, and changes in the design lead to even more changes in the code and test cases.

What Is Configuration Management?

Configuration management is the practice of identifying project artifacts and handling changes systematically so that a system can maintain its integrity over time. Another name for it is "change control." It includes techniques for evaluating proposed changes, tracking changes, and keeping copies of the system as it existed at various points in time.

If you don't control changes to requirements, you can end up writing code for parts of the system that are eventually eliminated. You can write code that's incompatible with new parts of the system. You might not detect many of the incompatibilities until integration time, which will become finger-pointing time because nobody will really know what's going on.

If changes to code aren't controlled, you might change a routine that someone else is changing at the same time; successfully combining your changes with theirs will be problematic. Uncontrolled code changes can make code seem more tested than it is. The version that's been tested will probably be the old, unchanged version; the modified version might not have been tested. Without good change control, you can make changes to a routine, find new errors, and not be able to back up to the old, working routine.

The problems go on indefinitely. If changes aren't handled systematically, you're taking random steps in the fog rather than moving directly toward a clear destination. Without good change control, rather than developing code you're wasting your time thrashing. Configuration management helps you use your time effectively.

HARD DATA

In spite of the obvious need for configuration management, many programmers have been avoiding it for decades. A survey more than 20 years ago found that over a third of programmers weren't even familiar with the idea (Beck and Perkins 1983), and there's little indication that that has changed. A more recent study by the Software Engineering Institute found that, of organizations using informal software-development practices, less than 20 percent had adequate configuration management (SEI 2003).

Configuration management wasn't invented by programmers, but because programming projects are so volatile, it's especially useful to programmers. Applied to software projects, configuration management is usually called "software configuration management" (SCM). SCM focuses on a program's requirements, source code, documentation, and test data.

The systemic problem with SCM is overcontrol. The surest way to stop car accidents is to prevent everyone from driving, and one sure way to prevent software-development problems is to stop all software development. Although that's one way to control changes, it's a terrible way to develop software. You have to plan SCM carefully so that it's an asset rather than an albatross around your neck.

Cross-Reference For details on the effects of project size on construction, see Chapter 27, "How Program Size Affects Construction."

On a small, one-person project, you can probably do well with no SCM beyond planning for informal periodic backups. Nonetheless, configuration management is still useful (and, in fact, I used configuration management in creating this manuscript). On a large, 50-person project, you'll probably need a full-blown SCM scheme, including fairly formal procedures for backups, change control for requirements and design, and control over documents, source code, content, test cases, and other project artifacts. If your project is neither very large nor very small, you'll have to settle on a degree of formality somewhere between the two extremes. The following subsections describe some of the options in implementing SCM.

Requirements and Design Changes

Cross-Reference Some development approaches support changes better than others. For details, see Section 3.2, "Determine the Kind of Software You're Working On."

During development, you're bound to be bristling with ideas about how to improve the system. If you implement each change as it occurs to you, you'll soon find yourself walking on a software treadmill—for all that the system will be changing, it won't be moving closer to completion. Here are some guidelines for controlling design changes:

Follow a systematic change-control procedure   As Section 3.4 noted, a systematic change-control procedure is a godsend when you have a lot of change requests. By establishing a systematic procedure, you make it clear that changes will be considered in the context of what's best for the project overall.

Handle change requests in groups   It's tempting to implement easy changes as ideas arise. The problem with handling changes in this way is that good changes can get lost. If you think of a simple change 25 percent of the way through the project and you're on schedule, you'll make the change. If you think of another simple change 50 percent of the way through the project and you're already behind, you won't. When you start to run out of time at the end of the project, it won't matter that the second change is 10 times as good as the first—you won't be in a position to make any nonessential changes. Some of the best changes can slip through the cracks merely because you thought of them later rather than sooner.

A solution to this problem is to write down all ideas and suggestions, no matter how easy they would be to implement, and save them until you have time to work on them. Then, viewing them as a group, choose the ones that will be the most beneficial.

Estimate the cost of each change   Whenever your customer, your boss, or you are tempted to change the system, estimate the time it would take to make the change, including review of the code for the change and retesting the whole system. Include in your estimate time for dealing with the change's ripple effect through requirements to design to code to test to changes in the user documentation. Let all the interested parties know that software is intricately interwoven and that time estimation is necessary even if the change appears small at first glance.

Regardless of how optimistic you feel when the change is first suggested, refrain from giving an off-the-cuff estimate. Such estimates are often mistaken by a factor of 2 or more.

Cross-Reference For another angle on handling changes, see "Handling Requirements Changes During Construction" in Section 3.4. For advice on handling code changes safely when they do occur, see Chapter 24, "Refactoring."

Be wary of high change volumes   While some degree of change is inevitable, a high volume of change requests is a key warning sign that requirements, architecture, or top-level designs weren't done well enough to support effective construction. Backing up to work on requirements or architecture might seem expensive, but it won't be nearly as expensive as constructing the software more than once or throwing away code for features that you really didn't need.

Establish a change-control board or its equivalent in a way that makes sense for your project   The job of a change-control board is to separate the wheat from the chaff in change requests. Anyone who wants to propose a change submits the change request to the change-control board. The term "change request" refers to any request that would change the software: an idea for a new feature, a change to an existing feature, an "error report" that might or might not be reporting a real error, and so on. The board meets periodically to review proposed changes. It approves, disapproves, or defers each change. Change-control boards are considered a best practice for prioritizing and controlling requirements changes; however, they are still fairly uncommon in commercial settings (Jones 1998, Jones 2000).

Watch for bureaucracy, but don't let the fear of bureaucracy preclude effective change control   Lack of disciplined change control is one of the biggest management problems facing the software industry today. A significant percentage of the projects that are perceived to be late would actually be on time if they accounted for the impact of untracked but agreed-upon changes. Poor change control allows changes to accumulate off the books, which undermines status visibility, long-range predictability, project planning, risk management specifically, and project management generally.

Change control tends to drift toward bureaucracy, so it's important to look for ways to streamline the change-control process. If you'd rather not use traditional change requests, set up a simple "ChangeBoard" e-mail alias and have people e-mail change requests to the address. Or have people present change proposals interactively at a change board meeting. An especially powerful approach is to log change requests as defects in your defect-tracking software. Purists will classify such changes as "requirements defects," or you could classify them as changes rather than defects.

You can implement the Change-Control Board itself formally, or you can define a Product Planning Group or War Council that carries the traditional responsibilities of a change-control board. Or you can identify a single person to be the Change Czar. But whatever you call it, do it!

KEY POINT

I occasionally see projects suffering from ham-handed implementations of change control. But 10 times as often I see projects suffering from no meaningful change control at all. The substance of change control is what's important, so don't let fear of bureaucracy stop you from realizing its many benefits.

Software Code Changes

Another configuration-management issue is controlling source code. If you change the code and a new error surfaces that seems unrelated to the change you made, you'll probably want to compare the new version of the code to the old in your search for the source of the error. If that doesn't tell you anything, you might want to look at a version that's even older. This kind of excursion through history is easy if you have version-control tools that keep track of multiple versions of source code.

Version-control software   Good version-control software works so easily that you barely notice you're using it. It's especially helpful on team projects. One style of version control locks source files so that only one person can modify a file at a time. Typically, when you need to work on source code in a particular file, you check the file out of version control. If someone else has already checked it out, you're notified that you can't check it out. When you can check the file out, you work on it just as you would without version control until you're ready to check it in. Another style allows multiple people to work on files simultaneously and handles the issue of merging changes when the code is checked in. In either case, when you check the file in, version control asks why you changed it, and you type in a reason.

For this modest investment of effort, you get several big benefits:

- You don't step on anyone's toes by working on a file while someone else is working on it (or at least you'll know about it if you do).

- You can easily update your copies of all the project's files to the current versions, usually by issuing a single command.

- You can backtrack to any version of any file that was ever checked into version control.

- You can get a list of the changes made to any version of any file.

- You don't have to worry about personal backups because the version-control copy is a safety net.

Version control is indispensable on team projects. It becomes even more powerful when version control, defect tracking, and change management are integrated. The applications division of Microsoft found its proprietary version-control tool to be a "major competitive advantage" (Moore 1992).

Tool Versions

For some kinds of projects, it may be necessary to be able to reconstruct the exact environment used to create each specific version of the software, including compilers, linkers, code libraries, and so on. In that case, you should put all of those tools into version control, too.

Machine Configurations

Many companies (including my company) have experienced good results from creating standardized development machine configurations. A disk image is created of a standard developer workstation, including all the common developer tools, office applications, and so on. That image is loaded onto each developer's machine. Having standardized configurations helps to avoid a raft of problems associated with slightly different configuration settings, different versions of tools used, and so on. A standardized disk image also greatly streamlines setting up new machines compared to having to install each piece of software individually.

Backup Plan

A backup plan isn't a dramatic new concept; it's the idea of backing up your work periodically. If you were writing a book by hand, you wouldn't leave the pages in a pile on your porch. If you did, they might get rained on or blown away, or your neighbor's dog might borrow them for a little bedtime reading. You'd put them somewhere safe. Software is less tangible, so it's easier to forget that you have something of enormous value on one machine.

Many things can happen to computerized data: a disk can fail; you or someone else can delete key files accidentally; an angry employee can sabotage your machine; or you could lose a machine to theft, flood, or fire. Take steps to safeguard your work. Your backup plan should include making backups on a periodic basis and periodic transfer of backups to off-site storage, and it should encompass all the important materials on your project—documents, graphics, and notes—in addition to source code.

One often-overlooked aspect of devising a backup plan is a test of your backup procedure. Try doing a restore at some point to make sure that the backup contains everything you need and that the recovery works.

When you finish a project, make a project archive. Save a copy of everything: source code, compilers, tools, requirements, design, documentation—everything you need to re-create the product. Keep it all in a safe place.

cc2e.com/2843

> ## CHECKLIST: Configuration Management
> ### General
> ❑ Is your software configuration management plan designed to help programmers and minimize overhead?
>
> ❑ Does your SCM approach avoid overcontrolling the project?
>
> ❑ Do you group change requests, either through informal means (such as a list of pending changes) or through a more systematic approach (such as a change-control board)?
>
> ❑ Do you systematically estimate the cost, schedule, and quality impact of each proposed change?
>
> ❑ Do you view major changes as a warning that requirements development isn't yet complete?

Tools

- ❑ Do you use version-control software to facilitate configuration management?
- ❑ Do you use version-control software to reduce coordination problems of working in teams?

Backup

- ❑ Do you back up all project materials periodically?
- ❑ Are project backups transferred to off-site storage periodically?
- ❑ Are all materials backed up, including source code, documents, graphics, and important notes?
- ❑ Have you tested the backup-recovery procedure?

Additional Resources on Configuration Management

cc2e.com/2850

Because this book is about construction, this section has focused on change control from a construction point of view. But changes affect projects at all levels, and a comprehensive change-control strategy needs to do the same.

Hass, Anne Mette Jonassen. *Configuration Management Principles and Practices*. Boston, MA: Addison-Wesley, 2003. This book provides the big-picture view of software configuration management and practical details on how to incorporate it into your software-development process. It focuses on managing and controlling configuration items.

Berczuk, Stephen P. and Brad Appleton. *Software Configuration Management Patterns: Effective Teamwork, Practical Integration*. Boston, MA: Addison-Wesley, 2003. Like Hass's book, this book provides a SCM overview and is practical. It complements Hass's book by providing practical guidelines that allow teams of developers to isolate and coordinate their work.

cc2e.com/2857

SPMN. *Little Book of Configuration Management*. Arlington, VA: Software Program Managers Network, 1998. This pamphlet is an introduction to configuration management activities and defines critical success factors. It's available as a free download from the SPMN website at *www.spmn.com/products_guidebooks.html*.

Bays, Michael. *Software Release Methodology*. Englewood Cliffs, NJ: Prentice Hall, 1999. This book discusses software configuration management with an emphasis on releasing software into production.

Bersoff, Edward H., and Alan M. Davis. "Impacts of Life Cycle Models on Software Configuration Management." *Communications of the ACM 34*, no. 8 (August 1991): 104–118. This article describes how SCM is affected by newer approaches to software development, especially prototyping approaches. The article is especially applicable in environments that are using agile development practices.

28.3 Estimating a Construction Schedule

HARD DATA

Managing a software project is one of the formidable challenges of the twenty-first century, and estimating the size of a project and the effort required to complete it is one of the most challenging aspects of software-project management. The average large software project is one year late and 100 percent over budget (Standish Group 1994, Jones 1997, Johnson 1999). At the individual level, surveys of estimated vs. actual schedules have found that developers' estimates tend to have an optimism factor of 20 to 30 percent (van Genuchten 1991). This has as much to do with poor size and effort estimates as with poor development efforts. This section outlines the issues involved in estimating software projects and indicates where to look for more information.

Estimation Approaches

Further Reading For further reading on schedule-estimation techniques, see Chapter 8 of *Rapid Development* (McConnell 1996) and *Software Cost Estimation with Cocomo II* (Boehm et al. 2000).

You can estimate the size of a project and the effort required to complete it in any of several ways:

- Use estimating software.
- Use an algorithmic approach, such as Cocomo II, Barry Boehm's estimation model (Boehm et al. 2000).
- Have outside estimation experts estimate the project.
- Have a walk-through meeting for estimates.
- Estimate pieces of the project, and then add the pieces together.
- Have people estimate their own tasks, and then add the task estimates together.
- Refer to experience on previous projects.
- Keep previous estimates and see how accurate they were. Use them to adjust new estimates.

Pointers to more information on these approaches are given in "Additional Resources on Software Estimation" at the end of this section. Here's a good approach to estimating a project:

Further Reading This approach is adapted from *Software Engineering Economics* (Boehm 1981).

Establish objectives   Why do you need an estimate? What are you estimating? Are you estimating only construction activities, or all of development? Are you estimating only the effort for your project, or your project plus vacations, holidays, training, and other nonproject activities? How accurate does the estimate need to be to meet your objectives? What degree of certainty needs to be associated with the estimate? Would an optimistic or a pessimistic estimate produce substantially different results?

Allow time for the estimate, and plan it   Rushed estimates are inaccurate estimates. If you're estimating a large project, treat estimation as a miniproject and take the time to miniplan the estimate so that you can do it well.

Cross-Reference For more information on software requirements, see Section 3.4, "Requirements Prerequisite."

Spell out software requirements Just as an architect can't estimate how much a "pretty big" house will cost, you can't reliably estimate a "pretty big" software project. It's unreasonable for anyone to expect you to be able to estimate the amount of work required to build something when "something" has not yet been defined. Define requirements or plan a preliminary exploration phase before making an estimate.

Estimate at a low level of detail Depending on the objectives you identified, base the estimate on a detailed examination of project activities. In general, the more detailed your examination is, the more accurate your estimate will be. The Law of Large Numbers says that a 10 percent error on one big piece will be 10 percent high or 10 percent low. On 50 small pieces, some of the 10 percent errors in the pieces will be high and some will be low, and the errors will tend to cancel each other out.

Cross-Reference It's hard to find an area of software development in which iteration is not valuable. Estimation is one case in which iteration is useful. For a summary of iterative techniques, see Section 34.8, "Iterate, Repeatedly, Again and Again."

Use several different estimation techniques, and compare the results The list of estimation approaches at the beginning of the section identified several techniques. They won't all produce the same results, so try several of them. Study the different results from the different approaches. Children learn early that if they ask each parent individually for a third bowl of ice cream, they have a better chance of getting at least one "yes" than if they ask only one parent. Sometimes the parents wise up and give the same answer; sometimes they don't. See what different answers you can get from different estimation techniques.

No approach is best in all circumstances, and the differences among them can be illuminating. For example, for the first edition of this book, my original eyeball estimate for the length of the book was 250–300 pages. When I finally did an in-depth estimate, the estimate came out to 873 pages. "That can't be right," I thought. So I estimated it using a completely different technique. The second estimate came out to 828 pages. Considering that these estimates were within about five percent of each other, I concluded that the book was going to be much closer to 850 pages than to 250 pages, and I was able to adjust my writing plans accordingly.

Reestimate periodically Factors on a software project change after the initial estimate, so plan to update your estimates periodically. As Figure 28-2 illustrates, the accuracy of your estimates should improve as you move toward completing the project. From time to time, compare your actual results to your estimated results, and use that evaluation to refine estimates for the remainder of the project.

cc2e.com/2864

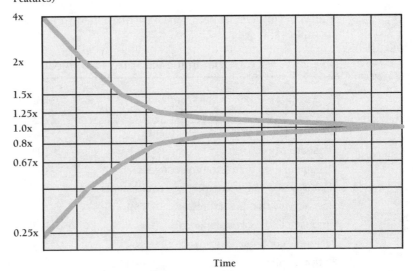

Figure 28-2 Estimates created early in a project are inherently inaccurate. As the project progresses, estimates can become more accurate. Reestimate periodically throughout a project, and use what you learn during each activity to improve your estimate for the next activity.

Estimating the Amount of Construction

Cross-Reference For details on the amount of coding for projects of various sizes, see "Activity Proportions and Size" in Section 27.5.

The extent to which construction will be a major influence on a project's schedule depends in part on the proportion of the project that will be devoted to construction—understood as detailed design, coding and debugging, and unit testing. Take another look at Figure 27-3 on page 654. As the figure shows, the proportion varies by project size. Until your company has project-history data of its own, the proportion of time devoted to each activity shown in the figure is a good place to start estimates for your projects.

The best answer to the question of how much construction a project will call for is that the proportion will vary from project to project and organization to organization. Keep records of your organization's experience on projects, and use them to estimate the time future projects will take.

Influences on Schedule

Cross-Reference The effect of a program's size on productivity and quality isn't always intuitively apparent. See Chapter 27, "How Program Size Affects Construction," for an explanation of how size affects construction.

The largest influence on a software project's schedule is the size of the program to be produced. But many other factors also influence a software-development schedule. Studies of commercial programs have quantified some of the factors, and they're shown in Table 28-1.

Table 28-1   Factors That Influence Software-Project Effort

Factor	Potential Helpful Influence	Potential Harmful Influence
Co-located vs. multisite development	-14%	22%
Database size	-10%	28%
Documentation match to project needs	-19%	23%
Flexibility allowed in interpreting requirements	-9%	10%
How actively risks are addressed	-12%	14%
Language and tools experience	-16%	20%
Personnel continuity (turnover)	-19%	29%
Platform volatility	-13%	30%
Process maturity	-13%	15%
Product complexity	-27%	74%
Programmer capability	-24%	34%
Reliability required	-18%	26%
Requirements analyst capability	-29%	42%
Reuse requirements	-5%	24%
State-of-the-art application	-11%	12%
Storage constraint (how much of available storage will be consumed)	0%	46%
Team cohesion	-10%	11%
Team's experience in the applications area	-19%	22%
Team's experience on the technology platform	-15%	19%
Time constraint (of the application itself)	0%	63%
Use of software tools	-22%	17%

Source: *Software Cost Estimation with Cocomo II* (Boehm et al. 2000).

Here are some of the less easily quantified factors that can influence a software-development schedule. These factors are drawn from Barry Boehm's *Software Cost Estimation with Cocomo II* (2000) and Capers Jones's *Estimating Software Costs* (1998).

■ Requirements developer experience and capability

■ Programmer experience and capability

- Team motivation
- Management quality
- Amount of code reused
- Personnel turnover
- Requirements volatility
- Quality of relationship with customer
- User participation in requirements
- Customer experience with the type of application
- Extent to which programmers participate in requirements development
- Classified security environment for computer, programs, and data
- Amount of documentation
- Project objectives (schedule vs. quality vs. usability vs. the many other possible objectives)

Each of these factors can be significant, so consider them along with the factors shown in Table 28-1 (which includes some of these factors).

Estimation vs. Control

The important question is, do you want prediction, or do you want control?
—Tom Gilb

Estimation is an important part of the planning needed to complete a software project on time. Once you have a delivery date and a product specification, the main problem is how to control the expenditure of human and technical resources for an on-time delivery of the product. In that sense, the accuracy of the initial estimate is much less important than your subsequent success at controlling resources to meet the schedule.

What to Do If You're Behind

The average project overruns its planned schedule by about 100 percent, as mentioned earlier in this chapter. When you're behind, increasing the amount of time usually isn't an option. If it is, do it. Otherwise, you can try one or more of these solutions:

HARD DATA

Hope that you'll catch up   Hopeful optimism is a common response to a project's falling behind schedule. The rationalization typically goes like this: "Requirements took a little longer than we expected, but now they're solid, so we're bound to save time later. We'll make up the shortfall during coding and testing." This is hardly ever the case. One survey of over 300 software projects concluded that delays and overruns generally increase toward the end of a project (van Genuchten 1991). Projects don't make up lost time later; they fall further behind.

Expand the team   According to Fred Brooks's law, adding people to a late software project makes it later (Brooks 1995). It's like adding gas to a fire. Brooks's explanation is convincing: new people need time to familiarize themselves with a project before they can become productive. Their training takes up the time of the people who have already been trained. And merely increasing the number of people increases the complexity and amount of project communication. Brooks points out that the fact that one woman can have a baby in nine months does not imply that nine women can have a baby in one month.

Undoubtedly the warning in Brooks's law should be heeded more often than it is. It's tempting to throw people at a project and hope that they'll bring it in on time. Managers need to understand that developing software isn't like riveting sheet metal: more workers working doesn't necessarily mean more work will get done.

The simple statement that adding programmers to a late project makes it later, however, masks the fact that under some circumstances it's possible to add people to a late project and speed it up. As Brooks points out in the analysis of his law, adding people to software projects in which the tasks can't be divided and performed independently doesn't help. But if a project's tasks are partitionable, you can divide them further and assign them to different people, even to people who are added late in the project. Other researchers have formally identified circumstances under which you can add people to a late project without making it later (Abdel-Hamid 1989, McConnell 1999).

Further Reading For an argument in favor of building only the most-needed features, see Chapter 14, "Feature-Set Control," in *Rapid Development* (McConnell 1996).

Reduce the scope of the project   The powerful technique of reducing the scope of the project is often overlooked. If you eliminate a feature, you eliminate the design, coding, debugging, testing, and documentation of that feature. You eliminate that feature's interface to other features.

When you plan the product initially, partition the product's capabilities into "must haves," "nice to haves," and "optionals." If you fall behind, prioritize the "optionals" and "nice to haves" and drop the ones that are the least important.

Short of dropping a feature altogether, you can provide a cheaper version of the same functionality. You might provide a version that's on time but that hasn't been tuned for performance. You might provide a version in which the least important functionality is implemented crudely. You might decide to back off on a speed requirement because it's much easier to provide a slow version. You might back off on a space requirement because it's easier to provide a memory-intensive version.

Reestimate development time for the least important features. What functionality can you provide in two hours, two days, or two weeks? What do you gain by building the two-week version rather than the two-day version, or the two-day version rather than the two-hour version?

Additional Resources on Software Estimation

cc2e.com/2871 Here are some additional references about software estimation:

Boehm, Barry, et al. *Software Cost Estimation with Cocomo II.* Boston, MA: Addison-Wesley, 2000. This book describes the ins and outs of the Cocomo II estimating model, which is undoubtedly the most popular model in use today.

Boehm, Barry W. *Software Engineering Economics.* Englewood Cliffs, NJ: Prentice Hall, 1981. This older book contains an exhaustive treatment of software-project estimation considered more generally than in Boehm's newer book.

Humphrey, Watts S. *A Discipline for Software Engineering.* Reading, MA: Addison-Wesley, 1995. Chapter 5 of this book describes Humphrey's Probe method, which is a technique for estimating work at the individual developer level.

Conte, S. D., H. E. Dunsmore, and V. Y. Shen. *Software Engineering Metrics and Models.* Menlo Park, CA: Benjamin/Cummings, 1986. Chapter 6 contains a good survey of estimation techniques, including a history of estimation, statistical models, theoretically based models, and composite models. The book also demonstrates the use of each estimation technique on a database of projects and compares the estimates to the projects' actual lengths.

Gilb, Tom. *Principles of Software Engineering Management.* Wokingham, England: Addison-Wesley, 1988. The title of Chapter 16, "Ten Principles for Estimating Software Attributes," is somewhat tongue-in-cheek. Gilb argues against project estimation and in favor of project control. Pointing out that people don't really want to predict accurately but do want to control final results, Gilb lays out 10 principles you can use to steer a project to meet a calendar deadline, a cost goal, or another project objective.

28.4 Measurement

Software projects can be measured in numerous ways. Here are two solid reasons to measure your process:

KEY POINT

For any project attribute, it's possible to measure that attribute in a way that's superior to not measuring it at all The measurement might not be perfectly precise, it might be difficult to make, and it might need to be refined over time, but measurement will give you a handle on your software-development process that you don't have without it (Gilb 2004).

If data is to be used in a scientific experiment, it must be quantified. Can you imagine a scientist recommending a ban on a new food product because a group of white rats "just seemed to get sicker" than another group? That's absurd. You'd demand a quantified reason, like "Rats that ate the new food product were sick 3.7 more days per month than rats that didn't." To evaluate software-development methods, you must measure them. Statements like "This new method seems more productive" aren't good enough.

What gets measured, gets done.
—Tom Peters

Be aware of measurement side effects Measurement has a motivational effect. People pay attention to whatever is measured, assuming that it's used to evaluate them. Choose what you measure carefully. People tend to focus on work that's measured and to ignore work that isn't.

To argue against measurement is to argue that it's better not to know what's really happening on your project When you measure an aspect of a project, you know something about it that you didn't know before. You can see whether the aspect gets bigger or smaller or stays the same. The measurement gives you a window into at least that aspect of your project. The window might be small and cloudy until you refine your measurements, but it will be better than no window at all. To argue against all measurements because some are inconclusive is to argue against windows because some happen to be cloudy.

You can measure virtually any aspect of the software-development process. Table 28-2 lists some measurements that other practitioners have found to be useful.

Table 28-2   Useful Software-Development Measurements

Size	Overall Quality
Total lines of code written	Total number of defects
Total comment lines	Number of defects in each class or routine
Total number of classes or routines	Average defects per thousand lines of code
Total data declarations	Mean time between failures
Total blank lines	Compiler-detected errors

Defect Tracking	Maintainability
Severity of each defect	Number of public routines on each class
Location of each defect (class or routine)	Number of parameters passed to each routine
Origin of each defect (requirements, design, construction, test)	Number of private routines and/or variables on each class
Way in which each defect is corrected	Number of local variables used by each routine
Person responsible for each defect	Number of routines called by each class or routine
Number of lines affected by each defect correction	Number of decision points in each routine
Work hours spent correcting each defect	Control-flow complexity in each routine
Average time required to find a defect	Lines of code in each class or routine
Average time required to fix a defect	Lines of comments in each class or routine
Number of attempts made to correct each defect	Number of data declarations in each class or routine
Number of new errors resulting from defect correction	Number of blank lines in each class or routine
	Number of *gotos* in each class or routine
	Number of input or output statements in each class or routine

Productivity
Work-hours spent on the project
Work-hours spent on each class or routine
Number of times each class or routine changed
Dollars spent on project
Dollars spent per line of code
Dollars spent per defect

You can collect most of these measurements with software tools that are currently available. Discussions throughout the book indicate the reasons that each measurement is useful. At this time, most of the measurements aren't useful for making fine distinctions among programs, classes, and routines (Shepperd and Ince 1989). They're useful mainly for identifying routines that are "outliers"; abnormal measurements in a routine are a warning sign that you should reexamine that routine, checking for unusually low quality.

Don't start by collecting data on all possible measurements—you'll bury yourself in data so complex that you won't be able to figure out what any of it means. Start with a simple set of measurements, such as the number of defects, the number of work-months, the total dollars, and the total lines of code. Standardize the measurements across your projects, and then refine them and add to them as your understanding of what you want to measure improves (Pietrasanta 1990).

Make sure you're collecting data for a reason. Set goals, determine the questions you need to ask to meet the goals, and then measure to answer the questions (Basili and Weiss 1984). Be sure that you ask for only as much information as is feasible to obtain, and keep in mind that data collection will always take a back seat to deadlines (Basili et al. 2002).

Additional Resources on Software Measurement

cc2e.com/2878 Here are addtional resources:

Oman, Paul and Shari Lawrence Pfleeger, eds. *Applying Software Metrics*. Los Alamitos, CA: IEEE Computer Society Press, 1996. This volume collects more than 25 key papers on software measurement under one cover.

Jones, Capers. *Applied Software Measurement: Assuring Productivity and Quality,* 2d ed. New York, NY: McGraw-Hill, 1997. Jones is a leader in software measurement, and his book is an accumulation of knowledge in this area. It provides the definitive theory and practice of current measurement techniques and describes problems with traditional measurements. It lays out a full program for collecting "function-point metrics." Jones has collected and analyzed a huge amount of quality and productivity data, and this book distills the results in one place—including a fascinating chapter on averages for U.S. software development.

Grady, Robert B. *Practical Software Metrics for Project Management and Process Improvement.* Englewood Cliffs, NJ: Prentice Hall PTR, 1992. Grady describes lessons learned from establishing a software-measurement program at Hewlett-Packard and tells you how to establish a software-measurement program in your organization.

Conte, S. D., H. E. Dunsmore, and V. Y. Shen. *Software Engineering Metrics and Models.* Menlo Park, CA: Benjamin/Cummings, 1986. This book catalogs current knowledge of software measurement circa 1986, including commonly used measurements, experimental techniques, and criteria for evaluating experimental results.

Basili, Victor R., et al. 2002. "Lessons learned from 25 years of process improvement: The Rise and Fall of the NASA Software Engineering Laboratory," *Proceedings of the 24th International Conference on Software Engineering.* Orlando, FL, 2002. This paper catalogs lessons learned by one of the world's most sophisticated software-development organizations. The lessons focus on measurement topics.

cc2e.com/2892

NASA Software Engineering Laboratory. *Software Measurement Guidebook*, June 1995, NASA-GB-001-94. This guidebook of about 100 pages is probably the best source of practical information on how to set up and run a measurement program. It can be downloaded from NASA's website.

cc2e.com/2899

Gilb, Tom. *Competitive Engineering.* Boston, MA: Addison-Wesley, 2004. This book presents a measurement-focused approach to defining requirements, evaluating designs, measuring quality, and, in general, managing projects. It can be downloaded from Gilb's website.

28.5 Treating Programmers as People

KEY POINT

The abstractness of the programming activity calls for an offsetting naturalness in the office environment and rich contacts among coworkers. Highly technical companies offer parklike corporate campuses, organic organizational structures, comfortable offices, and other "high-touch" environmental features to balance the intense, sometimes arid intellectuality of the work itself. The most successful technical companies combine elements of high-tech and high-touch (Naisbitt 1982). This section describes ways in which programmers are more than organic reflections of their silicon alter egos.

How Do Programmers Spend Their Time?

Programmers spend their time programming, but they also spend time in meetings, on training, on reading their mail, and on just thinking. A 1964 study at Bell Laboratories found that programmers spent their time this way as described in Table 28-3.

Table 28-3   One View of How Programmers Spend Their Time

Activity	Source Code	Business	Personal	Meetings	Training	Mail/Misc. Documents	Technical Manuals	Operating Procedures, Misc.	Program Test	Totals
Talk or listen	4%	17%	7%	3%				1%		32%
Talk with manager		1%								1%
Telephone		2%	1%							3%
Read	14%					2%	2%			18%
Write/record	13%					1%				14%
Away or out		4%	1%	4%	6%					15%
Walking	2%	2%	1%			1%				6%
Miscellaneous	2%	3%	3%			1%		1%	1%	11%
Totals	**35%**	**29%**	**13%**	**7%**	**6%**	**5%**	**2%**	**2%**	**1%**	**100%**

Source: "Research Studies of Programmers and Programming" (Bairdain 1964, reported in Boehm 1981).

This data is based on a time-and-motion study of 70 programmers. The data is old, and the proportions of time spent in the different activities would vary among programmers, but the results are nonetheless thought-provoking. About 30 percent of a programmer's time is spent in nontechnical activities that don't directly help the project: walking, personal business, and so on. Programmers in this study spent six percent of their time walking; that's about 2.5 hours a week, about 125 hours a year. That might not seem like much until you realize that programmers spend as much time each year walking as they spend in training, three times as much time as they spend reading technical manuals, and six times as much as they spend talking with their managers. I personally have not seen much change in this pattern today.

Variation in Performance and Quality

HARD DATA

Talent and effort among individual programmers vary tremendously, as they do in all fields. One study found that in a variety of professions—writing, football, invention, police work, and aircraft piloting—the top 20 percent of the people produced about 50 percent of the output (Augustine 1979). The results of the study are based on an analysis of productivity data, such as touchdowns, patents, solved cases, and so on. Since some people make no tangible contribution whatsoever and weren't considered in the study (quarterbacks who make no touchdowns, inventors who own no patents, detectives who don't close cases, and so on), the data probably understates the actual variation in productivity.

In programming specifically, many studies have shown order-of-magnitude differences in the quality of the programs written, the sizes of the programs written, and the productivity of programmers.

Individual Variation

HARD DATA

The original study that showed huge variations in individual programming productivity was conducted in the late 1960s by Sackman, Erikson, and Grant (1968). They studied professional programmers with an average of 7 years' experience and found that the ratio of initial coding time between the best and worst programmers was about 20 to 1, the ratio of debugging times over 25 to 1, of program size 5 to 1, and of program execution speed about 10 to 1. They found no relationship between a programmer's amount of experience and code quality or productivity.

HARD DATA

Although specific ratios such as 25 to 1 aren't particularly meaningful, more general statements such as "There are order-of-magnitude differences among programmers" are meaningful and have been confirmed by many other studies of professional programmers (Curtis 1981, Mills 1983, DeMarco and Lister 1985, Curtis et al. 1986, Card 1987, Boehm and Papaccio 1988, Valett and McGarry 1989, Boehm et al. 2000).

Team Variation

Programming teams also exhibit sizable differences in software quality and productivity. Good programmers tend to cluster, as do bad programmers, an observation that has been confirmed by a study of 166 professional programmers from 18 organizations (Demarco and Lister 1999).

HARD DATA

In one study of seven identical projects, the efforts expended varied by a factor of 3.4 to 1 and program sizes by a factor of 3 to 1 (Boehm, Gray, and Seewaldt 1984). In spite of the productivity range, the programmers in this study were not a diverse group. They were all professional programmers with several years of experience who were enrolled in a computer-science graduate program. It's reasonable to assume that a study of a less homogeneous group would turn up even greater differences.

An earlier study of programming teams observed a 5-to-1 difference in program size and a 2.6-to-1 variation in the time required for a team to complete the same project (Weinberg and Schulman 1974).

HARD DATA

After reviewing more than 20 years of data in constructing the Cocomo II estimation model, Barry Boehm and other researchers concluded that developing a program with a team in the 15th percentile of programmers ranked by ability typically requires about 3.5 times as many work-months as developing a program with a team in the 90th percentile (Boehm et al. 2000). Boehm and other researchers have found that 80 percent of the contribution comes from 20 percent of the contributors (Boehm 1987b).

The implication for recruiting and hiring is clear. If you have to pay more to get a top-10-percent programmer rather than a bottom-10-percent programmer, jump at the chance. You'll get an immediate payoff in the quality and productivity of the programmer you hire, and you'll get a residual effect in the quality and productivity of the other programmers your organization is able to retain because good programmers tend to cluster.

Religious Issues

Managers of programming projects aren't always aware that certain programming issues are matters of religion. If you're a manager and you try to require compliance with certain programming practices, you're inviting your programmers' ire. Here's a list of religious issues:

- Programming language
- Indentation style
- Placing of braces
- Choice of IDE
- Commenting style
- Efficiency vs. readability tradeoffs
- Choice of methodology—for example, Scrum vs. Extreme Programming vs. evolutionary delivery
- Programming utilities
- Naming conventions
- Use of *gotos*
- Use of global variables
- Measurements, especially productivity measures such as lines of code per day

The common denominator among these topics is that a programmer's position on each is a reflection of personal style. If you think you need to control a programmer in any of these religious areas, consider these points:

Be aware that you're dealing with a sensitive area   Sound out the programmer on each emotional topic before jumping in with both feet.

Use "suggestions" or "guidelines" with respect to the area   Avoid setting rigid "rules" or "standards."

Finesse the issues you can by sidestepping explicit mandates   To finesse indentation style or brace placement, require source code to be run through a pretty-printer formatter before it's declared finished. Let the pretty printer do the formatting. To finesse commenting style, require that all code be reviewed and that unclear code be modified until it's clear.

Have your programmers develop their own standards As mentioned elsewhere, the details of a specific standard are often less important than the fact that some standard exists. Don't set standards for your programmers, but do insist they standardize in the areas that are important to you.

Which of the religious topics are important enough to warrant going to the mat? Conformity in minor matters of style in any area probably won't produce enough benefit to offset the effects of lower morale. If you find indiscriminate use of *goto*s or global variables, unreadable styles, or other practices that affect whole projects, be prepared to put up with some friction to improve code quality. If your programmers are conscientious, this is rarely a problem. The biggest battles tend to be over nuances of coding style, and you can stay out of those with no loss to the project.

Physical Environment

Here's an experiment: go out to the country, find a farm, find a farmer, and ask how much money in equipment the farmer has for each worker. The farmer will look at the barn and see a few tractors, some wagons, a combine for wheat, and a peaviner for peas and will tell you that it's over $100,000 per employee.

Next go to the city, find a programming shop, find a programming manager, and ask how much money in equipment the programming manager has for each worker. The programming manager will look at an office and see a desk, a chair, a few books, and a computer and will tell you that it's under $25,000 per employee.

Physical environment makes a big difference in productivity. DeMarco and Lister asked 166 programmers from 35 organizations about the quality of their physical environments. Most employees rated their workplaces as not acceptable. In a subsequent programming competition, the programmers who performed in the top 25 percent had bigger, quieter, more private offices and fewer interruptions from people and phone calls. Here's a summary of the differences in office space between the best and worst performers:

Environmental Factor	Top 25%	Bottom 25%
Dedicated floor space	78 sq. ft.	46 sq. ft.
Acceptably quiet workspace	57% yes	29% yes
Acceptably private workspace	62% yes	19% yes
Ability to silence phone	52% yes	10% yes
Ability to divert calls	76% yes	19% yes
Frequent needless interruptions	38% yes	76% yes
Workspace that makes programmer feel appreciated	57% yes	29% yes

Source: *Peopleware* (DeMarco and Lister 1999).

HARD DATA

The data shows a strong correlation between productivity and the quality of the workplace. Programmers in the top 25 percent were 2.6 times more productive than programmers in the bottom 25 percent. DeMarco and Lister thought that the better programmers might naturally have better offices because they had been promoted, but further examination revealed that this wasn't the case. Programmers from the same organizations had similar facilities, regardless of differences in their performance.

Large software-intensive organizations have had similar experiences. Xerox, TRW, IBM, and Bell Labs have indicated that they realize significantly improved productivity with a $10,000 to $30,000 capital investment per person, sums that were more than recaptured in improved productivity (Boehm 1987a). With "productivity offices," self-reported estimates ranged from 39 to 47 percent improvement in productivity (Boehm et al. 1984).

In summary, if your workplace is a bottom-25 percent environment, you can realize about a 100 percent improvement in productivity by making it a top-25 percent environment. If your workplace is average, you can still realize a productivity improvement of 40 percent or more by making it a top-25 percent environment.

Additional Resources on Programmers as Human Beings

cc2e.com/2806

Here are additional resources:

Weinberg, Gerald M. *The Psychology of Computer Programming*, 2d ed. New York, NY: Van Nostrand Reinhold, 1998. This is the first book to explicitly identify programmers as human beings, and it's still the best on programming as a human activity. It's crammed with acute observations about the human nature of programmers and its implications.

DeMarco, Tom and Timothy Lister. *Peopleware: Productive Projects and Teams*, 2d ed. New York, NY: Dorset House, 1999. As the title suggests, this book also deals with the human factor in the programming equation. It's filled with anecdotes about managing people, the office environment, hiring and developing the right people, growing teams, and enjoying work. The authors lean on the anecdotes to support some uncommon viewpoints and their logic is thin in places, but the people-centered spirit of the book is what's important and the authors deliver that message without faltering.

cc2e.com/2820

McCue, Gerald M. "IBM's Santa Teresa Laboratory—Architectural Design for Program Development," *IBM Systems Journal* 17, no. 1 (1978): 4–25. McCue describes the process that IBM used to create its Santa Teresa office complex. IBM studied programmer needs, created architectural guidelines, and designed the facility with programmers in mind. Programmers participated throughout. The result is that in annual opinion surveys each year, the physical facilities at the Santa Teresa facility are rated the highest in the company.

McConnell, Steve. *Professional Software Development*. Boston, MA: Addison-Wesley, 2004. Chapter 7, "Orphans Preferred," summarizes studies on programmer demographics, including personality types, educational backgrounds, and job prospects.

Carnegie, Dale. *How to Win Friends and Influence People*, Revised Edition. New York, NY: Pocket Books, 1981. When Dale Carnegie wrote the title for the first edition of this book in 1936, he couldn't have realized the connotation it would carry today. It sounds like a book Machiavelli would have displayed on his shelf. The spirit of the book is diametrically opposed to Machiavellian manipulation, however, and one of Carnegie's key points is the importance of developing a genuine interest in other people. Carnegie has a keen insight into everyday relationships and explains how to work with other people by understanding them better. The book is filled with memorable anecdotes, sometimes two or three to a page. Anyone who works with people should read it at some point, and anyone who manages people should read it *now*.

28.6 Managing Your Manager

In software development, nontechnical managers are common, as are managers who have technical experience but who are 10 years behind the times. Technically competent, technically current managers are rare. If you work for one, do whatever you can to keep your job. It's an unusual treat.

In a hierarchy, every employee tends to rise to his level of incompetence.
—The Peter Principle

If your manager is more typical, you're faced with the unenviable task of managing your manager. "Managing your manager" means that you need to tell your manager what to do rather than the other way around. The trick is to do it in a way that allows your manager to continue believing that you are the one being managed. Here are some approaches to dealing with your manager:

- Plant ideas for what you want to do, and then wait for your manager to have a brainstorm (your idea) about doing what you want to do.

- Educate your manager about the right way to do things. This is an ongoing job because managers are often promoted, transferred, or fired.

- Focus on your manager's interests, doing what he or she really wants you to do, and don't distract your manager with unnecessary implementation details. (Think of it as "encapsulation" of your job.)

- Refuse to do what your manager tells you, and insist on doing your job the right way.

- Find another job.

The best long-term solution is to try to educate your manager. That's not always an easy task, but one way you can prepare for it is by reading Dale Carnegie's *How to Win Friends and Influence People*.

Additional Resources on Managing Construction

cc2e.com/2813

Here are a few books that cover issues of general concern in managing software projects:

Gilb, Tom. *Principles of Software Engineering Management*. Wokingham, England: Addison-Wesley, 1988. Gilb has charted his own course for thirty years, and most of the time he's been ahead of the pack whether or not the pack realizes it. This book is a good example. This was one of the first books to discuss evolutionary development practices, risk management, and the use of formal inspections. Gilb is keenly aware of leading-edge approaches; indeed, this book published more than 15 years ago contains most of the good practices currently flying under the "Agile" banner. Gilb is incredibly pragmatic, and the book is still one of the best software-management books.

McConnell, Steve. *Rapid Development*. Redmond, WA: Microsoft Press, 1996. This book covers project-leadership and project-management issues from the perspective of projects that are experiencing significant schedule pressure, which in my experience is most projects.

Brooks, Frederick P., Jr. *The Mythical Man-Month: Essays on Software Engineering, Anniversary Edition* (2d ed). Reading, MA: Addison-Wesley, 1995. This book is a hodgepodge of metaphors and folklore related to managing programming projects. It's entertaining, and it will give you many illuminating insights into your own projects. It's based on Brooks's challenges in developing the OS/360 operating system, which gives me some reservations. It's full of advice along the lines of "We did this and it failed" and "We should have done this because it would have worked." Brooks's observations about techniques that failed are well grounded, but his claims that other techniques would have worked are too speculative. Read the book critically to separate the observations from the speculations. This warning doesn't diminish the book's basic value. It's still cited in computing literature more often than any other book, and even though it was originally published in 1975, it seems fresh today. It's hard to read it without saying "Right on!" every couple of pages.

Relevant Standards

IEEE Std 1058-1998, Standard for Software Project Management Plans.

IEEE Std 12207-1997, Information Technology–Software Life Cycle Processes.

IEEE Std 1045-1992, Standard for Software Productivity Metrics.

IEEE Std 1062-1998, Recommended Practice for Software Acquisition.

IEEE Std 1540-2001, Standard for Software Life Cycle Processes–Risk Management.

IEEE Std 828-1998, Standard for Software Configuration Management Plans

IEEE Std 1490-1998, Guide–Adoption of PMI Standard–A Guide to the Project Management Body of Knowledge.

Key Points

- Good coding practices can be achieved either through enforced standards or through more light-handed approaches.

- Configuration management, when properly applied, makes programmers' jobs easier. This especially includes change control.

- Good software estimation is a significant challenge. Keys to success are using multiple approaches, tightening down your estimates as you work your way into the project, and making use of data to create the estimates.

- Measurement is a key to successful construction management. You can find ways to measure any aspect of a project that are better than not measuring it at all. Accurate measurement is a key to accurate scheduling, to quality control, and to improving your development process.

- Programmers and managers are people, and they work best when treated as such.

Chapter 29

Integration

cc2e.com/2985

Contents

Related Topics

The term "integration" refers to the software-development activity in which you combine separate software components into a single system. On small projects, integration might consist of a morning spent hooking a handful of classes together. On large projects, it might consist of weeks or months of hooking sets of programs together. Regardless of the size of the task, common principles apply.

The topic of integration is intertwined with the topic of construction sequence. The order in which you build classes or components affects the order in which you can integrate them—you can't integrate something that hasn't been built yet. Both integration and construction sequence are important topics. This chapter addresses both topics from the integration point of view.

29.1 Importance of the Integration Approach

In engineering fields other than software, the importance of proper integration is well known. The Pacific Northwest, where I live, saw a dramatic illustration of the hazards of poor integration when the football stadium at the University of Washington collapsed partway through construction, as shown in Figure 29-1.

Figure 29-1   The football stadium add-on at the University of Washington collapsed because it wasn't strong enough to support itself during construction. It likely would have been strong enough when completed, but it was constructed in the wrong order—an integration error.

It doesn't matter that the stadium would have been strong enough by the time it was done; it needed to be strong enough at each step. If you construct and integrate software in the wrong order, it's harder to code, harder to test, and harder to debug. If none of it will work until all of it works, it can seem as though it will never be finished. It too can collapse under its own weight during construction—the bug count might seem insurmountable, progress might be invisible, or the complexity might be overwhelming—even though the finished product would have worked.

Because it's done after a developer has finished developer testing and in conjunction with system testing, integration is sometimes thought of as a testing activity. It's complex enough, however, that it should be viewed as an independent activity.

KEY POINT

You can expect some of these benefits from careful integration:

- Easier defect diagnosis
- Fewer defects
- Less scaffolding
- Shorter time to first working product
- Shorter overall development schedules
- Better customer relations
- Improved morale
- Improved chance of project completion
- More reliable schedule estimates
- More accurate status reporting
- Improved code quality
- Less documentation

These might seem like elevated claims for system testing's forgotten cousin, but the fact that it's overlooked in spite of its importance is precisely the reason integration has its own chapter in this book.

29.2 Integration Frequency—Phased or Incremental?

Programs are integrated by means of either the phased or the incremental approach.

Phased Integration

Until a few years ago, phased integration was the norm. It follows these well-defined steps, or phases:

1. Design, code, test, and debug each class. This step is called "unit development."

2. Combine the classes into one whopping-big system ("system integration").

3. Test and debug the whole system. This is called "system dis-integration." (Thanks to Meilir Page-Jones for this witty observation.)

One problem with phased integration is that when the classes in a system are put together for the first time, new problems inevitably surface and the causes of the problems could be anywhere. Since you have a large number of classes that have never worked together before, the culprit might be a poorly tested class, an error in the interface between two classes, or an error caused by an interaction between two classes. All classes are suspect.

The uncertainty about the location of any of the specific problems is compounded by the fact that all the problems suddenly present themselves at once. This forces you to deal not only with problems caused by interactions between classes but with problems that are hard to diagnose because the problems themselves interact. For this reason, another name for phased integration is "big bang integration," as shown in Figure 29-2.

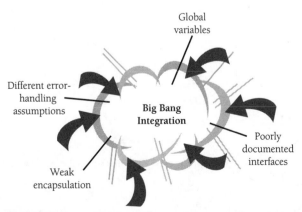

Figure 29-2   Phased integration is also called "big bang" integration for a good reason!

Phased integration can't begin until late in the project, after all the classes have been developer-tested. When the classes are finally combined and errors surface by the score, programmers immediately go into panicky debugging mode rather than methodical error detection and correction.

For small programs—no, for tiny programs—phased integration might be the best approach. If the program has only two or three classes, phased integration might save you time, if you're lucky. But in most cases, another approach is better.

Incremental Integration

Cross-Reference Metaphors appropriate for incremental integration are discussed in "Software Oyster Farming: System Accretion" and "Software Construction: Building Software," both in Section 2.3.

In incremental integration, you write and test a program in small pieces and then combine the pieces one at a time. In this one-piece-at-a-time approach to integration, you follow these steps:

1. Develop a small, functional part of the system. It can be the smallest functional part, the hardest part, a key part, or some combination. Thoroughly test and debug it. It will serve as a skeleton on which to hang the muscles, nerves, and skin that make up the remaining parts of the system.

2. Design, code, test, and debug a class.

3. Integrate the new class with the skeleton. Test and debug the combination of skeleton and new class. Make sure the combination works before you add any new classes. If work remains to be done, repeat the process starting at step 2.

Occasionally, you might want to integrate units larger than a single class. If a component has been thoroughly tested, for example, and each of its classes put through a mini-integration, you can integrate the whole component and still be doing incremental integration. As you add pieces to it, the system grows and gains momentum in the same way that a snowball grows and gains momentum when it rolls down a hill, as shown in Figure 29-3.

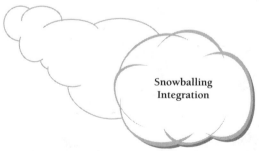

Figure 29-3 Incremental integration helps a project build momentum, like a snowball going down a hill.

Benefits of Incremental Integration

The incremental approach offers many advantages over the traditional phased approach regardless of which incremental strategy you use:

HARD DATA

Errors are easy to locate   When new problems surface during incremental integration, the new class is obviously involved. Either its interface to the rest of the program contains an error or its interaction with a previously integrated class produces an error. Either way, as suggested by Figure 29-4, you know exactly where to look. Moreover, simply because you have fewer problems at once, you reduce the risk that multiple problems will interact or that one problem will mask another. The more interface errors you tend to have, the more this benefit of incremental integration will help your projects. An accounting of errors for one project revealed that 39 percent were intermodule interface errors (Basili and Perricone 1984). Because developers on many projects spend up to 50 percent of their time debugging, maximizing debugging effectiveness by making errors easy to locate provides benefits in quality and productivity.

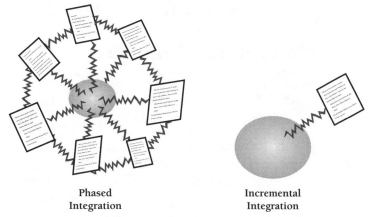

**Phased
Integration**

**Incremental
Integration**

Figure 29-4   In phased integration, you integrate so many components at once that it's hard to know where the error is. It might be in any of the components or in any of their connections. In incremental integration, the error is usually either in the new component or in the connection between the new component and the system.

The system succeeds early in the project   When code is integrated and running, even if the system isn't usable, it's apparent that it soon will be. With incremental integration, programmers see early results from their work, so their morale is better than when they suspect that their project will never draw its first breath.

You get improved progress monitoring   When you integrate frequently, the features that are present and not present are obvious. Management will have a better sense of progress from seeing 50 percent of a system's capability working than from hearing that coding is "99 percent complete."

You'll improve customer relations   If frequent integration has an effect on developer morale, it also has an effect on customer morale. Customers like signs of progress, and incremental builds provide signs of progress frequently.

The units of the system are tested more fully   Integration starts early in the project. You integrate each class as it's developed, rather than waiting for one magnificent binge of integration at the end. Classes are developer-tested in both cases, but each class is exercised as a part of the overall system more often with incremental integration than it is with phased integration.

You can build the system with a shorter development schedule   If integration is planned carefully, you can design part of the system while another part is being coded. This doesn't reduce the total number of work-hours required to develop the complete design and code, but it allows some work to be done in parallel, an advantage when calendar time is at a premium.

Incremental integration supports and encourages other incremental strategies. The advantages of incrementalism applied to integration are the tip of the iceberg.

29.3 Incremental Integration Strategies

With phased integration, you don't have to plan the order in which project components are built. All components are integrated at the same time, so you can build them in any order as long as they're all ready by D-day.

With incremental integration, you have to plan more carefully. Most systems will call for the integration of some components before the integration of others. Planning for integration thus affects planning for construction; the order in which components are constructed has to support the order in which they will be integrated.

Integration-order strategies come in a variety of shapes and sizes, and none is best in every case. The best integration approach varies from project to project, and the best solution is always the one that you create to meet the specific demands of a specific project. Knowing the points on the methodological number line will give you insight into the possible solutions.

Top-Down Integration

In top-down integration, the class at the top of the hierarchy is written and integrated first. The top is the main window, the applications control loop, the object that contains *main()* in Java, *WinMain()* for Microsoft Windows programming, or similar. Stubs have to be written to exercise the top class. Then, as classes are integrated from the top down, stub classes are replaced with real ones. This kind of integration proceeds as illustrated in Figure 29-5.

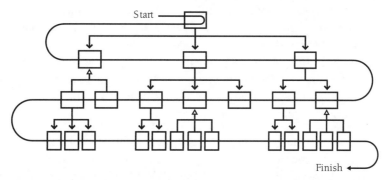

Figure 29-5   In top-down integration, you add classes at the top first, at the bottom last.

An important aspect of top-down integration is that the interfaces between classes must be carefully specified. The most troublesome errors to debug are not the ones that affect single classes but those that arise from subtle interactions between classes. Careful interface specification can reduce the problem. Interface specification isn't an integration activity, but making sure that the interfaces have been specified well is.

In addition to the advantages you get from any kind of incremental integration, an advantage of top-down integration is that the control logic of the system is tested relatively early. All the classes at the top of the hierarchy are exercised a lot so that big, conceptual, design problems are exposed quickly.

Another advantage of top-down integration is that, if you plan it carefully, you can complete a partially working system early in the project. If the user-interface parts are at the top, you can get a basic interface working quickly and flesh out the details later. The morale of both users and programmers benefits from getting something visible working early.

Top-down incremental integration also allows you to begin coding before the low-level design details are complete. Once the design has been driven down to a fairly low level of detail in all areas, you can begin implementing and integrating the classes at the higher levels without waiting to dot every "i" and cross every "t."

In spite of these advantages, pure top-down integration usually involves disadvantages that are more troublesome than you'll want to put up with. Pure top-down integration leaves exercising the tricky system interfaces until last. If system interfaces are buggy or a performance problem, you'd usually like to get to them long before the end of the project. It's not unusual for a low-level problem to bubble its way to the top of the system, causing high-level changes and reducing the benefit of earlier integration work. Minimize the bubbling problem through careful, early developer testing and performance analysis of the classes that exercise system interfaces.

Another problem with pure top-down integration is that you need a dump truck full of stubs to integrate from the top down. Many low-level classes haven't been integrated, which implies that a large number of stubs will be needed during intermediate steps in integration. Stubs are problematic in that, as test code, they're more likely to contain errors than the more carefully designed production code. Errors in the new stubs that support a new class defeat the purpose of incremental integration, which is to restrict the source of errors to one new class.

Cross-Reference Top-down integration is related to top-down design in name only. For details on top-down design, see "Top-Down and Bottom-Up Design Approaches" in Section 5.4.

Top-down integration is also nearly impossible to implement purely. In top-down integration done by the book, you start at the top—call it Level 1—and then integrate all the classes at the next level (Level 2). When you've integrated all the classes from Level 2, and not before, you integrate the classes from Level 3. The rigidity in pure top-down integration is completely arbitrary. It's hard to imagine anyone going to the trouble of using pure top-down integration. Most people use a hybrid approach, such as integrating from the top down in sections instead.

Finally, you can't use top-down integration if the collection of classes doesn't have a top. In many interactive systems, the location of the "top" is subjective. In many systems, the user interface is the top. In other systems, *main()* is the top.

A good alternative to pure top-down integration is the vertical-slice approach shown in Figure 29-6. In this approach, the system is implemented top-down in sections, perhaps fleshing out areas of functionality one by one and then moving to the next area.

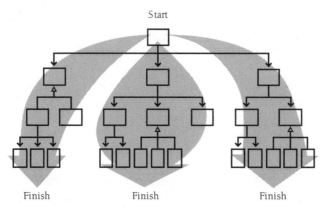

Figure 29-6   As an alternative to proceeding strictly top to bottom, you can integrate from the top down in vertical slices.

Even though pure top-down integration isn't workable, thinking about it will help you decide on a general approach. Some of the benefits and hazards that apply to a pure top-down approach apply, less obviously, to looser top-down approaches like vertical-slice integration, so keep them in mind.

Bottom-Up Integration

In bottom-up integration, you write and integrate the classes at the bottom of the hierarchy first. Adding the low-level classes one at a time rather than all at once is what makes bottom-up integration an incremental integration strategy. You write test drivers to exercise the low-level classes initially and add classes to the test-driver scaffolding as they're developed. As you add higher-level classes, you replace driver classes with real ones. Figure 29-7 shows the order in which classes are integrated in the bottom-up approach.

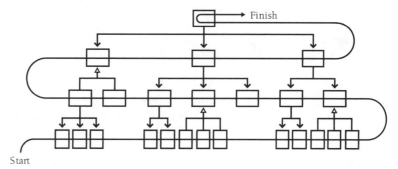

Figure 29-7 In bottom-up integration, you integrate classes at the bottom first, at the top last.

Bottom-up integration provides a limited set of incremental integration advantages. It restricts the possible sources of error to the single class being integrated, so errors are easy to locate. Integration can start early in the project. Bottom-up integration also exercises potentially troublesome system interfaces early. Since system limitations often determine whether you can meet the system's goals, making sure the system has done a full set of calisthenics is worth the trouble.

The main problem with bottom-up integration is that it leaves integration of the major, high-level system interfaces until last. If the system has conceptual design problems at the higher levels, construction won't find them until all the detailed work has been done. If the design must be changed significantly, some of the low-level work might have to be discarded.

Bottom-up integration requires you to complete the design of the whole system before you start integration. If you don't, assumptions that needn't have controlled the design might end up deeply embedded in low-level code, giving rise to the awkward situation in which you design high-level classes to work around problems in low-level ones. Letting low-level details drive the design of higher-level classes contradicts principles of information hiding and object-oriented design. The problems of integrating higher-level classes are but a teardrop in a rainstorm compared to the problems you'll have if you don't complete the design of high-level classes before you begin low-level coding.

As with top-down integration, pure bottom-up integration is rare, and you can use a hybrid approach instead, including integrating in slices as shown in Figure 29-8.

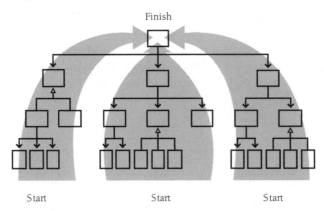

Figure 29-8 As an alternative to proceeding purely bottom to top, you can integrate from the bottom up in sections. This blurs the line between bottom-up integration and feature-oriented integration, which is described later in this chapter.

Sandwich Integration

The problems with pure top-down and pure bottom-up integration have led some experts to recommend a sandwich approach (Myers 1976). You first integrate the high-level business-object classes at the top of the hierarchy. Then you integrate the device-interface classes and widely used utility classes at the bottom. These high-level and low-level classes are the bread of the sandwich.

You leave the middle-level classes until later. These make up the meat, cheese, and tomatoes of the sandwich. If you're a vegetarian, they might make up the tofu and bean sprouts of the sandwich, but the author of sandwich integration is silent on this point—maybe his mouth was full. Figure 29-9 offers an illustration of the sandwich approach.

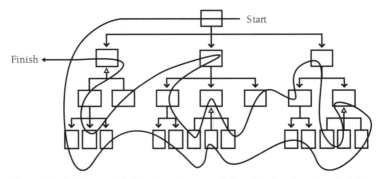

Figure 29-9 In sandwich integration, you integrate top-level and widely used bottom-level classes first and you save middle-level classes for last.

This approach avoids the rigidity of pure bottom-up or top-down integration. It integrates the often-troublesome classes first and has the potential to minimize the amount of scaffolding you'll need. It's a realistic, practical approach. The next approach is similar but has a different emphasis.

Risk-Oriented Integration

Risk-oriented integration is also called "hard part first integration." It's like sandwich integration in that it seeks to avoid the problems inherent in pure top-down or pure bottom-up integration. Coincidentally, it also tends to integrate the classes at the top and the bottom first, saving the middle-level classes for last. The motivation, however, is different.

In risk-oriented integration, you identify the level of risk associated with each class. You decide which will be the most challenging parts to implement, and you implement them first. Experience indicates that top-level interfaces are risky, so they are often at the top of the risk list. System interfaces, usually at the bottom level of the hierarchy, are also risky, so they're also at the top of the risk list. In addition, you might know of classes in the middle that will be challenging. Perhaps a class implements a poorly understood algorithm or has ambitious performance goals. Such classes can also be identified as high risks and integrated relatively early.

The remainder of the code, the easy stuff, can wait until later. Some of it will probably turn out to be harder than you thought, but that's unavoidable. Figure 29-10 presents an illustration of risk-oriented integration.

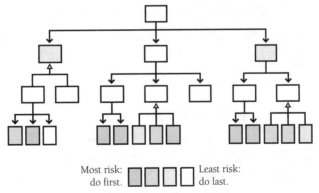

Most risk: do first.   Least risk: do last.

Figure 29-10   In risk-oriented integration, you integrate classes that you expect to be most troublesome first; you implement easier classes later.

Feature-Oriented Integration

Another approach is to integrate one feature at a time. The term "feature" doesn't refer to anything fancy, just an identifiable function of the system you're integrating. If you're writing a word processor, a feature might be displaying underlining on the screen or reformatting the document automatically—something like that.

When the feature to be integrated is bigger than a single class, the "increment" in incremental integration is bigger than a single class. This diminishes the benefit of incrementalism a little in that it reduces your certainty about the source of new errors, but if you have thoroughly tested the classes that implement the new feature before you integrate them, that's only a small disadvantage. You can use the incremental integration strategies recursively by integrating small pieces to form features and then incrementally integrating features to form a system.

You'll usually want to start with a skeleton you've chosen for its ability to support the other features. In an interactive system, the first feature might be the interactive menu system. You can hang the rest of the features on the feature that you integrate first. Figure 29-11 shows how it looks graphically.

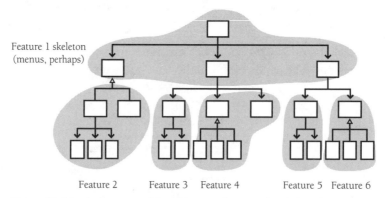

Figure 29-11   In feature-oriented integration, you integrate classes in groups that make up identifiable features—usually, but not always, multiple classes at a time.

Components are added in "feature trees," hierarchical collections of classes that make up a feature. Integration is easier if each feature is relatively independent, perhaps calling the same low-level library code as the classes for other features but having no calls to middle-level code in common with other features. (The shared, low-level library classes aren't shown in Figure 29-11.)

Feature-oriented integration offers three main advantages. First, it eliminates scaffolding for virtually everything except low-level library classes. The skeleton might need a little scaffolding, or some parts of the skeleton might simply not be operational until particular features have been added. When each feature has been hung on the structure, however, no additional scaffolding is needed. Since each feature is self-contained, each feature contains all the support code it needs.

The second main advantage is that each newly integrated feature brings about an incremental addition in functionality. This provides evidence that the project is moving steadily forward. It also creates functional software that you can provide to your customers for evaluation or that you can release earlier and with less functionality than originally planned.

A third advantage is that feature-oriented integration works well with object-oriented design. Objects tend to map well to features, which makes feature-oriented integration a natural choice for object-oriented systems.

Pure feature-oriented integration is as difficult to pursue as pure top-down or bottom-up integration. Usually some of the low-level code must be integrated before certain significant features can be.

T-Shaped Integration

A final approach that often addresses the problems associated with top-down and bottom-up integration is called "T-shaped integration." In this approach, one specific vertical slice is selected for early development and integration. That slice should exercise the system end-to-end and should be capable of flushing out any major problems in the system's design assumptions. Once that vertical slice has been implemented—and any associated problems have been corrected—the overall breadth of the system can be developed (such as the menu system in a desktop application). This approach, illustrated in Figure 29-12, is often combined with risk-oriented or feature-oriented integration.

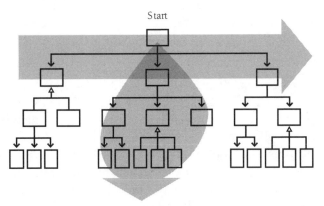

Figure 29-12   In T-shaped integration, you build and integrate a deep slice of the system to verify architectural assumptions, and then you build and integrate the breadth of the system to provide a framework for developing the remaining functionality.

Summary of Integration Approaches

Bottom-up, top-down, sandwich, risk-oriented, feature-oriented, T-shaped—do you get the feeling that people are making these names up as they go along? They are. None of these approaches are robust procedures that you should follow methodically from step 1 to step 47 and then declare yourself to be done. Like software-design approaches, they are heuristics more than algorithms, and rather than following any procedure dogmatically, you come out ahead by making up a unique strategy tailored to your specific project.

29.4 Daily Build and Smoke Test

Further Reading Much of this discussion is adapted from Chapter 18 of *Rapid Development* (McConnell 1996). If you've read that discussion, you might skip ahead to the "Continuous Integration" section.

Whatever integration strategy you select, a good approach to integrating the software is the "daily build and smoke test." Every file is compiled, linked, and combined into an executable program every day, and the program is then put through a "smoke test," a relatively simple check to see whether the product "smokes" when it runs.

This simple process produces several significant benefits. It reduces the risk of low quality, which is a risk related to the risk of unsuccessful or problematic integration. By smoke-testing all the code daily, quality problems are prevented from taking control of the project. You bring the system to a known, good state, and then you keep it there. You simply don't allow it to deteriorate to the point where time-consuming quality problems can occur.

This process also supports easier defect diagnosis. When the product is built and tested every day, it's easy to pinpoint why the product is broken on any given day. If the product worked on Day 17 and is broken on Day 18, something that happened between the two builds broke the product.

It improves morale. Seeing a product work provides an incredible boost to morale. It almost doesn't matter what the product does. Developers can be excited just to see it display a rectangle! With daily builds, a bit more of the product works every day, and that keeps morale high.

One side effect of frequent integration is that it surfaces work that can otherwise accumulate unseen until it appears unexpectedly at the end of the project. That accumulation of unsurfaced work can turn into an end-of-project tar pit that takes weeks or months to struggle out of. Teams that haven't used the daily build process sometimes feel that daily builds slow their progress to a snail's crawl. What's really happening is that daily builds amortize work more steadily throughout the project, and the project team is just getting a more accurate picture of how fast it's been working all along.

Here are some of the ins and outs of using daily builds:

Build daily The most fundamental part of the daily build is the "daily" part. As Jim McCarthy says, treat the daily build as the heartbeat of the project (McCarthy 1995).

If there's no heartbeat, the project is dead. A little less metaphorically, Michael Cusumano and Richard W. Selby describe the daily build as the sync pulse of a project (Cusumano and Selby 1995). Different developers' code is allowed to get a little out of sync between these pulses, but every time there's a sync pulse, the code has to come back into alignment. When you insist on keeping the pulses close together, you prevent developers from getting out of sync entirely.

Some organizations build every week, rather than every day. The problem with this is that if the build is broken one week, you might go for several weeks before the next good build. When that happens, you lose virtually all of the benefit of frequent builds.

Check for broken builds   For the daily-build process to work, the software that's built has to work. If the software isn't usable, the build is considered to be broken and fixing it becomes top priority.

Each project sets its own standard for what constitutes "breaking the build." The standard needs to set a quality level that's strict enough to keep showstopper defects out but lenient enough to disregard trivial defects, which can paralyze progress if given undue attention.

At a minimum, a "good" build should

- Compile all files, libraries, and other components successfully.
- Link all files, libraries, and other components successfully.
- Not contain any showstopper bugs that prevent the program from being launched or that make it hazardous to operate; in other words, a good build should pass the smoke test.

Smoke test daily   The smoke test should exercise the entire system from end to end. It does not have to be exhaustive, but it should be capable of exposing major problems. The smoke test should be thorough enough that if the build passes, you can assume that it is stable enough to be tested more thoroughly.

The daily build has little value without the smoke test. The smoke test is the sentry that guards against deteriorating product quality and creeping integration problems. Without it, the daily build becomes just a time-wasting exercise in ensuring that you have a clean compile every day.

Keep the smoke test current   The smoke test must evolve as the system evolves. At first, the smoke test will probably test something simple, such as whether the system can say "Hello, World." As the system develops, the smoke test will become more thorough. The first test might take a matter of seconds to run; as the system grows, the smoke test can grow to 10 minutes, an hour, or more. If the smoke test isn't kept current, the daily build can become an exercise in self-deception, in which a fractional set of test cases creates a false sense of confidence in the product's quality.

Automate the daily build and smoke test   Care and feeding of the build can become time-consuming. Automating the build and smoke test helps ensure that the code gets built and the smoke test gets run. It isn't practical to build and smoke test daily without automation.

Establish a build group   On most projects, tending the daily build and keeping the smoke test up to date becomes a big enough task to be an explicit part of someone's job. On large projects, it can become a full-time job for more than one person. On the first release of Microsoft Windows NT, for example, there were four full-time people in the build group (Zachary 1994).

Add revisions to the build only when it makes sense to do so...   Individual developers usually don't write code quickly enough to add meaningful increments to the system on a daily basis. They should work on a chunk of code and then integrate it when they have a collection of code in a consistent state—usually once every few days.

...but don't wait too long to add a set of revisions   Beware of checking in code infrequently. It's possible for a developer to become so embroiled in a set of revisions that every file in the system seems to be involved. That undermines the value of the daily build. The rest of the team will continue to realize the benefit of incremental integration, but that particular developer will not. If a developer goes more than a couple of days without checking in a set of changes, consider that developer's work to be at risk. As Kent Beck points out, frequent integration sometimes forces you to break the construction of a single feature into multiple episodes. That overhead is an acceptable price to pay for the reduced integration risk, improved status visibility, improved testability, and other benefits of frequent integration (Beck 2000).

Require developers to smoke test their code before adding it to the system   Developers need to test their own code before they add it to the build. A developer can do this by creating a private build of the system on a personal machine, which the developer then tests individually. Or the developer can release a private build to a "testing buddy," a tester who focuses on that developer's code. The goal in either case is to be sure that the new code passes the smoke test before it's allowed to influence other parts of the system.

Create a holding area for code that's to be added to the build   Part of the success of the daily build process depends on knowing which builds are good and which are not. In testing their own code, developers need to be able to rely on a known good system.

Most groups solve this problem by creating a holding area for code that developers think is ready to be added to the build. New code goes into the holding area, the new build is built, and if the build is acceptable, the new code is migrated into the master sources.

On small and medium-sized projects, a version-control system can serve this function. Developers check new code into the version-control system. Developers who want to use a known good build simply set a date flag in their version-control options file that tells the system to retrieve files based on the date of the last-known good build.

On large projects or projects that use unsophisticated version-control software, the holding area function has to be handled manually. The author of a set of new code sends e-mail to the build group to tell them where to find the new files to be checked in. Or the group establishes a "check-in" area on a file server where developers put new versions of their source files. The build group then assumes responsibility for checking new code into version control after they have verified that the new code doesn't break the build.

Create a penalty for breaking the build   Most groups that use daily builds create a penalty for breaking the build. Make it clear from the beginning that keeping the build healthy is one of the project's top priorities. A broken build should be the exception, not the rule. Insist that developers who have broken the build stop all other work until they've fixed it. If the build is broken too often, it's hard to take seriously the job of not breaking the build.

A light-hearted penalty can help to emphasize this priority. Some groups give out lollipops to each "sucker" who breaks the build. This developer then has to tape the sucker to his office door until he fixes the problem. Other groups have guilty developers wear goat horns or contribute $5 to a morale fund.

Some projects establish a penalty with more bite. Microsoft developers on high-profile projects such as Windows 2000 and Microsoft Office have taken to wearing beepers in the late stages of their projects. If they break the build, they get called in to fix it even if their defect is discovered at 3 a.m.

Release builds in the morning   Some groups have found that they prefer to build overnight, smoke test in the early morning, and release new builds in the morning rather than the afternoon. Smoke testing and releasing builds in the morning has several advantages.

First, if you release a build in the morning, testers can test with a fresh build that day. If you generally release builds in the afternoon, testers feel compelled to launch their automated tests before they leave for the day. When the build is delayed, which it often is, the testers have to stay late to launch their tests. Because it's not their fault that they have to stay late, the build process becomes demoralizing.

When you complete the build in the morning, you have more reliable access to developers when there are problems with the build. During the day, developers are down the hall. During the evening, developers can be anywhere. Even when developers are given beepers, they're not always easy to locate.

It might be more macho to start smoke testing at the end of the day and call people in the middle of the night when you find problems, but it's harder on the team, it wastes time, and in the end you lose more than you gain.

Build and smoke test even under pressure   When schedule pressure becomes intense, the work required to maintain the daily build can seem like extravagant overhead. The opposite is true. Under stress, developers lose some of their discipline. They feel pressure to take construction shortcuts that they would not take under less stressful circumstances. They review and test their own code less carefully than usual. The code tends toward a state of entropy more quickly than it does during less stressful times.

Against this backdrop, daily builds enforce discipline and keep pressure-cooker projects on track. The code still tends toward a state of entropy, but the build process brings that tendency to heel every day.

What Kinds of Projects Can Use the Daily Build Process?

Some developers protest that it's impractical to build every day because their projects are too large. But what was perhaps the most complex software project in recent history used daily builds successfully. By the time it was released, Microsoft Windows 2000 consisted of about 50 million lines of code spread across tens of thousands of source files. A complete build took as many as 19 hours on several machines, but the Windows 2000 development team still managed to build every day. Far from being a nuisance, the Windows 2000 team attributed much of its success on that huge project to their daily builds. The larger the project, the more important incremental integration becomes.

HARD DATA

A review of 104 projects in the U.S., India, Japan, and Europe found that only 20–25 percent of projects used daily builds at either the beginning or middle of their projects (Cusumano et al. 2003), so this represents a significant opportunity for improvement.

Continuous Integration

Some software writers have taken daily builds as a jumping-off point and recommend integrating *continuously* (Beck 2000). Most of the published references to continuous integration use the word "continuous" to mean "at least daily" (Beck 2000), which I think is reasonable. But I occasionally encounter people who take the word "continuous" literally. They aim to integrate each change with the latest build every couple of hours. For most projects, I think literal continuous integration is too much of a good thing.

HARD DATA

In my free time, I operate a discussion group consisting of the top technical executives from companies like Amazon.com, Boeing, Expedia, Microsoft, Nordstrom, and other Seattle-area companies. In a poll of these top technical executives, *none* of them thought that continuous integration was superior to daily integration. On medium-sized and large projects, there is value in letting the code get out of sync for short periods. Developers frequently get out of sync when they make larger-scale changes. They can then resynchronize after a short time. Daily builds allow the project team rendezvous points that are frequently enough. As long as the team syncs up every day, they don't need to rendezvous continuously.

cc2e.com/2992

CHECKLIST: Integration

Integration Strategy

❑ Does the strategy identify the optimal order in which subsystems, classes, and routines should be integrated?

❑ Is the integration order coordinated with the construction order so that classes will be ready for integration at the right time?

❑ Does the strategy lead to easy diagnosis of defects?

❑ Does the strategy keep scaffolding to a minimum?

❑ Is the strategy better than other approaches?

❑ Have the interfaces between components been specified well? (Specifying interfaces isn't an integration task, but verifying that they have been specified well is.)

Daily Build and Smoke Test

❑ Is the project building frequently—ideally, daily—to support incremental integration?

❑ Is a smoke test run with each build so that you know whether the build works?

❑ Have you automated the build and the smoke test?

❑ Do developers check in their code frequently—going no more than a day or two between check-ins?

❑ Is the smoke test kept up to date with the code, expanding as the code expands?

❑ Is a broken build a rare occurrence?

❑ Do you build and smoke test the software even when you're under pressure?

Additional Resources

cc2e.com/2999

Following are additional resources related to this chapter's subjects:

Integration

Lakos, John. *Large-Scale C++ Software Design*. Boston, MA: Addison-Wesley, 1996. Lakos argues that a system's "physical design"—its hierarchy of files, directories, and libraries—significantly affects a development team's ability to build software. If you don't pay attention to the physical design, build times will become long enough to undermine frequent integration. Lakos's discussion focuses on C++, but the insights related to "physical design" apply just as much to projects in other languages.

Myers, Glenford J. *The Art of Software Testing*. New York, NY: John Wiley & Sons, 1979. This classic testing book discusses integration as a testing activity.

Incrementalism

McConnell, Steve. *Rapid Development*. Redmond, WA: Microsoft Press, 1996. Chapter 7, "Lifecycle Planning," goes into much detail about the tradeoffs involved with more-flexible and less-flexible life-cycle models. Chapters 20, 21, 35, and 36 discuss specific life-cycle models that support various degrees of incrementalism. Chapter 19 describes "designing for change," a key activity needed to support iterative and incremental development models.

Boehm, Barry W. "A Spiral Model of Software Development and Enhancement." *Computer*, May 1988: 61–72. In this paper, Boehm describes his "spiral model" of software development. He presents the model as an approach to managing risk in a software-development project, so the paper is about development generally rather than about integration specifically. Boehm is one of the world's foremost experts on the big-picture issues of software development, and the clarity of his explanations reflects the quality of his understanding.

Gilb, Tom. *Principles of Software Engineering Management*. Wokingham, England: Addison-Wesley, 1988. Chapters 7 and 15 contain thorough discussions of evolutionary delivery, one of the first incremental development approaches.

Beck, Kent. *Extreme Programming Explained: Embrace Change*. Reading, MA: Addison-Wesley, 2000. This book contains a more modern, more concise, and more evangelical presentation of many of the ideas in Gilb's book. I personally prefer the depth of analysis presented in Gilb's book, but some readers may find Beck's presentation more accessible or more directly applicable to the kind of project they're working on.

Key Points

- The construction sequence and integration approach affect the order in which classes are designed, coded, and tested.

- A well-thought-out integration order reduces testing effort and eases debugging.

- Incremental integration comes in several varieties, and, unless the project is trivial, any one of them is better than phased integration.

- The best integration approach for any specific project is usually a combination of top-down, bottom-up, risk-oriented, and other integration approaches. T-shaped integration and vertical-slice integration are two approaches that often work well.

- Daily builds can reduce integration problems, improve developer morale, and provide useful project management information.

Chapter 30

Programming Tools

cc2e.com/3084

Contents

Related Topics

Modern programming tools decrease the amount of time required for construction. Use of a leading-edge tool set—and familiarity with the tools used—can increase productivity by 50 percent or more (Jones 2000; Boehm et al. 2000). Programming tools can also reduce the amount of tedious detail work that programming requires.

HARD DATA

A dog might be man's best friend, but a few good tools are a programmer's best friends. As Barry Boehm discovered long ago, 20 percent of the tools tend to account for 80 percent of the tool usage (1987b). If you're missing one of the more helpful tools, you're missing something that you could use a lot.

This chapter is focused in two ways. First, it covers only construction tools. Requirements-specification, management, and end-to-end-development tools are outside the scope of the book. Refer to the "Additional Resources" section at the end of the chapter for more information on tools for those aspects of software development. Second, this chapter covers kinds of tools rather than specific brands. A few tools are so common that they're discussed by name, but specific versions, products, and companies change so quickly that information about most of them would be out of date before the ink on these pages was dry.

A programmer can work for many years without discovering some of the most valuable tools available. The mission of this chapter is to survey available tools and help you determine whether you've overlooked any tools that might be useful. If you're a tool expert, you won't find much new information in this chapter. You might skim the earlier parts of the chapter, read Section 30.6 on "Tool Fantasyland," and then move on to the next chapter.

30.1 Design Tools

Cross-Reference For details on design, see Chapters 5 through 9.

Current design tools consist mainly of graphical tools that create design diagrams. Design tools are sometimes embedded in a computer-aided software engineering (CASE) tool with broader functions; some vendors advertise standalone design tools as CASE tools. Graphical design tools generally allow you to express a design in common graphical notations: UML, architecture block diagrams, hierarchy charts, entity relationship diagrams, or class diagrams. Some graphical design tools support only one notation. Others support a variety.

In one sense, these design tools are just fancy drawing packages. Using a simple graphics package or pencil and paper, you can draw everything that the tool can draw. But the tools offer valuable capabilities that a simple graphics package can't. If you've drawn a bubble chart and you delete a bubble, a graphical design tool will automatically rearrange the other bubbles, including connecting arrows and lower-level bubbles connected to the bubble. The tool takes care of the housekeeping when you add a bubble, too. A design tool can enable you to move between higher and lower levels of abstraction. A design tool will check the consistency of your design, and some tools can create code directly from your design.

30.2 Source-Code Tools

The tools available for working with source code are richer and more mature than the tools available for working with designs.

Editing

This group of tools relates to editing source code.

Integrated Development Environments (IDEs)

HARD DATA

Some programmers estimate that they spend as much as 40 percent of their time editing source code (Parikh 1986, Ratliff 1987). If that's the case, spending a few extra dollars for the best possible IDE is a good investment.

In addition to basic word-processing functions, good IDEs offer these features:

- Compilation and error detection from within the editor
- Integration with source-code control, build, test, and debugging tools

- Compressed or outline views of programs (class names only or logical structures without the contents, also known as "folding")

- Jump to definitions of classes, routines, and variables

- Jump to all places where a class, routine, or variable is used

- Language-specific formatting

- Interactive help for the language being edited

- Brace (*begin-end*) matching

- Templates for common language constructs (the editor completing the structure of a *for* loop after the programmer types *for*, for example)

- Smart indenting (including easily changing the indentation of a block of statements when logic changes)

- Automated code transforms or refactorings

- Macros programmable in a familiar programming language

- Listing of search strings so that commonly used strings don't need to be retyped

- Regular expressions in search-and-replace

- Search-and-replace across a group of files

- Editing multiple files simultaneously

- Side-by-side diff comparisons

- Multilevel undo

Considering some of the primitive editors still in use, you might be surprised to learn that several editors include all these capabilities.

Multiple-File String Searching and Replacing

If your editor doesn't support search-and-replace across multiple files, you can still find supplementary tools to do that job. These tools are useful for search for all occurrences of a class name or routine name. When you find an error in your code, you can use such tools to check for similar errors in other files.

You can search for exact strings, similar strings (ignoring differences in capitalization), or regular expressions. Regular expressions are particularly powerful because they let you search for complex string patterns. If you wanted to find all the array references containing magic numbers (digits "0" through "9"), you could search for "[", followed by zero or more spaces, followed by one or more digits, followed by zero or more spaces, followed by "]". One widely available search tool is called "grep." A grep query for magic numbers would look like this:

```
grep "\[ *[0-9]+ *\]" *.cpp
```

You can make the search criteria more sophisticated to fine-tune the search.

It's often helpful to be able to change strings across multiple files. For example, if you want to give a routine, constant, or global variable a better name, you might have to change the name in several files. Utilities that allow string changes across multiple files make that easy to do, which is good because you should have as few obstructions as possible to creating excellent class names, routine names, and constant names. Common tools for handling multiple-file string changes include Perl, AWK, and sed.

Diff Tools

Programmers often need to compare two files. If you make several attempts to correct an error and need to remove the unsuccessful attempts, a file comparator will make a comparison of the original and modified files and list the lines you've changed. If you're working on a program with other people and want to see the changes they have made since the last time you worked on the code, a comparator tool such as Diff will make a comparison of the current version with the last version of the code you worked on and show the differences. If you discover a new defect that you don't remember encountering in an older version of a program, rather than seeing a neurologist about amnesia, you can use a comparator to compare current and old versions of the source code, determine exactly what changed, and find the source of the problem. This functionality is often built into revision-control tools.

Merge Tools

One style of revision control locks source files so that only one person can modify a file at a time. Another style allows multiple people to work on files simultaneously and handles merging changes at check-in time. In this working mode, tools that merge changes are critical. These tools typically perform simple merges automatically and query the user for merges that conflict with other merges or that are more involved.

Source-Code Beautifiers

Cross-Reference For details on program layout, see Chapter 31, "Layout and Style."

Source-code beautifiers spruce up your source code so that it looks consistent. They highlight class and routine names, standardize your indentation style, format comments consistently, and perform other similar functions. Some beautifiers can put each routine onto a separate Web page or printed page or perform even more dramatic formatting. Many beautifiers let you customize the way in which the code is beautified.

There are at least two classes of source-code beautifiers. One class takes the source code as input and produces much better looking output without changing the original source code. Another kind of tool changes the source code itself—standardizing indentation, parameter list formatting, and so on. This capability is useful when working with large quantities of legacy code. The tool can do much of the tedious formatting work needed to make the legacy code conform to your coding style conventions.

Interface Documentation Tools

Some tools extract detailed programmer-interface documentation from source-code files. The code inside the source file uses clues such as @*tag* fields to identify text that should be extracted. The interface documentation tool then extracts that tagged text and presents it with nice formatting. Javadoc is a prominent example of this kind of tool.

Templates

Templates help you exploit the simple idea of streamlining keyboarding tasks that you do often and want to do consistently. Suppose you want a standard comment prolog at the beginning of your routines. You could build a skeleton prolog with the correct syntax and places for all the items you want in the standard prolog. This skeleton would be a "template" you'd store in a file or a keyboard macro. When you created a new routine, you could easily insert the template into your source file. You can use the template technique for setting up larger entities, such as classes and files, or smaller entities, such as loops.

If you're working on a group project, templates are an easy way to encourage consistent coding and documentation styles. Make templates available to the whole team at the beginning of the project, and the team will use them because they make its job easier—you get the consistency as a side benefit.

Cross-Reference Tools

A cross-reference tool lists variables and routines and all the places in which they're used—typically on Web pages.

Class Hierarchy Generators

A class-hierarchy generator produces information about inheritance trees. This is sometimes useful in debugging but is more often used for analyzing a program's structure or modularizing a program into packages or subsystems. This functionality is also available in some IDEs.

Analyzing Code Quality

Tools in this category examine the static source code to assess its quality.

Picky Syntax and Semantics Checkers

Syntax and semantics checkers supplement your compiler by checking code more thoroughly than the compiler normally does. Your compiler might check for only rudimentary syntax errors. A picky syntax checker might use nuances of the language to check for more subtle errors—things that aren't wrong from a compiler's point of view but that you probably didn't intend to write. For example, in C++, the statement

```
while ( i = 0 ) ...
```

is a perfectly legal statement, but it's usually meant to be

```
while ( i == 0 ) ...
```

The first line is syntactically correct, but switching = and == is a common mistake and the line is probably wrong. Lint is a picky syntax and semantics checker you can find in many C/C++ environments. Lint warns you about uninitialized variables, completely unused variables, variables that are assigned values and never used, parameters of a routine that are passed out of the routine without being assigned a value, suspicious pointer operations, suspicious logical comparisons (like the one in the example just shown), inaccessible code, and many other common problems. Other languages offer similar tools.

Metrics Reporters

Cross-Reference For more information on metrics, see Section 28.4, "Measurement."

Some tools analyze your code and report on its quality. For example, you can obtain tools that report on the complexity of each routine so that you can target the most complicated routines for extra review, testing, or redesign. Some tools count lines of code, data declarations, comments, and blank lines in either entire programs or individual routines. They track defects and associate them with the programmers who made them, the changes that correct them, and the programmers who make the corrections. They count modifications to the software and note the routines that are modified the most often. Complexity analysis tools have been found to have about a 20 percent positive impact on maintenance productivity (Jones 2000).

Refactoring Source Code

A few tools aid in converting source code from one format to another.

Refactorers

Cross-Reference For more on refactoring, see Chapter 24, "Refactoring."

A refactoring program supports common code refactorings either on a standalone basis or integrated into an IDE. Refactoring browsers allow you to change the name of a class across an entire code base easily. They allow you to extract a routine simply by highlighting the code you'd like to turn into a new routine, entering the new routine's name, and ordering parameters in a parameter list. Refactorers make code changes quicker and less error-prone. They're available for Java and Smalltalk and are becoming available for other languages. For more about refactoring tools, see Chapter 14, "Refactoring Tools" in *Refactoring* (Fowler 1999).

Restructurers

A restructurer will convert a plate of spaghetti code with *goto*s to a more nutritious entrée of better-structured code without *goto*s. Capers Jones reports that in maintenance environments code restructuring tools can have a 25–30 percent positive impact on maintenance productivity (Jones 2000). A restructurer has to make a lot of assumptions when it converts code, and if the logic is terrible in the original, it will still be terrible in the converted version. If you're doing a conversion manually, however, you can use a restructurer for the general case and hand-tune the hard cases. Alternatively, you can run the code through the restructurer and use it for inspiration for the hand conversion.

Code Translators

Some tools translate code from one language to another. A translator is useful when you have a large code base that you're moving to another environment. The hazard in using a language translator is that if you start with bad code the translator simply translates the bad code into an unfamiliar language.

Version Control

Cross-Reference These tools and their benefits are described in "Software Code Changes" in Section 28.2. You can deal with proliferating software versions by using version-control tools for

- Source-code control
- Dependency control like that offered by the make utility associated with UNIX
- Project documentation versioning
- Relating project artifacts like requirements, code, and test cases so that when a requirement changes, you can find the code and tests that are affected

Data Dictionaries

A data dictionary is a database that describes all the significant data in a project. In many cases, the data dictionary focuses primarily on database schemas. On large projects, a data dictionary is also useful for keeping track of the hundreds or thousands of class definitions. On large team projects, it's useful for avoiding naming clashes. A clash might be a direct, syntactic clash, in which the same name is used twice, or it might be a more subtle clash (or gap) in which different names are used to mean the same thing or the same name is used to mean subtly different things. For each data item (database table or class), the data dictionary contains the item's name and description. The dictionary might also contain notes about how the item is used.

30.3 Executable-Code Tools

Tools for working with executable code are as rich as the tools for working with source code.

Code Creation

The tools described in this section help with code creation.

Compilers and Linkers

Compilers convert source code to executable code. Most programs are written to be compiled, although some are still interpreted.

A standard linker links one or more object files, which the compiler has generated from your source files, with the standard code needed to make an executable program. Linkers typically can link files from multiple languages, allowing you to choose the language that's most appropriate for each part of your program without your having to handle the integration details yourself.

An overlay linker helps you put 10 pounds in a five-pound sack by developing programs that execute in less memory than the total amount of space they consume. An overlay linker creates an executable file that loads only part of itself into memory at any one time, leaving the rest on a disk until it's needed.

Build Tools

The purpose of a build tool is to minimize the time needed to build a program using current versions of the program's source files. For each target file in your project, you specify the source files that the target file depends on and how to make it. Build tools also eliminate errors related to sources being in inconsistent states; the build tool ensures they are all brought to a consistent state. Common build tools include the make utility that's associated with UNIX and the ant tool that's used for Java programs.

Suppose you have a target file named *userface.obj*. In the make file, you indicate that to make *userface.obj*, you have to compile the file *userface.cpp*. You also indicate that *userface.cpp* depends on *userface.h*, *stdlib.h*, and *project.h*. The concept of "depends on" simply means that if *userface.h*, *stdlib.h*, or *project.h* changes, *userface.cpp* needs to be recompiled.

When you build your program, the make tool checks all the dependencies you've described and determines the files that need to be recompiled. If five of your 250 source files depend on data definitions in *userface.h* and it changes, make automatically recompiles the five files that depend on it. It doesn't recompile the 245 files that don't depend on *userface.h*. Using make or ant beats the alternatives of recompiling all

250 files or recompiling each file manually, forgetting one, and getting weird out-of-synch errors. Overall, build tools like make or ant substantially improve the time and reliability of the average compile-link-run cycle.

Some groups have found interesting alternatives to dependency-checking tools like make. For example, the Microsoft Word group found that simply rebuilding all source files was faster than performing extensive dependency checking with make as long as the source files themselves were optimized (header file contents and so on). With this approach, the average developer's machine on the Word project could rebuild the entire Word executable—several million lines of code—in about 13 minutes.

Code Libraries

A good way to write high-quality code in a short amount of time is not to write it all but to find an open source version or buy it instead. You can find high-quality libraries in at least these areas:

- Container classes
- Credit card transaction services (e-commerce services)
- Cross-platform development tools. You might write code that executes in Microsoft Windows, Apple Macintosh, and the X Window System just by recompiling for each environment.
- Data compression tools
- Data types and algorithms
- Database operations and data-file manipulation tools
- Diagramming, graphing, and charting tools
- Imaging tools
- License managers
- Mathematical operations
- Networking and internet communications tools
- Report generators and report query builders
- Security and encryption tools
- Spreadsheet and grid tools
- Text and spelling tools
- Voice, phone, and fax tools

Code-Generation Wizards

If you can't find the code you want, how about getting someone else to write it instead? You don't have to put on your yellow plaid jacket and slip into a car salesman's patter to con someone else into writing your code. You can find tools that write code for you, and such tools are often integrated into IDEs.

Code-generating tools tend to focus on database applications, but that includes a lot of applications. Commonly available code generators write code for databases, user interfaces, and compilers. The code they generate is rarely as good as code generated by a human programmer, but many applications don't require handcrafted code. It's worth more to some users to have 10 working applications than to have one that works exceptionally well.

Code generators are also useful for making prototypes of production code. Using a code generator, you might be able to hack out a prototype in a few hours that demonstrates key aspects of a user interface or you might be able to experiment with various design approaches. It might take you several weeks to hand-code as much functionality. If you're just experimenting, why not do it in the cheapest possible way?

The common drawback of code generators is that they tend to generate code that's nearly unreadable. If you ever have to maintain such code, you can regret not writing it by hand in the first place.

Setup and Installation

Numerous vendors provide tools that support creation of setup programs. These tools typically support the creation of disks, CDs, or DVDs or installation over the Web. They check whether common library files already exist on the target installation machine, perform version checking, and so on.

Preprocessors

Cross-Reference For details on moving debugging aids in and out of the code, see "Plan to Remove Debugging Aids" in Section 8.6.

Preprocessors and preprocessor macro functions are useful for debugging because they make it easy to switch between development code and production code. During development, if you want to check memory fragmentation at the beginning of each routine, you can use a macro at the beginning of each routine. You might not want to leave the checks in production code, so for the production code you can redefine the macro so that it doesn't generate any code at all. For similar reasons, preprocessor macros are good for writing code that's targeted to be compiled in multiple environments—for example, in both Windows and Linux.

If you use a language with primitive control constructs, such as assembler, you can write a control-flow preprocessor to emulate the structured constructs of *if-then-else* and *while* loops in your language.

cc2e.com/3091

If your language doesn't have a preprocessor, you can use a standalone preprocessor as part of your build process. One readily available preprocessor is M4, available from *www.gnu.org/software/m4/*.

Debugging

Cross-Reference These tools and their benefits are described in Section 23.5, "Debugging Tools—Obvious and Not-So-Obvious."

These tools help in debugging:

- Compiler warning messages
- Test scaffolding
- Diff tools (for comparing different versions of source-code files)
- Execution profilers
- Trace monitors
- Interactive debuggers—both software and hardware

Testing tools, discussed next, are related to debugging tools.

Testing

Cross-Reference These tools and their benefits are described in Section 22.5, "Test-Support Tools."

These features and tools can help you do effective testing:

- Automated test frameworks like JUnit, NUnit, CppUnit, and so on
- Automated test generators
- Test-case record and playback utilities
- Coverage monitors (logic analyzers and execution profilers)
- Symbolic debuggers
- System perturbers (memory fillers, memory shakers, selective memory failers, memory-access checkers)
- Diff tools (for comparing data files, captured output, and screen images)
- Scaffolding
- Defect-injection tools
- Defect-tracking software

Code Tuning

These tools can help you fine-tune your code.

Execution Profilers

An execution profiler watches your code while it runs and tells you how many times each statement is executed or how much time the program spends on each statement or execution path. Profiling your code while it's running is like having a doctor press a stethoscope to your chest and tell you to cough. It gives you insight into how your program works, where the hot spots are, and where you should focus your code-tuning efforts.

Assembler Listings and Disassemblers

Some day you might want to look at the assembler code generated by your high-level language. Some high-level-language compilers generate assembler listings. Others don't, and you have to use a disassembler to re-create the assembler from the machine code that the compiler generates. Looking at the assembler code generated by your compiler shows you how efficiently your compiler translates high-level-language code into machine code. It can tell you why high-level code that looks fast runs slowly. In Chapter 26, "Code-Tuning Techniques," several of the benchmark results are counter-intuitive. While benchmarking that code, I frequently referred to the assembler listings to better understand the results that didn't make sense in the high-level language.

If you're not comfortable with assembly language and you want an introduction, you won't find a better one than comparing each high-level-language statement you write to the assembler instructions generated by the compiler. A first exposure to assembler is often a loss of innocence. When you see how much code the compiler creates—how much more than it needs to—you'll never look at your compiler in quite the same way again.

Conversely, in some environments the compiler must generate extremely complex code. Studying the compiler output can foster an appreciation for just how much work would be required to program in a lower level language.

30.4 Tool-Oriented Environments

Some environments have proven to be better suited to tool-oriented programming than others.

The UNIX environment is famous for its collection of small tools with funny names that work well together: grep, diff, sort, make, crypt, tar, lint, ctags, sed, awk, vi, and others. The C and C++ languages, closely coupled with UNIX, embody the same philosophy; the standard C++ library is composed of small functions that can easily be composed into larger functions because they work so well together.

cc2e.com/3026 Some programmers work so productively in UNIX that they take it with them. They use UNIX work-alike tools to support their UNIX habits in Windows and other environments. One tribute to the success of the UNIX paradigm is the availability of tools that put a UNIX costume on other machines. For example, cygwin provides UNIX-equivalent tools that work under Windows (*www.cygwin.com*).

Eric Raymond's *The Art of Unix Programming* (2004) contains an insightful discussion of the UNIX programming culture.

30.5 Building Your Own Programming Tools

Suppose you're given five hours to do the job and you have a choice:

- Do the job comfortably in five hours, or

- Spend four hours and 45 minutes feverishly building a tool to do the job, and then have the tool do the job in 15 minutes.

Most good programmers would choose the first option one time out of a million and the second option in every other case. Building tools is part of the warp and woof of programming. Nearly all large organizations (organizations with more than 1000 programmers) have internal tool and support groups. Many have proprietary requirements and design tools that are superior to those on the market (Jones 2000).

You can write many of the tools described in this chapter. Doing so might not be cost-effective, but there aren't any mountainous technical barriers to doing it.

Project-Specific Tools

Most medium-sized and large projects need special tools unique to the project. For example, you might need tools to generate special kinds of test data, to verify the quality of data files, or to emulate hardware that isn't yet available. Here are some examples of project-specific tool support:

- An aerospace team was responsible for developing in-flight software to control an infrared sensor and analyze its data. To verify the performance of the software, an in-flight data recorder documented the actions of the in-flight software. Engineers wrote custom data-analysis tools to analyze the performance of the in-flight systems. After each flight, they used the custom tools to check the primary systems.

- Microsoft planned to include a new font technology in a release of its Windows graphical environment. Since both the font data files and the software to display the fonts were new, errors could have arisen from either the data or the software. Microsoft developers wrote several custom tools to check for errors in the data files, which improved their ability to discriminate between font data errors and software errors.

■ An insurance company developed an ambitious system to calculate its rate increases. Because the system was complicated and accuracy was essential, hundreds of computed rates needed to be checked carefully, even though hand calculating a single rate took several minutes. The company wrote a separate software tool to compute rates one at a time. With the tool, the company could compute a single rate in a few seconds and check rates from the main program in a small fraction of the time it would have taken to check the main program's rates by hand.

Part of planning for a project should be thinking about the tools that might be needed and allocating time for building them.

Scripts

A script is a tool that automates a repetitive chore. In some systems, scripts are called batch files or macros. Scripts can be simple or complex, and some of the most useful are the easiest to write. For example, I keep a journal, and to protect my privacy, I encrypt it except when I'm writing in it. To make sure that I always encrypt and decrypt it properly, I have a script that decrypts my journal, executes the word processor, and then encrypts the journal. The script looks like this:

```
crypto c:\word\journal.* %1 /d /Es /s
word c:\word\journal.doc
crypto c:\word\journal.* %1 /Es /s
```

The *%1* is the field for my password which, for obvious reasons, isn't included in the script. The script saves me the work of typing (and mistyping) all the parameters and ensures that I always perform all the operations and perform them in the right order.

If you find yourself typing something longer than about five characters more than a few times a day, it's a good candidate for a script or batch file. Examples include compile/link sequences, backup commands, and any command with a lot of parameters.

30.6 Tool Fantasyland

Cross-Reference Tool availability depends partly on the maturity of the technical environment. For more on this, see Section 4.3, "Your Location on the Technology Wave."

For decades, tool vendors and industry pundits have promised that the tools needed to eliminate programming are just over the horizon. The first, and perhaps most ironic, tool to receive this moniker was Fortran. Fortran or "Formula Translation Language" was conceived so that scientists and engineers could simply type in formulas, thus supposedly eliminating the need for programmers.

Fortran did succeed in making it possible for scientists and engineers to write programs, but from our vantage point today, Fortran appears to be a comparatively low-level programming language. It hardly eliminated the need for programmers, and what the industry experienced with Fortran is indicative of progress in the software industry as a whole.

The software industry constantly develops new tools that reduce or eliminate some of the most tedious aspects of programming: details of laying out source statements; steps needed to edit, compile, link, and run a program; work needed to find mismatched braces; the number of steps needed to create standard message boxes; and so on. As each of these new tools begins to demonstrate incremental gains in productivity, pundits extrapolate those gains out to infinity, assuming that the gains will eventually "eliminate the need for programming." But what's happening in reality is that each new programming innovation arrives with a few blemishes. As time goes by, the blemishes are removed and that innovation's full potential is realized. However, once the fundamental tool concept is realized, further gains are achieved by stripping away the accidental difficulties that were created as side effects of creating the new tool. Elimination of these accidental difficulties does not increase productivity per se; it simply eliminates the "one step back" from the typical "two steps forward, one step back" equation.

Over the past several decades, programmers have seen numerous tools that were supposed to eliminate programming. First it was third-generation languages. Then it was fourth generation languages. Then it was automatic programming. Then it was CASE tools. Then it was visual programming. Each of these advances spun off valuable, incremental improvements to computer programming—and collectively they have made programming unrecognizable to anyone who learned programming before these advances. But none of these innovations succeeded in eliminating programming.

Cross-Reference Reasons for the difficulty of programming are described in "Accidental and Essential Difficulties" in Section 5.2.

The reason for this dynamic is that, at its essence, programming is fundamentally *hard*—even with good tool support. No matter what tools are available, programmers will have to wrestle with the messy real world; we will have to think rigorously about sequences, dependencies, and exceptions; and we'll have to deal with end users who can't make up their minds. We will always have to wrestle with ill-defined interfaces to other software and hardware, and we'll have to account for regulations, business rules, and other sources of complexity that arise from outside the world of computer programming.

We will always need people who can bridge the gap between the real-world problem to be solved and the computer that is supposed to be solving the problem. These people will be called programmers regardless of whether we're manipulating machine registers in assembler or dialog boxes in Microsoft Visual Basic. As long as we have computers, we'll need people who tell the computers what to do, and that activity will be called programming.

When you hear a tool vendor claim "This new tool will eliminate computer programming," run! Or at least smile to yourself at the vendor's naive optimism.

Additional Resources

cc2e.com/3098 Take a look at these additional resources for more on programming tools:

cc2e.com/3005 *www.sdmagazine.com/jolts. Software Development Magazine*'s annual Jolt Productivity award website is a good source of information about the best current tools.

Hunt, Andrew and David Thomas. *The Pragmatic Programmer*. Boston, MA: Addison-Wesley, 2000. Section 3 of this book provides an in-depth discussion of programming tools, including editors, code generators, debuggers, source-code control, and related tools.

cc2e.com/3012 Vaughn-Nichols, Steven. "Building Better Software with Better Tools," *IEEE Computer*, September 2003, pp. 12–14. This article surveys tool initiatives led by IBM, Microsoft Research, and Sun Research.

Glass, Robert L. *Software Conflict: Essays on the Art and Science of Software Engineering*. Englewood Cliffs, NJ: Yourdon Press, 1991. The chapter titled "Recommended: A Minimum Standard Software Toolset" provides a thoughtful counterpoint to the more-tools-is-better view. Glass argues for the identification of a minimum set of tools that should be available to all developers and proposes a starting kit.

Jones, Capers. *Estimating Software Costs*. New York, NY: McGraw-Hill, 1998.

Boehm, Barry, et al. *Software Cost Estimation with Cocomo II*. Reading, MA: Addison-Wesley, 2000. Both the Jones and the Boehm books devote sections to the impact of tool use on productivity.

cc2e.com/3019

Checklist: Programming Tools

- ❑ Do you have an effective IDE?

- ❑ Does your IDE support integration with source-code control; build, test, and debugging tools; and other useful functions?

- ❑ Do you have tools that automate common refactorings?

- ❑ Are you using version control to manage source code, content, requirements, designs, project plans, and other project artifacts?

- ❑ If you're working on a very large project, are you using a data dictionary or some other central repository that contains authoritative descriptions of each class used in the system?

- ❑ Have you considered code libraries as alternatives to writing custom code, where available?

- ❏ Are you making use of an interactive debugger?

- ❏ Do you use make or other dependency-control software to build programs efficiently and reliably?

- ❏ Does your test environment include an automated test framework, automated test generators, coverage monitors, system perturbers, diff tools, and defect-tracking software?

- ❏ Have you created any custom tools that would help support your specific project's needs, especially tools that automate repetitive tasks?

- ❏ Overall, does your environment benefit from adequate tool support?

Key Points

- ■ Programmers sometimes overlook some of the most powerful tools for years before discovering them.

- ■ Good tools can make your life a lot easier.

- ■ Tools are readily available for editing, analyzing code quality, refactoring, version control, debugging, testing, and code tuning.

- ■ You can make many of the special-purpose tools you need.

- ■ Good tools can reduce the more tedious aspects of software development, but they can't eliminate the need for programming, although they will continue to reshape what we mean by "programming."

Part VII
Software Craftsmanship

Chapter 31
Layout and Style

Contents

- 31.1 Layout Fundamentals: page 730
- 31.2 Layout Techniques: page 736
- 31.3 Layout Styles: page 738
- 31.4 Laying Out Control Structures: page 745
- 31.5 Laying Out Individual Statements: page 753
- 31.6 Laying Out Comments: page 763
- 31.7 Laying Out Routines: page 766
- 31.8 Laying Out Classes: page 768

Related Topics

- Self-documenting code: Chapter 32
- Code formatting tools: "Editing" in Section 30.2

This chapter turns to an aesthetic aspect of computer programming: the layout of program source code. The visual and intellectual enjoyment of well-formatted code is a pleasure that few nonprogrammers can appreciate. But programmers who take pride in their work derive great artistic satisfaction from polishing the visual structure of their code.

The techniques in this chapter don't affect execution speed, memory use, or other aspects of a program that are visible from outside the program. They affect how easy it is to understand the code, review it, and revise it months after you write it. They also affect how easy it is for others to read, understand, and modify once you're out of the picture.

This chapter is full of the picky details that people refer to when they talk about "attention to detail." Over the life of a project, attention to such details makes a difference in the initial quality and the ultimate maintainability of the code you write. Such details are too integral to the coding process to be changed effectively later. If they're to be done at all, they must be done during initial construction. If you're working on a team project, have your team read this chapter and agree on a team style before you begin coding.

You might not agree with everything you read here, but my point is less to win your agreement than to convince you to consider the issues involved in formatting style. If you have high blood pressure, move on to the next chapter—it's less controversial.

31.1 Layout Fundamentals

This section explains the theory of good layout. The rest of the chapter explains the practice.

Layout Extremes

Consider the routine shown in Listing 31-1:

Listing 31-1   Java layout example #1.

CODING
HORROR

```
/* Use the insertion sort technique to sort the "data" array in ascending order.
This routine assumes that data[ firstElement ] is not the first element in data and
that data[ firstElement-1 ] can be accessed. */ public void InsertionSort( int[]
data, int firstElement, int lastElement ) { /* Replace element at lower boundary
with an element guaranteed to be first in a sorted list. */ int lowerBoundary =
data[ firstElement-1 ]; data[ firstElement-1 ] = SORT_MIN; /* The elements in
positions firstElement through sortBoundary-1 are always sorted. In each pass
through the loop, sortBoundary is increased, and the element at the position of the
new sortBoundary probably isn't in its sorted place in the array, so it's inserted
into the proper place somewhere between firstElement and sortBoundary. */ for (
int sortBoundary = firstElement+1; sortBoundary <= lastElement; sortBoundary++  )
{ int insertVal = data[ sortBoundary ]; int insertPos = sortBoundary; while (
insertVal < data[ insertPos-1 ] ) { data[ insertPos ] = data[ insertPos-1 ];
insertPos = insertPos-1; } data[ insertPos ] = insertVal; } /* Replace original
lower-boundary element */ data[ firstElement-1 ] = lowerBoundary; }
```

The routine is syntactically correct. It's thoroughly commented and has good variable names and clear logic. If you don't believe that, read it and find a mistake! What the routine doesn't have is good layout. This is an extreme example, headed toward "negative infinity" on the number line of bad-to-good layout. Listing 31-2 is a less extreme example:

Listing 31-2   Java layout example #2.

CODING
HORROR

```
/* Use the insertion sort technique to sort the "data" array in ascending
order. This routine assumes that data[ firstElement ] is not the
first element in data and that data[ firstElement-1 ] can be accessed. */
public void InsertionSort( int[] data, int firstElement, int lastElement ) {
/* Replace element at lower boundary with an element guaranteed to be first in a
sorted list. */
int lowerBoundary = data[ firstElement-1 ];
data[ firstElement-1 ] = SORT_MIN;
/* The elements in positions firstElement through sortBoundary-1 are
always sorted. In each pass through the loop, sortBoundary
is increased, and the element at the position of the
new sortBoundary probably isn't in its sorted place in the
array, so it's inserted into the proper place somewhere
between firstElement and sortBoundary. */
for (
int sortBoundary = firstElement+1;
sortBoundary <= lastElement;
```

```
sortBoundary++
) {
int insertVal = data[ sortBoundary ];
int insertPos = sortBoundary;
while ( insertVal < data[ insertPos-1 ] ) {
data[ insertPos ] = data[ insertPos-1 ];
insertPos = insertPos-1;
}
data[ insertPos ] = insertVal;
}
/* Replace original lower-boundary element */
data[ firstElement-1 ] = lowerBoundary;
}
```

This code is the same as Listing 31-1's. Although most people would agree that the code's layout is much better than the first example's, the code is still not very readable. The layout is still crowded and offers no clue to the routine's logical organization. It's at about 0 on the number line of bad-to-good layout. The first example was contrived, but the second one isn't at all uncommon. I've seen programs several thousand lines long with layout at least as bad as this. With no documentation and bad variable names, overall readability was worse than in this example. This code is formatted for the computer; there's no evidence that the author expected the code to be read by humans. Listing 31-3 is an improvement.

Listing 31-3   Java layout example #3.

```
/* Use the insertion sort technique to sort the "data" array in ascending
order. This routine assumes that data[ firstElement ] is not the
first element in data and that data[ firstElement-1 ] can be accessed.
*/

public void InsertionSort( int[] data, int firstElement, int lastElement ) {
   // Replace element at lower boundary with an element guaranteed to be
   // first in a sorted list.
   int lowerBoundary = data[ firstElement-1 ];
   data[ firstElement-1 ] = SORT_MIN;

   /* The elements in positions firstElement through sortBoundary-1 are
   always sorted. In each pass through the loop, sortBoundary
   is increased, and the element at the position of the
   new sortBoundary probably isn't in its sorted place in the
   array, so it's inserted into the proper place somewhere
   between firstElement and sortBoundary.
   */
   for ( int sortBoundary = firstElement + 1; sortBoundary <= lastElement;
      sortBoundary++ ) {
      int insertVal = data[ sortBoundary ];
      int insertPos = sortBoundary;
      while ( insertVal < data[ insertPos - 1 ] ) {
         data[ insertPos ] = data[ insertPos - 1 ];
         insertPos = insertPos - 1;
      }
```

```
        data[ insertPos ] = insertVal;
    }

    // Replace original lower-boundary element
    data[ firstElement - 1 ] = lowerBoundary;
}
```

This layout of the routine is a strong positive on the number line of bad-to-good layout. The routine is now laid out according to principles that are explained throughout this chapter. The routine has become much more readable, and the effort that has been put into documentation and good variable names is now evident. The variable names were just as good in the earlier examples, but the layout was so poor that they weren't helpful.

The only difference between this example and the first two is the use of white space—the code and comments are exactly the same. White space is of use only to human readers—your computer could interpret any of the three fragments with equal ease. Don't feel bad if you can't do as well as your computer!

The Fundamental Theorem of Formatting

The Fundamental Theorem of Formatting says that good visual layout shows the logical structure of a program.

KEY POINT

Making the code look pretty is worth something, but it's worth less than showing the code's structure. If one technique shows the structure better and another looks better, use the one that shows the structure better. This chapter presents numerous examples of formatting styles that look good but that misrepresent the code's logical organization. In practice, prioritizing logical representation usually doesn't create ugly code—unless the logic of the code is ugly. Techniques that make good code look good and bad code look bad are more useful than techniques that make all code look good.

Human and Computer Interpretations of a Program

> Any fool can write code that a computer can understand. Good programmers write code that humans can understand.
> —*Martin Fowler*

Layout is a useful clue to the structure of a program. Whereas the computer might care exclusively about braces or *begin* and *end*, a human reader is apt to draw clues from the visual presentation of the code. Consider the code fragment in Listing 31-4, in which the indentation scheme makes it look to a human as if three statements are executed each time the loop is executed.

Listing 31-4 Java example of layout that tells different stories to humans and computers.

```
// swap left and right elements for whole array
for ( i = 0; i < MAX_ELEMENTS; i++ )
    leftElement = left[ i ];
    left[ i ]  = right[ i ];
    right[ i ] = leftElement;
```

If the code has no enclosing braces, the compiler will execute the first statement *MAX_ELEMENTS* times and the second and third statements one time each. The indentation makes it clear to you and me that the author of the code wanted all three statements to be executed together and intended to put braces around them. That won't be clear to the compiler. Listing 31-5 is another example:

Listing 31-5   Another Java example of layout that tells different stories to humans and computers.

```
x = 3+4 * 2+7;
```

A human reader of this code would be inclined to interpret the statement to mean that *x* is assigned the value *(3+4) * (2+7)*, or *63*. The computer will ignore the white space and obey the rules of precedence, interpreting the expression as *3 + (4*2) + 7*, or *18*. The point is that a good layout scheme would make the visual structure of a program match the logical structure, or tell the same story to the human that it tells to the computer.

How Much Is Good Layout Worth?

Our studies support the claim that knowledge of programming plans and rules of programming discourse can have a significant impact on program comprehension. In their book called [The] Elements of [Programming] Style, Kernighan and Plauger also identify what we would call discourse rules. Our empirical results put teeth into these rules: It is not merely a matter of aesthetics that programs should be written in a particular style. Rather there is a psychological basis for writing programs in a conventional manner: programmers have strong expectations that other programmers will follow these discourse rules. If the rules are violated, then the utility afforded by the expectations that programmers have built up over time is effectively nullified. The results from the experiments with novice and advanced student programmers and with professional programmers described in this paper provide clear support for these claims.

—Elliot Soloway and Kate Ehrlich

Cross-Reference Good layout is one key to readability. For details on the value of readability, see Section 34.3, "Write Programs for People First, Computers Second."

In layout, perhaps more than in any other aspect of programming, the difference between communicating with the computer and communicating with human readers comes into play. The smaller part of the job of programming is writing a program so that the computer can read it; the larger part is writing it so that other humans can read it.

In their classic paper "Perception in Chess," Chase and Simon reported on a study that compared the abilities of experts and novices to remember the positions of pieces in chess (1973). When pieces were arranged on the board as they might be during a game, the experts' memories were far superior to the novices'. When the pieces were arranged randomly, there was little difference between the memories of the experts and the novices. The traditional interpretation of this result is that an expert's memory is not inherently better than a novice's but that the expert has a knowledge structure that helps him or her remember particular kinds of information. When new information corresponds to the knowledge structure—in this case, the sensible placement of chess pieces—the expert can remember it easily. When new information doesn't correspond to a knowledge structure—the chess pieces are randomly positioned—the expert can't remember it any better than the novice.

A few years later, Ben Shneiderman duplicated Chase and Simon's results in the computer-programming arena and reported his results in a paper called "Exploratory Experiments in Programmer Behavior" (1976). Shneiderman found that when program statements were arranged in a sensible order, experts were able to remember them better than novices. When statements were shuffled, the experts' superiority was reduced. Shneiderman's results have been confirmed in other studies (McKeithen et al. 1981, Soloway and Ehrlich 1984). The basic concept has also been confirmed in the games Go and bridge and in electronics, music, and physics (McKeithen et al. 1981).

After I published the first edition of this book, Hank, one of the programmers who reviewed the manuscript, said "I was surprised that you didn't argue more strongly in favor of a brace style that looks like this:

```
for ( ...)
   {
   }
```

"I was surprised that you even included the brace style that looked like this:

```
for ( ...) {
}
```

"I thought that, with both Tony and me arguing for the first style, you'd prefer that."

I responded, "You mean you were arguing for the first style, and Tony was arguing for the second style, don't you? Tony argued for the second style, not the first."

Hank responded, "That's funny. The last project Tony and I worked on together, I preferred style #2, and Tony preferred style #1. We spent the whole project arguing about which style was best. I guess we talked one another into preferring each other's styles!"

This experience, as well as the studies cited above, suggest that structure helps experts to perceive, comprehend, and remember important features of programs. Expert programmers often cling to their own styles tenaciously, even when they're vastly different from other styles used by other expert programmers. The bottom line is that the details of a specific method of structuring a program are much less important than the fact that the program is structured consistently.

KEY POINT

Layout as Religion

The importance to comprehension and memory of structuring one's environment in a familiar way has led some researchers to hypothesize that layout might harm an expert's ability to read a program if the layout is different from the scheme the expert uses (Sheil 1981, Soloway and Ehrlich 1984). That possibility, compounded by the fact that layout is an aesthetic as well as a logical exercise, means that debates about program formatting often sound more like religious wars than philosophical discussions.

Cross-Reference If you're mixing software and religion, you might read Section 34.9, "Thou Shalt Rend Software and Religion Asunder" before reading the rest of this chapter.

At a coarse level, it's clear that some forms of layout are better than others. The successively better layouts of the same code at the beginning of this chapter made that evident. This book won't steer clear of the finer points of layout just because they're controversial. Good programmers should be open-minded about their layout practices and accept practices proven to be better than the ones they're used to, even if adjusting to a new method results in some initial discomfort.

Objectives of Good Layout

The results point out the fragility of programming expertise: advanced programmers have *strong* expectations about what programs should look like, and when those expectations are violated— in seemingly innocuous ways—their performance drops drastically.
—*Elliot Soloway and Kate Ehrlich*

Many decisions about layout details are a matter of subjective aesthetics; often, you can accomplish the same goal in many ways. You can make debates about subjective issues less subjective if you explicitly specify the criteria for your preferences. Explicitly, then, a good layout scheme should do the following:

Accurately represent the logical structure of the code   That's the Fundamental Theorem of Formatting again: the primary purpose of good layout is to show the logical structure of the code. Typically, programmers use indentation and other white space to show the logical structure.

Consistently represent the logical structure of the code   Some styles of layout have rules with so many exceptions that it's hard to follow the rules consistently. A good style applies to most cases.

Improve readability   An indentation strategy that's logical but that makes the code harder to read is useless. A layout scheme that calls for spaces only where they are required by the compiler is logical but not readable. A good layout scheme makes code easier to read.

Withstand modifications The best layout schemes hold up well under code modification. Modifying one line of code shouldn't require modifying several others.

In addition to these criteria, minimizing the number of lines of code needed to implement a simple statement or block is also sometimes considered.

How to Put the Layout Objectives to Use

KEY POINT

You can use the criteria for a good layout scheme to ground a discussion of layout so that the subjective reasons for preferring one style over another are brought into the open.

Weighting the criteria in different ways might lead to different conclusions. For example, if you feel strongly that minimizing the number of lines used on the screen is important—perhaps because you have a small computer screen—you might criticize one style because it uses two more lines for a routine parameter list than another.

31.2 Layout Techniques

You can achieve good layout by using a few layout tools in several different ways. This section describes each of them.

White Space

Usewhitespacetoenhancereadability. White space, including spaces, tabs, line breaks, and blank lines, is the main tool available to you for showing a program's structure.

Cross-Reference Some researchers have explored the similarity between the structure of a book and the structure of a program. For information, see "The Book Paradigm for Program Documentation" in Section 32.5.

You wouldn't think of writing a book with no spaces between words, no paragraph breaks, and no divisions into chapters. Such a book might be readable cover to cover, but it would be virtually impossible to skim it for a line of thought or to find an important passage. Perhaps more important, the book's layout wouldn't show the reader how the author intended to organize the information. The author's organization is an important clue to the topic's logical organization.

Breaking a book into chapters, paragraphs, and sentences shows a reader how to mentally organize a topic. If the organization isn't evident, the reader has to provide the organization, which puts a much greater burden on the reader and adds the possibility that the reader may never figure out how the topic is organized.

The information contained in a program is denser than the information contained in most books. Whereas you might read and understand a page of a book in a minute or two, most programmers can't read and understand a naked program listing at anything close to that rate. A program should give more organizational clues than a book, not fewer.

Grouping   From the other side of the looking glass, white space is grouping, making sure that related statements are grouped together.

In writing, thoughts are grouped into paragraphs. A well-written paragraph contains only sentences that relate to a particular thought. It shouldn't contain extraneous sentences. Similarly, a paragraph of code should contain statements that accomplish a single task and that are related to each other.

Blank lines   Just as it's important to group related statements, it's important to separate unrelated statements from each other. The start of a new paragraph in English is identified with indentation or a blank line. The start of a new paragraph of code should be identified with a blank line.

Using blank lines is a way to indicate how a program is organized. You can use them to divide groups of related statements into paragraphs, to separate routines from one another, and to highlight comments.

Although this particular statistic may be hard to put to work, a study by Gorla, Benander, and Benander found that the optimal number of blank lines in a program is about 8 to 16 percent. Above 16 percent, debug time increases dramatically (1990).

Indentation   Use indentation to show the logical structure of a program. As a rule, you should indent statements under the statement to which they are logically subordinate.

Indentation has been shown to be correlated with increased programmer comprehension. The article "Program Indentation and Comprehensibility" reported that several studies found correlations between indentation and improved comprehension (Miaria et al. 1983). Subjects scored 20 to 30 percent higher on a test of comprehension when programs had a two-to-four-spaces indentation scheme than they did when programs had no indentation at all.

The same study found that it was important to neither underemphasize nor overemphasize a program's logical structure. The lowest comprehension scores were achieved on programs that were not indented at all. The second lowest were achieved on programs that used six-space indentation. The study concluded that two-to-four-space indentation was optimal. Interestingly, many subjects in the experiment felt that the six-space indentation was easier to use than the smaller indentations, even though their scores were lower. That's probably because six-space indentation looks pleasing. But regardless of how pretty it looks, six-space indentation turns out to be less readable. This is an example of a collision between aesthetic appeal and readability.

Parentheses

Use more parentheses than you think you need. Use parentheses to clarify expressions that involve more than two terms. They may not be needed, but they add clarity and they don't cost you anything. For example, how are the following expressions evaluated?

C++ version: `12 + 4 % 3 * 7 / 8`

Microsoft Visual Basic version: `12 + 4 mod 3 * 7 / 8`

The key question is, did you have to think about how the expressions are evaluated? Can you be confident in your answer without checking some references? Even experienced programmers don't answer confidently, and that's why you should use parentheses whenever there's any doubt about how an expression is evaluated.

31.3 Layout Styles

Most layout issues have to do with laying out blocks, the groups of statements below control statements. A block is enclosed between braces or keywords: { and } in C++ and Java, *if-then-endif* in Visual Basic, and other similar structures in other languages. For simplicity, much of this discussion uses *begin* and *end* generically, assuming that you can figure out how the discussion applies to braces in C++ and Java or other blocking mechanisms in other languages. The following sections describe four general styles of layout:

- Pure blocks
- Emulating pure blocks
- Using *begin-end* pairs (braces) to designate block boundaries
- Endline layout

Pure Blocks

Much of the layout controversy stems from the inherent awkwardness of the more popular programming languages. A well-designed language has clear block structures that lend themselves to a natural indentation style. In Visual Basic, for example, each control construct has its own terminator and you can't use a control construct without using the terminator. Code is blocked naturally. Some examples in Visual Basic are shown in Listing 31-6, Listing 31-7, and Listing 31-8:

Listing 31-6 Visual Basic example of a pure *if* block.

```
If pixelColor = Color_Red Then
    statement1
    statement2
    ...
End If
```

Listing 31-7 Visual Basic example of a pure *while* block.

```
While pixelColor = Color_Red
    statement1
    statement2
    ...
Wend
```

Listing 31-8 Visual Basic example of a pure *case* block.

```
Select Case pixelColor
    Case Color_Red
        statement1
        statement2
        ...
    Case Color_Green
        statement1
        statement2
        ...
    Case Else
        statement1
        statement2
        ...
End Select
```

A control construct in Visual Basic always has a beginning statement—*If-Then*, *While*, and *Select-Case* in the examples—and it always has a corresponding *End* statement. Indenting the inside of the structure isn't a controversial practice, and the options for aligning the other keywords are somewhat limited. Listing 31-9 is an abstract representation of how this kind of formatting works:

Listing 31-9 Abstract example of the pure-block layout style.

In this example, statement A begins the control construct and statement D ends the control construct. The alignment between the two provides solid visual closure.

The controversy about formatting control structures arises in part from the fact that some languages don't *require* block structures. You can have an *if-then* followed by a single statement and not have a formal block. You have to add a *begin-end* pair or opening and closing braces to create a block rather than getting one automatically with each control construct. Uncoupling *begin* and *end* from the control structure–as languages like C++ and Java do with { and }–leads to questions about where to put the *begin* and *end*. Consequently, many indentation problems are problems only because you have to compensate for poorly designed language structures. Various ways to compensate are described in the following sections.

Emulating Pure Blocks

A good approach in languages that don't have pure blocks is to view the *begin* and *end* keywords (or { and } tokens) as extensions of the control construct they're used with. Then it's sensible to try to emulate the Visual Basic formatting in your language. Listing 31-10 is an abstract view of the visual structure you're trying to emulate:

Listing 31-10 Abstract example of the pure-block layout style.

In this style, the control structure opens the block in statement A and finishes the block in statement D. This implies that the *begin* should be at the end of statement A and the *end* should be statement D. In the abstract, to emulate pure blocks, you'd have to do something like Listing 31-11:

Listing 31-11 Abstract example of emulating the pure-block style.

Some examples of how the style looks in C++ are shown in Listing 31-12, Listing 31-13, and Listing 31-14:

Listing 31-12   C++ example of emulating a pure *if* block.

```
if ( pixelColor == Color_Red ) {
    statement1;
    statement2;
    ...
}
```

Listing 31-13   C++ example of emulating a pure *while* block.

```
while ( pixelColor == Color_Red ) {
    statement1;
    statement2;
    ...
}
```

Listing 31-14   C++ example of emulating a pure *switch/case* block.

```
switch ( pixelColor ) {
    case Color_Red:
        statement1;
        statement2;
        ...
    break;
    case Color_Green:
        statement1;
        statement2;
        ...
    break;
    default:
        statement1;
        statement2;
        ...
    break;
}
```

This style of alignment works pretty well. It looks good, you can apply it consistently, and it's maintainable. It supports the Fundamental Theorem of Formatting in that it helps to show the logical structure of the code. It's a reasonable style choice. This style is standard in Java and common in C++.

Using *begin-end* Pairs (Braces) to Designate Block Boundaries

A substitute for a pure-block structure is to view *begin-end* pairs as block boundaries. (The following discussion uses *begin-end* to refer generically to *begin-end* pairs, braces, and other equivalent language structures.) If you take that approach, you view the *begin* and the *end* as statements that follow the control construct rather than as fragments that are part of it. Graphically, this is the ideal, just as it was with the pure-block emulation shown again in Listing 31-15:

Listing 31-15   Abstract example of the pure-block layout style.

But in this style, to treat the *begin* and the *end* as parts of the block structure rather than the control statement, you have to put the *begin* at the beginning of the block (rather than at the end of the control statement) and the *end* at the end of the block (rather than terminating the control statement). In the abstract, you'll have to do something like what's done in Listing 31-16:

Listing 31-16   Abstract example of using *begin* and *end* as block boundaries.

Some examples of how using *begin* and *end* as block boundaries looks in C++ are shown in Listing 31-17, Listing 31-18, and Listing 31-19:

Listing 31-17   C++ example of using *begin* and *end* as block boundaries in an *if* block.

```
if ( pixelColor == Color_Red )
    {
    statement1;
    statement2;
    ...
    }
```

Listing 31-18   C++ example of using *begin* and *end* as block boundaries in a *while* block.

```
while ( pixelColor == Color_Red )
    {
    statement1;
    statement2;
    ...
    }
```

Listing 31-19 C++ example of using *begin* and *end* as block boundaries in a *switch/case* block.

```
switch ( pixelColor )
    {
    case Color_Red:
        statement1;
        statement2;
        ...
        break;
    case Color_Green:
        statement1;
        statement2;
        ...
        break;
    default:
        statement1;
        statement2;
        ...
        break;
    }
```

This alignment style works well; it supports the Fundamental Theorem of Formatting (once again, by exposing the code's underlying logical structure). Its only limitation is that it can't be applied literally in *switch/case* statements in C++ and Java, as shown by Listing 31-19. (The *break* keyword is a substitute for the closing brace, but there is no equivalent to the opening brace.)

Endline Layout

Another layout strategy is "endline layout," which refers to a large group of layout strategies in which the code is indented to the middle or end of the line. The endline indentation is used to align a block with the keyword that began it, to make a routine's subsequent parameters line up under its first parameter, to line up cases in a *case* statement, and for other similar purposes. Listing 31-20 is an abstract example:

Listing 31-20 Abstract example of the endline layout style.

In this example, statement A begins the control construct and statement D ends it. Statements B, C, and D are aligned under the keyword that began the block in statement A.

The uniform indentation of B, C, and D shows that they're grouped together. Listing 31-21 is a less abstract example of code formatted using this strategy:

Listing 31-21   Visual Basic example of endline layout of a *while* block.

```
While ( pixelColor = Color_Red )
        statement1;
        statement2;
        ...
        Wend
```

In the example, the *begin* is placed at the end of the line rather than under the corresponding keyword. Some people prefer to put *begin* under the keyword, but choosing between those two fine points is the least of this style's problems.

The endline layout style works acceptably in a few cases. Listing 31-22 is an example in which it works:

Listing 31-22   A rare Visual Basic example in which endline layout seems appealing.

```
If ( soldCount > 1000 ) Then
                            markdown = 0.10
                            profit = 0.05
                        Else
                            markdown = 0.05
                        End If
```

> The *else* keyword is aligned with the *then* keyword above it.

In this case, the *Then*, *Else*, and *End If* keywords are aligned and the code following them is also aligned. The visual effect is a clear logical structure.

If you look critically at the earlier *case*-statement example, you can probably predict the unraveling of this style. As the conditional expression becomes more complicated, the style will give useless or misleading clues about the logical structure. Listing 31-23 is an example of how the style breaks down when it's used with a more complicated conditional:

Listing 31-23   A more typical Visual Basic example, in which endline layout breaks down.

CODING HORROR

```
If ( soldCount > 10 And prevMonthSales > 10 ) Then
   If ( soldCount > 100 And prevMonthSales > 10 ) Then
      If ( soldCount > 1000 ) Then
                            markdown = 0.1
                            profit = 0.05
                        Else
                            markdown = 0.05
                        End If
                                        Else
                                            markdown = 0.025
                                        End If
                    Else
                        markdown = 0.0
                    End If
```

What's the reason for the bizarre formatting of the *Else* clauses at the end of the example? They're consistently indented under the corresponding keywords, but it's hard to argue that their indentations clarify the logical structure. And if the code were modified so that the length of the first line changed, the endline style would require that the indentation of corresponding statements be changed. This poses a maintenance problem that pure block, pure-block emulation, and using *begin-end* to designate block boundaries do not.

You might think that these examples are contrived just to make a point, but this style has been persistent despite its drawbacks. Numerous textbooks and programming references have recommended this style. The earliest book I saw that recommended this style was published in the mid-1970s, and the most recent was published in 2003.

Overall, endline layout is inaccurate, hard to apply consistently, and hard to maintain. You'll see other problems with endline layout throughout the chapter.

Which Style Is Best?

If you're working in Visual Basic, use pure-block indentation. (The Visual Basic IDE makes it hard not to use this style anyway.)

In Java, standard practice is to use pure-block indentation.

In C++, you might simply choose the style you like or the one that is preferred by the majority of people on your team. Either pure-block emulation or *begin-end* block boundaries work equally well. The only study that has compared the two styles found no statistically significant difference between the two as far as understandability is concerned (Hansen and Yim 1987).

Neither of the styles is foolproof, and each requires an occasional "reasonable and obvious" compromise. You might prefer one or the other for aesthetic reasons. This book uses pure-block style in its code examples, so you can see many more illustrations of how that style works just by skimming through its examples. Once you've chosen a style, you reap the most benefit from good layout when you apply it consistently.

31.4 Laying Out Control Structures

Cross-Reference For details on documenting control structures, see "Commenting Control Structures" in Section 32.5. For a discussion of other aspects of control structures, see Chapters 14 through 19.

The layout of some program elements is primarily a matter of aesthetics. Layout of control structures, however, affects readability and comprehensibility and is therefore a practical priority.

Fine Points of Formatting Control-Structure Blocks

Working with control-structure blocks requires attention to some fine details. Here are some guidelines:

Avoid unindented* begin-end *pairs In the style shown in Listing 31-24, the *begin-end* pair is aligned with the control structure, and the statements that *begin* and *end* enclose are indented under *begin*.

Listing 31-24 Java example of unindented *begin-end* pairs.

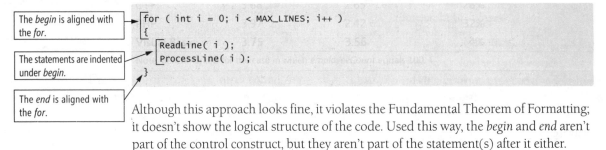

The *begin* is aligned with the *for*.

The statements are indented under *begin*.

The *end* is aligned with the *for*.

```
for ( int i = 0; i < MAX_LINES; i++ )
{
    ReadLine( i );
    ProcessLine( i );
}
```

Although this approach looks fine, it violates the Fundamental Theorem of Formatting; it doesn't show the logical structure of the code. Used this way, the *begin* and *end* aren't part of the control construct, but they aren't part of the statement(s) after it either.

Listing 31-25 is an abstract view of this approach:

Listing 31-25 Abstract example of misleading indentation.

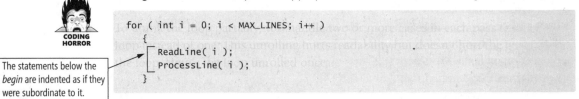

In this example, is statement B subordinate to statement A? It doesn't look like part of statement A, and it doesn't look as if it's subordinate to it either. If you have used this approach, change to one of the two layout styles described earlier and your formatting will be more consistent.

***Avoid double indentation with* begin *and* end** A corollary to the rule against nonindented *begin-end* pairs is the rule against doubly indented *begin-end* pairs. In this style, shown in Listing 31-26, *begin* and *end* are indented and the statements they enclose are indented again:

Listing 31-26 Java example of inappropriate double indentation of *begin-end* block.

CODING HORROR

```
for ( int i = 0; i < MAX_LINES; i++ )
    {
        ReadLine( i );
        ProcessLine( i );
    }
```

The statements below the *begin* are indented as if they were subordinate to it.

This is another example of a style that looks fine but violates the Fundamental Theorem of Formatting. One study showed no difference in comprehension between programs that are singly indented and programs that are doubly indented (Miaria et al. 1983), but this style doesn't accurately show the logical structure of the program. *ReadLine()* and *ProcessLine()* are shown as if they are logically subordinate to the *begin-end* pair, and they aren't.

The approach also exaggerates the complexity of a program's logical structure. Which of the structures shown in Listing 31-27 and Listing 31-28 looks more complicated?

Listing 31-27   Abstract Structure 1.

Listing 31-28   Abstract Structure 2.

Both are abstract representations of the structure of the *for* loop. Abstract Structure 1 looks more complicated even though it represents the same code as Abstract Structure 2. If you were to nest statements to two or three levels, double indentation would give you four or six levels of indentation. The layout that resulted would look more complicated than the actual code would be. Avoid the problem by using pure-block emulation or by using *begin* and *end* as block boundaries and aligning *begin* and *end* with the statements they enclose.

Other Considerations

Although indentation of blocks is the major issue in formatting control structures, you'll run into a few other kinds of issues, so here are some more guidelines:

Use blank lines between paragraphs   Some blocks of code aren't demarcated with *begin-end* pairs. A logical block—a group of statements that belong together—should be treated the way paragraphs in English are. Separate them from one another with blank lines. Listing 31-29 shows an example of paragraphs that should be separated:

Listing 31-29 C++ example of code that should be grouped and separated.

```
cursor.start = startingScanLine;
cursor.end   = endingScanLine;
window.title = editWindow.title;
window.dimensions       = editWindow.dimensions;
window.foregroundColor = userPreferences.foregroundColor;
cursor.blinkRate        = editMode.blinkRate;
window.backgroundColor = userPreferences.backgroundColor;
SaveCursor( cursor );
SetCursor( cursor );
```

Cross-Reference If you use the Pseudocode Programming Process, your blocks of code will be separated automatically. For details, see Chapter 9, "The Pseudocode Programming Process."

This code looks all right, but blank lines would improve it in two ways. First, when you have a group of statements that don't have to be executed in any particular order, it's tempting to lump them all together this way. You don't need to further refine the statement order for the computer, but human readers appreciate more clues about which statements need to be performed in a specific order and which statements are just along for the ride. The discipline of putting blank lines throughout a program makes you think harder about which statements really belong together. The revised fragment in Listing 31-30 shows how this collection should really be organized.

Listing 31-30 C++ example of code that is appropriately grouped and separated.

These lines set up a text window.

These lines set up a cursor and should be separated from the preceding lines.

```
window.dimensions = editWindow.dimensions;
window.title = editWindow.title;
window.backgroundColor = userPreferences.backgroundColor;
window.foregroundColor = userPreferences.foregroundColor;

cursor.start = startingScanLine;
cursor.end = endingScanLine;
cursor.blinkRate = editMode.blinkRate;
SaveCursor( cursor );
SetCursor( cursor );
```

The reorganized code shows that two things are happening. In the first example, the lack of statement organization and blank lines, and the old aligned-equals signs trick, make the statements look more related than they are.

The second way in which using blank lines tends to improve code is that it opens up natural spaces for comments. In Listing 31-30, a comment above each block would nicely supplement the improved layout.

Format single-statement blocks consistently A single-statement block is a single statement following a control structure, such as one statement following an *if* test. In such a case, *begin* and *end* aren't needed for correct compilation and you have the three style options shown in Listing 31-31:

Listing 31-31   Java example of style options for single-statement blocks.

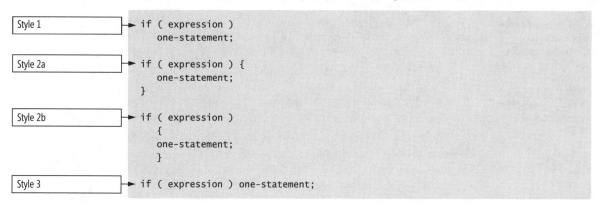

There are arguments in favor of each of these approaches. Style 1 follows the indentation scheme used with blocks, so it's consistent with other approaches. Style 2 (either 2a or 2b) is also consistent, and the *begin-end* pair reduces the chance that you'll add statements after the *if* test and forget to add *begin* and *end*. This would be a particularly subtle error because the indentation would tell you that everything is OK, but the indentation wouldn't be interpreted the same way by the compiler. Style 3's main advantage over Style 2 is that it's easier to type. Its advantage over Style 1 is that if it's copied to another place in the program, it's more likely to be copied correctly. Its disadvantage is that in a line-oriented debugger, the debugger treats the line as one line and the debugger doesn't show you whether it executes the statement after the *if* test.

I've used Style 1 and have been the victim of incorrect modification many times. I don't like the exception to the indentation strategy caused by Style 3, so I avoid it altogether. On a group project, I favor either variation of Style 2 for its consistency and safe modifiability. Regardless of the style you choose, use it consistently and use the same style for *if* tests and all loops.

For complicated expressions, put separate conditions on separate lines   Put each part of a complicated expression on its own line. Listing 31-32 shows an expression that's formatted without any attention to readability:

Listing 31-32   Java example of an essentially unformatted (and unreadable) complicated expression.

```
if ((('0' <= inChar) && (inChar <= '9')) || (('a' <= inChar) &&
    (inChar <= 'z')) || (('A' <= inChar) && (inChar <= 'Z')))
    ...
```

This is an example of formatting for the computer instead of for human readers. By breaking the expression into several lines, as in Listing 31-33, you can improve readability.

Listing 31-33 Java example of a readable complicated expression.

Cross-Reference Another technique for making complicated expressions readable is to put them into boolean functions. For details on that technique and other readability techniques, see Section 19.1, "Boolean Expressions."

```
if ( ( ( '0' <= inChar ) && ( inChar <= '9' ) ) ||
     ( ( 'a' <= inChar ) && ( inChar <= 'z' ) ) ||
     ( ( 'A' <= inChar ) && ( inChar <= 'Z' ) ) )
     ...
```

The second fragment uses several formatting techniques—indentation, spacing, number-line ordering, and making each incomplete line obvious—and the result is a readable expression. Moreover, the intent of the test is clear. If the expression contained a minor error, such as using a z instead of a Z, it would be obvious in code formatted this way, whereas the error wouldn't be clear with less careful formatting.

Cross-Reference For details on the use of *goto*s, see Section 17.3, "goto."

***Avoid* gotos**   The original reason to avoid *goto*s was that they made it difficult to prove that a program was correct. That's a nice argument for all the people who want to prove their programs correct, which is practically no one. The more pressing problem for most programmers is that *goto*s make code hard to format. Do you indent all the code between the *goto* and the label it goes to? What if you have several *goto*s to the same label? Do you indent each new one under the previous one? Here's some advice for formatting *goto*s:

Goto labels should be left-aligned in all caps and should include the programmer's name, home phone number, and credit card number.
—*Abdul Nizar*

- Avoid *goto*s. This sidesteps the formatting problem altogether.

- Use a name in all caps for the label the code goes to. This makes the label obvious.

- Put the statement containing the *goto* on a line by itself. This makes the *goto* obvious.

- Put the label the *goto* goes to on a line by itself. Surround it with blank lines. This makes the label obvious. Outdent the line containing the label to the left margin to make the label as obvious as possible.

Listing 31-34 shows these *goto* layout conventions at work.

Cross-Reference For other methods of addressing this problem, see "Error Processing and *goto*s" in Section 17.3.

Listing 31-34 C++ example of making the best of a bad situation (using *goto*).

```
void PurgeFiles( ErrorCode & errorCode ) {
   FileList fileList;
   int numFilesToPurge = 0;
   MakePurgeFileList( fileList, numFilesToPurge );

   errorCode = FileError_Success;
   int fileIndex = 0;
   while ( fileIndex < numFilesToPurge ) {
      DataFile fileToPurge;
      if ( !FindFile( fileList[ fileIndex ], fileToPurge ) ) {
         errorCode = FileError_NotFound;
         goto END_PROC;
      }
```

Here's a *goto*.

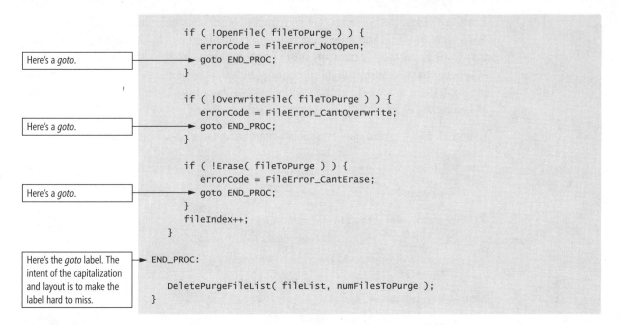

Here's a *goto*.

Here's a *goto*.

Here's a *goto*.

Here's the *goto* label. The intent of the capitalization and layout is to make the label hard to miss.

```
        if ( !OpenFile( fileToPurge ) ) {
            errorCode = FileError_NotOpen;
            goto END_PROC;
        }

        if ( !OverwriteFile( fileToPurge ) ) {
            errorCode = FileError_CantOverwrite;
            goto END_PROC;
        }

        if ( !Erase( fileToPurge ) ) {
            errorCode = FileError_CantErase;
            goto END_PROC;
        }
        fileIndex++;
    }

END_PROC:

    DeletePurgeFileList( fileList, numFilesToPurge );
}
```

Cross-Reference For details on using *case* statements, see Section 15.2, "*case* Statements."

The C++ example in Listing 31-34 is relatively long so that you can see a case in which an expert programmer might conscientiously decide that a *goto* is the best design choice. In such a case, the formatting shown is about the best you can do.

No endline exception for* case *statements   One of the hazards of endline layout comes up in the formatting of *case* statements. A popular style of formatting *cases* is to indent them to the right of the description of each case, as shown in Listing 31-35. The big problem with this style is that it's a maintenance headache.

Listing 31-35   C++ example of hard-to-maintain endline layout of a *case* statement.

```
switch ( ballColor ) {
   case BallColor_Blue:             Rollout();
                                    break;
   case BallColor_Orange:           SpinOnFinger();
                                    break;
   case BallColor_FluorescentGreen: Spike();
                                    break;
   case BallColor_White:            KnockCoverOff();
                                    break;
   case BallColor_WhiteAndBlue:     if ( mainColor == BallColor_White ) {
                                       KnockCoverOff();
                                    }
                                    else if ( mainColor == BallColor_Blue ) {
                                       Rollout();
                                    }
                                    break;
   default:                         FatalError( "Unrecognized kind of ball." );
                                    break;
}
```

If you add a case with a longer name than any of the existing names, you have to shift out all the cases and the code that goes with them. The large initial indentation makes it awkward to accommodate any more logic, as shown in the *WhiteAndBlue* case. The solution is to switch to your standard indentation increment. If you indent statements in a loop three spaces, indent cases in a *case* statement the same number of spaces, as in Listing 31-36:

Listing 31-36 C++ example of good standard indentation of a *case* statement.

```
switch ( ballColor ) {
   case BallColor_Blue:
      Rollout();
      break;
   case BallColor_Orange:
      SpinOnFinger();
      break;
   case BallColor_FluorescentGreen:
      Spike();
      break;
   case BallColor_White:
      KnockCoverOff();
      break;
   case BallColor_WhiteAndBlue:
      if ( mainColor == BallColor_White ) {
         KnockCoverOff();
      }
      else if ( mainColor == BallColor_Blue ) {
         Rollout();
      }
      break;
   default:
      FatalError( "Unrecognized kind of ball." );
      break;
}
```

This is an instance in which many people might prefer the looks of the first example. For the ability to accommodate longer lines, consistency, and maintainability, however, the second approach wins hands down.

If you have a *case* statement in which all the cases are exactly parallel and all the actions are short, you could consider putting the case and action on the same line. In most instances, however, you'll live to regret it. The formatting is a pain initially and breaks under modification, and it's hard to keep the structure of all the cases parallel as some of the short actions become longer ones.

31.5 Laying Out Individual Statements

This section explains many ways to improve individual statements in a program.

Statement Length

Cross-Reference For details on documenting individual statements, see "Commenting Individual Lines" in Section 32.5.

A common and somewhat outdated rule is to limit statement line length to 80 characters. Here are the reasons:

■ Lines longer than 80 characters are hard to read.

■ The 80-character limitation discourages deep nesting.

■ Lines longer than 80 characters often won't fit on 8.5" x 11" paper, especially when code is printed "2 up" (2 pages of code to each physical printout page).

With larger screens, narrow typefaces, and landscape mode, the 80-character limit appears increasingly arbitrary. A single 90-character-long line is usually more readable than one that has been broken in two just to avoid spilling over the 80th column. With modern technology, it's probably all right to exceed 80 columns occasionally.

Using Spaces for Clarity

Add white space within a statement for the sake of readability:

Use spaces to make logical expressions readable   The expression

```
while(pathName[startPath+position]<>';') and
   ((startPath+position)<length(pathName)) do
```

is about as readable as Idareyoutoreadthis.

As a rule, you should separate identifiers from other identifiers with spaces. If you use this rule, the *while* expression looks like this:

```
while ( pathName[ startPath+position ] <> ';' ) and
   (( startPath + position ) < length( pathName )) do
```

Some software artists might recommend enhancing this particular expression with additional spaces to emphasize its logical structure, this way:

```
while ( pathName[ startPath + position ] <> ';' ) and
   ( ( startPath + position ) < length( pathName ) ) do
```

This is fine, although the first use of spaces was sufficient to ensure readability. Extra spaces hardly ever hurt, however, so be generous with them.

Use spaces to make array references readable The expression

```
grossRate[census[groupId].gender,census[groupId].ageGroup]
```

is no more readable than the earlier dense *while* expression. Use spaces around each index in the array to make the indexes readable. If you use this rule, the expression looks like this:

```
grossRate[ census[ groupId ].gender, census[ groupId ].ageGroup ]
```

Use spaces to make routine arguments readable What is the fourth argument to the following routine?

```
ReadEmployeeData(maxEmps,empData,inputFile,empCount,inputError);
```

Now, what is the fourth argument to the following routine?

```
GetCensus( inputFile, empCount, empData, maxEmps, inputError );
```

Which one was easier to find? This is a realistic, worthwhile question because argument positions are significant in all major procedural languages. It's common to have a routine specification on one half of your screen and the call to the routine on the other half, and to compare each formal parameter with each actual parameter.

Formatting Continuation Lines

One of the most vexing problems of program layout is deciding what to do with the part of a statement that spills over to the next line. Do you indent it by the normal indentation amount? Do you align it under the keyword? What about assignments?

Here's a sensible, consistent approach that's particularly useful in Java, C, C++, Visual Basic, and other languages that encourage long variable names:

Make the incompleteness of a statement obvi . Sometimes a statement must be broken across lines, either because it's longer than programming standards allow or because it's too absurdly long to put on one line. Make it obvious that the part of the statement on the first line is only part of a statement. The easiest way to do that is to break up the statement so that the part on the first line is blatantly incorrect syntactically if it stands alone. Some examples are shown in Listing 31-37:

Listing 31-37 Java examples of obviously incomplete statements.

The && signals that the statement isn't complete.	```while (pathName[startPath + position] != ';') && ((startPath + position) <= pathName.length()) ...```
The plus sign (+) signals that the statement isn't complete.	```totalBill = totalBill + customerPurchases[customerID] + SalesTax(customerPurchases[customerID]); ...```
The comma (,) signals that the statement isn't complete.	```DrawLine(window.north, window.south, window.east, window.west, currentWidth, currentAttribute); ...```

In addition to telling the reader that the statement isn't complete on the first line, the break helps prevent incorrect modifications. If the continuation of the statement were deleted, the first line wouldn't look as if you had merely forgotten a parenthesis or semicolon—it would clearly need something more.

An alternative approach that also works well is to put the continuation character at the beginning of the continuation line, as shown in Listing 31-38.

Listing 31-38   Java examples of obviously incomplete statements—alternate style.

```
while ( pathName[ startPath + position ] != ';' )
   && ( ( startPath + position ) <= pathName.length() )
...

totalBill = totalBill + customerPurchases[ customerID ]
   + SalesTax( customerPurchases[ customerID ] );
```

While this style won't induce a syntax error with a hanging *&&* or *+*, it does make it easier to scan for operators at the left edge of the column, where the text is aligned, than at the right edge, where it's ragged. It has the additional advantage of illuminating the structure of operations, as illustrated in Listing 31-39.

Listing 31-39   Java example of a style that illuminates complex operations.

```
totalBill = totalBill
   + customerPurchases[ customerID ]
   + CitySalesTax( customerPurchases[ customerID ] )
   + StateSalesTax( customerPurchases[ customerID ] )
   + FootballStadiumTax()
   - SalesTaxExemption( customerPurchases[ customerID ] );
```

Keep closely related elements together   When you break a line, keep things together that belong together: array references, arguments to a routine, and so on. The example shown in Listing 31-40 is poor form:

Listing 31-40   Java example of breaking a line poorly.

```
customerBill = PreviousBalance( paymentHistory[ customerID ] ) + LateCharge(
   paymentHistory[ customerID ] );
```

CODING HORROR

Admittedly, this line break follows the guideline of making the incompleteness of the statement obvious, but it does so in a way that makes the statement unnecessarily hard to read. You might find a case in which the break is necessary, but in this case it isn't. It's better to keep the array references all on one line. Listing 31-41 shows better formatting:

Listing 31-41 Java example of breaking a line well.

```
customerBill = PreviousBalance( paymentHistory[ customerID ] ) +
   LateCharge( paymentHistory[ customerID ] );
```

Indent routine-call continuation lines the standard amount If you normally indent three spaces for statements in a loop or a conditional, indent the continuation lines for a routine by three spaces. Some examples are shown in Listing 31-42:

Listing 31-42 Java examples of indenting routine-call continuation lines using the standard indentation increment.

```
DrawLine( window.north, window.south, window.east, window.west,
   currentWidth, currentAttribute );
SetFontAttributes( faceName[ fontId ], size[ fontId ], bold[ fontId ],
   italic[ fontId ], syntheticAttribute[ fontId ].underline,
   syntheticAttribute[ fontId ].strikeout );
```

One alternative to this approach is to line up the continuation lines under the first argument to the routine, as shown in Listing 31-43:

Listing 31-43 Java examples of indenting a routine-call continuation line to emphasize routine names.

```
DrawLine( window.north, window.south, window.east, window.west,
          currentWidth, currentAttribute );
SetFontAttributes( faceName[ fontId ], size[ fontId ], bold[ fontId ],
                   italic[ fontId ], syntheticAttribute[ fontId ].underline,
                   syntheticAttribute[ fontId ].strikeout );
```

From an aesthetic point of view, this looks a little ragged compared to the first approach. It is also difficult to maintain as routine names change, argument names change, and so on. Most programmers tend to gravitate toward the first style over time.

Make it easy to find the end of a continuation line One problem with the approach shown above is that you can't easily find the end of each line. Another alternative is to put each argument on a line of its own and indicate the end of the group with a closing parenthesis. Listing 31-44 shows how it looks.

Listing 31-44 Java examples of formatting routine-call continuation lines one argument to a line.

```
DrawLine(
   window.north,
   window.south,
   window.east,
   window.west,
   currentWidth,
```

```
        currentAttribute
);

SetFontAttributes(
    faceName[ fontId ],
    size[ fontId ],
    bold[ fontId ],
    italic[ fontId ],
    syntheticAttribute[ fontId ].underline,
    syntheticAttribute[ fontId ].strikeout
);
```

Obviously, this approach takes up a lot of real estate. If the arguments to a routine are long object-field references or pointer names, however, as the last two are, using one argument per line improves readability substantially. The); at the end of the block makes the end of the call clear. You also don't have to reformat when you add a parameter; you just add a new line.

In practice, usually only a few routines need to be broken into multiple lines. You can handle others on one line. Any of the three options for formatting multiple-line routine calls works all right if you use it consistently.

Indent control-statement continuation lines the standard amount   If you run out of room for a *for* loop, a *while* loop, or an *if* statement, indent the continuation line by the same amount of space that you indent statements in a loop or after an *if* statement. Two examples are shown in Listing 31-45:

Listing 31-45   Java examples of indenting control-statement continuation lines.

This continuation line is indented the standard number of spaces...

...as is this one.

```
while ( ( pathName[ startPath + position ] != ';' ) &&
    ( ( startPath + position ) <= pathName.length() ) ) {
    ...
}

for ( int employeeNum = employee.first + employee.offset;
    employeeNum < employee.first + employee.offset + employee.total;
    employeeNum++ ) {
    ...
}
```

Cross-Reference Sometimes the best solution to a complicated test is to put it into a boolean function. For examples, see "Making Complicated Expressions Simple" in Section 19.1.

This meets the criteria set earlier in the chapter. The continuation part of the statement is done logically—it's always indented underneath the statement it continues. The indentation can be done consistently—it uses only a few more spaces than the original line. It's as readable as anything else, and it's as maintainable as anything else. In some cases you might be able to improve readability by fine-tuning the indentation or spacing, but be sure to keep the maintainability tradeoff in mind when you consider fine-tuning.

Do not align right sides of assignment statements In the first edition of this book I recommended aligning the right sides of statements containing assignments as shown in Listing 31-46:

Listing 31-46 Java example of endline layout used for assignment-statement continuation—bad practice.

```
customerPurchases = customerPurchases + CustomerSales( CustomerID );
customerBill      = customerBill + customerPurchases;
totalCustomerBill = customerBill + PreviousBalance( customerID ) +
                    LateCharge( customerID );
customerRating    = Rating( customerID, totalCustomerBill );
```

With the benefit of 10 years' hindsight, I have found that, while this indentation style might look attractive, it becomes a headache to maintain the alignment of the equals signs as variable names change and code is run through tools that substitute tabs for spaces and spaces for tabs. It is also hard to maintain as lines are moved among different parts of the program that have different levels of indentation.

For consistency with the other indentation guidelines as well as maintainability, treat groups of statements containing assignment operations just as you would treat other statements, as Listing 31-47 shows:

Listing 31-47 Java example of standard indentation for assignment-statement continuation—good practice.

```
customerPurchases = customerPurchases + CustomerSales( CustomerID );
customerBill = customerBill + customerPurchases;
totalCustomerBill = customerBill + PreviousBalance( customerID ) +
    LateCharge( customerID );
customerRating = Rating( customerID, totalCustomerBill );
```

Indent assignment-statement continuation lines the standard amount In Listing 31-47, the continuation line for the third assignment statement is indented the standard amount. This is done for the same reasons that assignment statements in general are not formatted in any special way: general readability and maintainability.

Using Only One Statement Per Line

Modern languages such as C++ and Java allow multiple statements per line. The power of free formatting is a mixed blessing, however, when it comes to putting multiple statements on a line. This line contains several statements that could logically be separated onto lines of their own:

```
i = 0; j = 0; k = 0; DestroyBadLoopNames( i, j, k );
```

One argument in favor of putting several statements on one line is that it requires fewer lines of screen space or printer paper, which allows more of the code to be viewed at once. It's also a way to group related statements, and some programmers believe that it provides optimization clues to the compiler.

These are good reasons, but the reasons to limit yourself to one statement per line are more compelling:

- Putting each statement on a line of its own provides an accurate view of a program's complexity. It doesn't hide complexity by making complex statements look trivial. Statements that are complex look complex. Statements that are easy look easy.

Cross-Reference Code-level performance optimizations are discussed in Chapter 25, "Code-Tuning Strategies," and Chapter 26, "Code-Tuning Techniques."

- Putting several statements on one line doesn't provide optimization clues to modern compilers. Today's optimizing compilers don't depend on formatting clues to do their optimizations. This is illustrated later in this section.

- With statements on their own lines, the code reads from top to bottom, instead of top to bottom and left to right. When you're looking for a specific line of code, your eye should be able to follow the left margin of the code. It shouldn't have to dip into each and every line just because a single line might contain two statements.

- With statements on their own lines, it's easy to find syntax errors when your compiler provides only the line numbers of the errors. If you have multiple statements on a line, the line number doesn't tell you which statement is in error.

- With one statement to a line, it's easy to step through the code with line-oriented debuggers. If you have several statements on a line, the debugger executes them all at once and you have to switch to assembler to step through individual statements.

- With one to a line, it's easy to edit individual statements—to delete a line or temporarily convert a line to a comment. If you have multiple statements on a line, you have to do your editing between other statements.

In C++, avoid using multiple operations per line (side effects)   Side effects are consequences of a statement other than its main consequence. In C++, the ++ operator on a line that contains other operations is a side effect. Likewise, assigning a value to a variable and using the left side of the assignment in a conditional is a side effect.

Side effects tend to make code difficult to read. For example, if *n* equals 4, what is the printout of the statement shown in Listing 31-48?

Listing 31-48   C++ example of an unpredictable side effect.

```
PrintMessage( ++n, n + 2 );
```

Is it 4 and 6? Is it 5 and 7? Is it 5 and 6? The answer is "None of the above." The first argument, ++n, is 5. But the C++ language does not define the order in which terms in an expression or arguments to a routine are evaluated. So the compiler can evaluate the second argument, n + 2, either before or after the first argument; the result might be either 6 or 7, depending on the compiler. Listing 31-49 shows how you should rewrite the statement so that the intent is clear:

Listing 31-49   C++ example of avoiding an unpredictable side effect.

```
++n;
PrintMessage( n, n + 2 );
```

If you're still not convinced that you should put side effects on lines by themselves, try to figure out what the routine shown in Listing 31-50 does:

Listing 31-50   C example of too many operations on a line.

```
strcpy( char * t, char * s ) {
   while ( *++t = *++s )
      ;
}
```

Some experienced C programmers don't see the complexity in that example because it's a familiar function. They look at it and say, "That's *strcpy()*." In this case, however, it's not quite *strcpy()*. It contains an error. If you said, "That's *strcpy()*" when you saw the code, you were recognizing the code, not reading it. This is exactly the situation you're in when you debug a program: the code that you overlook because you "recognize" it rather than read it can contain the error that's harder to find than it needs to be.

The fragment shown in Listing 31-51 is functionally identical to the first and is more readable:

Listing 31-51   C example of a readable number of operations on each line.

```
strcpy( char * t, char * s ) {
   do {
      ++t;
      ++s;
      *t = *s;
   }
   while ( *t != '\0' );
}
```

In the reformatted code, the error is apparent. Clearly, t and s are incremented before *s is copied to *t. The first character is missed.

The second example looks more elaborate than the first, even though the operations performed in the second example are identical. The reason it looks more elaborate is that it doesn't hide the complexity of the operations.

Cross-Reference For details on code tuning, see Chapter 25, "Code-Tuning Strategies," and Chapter 26, "Code-Tuning Techniques."

Improved performance doesn't justify putting multiple operations on the same line either. Because the two *strcpy()* routines are logically equivalent, you would expect the compiler to generate identical code for them. When both versions of the routine were profiled, however, the first version took 4.81 seconds to copy 5,000,000 strings and the second took 4.35 seconds.

In this case, the "clever" version carries an 11 percent speed penalty, which makes it look a lot less clever. The results vary from compiler to compiler, but in general they suggest that until you've measured performance gains, you're better off striving for clarity and correctness first, performance second.

Even if you read statements with side effects easily, take pity on other people who will read your code. Most good programmers need to think twice to understand expressions with side effects. Let them use their brain cells to understand the larger questions of how your code works rather than the syntactic details of a specific expression.

Laying Out Data Declarations

Cross-Reference For details on documenting data declarations, see "Commenting Data Declarations" in Section 32.5. For aspects of data use, see Chapters 10 through 13.

Use only one data declaration per line   As shown in the previous examples, you should give each data declaration its own line. It's easier to put a comment next to each declaration if each one is on its own line. It's easier to modify declarations because each declaration is self-contained. It's easier to find specific variables because you can scan a single column rather than reading each line. It's easier to find and fix syntax errors because the line number the compiler gives you has only one declaration on it.

Quickly—in the data declaration in Listing 31-52, what type of variable is *currentBottom*?

Listing 31-52   C++ example of crowding more than one variable declaration onto a line.

```
int rowIndex, columnIdx; Color previousColor, currentColor, nextColor; Point
previousTop, previousBottom, currentTop, currentBottom, nextTop, nextBottom; Font
previousTypeface, currentTypeface, nextTypeface; Color choices[ NUM_COLORS ];
```

This is an extreme example, but it's not too far removed from a much more common style shown in Listing 31-53:

Listing 31-53   C++ example of crowding more than one variable declaration onto a line.

```
int rowIndex, columnIdx;
Color previousColor, currentColor, nextColor;
Point previousTop, previousBottom, currentTop, currentBottom, nextTop,
nextBottom;
Font previousTypeface, currentTypeface, nextTypeface;
Color choices[ NUM_COLORS ];
```

This is not an uncommon style of declaring variables, and the variable is still hard to find because all the declarations are jammed together. The variable's type is hard to find, too. Now, what is *nextColor*'s type in Listing 31-54?

Listing 31-54   C++ example of readability achieved by putting only one variable declaration on each line.

```
int rowIndex;
int columnIdx;
Color previousColor;
Color currentColor;
Color nextColor;
Point previousTop;
Point previousBottom;
Point currentTop;
Point currentBottom;
Point nextTop;
Point nextBottom;
Font previousTypeface;
Font currentTypeface;
Font nextTypeface;
Color choices[ NUM_COLORS ];
```

The variable *nextColor* was probably easier to find than *nextTypeface* was in Listing 31-53. This style is characterized by one declaration per line and a complete declaration, including the variable type, on each line.

Admittedly, this style chews up a lot of screen space—20 lines instead of the three in the first example, although those three lines were pretty ugly. I can't point to any studies that show that this style leads to fewer bugs or greater comprehension. If Sally Programmer, Jr., asked me to review her code, however, and her data declarations looked like the first example, I'd say "No way—too hard to read." If they looked like the second example, I'd say "Uh...maybe I'll get back to you." If they looked like the final example, I would say "Certainly—it's a pleasure."

Declare variables close to where they're first used   A style that's preferable to declaring all variables in a big block is to declare each variable close to where it's first used. This reduces "span" and "live time" and facilitates refactoring code into smaller routines when necessary. For more details, see "Keep Variables 'Live' for as Short a Time as Possible" in Section 10.4.

Order declarations sensibly   In Listing 31-54, the declarations are grouped by types. Grouping by types is usually sensible since variables of the same type tend to be used in related operations. In other cases, you might choose to order them alphabetically by variable name. Although alphabetical ordering has many advocates, my feeling is that it's too much work for what it's worth. If your list of variables is so long that alphabetical ordering helps, your routine is probably too big. Break it up so that you have smaller routines with fewer variables.

In C++, put the asterisk next to the variable name in pointer declarations or declare pointer types   It's common to see pointer declarations that put the asterisk next to the type, as in Listing 31-55:

Listing 31-55   C++ example of asterisks in pointer declarations.

```
EmployeeList* employees;
File* inputFile;
```

The problem with putting the asterisk next to the type name rather than the variable name is that, when you put more than one declaration on a line, the asterisk will apply only to the first variable even though the visual formatting suggests it applies to all variables on the line. You can avoid this problem by putting the asterisk next to the variable name rather than the type name, as in Listing 31-56:

Listing 31-56   C++ example of using asterisks in pointer declarations.

```
EmployeeList *employees;
File *inputFile;
```

This approach has the weakness of suggesting that the asterisk is part of the variable name, which it isn't. The variable can be used either with or without the asterisk.

The best approach is to declare a type for the pointer and use that instead. An example is shown in Listing 31-57:

Listing 31-57   C++ example of good uses of a pointer type in declarations.

```
EmployeeListPointer employees;
FilePointer inputFile;
```

The particular problem addressed by this approach can be solved either by requiring all pointers to be declared using pointer types, as shown in Listing 31-57, or by requiring no more than one variable declaration per line. Be sure to choose at least one of these solutions!

31.6 Laying Out Comments

Cross-Reference For details on other aspects of comments, see Chapter 32, "Self-Documenting Code."

Comments done well can greatly enhance a program's readability; comments done poorly can actually hurt it. The layout of comments plays a large role in whether they help or hinder readability.

Indent a comment with its corresponding code   Visual indentation is a valuable aid to understanding a program's logical structure, and good comments don't interfere with the visual indentation. For example, what is the logical structure of the routine shown in Listing 31-58?

Listing 31-58   Visual Basic example of poorly indented comments.

CODING HORROR

```
For transactionId = 1 To totalTransactions
' get transaction data
  GetTransactionType( transactionType )
  GetTransactionAmount( transactionAmount )

' process transaction based on transaction type
  If transactionType = Transaction_Sale Then
     AcceptCustomerSale( transactionAmount )

  Else
     If transactionType = Transaction_CustomerReturn Then

' either process return automatically or get manager approval, if required
        If transactionAmount >= MANAGER_APPROVAL_LEVEL Then

' try to get manager approval and then accept or reject the return
' based on whether approval is granted
           GetMgrApproval( isTransactionApproved )
           If ( isTransactionApproved ) Then
              AcceptCustomerReturn( transactionAmount )
           Else
              RejectCustomerReturn( transactionAmount )
           End If
        Else

' manager approval not required, so accept return
           AcceptCustomerReturn( transactionAmount )
        End If
     End If
  End If
Next
```

In this example, you don't get much of a clue to the logical structure because the comments completely obscure the visual indentation of the code. You might find it hard to believe that anyone ever makes a conscious decision to use such an indentation style, but I've seen it in professional programs and know of at least one textbook that recommends it.

The code shown in Listing 31-59 is exactly the same as that in Listing 31-58, except for the indentation of the comments.

Listing 31-59 Visual Basic example of nicely indented comments.

```
For transactionId = 1 To totalTransactions
    ' get transaction data
    GetTransactionType( transactionType )
    GetTransactionAmount( transactionAmount )

    ' process transaction based on transaction type
    If transactionType = Transaction_Sale Then
        AcceptCustomerSale( transactionAmount )

    Else
        If transactionType = Transaction_CustomerReturn Then

            ' either process return automatically or get manager approval, if required
            If transactionAmount >= MANAGER_APPROVAL_LEVEL Then

                ' try to get manager approval and then accept or reject the return
                ' based on whether approval is granted
                GetMgrApproval( isTransactionApproved )
                If ( isTransactionApproved ) Then
                    AcceptCustomerReturn( transactionAmount )
                Else
                    RejectCustomerReturn( transactionAmount )
                End If
            Else
                ' manager approval not required, so accept return
                AcceptCustomerReturn( transactionAmount )
            End If
        End If
    End If
Next
```

In Listing 31-59, the logical structure is more apparent. One study of the effectiveness of commenting found that the benefit of having comments was not conclusive, and the author speculated that it was because they "disrupt visual scanning of the program" (Shneiderman 1980). From these examples, it's obvious that the *style* of commenting strongly influences whether comments are disruptive.

Set off each comment with at least one blank line   If someone is trying to get an overview of your program, the most effective way to do it is to read the comments without reading the code. Setting comments off with blank lines helps a reader scan the code. An example is shown in Listing 31-60:

Listing 31-60 Java example of setting off a comment with a blank line.

```
// comment zero
CodeStatementZero;
CodeStatementOne;

// comment one
CodeStatementTwo;
CodeStatementThree;
```

Some people use a blank line both before and after the comment. Two blanks use more display space, but some people think the code looks better than with just one. An example is shown in Listing 31-61:

Listing 31-61   Java example of setting off a comment with two blank lines.

```
// comment zero

CodeStatementZero;
CodeStatementOne;

// comment one

CodeStatementTwo;
CodeStatementThree;
```

Unless your display space is at a premium, this is a purely aesthetic judgment and you can make it accordingly. In this, as in many other areas, the fact that a convention exists is more important than the convention's specific details.

31.7 Laying Out Routines

Cross-Reference For details on documenting routines, see "Commenting Routines" in Section 32.5. For details on the process of writing a routine, see Section 9.3, "Constructing Routines by Using the PPP." For a discussion of the differences between good and bad routines, see Chapter 7, "High-Quality Routines."

Routines are composed of individual statements, data, control structures, comments—all the things discussed in the other parts of the chapter. This section provides layout guidelines unique to routines.

Use blank lines to separate parts of a routine   Use blank lines between the routine header, its data and named-constant declarations (if any), and its body.

Use standard indentation for routine arguments   The options with routine-header layout are about the same as they are in a lot of other areas of layout: no conscious layout, endline layout, or standard indentation. As in most other cases, standard indentation does better in terms of accuracy, consistency, readability, and modifiability. Listing 31-62 shows two examples of routine headers with no conscious layout:

Listing 31-62   C++ examples of routine headers with no conscious layout.

```
bool ReadEmployeeData(int maxEmployees,EmployeeList *employees,
   EmployeeFile *inputFile,int *employeeCount,bool  *isInputError)
...

void InsertionSort(SortArray data,int firstElement,int lastElement)
```

These routine headers are purely utilitarian. The computer can read them as well as it can read headers in any other format, but they cause trouble for humans. Without a conscious effort to make the headers hard to read, how could they be any worse?

The second approach in routine-header layout is the endline layout, which usually works all right. Listing 31-63 shows the same routine headers reformatted:

Listing 31-63   C++ example of routine headers with mediocre endline layout.

```
bool ReadEmployeeData( int            maxEmployees,
                       EmployeeList   *employees,
                       EmployeeFile   *inputFile,
                       int            *employeeCount,
                       bool           *isInputError )
...
void InsertionSort( SortArray   data,
                    int         firstElement,
                    int         lastElement )
```

Cross-Reference For more details on using routine parameters, see Section 7.5, "How to Use Routine Parameters."

The endline approach is neat and aesthetically appealing. The main problem is that it takes a lot of work to maintain, and styles that are hard to maintain aren't maintained. Suppose that the function name changes from *ReadEmployeeData()* to *ReadNewEmployeeData()*. That would throw the alignment of the first line off from that of the other four lines. You'd have to reformat the other four lines of the parameter list to align with the new position of *maxEmployees* caused by the longer function name. And you'd probably run out of space on the right side since the elements are so far to the right already.

The examples shown in Listing 31-64, formatted using standard indentation, are just as appealing aesthetically but take less work to maintain.

Listing 31-64   C++ example of routine headers with readable, maintainable standard indentation.

```
public bool ReadEmployeeData(
    int maxEmployees,
    EmployeeList *employees,
    EmployeeFile *inputFile,
    int *employeeCount,
    bool *isInputError
)
...

public void InsertionSort(
    SortArray data,
    int firstElement,
    int lastElement
)
```

This style holds up better under modification. If the routine name changes, the change has no effect on any of the parameters. If parameters are added or deleted, only one line has to be modified—plus or minus a comma. The visual cues are similar to those in the indentation scheme for a loop or an *if* statement. Your eye doesn't have to scan different parts of the page for every individual routine to find meaningful information; it knows where the information is every time.

This style translates to Visual Basic in a straightforward way, though it requires the use of line-continuation characters, as shown in Listing 31-65:

Listing 31-65   Visual Basic example of routine headers with readable, maintainable standard indentation.

Here's the "_" character used as a line-continuation character.

```
Public Sub ReadEmployeeData ( _
    ByVal maxEmployees As Integer, _
    ByRef employees As EmployeeList, _
    ByRef inputFile As EmployeeFile, _
    ByRef employeeCount As Integer, _
    ByRef isInputError As Boolean _
)
```

31.8 Laying Out Classes

This section presents guidelines for laying out code in classes. The first subsection describes how to lay out the class interface. The second subsection describes how to lay out the class implementations. The final subsection discusses laying out files and programs.

Laying Out Class Interfaces

Cross-Reference For details on documenting classes, see "Commenting Classes, Files, and Programs" in Section 32.5. For a discussion of the differences between good and bad classes, see Chapter 6, "Working Classes."

In laying out class interfaces, the convention is to present the class members in the following order:

1. Header comment that describes the class and provides any notes about the overall usage of the class

2. Constructors and destructors

3. Public routines

4. Protected routines

5. Private routines and member data

Laying Out Class Implementations

Class implementations are generally laid out in this order:

1. Header comment that describes the contents of the file the class is in

2. Class data

3. Public routines

4. Protected routines

5. Private routines

If you have more than one class in a file, identify each class clearly   Routines that are related should be grouped together into classes. A reader scanning your code should be able to tell easily which class is which. Identify each class clearly by using several blank lines between it and the classes next to it. A class is like a chapter in a book. In a book, you start each chapter on a new page and use big print for the chapter title. Emphasize the start of each class similarly. An example of separating classes is shown in Listing 31-66:

Listing 31-66   C++ example of formatting the separation between classes.

This is the last routine in a class.

```cpp
// create a string identical to sourceString except that the
// blanks are replaced with underscores.
void EditString::ConvertBlanks(
   char *sourceString,
   char *targetString
   ) {
   Assert( strlen( sourceString ) <= MAX_STRING_LENGTH );
   Assert( sourceString != NULL );
   Assert( targetString != NULL );
   int charIndex = 0;
   do {
      if ( sourceString[ charIndex ] == " " ) {
         targetString[ charIndex ] = '_';
      }
      else {
         targetString[ charIndex ] = sourceString[ charIndex ];
      }
      charIndex++;
   } while sourceString[ charIndex ] != '\0';
}
```

The beginning of the new class is marked with several blank lines and the name of the class.

```cpp
//-------------------------------------------------------------------
// MATHEMATICAL FUNCTIONS
//
// This class contains the program's mathematical functions.
//-------------------------------------------------------------------
```

This is the first routine in a new class.

```cpp
// find the arithmetic maximum of arg1 and arg2
int Math::Max( int arg1, int arg2 ) {
   if ( arg1 > arg2 ) {
      return arg1;
   }
   else {
      return arg2;
   }
}
```

This routine is separated from the previous routine by blank lines only.

```cpp
// find the arithmetic minimum of arg1 and arg2
int Math::Min( int arg1, int arg2 ) {
   if ( arg1 < arg2 ) {
      return arg1;
   }
   else {
      return arg2;
   }
}
```

Avoid overemphasizing comments within classes. If you mark every routine and comment with a row of asterisks instead of blank lines, you'll have a hard time coming up with a device that effectively emphasizes the start of a new class. An example is shown in Listing 31-67:

Listing 31-67   C++ example of overformatting a class.

```cpp
//***********************************************************************************
//***********************************************************************************
// MATHEMATICAL FUNCTIONS
//
// This class contains the program's mathematical functions.
//***********************************************************************************
//***********************************************************************************


//***********************************************************************************
// find the arithmetic maximum of arg1 and arg2
//***********************************************************************************
int Math::Max( int arg1, int arg2 ) {
//***********************************************************************************
    if ( arg1 > arg2 ) {
        return arg1;
    }
    else {
        return arg2;
    }
}


//***********************************************************************************
// find the arithmetic minimum of arg1 and arg2
//***********************************************************************************
int Math::Min( int arg1, int arg2 ) {
//***********************************************************************************
    if ( arg1 < arg2 ) {
        return arg1;
    }
    else {
        return arg2;
    }
}
```

In this example, so many things are highlighted with asterisks that nothing is really emphasized. The program becomes a dense forest of asterisks. Although it's more an aesthetic than a technical judgment, in formatting, less is more.

If you must separate parts of a program with long lines of special characters, develop a hierarchy of characters (from densest to lightest) instead of relying exclusively on asterisks. For example, use asterisks for class divisions, dashes for routine divisions, and blank lines for important comments. Refrain from putting two rows of asterisks or dashes together. An example is shown in Listing 31-68:

Listing 31-68   C++ example of good formatting with restraint.

```
//*************************************************************************
// MATHEMATICAL FUNCTIONS
//
// This class contains the program's mathematical functions.
//*************************************************************************

//-----------------------------------------------------------------------
// find the arithmetic maximum of arg1 and arg2
//-----------------------------------------------------------------------
int Math::Max( int arg1, int arg2 ) {
   if ( arg1 > arg2 ) {
      return arg1;
   }
   else {
      return arg2;
   }
}


//-----------------------------------------------------------------------
// find the arithmetic minimum of arg1 and arg2
//-----------------------------------------------------------------------
int Math::Min( int arg1, int arg2 ) {
   if ( arg1 < arg2 ) {
      return arg1;
   }
   else {
      return arg2;
   }
}
```

> The lightness of this line compared to the line of asterisks visually reinforces the fact that the routine is subordinate to the class.

This advice about how to identify multiple classes within a single file applies only when your language restricts the number of files you can use in a program. If you're using C++, Java, Visual Basic, or other languages that support multiple source files, put only one class in each file unless you have a compelling reason to do otherwise (such as including a few small classes that make up a single pattern). Within a single class, however, you might still have subgroups of routines, and you can group them using techniques such as the ones shown here.

Laying Out Files and Programs

Cross-Reference For documentation details, see "Commenting Classes, Files, and Programs" in Section 32.5.

Beyond the formatting techniques for classes is a larger formatting issue: how do you organize classes and routines within a file, and how do you decide which classes to put in a file in the first place?

Put one class in one file   A file isn't just a bucket that holds some code. If your language allows it, a file should hold a collection of routines that supports one and only one purpose. A file reinforces the idea that a collection of routines are in the same class.

Cross-Reference For details on the differences between classes and routines and how to make a collection of routines into a class, see Chapter 6, "Working Classes."

All the routines within a file make up the class. The class might be one that the program really recognizes as such, or it might be just a logical entity that you've created as part of your design.

Classes are a semantic language concept. Files are a physical operating-system concept. The correspondence between classes and files is coincidental and continues to weaken over time as more environments support putting code into databases or otherwise obscuring the relationship between routines, classes, and files.

Give the file a name related to the class name   Most projects have a one-to-one correspondence between class names and file names. A class named *CustomerAccount* would have files named *CustomerAccount.cpp* and *CustomerAccount.h*, for example.

Separate routines within a file clearly   Separate each routine from other routines with at least two blank lines. The blank lines are as effective as big rows of asterisks or dashes, and they're a lot easier to type and maintain. Use two or three to produce a visual difference between blank lines that are part of a routine and blank lines that separate routines. An example is shown in Listing 31-69:

Listing 31-69   Visual Basic example of using blank lines between routines.

```
'find the arithmetic maximum of arg1 and arg2
Function Max( arg1 As Integer, arg2 As Integer ) As Integer
   If ( arg1 > arg2 ) Then
      Max = arg1
   Else
      Max = arg2
   End If
End Function



'find the arithmetic minimum of arg1 and arg2
Function Min( arg1 As Integer, arg2 As Integer ) As Integer
   If ( arg1 < arg2 ) Then
      Min = arg1
   Else
      Min = arg2
   End If
end Function
```

At least two blank lines separate the two routines.

Blank lines are easier to type than any other kind of separator and look at least as good. Three blank lines are used in this example so that the separation between routines is more noticeable than the blank lines within each routine.

Sequence routines alphabetically   An alternative to grouping related routines in a file is to put them in alphabetical order. If you can't break a program up into classes or if your editor doesn't allow you to find functions easily, the alphabetical approach can save search time.

In C++, order the source file carefully   Here's a typical order of source-file contents in C++:

1. File-description comment

2. *#include* files

3. Constant definitions that apply to more than one class (if more than one class in the file)

4. Enums that apply to more than one class (if more than one class in the file)

5. Macro function definitions

6. Type definitions that apply to more than one class (if more than one class in the file)

7. Global variables and functions imported

8. Global variables and functions exported

9. Variables and functions that are private to the file

10. Classes, including constant definitions, enums, and type definitions within each class

cc2e.com/3194

CHECKLIST: Layout

General

❏ Is formatting done primarily to illuminate the logical structure of the code?

❏ Can the formatting scheme be used consistently?

❏ Does the formatting scheme result in code that's easy to maintain?

❏ Does the formatting scheme improve code readability?

Control Structures

❏ Does the code avoid doubly indented *begin-end* or *{}* pairs?

❏ Are sequential blocks separated from each other with blank lines?

❏ Are complicated expressions formatted for readability?

❏ Are single-statement blocks formatted consistently?

❏ Are *case* statements formatted in a way that's consistent with the formatting of other control structures?

❏ Have *goto*s been formatted in a way that makes their use obvious?

Individual Statements

❑ Is white space used to make logical expressions, array references, and routine arguments readable?

❑ Do incomplete statements end the line in a way that's obviously incorrect?

❑ Are continuation lines indented the standard indentation amount?

❑ Does each line contain at most one statement?

❑ Is each statement written without side effects?

❑ Is there at most one data declaration per line?

Comments

❑ Are the comments indented the same number of spaces as the code they comment?

❑ Is the commenting style easy to maintain?

Routines

❑ Are the arguments to each routine formatted so that each argument is easy to read, modify, and comment?

❑ Are blank lines used to separate parts of a routine?

Classes, Files and Programs

❑ Is there a one-to-one relationship between classes and files for most classes and files?

❑ If a file does contain multiple classes, are all the routines in each class grouped together and is each class clearly identified?

❑ Are routines within a file clearly separated with blank lines?

❑ In lieu of a stronger organizing principle, are all routines in alphabetical sequence?

Additional Resources

cc2e.com/3101

Most programming textbooks say a few words about layout and style, but thorough discussions of programming style are rare; discussions of layout are rarer still. The following books talk about layout and programming style:

Kernighan, Brian W. and Rob Pike. *The Practice of Programming* Reading, MA: Addison-Wesley, 1999. Chapter 1 of this book discusses programming style focusing on C and C++.

Vermeulen, Allan, et al. *The Elements of Java Style*. Cambridge University Press, 2000.

Misfeldt, Trevor, Greg Bumgardner, and Andrew Gray. *The Elements of C++ Style*. Cambridge University Press, 2004.

Kernighan, Brian W., and P. J. Plauger. *The Elements of Programming Style*, 2d ed. New York, NY: McGraw-Hill, 1978. This is the classic book on programming style—the first in the genre of programming-style books.

For a substantially different approach to readability, take a look at the following book:

Knuth, Donald E. *Literate Programming*. Cambridge University Press, 2001. This is a collection of papers describing the "literate programming" approach of combining a programming language and a documentation language. Knuth has been writing about the virtues of literate programming for about 20 years, and in spite of his strong claim to the title Best Programmer on the Planet, literate programming isn't catching on. Read some of his code to form your own conclusions about the reason.

Key Points

- The first priority of visual layout is to illuminate the logical organization of the code. Criteria used to assess whether that priority is achieved include accuracy, consistency, readability, and maintainability.

- Looking good is secondary to the other criteria—a distant second. If the other criteria are met and the underlying code is good, however, the layout will look fine.

- Visual Basic has pure blocks and the conventional practice in Java is to use pure-block style, so you can use a pure-block layout if you program in those languages. In C++, either pure-block emulation or *begin-end* block boundaries work well.

- Structuring code is important for its own sake. The specific convention you follow is less important than the fact that you follow some convention consistently. A layout convention that's followed inconsistently can actually hurt readability.

- Many aspects of layout are religious issues. Try to separate objective preferences from subjective ones. Use explicit criteria to help ground your discussions about style preferences.

Chapter 32

Self-Documenting Code

cc2e.com/3245

Contents

Related Topics

> Code as if whoever maintains your program is a violent psychopath who knows where you live.
> —*Anonymous*

Most programmers enjoy writing documentation if the documentation standards aren't unreasonable. Like layout, good documentation is a sign of the professional pride a programmer puts into a program. Software documentation can take many forms, and, after describing the sweep of the documentation landscape, this chapter cultivates the specific patch of documentation known as "comments."

32.1 External Documentation

Cross-Reference For more on external documentation, see Section 32.6, "IEEE Standards."

Documentation on a software project consists of information both inside the source-code listings and outside them—usually in the form of separate documents or unit development folders. On large, formal projects, most of the documentation is outside the source code (Jones 1998). External construction documentation tends to be at a high level compared to the code, at a low level compared to the documentation from the problem definition, requirements, and architecture activities.

Further Reading For a detailed description, see "The Unit Development Folder (UDF): An Effective Management Tool for Software Development" (Ingrassia 1976) or "The Unit Development Folder (UDF): A Ten-Year Perspective" (Ingrassia 1987).

Unit development folders   A unit-development folder (UDF), or software-development folder (SDF), is an informal document that contains notes used by a developer during construction. A "unit" is loosely defined, usually to mean a class, although it could also mean a package or a component. The main purpose of a UDF is to provide a trail of design decisions that aren't documented elsewhere. Many projects have standards that specify the minimum content of a UDF, such as copies of the relevant requirements, the parts of the top-level design the unit implements, a copy of the development standards, a current code listing, and design notes from the unit's developer. Sometimes the customer requires a software developer to deliver the project's UDFs; often they are for internal use only.

Detailed-design document   The detailed-design document is the low-level design document. It describes the class-level or routine-level design decisions, the alternatives that were considered, and the reasons for selecting the approaches that were selected. Sometimes this information is contained in a formal document. In such cases, detailed design is usually considered to be separate from construction. Sometimes it consists mainly of developers' notes collected into a UDF. And sometimes—often—it exists only in the code itself.

32.2 Programming Style as Documentation

In contrast to external documentation, internal documentation is found within the program listing itself. It's the most detailed kind of documentation, at the source-statement level. Because it's most closely associated with the code, internal documentation is also the kind of documentation most likely to remain correct as the code is modified.

The main contributor to code-level documentation isn't comments, but good programming style. Style includes good program structure, use of straightforward and easily understandable approaches, good variable names, good routine names, use of named constants instead of literals, clear layout, and minimization of control-flow and data-structure complexity.

Here's a code fragment with poor style:

CODING
HORROR

Java Example of Poor Documentation Resulting from Bad Programming Style
```java
for ( i = 2; i <= num; i++ ) {
meetsCriteria[ i ] = true;
}
for ( i = 2; i <= num / 2; i++ ) {
j = i + i;
while ( j <= num ) {
```

```
meetsCriteria[ j ] = false;
j = j + i;
}
}
for ( i = 2; i <= num; i++ ) {
if ( meetsCriteria[ i ] ) {
System.out.println ( i + " meets criteria." );
}
}
```

What do you think this routine does? It's unnecessarily cryptic. It's poorly documented not because it lacks comments, but because it lacks good programming style. The variable names are uninformative, and the layout is crude. Here's the same code improved—just improving the programming style makes its meaning much clearer:

Java Example of Documentation Without Comments (with Good Style)

```
for ( primeCandidate = 2; primeCandidate <= num; primeCandidate++ ) {
    isPrime[ primeCandidate ] = true;
}

for ( int factor = 2; factor < ( num / 2 ); factor++ ) {
    int factorableNumber = factor + factor;
    while ( factorableNumber <= num ) {
        isPrime[ factorableNumber ] = false;
        factorableNumber = factorableNumber + factor;
    }
}

for ( primeCandidate = 2; primeCandidate <= num; primeCandidate++ ) {
    if ( isPrime[ primeCandidate ] ) {
        System.out.println( primeCandidate + " is prime." );
    }
}
```

Cross-Reference In this code, the variable *factorableNumber* is added solely for the sake of clarifying the operation. For details on adding variables to clarify operations, see "Making Complicated Expressions Simple" in Section 19.1.

Unlike the first piece of code, this one lets you know at first glance that it has something to do with prime numbers. A second glance reveals that it finds the prime numbers between *1* and *Num*. With the first code fragment, it takes more than two glances just to figure out where the loops end.

The difference between the two code fragments has nothing to do with comments—neither fragment has any. The second one is much more readable, however, and approaches the Holy Grail of legibility: self-documenting code. Such code relies on good programming style to carry the greater part of the documentation burden. In well-written code, comments are the icing on the readability cake.

cc2e.com/3252

CHECKLIST: Self-Documenting Code

Classes

- ❑ Does the class's interface present a consistent abstraction?
- ❑ Is the class well named, and does its name describe its central purpose?
- ❑ Does the class's interface make obvious how you should use the class?
- ❑ Is the class's interface abstract enough that you don't have to think about how its services are implemented? Can you treat the class as a black box?

Routines

- ❑ Does each routine's name describe exactly what the routine does?
- ❑ Does each routine perform one well-defined task?
- ❑ Have all parts of each routine that would benefit from being put into their own routines been put into their own routines?
- ❑ Is each routine's interface obvious and clear?

Data Names

- ❑ Are type names descriptive enough to help document data declarations?
- ❑ Are variables named well?
- ❑ Are variables used only for the purpose for which they're named?
- ❑ Are loop counters given more informative names than i, j, and k?
- ❑ Are well-named enumerated types used instead of makeshift flags or boolean variables?
- ❑ Are named constants used instead of magic numbers or magic strings?
- ❑ Do naming conventions distinguish among type names, enumerated types, named constants, local variables, class variables, and global variables?

Data Organization

- ❑ Are extra variables used for clarity when needed?
- ❑ Are references to variables close together?
- ❑ Are data types simple so that they minimize complexity?
- ❑ Is complicated data accessed through abstract access routines (abstract data types)?

Control

- ❑ Is the nominal path through the code clear?
- ❑ Are related statements grouped together?

- ❏ Have relatively independent groups of statements been packaged into their own routines?

- ❏ Does the normal case follow the *if* rather than the *else*?

- ❏ Are control structures simple so that they minimize complexity?

- ❏ Does each loop perform one and only one function, as a well-defined routine would?

- ❏ Is nesting minimized?

- ❏ Have boolean expressions been simplified by using additional boolean variables, boolean functions, and decision tables?

Layout

- ❏ Does the program's layout show its logical structure?

Design

- ❏ Is the code straightforward, and does it avoid cleverness?

- ❏ Are implementation details hidden as much as possible?

- ❏ Is the program written in terms of the problem domain as much as possible rather than in terms of computer-science or programming-language structures?

32.3 To Comment or Not to Comment

Comments are easier to write poorly than well, and commenting can be more damaging than helpful. The heated discussions over the virtues of commenting often sound like philosophical debates over moral virtues, which makes me think that if Socrates had been a computer programmer, he and his students might have had the following discussion.

The Commento

Characters:

THRASYMACHUS   A green, theoretical purist who believes everything he reads

CALLICLES   A battle-hardened veteran from the old school—a "real" programmer

GLAUCON   A young, confident, hot-shot computer jock

ISMENE   A senior programmer tired of big promises, just looking for a few practices that work

SOCRATES   The wise old programmer

Setting:

END OF THE TEAM'S DAILY STANDUP MEETING

"Does anyone have any other issues before we get back to work?" Socrates asked.

"I want to suggest a commenting standard for our projects," Thrasymachus said. "Some of our programmers barely comment their code, and everyone knows that code without comments is unreadable."

"You must be fresher out of college than I thought," Callicles responded. "Comments are an academic panacea, but everyone who's done any real programming knows that comments make the code harder to read, not easier. English is less precise than Java or Visual Basic and makes for a lot of excess verbiage. Programming-language statements are short and to the point. If you can't make the code clear, how can you make the comments clear? Plus, comments get out of date as the code changes. If you believe an out-of-date comment, you're sunk."

"I agree with that," Glaucon joined in. "Heavily commented code is harder to read because it means more to read. I already have to read the code; why should I have to read a lot of comments, too?"

"Wait a minute," Ismene said, putting down her coffee mug to put in her two drachmas' worth. "I know that commenting can be abused, but good comments are worth their weight in gold. I've had to maintain code that had comments and code that didn't, and I'd rather maintain code with comments. I don't think we should have a standard that says use one comment for every *x* lines of code, but we should encourage everyone to comment."

"If comments are a waste of time, why does anyone use them, Callicles?" Socrates asked.

"Either because they're required to or because they read somewhere that they're useful. No one who's thought about it could ever decide they're useful."

"Ismene thinks they're useful. She's been here three years, maintaining your code without comments and other code with comments, and she prefers the code with comments. What do you make of that?"

"Comments are useless because they just repeat the code in a more verbose—"

KEY POINT

"Wait right there," Thrasymachus interrupted. "Good comments don't repeat the code or explain it. They clarify its intent. Comments should explain, at a higher level of abstraction than the code, what you're trying to do."

"Right," Ismene said. "I scan the comments to find the section that does what I need to change or fix. You're right that comments that repeat the code don't help at all because the code says everything already. When I read comments, I want it to be like reading headings in a book or a table of contents. Comments help me find the right section, and then I start reading the code. It's a lot faster to read one sentence in English than it is to parse 20 lines of code in a programming language." Ismene poured herself another cup of coffee.

"I think that people who refuse to write comments (1) think their code is clearer than it could possibly be, (2) think that other programmers are far more interested in their code than they really are, (3) think other programmers are smarter than they really are, (4) are lazy, or (5) are afraid someone else might figure out how their code works.

"Code reviews would be a big help here, Socrates," Ismene continued. "If someone claims they don't need to write comments and are bombarded by questions during a review—when several peers start saying, 'What the heck are you trying to do in this piece of code?'—then they'll start putting in comments. If they don't do it on their own, at least their manager will have the ammo to make them do it.

"I'm not accusing you of being lazy or afraid that people will figure out your code, Callicles. I've worked on your code and you're one of the best programmers in the company. But have a heart, huh? Your code would be easier for me to work on if you used comments."

"But they're a waste of resources," Callicles countered. "A good programmer's code should be self-documenting; everything you need to know should be in the code."

"No way!" Thrasymachus was out of his chair. "Everything the compiler needs to know is in the code! You might as well argue that everything you need to know is in the binary executable file! If you were smart enough to read it! What is *meant* to happen is not in the code."

Thrasymachus realized he was standing up and sat down. "Socrates, this is ridiculous. Why do we have to argue about whether comments are valuable? Everything I've ever read says they're valuable and should be used liberally. We're wasting our time."

"Cool down, Thrasymachus. Ask Callicles how long he's been programming."

"How long, Callicles?"

"Well, I started on the Acropolis IV about 15 years ago. I guess I've seen about a dozen major systems from the time they were born to the time we gave them a cup of hemlock. And I've worked on major parts of a dozen more. Two of those systems had over half a million lines of code, so I know what I'm talking about. Comments are pretty useless."

Socrates looked at the younger programmer. "As Callicles says, comments have a lot of legitimate problems, and you won't realize that without more experience. If they're not done right, they're worse than useless."

Clearly, at some level comments *have* to be useful. To believe otherwise would be to believe that the comprehensibility of a program is independent of how much information the reader might already have about it.
—*B. A. Sheil*

"Even when they're done right, they're useless," Callicles said. "Comments are less precise than a programming language. I'd rather not have them at all."

"Wait a minute," Socrates said. "Ismene agrees that comments are less precise. Her point is that comments give you a higher level of abstraction, and we all know that levels of abstraction are one of a programmer's most powerful tools."

"I don't agree with that," Glaucon replied. "Instead of focusing on commenting, you should focus on making code more readable. Refactoring eliminates most of my comments. Once I've refactored, my code might have 20 or 30 routine calls without needing any comments. A good programmer can read the intent from the code itself, and what good does it do to read about somebody's intent when you know the code has an error?" Glaucon was pleased with his contribution. Callicles nodded.

"It sounds like you guys have never had to modify someone else's code," Ismene said. Callicles suddenly seemed very interested in the pencil marks on the ceiling tiles. "Why don't you try reading your own code six months or a year after you write it? You can improve your code-reading ability and your commenting. You don't have to choose one or the other. If you're reading a novel, you might not want section headings. But if you're reading a technical book, you'd like to be able to find what you're looking for quickly. I shouldn't have to switch into ultra-concentration mode and read hundreds of lines of code just to find the two lines I want to change."

"All right, I can see that it would be handy to be able to scan code," Glaucon said. He'd seen some of Ismene's programs and had been impressed. "But what about Callicles' other point, that comments get out of date as the code changes? I've only been programming for a couple of years, but even I know that nobody updates their comments."

"Well, yes and no," Ismene said. "If you take the comment as sacred and the code as suspicious, you're in deep trouble. Actually, finding a disagreement between the comment and the code tends to mean both are wrong. The fact that some comments are bad doesn't mean that commenting is bad. I'm going to the lunchroom to get another pot of coffee." Ismene left the room.

"My main objection to comments," Callicles said, "is that they're a waste of resources."

"Can anyone think of ways to minimize the time it takes to write the comments?" Socrates asked.

"Design routines in pseudocode, and then convert the pseudocode to comments and fill in the code between them," Glaucon said.

"OK, that would work as long as the comments don't repeat the code," Callicles said.

"Writing a comment makes you think harder about what your code is doing," Ismene said, returning from the lunchroom. "If it's hard to comment, either it's bad code or you don't understand it well enough. Either way, you need to spend more time on the code, so the time you spent commenting wasn't wasted because it pointed you to required work."

"All right," Socrates said. "I can't think of any more questions, and I think Ismene got the best of you guys today. We'll encourage commenting, but we won't be naive about it. We'll have code reviews so that everyone will get a good sense of the kind of comments that actually help. If you have trouble understanding someone else's code, let them know how they can improve it."

32.4 Keys to Effective Comments

As long as there are ill-defined goals, bizarre bugs, and unrealistic schedules, there will be Real Programmers willing to jump in and Solve The Problem, saving the documentation for later. Long live Fortran!
—Ed Post

What does the following routine do?

Java Mystery Routine Number One
```java
// write out the sums 1..n for all n from 1 to num
current = 1;
previous = 0;
sum = 1;
for ( int i = 0; i < num; i++ ) {
    System.out.println( "Sum = " + sum );
    sum = current + previous;
    previous = current;
    current = sum;
}
```

Your best guess?

This routine computes the first *num* Fibonacci numbers. Its coding style is a little better than the style of the routine at the beginning of the chapter, but the comment is wrong, and if you blindly trust the comment, you head down the primrose path in the wrong direction.

What about this one?

Java Mystery Routine Number Two
```java
// set product to "base"
product = base;

// loop from 2 to "num"
for ( int i = 2; i <= num; i++ ) {
    // multiply "base" by "product"
    product = product * base;
}
System.out.println( "Product = " + product );
```

This routine raises an integer *base* to the integer power *num*. The comments in this routine are accurate, but they add nothing to the code. They are merely a more verbose version of the code itself.

Here's one last routine:

Java Mystery Routine Number Three

```java
// compute the square root of Num using the Newton-Raphson approximation
r = num / 2;
while ( abs( r - (num/r) ) > TOLERANCE ) {
   r = 0.5 * ( r + (num/r) );
}
System.out.println( "r = " + r );
```

This routine computes the square root of *num*. The code isn't great, but the comment is accurate.

Which routine was easiest for you to figure out correctly? None of the routines is particularly well written—the variable names are especially poor. In a nutshell, however, these routines illustrate the strengths and weaknesses of internal comments. Routine One has an incorrect comment. Routine Two's commenting merely repeats the code and is therefore useless. Only Routine Three's commenting earns its rent. Poor comments are worse than no comments. Routines One and Two would be better with no comments than with the poor comments they have.

The following subsections describe keys to writing effective comments.

Kinds of Comments

Comments can be classified into six categories:

Repeat of the Code

A repetitious comment restates what the code does in different words. It merely gives the reader of the code more to read without providing additional information.

Explanation of the Code

Explanatory comments are typically used to explain complicated, tricky, or sensitive pieces of code. In such situations they are useful, but usually that's only because the code is confusing. If the code is so complicated that it needs to be explained, it's nearly always better to improve the code than it is to add comments. Make the code itself clearer, and then use summary or intent comments.

Marker in the Code

A marker comment is one that isn't intended to be left in the code. It's a note to the developer that the work isn't done yet. Some developers type in a marker that's syntactically incorrect (******, for example) so that the compiler flags it and reminds them that they have more work to do. Other developers put a specified set of characters in comments that don't interfere with compilation so that they can search for them.

Few feelings are worse than having a customer report a problem in the code, debugging the problem, and tracing it to a section of code where you find something like this:

```
return NULL; // ****** NOT DONE! FIX BEFORE RELEASE!!!
```

Releasing defective code to customers is bad enough; releasing code that you *knew* was defective is even worse.

I've found that standardizing the style of marker comments is helpful. If you don't standardize, some programmers will use *******, some will use *!!!!!!*, some will use *TBD*, and some will use various other conventions. Using a variety of notations makes mechanical searching for incomplete code error-prone or impossible. Standardizing on one specific marker style allows you to do a mechanical search for incomplete sections of code as one of the steps in a release checklist, which avoids the *FIX BEFORE RELEASE!!!* problem. Some editors support "to do" tags and allow you to navigate to them easily.

Summary of the Code

A comment that summarizes code does just that: it distills a few lines of code into one or two sentences. Such comments are more valuable than comments that merely repeat the code because a reader can scan them more quickly than the code. Summary comments are particularly useful when someone other than the code's original author tries to modify the code.

Description of the Code's Intent

A comment at the level of intent explains the purpose of a section of code. Intent comments operate more at the level of the problem than at the level of the solution. For example,

```
-- get current employee information
```

is an intent comment, whereas

```
-- update employeeRecord object
```

is a summary comment in terms of the solution. A six-month study conducted by IBM found that maintenance programmers "most often said that understanding the original programmer's intent was the most difficult problem" (Fjelstad and Hamlen 1979). The distinction between intent and summary comments isn't always clear, and it's usually not important. Examples of intent comments are given throughout this chapter.

Information That Cannot Possibly Be Expressed by the Code Itself

Some information can't be expressed in code but must still be in the source code. This category of comments includes copyright notices, confidentiality notices, version numbers, and other housekeeping details; notes about the code's design; references to related requirements or architecture documentation; pointers to online references; optimization notes; comments required by editing tools such as Javadoc and Doxygen; and so on.

The three kinds of comments that are acceptable for completed code are information that can't be expressed in code, intent comments, and summary comments.

Commenting Efficiently

Effective commenting isn't that time-consuming. Too many comments are as bad as too few, and you can achieve a middle ground economically.

Comments can take a lot of time to write for two common reasons. First, the commenting style might be time-consuming or tedious. If it is, find a new style. A commenting style that requires a lot of busy work is a maintenance headache. If the comments are hard to change, they won't be changed and they'll become inaccurate and misleading, which is worse than having no comments at all.

Second, commenting might be difficult because the words to describe what the program is doing don't come easily. That's usually a sign that you don't understand what the program does. The time you spend "commenting" is really time spent understanding the program better, which is time that needs to be spent regardless of whether you comment.

Following are guidelines for commenting efficiently:

Use styles that don't break down or discourage modification Any style that's too fancy is annoying to maintain. For example, pick out the part of the comment below that won't be maintained:

Java Example of a Commenting Style That's Hard to Maintain
```java
//    Variable        Meaning
//    --------        -------
//    xPos .......... XCoordinate Position (in meters)
//    yPos .......... YCoordinate Position (in meters)
```

```
//  ndsCmptng...... Needs Computing (= 0 if no computation is needed,
//                                  = 1 if computation is needed)
//  ptGrdTtl....... Point Grand Total
//  ptValMax....... Point Value Maximum
//  psblScrMax..... Possible Score Maximum
```

If you said that the leader dots (.....) will be hard to maintain, you're right! They look nice, but the list is fine without them. They add busy work to the job of modifying comments, and you'd rather have accurate comments than nice-looking ones, if that's the choice—and it usually is.

Here's another example of a common style that's hard to maintain:

C++ Example of a Commenting Style That's Hard to Maintain

```
/***********************************************************************
 * class:  GigaTron (GIGATRON.CPP)                                     *
 *                                                                     *
 * author: Dwight K. Coder                                             *
 * date:   July 4, 2014                                                *
 *                                                                     *
 * Routines to control the twenty-first century's code evaluation      *
 * tool. The entry point to these routines is the EvaluateCode()       *
 * routine at the bottom of this file.                                 *
 ***********************************************************************/
```

This is a nice-looking block comment. It's clear that the whole block belongs together, and the beginning and ending of the block are obvious. What isn't clear about this block is how easy it is to change. If you have to add the name of a file to the bottom of the comment, chances are pretty good that you'll have to fuss with the pretty column of asterisks at the right. If you need to change the paragraph comments, you'll have to fuss with asterisks on both the left and the right. In practice, this means that the block won't be maintained because it will be too much work. If you can press a key and get neat columns of asterisks, that's great. Use it. The problem isn't the asterisks but that they're hard to maintain. The following comment looks almost as good and is a cinch to maintain:

C++ Example of a Commenting Style That's Easy to Maintain

```
/***********************************************************************
   class:  GigaTron (GIGATRON.CPP)

   author: Dwight K. Coder
   date:   July 4, 2014

   Routines to control the twenty-first century's code evaluation
   tool. The entry point to these routines is the EvaluateCode()
   routine at the bottom of this file.
 ***********************************************************************/
```

Here's a particularly difficult style to maintain:

CODING HORROR

> **Microsoft Visual Basic Example of a Commenting Style That's Hard to Maintain**
>
> ```
> '   set up Color enumerated type
> '   +-------------------------+
>     ...
>
> '   set up Vegetable enumerated type
> '   +-----------------------------+
>     ...
> ```

It's hard to know what value the plus sign at the beginning and end of each dashed line adds to the comment, but it's easy to guess that every time a comment changes, the underline has to be adjusted so that the ending plus sign is in precisely the right place. And what do you do when a comment spills over into two lines? How do you align the plus signs? Take words out of the comment so that it takes up only one line? Make both lines the same length? The problems with this approach multiply when you try to apply it consistently.

A common guideline for Java and C++ that arises from a similar motivation is to use // syntax for single-line comments and /* ... */ syntax for longer comments, as shown here:

> **Java Example of Using Different Comment Syntaxes for Different Purposes**
>
> ```
> // This is a short comment
>     ...
> /* This is a much longer comment. Four score and seven years ago our fathers
> brought forth on this continent a new nation, conceived in liberty and dedicated to
> the proposition that all men are created equal. Now we are engaged in a great civil
> war, testing whether that nation or any nation so conceived and so dedicated can
> long endure. We are met on a great battlefield of that war. We have come to
> dedicate a portion of that field as a final resting-place for those who here gave
> their lives that that nation might live. It is altogether fitting and proper that
> we should do this.
> */
> ```

The first comment is easy to maintain as long as it's kept short. For longer comments, the task of creating long columns of double slashes, manually breaking lines of text between rows, and similar activities is not very rewarding, and so the /* ... */ syntax is more appropriate for multiline comments.

KEY POINT

The point is that you should pay attention to how you spend your time. If you spend a lot of time entering and deleting dashes to make plus signs line up, you're not programming; you're wasting time. Find a more efficient style. In the case of the underlines with plus signs, you could choose to have just the comments without any underlining. If you need to use underlines for emphasis, find some way other than underlines with plus signs to emphasize those comments. One way would be to have a standard underline that's always the same length regardless of the length of the comment. Such a line requires no maintenance, and you can use a text-editor macro to enter it in the first place.

Cross-Reference For details on the Pseudocode Programming Process, see Chapter 9, "The Pseudocode Programming Process."

Use the Pseudocode Programming Process to reduce commenting time   If you outline the code in comments before you write it, you win in several ways. When you finish the code, the comments are done. You don't have to dedicate time to comments. You also gain all the design benefits of writing in high-level pseudocode before filling in the low-level programming-language code.

Integrate commenting into your development style   The alternative to integrating commenting into your development style is leaving commenting until the end of the project, and that has too many disadvantages. It becomes a task in its own right, which makes it seem like more work than when it's done a little bit at a time. Commenting done later takes more time because you have to remember or figure out what the code is doing instead of just writing down what you're already thinking about. It's also less accurate because you tend to forget assumptions or subtleties in the design.

The common argument against commenting as you go along is "When you're concentrating on the code, you shouldn't break your concentration to write comments." The appropriate response is that, if you have to concentrate so hard on writing code that commenting interrupts your thinking, you need to design in pseudocode first and then convert the pseudocode to comments. Code that requires that much concentration is a warning sign.

KEY POINT

If your design is hard to code, simplify the design before you worry about comments or code. If you use pseudocode to clarify your thoughts, coding is straightforward and the comments are automatic.

Performance is not a good reason to avoid commenting   One recurring attribute of the rolling wave of technology discussed in Section 4.3, "Your Location on the Technology Wave," is interpreted environments in which commenting imposes a measurable performance penalty. In the 1980s, comments in Basic programs on the original IBM PC slowed programs. In the 1990s, *.asp* pages did the same thing. In the 2000s, JavaScript code and other code that needs to be sent across network connections presents a similar problem.

In each of these cases, the ultimate solution has not been to avoid commenting; it's been to create a release version of the code that's different from the development version. This is typically accomplished by running the code through a tool that strips out comments as part of the build process.

Optimum Number of Comments

HARD DATA

Capers Jones points out that studies at IBM found that a commenting density of one comment roughly every 10 statements was the density at which clarity seemed to peak. Fewer comments made the code hard to understand. More comments also reduced code understandability (Jones 2000).

This kind of research can be abused, and projects sometimes adopt a standard such as "programs must have one comment at least every five lines." This standard addresses the symptom of programmers' not writing clear code, but it doesn't address the cause.

If you use the Pseudocode Programming Process effectively, you'll probably end up with a comment for every few lines of code. The number of comments, however, will be a side effect of the process itself. Rather than focusing on the number of comments, focus on whether each comment is efficient. If the comments describe why the code was written and meet the other criteria established in this chapter, you'll have enough comments.

32.5 Commenting Techniques

Commenting is amenable to several different techniques depending on the level to which the comments apply: program, file, routine, paragraph, or individual line.

Commenting Individual Lines

In good code, the need to comment individual lines of code is rare. Here are two possible reasons a line of code would need a comment:

- The single line is complicated enough to need an explanation.
- The single line once had an error, and you want a record of the error.

Here are some guidelines for commenting a line of code:

Avoid self-indulgent comments Many years ago, I heard the story of a maintenance programmer who was called out of bed to fix a malfunctioning program. The program's author had left the company and couldn't be reached. The maintenance programmer hadn't worked on the program before, and after examining the documentation carefully, he found only one comment. It looked like this:

```
MOV AX, 723h    ; R. I. P. L. V. B.
```

After working with the program through the night and puzzling over the comment, the programmer made a successful patch and went home to bed. Months later, he met the program's author at a conference and found out that the comment stood for "Rest in peace, Ludwig van Beethoven." Beethoven died in 1827 (decimal), which is 723 (hexadecimal). The fact that 723h was needed in that spot had nothing to do with the comment. Aaarrrghhhhh!

Endline Comments and Their Problems

Endline comments are comments that appear at the ends of lines of code:

```
Visual Basic Example of Endline Comments
For employeeId = 1 To employeeCount
   GetBonus( employeeId, employeeType, bonusAmount )
   If employeeType = EmployeeType_Manager Then
      PayManagerBonus( employeeId, bonusAmount ) ' pay full amount
   Else
      If employeeType = EmployeeType_Programmer Then
         If bonusAmount >= MANAGER_APPROVAL_LEVEL Then
            PayProgrammerBonus( employeeId, StdAmt() ) ' pay std. amount
         Else
            PayProgrammerBonus( employeeId, bonusAmount ) ' pay full amount
         End If
      End If
   End If
Next
```

Although useful in some circumstances, endline comments pose several problems. The comments have to be aligned to the right of the code so that they don't interfere with the visual structure of the code. If you don't align them neatly, they'll make your listing look like it's been through the washing machine. Endline comments tend to be hard to format. If you use many of them, it takes time to align them. Such time is not spent learning more about the code; it's dedicated solely to the tedious task of pressing the spacebar or the Tab key.

Endline comments are also hard to maintain. If the code on any line containing an endline comment grows, it bumps the comment farther out and all the other endline comments will have to be bumped out to match. Styles that are hard to maintain aren't maintained, and the commenting deteriorates under modification rather than improving.

Endline comments also tend to be cryptic. The right side of the line usually doesn't offer much room, and the desire to keep the comment on one line means that the comment must be short. Work then goes into making the line as short as possible instead of as clear as possible.

Avoid endline comments on single lines   In addition to their practical problems, endline comments pose several conceptual problems. Here's an example of a set of endline comments:

The comments merely repeat the code.

```
C++ Example of Useless Endline Comments
memoryToInitialize = MemoryAvailable();        // get amount of memory available
pointer = GetMemory( memoryToInitialize ); // get a ptr to the available memory
ZeroMemory( pointer, memoryToInitialize ); // set memory to 0
...
FreeMemory( pointer );                         // free memory allocated
```

A systemic problem with endline comments is that it's hard to write a meaningful comment for one line of code. Most endline comments just repeat the line of code, which hurts more than it helps.

Avoid endline comments for multiple lines of code If an endline comment is intended to apply to more than one line of code, the formatting doesn't show which lines the comment applies to:

CODING HORROR

> **Visual Basic Example of a Confusing Endline Comment on Multiple Lines of Code**
> ```
> For rateIdx = 1 to rateCount                  ' Compute discounted rates
>     LookupRegularRate( rateIdx, regularRate )
>     rate( rateIdx ) = regularRate * discount( rateIdx )
> Next
> ```

Even though the content of this particular comment is fine, its placement isn't. You have to read the comment and the code to know whether the comment applies to a specific statement or to the entire loop.

When to Use Endline Comments

Consider three exceptions to the recommendation against using endline comments:

Cross-Reference Other aspects of endline comments on data declarations are described in "Commenting Data Declarations," later in this section.

Use endline comments to annotate data declarations Endline comments are useful for annotating data declarations because they don't have the same systemic problems as endline comments on code, provided that you have enough width. With 132 columns, you can usually write a meaningful comment beside each data declaration:

> **Java Example of Good Endline Comments for Data Declarations**
> ```
> int boundary = 0;            // upper index of sorted part of array
> String insertVal = BLANK;    // data elmt to insert in sorted part of array
> int insertPos = 0;           // position to insert elmt in sorted part of array
> ```

Avoid using endline comments for maintenance notes Endline comments are sometimes used for recording modifications to code after its initial development. This kind of comment typically consists of a date and the programmer's initials, or possibly an error-report number. Here's an example:

```
for i = 1 to maxElmts - 1    -- fixed error #A423 10/1/05 (scm)
```

Adding such a comment can be gratifying after a late-night debugging session on software that's in production, but such comments really have no place in production code. Such comments are handled better by version-control software. Comments should explain why the code works *now*, not why the code didn't work at some point in the past.

Cross-Reference Use of endline comments to mark ends of blocks is described further in "Commenting Control Structures," later in this section.

Use endline comments to mark ends of blocks   An endline comment is useful for marking the end of a long block of code—the end of a *while* loop or an *if* statement, for example. This is described in more detail later in this chapter.

Aside from a couple of special cases, endline comments have conceptual problems and tend to be used for code that's too complicated. They are also difficult to format and maintain. Overall, they're best avoided.

Commenting Paragraphs of Code

Most comments in a well-documented program are one-sentence or two-sentence comments that describe paragraphs of code:

Java Example of a Good Comment for a Paragraph of Code
```java
// swap the roots
oldRoot = root[0];
root[0] = root[1];
root[1] = oldRoot;
```

The comment doesn't repeat the code—it describes the code's intent. Such comments are relatively easy to maintain. Even if you find an error in the way the roots are swapped, for example, the comment won't need to be changed. Comments that aren't written at the level of intent are harder to maintain.

Write comments at the level of the code's intent   Describe the purpose of the block of code that follows the comment. Here's an example of a comment that's ineffective because it doesn't operate at the level of intent:

Cross-Reference This code that performs a simple string search is used only for purposes of illustration. For real code, you'd use Java's built-in string library functions instead. For more on the importance of understanding your language's capabilities, see "Read!" in Section 33.3.

Java Example of an Ineffective Comment
```java
/* check each character in "inputString" until a dollar sign
is found or all characters have been checked
*/
done = false;
maxLen = inputString.length();
i = 0;
while ( !done && ( i < maxLen ) ) {
    if ( inputString[ i ] == '$' ) {
        done = true;
    }
    else {
        i++;
    }
}
```

You can figure out that the loop looks for a $ by reading the code, and it's somewhat helpful to have that summarized in the comment. The problem with this comment is that it merely repeats the code and doesn't give you any insight into what the code is supposed to be doing. This comment would be a little better:

```
// find '$' in inputString
```

This comment is better because it indicates that the goal of the loop is to find a $. But it still doesn't give you much insight into why the loop would need to find a $—in other words, into the deeper intent of the loop. Here's a comment that's better still:

```
// find the command-word terminator ($)
```

This comment actually contains information that the code listing does not, namely that the $ terminates a command word. In no way could you deduce that fact merely from reading the code fragment, so the comment is genuinely helpful.

Another way of thinking about commenting at the level of intent is to think about what you would name a routine that did the same thing as the code you want to comment. If you're writing paragraphs of code that have one purpose each, it isn't difficult. The comment in the previous code sample is a good example. *FindCommandWordTerminator()* would be a decent routine name. The other options, *Find$InInputString()* and *Check-EachCharacterInInputStrUntilADollarSignIsFoundOrAllCharactersHaveBeenChecked()*, are poor names (or invalid) for obvious reasons. Type the description without shortening or abbreviating it, as you might for a routine name. That description is your comment, and it's probably at the level of intent.

KEY POINT

Focus your documentation efforts on the code itself   For the record, the code itself is always the first documentation you should check. In the previous example, the literal, $, should be replaced with a named constant and the variables should provide more of a clue about what's going on. If you want to push the edge of the readability envelope, add a variable to contain the result of the search. Doing that clearly distinguishes between the loop index and the result of the loop. Here's the code rewritten with good comments and good style:

Java Example of a Good Comment and Good Code
```java
// find the command-word terminator
foundTheTerminator = false;
commandStringLength = inputString.length();
testCharPosition = 0;
while ( !foundTheTerminator && ( testCharPosition < commandStringLength ) ) {
    if ( inputString[ testCharPosition ] == COMMAND_WORD_TERMINATOR ) {
        foundTheTerminator = true;
        terminatorPosition = testCharPosition;
    }
    else {
        testCharPosition = testCharPosition + 1;
    }
}
```

Here's the variable that contains the result of the search.

If the code is good enough, it begins to read at close to the level of intent, encroaching on the comment's explanation of the code's intent. At that point, the comment and the code might become somewhat redundant, but that's a problem few programs have.

Cross-Reference For more on moving a section of code into its own routine, see "Extract routine/extract method" in Section 24.3.

Another good step for this code would be to create a routine called something like *FindCommandWordTerminator()* and move the code from the sample into that routine. A comment that describes that thought is useful but is more likely than a routine name to become inaccurate as the software evolves.

Focus paragraph comments on the why rather than the how Comments that explain how something is done usually operate at the programming-language level rather than the problem level. It's nearly impossible for a comment that focuses on how an operation is done to explain the intent of the operation, and comments that tell how are often redundant. What does the following comment tell you that the code doesn't?

Java Example of a Comment That Focuses on *How*
```java
// if account flag is zero
if ( accountFlag == 0 ) ...
```

The comment tells you nothing more than the code itself does. What about this comment?

Java Example of a Comment That Focuses on *Why*
```java
// if establishing a new account
if ( accountFlag == 0 ) ...
```

This comment is a lot better because it tells you something you couldn't infer from the code itself. The code itself could still be improved by use of a meaningful enumerated type name instead of *O* and a better variable name. Here's the best version of this comment and code:

Java Example of Using Good Style In Addition to a "Why" Comment
```java
// if establishing a new account
if ( accountType == AccountType.NewAccount ) ...
```

When code attains this level of readability, it's appropriate to question the value of the comment. In this case, the comment has been made redundant by the improved code, and it should probably be removed. Alternatively, the purpose of the comment could be subtly shifted, like this:

Java Example of Using a "Section Heading" Comment
```java
// establish a new account
if ( accountType == AccountType.NewAccount ) {
   ...
}
```

If this comment documents the whole block of code following the *if* test, it serves as a summary-level comment and it's appropriate to retain it as a section heading for the paragraph of code it references.

Use comments to prepare the reader for what is to follow   Good comments tell the person reading the code what to expect. A reader should be able to scan only the comments and get a good idea of what the code does and where to look for a specific activity. A corollary to this rule is that a comment should always precede the code it describes. This idea isn't always taught in programming classes, but it's a well-established convention in commercial practice.

Make every comment count   There's no virtue in excessive commenting—too many comments obscure the code they're meant to clarify. Rather than writing more comments, put the extra effort into making the code itself more readable.

Document surprises   If you find anything that isn't obvious from the code itself, put it into a comment. If you have used a tricky technique instead of a straightforward one to improve performance, use comments to point out what the straightforward technique would be and quantify the performance gain achieved by using the tricky technique. Here's an example:

```
C++ Example of Documenting a Surprise
for ( element = 0; element < elementCount; element++ ) {
   // Use right shift to divide by two. Substituting the
   // right-shift operation cuts the loop time by 75%.
   elementList[ element ] = elementList[ element ] >> 1;
}
```

The selection of the right shift in this example is intentional. Among experienced programmers, it's common knowledge that for integers, right shift is functionally equivalent to divide-by-two.

If it's common knowledge, why document it? Because the purpose of the operation is not to perform a right shift; it is to perform a divide-by-two. The fact that the code doesn't use the technique most suited to its purpose is significant. Moreover, most compilers optimize integer division-by-two to be a right shift anyway, meaning that the reduced clarity is usually unnecessary. In this particular case, the compiler evidently doesn't optimize the divide-by-two, and the time saved will be significant. With the documentation, a programmer reading the code would see the motivation for using the nonobvious technique. Without the comment, the same programmer would be inclined to grumble that the code is unnecessarily "clever" without any meaningful gain in performance. Usually such grumbling is justified, so it's important to document the exceptions.

Avoid abbreviations   Comments should be unambiguous, readable without the work of figuring out abbreviations. Avoid all but the most common abbreviations in comments. Unless you're using endline comments, using abbreviations isn't usually a temptation. If you are and it is, realize that abbreviations are another strike against a technique that struck out several pitches ago.

Differentiate between major and minor comments   In a few cases, you might want to differentiate between different levels of comments, indicating that a detailed comment is part of a previous, broader comment. You can handle this in a couple of ways. You can try underlining the major comment and not underlining the minor comment:

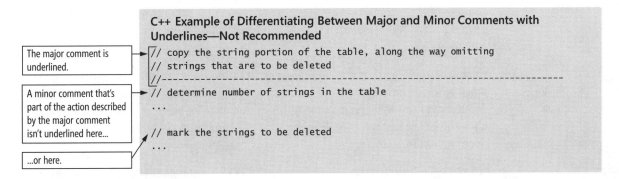

C++ Example of Differentiating Between Major and Minor Comments with Underlines—Not Recommended

The major comment is underlined.

A minor comment that's part of the action described by the major comment isn't underlined here...

...or here.

```
// copy the string portion of the table, along the way omitting
// strings that are to be deleted
//-------------------------------------------------------------------
// determine number of strings in the table
...

// mark the strings to be deleted
...
```

The weakness of this approach is that it forces you to underline more comments than you'd really like to. If you underline a comment, it's assumed that all the nonunderlined comments that follow it are subordinate to it. Consequently, when you write the first comment that isn't subordinate to the underlined comment, it too must be underlined and the cycle starts all over. The result is too much underlining or inconsistent underlining in some places and no underlining in others.

This theme has several variations that all have the same problem. If you put the major comment in all caps and the minor comments in lowercase, you substitute the problem of too many all-caps comments for too many underlined comments. Some programmers use an initial cap on major statements and no initial cap on minor ones, but that's a subtle visual cue too easily overlooked.

A better approach is to use ellipses in front of the minor comments:

C++ Example of Differentiating Between Major and Minor Comments with Ellipses

The major comment is formatted normally.

A minor comment that's part of the action described by the major comment is preceded by an ellipsis here...

...and here.

```
// copy the string portion of the table, along the way omitting
// strings that are to be deleted
// ... determine number of strings in the table
...

// ... mark the strings to be deleted
...
```

Another approach that's often best is to put the major-comment operation into its own routine. Routines should be logically "flat," with all their activities on about the same logical level. If your code differentiates between major and minor activities within a routine, the routine isn't flat. Putting the complicated group of activities into its own routine makes for two logically flat routines instead of one logically lumpy one.

This discussion of major and minor comments doesn't apply to indented code within loops and conditionals. In such cases, you'll often have a broad comment at the top of the loop and more detailed comments about the operations within the indented code. In those cases, the indentation provides the clue to the logical organization of the comments. This discussion applies only to sequential paragraphs of code in which several paragraphs make up a complete operation and some paragraphs are subordinate to others.

Comment anything that gets around an error or an undocumented feature in a language or an environment If it's an error, it probably isn't documented. Even if it's documented somewhere, it doesn't hurt to document it again in your code. If it's an undocumented feature, by definition it isn't documented elsewhere and it should be documented in your code.

Suppose you find that the library routine *WriteData(data, numItems, blockSize)* works properly except when *blockSize* equals *500*. It works fine for *499*, *501*, and every other value you've ever tried, but you've found that the routine has a defect that appears only when *blockSize* equals *500*. In code that uses *WriteData()*, document why you're making a special case when *blockSize* is *500*. Here's an example of how it could look:

Java Example of Documenting the Workaround for an Error

```java
blockSize = optimalBlockSize( numItems, sizePerItem );

/* The following code is necessary to work around an error in
WriteData() that appears only when the third parameter
equals 500. '500' has been replaced with a named constant
for clarity.
*/
if ( blockSize == WRITEDATA_BROKEN_SIZE ) {
   blockSize = WRITEDATA_WORKAROUND_SIZE;
}
WriteData ( file, data, blockSize );
```

Justify violations of good programming style   If you've had to violate good programming style, explain why. That will prevent a well-intentioned programmer from changing the code to a better style, possibly breaking your code. The explanation will make it clear that you knew what you were doing and weren't just sloppy—give yourself credit where credit is due!

Don't comment tricky code; rewrite it   Here's a comment from a project I worked on:

CODING HORROR

C++ Example of Commenting Clever Code

```
// VERY IMPORTANT NOTE:
// The constructor for this class takes a reference to a UiPublication.
// The UiPublication object MUST NOT BE DESTROYED before the DatabasePublication
// object. If it is, the DatabasePublication object will cause the program to
// die a horrible death.
```

This is a good example of one of the most prevalent and hazardous bits of programming folklore: that comments should be used to document especially "tricky" or "sensitive" sections of code. The reasoning is that people should know they need to be careful when they're working in certain areas.

This is a scary idea.

Commenting tricky code is exactly the wrong approach to take. Comments can't rescue difficult code. As Kernighan and Plauger emphasize, "Don't document bad code—rewrite it" (1978).

HARD DATA

One study found that areas of source code with large numbers of comments also tended to have the most defects and to consume the most development effort (Lind and Vairavan 1989). The authors hypothesized that programmers tended to comment difficult code heavily.

KEY POINT

When someone says, "This is really *tricky* code," I hear them say, "This is really *bad* code." If something seems tricky to you, it will be incomprehensible to someone else. Even something that doesn't seem all that tricky to you can seem impossibly convoluted to another person who hasn't seen the trick before. If you have to ask yourself "Is this tricky?" it is. You can always find a rewrite that's not tricky, so rewrite the code. Make your code so good that you don't need comments, and then comment it to make it even better.

This advice applies mainly to code you're writing for the first time. If you're maintaining a program and don't have the latitude to rewrite bad code, commenting the tricky parts is a good practice.

Commenting Data Declarations

Cross-Reference For details on formatting data, see "Laying Out Data Declarations" in Section 31.5. For details on how to use data effectively, see Chapters 10 through 13.

Comments for variable declarations describe aspects of the variable that the variable name can't describe. It's important to document data carefully; at least one company that studied its own practices has concluded that annotations on data are even more important than annotations on the processes in which the data is used (SDC, in Glass 1982). Here are some guidelines for commenting data:

Comment the units of numeric data If a number represents length, indicate whether the length is expressed in inches, feet, meters, or kilometers. If it's time, indicate whether it's expressed in elapsed seconds since 1-1-1980, milliseconds since the start of the program, and so on. If it's coordinates, indicate whether they represent latitude, longitude, and altitude and whether they're in radians or degrees; whether they represent an *X, Y, Z* coordinate system with its origin at the earth's center; and so on. Don't assume that the units are obvious. To a new programmer, they won't be. To someone who's been working on another part of the system, they won't be. After the program has been substantially modified, they won't be.

Alternatively, in many cases you should embed the units in the variable names rather than in comments. An expression like *distanceToSurface = marsLanderAltitude* looks like it's probably correct, but *distanceToSurfaceInMeters = marsLanderAltitudeInFeet* exposes an obvious error.

Cross-Reference A stronger technique for documenting allowable ranges of variables is to use assertions at the beginning and end of a routine to assert that the variable's values should be within a prescribed range. For more details, see Section 8.2, "Assertions."

Comment the range of allowable numeric values If a variable has an expected range of values, document the expected range. One of the powerful features of the Ada programming language was the ability to restrict the allowable values of a numeric variable to a range of values. If your language doesn't support that capability (and most languages don't), use a comment to document the expected range of values. For example, if a variable represents an amount of money in dollars, indicate that you expect it to be between $1 and $100. If a variable indicates a voltage, indicate that it should be between 105v and 125v.

Comment coded meanings If your language supports enumerated types—as C++ and Visual Basic do—use them to express coded meanings. If it doesn't, use comments to indicate what each value represents—and use a named constant rather than a literal for each of the values. If a variable represents kinds of electrical current, comment the fact that *1* represents alternating current, *2* represents direct current, and *3* represents *undefined*.

Here's an example of documenting variable declarations that illustrates the three preceding recommendations—all the range information is given in comments:

Visual Basic Example of Nicely Documented Variable Declarations

```
Dim cursorX As Integer    ' horizontal cursor position; ranges from 1..MaxCols
Dim cursorY As Integer    ' vertical cursor position; ranges from 1..MaxRows

Dim antennaLength As Long        ' length of antenna in meters; range is >= 2
Dim signalStrength As Integer    ' strength of signal in kilowatts; range is >= 1

Dim characterCode As Integer        ' ASCII character code; ranges from 0..255
Dim characterAttribute As Integer ' 0=Plain; 1=Italic; 2=Bold; 3=BoldItalic
Dim characterSize As Integer        ' size of character in points; ranges from 4..127
```

Comment limitations on input data   Input data might come from an input parameter, a file, or direct user input. The previous guidelines apply as much to routine-input parameters as to other kinds of data. Make sure that expected and unexpected values are documented. Comments are one way of documenting that a routine is never supposed to receive certain data. Assertions are another way to document valid ranges, and if you use them the code becomes that much more self-checking.

Document flags to the bit level   If a variable is used as a bit field, document the meaning of each bit:

Cross-Reference For details on naming flag variables, see "Naming Status Variables" in Section 11.2.

Visual Basic Example of Documenting Flags to the Bit Level

```
' The meanings of the bits in statusFlags are as follows, from most
' significant bit to least significant bit:
' MSB   0       error detected: 1=yes, 0=no
'       1-2     kind of error: 0=syntax, 1=warning, 2=severe, 3=fatal
'       3       reserved (should be 0)
'       4       printer status: 1=ready, 0=not ready
'       ...
'       14      not used (should be 0)
' LSB   15-32 not used (should be 0)
Dim statusFlags As Integer
```

If the example were written in C++, it would call for bit-field syntax so that the bit-field meanings would be self-documenting.

Stamp comments related to a variable with the variable's name   If you have comments that refer to a specific variable, make sure the comment is updated whenever the variable is updated. One way to improve the odds of a consistent modification is to stamp the comment with the variable name. That way, string searches for the variable name will find the comment as well as the variable.

Cross-Reference For details on using global data, see Section 13.3, "Global Data."

Document global data   If global data is used, annotate each piece well at the point at which it's declared. The annotation should indicate the purpose of the data and why it needs to be global. At each point at which the data is used, make it clear that the data is global. A naming convention is the first choice for highlighting a variable's global status. If a naming convention isn't used, comments can fill the gap.

Commenting Control Structures

Cross-Reference For other details on control structures, see Section 31.3, "Layout Styles," Section 31.4, "Laying Out Control Structures," and Chapters 14 through 19.

The space before a control structure is usually a natural place to put a comment. If it's an *if* or a *case* statement, you can provide the reason for the decision and a summary of the outcome. If it's a loop, you can indicate the purpose of the loop.

C++ Example of Commenting the Purpose of a Control Structure

Purpose of the following loop. →
```cpp
// copy input field up to comma
while ( ( *inputString != ',' ) && ( *inputString != END_OF_STRING ) ) {
   *field = *inputString;
   field++;
   inputString++;
```
End of the loop (useful for longer, nested loops—although the need for such a comment indicates overly complicated code). →
```cpp
} // while -- copy input field

*field = END_OF_STRING;

if ( *inputString != END_OF_STRING ) {
```
Purpose of the loop. Position of comment makes it clear that *inputString* is being set up for the loop.
```cpp
   // read past comma and subsequent blanks to get to the next input field
   inputString++;
   while ( ( *inputString == ' ' ) && ( *inputString != END_OF_STRING ) ) {
      inputString++;
   }
} // if -- at end of string
```

This example suggests some guidelines:

Put a comment before each* if, case, loop, *or block of statements Such a place is a natural spot for a comment, and these constructs often need explanation. Use a comment to clarify the purpose of the control structure.

Comment the end of each control structure Use a comment to show what ended—for example,

```
} // for clientIndex - process record for each client
```

A comment is especially helpful at the end of long loops and to clarify loop nesting. Here's a Java example of using comments to clarify the ends of loop structures:

Java Example of Using Comments to Show Nesting
```java
for ( tableIndex = 0; tableIndex < tableCount; tableIndex++ ) {
   while ( recordIndex < recordCount ) {
      if ( !IllegalRecordNumber( recordIndex ) ) {
         ...
```
These comments indicate which control structure is ending.
```java
      } // if
   } // while
} // for
```

This commenting technique supplements the visual clues about the logical structure given by the code's indentation. You don't need to use the technique for short loops that aren't nested. When the nesting is deep or the loops are long, however, the technique pays off.

Treat end-of-loop comments as a warning indicating complicated code   If a loop is complicated enough to need an end-of-loop comment, treat the comment as a warning sign: the loop might need to be simplified. The same rule applies to complicated *if* tests and *case* statements.

End-of-loop comments provide useful clues to logical structure, but writing them initially and then maintaining them can become tedious. The best way to avoid such tedious work is often to rewrite any code that's complicated enough to require tedious documentation.

Commenting Routines

Cross-Reference For details on formatting routines, see Section 31.7. For details on how to create high-quality routines, see Chapter 7.

Routine-level comments are the subject of some of the worst advice in typical computer-science textbooks. Many textbooks urge you to pile up a stack of information at the top of every routine, regardless of its size or complexity:

CODING HORROR

Visual Basic Example of a Monolithic, Kitchen-Sink Routine Prolog

```
'*********************************************************************
' Name: CopyString
'
' Purpose:      This routine copies a string from the source
'               string (source) to the target string (target).
'
' Algorithm:    It gets the length of "source" and then copies each
'               character, one at a time, into "target". It uses
'               the loop index as an array index into both "source"
'               and "target" and increments the loop/array index
'               after each character is copied.
'
' Inputs:       input    The string to be copied
'
' Outputs:      output   The string to receive the copy of "input"
'
' Interface Assumptions: None
'
' Modification History: None
'
' Author:       Dwight K. Coder
' Date Created: 10/1/04
' Phone:        (555) 222-2255
' SSN:          111-22-3333
' Eye Color:    Green
' Maiden Name:  None
' Blood Type:   AB-
' Mother's Maiden Name: None
' Favorite Car: Pontiac Aztek
' Personalized License Plate: "Tek-ie"
'*********************************************************************
```

This is ridiculous. *CopyString* is presumably a trivial routine—probably fewer than five lines of code. The comment is totally out of proportion to the scale of the routine. The parts about the routine's *Purpose* and *Algorithm* are strained because it's hard to describe something as simple as *CopyString* at a level of detail that's between "copy a string" and the code itself. The boilerplate comments *Interface Assumptions* and *Modification History* aren't useful either—they just take up space in the listing. Requiring the author's name is redundant with information that can be retrieved more accurately from the revision-control system. To require all these ingredients for every routine is a recipe for inaccurate comments and maintenance failure. It's a lot of make-work that never pays off.

Another problem with heavy routine headers is that they discourage good factoring of the code—the overhead to create a new routine is so high that programmers will tend to err on the side of creating fewer routines, not more. Coding conventions should encourage good practices; heavy routine headers do the opposite.

Here are some guidelines for commenting routines:

Keep comments close to the code they describe   One reason that the prolog to a routine shouldn't contain voluminous documentation is that such a practice puts the comments far away from the parts of the routine they describe. During maintenance, comments that are far from the code tend not to be maintained with the code. The comments and the code start to disagree, and suddenly the comments are worthless. Instead, follow the Principle of Proximity and put comments as close as possible to the code they describe. They're more likely to be maintained, and they'll continue to be worthwhile.

Several components of routine prologs are described below and should be included as needed. For your convenience, create a boilerplate documentation prolog. Just don't feel obliged to include all the information in every case. Fill out the parts that matter, and delete the rest.

Cross-Reference Good routine names are key to routine documentation. For details on how to create them, see Section 7.3, "Good Routine Names."

Describe each routine in one or two sentences at the top of the routine   If you can't describe the routine in a short sentence or two, you probably need to think harder about what it's supposed to do. Difficulty in creating a short description is a sign that the design isn't as good as it should be. Go back to the design drawing board and try again. The short summary statement should be present in virtually all routines except for simple *Get* and *Set* accessor routines.

Document parameters where they are declared   The easiest way to document input and output variables is to put comments next to the parameter declarations:

Java Example of Documenting Input and Output Data Where It's Declared—Good Practice

```java
public void InsertionSort(
    int[] dataToSort, // elements to sort in locations firstElement..lastElement
    int firstElement, // index of first element to sort (>=0)
    int lastElement // index of last element to sort (<= MAX_ELEMENTS)
)
```

Cross-Reference Endline comments are discussed in more detail in "Endline Comments and Their Problems," earlier in this section.

This practice is a good exception to the rule of not using endline comments; they are exceptionally useful in documenting input and output parameters. This occasion for commenting is also a good illustration of the value of using standard indentation rather than endline indentation for routine parameter lists—you wouldn't have room for meaningful endline comments if you used endline indentation. The comments in the example are strained for space even with standard indentation. This example also demonstrates that comments aren't the only form of documentation. If your variable names are good enough, you might be able to skip commenting them. Finally, the need to document input and output variables is a good reason to avoid global data. Where do you document it? Presumably, you document the globals in the monster prolog. That makes for more work and, unfortunately, in practice usually means that the global data doesn't get documented. That's too bad because global data needs to be documented at least as much as anything else.

Take advantage of code documentation utilities such as Javadoc If the code in the previous example were actually written in Java, you would have the additional ability to set up the code to take advantage of Java's document extraction utility, Javadoc. In that case, "documenting parameters where they are declared" would change to look like this:

Java Example of Documenting Input and Output Data To Take Advantage of Javadoc

```java
/**
 * ... <description of the routine> ...
 *
 * @param dataToSort  elements to sort in locations firstElement..lastElement
 * @param firstElement index of first element to sort (>=0)
 * @param lastElement  index of last element to sort (<= MAX_ELEMENTS)
 */
public void InsertionSort(
    int[] dataToSort,
    int firstElement,
    int lastElement
)
```

With a tool like Javadoc, the benefit of setting up the code to extract documentation outweighs the risks associated with separating the parameter description from the parameter's declaration. If you're not working in an environment that supports document extraction, like Javadoc, you're usually better off keeping the comments closer to the parameter names to avoid inconsistent edits and duplication of the names themselves.

Differentiate between input and output data   It's useful to know which data is used as input and which is used as output. Visual Basic makes it relatively easy to tell because output data is preceded by the *ByRef* keyword and input data is preceded by the *ByVal* keyword. If your language doesn't support such differentiation automatically, put it into comments. Here's an example in C++:

Cross-Reference The order of these parameters follows the standard order for C++ routines but conflicts with more general practices. For details, see "Put parameters in input-modify-output order" in Section 7.5. For details on using a naming convention to differentiate between input and output data, see Section 11.4.

C++ Example of Differentiating Between Input and Output Data
```cpp
void StringCopy(
    char *target,        // out: string to copy to
    const char *source  // in: string to copy from
)
...
```

C++-language routine declarations are a little tricky because some of the time the asterisk (*) indicates that the argument is an output argument and a lot of the time it just means that the variable is easier to handle as a pointer than as a nonpointer type. You're usually better off identifying input and output arguments explicitly.

If your routines are short enough and you maintain a clear distinction between input and output data, documenting the data's input or output status is probably unnecessary. If the routine is longer, however, it's a useful service to anyone who reads the routine.

Cross-Reference For details on other considerations for routine interfaces, see Section 7.5, "How to Use Routine Parameters." To document assumptions using assertions, see "Use assertions to document and verify preconditions and postconditions" in Section 8.2.

Document interface assumptions   Documenting interface assumptions might be viewed as a subset of the other commenting recommendations. If you have made any assumptions about the state of variables you receive—legal and illegal values, arrays being in sorted order, member data being initialized or containing only good data, and so on—document them either in the routine prolog or where the data is declared. This documentation should be present in virtually every routine.

Make sure that global data that's used is documented. A global variable is as much an interface to a routine as anything else and is all the more hazardous because it sometimes doesn't seem like one.

As you're writing the routine and realize that you're making an interface assumption, write it down immediately.

Comment on the routine's limitations   If the routine provides a numeric result, indicate the accuracy of the result. If the computations are undefined under some conditions, document the conditions. If the routine has a default behavior when it gets into trouble, document the behavior. If the routine is expected to work only on arrays or tables of a certain size, indicate that. If you know of modifications to the program that would break the routine, document them. If you ran into gotchas during the development of the routine, document those also.

Document the routine's global effects   If the routine modifies global data, describe exactly what it does to the global data. As mentioned in Section 13.3, "Global Data," modifying global data is at least an order of magnitude more dangerous than merely reading it, so modifications should be performed carefully, part of the care being clear documentation. As usual, if documenting becomes too onerous, rewrite the code to reduce global data.

Document the source of algorithms that are used   If you've used an algorithm from a book or magazine, document the volume and page number you took it from. If you developed the algorithm yourself, indicate where the reader can find the notes you've made about it.

Use comments to mark parts of your program   Some programmers use comments to mark parts of their program so that they can find them easily. One such technique in C++ and Java is to mark the top of each routine with a comment beginning with these characters:

/**

This allows you to jump from routine to routine by doing a string search for /** or to use your editor to jump automatically if it supports that.

A similar technique is to mark different kinds of comments differently, depending on what they describe. For example, in C++ you could use *@keyword*, where *keyword* is a code you use to indicate the kind of comment. The comment *@param* could indicate that the comment describes a parameter to a routine, *@version* could indicate file-version information, *@throws* could document the exceptions thrown by a routine, and so on. This technique allows you to use tools to extract different kinds of information from your source files. For example, you could search for *@throws* to retrieve documentation about all the exceptions thrown by all the routines in a program.

cc2e.com/3259   This C++ convention is based on the Javadoc convention, which is a well-established interface documentation convention for Java programs (*java.sun.com/j2se/javadoc/*). You can define your own conventions in other languages.

Commenting Classes, Files, and Programs

Cross-Reference For layout details, see Section 31.8, "Laying Out Classes." For details on using classes, see Chapter 6, "Working Classes."

Classes, files, and programs are all characterized by the fact that they contain multiple routines. A file or class should contain a collection of related routines. A program contains all the routines in a program. The documentation task in each case is to provide a meaningful, top-level view of the contents of the file, class, or program.

General Guidelines for Class Documentation

For each class, use a block comment to describe general attributes of the class:

Describe the design approach to the class   Overview comments that provide information that can't readily be reverse-engineered from coding details are especially useful. Describe the class's design philosophy, overall design approach, design alternatives that were considered and discarded, and so on.

Describe limitations, usage assumptions, and so on   Similar to routines, be sure to describe any limitations imposed by the class's design. Also describe assumptions about input and output data, error-handling responsibilities, global effects, sources of algorithms, and so on.

Comment the class interface   Can another programmer understand how to use a class without looking at the class's implementation? If not, class encapsulation is seriously at risk. The class's interface should contain all the information anyone needs to use the class. The Javadoc convention is to require, at a minimum, documentation for each parameter and each return value (Sun Microsystems 2000). This should be done for all exposed routines of each class (Bloch 2001).

Don't document implementation details in the class interface   A cardinal rule of encapsulation is that you expose information only on a need-to-know basis: if there is any question about whether information needs to be exposed, the default is to keep it hidden. Consequently, class interface files should contain information needed to use the class but not information needed to implement or maintain the inner workings of the class.

General Guidelines for File Documentation

At the top of a file, use a block comment to describe the contents of the file:

Describe the purpose and contents of each file   The file header comment should describe the classes or routines contained in a file. If all the routines for a program are in one file, the purpose of the file is pretty obvious—it's the file that contains the whole program. If the purpose of the file is to contain one specific class, the purpose is also obvious—it's the file that contains the class with a similar name.

If the file contains more than one class, explain why the classes need to be combined into a single file.

If the division into multiple source files is made for some reason other than modularity, a good description of the purpose of the file will be even more helpful to a programmer who is modifying the program. If someone is looking for a routine that does *x*, does the file's header comment help that person determine whether this file contains such a routine?

Put your name, e-mail address, and phone number in the block comment   Authorship and primary responsibility for specific areas of source code becomes important on large projects. Small projects (fewer than 10 people) can use collaborative development approaches, such as shared code ownership in which all team members are equally responsible for all sections of code. Larger systems require that programmers specialize in different areas of code, which makes full-team shared-code ownership impractical.

In that case, authorship is important information to have in a listing. It gives other programmers who work on the code a clue about the programming style, and it gives them someone to contact if they need help. Depending on whether you work on individual routines, classes, or programs, you should include author information at the routine, class, or program level.

Include a version-control tag   Many version-control tools will insert version information into a file. In CVS, for example, the characters

```
// $Id$
```

will automatically expand to

```
// $Id: ClassName.java,v 1.1 2004/02/05 00:36:43 ismene Exp $
```

This allows you to maintain current versioning information within a file without requiring any developer effort other than inserting the original *Id* comment.

Include legal notices in the block comment   Many companies like to include copyright statements, confidentiality notices, and other legal notices in their programs. If yours is one of them, include a line similar to the one below. Check with your company's legal advisor to determine what information, if any, to include in your files.

Java Example of a Copyright Statement
```
// (c) Copyright 1993-2004 Steven C. McConnell. All Rights Reserved.
...
```

Give the file a name related to its contents   Normally, the name of the file should be closely related to the name of the public class contained in the file. For example, if the class is named *Employee*, the file should be named *Employee.cpp*. Some languages, notably Java, require the file name to match the class name.

The Book Paradigm for Program Documentation

Further Reading This discussion is adapted from "The Book Paradigm for Improved Maintenance" (Oman and Cook 1990a) and "Typographic Style Is More Than Cosmetic" (Oman and Cook 1990b). A similar analysis is presented in detail in *Human Factors and Typography for More Readable Programs* (Baecker and Marcus 1990).

Most experienced programmers agree that the documentation techniques described in the previous section are valuable. The hard, scientific evidence for the value of any one of the techniques is still weak. When the techniques are combined, however, evidence of their effectiveness is strong.

In 1990, Paul Oman and Curtis Cook published a pair of studies on the "Book Paradigm" for documentation (1990a, 1990b). They looked for a coding style that would support several different styles of code reading. One goal was to support top-down, bottom-up, and focused searches. Another was to break up the code into chunks that programmers could remember more easily than a long listing of homogeneous code. Oman and Cook wanted the style to provide for both high-level and low-level clues about code organization.

They found that by thinking of code as a special kind of book and by formatting it accordingly, they could achieve their goals. In the Book Paradigm, code and its documentation are organized into several components similar to the components of a book to help programmers get a high-level view of the program.

The "preface" is a group of introductory comments such as those usually found at the beginning of a file. It functions as the preface to a book does. It gives the programmer an overview of the program.

The "table of contents" shows the top-level files, classes, and routines (chapters). They might be shown in a list, as a traditional book's chapters are, or graphically in a structure chart.

The "sections" are the divisions within routines—routine declarations, data declarations, and executable statements, for example.

The "cross-references" are cross-reference maps of the code, including line numbers.

The low-level techniques that Oman and Cook use to take advantage of the similarities between a book and a code listing are similar to the techniques described in Chapter 31, "Layout and Style," and in this chapter.

HARD DATA

The upshot of using their techniques to organize code was that when Oman and Cook gave a maintenance task to a group of experienced, professional programmers, the average time to perform a maintenance task in a 1000-line program was only about three-quarters of the time it took the programmers to do the same task in a traditional source listing (1990b). Moreover, the maintenance scores of programmers on code documented with the Book Paradigm averaged about 20 percent higher than on traditionally documented code. Oman and Cook concluded that by paying attention to the typographic principles of book design, you can get a 10 to 20 percent improvement in comprehension. A study with programmers at the University of Toronto produced similar results (Baecker and Marcus 1990).

The Book Paradigm emphasizes the importance of providing documentation that explains both the high-level and the low-level organization of your program.

32.6 IEEE Standards

For documentation beyond the source-code level, valuable sources of information are the IEEE (Institute for Electric and Electrical Engineers) Software Engineering Standards. IEEE standards are developed by groups composed of practitioners and academicians who are expert in a particular area. Each standard contains a summary of the area covered by the standard and typically contains the outline for the appropriate documentation for work in that area.

Several national and international organizations participate in standards work. The IEEE is a group that has taken the lead in defining software engineering standards. Some standards are jointly adopted by ISO (International Standards Organization), EIA (Electronic Industries Alliance), or IEC (International Engineering Consortium).

Standards names are composed of the standards number, the year the standard was adopted, and the name of the standard. So, *IEEE/EIA Std 12207-1997, Information Technology–Software Life Cycle Processes*, refers to standard number 12207.2, which was adopted in 1997 by the IEEE and EIA.

Here are some of the national and international standards most applicable to software projects:

cc2e.com/3266

The top-level standard is *ISO/IEC Std 12207, Information Technology–Software Life Cycle Processes*, which is the international standard that defines a life-cycle framework for developing and managing software projects. This standard was adopted in the United States as *IEEE/EIA Std 12207, Information Technology–Software Life Cycle Processes*.

Software-Development Standards

cc2e.com/3273

Here are software-development standards to consider:

IEEE Std 830-1998, Recommended Practice for Software Requirements Specifications

IEEE Std 1233-1998, Guide for Developing System Requirements Specifications

IEEE Std 1016-1998, Recommended Practice for Software Design Descriptions

IEEE Std 828-1998, Standard for Software Configuration Management Plans

IEEE Std 1063-2001, Standard for Software User Documentation

IEEE Std 1219-1998, Standard for Software Maintenance

Software Quality-Assurance Standards

cc2e.com/3280

And here are software quality-assurance standards:

IEEE Std 730-2002, Standard for Software Quality Assurance Plans

IEEE Std 1028-1997, Standard for Software Reviews

IEEE Std 1008-1987 (R1993), Standard for Software Unit Testing

IEEE Std 829-1998, Standard for Software Test Documentation

IEEE Std 1061-1998, Standard for a Software Quality Metrics Methodology

Management Standards

cc2e.com/3287

Here are some software-management standards:

IEEE Std 1058-1998, Standard for Software Project Management Plans

IEEE Std 1074-1997, Standard for Developing Software Life Cycle Processes

IEEE Std 1045-1992, Standard for Software Productivity Metrics

IEEE Std 1062-1998, Recommended Practice for Software Acquisition

IEEE Std 1540-2001, Standard for Software Life Cycle Processes - Risk Management

IEEE Std 1490-1998, Guide - Adoption of PMI Standard - A Guide to the Project Management Body of Knowledge

Overview of Standards

cc2e.com/3294

Here are sources that provide overviews of standards:

cc2e.com/3201

IEEE Software Engineering Standards Collection, 2003 Edition. New York, NY: Institute of Electrical and Electronics Engineers (IEEE). This comprehensive volume contains 40 of the most recent ANSI/IEEE standards for software development as of 2003. Each standard includes a document outline, a description of each component of the outline, and a rationale for that component. The document includes standards for quality-assurance plans, configuration-management plans, test documents, requirements specifications, verification and validation plans, design descriptions, project-management plans, and user documentation. The book is a distillation of the expertise of hundreds of people at the top of their fields and would be a bargain at virtually any price. Some of the standards are also available individually. All are available from the IEEE Computer Society in Los Alamitos, California and from *www.computer.org/cspress.*

Moore, James W. *Software Engineering Standards: A User's Road Map.* Los Alamitos, CA: IEEE Computer Society Press, 1997. Moore provides an overview of IEEE software engineering standards.

Additional Resources

cc2e.com/3208

In addition to the IEEE standards, numerous other resources are available on program documentation.

Spinellis, Diomidis. *Code Reading: The Open Source Perspective*. Boston, MA: Addison-Wesley, 2003. This book is a pragmatic exploration of techniques for reading code, including where to find code to read, tips for reading large code bases, tools that support code reading, and many other useful suggestions.

cc2e.com/3215

I wonder how many great novelists have never read someone else's work, how many great painters have never studied another's brush strokes, how many skilled surgeons never learned by looking over a colleague's shoulder.... And yet that's what we expect programmers to do.
—*Dave Thomas*

SourceForge.net. For decades, a perennial problem in teaching software development has been finding life-size examples of production code to share with students. Many people learn quickest from studying real-life examples, but most life-size code bases are treated as proprietary information by the companies that created them. This situation has improved dramatically through the combination of the Internet and open-source software. The Source Forge website contains code for thousands of programs in C, C++, Java, Visual Basic, PHP, Perl, Python, and many other languages, all which you can download for free. Programmers can benefit from wading through the code on the website to see much larger real-world examples than *Code Complete, Second Edition*, is able to show in its short code examples. Junior programmers who haven't previously seen extensive examples of production code will find this website especially valuable as a source of both good and bad coding practices.

cc2e.com/3222

Sun Microsystems. "How to Write Doc Comments for the Javadoc Tool," 2000. Available from *http://java.sun.com/j2se/javadoc/writingdoccomments/*. This article describes how to use Javadoc to document Java programs. It includes detailed advice about how to tag comments by using an *@tag* style notation. It also includes many specific details about how to wordsmith the comments themselves. The Javadoc conventions are probably the most fully developed code-level documentation standards currently available.

Here are sources of information on other topics in software documentation:

McConnell, Steve. *Software Project Survival Guide*. Redmond, WA: Microsoft Press, 1998. This book describes the documentation required by a medium-sized business-critical project. A related website provides numerous related document templates.

cc2e.com/3229

www.construx.com. This website (my company's website) contains numerous document templates, coding conventions, and other resources related to all aspects of software development, including software documentation.

cc2e.com/3236

Post, Ed. "Real Programmers Don't Use Pascal," *Datamation*, July 1983, pp. 263–265. This tongue-in-cheek paper argues for a return to the "good old days" of Fortran programming when programmers didn't have to worry about pesky issues like readability.

cc2e.com/3243

CHECKLIST: Good Commenting Technique

General

- ❑ Can someone pick up the code and immediately start to understand it?
- ❑ Do comments explain the code's intent or summarize what the code does, rather than just repeating the code?
- ❑ Is the Pseudocode Programming Process used to reduce commenting time?
- ❑ Has tricky code been rewritten rather than commented?
- ❑ Are comments up to date?
- ❑ Are comments clear and correct?
- ❑ Does the commenting style allow comments to be easily modified?

Statements and Paragraphs

- ❑ Does the code avoid endline comments?
- ❑ Do comments focus on *why* rather than *how*?
- ❑ Do comments prepare the reader for the code to follow?
- ❑ Does every comment count? Have redundant, extraneous, and self-indulgent comments been removed or improved?
- ❑ Are surprises documented?
- ❑ Have abbreviations been avoided?
- ❑ Is the distinction between major and minor comments clear?
- ❑ Is code that works around an error or undocumented feature commented?

Data Declarations

- ❑ Are units on data declarations commented?
- ❑ Are the ranges of values on numeric data commented?
- ❑ Are coded meanings commented?
- ❑ Are limitations on input data commented?
- ❑ Are flags documented to the bit level?
- ❑ Has each global variable been commented where it is declared?
- ❑ Has each global variable been identified as such at each usage, by a naming convention, a comment, or both?
- ❑ Are magic numbers replaced with named constants or variables rather than just documented?

Control Structures

❑ Is each control statement commented?

❑ Are the ends of long or complex control structures commented or, when possible, simplified so that they don't need comments?

Routines

❑ Is the purpose of each routine commented?

❑ Are other facts about each routine given in comments, when relevant, including input and output data, interface assumptions, limitations, error corrections, global effects, and sources of algorithms?

Files, Classes, and Programs

❑ Does the program have a short document, such as that described in the Book Paradigm, that gives an overall view of how the program is organized?

❑ Is the purpose of each file described?

❑ Are the author's name, e-mail address, and phone number in the listing?

Key Points

■ The question of whether to comment is a legitimate one. Done poorly, commenting is a waste of time and sometimes harmful. Done well, commenting is worthwhile.

■ The source code should contain most of the critical information about the program. As long as the program is running, the source code is more likely than any other resource to be kept current, and it's useful to have important information bundled with the code.

■ Good code is its own best documentation. If the code is bad enough to require extensive comments, try first to improve the code so that it doesn't need extensive comments.

■ Comments should say things about the code that the code can't say about itself—at the summary level or the intent level.

■ Some commenting styles require a lot of tedious clerical work. Develop a style that's easy to maintain.

Chapter 33
Personal Character

Contents

- 33.1 Isn't Personal Character Off the Topic?: page 820

- 33.2 Intelligence and Humility: page 821

- 33.3 Curiosity: page 822

- 33.4 Intellectual Honesty: page 826

- 33.5 Communication and Cooperation: page 828

- 33.6 Creativity and Discipline: page 829

- 33.7 Laziness: page 830

- 33.8 Characteristics That Don't Matter As Much As You Might Think: page 830

- 33.9 Habits: page 833

Related Topics

- Themes in software craftsmanship: Chapter 34

- Complexity: Sections 5.2 and 19.6

Personal character has received a rare degree of attention in software development. Ever since Edsger Dijkstra's landmark 1965 article, "Programming Considered as a Human Activity," programmer character has been regarded as a legitimate and fruitful area of inquiry. Titles such as *The Psychology of Bridge Construction* and "Exploratory Experiments in Attorney Behavior" might seem absurd, but in the computer field *The Psychology of Computer Programming*, "Exploratory Experiments in Programmer Behavior," and similar titles are classics.

Engineers in every discipline learn the limits of the tools and materials they work with. If you're an electrical engineer, you know the conductivity of various metals and a hundred ways to use a voltmeter. If you're a structural engineer, you know the load-bearing properties of wood, concrete, and steel.

If you're a software engineer, your basic building material is human intellect and your primary tool is *you*. Rather than designing a structure to the last detail and then handing the blueprints to someone else for construction, you know that once you've designed a piece of software to the last detail, it's done. The whole job of programming is building air castles—it's one of the most purely mental activities you can do.

Consequently, when software engineers study the essential properties of their tools and raw materials, they find that they're studying people: intellect, character, and other attributes that are less tangible than wood, concrete, and steel.

If you're looking for concrete programming tips, this chapter might seem too abstract to be useful. Once you've absorbed the specific advice in the rest of the book, however, this chapter spells out what you need to do to continue improving. Read the next section, and then decide whether you want to skip the chapter.

33.1 Isn't Personal Character Off the Topic?

The intense inwardness of programming makes personal character especially important. You know how difficult it is to put in eight concentrated hours in one day. You've probably had the experience of being burned out one day from concentrating too hard the day before or burned out one month from concentrating too hard the month before. You've probably had days on which you've worked well from 8:00 A.M. to 2:00 P.M. and then felt like quitting. You didn't quit, though; you pushed on from 2:00 P.M. to 5:00 P.M. and then spent the rest of the week fixing what you wrote from 2:00 to 5:00.

Programming work is essentially unsupervisable because no one ever really knows what you're working on. We've all had projects in which we spent 80 percent of the time working on a small piece we found interesting and 20 percent of the time building the other 80 percent of the program.

Your employer can't force you to be a good programmer; a lot of times your employer isn't even in a position to judge whether you're good. If you want to be great, you're responsible for making yourself great. It's a matter of your personal character.

HARD DATA

Once you decide to make yourself a superior programmer, the potential for improvement is huge. Study after study has found differences on the order of 10 to 1 in the time required to create a program. They have also found differences on the order of 10 to 1 in the time required to debug a program and 10 to 1 in the resulting size, speed, error rate, and number of errors detected (Sackman, Erikson, and Grant 1968; Curtis 1981; Mills 1983; DeMarco and Lister 1985; Curtis et al. 1986; Card 1987; Valett and McGarry 1989).

You can't do anything about your intelligence, so the classical wisdom goes, but you can do something about your character. And it turns out that character is the more decisive factor in the makeup of a superior programmer.

33.2 Intelligence and Humility

We become authorities and experts in the practical and scientific spheres by so many separate acts and hours of work. If a person keeps faithfully busy each hour of the working day, he can count on waking up some morning to find himself one of the competent ones of his generation.
—*William James*

Intelligence doesn't seem like an aspect of personal character, and it isn't. Coincidentally, great intelligence is only loosely connected to being a good programmer.

What? You don't have to be superintelligent?

No, you don't. Nobody is really smart enough to program computers. Fully understanding an average program requires an almost limitless capacity to absorb details and an equal capacity to comprehend them all at the same time. The way you focus your intelligence is more important than how much intelligence you have.

As Chapter 5 ("Design in Construction") mentioned, at the 1972 Turing Award Lecture, Edsger Dijkstra delivered a paper titled "The Humble Programmer." He argued that most of programming is an attempt to compensate for the strictly limited size of our skulls. The people who are best at programming are the people who realize how small their brains are. They are humble. The people who are the worst at programming are the people who refuse to accept the fact that their brains aren't equal to the task. Their egos keep them from being great programmers. The more you learn to compensate for your small brain, the better a programmer you'll be. The more humble you are, the faster you'll improve.

The purpose of many good programming practices is to reduce the load on your gray cells. Here are a few examples:

- The point of "decomposing" a system is to make it simpler to understand. (See "Levels of Design" in Section 5.2 for more details.)

- Conducting reviews, inspections, and tests is a way of compensating for anticipated human fallibilities. These review techniques originated as part of "egoless programming" (Weinberg 1998). If you never made mistakes, you wouldn't need to review your software. But you know that your intellectual capacity is limited, so you augment it with someone else's.

- Keeping routines short reduces the load on your brain.

- Writing programs in terms of the problem domain rather than in terms of low-level implementation details reduces your mental workload.

- Using conventions of all sorts frees your brain from the relatively mundane aspects of programming, which offer little payback.

You might think that the high road would be to develop better mental abilities so that you wouldn't need these programming crutches. You might think that a programmer who uses mental crutches is taking the low road. Empirically, however, it's been shown that humble programmers who compensate for their fallibilities write code that's easier for themselves and others to understand and that has fewer errors. The real low road is the road of errors and delayed schedules.

33.3 Curiosity

Once you admit that your brain is too small to understand most programs and you realize that effective programming is a search for ways to offset that fact, you begin a career-long search for ways to compensate. In the development of a superior programmer, curiosity about technical subjects must be a priority. The relevant technical information changes continually. Many Web programmers have never had to program in Microsoft Windows, and many Windows programmers never had to deal with DOS or UNIX or punch cards. Specific features of the technical environment change every 5 to 10 years. If you aren't curious enough to keep up with the changes, you might find yourself down at the old-programmers' home playing cards with T-Bone Rex and the Brontosaurus sisters.

Programmers are so busy working they often don't have time to be curious about how they might do their jobs better. If this is true for you, you're not alone. The following subsections describe a few specific actions you can take to exercise your curiosity and make learning a priority.

Cross-Reference For a fuller discussion of the importance of process in software development, see Section 34.2, "Pick Your Process."

Build your awareness of the development process The more aware you are of the development process, whether from reading or from your own observations about software development, the better position you're in to understand changes and to move your group in a good direction.

If your workload consists entirely of short-term assignments that don't develop your skills, be dissatisfied. If you're working in a competitive software market, half of what you now need to know to do your job will be out of date in three years. If you're not learning, you're turning into a dinosaur.

HARD DATA

You're in too much demand to spend time working for management that doesn't have your interests in mind. Despite some ups and downs and some jobs moving overseas, the average number of software jobs available in the U.S. is expected to increase dramatically between 2002 and 2012. Jobs for systems analysts are expected to increase by about 60 percent and for software engineers by about 50 percent. For all computer-job categories combined, about 1 million new jobs will be created beyond the 3 million that currently exist (Hecker 2001, BLS 2004). If you can't learn at your job, find a new one.

Cross-Reference Several key aspects of programming revolve around the idea of experimentation. For details, see "Experimentation" in Section 34.9.

Experiment One effective way to learn about programming is to experiment with programming and the development process. If you don't know how a feature of your language works, write a short program to exercise the feature and see how it works. Prototype! Watch the program execute in the debugger. You're better off working with a short program to test a concept than you are writing a larger program with a feature you don't quite understand.

What if the short program shows that the feature doesn't work the way you want it to? That's what you wanted to find out. Better to find it out in a small program than a large one. One key to effective programming is learning to make mistakes quickly, learning from them each time. Making a mistake is no sin. Failing to learn from a mistake is.

Further Reading A great book that teaches problem solving is James Adams's *Conceptual Blockbusting* (2001).

Read about problem solving   Problem solving is the core activity in building computer software. Herbert Simon reported a series of experiments on human problem solving. They found that human beings don't always discover clever problem-solving strategies themselves, even though the same strategies could readily be taught to the same people (Simon 1996). The implication is that even if you want to reinvent the wheel, you can't count on success. You might reinvent the square instead.

Analyze and plan before you act   You'll find that there's a tension between analysis and action. At some point you have to quit gathering data and act. The problem for most programmers, however, isn't an excess of analysis. The pendulum is currently so far on the "acting" side of the arc that you can wait until it's at least partway to the middle before worrying about getting stuck on the "analysis-paralysis" side.

cc2e.com/3320

Learn about successful projects   One especially good way to learn about programming is to study the work of the great programmers. Jon Bentley thinks that you should be able to sit down with a glass of brandy and a good cigar and read a program the way you would a good novel. That might not be as far-fetched as it sounds. Most people wouldn't want to use their recreational time to scrutinize a 500-page source listing, but many people would enjoy studying a high-level design and dipping into more detailed source listings for selected areas.

The software-engineering field makes extraordinarily limited use of examples of past successes and failures. If you were interested in architecture, you'd study the drawings of Louis Sullivan, Frank Lloyd Wright, and I. M. Pei. You'd probably visit some of their buildings. If you were interested in structural engineering, you'd study the Brooklyn Bridge; the Tacoma Narrows Bridge; and a variety of other concrete, steel, and wood structures. You would study examples of successes and failures in your field.

Thomas Kuhn points out that a part of any mature science is a set of solved problems that are commonly recognized as examples of good work in the field and that serve as examples for future work (Kuhn 1996). Software engineering is only beginning to mature to this level. In 1990, the Computer Science and Technology Board concluded that there were few documented case studies of either successes or failures in the software field (CSTB 1990).

An article in the *Communications of the ACM* argued for learning from case studies of programming problems (Linn and Clancy 1992). The fact that someone has to argue for this is significant. That one of the most popular computing columns, "Programming Pearls," was built around case studies of programming problems is also suggestive. And one of the most popular books in software engineering is *The Mythical Man-Month*, a case study in programming management of the IBM OS/360 project.

With or without a book of case studies in programming, find code written by superior programmers and read it. Ask to look at the code of programmers you respect. Ask to look at the code of programmers you don't. Compare their code, and compare their code to your own. What are the differences? Why are they different? Which way is better? Why?

In addition to reading other people's code, develop a desire to know what expert programmers think about your code. Find world-class programmers who'll give you their criticism. As you listen to the criticism, filter out points that have to do with their personal idiosyncrasies and concentrate on the points that matter. Then change your programming so that it's better.

Read!   Documentation phobia is rampant among programmers. Computer documentation tends to be poorly written and poorly organized, but for all its problems, there's much to gain from overcoming an excessive fear of computer-screen photons or paper products. Documentation contains the keys to the castle, and it's worth spending time reading it. Overlooking information that's readily available is such a common oversight that a familiar acronym on newsgroups and bulletin boards is "RTFM!" which stands for "Read the !#*%*@ Manual!"

A modern language product is usually bundled with an enormous set of library code. Time spent browsing through the library documentation is well invested. Often the company that provides the language product has already created many of the classes you need. If it has, make sure you know about them. Skim the documentation every couple of months.

Cross-Reference For books you can use in a personal reading program, see Section 35.4, "A Software Developer's Reading Plan."

Read other books and periodicals   Pat yourself on the back for reading this book. You're already learning more than most people in the software industry because one book is more than most programmers read each year (DeMarco and Lister 1999). A little reading goes a long way toward professional advancement. If you read even one good programming book every two months, roughly 35 pages a week, you'll soon have a firm grasp on the industry and distinguish yourself from nearly everyone around you.

Affiliate with other professionals   Find other people who care about sharpening their software-development skills. Attend a conference, join a local user group, or participate in an online discussion group.

Further Reading For other discussions of programmer levels, see "Construx's Professional Development Program" (Chapter 16) in *Professional Software Development* (McConnell 2004).

Make a commitment to professional development   Good programmers constantly look for ways to become better. Consider the following professional development ladder used at my company and several others:

- **Level 1: Beginning**   A beginner is a programmer capable of using the basic capabilities of one language. Such a person can write classes, routines, loops, and conditionals and use many of the features of a language.

- **Level 2: Introductory**   An intermediate programmer who has moved past the beginner phase is capable of using the basic capabilities of multiple languages and is very comfortable in at least one language.

- **Level 3: Competency**   A competent programmer has expertise in a language or an environment or both. A programmer at this level might know all the intricacies of J2EE or have the *Annotated C++ Reference Manual* memorized. Programmers at this level are valuable to their companies, and many programmers never move beyond this level.

- **Level 4: Leadership**   A leader has the expertise of a Level 3 programmer and recognizes that programming is only 15 percent communicating with the computer and 85 percent communicating with people. Only 30 percent of an average programmer's time is spent working alone (McCue 1978). Even less time is spent communicating with the computer. The guru writes code for an audience of people rather than machines. True guru-level programmers write code that's crystal-clear, and they document it, too. They don't want to waste their valuable gray cells reconstructing the logic of a section of code that they could have read in a one-sentence comment.

A great coder who doesn't emphasize readability is probably stuck at Level 3, but even that isn't usually the case. In my experience, the main reason people write unreadable code is that their code is bad. They don't say to themselves, "My code is bad, so I'll make it hard to read." They just don't understand their code well enough to make it readable, which locks them into one of the lower levels.

The worst code I've ever seen was written by someone who wouldn't let anyone go near her programs. Finally, her manager threatened to fire her if she didn't cooperate. Her code was uncommented and littered with variables like *x, xx, xxx, xx1,* and *xx2,* all of which were global. Her manager's boss thought she was a great programmer because she fixed errors quickly. The quality of her code gave her abundant opportunities to demonstrate her error-correcting ability.

It's no sin to be a beginner or an intermediate. It's no sin to be a competent programmer instead of a leader. The sin is in how long you remain a beginner or intermediate after you know what you have to do to improve.

33.4 Intellectual Honesty

Part of maturing as a programming professional is developing an uncompromising sense of intellectual honesty. Intellectual honesty commonly manifests itself in several ways:

- Refusing to pretend you're an expert when you're not

- Readily admitting your mistakes

- Trying to understand a compiler warning rather than suppressing the message

- Clearly understanding your program—not compiling it to see if it works

- Providing realistic status reports

- Providing realistic schedule estimates and holding your ground when management asks you to adjust them

The first two items on this list—admitting that you don't know something or that you made a mistake—echo the theme of intellectual humility discussed earlier. How can you learn anything new if you pretend that you know everything already? You'd be better off pretending that you don't know anything. Listen to people's explanations, learn something new from them, and assess whether *they* know what *they* are talking about.

Be ready to quantify your degree of certainty on any issue. If it's usually 100 percent, that's a warning sign.

> Any fool can defend his or her mistakes—and most fools do.
> —*Dale Carnegie*

Refusing to admit mistakes is a particularly annoying habit. If Sally refuses to admit a mistake, she apparently believes that not admitting the mistake will trick others into believing that she didn't make it. The opposite is true. Everyone will know she made a mistake. Mistakes are accepted as part of the ebb and flow of complex intellectual activities, and as long as she hasn't been negligent, no one will hold mistakes against her.

If she refuses to admit a mistake, the only person she'll fool is herself. Everyone else will learn that they're working with a prideful programmer who's not completely honest. That's a more damning fault than making a simple error. If you make a mistake, admit it quickly and emphatically.

Pretending to understand compiler messages when you don't is another common blind spot. If you don't understand a compiler warning or if you think you know what it means but are too pressed for time to check it, guess what's really a waste of time? You'll probably end up trying to solve the problem from the ground up while the compiler waves the solution in your face. I've had several people ask for help in debugging programs. I'll ask if they have a clean compile, and they'll say yes. Then they'll start to explain the symptoms of the problem, and I'll say, "Hmmmm. That sounds like it would be an uninitialized pointer, but the compiler should have warned you about that." Then they'll say, "Oh yeah—it did warn about that. We thought it meant something else." It's hard to fool other people about your mistakes. It's even harder to fool the computer, so don't waste your time trying.

A related kind of intellectual sloppiness occurs when you don't quite understand your program and "just compile it to see if it works." One example is running the program to see whether you should use < or <=. In that situation, it doesn't really matter whether the program works because you don't understand it well enough to know why it works. Remember that testing can show only the presence of errors, not their absence. If you don't understand the program, you can't test it thoroughly. Feeling tempted to compile a program to "see what happens" is a warning sign. It might mean that you need to back up to design or that you began coding before you were sure you knew what you were doing. Make sure you have a strong intellectual grip on the program before you relinquish it to the compiler.

> The first 90 percent of the code accounts for the first 90 percent of the development time. The remaining 10 percent of the code accounts for the other 90 percent of the development time.
> —*Tom Cargill*

Status reporting is an area of scandalous duplicity. Programmers are notorious for saying that a program is "90 percent complete" during the last 50 percent of the project. If your problem is that you have a poor sense of your own progress, you can solve it by learning more about how you work. But if your problem is that you don't speak your mind because you want to give the answer your manager wants to hear, that's a different story. A manager usually appreciates honest observations about the status of a project, even if they're not the opinions the manager wants to hear. If your observations are well thought out, give them as dispassionately as you can and in private. Management needs to have accurate information to coordinate development activities, and full cooperation is essential.

cc2e.com/3341

An issue related to inaccurate status reporting is inaccurate estimation. The typical scenario goes like this: Management asks Bert for an estimate of how long it would take to develop a new database product. Bert talks to a few programmers, crunches some numbers, and comes back with an estimate of eight programmers and six months. His manager says, "That's not really what we're looking for. Can you do it in a shorter time, with fewer programmers?" Bert goes away and thinks about it and decides that for a short period he could cut training and vacation time and have everyone work a little overtime. He comes back with an estimate of six programmers and four months. His manager says, "That's great. This is a relatively low-priority project, so try to keep it on time without any overtime because the budget won't allow it."

The mistake Bert made was not realizing that estimates aren't negotiable. He can revise an estimate to be more accurate, but negotiating with his boss won't change the time it takes to develop a software project. IBM's Bill Weimer says, "We found that technical people, in general, were actually very good at estimating project requirements and schedules. The problem they had was defending their decisions; they needed to learn how to hold their ground" (Weimer in Metzger and Boddie 1996). Bert's not going to make his manager any happier by promising to deliver a project in four months and delivering it in six than he would by promising and delivering it in six. He'll lose credibility by compromising, and he'll gain respect by standing firm on his estimate.

If management applies pressure to change your estimate, realize that ultimately the decision whether to do a project rests with management: "Look. This is how much it's going to cost. I can't say whether it's worth this price to the company—that's your job. But I can tell you how long it takes to develop a piece of software—that's my job. I can't 'negotiate' how long it will take; that's like negotiating how many feet are in a mile. You can't negotiate laws of nature. We can, however, negotiate other aspects of the project that affect the schedule and then reestimate the schedule. We can eliminate features, reduce performance, develop the project in increments, or use fewer people and a longer schedule or more people and a shorter schedule."

One of the scariest exchanges I've ever heard was at a lecture on managing software projects. The speaker was the author of a best-selling software-project-management book. A member of the audience asked, "What do you do if management asks for an estimate and you know that if you give them an accurate estimate they'll say it's too high and decide not to do the project?" The speaker responded that that was one of those tricky areas in which you had to get management to buy into the project by underestimating it. He said that once they'd invested in the first part of the project, they'd see it through to the end.

Wrong answer! Management is responsible for the big-picture issues of running a company. If a certain software capability is worth $250K to a company and you estimate it will cost $750K to develop, the company shouldn't develop the software. It's management's responsibility to make such judgments. When the speaker advocated lying about the project's cost, telling management it would cost less than it really would, he advocated covertly stealing management's authority. If you think a project is interesting, breaks important new ground for the company, or provides valuable training, say so. Management can weigh those factors, too. But tricking management into making the wrong decision could literally cost the company hundreds of thousands of dollars. If it costs you your job, you'll have gotten what you deserve.

33.5 Communication and Cooperation

Truly excellent programmers learn how to work and play well with others. Writing readable code is part of being a team player. The computer probably reads your program as often as other people do, but it's a lot better at reading poor code than people are. As a readability guideline, keep the person who has to modify your code in mind. Programming is communicating with another programmer first and communicating with the computer second.

33.6 Creativity and Discipline

When I got out of school, I thought I was the best programmer in the world. I could write an unbeatable tic-tac-toe program, use five different computer languages, and create 1000-line programs that WORKED (really!). Then I got out into the Real World. My first task in the Real World was to read and understand a 200,000-line Fortran program and then speed it up by a factor of two. Any Real Programmer will tell you that all the Structured Coding in the world won't help you solve a problem like that—it takes actual talent.
—Ed Post

It's hard to explain to a fresh computer-science graduate why you need conventions and engineering discipline. When I was an undergraduate, the largest program I wrote was about 500 lines of executable code. As a professional, I've written dozens of utilities that have been smaller than 500 lines, but the average main-project size has been 5,000 to 25,000 lines, and I've participated in projects with over a half million lines of code. This type of effort requires not the same skills on a larger scale, but a new set of skills altogether.

Some creative programmers view the discipline of standards and conventions as stifling to their creativity. The opposite is true. Can you imagine a website on which each page used different fonts, colors, text alignment, graphics styles, and navigation clues? The effect would be chaotic, not creative. Without standards and conventions on large projects, project completion itself is impossible. Creativity isn't even imaginable. Don't waste your creativity on things that don't matter. Establish conventions in noncritical areas so that you can focus your creative energies in the places that count.

In a 15-year retrospective on work at NASA's Software Engineering Laboratory, McGarry and Pajerski reported that methods and tools that emphasize human discipline have been especially effective (1990). Many highly creative people have been extremely disciplined. "Form is liberating," as the saying goes. Great architects work within the constraints of physical materials, time, and cost. Great artists do, too. Anyone who has examined Leonardo's drawings has to admire his disciplined attention to detail. When Michelangelo designed the ceiling of the Sistine Chapel, he divided it into symmetric collections of geometric forms, such as triangles, circles, and squares. He designed it in three zones corresponding to three Platonic stages. Without this self-imposed structure and discipline, the 300 human figures would have been merely chaotic rather than the coherent elements of an artistic masterpiece.

A programming masterpiece requires just as much discipline. If you don't try to analyze requirements and design before you begin coding, much of your learning about the project will occur during coding and the result of your labors will look more like a three-year-old's finger painting than a work of art.

33.7 Laziness

Laziness: The quality that makes you go to great effort to reduce overall energy expenditure. It makes you write labor-saving programs that other people will find useful, and document what you wrote so that you don't have to answer so many questions about it.
—*Larry Wall*

Laziness manifests itself in several ways:

- Deferring an unpleasant task
- Doing an unpleasant task quickly to get it out of the way
- Writing a tool to do the unpleasant task so that you never have to do the task again

Some of these manifestations of laziness are better than others. The first is hardly ever beneficial. You've probably had the experience of spending several hours futzing with jobs that didn't really need to be done so that you wouldn't have to face a relatively minor job that you couldn't avoid. I detest data entry, and many programs require a small amount of data entry. I've been known to delay working on a program for days just to delay the inevitable task of entering several pages of numbers by hand. This habit is "true laziness." It manifests itself again in the habit of compiling a class to see if it works so that you can avoid the exercise of checking the class with your mind.

The small tasks are never as bad as they seem. If you develop the habit of doing them right away, you can avoid the procrastinating kind of laziness. This habit is "enlightened laziness"—the second kind of laziness. You're still lazy, but you're getting around the problem by spending the smallest possible amount of time on something that's unpleasant.

The third option is to write a tool to do the unpleasant task. This is "long-term laziness." It is undoubtedly the most productive kind of laziness (provided that you ultimately save time by having written the tool). In these contexts, a certain amount of laziness is beneficial.

When you step through the looking glass, you see the other side of the laziness picture. "Hustle" or "making an effort" doesn't have the rosy glow it does in high-school physical education class. Hustle is extra, unnecessary effort. It shows that you're eager but not that you're getting your work done. It's easy to confuse motion with progress, busy-ness with being productive. The most important work in effective programming is thinking, and people tend not to look busy when they're thinking. If I worked with a programmer who looked busy all the time, I'd assume that he was not a good programmer because he wasn't using his most valuable tool, his brain.

33.8 Characteristics That Don't Matter As Much As You Might Think

Hustle isn't the only characteristic that you might admire in other aspects of your life but that doesn't work very well in software development.

Persistence

Depending on the situation, persistence can be either an asset or a liability. Like most value-laden concepts, it's identified by different words depending on whether you think it's a good quality or a bad one. If you want to identify persistence as a bad quality, you say it's "stubbornness" or "pigheadedness." If you want it to be a good quality, you call it "tenacity" or "perseverance."

Most of the time, persistence in software development is pigheadedness—it has little value. Persistence when you're stuck on a piece of new code is hardly ever a virtue. Try redesigning the class, try an alternative coding approach, or try coming back to it later. When one approach isn't working, that's a good time to try an alternative (Pirsig 1974).

Cross-Reference For a more detailed discussion of persistence in debugging, see "Tips for Finding Defects" in Section 23.2.

In debugging, it can be mighty satisfying to track down the error that has been annoying you for four hours, but it's often better to give up on the error after a certain amount of time with no progress—say 15 minutes. Let your subconscious chew on the problem for a while. Try to think of an alternative approach that would circumvent the problem altogether. Rewrite the troublesome section of code from scratch. Come back to it later when your mind is fresh. Fighting computer problems is no virtue. Avoiding them is better.

It's hard to know when to give up, but it's essential that you ask. When you notice that you're frustrated, that's a good time to ask the question. Asking doesn't necessarily mean that it's time to give up, but it probably means that it's time to set some parameters on the activity: "If I don't solve the problem using this approach within the next 30 minutes, I'll take 10 minutes to brainstorm about different approaches and try the best one for the next hour."

Experience

The value of hands-on experience as compared to book learning is smaller in software development than in many other fields for several reasons. In many other fields, basic knowledge changes slowly enough that someone who graduated from college 10 years after you did probably learned the same basic material that you did. In software development, even basic knowledge changes rapidly. The person who graduated from college 10 years after you did probably learned twice as much about effective programming techniques. Older programmers tend to be viewed with suspicion not just because they might be out of touch with specific technology but because they might never have been exposed to basic programming concepts that became well known after they left school.

In other fields, what you learn about your job today is likely to help you in your job tomorrow. In software, if you can't shake the habits of thinking you developed while using your former programming language or the code-tuning techniques that worked on your old machine, your experience will be worse than none at all. A lot of software people spend their time preparing to fight the last war rather than the next one. If you can't change with the times, experience is more a handicap than a help.

Aside from the rapid changes in software development, people often draw the wrong conclusions from their experiences. It's hard to view your own life objectively. You can overlook key elements of your experience that would cause you to draw different conclusions if you recognized them. Reading studies of other programmers is helpful because the studies reveal other people's experience—filtered enough that you can examine it objectively.

People also put an absurd emphasis on the *amount* of experience programmers have. "We want a programmer with five years of C programming experience" is a silly statement. If a programmer hasn't learned C after a year or two, the next three years won't make much difference. This kind of "experience" has little relationship to performance.

The fact that information changes quickly in programming makes for weird dynamics in the area of "experience." In many fields, a professional who has a history of achievement can coast, relaxing and enjoying the respect earned by a string of successes. In software development, anyone who coasts quickly becomes out of touch. To stay valuable, you have to stay current. For young, hungry programmers, this is an advantage. Older programmers sometimes feel they've already earned their stripes and resent having to prove themselves year after year.

The bottom line on experience is this: if you work for 10 years, do you get 10 years of experience or do you get 1 year of experience 10 times? You have to reflect on your activities to get true experience. If you make learning a continuous commitment, you'll get experience. If you don't, you won't, no matter how many years you have under your belt.

Gonzo Programming

> *If you haven't spent at least a month working on the same program—working 16 hours a day, dreaming about it during the remaining 8 hours of restless sleep, working several nights straight through trying to eliminate that "one last bug" from the program—then you haven't really written a complicated computer program. And you may not have the sense that there is something exhilarating about programming.*
>
> –Edward Yourdon

This lusty tribute to programming machismo is pure B.S. and an almost certain recipe for failure. Those all-night programming stints make you feel like the greatest programmer in the world, but then you have to spend several weeks correcting the defects you installed during your blaze of glory. By all means, get excited about programming. But excitement is no substitute for competency. Remember which is more important.

33.9 Habits

The moral virtues, then, are engendered in us neither by nor contrary to nature....their full development in us is due to habit....Anything that we have to learn to do we learn by the actual doing of it....Men will become good builders as a result of building well and bad ones as a result of building badly....So it is a matter of no little importance what sort of habits we form from the earliest age—it makes a vast difference, or rather all the difference in the world.

—Aristotle

Good habits matter because most of what you do as a programmer you do without consciously thinking about it. For example, at one time, you might have thought about how you wanted to format indented loops, but now you don't think about it again each time you write a new loop. You do it the way you do it out of habit. This is true of virtually all aspects of program formatting. When was the last time you seriously questioned your formatting style? Chances are good that if you've been programming for five years, you last questioned it four and a half years ago. The rest of the time you've relied on habit.

Cross-Reference For details on errors in assignment statements, see "Errors by Classification" in Section 22.4.

You have habits in many areas. For example, programmers tend to check loop indexes carefully and not to check assignment statements, which makes errors in assignment statements much harder to find than errors in loop indexes (Gould 1975). You respond to criticism in a friendly way or in an unfriendly way. You're always looking for ways to make code readable or fast, or you're not. If you have to choose between making code fast and making it readable, and you make the same choice every time, you're not really choosing—you're responding out of habit.

Study the quotation from Aristotle and substitute "programming virtues" for "moral virtues." He points out that you are not predisposed to either good or bad behavior but are constituted in such a way that you can become either a good or a bad programmer. The main way you become good or bad at what you do is by doing—builders by building and programmers by programming. What you do becomes habit, and over time your good and bad habits determine whether you're a good or a bad programmer.

Bill Gates says that any programmer who will ever be good is good in the first few years. After that, whether a programmer is good or not is cast in concrete (Lammers 1986). After you've been programming a long time, it's hard to suddenly start saying, "How do I make this loop faster?" or "How do I make this code more readable?" These are habits that good programmers develop early.

When you first learn something, learn it the right way. When you first do it, you're actively thinking about it and you still have an easy choice between doing it in a good way and doing it in a bad way. After you've done it a few times, you pay less attention to what you're doing and "force of habit" takes over. Make sure that the habits that take over are the ones you want to have.

What if you don't already have the most effective habits? How do you change a bad habit? If I had the definitive answer to that, I could sell self-help tapes on late-night TV. But here's at least part of an answer. You can't replace a bad habit with no habit at all. That's why people who suddenly stop smoking or swearing or overeating have such a hard time unless they substitute something else, like chewing gum. It's easier to replace an old habit with a new one than it is to eliminate one altogether. In programming, try to develop new habits that work. Develop the habits of writing a class in pseudocode before coding it and carefully reading the code before compiling it, for instance. You won't have to worry about losing the bad habits; they'll naturally drop by the wayside as new habits take their places.

Additional Resources

cc2e.com/3327

Following are additional resources on the human aspects of software development:

cc2e.com/3334

Dijkstra, Edsger. "The Humble Programmer." Turing Award Lecture. *Communications of the ACM* 15, no. 10 (October 1972): 859–66. This classic paper helped begin the inquiry into how much computer programming depends on the programmer's mental abilities. Dijkstra has persistently stressed the message that the essential task of programming is mastering the enormous complexity of computer science. He argues that programming is the only activity in which humans have to master nine orders of magnitude of difference between the lowest level of detail and the highest. This paper would be interesting reading solely for its historical value, but many of its themes sound fresh decades later. It also conveys a good sense of what it was like to be a programmer in the early days of computer science.

Weinberg, Gerald M. *The Psychology of Computer Programming: Silver Anniversary Edition.* New York, NY: Dorset House, 1998. This classic book contains a detailed exposition of the idea of egoless programming and of many other aspects of the human side of computer programming. It contains many entertaining anecdotes and is one of the most readable books yet written about software development.

Pirsig, Robert M. *Zen and the Art of Motorcycle Maintenance: An Inquiry into Values.* William Morrow, 1974. Pirsig provides an extended discussion of "quality," ostensibly as it relates to motorcycle maintenance. Pirsig was working as a software technical writer when he wrote *ZAMM*, and his insightful comments apply as much to the psychology of software projects as to motorcycle maintenance.

Curtis, Bill, ed. *Tutorial: Human Factors in Software Development.* Los Angeles, CA: IEEE Computer Society Press, 1985. This is an excellent collection of papers that address the human aspects of creating computer programs. The 45 papers are divided into sections on mental models of programming knowledge, learning to program, problem solving and design, effects of design representations, language characteristics, error diagnosis, and methodology. If programming is one of the most difficult intellectual challenges that humankind has ever faced, learning more about human mental capacities is critical to the success of the endeavor. These papers about psychological factors also help you to turn your mind inward and learn about how you individually can program more effectively.

McConnell, Steve. *Professional Software Development*. Boston, MA: Addison-Wesley, 2004. Chapter 7, "Orphans Preferred," provides more details on programmer personalities and the role of personal character.

Key Points

- Your personal character directly affects your ability to write computer programs.

- The characteristics that matter most are humility, curiosity, intellectual honesty, creativity and discipline, and enlightened laziness.

- The characteristics of a superior programmer have almost nothing to do with talent and everything to do with a commitment to personal development.

- Surprisingly, raw intelligence, experience, persistence, and guts hurt as much as they help.

- Many programmers don't actively seek new information and techniques and instead rely on accidental, on-the-job exposure to new information. If you devote a small percentage of your time to reading and learning about programming, after a few months or years you'll dramatically distinguish yourself from the programming mainstream.

- Good character is mainly a matter of having the right habits. To be a great programmer, develop the right habits and the rest will come naturally.

Chapter 34

Themes in Software Craftsmanship

cc2e.com/3444

Contents

Related Topics

- The whole book

This book is mostly about the details of software construction: high-quality classes, variable names, loops, source-code layout, system integration, and so on. This book has deemphasized abstract topics to emphasize subjects that are more concrete.

Once the earlier parts of the book have put the concrete topics on the table, all you have to do to appreciate the abstract concepts is to pick up the topics from the various chapters and see how they're related. This chapter makes the abstract themes explicit: complexity, abstraction, process, readability, iteration, and so on. These themes account in large part for the difference between hacking and software craftsmanship.

34.1 Conquer Complexity

Cross-Reference For details on the importance of attitude in conquering complexity, see Section 33.2, "Intelligence and Humility."

The drive to reduce complexity is at the heart of software development, to such a degree that Chapter 5, "Design in Construction," described managing complexity as Software's Primary Technical Imperative. Although it's tempting to try to be a hero and deal with computer-science problems at all levels, no one's brain is really capable of spanning nine orders of magnitude of detail. Computer science and software engineering have developed many intellectual tools for handling such complexity, and discussions of other topics in this book have brushed up against several of them:

- Dividing a system into subsystems at the architecture level so that your brain can focus on a smaller amount of the system at one time.

- Carefully defining class interfaces so that you can ignore the internal workings of the class.

- Preserving the abstraction represented by the class interface so that your brain doesn't have to remember arbitrary details.

- Avoiding global data, because global data vastly increases the percentage of the code you need to juggle in your brain at any one time.

- Avoiding deep inheritance hierarchies because they are intellectually demanding.

- Avoiding deep nesting of loops and conditionals because they can be replaced by simpler control structures that burn up fewer gray cells.

- Avoiding *goto*s because they introduce nonlinearity that has been found to be difficult for most people to follow.

- Carefully defining your approach to error handling rather than using an arbitrary proliferation of different error-handling techniques.

- Being systematic about the use of the built-in exception mechanism, which can become a nonlinear control structure that's about as hard to understand as *goto*s if not used with discipline.

- Not allowing classes to grow into monster classes that amount to whole programs in themselves.

- Keeping routines short.

- Using clear, self-explanatory variable names so that your brain doesn't have to waste cycles remembering details like "*i* stands for the account index, and *j* stands for the customer index, or was it the other way around?"

- Minimizing the number of parameters passed to a routine, or, more important, passing only the parameters needed to preserve the routine interface's abstraction.

- Using conventions to spare your brain the challenge of remembering arbitrary, accidental differences between different sections of code.

- In general, attacking what Chapter 5 describes as "accidental difficulties" wherever possible.

When you put a complicated test into a boolean function and abstract the purpose of the test, you make the code less complex. When you substitute a table lookup for a complicated chain of logic, you do the same thing. When you create a well-defined, consistent class interface, you eliminate the need to worry about implementation details of the class and you simplify your job overall.

The point of having coding conventions is also mainly to reduce complexity. When you can standardize decisions about formatting, loops, variable names, modeling notations, and so on, you release mental resources that you need to focus on more challenging aspects of the programming problem. One reason coding conventions are so controversial is that choices among the options have some limited aesthetic base but are essentially arbitrary. People have the most heated arguments over their smallest differences. Conventions are the most useful when they spare you the trouble of making and defending arbitrary decisions. They're less valuable when they impose restrictions in more meaningful areas.

Abstraction in its various forms is a particularly powerful tool for managing complexity. Programming has advanced largely through increasing the abstractness of program components. Fred Brooks argues that the biggest single gain ever made in computer science was in the jump from machine language to higher-level languages—it freed programmers from worrying about the detailed quirks of individual pieces of hardware and allowed them to focus on programming (Brooks 1995). The idea of routines was another big step, followed by classes and packages.

Naming variables functionally, for the "what" of the problem rather than the "how" of the implementation-level solution, increases the level of abstraction. If you say, "OK, I'm popping the stack and that means that I'm getting the most recent employee," abstraction can save you the mental step "I'm popping the stack." You simply say, "I'm getting the most recent employee." This is a small gain, but when you're trying to reduce a range in complexity of 1 to 10^9, every step counts. Using named constants rather than literals also increases the level of abstraction. Object-oriented programming provides a level of abstraction that applies to algorithms and data at the same time, a kind of abstraction that functional decomposition alone didn't provide.

In summary, a primary goal of software design and construction is conquering complexity. The motivation behind many programming practices is to reduce a program's complexity, and reducing complexity is arguably the most important key to being an effective programmer.

34.2 Pick Your Process

A second major thread in this book is the idea that the process you use to develop software matters a surprising amount. On a small project, the talents of the individual programmer are the biggest influence on the quality of the software. Part of what makes an individual programmer successful is his or her choice of processes.

On projects with more than one programmer, organizational characteristics make a bigger difference than the skills of the individuals involved do. Even if you have a great team, its collective ability isn't simply the sum of the team members' individual abilities. The way in which people work together determines whether their abilities are added to each other or subtracted from each other. The process the team uses determines whether one person's work supports the work of the rest of the team or undercuts it.

Cross-Reference For details on making requirements stable, see Section 3.4, "Requirements Prerequisite." For details on variations in development approaches, see Section 3.2, "Determine the Kind of Software You're Working On."

One example of the way in which process matters is the consequence of not making requirements stable before you begin designing and coding. If you don't know what you're building, you can't very well create a superior design for it. If the requirements and subsequently the design change while the software is under development, the code must change too, which risks degrading the quality of the system.

"Sure," you say, "but in the real world, you never really have stable requirements, so that's a red herring." Again, the process you use determines both how stable your requirements are and how stable they need to be. If you want to build more flexibility into the requirements, you can set up an incremental development approach in which you plan to deliver the software in several increments rather than all at once. This is an attention to process, and it's the process you use that ultimately determines whether your project succeeds or fails. Table 3-1 in Section 3.1 makes it clear that requirements errors are far more costly than construction errors, so focusing on that part of the process also affects cost and schedule.

My message to the serious programmer is: spend a part of your working day examining and refining your own methods. Even though programmers are always struggling to meet some future or past deadline, methodological abstraction is a wise long-term investment.
—*Robert W. Floyd*

The same principle of consciously attending to process applies to design. You have to lay a solid foundation before you can begin building on it. If you rush to coding before the foundation is complete, it will be harder to make fundamental changes in the system's architecture. People will have an emotional investment in the design because they will have already written code for it. It's hard to throw away a bad foundation once you've started building a house on it.

The main reason the process matters is that in software, quality must be built in from the first step onward. This flies in the face of the folk wisdom that you can code like hell and then test all the mistakes out of the software. That idea is dead wrong. Testing merely tells you the specific ways in which your software is defective. Testing won't make your program more usable, faster, smaller, more readable, or more extensible.

Premature optimization is another kind of process error. In an effective process, you make coarse adjustments at the beginning and fine adjustments at the end. If you were a sculptor, you'd rough out the general shape before you started polishing individual features. Premature optimization wastes time because you spend time polishing sections of code that don't need to be polished. You might polish sections that are small enough and fast enough as they are, you might polish code that you later throw away, and you might fail to throw away bad code because you've already spent time polishing it. Always be thinking, "Am I doing this in the right order? Would changing the order make a difference?" Consciously follow a good process.

Cross-Reference For details on iteration, see Section 34.8, "Iterate, Repeatedly, Again and Again," later in this chapter.

Low-level processes matter, too. If you follow the process of writing pseudocode and then filling in the code around the pseudocode, you reap the benefits of designing from the top down. You're also guaranteed to have comments in the code without having to put them in later.

Observing large processes and small processes means pausing to pay attention to how you create software. It's time well spent. Saying that "code is what matters; you have to focus on how good the code is, not some abstract process" is shortsighted and ignores mountains of experimental and practical evidence to the contrary. Software development is a creative exercise. If you don't understand the creative process, you're not getting the most out of the primary tool you use to create software—your brain. A bad process wastes your brain cycles. A good process leverages them to maximum advantage.

34.3 Write Programs for People First, Computers Second

> ***your program*** *n. A maze of non sequiturs littered with clever-clever tricks and irrelevant comments. Compare MY PROGRAM.*
>
> ***my program*** *n. A gem of algoristic precision, offering the most sublime balance between compact, efficient coding on the one hand and fully commented legibility for posterity on the other. Compare YOUR PROGRAM.*
>
> *—Stan Kelly-Bootle*

Another theme that runs throughout this book is an emphasis on code readability. Communication with other people is the motivation behind the quest for the Holy Grail of self-documenting code.

The computer doesn't care whether your code is readable. It's better at reading binary machine instructions than it is at reading high-level-language statements. You write readable code because it helps other people to read your code. Readability has a positive effect on all these aspects of a program:

- Comprehensibility
- Reviewability
- Error rate
- Debugging
- Modifiability
- Development time—a consequence of all of the above
- External quality—a consequence of all of the above

In the early years of programming, a program was regarded as the private property of the programmer. One would no more think of reading a colleague's program unbidden than of picking up a love letter and reading it. This is essentially what a program was, a love letter from the programmer to the hardware, full of the intimate details known only to partners in an affair. Consequently, programs became larded with the pet names and verbal shorthand so popular with lovers who live in the blissful abstraction that assumes that theirs is the only existence in the universe. Such programs are unintelligible to those outside the partnership.
—*Michael Marcotty*

Readable code doesn't take any longer to write than confusing code does, at least not in the long run. It's easier to be sure your code works if you can easily read what you wrote. That should be a sufficient reason to write readable code. But code is also read during reviews. It's read when you or someone else fixes an error. It's read when the code is modified. It's read when someone tries to use part of your code in a similar program.

Making code readable is not an optional part of the development process, and favoring write-time convenience over read-time convenience is a false economy. You should go to the effort of writing good code, which you can do once, rather than the effort of reading bad code, which you'd have to do again and again.

"What if I'm just writing code for myself? Why should I make it readable?" Because a week or two from now you're going to be working on another program and think, "Hey! I already wrote this class last week. I'll just drop in my old tested, debugged code and save some time." If the code isn't readable, good luck!

The idea of writing unreadable code because you're the only person working on a project sets a dangerous precedent. Your mother used to say, "What if your face froze in that expression?" And your dad used to say, "You play how you practice." Habits affect all your work; you can't turn them on and off at will, so be sure that what you're doing is something you want to become a habit. A professional programmer writes readable code, period.

It's also good to recognize that whether a piece of code ever belongs exclusively to you is debatable. Douglas Comer came up with a useful distinction between private and public programs (Comer 1981): "Private programs" are programs for a programmer's own use. They aren't used by others. They aren't modified by others. Others don't even know the programs exist. They are usually trivial, and they are the rare exception. "Public programs" are programs used or modified by someone other than the author.

Standards for public and for private programs can be different. Private programs can be sloppily written and full of limitations without affecting anyone but the author. Public programs must be written more carefully: their limitations should be documented, they should be reliable, and they should be modifiable. Beware of a private program's becoming public, as private programs often do. You need to convert the program to a public program before it goes into general circulation. Part of making a private program public is making it readable.

HARD DATA

Even if you think you're the only one who will read your code, in the real world chances are good that someone else will need to modify your code. One study found that 10 generations of maintenance programmers work on an average program before it gets rewritten (Thomas 1984). Maintenance programmers spend 50 to 60 percent of their time trying to understand the code they have to maintain, and they appreciate the time you put into documenting it (Parikh and Zvegintzov 1983).

Earlier chapters in this book examined the techniques that help you achieve readability: good class, routine, and variable names, careful formatting, small routines, hiding complex boolean tests in boolean functions, assigning intermediate results to variables for clarity in complicated calculations, and so on. No individual application of a technique can make the difference between a readable program and an illegible one, but the accumulation of many small readability improvements will be significant.

If you think you don't need to make your code readable because no one else ever looks at it, make sure you're not confusing cause and effect.

34.4 Program into Your Language, Not in It

Don't limit your programming thinking only to the concepts that are supported automatically by your language. The best programmers think of what they want to do, and then they assess how to accomplish their objectives with the programming tools at their disposal.

Should you use a class member routine that's inconsistent with the class's abstraction just because it's more convenient than using one that provides more consistency? You should write code in a way that preserves the abstraction represented by the class's interface as much as possible. You don't need to use global data or *goto*s just because your language supports them. You can choose not to use those hazardous programming capabilities and instead use programming conventions to make up for weaknesses of the language. Programming using the most obvious path amounts to programming *in* a language rather than programming *into* a language; it's the programmer's equivalent of "If Freddie jumped off a bridge, would you jump off a bridge, too?" Think about your technical goals, and then decide how best to accomplish those goals by programming *into* your language.

Your language doesn't support assertions? Write your own *assert()* routine. It might not function exactly the same as a built-in *assert()*, but you can still realize most of *assert()*'s benefits by writing your own routine. Your language doesn't support enumerated types or named constants? That's fine; you can define your own enumerations and named constants with a disciplined use of global variables supported by clear naming conventions.

In extreme cases, especially in new-technology environments, your tools might be so primitive that you're forced to change your desired programming approach significantly. In such cases, you might have to balance your desire to program into the language with the accidental difficulties that are created when the language makes your desired approach too cumbersome. But in such cases, you'll benefit even more from programming conventions that help you steer clear of those environments' most hazardous features. In more typical cases, the gap between what you want to do and what your tools will readily support will require you to make only relatively minor concessions to your environment.

34.5 Focus Your Attention with the Help of Conventions

Cross-Reference For an analysis of the value of conventions as they apply to program layout, see "How Much Is Good Layout Worth?" and "Objectives of Good Layout" in Section 31.1.

A set of conventions is one of the intellectual tools used to manage complexity. Earlier chapters talk about specific conventions. This section lays out the benefits of conventions with many examples.

Many of the details of programming are somewhat arbitrary. How many spaces do you indent a loop? How do you format a comment? How should you order class routines? Most of the questions like these have several correct answers. The specific way in which such a question is answered is less important than that it be answered consistently each time. Conventions save programmers the trouble of answering the same questions—making the same arbitrary decisions—again and again. On projects with many programmers, using conventions prevents the confusion that results when different programmers make the arbitrary decisions differently.

A convention conveys important information concisely. In naming conventions, a single character can differentiate among local, class, and global variables; capitalization can concisely differentiate among types, named constants, and variables. Indentation conventions can concisely show the logical structure of a program. Alignment conventions can indicate concisely that statements are related.

Conventions protect against known hazards. You can establish conventions to eliminate the use of dangerous practices, to restrict such practices to cases in which they're needed, or to compensate for their known hazards. You could eliminate a dangerous practice, for example, by prohibiting global variables or prohibiting multiple statements on a line. You could compensate for a hazardous practice by requiring parentheses around complicated expressions or requiring pointers to be set to NULL immediately after they're deleted to help prevent dangling pointers.

Conventions add predictability to low-level tasks. Having conventional ways of handling memory requests, error processing, input/output, and class interfaces adds a meaningful structure to your code and makes it easier for another programmer to figure out—as long as the programmer knows your conventions. As mentioned in an earlier chapter, one of the biggest benefits of eliminating global data is that you eliminate potential interactions among different classes and subsystems. A reader knows roughly what to expect from local and class data. But it's hard to tell when changing global data will break some bit of code four subsystems away. Global data increases the reader's uncertainty. With good conventions, you and your readers can take more for granted. The amount of detail that has to be assimilated will be reduced, and that in turn will improve program comprehension.

Conventions can compensate for language weaknesses. In languages that don't support named constants (such as Python, Perl, UNIX shell script, and so on), a convention can differentiate between variables intended to be both read and written and those that are intended to emulate read-only constants. Conventions for the disciplined use of global data and pointers are other examples of compensating for language weaknesses with conventions.

Programmers on large projects sometimes go overboard with conventions. They establish so many standards and guidelines that remembering them becomes a full-time job. But programmers on small projects tend to go "underboard," not realizing the full benefits of intelligently conceived conventions. You should understand their real value and take advantage of them; you should use them to provide structure in areas in which structure is needed.

34.6 Program in Terms of the Problem Domain

Another specific method of dealing with complexity is to work at the highest possible level of abstraction. One way of working at a high level of abstraction is to work in terms of the programming problem rather than the computer-science solution.

Top-level code shouldn't be filled with details about files and stacks and queues and arrays and characters whose parents couldn't think of better names for them than i, j, and k. Top-level code should describe the problem that's being solved. It should be packed with descriptive class names and routine calls that indicate exactly what the program is doing, not cluttered with details about opening a file as "read only." Top-level code shouldn't contain clumps of comments that say "i is a variable that represents the index of the record from the employee file here, and then a little later it's used to index the client account file there."

That's clumsy programming practice. At the top level of the program, you don't need to know that the employee data comes as records or that it's stored as a file. Information at that level of detail should be hidden. At the highest level, you shouldn't have any idea how the data is stored. Nor do you need to read a comment that explains what i means and that it's used for two purposes. You should see different variable names for the two purposes instead, and they should also have distinctive names such as *employeeIndex* and *clientIndex*.

Separating a Program into Levels of Abstraction

Obviously, you have to work in implementation-level terms at some level, but you can isolate the part of the program that works in implementation-level terms from the part that works in problem-domain terms. If you're designing a program, consider the levels of abstraction shown in Figure 34-1.

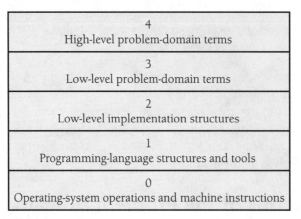

Figure 34-1   Programs can be divided into levels of abstraction. A good design will allow you to spend much of your time focusing on only the upper layers and ignoring the lower layers.

Level 0: Operating-System Operations and Machine Instructions

If you're working in a high-level language, you don't have to worry about the lowest level—your language takes care of it automatically. If you're working in a low-level language, you should try to create higher layers for yourself to work in, even though many programmers don't do that.

Level 1: Programming-Language Structures and Tools

Programming-language structures are the language's primitive data types, control structures, and so on. Most common languages also provide additional libraries, access to operating system calls, and so on. Using these structures and tools comes naturally since you can't program without them. Many programmers never work above this level of abstraction, which makes their lives much harder than they need to be.

Level 2: Low-Level Implementation Structures

Low-level implementation structures are slightly higher-level structures than those provided by the language itself. They tend to be the operations and data types you learn about in college courses in algorithms and data types: stacks, queues, linked lists, trees, indexed files, sequential files, sort algorithms, search algorithms, and so on. If your program consists entirely of code written at this level, you'll be awash in too much detail to win the battle against complexity.

Level 3: Low-Level Problem-Domain Terms

At this level, you have the primitives you need to work in terms of the problem domain. It's a glue layer between the computer-science structures below and the high-level problem-domain code above. To write code at this level, you need to figure out the vocabulary of the problem area and create building blocks you can use to work with the problem the program solves. In many applications, this will be the business objects layer or a services layer. Classes at this level provide the vocabulary and the building blocks. The classes might be too primitive to be used to solve the problem directly at this level, but they provide a framework that higher-level classes can use to build a solution to the problem.

Level 4: High-Level Problem-Domain Terms

This level provides the abstractive power to work with a problem on its own terms. Your code at this level should be somewhat readable by someone who's not a computer-science whiz, perhaps even by your nontechnical customer. Code at this level won't depend much on the specific features of your programming language because you'll have built your own set of tools to work with the problem. Consequently, at this level your code depends more on the tools you've built for yourself at Level 3 than on the capabilities of the language you're using.

Implementation details should be hidden two layers below this one, in a layer of computer-science structures, so that changes in hardware or the operating system don't affect this layer at all. Embody the user's view of the world in the program at this level because when the program changes, it will change in terms of the user's view. Changes in the problem domain should affect this layer a lot, but they should be easy to accommodate by programming in the problem-domain building blocks from the layer below.

In addition to these conceptual layers, many programmers find it useful to break a program up into other "layers" that cut across the layers described here. For example, the typical three-tier architecture cuts across the levels described here and provides further tools for making the design and code intellectually manageable.

Low-Level Techniques for Working in the Problem Domain

Even without a complete, architectural approach to working in the problem area's vocabulary, you can use many of the techniques in this book to work in terms of the real-world problem rather than the computer-science solution:

- Use classes to implement structures that are meaningful in problem-domain terms.

- Hide information about the low-level data types and their implementation details.

- Use named constants to document the meanings of strings and of numeric literals.

- Assign intermediate variables to document the results of intermediate calculations.

- Use boolean functions to clarify complex boolean tests.

34.7 Watch for Falling Rocks

Programming is neither fully an art nor fully a science. As it's typically practiced, it's a "craft" that's somewhere between art and science. At its best, it's an engineering discipline that arises from the synergistic fusion of art and science (McConnell 2004). Whether art, science, craft, or engineering, it still takes plenty of individual judgment to create a working software product. And part of having good judgment in computer programming is being sensitive to a wide array of warning signs, subtle indications of problems in your program. Warning signs in programming alert you to the possibility of problems, but they're usually not as blatant as a road sign that says "Watch for falling rocks."

When you or someone else says "This is really tricky code," that's a warning sign, usually of poor code. "Tricky code" is a code phrase for "bad code." If you think code is tricky, think about rewriting it so that it's not.

A class's having more errors than average is a warning sign. A few error-prone classes tend to be the most expensive part of a program. If you have a class that has had more errors than average, it will probably continue to have more errors than average. Think about rewriting it.

If programming were a science, each warning sign would imply a specific, well-defined corrective action. Because programming is still a craft, however, a warning sign merely points to an issue that you should consider. You can't necessarily rewrite tricky code or improve an error-prone class.

Just as an abnormal number of defects in a class warns you that the class has low quality, an abnormal number of defects in a program implies that your process is defective. A good process wouldn't allow error-prone code to be developed. It would include the checks and balances of architecture followed by architecture reviews, design followed by design reviews, and code followed by code reviews. By the time the code was ready for testing, most errors would have been eliminated. Exceptional performance requires working smart in addition to working hard. Lots of debugging on a project is a warning sign that implies people aren't working smart. Writing a lot of code in a day and then spending two weeks debugging it is not working smart.

You can use design metrics as another kind of warning sign. Most design metrics are heuristics that give an indication of the quality of a design. The fact that a class contains more than seven members doesn't necessarily mean that it's poorly designed, but it's a warning that the class is complicated. Similarly, more than about 10 decision points in a routine, more than three levels of logical nesting, an unusual number of variables, high coupling to other classes, or low class or routine cohesion should raise a warning flag. None of these signs necessarily means that a class is poorly designed, but the presence of any of them should cause you to look at the class skeptically.

Any warning sign should cause you to doubt the quality of your program. As Charles Saunders Peirce says, "Doubt is an uneasy and dissatisfied state from which we struggle to free ourselves and pass into the state of belief." Treat a warning sign as an "irritation of doubt" that prompts you to look for the more satisfied state of belief.

If you find yourself working on repetitious code or making similar modifications in several areas, you should feel "uneasy and dissatisfied," doubting that control has been adequately centralized in classes or routines. If you find it hard to create scaffolding for test cases because you can't use an individual class easily, you should feel the "irritation of doubt" and ask whether the class is coupled too tightly to other classes. If you can't reuse code in other programs because some classes are too interdependent, that's another warning sign that the classes are coupled too tightly.

When you're deep into a program, pay attention to warning signs that indicate that part of the program design isn't defined well enough to code. Difficulties in writing comments, naming variables, and decomposing the problem into cohesive classes with clear interfaces all indicate that you need to think harder about the design before coding. Wishy-washy names and difficulty in describing sections of code in concise comments are other signs of trouble. When the design is clear in your mind, the low-level details come easily.

Be sensitive to indications that your program is hard to understand. Any discomfort is a clue. If it's hard for you, it will be even harder for the next programmers. They'll appreciate the extra effort you make to improve it. If you're figuring out code instead of reading it, it's too complicated. If it's hard, it's wrong. Make it simpler.

HARD DATA

If you want to take full advantage of warning signs, program in such a way that you create your own warnings. This is useful because even after you know what the signs are, it's surprisingly easy to overlook them. Glenford Myers conducted a study of defect correction in which he found that the single most common cause of not finding errors was simply overlooking them. The errors were visible on test output but not noticed (Myers 1978b).

Make it hard to overlook problems in your program. One example is setting pointers to null after you free them so that they'll cause ugly problems if you mistakenly use one. A freed pointer might point to a valid memory location even after it's been freed. Setting it to null guarantees that it points to an invalid location, making the error harder to overlook.

Compiler warnings are literal warning signs that are often overlooked. If your program generates warnings or errors, fix it so that it doesn't. You don't have much chance of noticing subtle warning signs when you're ignoring those that have "WARNING" printed directly on them.

Why is paying attention to intellectual warning signs especially important in software development? The quality of the thinking that goes into a program largely determines the quality of the program, so paying attention to warnings about the quality of thinking directly affects the final product.

34.8 Iterate, Repeatedly, Again and Again

Iteration is appropriate for many software-development activities. During your initial specification of a system, you work with the user through several versions of requirements until you're sure you agree on them. That's an iterative process. When you build flexibility into your process by building and delivering a system in several increments, that's an iterative process. If you use prototyping to develop several alternative solutions quickly and cheaply before crafting the final product, that's another form of iteration. Iterating on requirements is perhaps as important as any other aspect of the software-development process. Projects fail because they commit themselves to a solution before exploring alternatives. Iteration provides a way to learn about a product before you build it.

As Chapter 28, "Managing Construction," points out, schedule estimates during initial project planning can vary greatly depending on the estimation technique you use. Using an iterative approach for estimation produces a more accurate estimate than relying on a single technique.

Software design is a heuristic process and, like all heuristic processes, is subject to iterative revision and improvement. Software tends to be validated rather than proven, which means that it's tested and developed iteratively until it answers questions correctly. Both high-level and low-level design attempts should be repeated. A first attempt might produce a solution that works, but it's unlikely to produce the best solution. Taking several repeated and different approaches produces insight into the problem that's unlikely with a single approach.

The idea of iteration appears again in code tuning. Once the software is operational, you can rewrite small parts of it to greatly improve overall system performance. Many of the attempts at optimization, however, hurt the code more than they help it. It's not an intuitive process, and some techniques that seem likely to make a system smaller and faster actually make it larger and slower. The uncertainty about the effect of any optimization technique creates a need for tuning, measuring, and tuning again. If a bottleneck is critical to system performance, you can tune the code several times, and several of your later attempts may be more successful than your first.

Reviews cut across the grain of the development process, inserting iterations at any stage in which they're conducted. The purpose of a review is to check the quality of the work at a particular point. If the product fails the review, it's sent back for rework. If it succeeds, it doesn't need further iteration.

One definition of engineering is to do for a dime what anyone can do for a dollar. Iterating in the late stages is doing for two dollars what anyone can do for one dollar. Fred Brooks suggested that you "build one to throw away; you will, anyhow" (Brooks 1995). The trick of software engineering is to build the disposable parts as quickly and inexpensively as possible, which is the point of iterating in the early stages.

34.9 Thou Shalt Rend Software and Religion Asunder

Religion appears in software development in numerous incarnations—as dogmatic adherence to a single design method, as unswerving belief in a specific formatting or commenting style, or as a zealous avoidance of global data. Whatever the case, it's always inappropriate.

Software Oracles

Cross-Reference For details on handling programming religion as a manager, see "Religious Issues" in Section 28.5.

Unfortunately, the zealous attitude is decreed from on high by some of the more prominent people in the profession. It's important to publicize innovations so that practitioners can try out promising new methods. Methods have to be tried before they can be fully proven or disproved. The dissemination of research results to practitioners is called "technology transfer" and is important for advancing the state of the practice of software development. There's a difference, however, between disseminating a new methodology and selling software snake oil. The idea of technology transfer is poorly served by dogmatic methodology peddlers who try to convince you that their new one-size-fits-all, high-tech cow pies will solve all your problems. Forget everything you've already learned because this new method is so great it will improve your productivity 100 percent in everything!

Rather than latching on to the latest miracle fad, use a mixture of methods. Experiment with the exciting, recent methods, but bank on the old and dependable ones.

Eclecticism

Cross-Reference For more on the difference between algorithmic and heuristic approaches, see Section 2.2, "How to Use Software Metaphors." For information on eclecticism in design, see "Iterate" in Section 5.4.

Blind faith in one method precludes the selectivity you need if you're to find the most effective solutions to programming problems. If software development were a deterministic, algorithmic process, you could follow a rigid methodology to your solution. But software development isn't a deterministic process; it's heuristic, which means that rigid processes are inappropriate and have little hope of success. In design, for example, sometimes top-down decomposition works well. Sometimes an object-oriented approach, a bottom-up composition, or a data-structure approach works better. You have to be willing to try several approaches, knowing that some will fail and some will succeed but not knowing which ones will work until after you try them. You have to be eclectic.

Adherence to a single method is also harmful in that it makes you force-fit the problem to the solution. If you decide on the solution method before you fully understand the problem, you act prematurely. Over-constrain the set of possible solutions, and you might rule out the most effective solution.

You'll be uncomfortable with any new methodology initially, and the advice that you avoid religion in programming isn't meant to suggest that you should stop using a new method as soon as you have a little trouble solving a problem with it. Give the new method a fair shake, but give the old methods their fair shakes, too.

Cross-Reference For a more detailed description of the toolbox metaphor, see "Applying Software Techniques: The Intellectual Toolbox" in Section 2.3.

Eclecticism is a useful attitude to bring to the techniques presented in this book as much as to techniques described in other sources. Discussions of several topics presented here have advanced alternative approaches that you can't use at the same time. You have to choose one or the other for each specific problem. You have to treat the techniques as tools in a toolbox and use your own judgment to select the best tool for the job. Most of the time, the tool choice doesn't matter very much. You can use a box wrench, vise-grip pliers, or a crescent wrench. In some cases, however, the tool selection matters a lot, so you should always make your selection carefully. Engineering is in part a discipline of making tradeoffs among competing techniques. You can't make a tradeoff if you've prematurely limited your choices to a single tool.

The toolbox metaphor is useful because it makes the abstract idea of eclecticism concrete. Suppose you were a general contractor and your buddy Simple Simon always used vise-grip pliers. Suppose he refused to use a box wrench or a crescent wrench. You'd probably think he was odd because he wouldn't use all the tools at his disposal. The same is true in software development. At a high level, you have alternative design methods. At a more detailed level, you can choose one of several data types to represent any given design. At an even more detailed level, you can choose several different schemes for formatting and commenting code, naming variables, defining class interfaces, and passing routine parameters.

A dogmatic stance conflicts with the eclectic toolbox approach to software construction. It's incompatible with the attitude needed to build high-quality software.

Experimentation

Eclecticism has a close relative in experimentation. You need to experiment throughout the development process, but zealous inflexibility hobbles the impulse. To experiment effectively, you must be willing to change your beliefs based on the results of the experiment. If you're not willing, experimentation is a gratuitous waste of time.

Many of the inflexible approaches to software development are based on a fear of making mistakes. A blanket attempt to avoid mistakes is the biggest mistake of all. Design is a process of carefully planning small mistakes in order to avoid making big ones. Experimentation in software development is a process of setting up tests so that you learn whether an approach fails or succeeds—the experiment itself is a success as long as it resolves the issue.

Experimentation is appropriate at as many levels as eclecticism is. At each level at which you are ready to make an eclectic choice, you can probably come up with a corresponding experiment to determine which approach works best. At the architectural-design level, an experiment might consist of sketching software architectures using three different design approaches. At the detailed-design level, an experiment might consist of following the implications of a higher-level architecture using three different low-level design approaches. At the programming-language level, an experiment might consist of writing a short experimental program to exercise the operation of a part of the language you're not completely familiar with. The experiment might consist of tuning a piece of code and benchmarking it to verify that it's really smaller or faster. At the overall software-development-process level, an experiment might consist of collecting quality and productivity data so that you can see whether inspections really find more errors than walk-throughs.

The point is that you have to keep an open mind about all aspects of software development. You have to get technical about your process as well as your product. Open-minded experimentation and religious adherence to a predefined approach don't mix.

Key Points

- One primary goal of programming is managing complexity.

- The programming process significantly affects the final product.

- Team programming is more an exercise in communicating with people than in communicating with a computer. Individual programming is more an exercise in communicating with yourself than with a computer.

- When abused, a programming convention can be a cure that's worse than the disease. Used thoughtfully, a convention adds valuable structure to the development environment and helps with managing complexity and communication.

- Programming in terms of the problem rather than the solution helps to manage complexity.

- Paying attention to intellectual warning signs like the "irritation of doubt" is especially important in programming because programming is almost purely a mental activity.

- The more you iterate in each development activity, the better the product of that activity will be.

- Dogmatic methodologies and high-quality software development don't mix. Fill your intellectual toolbox with programming alternatives, and improve your skill at choosing the right tool for the job.

Chapter 35

Where to Find More Information

Contents

Related Topics

- Web resources: *www.cc2e.com*

If you've read this far, you already know that a lot has been written about effective software-development practices. Much more information is available than most people realize. People have already made all the mistakes that you're making now, and unless you're a glutton for punishment, you'll prefer reading their books and avoiding their mistakes to inventing new versions of old problems.

Because this book describes hundreds of other books and articles that contain information on software development, it's hard to know what to read first. A software-development library is made up of several kinds of information. A core of programming books explains fundamental concepts of effective programming. Related books explain the larger technical, management, and intellectual contexts within which programming goes on. And detailed references on languages, operating systems, environments, and hardware contain information that's useful for specific projects.

Books in the last category generally have a life span of about one project; they're more or less temporary and aren't discussed here. Of the other kinds of books, it's useful to have a core set that discusses each of the major software-development activities in depth: books on requirements, design, construction, management, testing, and so on. The following sections describe construction resources in depth and then provide an overview of materials available in other software knowledge areas. Section 35.4 wraps these resources into a neat package by defining a software developer's reading program.

35.1 Information About Software Construction

cc2e.com/3588

I originally wrote this book because I couldn't find a thorough discussion of software construction. In the years since I published the first edition, several good books have appeared.

Pragmatic Programmer (Hunt and Thomas 2000) focuses on the activities most closely associated with coding, including testing, debugging, use of assertions, and so on. It does not dive deeply into code itself but contains numerous principles related to creating good code.

Jon Bentley's *Programming Pearls*, 2d ed. (Bentley 2000) discusses the art and science of software design in the small. The book is organized as a set of essays that are very well written and express a great deal of insight into effective construction techniques as well as genuine enthusiasm for software construction. I use something I learned from Bentley's essays nearly every day that I program.

Cross-Reference For more in the economics of Extreme Programming and agile programming, see *cc2e.com/ 3545*.

Kent Beck's *Extreme Programming Explained: Embrace Change* (Beck 2000) defines a construction-centric approach to software development. As Section 3.1 ("Importance of Prerequisites") explained, the book's assertions about the economics of Extreme Programming are not borne out by industry research, but many of its recommendations are useful during construction regardless of whether a team is using Extreme Programming or some other approach.

A more specialized book is Steve Maguire's *Writing Solid Code – Microsoft's Techniques for Developing Bug-Free C Software* (Maguire 1993). It focuses on construction practices for commercial-quality software applications, mostly based on the author's experiences working on Microsoft's Office applications. It focuses on techniques applicable in C. It is largely oblivious to object-oriented programming issues, but most of the topics it addresses are relevant in any environment.

Another more specialized book is *The Practice of Programming*, by Brian Kernighan and Rob Pike (Kernighan and Pike 1999). This book focuses on nitty-gritty, practical aspects of programming, bridging the gap between academic computer-science knowledge and hands-on lessons. It includes discussions of programming style, design, debugging, and testing. It assumes familiarity with C/C++.

cc2e.com/3549

Although it's out of print and hard to find, *Programmers at Work*, by Susan Lammers (1986), is worth the search. It contains interviews with the industry's high-profile programmers. The interviews explore their personalities, work habits, and programming philosophies. The luminaries interviewed include Bill Gates (founder of Microsoft), John Warnock (founder of Adobe), Andy Hertzfeld (principal developer of the Macintosh operating system), Butler Lampson (a senior engineer at DEC, now at Microsoft), Wayne Ratliff (inventor of dBase), Dan Bricklin (inventor of VisiCalc), and a dozen others.

35.2 Topics Beyond Construction

Beyond the core books described in the previous section, here are some books that range further afield from the topic of software construction.

Overview Material

cc2e.com/3595

The following books provide software-development overviews from a variety of vantage points:

Robert L. Glass's *Facts and Fallacies of Software Engineering* (2003) provides a readable introduction to the conventional wisdom of software development dos and don'ts. The book is well researched and provides numerous pointers to additional resources.

My own *Professional Sofware Development* (2004) surveys the field of software development as it is practiced now and as it could be if it were routinely practiced at its best.

The *Swebok: Guide to the Software Engineering Body of Knowledge* (Abran 2001) provides a detailed decomposition of the software-engineering body of knowledge. This book has dived into detail in the software-construction area. The Guide to the Swebok shows just how much more knowledge exists in the field.

Gerald Weinberg's *The Psychology of Computer Programming* (Weinberg 1998) is packed with fascinating anecdotes about programming. It's far-ranging because it was written at a time when anything related to software was considered to be about programming. The advice in the original review of the book in the *ACM Computing Reviews* is as good today as it was when the review was written:

> *Every manager of programmers should have his own copy. He should read it, take it to heart, act on the precepts, and leave the copy on his desk to be stolen by his programmers. He should continue replacing the stolen copies until equilibrium is established (Weiss 1972).*

If you can't find *The Psychology of Computer Programming*, look for *The Mythical Man-Month* (Brooks 1995) or *PeopleWare* (DeMarco and Lister 1999). They both drive home the theme that programming is first and foremost something done by people and only secondarily something that happens to involve computers.

A final excellent overview of issues in software development is *Software Creativity* (Glass 1995). This book should have been a breakthrough book on software creativity the way that *Peopleware* was on software teams. Glass discusses creativity versus discipline, theory versus practice, heuristics versus methodology, process versus product, and many of the other dichotomies that define the software field. After years of discussing this book with programmers who work for me, I have concluded that the difficulty with the book is that it is a collection of essays edited by Glass but not entirely written by him. For some readers, this gives the book an unfinished feel. Nonetheless, I still require every developer in my company to read it. The book is out of print and hard to find but worth the effort if you are able to find it.

Software-Engineering Overviews

Every practicing computer programmer or software engineer should have a high-level reference on software engineering. Such books survey the methodological landscape rather than painting specific features in detail. They provide an overview of effective software-engineering practices and capsule descriptions of specific software-engineering techniques. The capsule descriptions aren't detailed enough to train you in the techniques, but a single book would have to be several thousand pages long to do that. They provide enough information so that you can learn how the techniques fit together and can choose techniques for further investigation.

Roger S. Pressman's *Software Engineering: A Practitioner's Approach*, 6th ed. (Pressman 2004), is a balanced treatment of requirements, design, quality validation, and management. Its 900 pages pay little attention to programming practices, but that's a minor limitation, especially if you already have a book on construction such as the one you're reading.

The sixth edition of Ian Sommerville's *Software Engineering* (Sommerville 2000) is comparable to Pressman's book, and it also provides a good high-level overview of the software-development process.

Other Annotated Bibliographies

cc2e.com/3502

Good computing bibliographies are rare. Here are a few that justify the effort it takes to obtain them:

ACM Computing Reviews is a special-interest publication of the Association for Computing Machinery (ACM) that's dedicated to reviewing books about all aspects of computers and computer programming. The reviews are organized according to an extensive classification scheme, making it easy to find books in your area of interest. For information on this publication and on membership in the ACM, see *www.acm.org*.

cc2e.com/3509

Construx Software's Professional Development Ladder (*www.construx.com/ladder/*). This website provides recommended reading programs for software developers, testers, and managers.

35.3 Periodicals

Lowbrow Programmer Magazines

These magazines are often available at local newsstands:

cc2e.com/3516

Software Development. www.sdmagazine.com. This magazine focuses on programming issues—less on tips for specific environments than on the general issues you face as a professional programmer. The quality of the articles is quite good. It also includes product reviews.

cc2e.com/3523

Dr. Dobb's Journal. www.ddj.com. This magazine is oriented toward hard-core programmers. Its articles tend to deal with detailed issues and include lots of code.

If you can't find these magazines at your local newsstand, many publishers will send you a complimentary issue, and many articles are available online.

Highbrow Programmer Journals

You don't usually buy these magazines at the newsstand. You usually have to go to a major university library or subscribe to them for yourself or your company:

cc2e.com/3530

IEEE Software. www.computer.org/software/. This bimonthly magazine focuses on software construction, management, requirements, design and other leading-edge software topics. Its mission is to "build the community of leading software practitioners." In 1993, I wrote that it's "the most valuable magazine a programmer can subscribe to." Since I wrote that, I've been Editor in Chief of the magazine, and I still believe it's the best periodical available for a serious software practitioner.

cc2e.com/3537

IEEE Computer. www.computer.org/computer/. This monthly magazine is the flagship publication of the IEEE (Institute of Electrical and Electronics Engineers) Computer Society. It publishes articles on a wide spectrum of computer topics and has scrupulous review standards to ensure the quality of the articles it publishes. Because of its breadth, you'll probably find fewer articles that interest you than you will in *IEEE Software*.

cc2e.com/3544

Communications of the ACM. www.acm.org/cacm/. This magazine is one of the oldest and most respected computer publications available. It has the broad charter of publishing about the length and breadth of computerology, a subject that's much vaster than it was even a few years ago. As with *IEEE Computer*, because of its breadth, you'll probably find that many of the articles are outside your area of interest. The magazine tends to have an academic flavor, which has both a bad side and a good side. The bad side is that some of the authors write in an obfuscatory academic style. The good side is that it contains leading-edge information that won't filter down to the lowbrow magazines for years.

Special-Interest Publications

Several publications provide in-depth coverage of specialized topics.

Professional Publications

cc2e.com/3551

The IEEE Computer Society publishes specialized journals on software engineering, security and privacy, computer graphics and animation, internet development, multimedia, intelligent systems, the history of computing, and other topics. See *www.computer.org* for more details.

cc2e.com/3558

The ACM also publishes special-interest publications in artificial intelligence, computers and human interaction, databases, embedded systems, graphics, programming languages, mathematical software, networking, software engineering, and other topics. See *www.acm.org* for more information.

Popular-Market Publications

cc2e.com/3565

These magazines all cover what their names suggest they cover.

The C/C++ Users Journal. www.cuj.com.

Java Developer's Journal. www.sys-con.com/java/.

Embedded Systems Programming. www.embedded.com.

Linux Journal. www.linuxjournal.com.

Unix Review. www.unixreview.com.

Windows Developer's Network. www.wd-mag.com.

35.4 A Software Developer's Reading Plan

cc2e.com/3507

This section describes the reading program that a software developer needs to work through to achieve full professional standing at my company, Construx Software. The plan described is a generic baseline plan for a software professional who wants to focus on development. Our mentoring program provides for further tailoring of the generic plan to support an individual's interests, and within Construx this reading is also supplemented with training and directed professional experiences.

Introductory Level

To move beyond "introductory" level at Construx, a developer must read the following books:

Adams, James L. *Conceptual Blockbusting: A Guide to Better Ideas*, 4th ed. Cambridge, MA: Perseus Publishing, 2001.

Bentley, Jon. *Programming Pearls*, 2d ed. Reading, MA: Addison-Wesley, 2000.

Glass, Robert L. *Facts and Fallacies of Software Engineering*. Boston, MA: Addison-Wesley, 2003.

McConnell, Steve. *Software Project Survival Guide*. Redmond, WA: Microsoft Press, 1998.

McConnell, Steve. *Code Complete*, 2d ed. Redmond, WA: Microsoft Press, 2004.

Practitioner Level

To achieve "intermediate" status at Construx, a programmer needs to read the following additional materials:

Berczuk, Stephen P. and Brad Appleton. *Software Configuration Management Patterns: Effective Teamwork, Practical Integration*. Boston, MA: Addison-Wesley, 2003.

Fowler, Martin. *UML Distilled: A Brief Guide to the Standard Object* Modeling Language, 3d ed. Boston, MA: Addison-Wesley, 2003.

Glass, Robert L. *Software Creativity*. Reading, MA: Addison-Wesley, 1995.

Kaner, Cem, Jack Falk, Hung Q. Nguyen. *Testing Computer Software*, 2d ed. New York, NY: John Wiley & Sons, 1999.

Larman, Craig. *Applying UML and Patterns: An Introduction to Object-Oriented Analysis and Design and the Unified Process*, 2d ed. Englewood Cliffs, NJ: Prentice Hall, 2001.

McConnell, Steve. *Rapid Development*. Redmond, WA: Microsoft Press, 1996.

Wiegers, Karl. *Software Requirements*, 2d ed. Redmond, WA: Microsoft Press, 2003.

cc2e.com/3514   "Manager's Handbook for Software Development," NASA Goddard Space Flight Center. Downloadable from *sel.gsfc.nasa.gov/website/documents/online-doc.htm*.

Professional Level

A software developer must read the following materials to achieve full professional standing at Construx ("leadership" level). Additional requirements are tailored to each individual developer; this section describes the generic requirements.

Bass, Len, Paul Clements, and Rick Kazman. *Software Architecture in Practice*, 2d ed. Boston, MA: Addison-Wesley, 2003.

Fowler, Martin. *Refactoring: Improving the Design of Existing Code*. Reading, MA: Addison-Wesley, 1999.

Gamma, Erich, et al. *Design Patterns*. Reading, MA: Addison-Wesley, 1995.

Gilb, Tom. *Principles of Software Engineering Management.* Wokingham, England: Addison-Wesley, 1988.

Maguire, Steve. *Writing Solid Code.* Redmond, WA: Microsoft Press, 1993.

Meyer, Bertrand. *Object-Oriented Software Construction*, 2d ed. New York, NY: Prentice Hall PTR, 1997.

cc2e.com/3521

"Software Measurement Guidebook," NASA Goddard Space Flight Center. Available from *sel.gsfc.nasa.gov/website/documents/online-doc.htm.*

cc2e.com/3528

For more details on this professional development program, as well as for up-to-date reading lists, see our professional development website at *www.construx.com /professionaldev/.*

35.5 Joining a Professional Organization

cc2e.com/3535

One of the best ways to learn more about programming is to get in touch with other programmers who are as dedicated to the profession as you are. Local user groups for specific hardware and language products are one kind of group. Other kinds are national and international professional organizations. The most practitioner-oriented organization is the IEEE Computer Society, which publishes the *IEEE Computer* and *IEEE Software* magazines. For membership information, see *www.computer.org.*

cc2e.com/3542

The original professional organization was the ACM, which publishes *Communications of the ACM* and many special-interest magazines. It tends to be somewhat more academically oriented than the IEEE Computer Society. For membership information, see *www.acm.org.*

Bibliography

"A C Coding Standard." 1991. *Unix Review* 9, no. 9 (September): 42–43.

Abdel-Hamid, Tarek K. 1989. "The Dynamics of Software Project Staffing: A System Dynamics Based Simulation Approach." *IEEE Transactions on Software Engineering* SE-15, no. 2 (February): 109–19.

Abran, Alain, et al. 2001. *Swebok: Guide to the Software Engineering Body of Knowledge: Trial Version 1.00-May 2001.* Los Alamitos, CA: IEEE Computer Society Press.

Abrash, Michael. 1992. "Flooring It: The Optimization Challenge." *PC Techniques* 2, no. 6 (February/March): 82–88.

Ackerman, A. Frank, Lynne S. Buchwald, and Frank H. Lewski. 1989. "Software Inspections: An Effective Verification Process." *IEEE Software*, May/June 1989, 31–36.

Adams, James L. 2001. *Conceptual Blockbusting: A Guide to Better Ideas*, 4th ed. Cambridge, MA: Perseus Publishing.

Aho, Alfred V., Brian W. Kernighan, and Peter J. Weinberg. 1977. *The AWK Programming Language.* Reading, MA: Addison-Wesley.

Aho, Alfred V., John E. Hopcroft, and Jeffrey D. Ullman. 1983. *Data Structures and Algorithms.* Reading, MA: Addison-Wesley.

Albrecht, Allan J. 1979. "Measuring Application Development Productivity." *Proceedings of the Joint SHARE/GUIDE/IBM Application Development Symposium, October 1979*: 83–92.

Ambler, Scott. 2003. *Agile Database Techniques.* New York, NY: John Wiley & Sons.

Anand, N. 1988. "Clarify Function!" *ACM Sigplan Notices* 23, no. 6 (June): 69–79.

Aristotle. *The Ethics of Aristotle: The Nicomachean Ethics.* Trans. by J.A.K. Thomson. Rev. by Hugh Tredennick. Harmondsworth, Middlesex, England: Penguin, 1976.

Armenise, Pasquale. 1989. "A Structured Approach to Program Optimization." *IEEE Transactions on Software Engineering* SE-15, no. 2 (February): 101–8.

Arnold, Ken, James Gosling, and David Holmes. 2000. *The Java Programming Language*, 3d ed. Boston, MA: Addison-Wesley.

Arthur, Lowell J. 1988. *Software Evolution: The Software Maintenance Challenge.* New York, NY: John Wiley & Sons.

Augustine, N. R. 1979. "Augustine's Laws and Major System Development Programs." *Defense Systems Management Review*: 50–76.

Babich, W. 1986. *Software Configuration Management.* Reading, MA: Addison-Wesley.

Bachman, Charles W. 1973. "The Programmer as Navigator." Turing Award Lecture. *Communications of the ACM* 16, no. 11 (November): 653.

Baecker, Ronald M., and Aaron Marcus. 1990. *Human Factors and Typography for More Readable Programs.* Reading, MA: Addison-Wesley.

Bairdain, E. F. 1964. "Research Studies of Programmers and Programming." Unpublished studies reported in Boehm 1981.

Baker, F. Terry, and Harlan D. Mills. 1973. "Chief Programmer Teams." *Datamation* 19, no. 12 (December): 58–61.

Barbour, Ian G. 1966. *Issues in Science and Religion.* New York, NY: Harper & Row.

Barbour, Ian G. 1974. *Myths, Models, and Paradigms: A Comparative Study in Science and Religion*. New York, NY: Harper & Row.

Barwell, Fred, et al. 2002. *Professional VB.NET*, 2d ed. Birmingham, UK: Wrox.

Basili, V. R., and B. T. Perricone. 1984. "Software Errors and Complexity: An Empirical Investigation." *Communications of the ACM* 27, no. 1 (January): 42–52.

Basili, Victor R., and Albert J. Turner. 1975. "Iterative Enhancement: A Practical Technique for Software Development." *IEEE Transactions on Software Engineering* SE-1, no. 4 (December): 390–96.

Basili, Victor R., and David M. Weiss. 1984. "A Methodology for Collecting Valid Software Engineering Data." *IEEE Transactions on Software Engineering* SE-10, no. 6 (November): 728–38.

Basili, Victor R., and Richard W. Selby. 1987. "Comparing the Effectiveness of Software Testing Strategies." *IEEE Transactions on Software Engineering* SE-13, no. 12 (December): 1278–96.

Basili, Victor R., et al. 2002. "Lessons learned from 25 years of process improvement: The Rise and Fall of the NASA Software Engineering Laboratory," *Proceedings of the 24th International Conference on Software Engineering*, Orlando, FL.

Basili, Victor R., Richard W. Selby, and David H. Hutchens. 1986. "Experimentation in Software Engineering." *IEEE Transactions on Software Engineering* SE-12, no. 7 (July): 733–43.

Basili, Victor, L. Briand, and W.L. Melo. 1996. "A Validation of Object-Oriented Design Metrics as Quality Indicators," *IEEE Transactions on Software Engineering*, October 1996, 751–761.

Bass, Len, Paul Clements, and Rick Kazman. 2003. *Software Architecture in Practice*, 2d ed. Boston, MA: Addison-Wesley.

Bastani, Farokh, and Sitharama Iyengar. 1987. "The Effect of Data Structures on the Logical Complexity of Programs." *Communications of the ACM* 30, no. 3 (March): 250–59.

Bays, Michael. 1999. *Software Release Methodology*. Englewood Cliffs, NJ: Prentice Hall.

Beck, Kent. 2000. *Extreme Programming Explained: Embrace Change*. Reading, MA: Addison-Wesley.

Beck, Kent. 2003. *Test-Driven Development: By Example*. Boston, MA: Addison-Wesley.

Beck, Kent. 1991. "Think Like An Object." *Unix Review* 9, no. 10 (October): 39–43.

Beck, Leland L., and Thomas E. Perkins. 1983. "A Survey of Software Engineering Practice: Tools, Methods, and Results." *IEEE Transactions on Software Engineering* SE-9, no. 5 (September): 541–61.

Beizer, Boris. 1990. *Software Testing Techniques*, 2d ed. New York, NY: Van Nostrand Reinhold.

Bentley, Jon, and Donald Knuth. 1986. "Literate Programming." *Communications of the ACM* 29, no. 5 (May): 364–69.

Bentley, Jon, Donald Knuth, and Doug McIlroy. 1986. "A Literate Program." *Communications of the ACM* 29, no. 5 (May): 471–83.

Bentley, Jon. 1982. *Writing Efficient Programs*. Englewood Cliffs, NJ: Prentice Hall.

Bentley, Jon. 1988. *More Programming Pearls: Confessions of a Coder*. Reading, MA: Addison-Wesley.

Bentley, Jon. 1991. "Software Exploratorium: Writing Efficient C Programs." *Unix Review* 9, no. 8 (August): 62–73.

Bentley, Jon. 2000. *Programming Pearls*, 2d ed. Reading, MA: Addison-Wesley.

Berczuk, Stephen P. and Brad Appleton. 2003. *Software Configuration Management Patterns: Effective Teamwork, Practical Integration*. Boston, MA: Addison-Wesley.

Berry, R. E., and B. A. E. Meekings. 1985. "A Style Analysis of C Programs." *Communications of the ACM* 28, no. 1 (January): 80–88.

Bersoff, Edward H. 1984. "Elements of Software Configuration Management." *IEEE Transactions on Software Engineering* SE-10, no. 1 (January): 79–87.

Bersoff, Edward H., and Alan M. Davis. 1991. "Impacts of Life Cycle Models on Software Configuration Management." *Communications of the ACM* 34, no. 8 (August): 104–18.

Bersoff, Edward H., et al. 1980. *Software Configuration Management*. Englewood Cliffs, NJ: Prentice Hall.

Birrell, N. D., and M. A. Ould. 1985. *A Practical Handbook for Software Development*. Cambridge, England: Cambridge University Press.

Bloch, Joshua. 2001. *Effective Java Programming Language Guide*. Boston, MA: Addison-Wesley.

BLS 2002. *Occupational Outlook Handbook 2002-03 Edition*, Bureau of Labor Statistics.

BLS 2004. *Occupational Outlook Handbook 2004-05 Edition*, Bureau of Labor Statistics.

Blum, Bruce I. 1989. "A Software Environment: Some Surprising Empirical Results." *Proceedings of the Fourteenth Annual Software Engineering Workshop, November 29, 1989*. Greenbelt, MD: Goddard Space Flight Center. Document SEL-89-007.

Boddie, John. 1987. *Crunch Mode*. New York, NY: Yourdon Press.

Boehm, Barry and Richard Turner. 2004. *Balancing Agility and Discipline: A Guide for the Perplexed*. Boston, MA: Addison-Wesley.

Boehm, Barry W. 1981. *Software Engineering Economics*. Englewood Cliffs, NJ: Prentice Hall.

Boehm, Barry W. 1984. "Software Engineering Economics." *IEEE Transactions on Software Engineering* SE-10, no. 1 (January): 4–21.

Boehm, Barry W. 1987a. "Improving Software Productivity." *IEEE Computer*, September, 43–57.

Boehm, Barry W. 1987b. "Industrial Software Metrics Top 10 List." *IEEE Software* 4, no. 9 (September): 84–85.

Boehm, Barry W. 1988. "A Spiral Model of Software Development and Enhancement." *Computer*, May, 61–72.

Boehm, Barry W., and Philip N. Papaccio. 1988. "Understanding and Controlling Software Costs." *IEEE Transactions on Software Engineering* SE-14, no. 10 (October): 1462–77.

Boehm, Barry W., ed. 1989. *Tutorial: Software Risk Management*. Washington, DC: IEEE Computer Society Press.

Boehm, Barry W., et al. 1978. *Characteristics of Software Quality*. New York, NY: North-Holland.

Boehm, Barry W., et al. 1984. "A Software Development Environment for Improving Productivity." *Computer*, June, 30–44.

Boehm, Barry W., T. E. Gray, and T. Seewaldt. 1984. "Prototyping Versus Specifying: A Multiproject Experiment." *IEEE Transactions on Software Engineering* SE-10, no. 3 (May): 290–303. Also in Jones 1986b.

Boehm, Barry, et al. 2000a. *Software Cost Estimation with Cocomo II*. Boston, MA: Addison-Wesley.

Boehm, Barry. 2000b. "Unifying Software Engineering and Systems Engineering," *IEEE Computer*, March 2000, 114–116.

Boehm-Davis, Deborah, Sylvia Sheppard, and John Bailey. 1987. "Program Design Languages: How Much Detail Should They Include?" *International Journal of Man-Machine Studies* 27, no. 4: 337–47.

Böhm, C., and G. Jacopini. 1966. "Flow Diagrams, Turing Machines and Languages with Only Two Formation Rules." *Communications of the ACM* 9, no. 5 (May): 366–71.

Booch, Grady. 1987. *Software Engineering with Ada*, 2d ed. Menlo Park, CA: Benjamin/Cummings.

Booch, Grady. 1994. *Object Oriented Analysis and Design with Applications*, 2d ed. Boston, MA: Addison-Wesley.

Booth, Rick. 1997. *Inner Loops : A Sourcebook for Fast 32-bit Software Development*. Boston, MA: Addison-Wesley.

Boundy, David. 1991. "A Taxonomy of Programmers." *ACM SIGSOFT Software Engineering Notes* 16, no. 4 (October): 23–30.

Brand, Stewart. 1995. *How Buildings Learn: What Happens After They're Built*. Penguin USA.

Branstad, Martha A., John C. Cherniavsky, and W. Richards Adrion. 1980. "Validation, Verification, and Testing for the Individual Programmer." *Computer*, December, 24–30.

Brockmann, R. John. 1990. *Writing Better Computer User Documentation: From Paper to Hypertext: Version 2.0*. New York, NY: John Wiley & Sons.

Brooks, Frederick P., Jr. 1987. "No Silver Bullets—Essence and Accidents of Software Engineering." *Computer*, April, 10–19.

Brooks, Frederick P., Jr. 1995. *The Mythical Man-Month: Essays on Software Engineering, Anniversary Edition* (2d ed.). Reading, MA: Addison-Wesley.

Brooks, Ruven. 1977. "Towards a Theory of the Cognitive Processes in Computer Programming." *International Journal of Man-Machine Studies* 9:737–51.

Brooks, W. Douglas. 1981. "Software Technology Payoff—Some Statistical Evidence." *The Journal of Systems and Software* 2:3–9.

Brown, A. R., and W. A. Sampson. 1973. *Program Debugging*. New York, NY: American Elsevier.

Buschman, Frank, et al. 1996. *Pattern-Oriented Software Architecture, Volume 1: A System of Patterns*. New York, NY: John Wiley & Sons.

Bush, Marilyn, and John Kelly. 1989. "The Jet Propulsion Laboratory's Experience with Formal Inspections." *Proceedings of the Fourteenth Annual Software Engineering Workshop, November 29, 1989*. Greenbelt, MD: Goddard Space Flight Center. Document SEL-89-007.

Caine, S. H., and E. K. Gordon. 1975. "PDL—A Tool for Software Design." *AFIPS Proceedings of the 1975 National Computer Conference 44*. Montvale, NJ: AFIPS Press, 271–76.

Card, David N. 1987. "A Software Technology Evaluation Program." *Information and Software Technology* 29, no. 6 (July/August): 291–300.

Card, David N., Frank E. McGarry, and Gerald T. Page. 1987. "Evaluating Software Engineering Technologies." *IEEE Transactions on Software Engineering* SE-13, no. 7 (July): 845–51.

Card, David N., Victor E. Church, and William W. Agresti. 1986. "An Empirical Study of Software Design Practices." *IEEE Transactions on Software Engineering* SE-12, no. 2 (February): 264–71.

Card, David N., with Robert L. Glass. 1990. *Measuring Software Design Quality*. Englewood Cliffs, NJ: Prentice Hall.

Card, David, Gerald Page, and Frank McGarry. 1985. "Criteria for Software Modularization." *Proceedings of the 8th International Conference on Software Engineering*. Washington, DC: IEEE Computer Society Press, 372–77.

Carnegie, Dale. 1981. *How to Win Friends and Influence People*, Revised Edition. New York, NY: Pocket Books.

Chase, William G., and Herbert A. Simon. 1973. "Perception in Chess." *Cognitive Psychology* 4:55–81.

Clark, R. Lawrence. 1973. "A Linguistic Contribution of GOTO-less Programming," *Datamation*, December 1973.

Clements, Paul, ed. 2003. *Documenting Software Architectures: Views and Beyond*. Boston, MA: Addison-Wesley.

Clements, Paul, Rick Kazman, and Mark Klein. 2002. *Evaluating Software Architectures: Methods and Case Studies*. Boston, MA: Addison-Wesley.

Coad, Peter, and Edward Yourdon. 1991. *Object-Oriented Design*. Englewood Cliffs, NJ: Yourdon Press.

Cobb, Richard H., and Harlan D. Mills. 1990. "Engineering Software Under Statistical Quality Control." *IEEE Software* 7, no. 6 (November): 45–54.

Cockburn, Alistair. 2000. *Writing Effective Use Cases*. Boston, MA: Addison-Wesley.

Cockburn, Alistair. 2002. *Agile Software Development*. Boston, MA: Addison-Wesley.

Collofello, Jim, and Scott Woodfield. 1989. "Evaluating the Effectiveness of Reliability Assurance Techniques." *Journal of Systems and Software* 9, no. 3 (March).

Comer, Douglas. 1981. "Principles of Program Design Induced from Experience with Small Public Programs." *IEEE Transactions on Software Engineering* SE-7, no. 2 (March): 169–74.

Constantine, Larry L. 1990a. "Comments on 'On Criteria for Module Interfaces.'" *IEEE Transactions on Software Engineering* SE-16, no. 12 (December): 1440.

Constantine, Larry L. 1990b. "Objects, Functions, and Program Extensibility." *Computer Language*, January, 34–56.

Conte, S. D., H. E. Dunsmore, and V. Y. Shen. 1986. *Software Engineering Metrics and Models*. Menlo Park, CA: Benjamin/Cummings.

Cooper, Doug, and Michael Clancy. 1982. *Oh! Pascal!* 2d ed. New York, NY: Norton.

Cooper, Kenneth G. and Thomas W. Mullen. 1993. "Swords and Plowshares: The Rework Cycles of Defense and Commercial Software Development Projects," *American Programmer*, May 1993, 41–51.

Corbató, Fernando J. 1991. "On Building Systems That Will Fail." 1991 Turing Award Lecture. *Communications of the ACM* 34, no. 9 (September): 72–81.

Cornell, Gary and Jonathan Morrison. 2002. *Programming VB .NET: A Guide for Experienced Programmers*, Berkeley, CA: Apress.

Corwin, Al. 1991. Private communication.

CSTB 1990. "Scaling Up: A Research Agenda for Software Engineering." Excerpts from a report by the Computer Science and Technology Board. *Communications of the ACM* 33, no. 3 (March): 281–93.

Curtis, Bill, ed. 1985. *Tutorial: Human Factors in Software Development*. Los Angeles, CA: IEEE Computer Society Press.

Curtis, Bill, et al. 1986. "Software Psychology: The Need for an Interdisciplinary Program." *Proceedings of the IEEE* 74, no. 8: 1092–1106.

Curtis, Bill, et al. 1989. "Experimentation of Software Documentation Formats." *Journal of Systems and Software* 9, no. 2 (February): 167–207.

Curtis, Bill, H. Krasner, and N. Iscoe. 1988. "A Field Study of the Software Design Process for Large Systems." *Communications of the ACM* 31, no. 11 (November): 1268–87.

Curtis, Bill. 1981. "Substantiating Programmer Variability." *Proceedings of the IEEE* 69, no. 7: 846.

Cusumano, Michael and Richard W. Selby. 1995. *Microsoft Secrets*. New York, NY: The Free Press.

Cusumano, Michael, et al. 2003. "Software Development Worldwide: The State of the Practice," *IEEE Software*, November/December 2003, 28–34.

Dahl, O. J., E. W. Dijkstra, and C. A. R. Hoare. 1972. *Structured Programming*. New York, NY: Academic Press.

Date, Chris. 1977. *An Introduction to Database Systems*. Reading, MA: Addison-Wesley.

Davidson, Jack W., and Anne M. Holler. 1992. "Subprogram Inlining: A Study of Its Effects on Program Execution Time." *IEEE Transactions on Software Engineering* SE-18, no. 2 (February): 89–102.

Davis, P. J. 1972. "Fidelity in Mathematical Discourse: Is One and One Really Two?" *American Mathematical Monthly*, March, 252–63.

DeGrace, Peter, and Leslie Stahl. 1990. *Wicked Problems, Righteous Solutions: A Catalogue of Modern Software Engineering Paradigms*. Englewood Cliffs, NJ: Yourdon Press.

DeMarco, Tom and Timothy Lister. 1999. *Peopleware: Productive Projects and Teams*, 2d ed. New York, NY: Dorset House.

DeMarco, Tom, and Timothy Lister. 1985. "Programmer Performance and the Effects of the Workplace." *Proceedings of the 8th International Conference on Software Engineering*. Washington, DC: IEEE Computer Society Press, 268–72.

DeMarco, Tom. 1979. *Structured Analysis and Systems Specification: Tools and Techniques*. Englewood Cliffs, NJ: Prentice Hall.

DeMarco, Tom. 1982. *Controlling Software Projects*. New York, NY: Yourdon Press.

DeMillo, Richard A., Richard J. Lipton, and Alan J. Perlis. 1979. "Social Processes and Proofs of Theorems and Programs." *Communications of the ACM* 22, no. 5 (May): 271–80.

Dijkstra, Edsger. 1965. "Programming Considered as a Human Activity." *Proceedings of the 1965 IFIP Congress*. Amsterdam: North-Holland, 213–17. Reprinted in Yourdon 1982.

Dijkstra, Edsger. 1968. "Go To Statement Considered Harmful." *Communications of the ACM* 11, no. 3 (March): 147–48.

Dijkstra, Edsger. 1969. "Structured Programming." Reprinted in Yourdon 1979.

Dijkstra, Edsger. 1972. "The Humble Programmer." *Communications of the ACM* 15, no. 10 (October): 859–66.

Dijkstra, Edsger. 1985. "Fruits of Misunderstanding." *Datamation*, February 15, 86–87.

Dijkstra, Edsger. 1989. "On the Cruelty of Really Teaching Computer Science." *Communications of the ACM* 32, no. 12 (December): 1397–1414.

Dunn, Robert H. 1984. *Software Defect Removal*. New York, NY: McGraw-Hill.

Ellis, Margaret A., and Bjarne Stroustrup. 1990. *The Annotated C++ Reference Manual*. Boston, MA: Addison-Wesley.

Elmasri, Ramez, and Shamkant B. Navathe. 1989. *Fundamentals of Database Systems*. Redwood City, CA: Benjamin/Cummings.

Elshoff, James L. 1976. "An Analysis of Some Commercial PL/I Programs." *IEEE Transactions on Software Engineering* SE-2, no. 2 (June): 113–20.

Elshoff, James L. 1977. "The Influence of Structured Programming on PL/I Program Profiles." *IEEE Transactions on Software Engineering* SE-3, no. 5 (September): 364–68.

Elshoff, James L., and Michael Marcotty. 1982. "Improving Computer Program Readability to Aid Modification." *Communications of the ACM* 25, no. 8 (August): 512–21.

Endres, Albert. 1975. "An Analysis of Errors and Their Causes in System Programs." *IEEE Transactions on Software Engineering* SE-1, no. 2 (June): 140–49.

Evangelist, Michael. 1984. "Program Complexity and Programming Style." *Proceedings of the First International Conference on Data Engineering.* New York, NY: IEEE Computer Society Press, 534–41.

Fagan, Michael E. 1976. "Design and Code Inspections to Reduce Errors in Program Development." *IBM Systems Journal* 15, no. 3: 182–211.

Fagan, Michael E. 1986. "Advances in Software Inspections." *IEEE Transactions on Software Engineering* SE-12, no. 7 (July): 744–51.

Federal Software Management Support Center. 1986. *Programmers Work-bench Handbook.* Falls Church, VA: Office of Software Development and Information Technology.

Feiman, J., and M. Driver. 2002. "Leading Programming Languages for IT Portfolio Planning," Gartner Research report SPA-17-6636, September 27, 2002.

Fetzer, James H. 1988. "Program Verification: The Very Idea." *Communications of the ACM* 31, no. 9 (September): 1048–63.

FIPS PUB 38, *Guidelines for Documentation of Computer Programs and Automated Data Systems.* 1976. U.S. Department of Commerce. National Bureau of Standards. Washington, DC: U.S. Government Printing Office, Feb. 15.

Fishman, Charles. 1996. "They Write the Right Stuff," *Fast Company*, December 1996.

Fjelstad, R. K., and W. T. Hamlen. 1979. "Applications Program Maintenance Study: Report to our Respondents." *Proceedings Guide 48*, Philadelphia. Reprinted in *Tutorial on Software Maintenance*, G. Parikh and N. Zvegintzov, eds. Los Alamitos, CA: CS Press, 1983: 13–27.

Floyd, Robert. 1979. "The Paradigms of Programming." *Communications of the ACM* 22, no. 8 (August): 455–60.

Fowler, Martin. 1999. *Refactoring: Improving the Design of Existing Code.* Reading, MA: Addison-Wesley.

Fowler, Martin. 2002. *Patterns of Enterprise Application Architecture.* Boston, MA: Addison-Wesley.

Fowler, Martin. 2003. *UML Distilled: A Brief Guide to the Standard Object Modeling Language,* 3d ed. Boston, MA: Addison-Wesley.

Fowler, Martin. 2004. *UML Distilled,* 3d ed. Boston, MA: Addison-Wesley.

Fowler, Priscilla J. 1986. "In-Process Inspections of Work Products at AT&T." *AT&T Technical Journal*, March/April, 102–12.

Foxall, James. 2003. *Practical Standards for Microsoft Visual Basic .NET.* Redmond, WA: Microsoft Press.

Freedman, Daniel P., and Gerald M. Weinberg. 1990. *Handbook of Walkthroughs, Inspections and Technical Reviews,* 3d ed. New York, NY: Dorset House.

Freeman, Peter, and Anthony I. Wasserman, eds. 1983. *Tutorial on Software Design Techniques,* 4th ed. Silver Spring, MD: IEEE Computer Society Press.

Gamma, Erich, et al. 1995. *Design Patterns.* Reading, MA: Addison-Wesley.

Gerber, Richard. 2002. *Software Optimization Cookbook: High-Performance Recipes for the Intel Architecture.* Intel Press.

Gibson, Elizabeth. 1990. "Objects—Born and Bred." *BYTE*, October, 245–54.

Gilb, Tom, and Dorothy Graham. 1993. *Software Inspection*. Wokingham, England: Addison-Wesley.

Gilb, Tom. 1977. *Software Metrics*. Cambridge, MA: Winthrop.

Gilb, Tom. 1988. *Principles of Software Engineering Management*. Wokingham, England: Addison-Wesley.

Gilb, Tom. 2004. *Competitive Engineering*. Boston, MA: Addison-Wesley. Downloadable from *www.result-planning.com*.

Ginac, Frank P. 1998. *Customer Oriented Software Quality Assurance*. Englewood Cliffs, NJ: Prentice Hall.

Glass, Robert L. 1982. *Modern Programming Practices: A Report from Industry*. Englewood Cliffs, NJ: Prentice Hall.

Glass, Robert L. 1988. *Software Communication Skills*. Englewood Cliffs, NJ: Prentice Hall.

Glass, Robert L. 1991. *Software Conflict: Essays on the Art and Science of Software Engineering*. Englewood Cliffs, NJ: Yourdon Press.

Glass, Robert L. 1995. *Software Creativity*. Reading, MA: Addison-Wesley.

Glass, Robert L. 1999. "Inspections—Some Surprising Findings," *Communications of the ACM*, April 1999, 17–19.

Glass, Robert L. 1999. "The realities of software technology payoffs," *Communications of the ACM*, February 1999, 74–79.

Glass, Robert L. 2003. *Facts and Fallacies of Software Engineering*. Boston, MA: Addison-Wesley.

Glass, Robert L., and Ronald A. Noiseux. 1981. *Software Maintenance Guidebook*. Englewood Cliffs, NJ: Prentice Hall.

Gordon, Ronald D. 1979. "Measuring Improvements in Program Clarity." *IEEE Transactions on Software Engineering* SE-5, no. 2 (March): 79–90.

Gordon, Scott V., and James M. Bieman. 1991. "Rapid Prototyping and Software Quality: Lessons from Industry." *Ninth Annual Pacific Northwest Software Quality Conference, October 7–8*. Oregon Convention Center, Portland, OR.

Gorla, N., A. C. Benander, and B. A. Benander. 1990. "Debugging Effort Estimation Using Software Metrics." *IEEE Transactions on Software Engineering* SE-16, no. 2 (February): 223–31.

Gould, John D. 1975. "Some Psychological Evidence on How People Debug Computer Programs." *International Journal of Man-Machine Studies* 7:151–82.

Grady, Robert B. 1987. "Measuring and Managing Software Maintenance." *IEEE Software* 4, no. 9 (September): 34–45.

Grady, Robert B. 1993. "Practical Rules of Thumb for Software Managers." *The Software Practitioner* 3, no. 1 (January/February): 4–6.

Grady, Robert B. 1999. "An Economic Release Decision Model: Insights into Software Project Management." In *Proceedings of the Applications of Software Measurement Conference*, 227–239. Orange Park, FL: Software Quality Engineering.

Grady, Robert B., and Tom Van Slack. 1994. "Key Lessons in Achieving Widespread Inspection Use," *IEEE Software*, July 1994.

Grady, Robert B. 1992. *Practical Software Metrics For Project Management And Process Improvement*. Englewood Cliffs, NJ: Prentice Hall.

Grady, Robert B., and Deborah L. Caswell. 1987. *Software Metrics: Establishing a Company-Wide Program*. Englewood Cliffs, NJ: Prentice Hall.

Green, Paul. 1987. "Human Factors in Computer Systems, Some Useful Readings." *Sigchi Bulletin* 19, no. 2: 15–20.

Gremillion, Lee L. 1984. "Determinants of Program Repair Maintenance Requirements." *Communications of the ACM* 27, no. 8 (August): 826–32.

Gries, David. 1981. *The Science of Programming.* New York, NY: Springer-Verlag.

Grove, Andrew S. 1983. *High Output Management.* New York, NY: Random House.

Haley, Thomas J. 1996. "Software Process Improvement at Raytheon." *IEEE Software,* November 1996.

Hansen, John C., and Roger Yim. 1987. "Indentation Styles in C." *SIGSMALL/PC Notes* 13, no. 3 (August): 20–23.

Hanson, Dines. 1984. *Up and Running.* New York, NY: Yourdon Press.

Harrison, Warren, and Curtis Cook. 1986. "Are Deeply Nested Conditionals Less Readable?" *Journal of Systems and Software* 6, no. 4 (November): 335–42.

Hasan, Jeffrey and Kenneth Tu. 2003. *Performance Tuning and Optimizing ASP.NET Applications.* Apress.

Hass, Anne Mette Jonassen. 2003. *Configuration Management Principles and Practices,* Boston, MA: Addison-Wesley.

Hatley, Derek J., and Imtiaz A. Pirbhai. 1988. *Strategies for Real-Time System Specification.* New York, NY: Dorset House.

Hecht, Alan. 1990. "Cute Object-oriented Acronyms Considered FOOlish." *Software Engineering Notes,* January, 48.

Heckel, Paul. 1994. *The Elements of Friendly Software Design.* Alameda, CA: Sybex.

Hecker, Daniel E. 2001. "Occupational Employment Projections to 2010." *Monthly Labor Review,* November 2001.

Hecker, Daniel E. 2004. "Occupational Employment Projections to 2012." *Monthly Labor Review,* February 2004, Vol. 127, No. 2, pp. 80-105.

Henry, Sallie, and Dennis Kafura. 1984. "The Evaluation of Software Systems' Structure Using Quantitative Software Metrics." *Software–Practice and Experience* 14, no. 6 (June): 561–73.

Hetzel, Bill. 1988. *The Complete Guide to Software Testing,* 2d ed. Wellesley, MA: QED Information Systems.

Highsmith, James A., III. 2000. *Adaptive Software Development: A Collaborative Approach to Managing Complex Systems.* New York, NY: Dorset House.

Highsmith, Jim. 2002. *Agile Software Development Ecosystems.* Boston, MA: Addison-Wesley.

Hildebrand, J. D. 1989. "An Engineer's Approach." *Computer Language,* October, 5–7.

Hoare, Charles Anthony Richard, 1981. "The Emperor's Old Clothes." *Communications of the ACM,* February 1981, 75–83.

Hollocker, Charles P. 1990. *Software Reviews and Audits Handbook.* New York, NY: John Wiley & Sons.

Houghton, Raymond C. 1990. "An Office Library for Software Engineering Professionals." *Software Engineering: Tools, Techniques, Practice,* May/June, 35–38.

Howard, Michael, and David LeBlanc. 2003. *Writing Secure Code,* 2d ed. Redmond, WA: Microsoft Press.

Hughes, Charles E., Charles P. Pfleeger, and Lawrence L. Rose. 1978. *Advanced Programming Techniques: A Second Course in Programming Using Fortran.* New York, NY: John Wiley & Sons.

Humphrey, Watts S. 1989. *Managing the Software Process.* Reading, MA: Addison-Wesley.

Humphrey, Watts S. 1995. *A Discipline for Software Engineering.* Reading, MA: Addison-Wesley.

Humphrey, Watts S., Terry R. Snyder, and Ronald R. Willis. 1991. "Software Process Improvement at Hughes Aircraft." *IEEE Software* 8, no. 4 (July): 11–23.

Humphrey, Watts. 1997. *Introduction to the Personal Software Process.* Reading, MA: Addison-Wesley.

Humphrey, Watts. 2002. *Winning with Software: An Executive Strategy*. Boston, MA: Addison-Wesley.

Hunt, Andrew, and David Thomas. 2000. *The Pragmatic Programmer*. Boston, MA: Addison-Wesley.

Ichbiah, Jean D., et al. 1986. *Rationale for Design of the Ada Programming Language*. Minneapolis, MN: Honeywell Systems and Research Center.

IEEE Software 7, no. 3 (May 1990).

IEEE Std 1008-1987 (R1993), Standard for Software Unit Testing

IEEE Std 1016-1998, Recommended Practice for Software Design Descriptions

IEEE Std 1028-1997, Standard for Software Reviews

IEEE Std 1045-1992, Standard for Software Productivity Metrics

IEEE Std 1058-1998, Standard for Software Project Management Plans

IEEE Std 1061-1998, Standard for a Software Quality Metrics Methodology

IEEE Std 1062-1998, Recommended Practice for Software Acquisition

IEEE Std 1063-2001, Standard for Software User Documentation

IEEE Std 1074-1997, Standard for Developing Software Life Cycle Processes

IEEE Std 1219-1998, Standard for Software Maintenance

IEEE Std 1233-1998, Guide for Developing System Requirements Specifications

IEEE Std 1233-1998. IEEE Guide for Developing System Requirements Specifications

IEEE Std 1471-2000. Recommended Practice for Architectural Description of Software Intensive Systems

IEEE Std 1490-1998, Guide - Adoption of PMI Standard - A Guide to the Project Management Body of Knowledge

IEEE Std 1540-2001, Standard for Software Life Cycle Processes - Risk Management

IEEE Std 730-2002, Standard for Software Quality Assurance Plans

IEEE Std 828-1998, Standard for Software Configuration Management Plans

IEEE Std 829-1998, Standard for Software Test Documentation

IEEE Std 830-1998, Recommended Practice for Software Requirements Specifications

IEEE Std 830-1998. IEEE Recommended Practice for Software Requirements Specifications. Los Alamitos, CA: IEEE Computer Society Press.

IEEE, 1991. *IEEE Software Engineering Standards Collection, Spring 1991 Edition*. New York, NY: Institute of Electrical and Electronics Engineers.

IEEE, 1992. "Rear Adm. Grace Hopper dies at 85." *IEEE Computer*, February, 84.

Ingrassia, Frank S. 1976. "The Unit Development Folder (UDF): An Effective Management Tool for Software Development." TRW Technical Report TRW-SS-76-11. Also reprinted in Reifer 1986, 366–79.

Ingrassia, Frank S. 1987. "The Unit Development Folder (UDF): A Ten-Year Perspective." *Tutorial: Software Engineering Project Management*, ed. Richard H. Thayer. Los Alamitos, CA: IEEE Computer Society Press, 405–15.

Jackson, Michael A. 1975. *Principles of Program Design*. New York, NY: Academic Press.

Jacobson, Ivar, Grady Booch, and James Rumbaugh. 1999. *The Unified Software Development Process*. Reading, MA: Addison-Wesley.

Johnson, Jim. 1999. "Turning Chaos into Success," *Software Magazine*, December 1999, 30–39.

Johnson, Mark. 1994a. "Dr. Boris Beizer on Software Testing: An Interview Part 1," *The Software QA Quarterly*, Spring 1994, 7–13.

Johnson, Mark. 1994b. "Dr. Boris Beizer on Software Testing: An Interview Part 2," *The Software QA Quarterly*, Summer 1994, 41–45.

Johnson, Walter L. 1987. "Some Comments on Coding Practice." *ACM SIGSOFT Software Engineering Notes* 12, no. 2 (April): 32–35.

Jones, T. Capers. 1977. "Program Quality and Programmer Productivity." *IBM Technical Report TR 02.764*, January, 42–78. Also in Jones 1986b.

Jones, Capers. 1986a. *Programming Productivity*. New York, NY: McGraw-Hill.

Jones, T. Capers, ed. 1986b. *Tutorial: Programming Productivity: Issues for the Eighties*, 2d ed. Los Angeles, CA: IEEE Computer Society Press.

Jones, Capers. 1996. "Software Defect-Removal Efficiency," *IEEE Computer*, April 1996.

Jones, Capers. 1997. *Applied Software Measurement: Assuring Productivity and Quality*, 2d ed. New York, NY: McGraw-Hill.

Jones, Capers. 1998. *Estimating Software Costs*. New York, NY: McGraw-Hill.

Jones, Capers. 2000. *Software Assessments, Benchmarks, and Best Practices*. Reading, MA: Addison-Wesley.

Jones, Capers. 2003. "Variations in Software Development Practices," *IEEE Software*, November/December 2003, 22–27.

Jonsson, Dan. 1989. "Next: The Elimination of GoTo-Patches?" *ACM Sigplan Notices* 24, no. 3 (March): 85–92.

Kaelbling, Michael. 1988. "Programming Languages Should NOT Have Comment Statements." *ACM Sigplan Notices* 23, no. 10 (October): 59–60.

Kaner, Cem, Jack Falk, and Hung Q. Nguyen. 1999. *Testing Computer Software*, 2d ed. New York, NY: John Wiley & Sons.

Kaner, Cem, James Bach, and Bret Pettichord. 2002. *Lessons Learned in Software Testing*. New York, NY: John Wiley & Sons.

Keller, Daniel. 1990. "A Guide to Natural Naming." *ACM Sigplan Notices* 25, no. 5 (May): 95–102.

Kelly, John C. 1987. "A Comparison of Four Design Methods for Real-Time Systems." *Proceedings of the Ninth International Conference on Software Engineering*. 238–52.

Kelly-Bootle, Stan. 1981. *The Devil's DP Dictionary*. New York, NY: McGraw-Hill.

Kernighan, Brian W., and Rob Pike. 1999. *The Practice of Programming*. Reading, MA: Addison-Wesley.

Kernighan, Brian W., and P. J. Plauger. 1976. *Software Tools*. Reading, MA: Addison-Wesley.

Kernighan, Brian W., and P. J. Plauger. 1978. *The Elements of Programming Style*. 2d ed. New York, NY: McGraw-Hill.

Kernighan, Brian W., and P. J. Plauger. 1981. *Software Tools in Pascal*. Reading, MA: Addison-Wesley.

Kernighan, Brian W., and Dennis M. Ritchie. 1988. *The C Programming Language*, 2d ed. Englewood Cliffs, NJ: Prentice Hall.

Killelea, Patrick. 2002. *Web Performance Tuning*, 2d ed. Sebastopol, CA: O'Reilly & Associates.

King, David. 1988. *Creating Effective Software: Computer Program Design Using the Jackson Methodology*. New York, NY: Yourdon Press.

Knuth, Donald. 1971. "An Empirical Study of FORTRAN programs," *Software–Practice and Experience* 1:105–33.

Knuth, Donald. 1974. "Structured Programming with go to Statements." In *Classics in Software Engineering*, edited by Edward Yourdon. Englewood Cliffs, NJ: Yourdon Press, 1979.

Knuth, Donald. 1986. *Computers and Typesetting, Volume B, TEX: The Program.* Reading, MA: Addison-Wesley.

Knuth, Donald. 1997a. *The Art of Computer Programming*, vol. 1, *Fundamental Algorithms*, 3d ed. Reading, MA: Addison-Wesley.

Knuth, Donald. 1997b. *The Art of Computer Programming*, vol. 2, *Seminumerical Algorithms*, 3d ed. Reading, MA: Addison-Wesley.

Knuth, Donald. 1998. *The Art of Computer Programming*, vol. 3, *Sorting and Searching*, 2d ed. Reading, MA: Addison-Wesley.

Knuth, Donald. 2001. *Literate Programming*. Cambridge University Press.

Korson, Timothy D., and Vijay K. Vaishnavi. 1986. "An Empirical Study of Modularity on Program Modifiability." In Soloway and Iyengar 1986: 168–86.

Kouchakdjian, Ara, Scott Green, and Victor Basili. 1989. "Evaluation of the Cleanroom Methodology in the Software Engineering Laboratory." *Proceedings of the Fourteenth Annual Software Engineering Workshop, November 29, 1989.* Greenbelt, MD: Goddard Space Flight Center. Document SEL-89-007.

Kovitz, Benjamin, L. 1998 *Practical Software Requirements: A Manual of Content and Style*, Manning Publications Company.

Kreitzberg, C. B., and B. Shneiderman. 1972. *The Elements of Fortran Style.* New York, NY: Harcourt Brace Jovanovich.

Kruchten, Philippe B. "The 4+1 View Model of Architecture." *IEEE Software*, pages 42–50, November 1995.

Kruchten, Philippe. 2000. *The Rational Unified Process: An Introduction, 2d Ed.,* Reading, MA: Addison-Wesley.

Kuhn, Thomas S. 1996. *The Structure of Scientific Revolutions*, 3d ed. Chicago: University of Chicago Press.

Lammers, Susan. 1986. *Programmers at Work.* Redmond, WA: Microsoft Press.

Lampson, Butler. 1984. "Hints for Computer System Design." *IEEE Software* 1, no. 1 (January): 11–28.

Larman, Craig and Rhett Guthrie. 2000. *Java 2 Performance and Idiom Guide.* Englewood Cliffs, NJ: Prentice Hall.

Larman, Craig. 2001. *Applying UML and Patterns: An Introduction to Object-Oriented Analysis and Design and the Unified Process*, 2d ed. Englewood Cliffs, NJ: Prentice Hall.

Larman, Craig. 2004. *Agile and Iterative Development: A Manager's Guide.* Boston, MA: Addison-Wesley, 2004.

Lauesen, Soren. *Software Requirements: Styles and Techniques.* Boston, MA: Addison-Wesley, 2002.

Laurel, Brenda, ed. 1990. *The Art of Human-Computer Interface Design.* Reading, MA: Addison-Wesley.

Ledgard, Henry F., with John Tauer. 1987a. *C With Excellence: Programming Proverbs.* Indianapolis: Hayden Books.

Ledgard, Henry F., with John Tauer. 1987b. *Professional Software*, vol. 2, *Programming Practice.* Indianapolis: Hayden Books.

Ledgard, Henry, and Michael Marcotty. 1986. *The Programming Language Landscape: Syntax, Semantics, and Implementation*, 2d ed. Chicago: Science Research Associates.

Ledgard, Henry. 1985. "Programmers: The Amateur vs. the Professional." *Abacus* 2, no. 4 (Summer): 29–35.

Leffingwell, Dean. 1997. "Calculating the Return on Investment from More Effective Requirements Management," *American Programmer*, 10(4):13–16.

Lewis, Daniel W. 1979. "A Review of Approaches to Teaching Fortran." *IEEE Transactions on Education*, E-22, no. 1: 23–25.

Lewis, William E. 2000. *Software Testing and Continuous Quality Improvement*, 2d ed. Auerbach Publishing.

Lieberherr, Karl J. and Ian Holland. 1989. "Assuring Good Style for Object-Oriented Programs." *IEEE Software*, September 1989, pp. 38f.

Lientz, B. P., and E. B. Swanson. 1980. *Software Maintenance Management*. Reading, MA: Addison-Wesley.

Lind, Randy K., and K. Vairavan. 1989. "An Experimental Investigation of Software Metrics and Their Relationship to Software Development Effort." *IEEE Transactions on Software Engineering* SE-15, no. 5 (May): 649–53.

Linger, Richard C., Harlan D. Mills, and Bernard I. Witt. 1979. *Structured Programming: Theory and Practice*. Reading, MA: Addison-Wesley.

Linn, Marcia C., and Michael J. Clancy. 1992. "The Case for Case Studies of Programming Problems." *Communications of the ACM* 35, no. 3 (March): 121–32.

Liskov, Barbara, and Stephen Zilles. 1974. "Programming with Abstract Data Types." *ACM Sigplan Notices* 9, no. 4: 50–59.

Liskov, Barbara. "Data Abstraction and Hierarchy," *ACM SIGPLAN Notices*, May 1988.

Littman, David C., et al. 1986. "Mental Models and Software Maintenance." In Soloway and Iyengar 1986: 80–98.

Longstreet, David H., ed. 1990. *Software Maintenance and Computers*. Los Alamitos, CA: IEEE Computer Society Press.

Loy, Patrick H. 1990. "A Comparison of Object-Oriented and Structured Development Methods." *Software Engineering Notes* 15, no. 1 (January): 44–48.

Mackinnon, Tim, Steve Freeman, and Philip Craig. 2000. "Endo-Testing: Unit Testing with Mock Objects," *eXtreme Programming* and Flexible Processes Software Engineering - XP2000 Conference.

Maguire, Steve. 1993. *Writing Solid Code*. Redmond, WA: Microsoft Press.

Mannino, P. 1987. "A Presentation and Comparison of Four Information System Development Methodologies." *Software Engineering Notes* 12, no. 2 (April): 26–29.

Manzo, John. 2002. "Odyssey and Other Code Science Success Stories." *Crosstalk*, October 2002.

Marca, David. 1981. "Some Pascal Style Guidelines." *ACM Sigplan Notices* 16, no. 4 (April): 70–80.

March, Steve. 1999. "Learning from Pathfinder's Bumpy Start." *Software Testing and Quality Engineering*, September/October 1999, pp. 10f.

Marcotty, Michael. 1991. *Software Implementation*. New York, NY: Prentice Hall.

Martin, Robert C. 2003. *Agile Software Development: Principles, Patterns, and Practices*. Upper Saddle River, NJ: Pearson Education.

McCabe, Tom. 1976. "A Complexity Measure." *IEEE Transactions on Software Engineering*, SE-2, no. 4 (December): 308–20.

McCarthy, Jim. 1995. *Dynamics of Software Development*. Redmond, WA: Microsoft Press.

McConnell, Steve. 1996. *Rapid Development*. Redmond, WA: Microsoft Press.

McConnell, Steve. 1997a. "The Programmer Writing," *IEEE Software*, July/August 1997.

McConnell, Steve. 1997b. "Achieving Leaner Software," *IEEE Software*, November/December 1997.

McConnell, Steve. 1998a. *Software Project Survival Guide*. Redmond, WA: Microsoft Press.

McConnell, Steve. 1998b. "Why You Should Use Routines, Routinely," *IEEE Software*, Vol. 15, No. 4, July/August 1998.

McConnell, Steve. 1999. "Brooks Law Repealed?" *IEEE Software*, November/December 1999.

McConnell, Steve. 2004. *Professional Software Development*. Boston, MA: Addison-Wesley.

McCue, Gerald M. 1978. "IBM's Santa Teresa Laboratory—Architectural Design for Program Development." *IBM Systems Journal* 17, no. 1:4–25.

McGarry, Frank, and Rose Pajerski. 1990. "Towards Understanding Software—15 Years in the SEL." *Proceedings of the Fifteenth Annual Software Engineering Workshop, November 28–29, 1990*. Greenbelt, MD: Goddard Space Flight Center. Document SEL-90-006.

McGarry, Frank, Sharon Waligora, and Tim McDermott. 1989. "Experiences in the Software Engineering Laboratory (SEL) Applying Software Measurement." *Proceedings of the Fourteenth Annual Software Engineering Workshop, November 29, 1989*. Greenbelt, MD: Goddard Space Flight Center. Document SEL-89-007.

McGarry, John, et al. 2001. *Practical Software Measurement: Objective Information for Decision Makers*. Boston, MA: Addison-Wesley.

McKeithen, Katherine B., et al. 1981. "Knowledge Organization and Skill Differences in Computer Programmers." *Cognitive Psychology* 13:307–25.

Metzger, Philip W., and John Boddie. 1996. *Managing a Programming Project: Processes and People*, 3d ed. Englewood Cliffs, NJ: Prentice Hall, 1996.

Meyer, Bertrand. 1997. *Object-Oriented Software Construction*, 2d ed. New York, NY: Prentice Hall.

Meyers, Scott. 1996. *More Effective C++: 35 New Ways to Improve Your Programs and Designs*. Reading, MA: Addison-Wesley.

Meyers, Scott. 1998. *Effective C++: 50 Specific Ways to Improve Your Programs and Designs*, 2d ed. Reading, MA: Addison-Wesley.

Miaria, Richard J., et al. 1983. "Program Indentation and Comprehensibility." *Communications of the ACM* 26, no. 11 (November): 861–67.

Michalewicz, Zbigniew, and David B. Fogel. 2000. *How to Solve It: Modern Heuristics*. Berlin: Springer-Verlag.

Miller, G. A. 1956. "The Magical Number Seven, Plus or Minus Two: Some Limits on Our Capacity for Processing Information." *The Psychological Review* 63, no. 2 (March): 81–97.

Mills, Harlan D. 1983. *Software Productivity*. Boston, MA: Little, Brown.

Mills, Harlan D. 1986. "Structured Programming: Retrospect and Prospect." *IEEE Software*, November, 58–66.

Mills, Harlan D., and Richard C. Linger. 1986. "Data Structured Programming: Program Design Without Arrays and Pointers." *IEEE Transactions on Software Engineering* SE-12, no. 2 (February): 192–97.

Mills, Harlan D., Michael Dyer, and Richard C. Linger. 1987. "Cleanroom Software Engineering." *IEEE Software*, September, 19–25.

Misfeldt, Trevor, Greg Bumgardner, and Andrew Gray. 2004. *The Elements of C++ Style*. Cambridge University Press.

Mitchell, Jeffrey, Joseph Urban, and Robert McDonald. 1987. "The Effect of Abstract Data Types on Program Development." *IEEE Computer* 20, no. 9 (September): 85–88.

Mody, R. P. 1991. "C in Education and Software Engineering." *SIGCSE Bulletin* 23, no. 3 (September): 45–56.

Moore, Dave. 1992. Private communication.

Moore, James W. 1997. *Software Engineering Standards: A User's Road Map*. Los Alamitos, CA: IEEE Computer Society Press.

Morales, Alexandra Weber. 2003. "The Consummate Coach: Watts Humphrey, Father of Cmm and Author of Winning with Software, Explains How to Get Better at What You Do," *SD Show Daily*, September 16, 2003.

Myers, Glenford J. 1976. *Software Reliability*. New York, NY: John Wiley & Sons.

Myers, Glenford J. 1978a. *Composite/Structural Design*. New York, NY: Van Nostrand Reinhold.

Myers, Glenford J. 1978b. "A Controlled Experiment in Program Testing and Code Walkthroughs/Inspections." *Communications of the ACM* 21, no. 9 (September): 760–68.

Myers, Glenford J. 1979. *The Art of Software Testing*. New York, NY: John Wiley & Sons.

Myers, Ware. 1992. "Good Software Practices Pay Off—Or Do They?" *IEEE Software*, March, 96–97.

Naisbitt, John. 1982. *Megatrends*. New York, NY: Warner Books.

NASA Software Engineering Laboratory, 1994. *Software Measurement Guidebook*, June 1995, NASA-GB-001-94. Available from *http://sel.gsfc.nasa.gov/website /documents/online-doc/94-102.pdf*.

NCES 2002. National Center for Education Statistics, *2001 Digest of Educational Statistics,* Document Number NCES 2002130, April 2002.

Nevison, John M. 1978. *The Little Book of BASIC Style*. Reading, MA: Addison-Wesley.

Newcomer, Joseph M. 2000. "Optimization: Your Worst Enemy," May 2000, *www.flounder.com/optimization.htm*.

Norcio, A. F. 1982. "Indentation, Documentation and Programmer Comprehension." *Proceedings: Human Factors in Computer Systems, March 15–17, 1982, Gaithersburg, MD*: 118–20.

Norman, Donald A. 1988. *The Psychology of Everyday Things*. New York, NY: Basic Books. (Also published in paperback as *The Design of Everyday Things*. New York, NY: Doubleday, 1990.)

Oman, Paul and Shari Lawrence Pfleeger, eds. 1996. *Applying Software Metrics*. Los Alamitos, CA: IEEE Computer Society Press.

Oman, Paul W., and Curtis R. Cook. 1990a. "The Book Paradigm for Improved Maintenance." *IEEE Software*, January, 39–45.

Oman, Paul W., and Curtis R. Cook. 1990b. "Typographic Style Is More Than Cosmetic." *Communications of the ACM* 33, no. 5 (May): 506–20.

Ostrand, Thomas J., and Elaine J. Weyuker. 1984. "Collecting and Categorizing Software Error Data in an Industrial Environment." *Journal of Systems and Software* 4, no. 4 (November): 289–300.

Page-Jones, Meilir. 2000. *Fundamentals of Object-Oriented Design in UML*. Boston, MA: Addison-Wesley.

Page-Jones, Meilir. 1988. *The Practical Guide to Structured Systems Design*. Englewood Cliffs, NJ: Yourdon Press.

Parikh, G., and N. Zvegintzov, eds. 1983. *Tutorial on Software Maintenance*. Los Alamitos, CA: IEEE Computer Society Press.

Parikh, Girish. 1986. *Handbook of Software Maintenance*. New York, NY: John Wiley & Sons.

Parnas, David L. 1972. "On the Criteria to Be Used in Decomposing Systems into Modules." *Communications of the ACM* 5, no. 12 (December): 1053–58.

Parnas, David L. 1976. "On the Design and Development of Program Families." *IEEE Transactions on Software Engineering* SE-2, 1 (March): 1–9.

Parnas, David L. 1979. "Designing Software for Ease of Extension and Contraction." *IEEE Transactions on Software Engineering* SE-5, no. 2 (March): 128–38.

Parnas, David L. 1999. ACM Fellow Profile: David Lorge Parnas," *ACM Software Engineering Notes*, May 1999, 10–14.

Parnas, David L., and Paul C. Clements. 1986. "A Rational Design Process: How and Why to Fake It." *IEEE Transactions on Software Engineering* SE-12, no. 2 (February): 251–57.

Parnas, David L., Paul C. Clements, and D. M. Weiss. 1985. "The Modular Structure of Complex Systems." *IEEE Transactions on Software Engineering* SE-11, no. 3 (March): 259–66.

Perrott, Pamela. 2004. Private communication.

Peters, L. J., and L. L. Tripp. 1976. "Is Software Design Wicked" *Datamation*, Vol. 22, No. 5 (May 1976), 127–136.

Peters, Lawrence J. 1981. *Handbook of Software Design: Methods and Techniques.* New York, NY: Yourdon Press.

Peters, Lawrence J., and Leonard L. Tripp. 1977. "Comparing Software Design Methodologies." *Datamation*, November, 89–94.

Peters, Tom. 1987. *Thriving on Chaos: Handbook for a Management Revolution.* New York, NY: Knopf.

Petroski, Henry. 1994. *Design Paradigms: Case Histories of Error and Judgment in Engineering.* Cambridge, U.K.: Cambridge University Press.

Pietrasanta, Alfred M. 1990. "Alfred M. Pietrasanta on Improving the Software Process." *Software Engineering: Tools, Techniques, Practices* 1, no. 1 (May/June): 29–34.

Pietrasanta, Alfred M. 1991a. "A Strategy for Software Process Improvement." *Ninth Annual Pacific Northwest Software Quality Conference, October 7–8, 1991.* Oregon Convention Center, Portland, OR

Pietrasanta, Alfred M. 1991b. "Implementing Software Engineering in IBM." Keynote address. *Ninth Annual Pacific Northwest Software Quality Conference, October 7–8, 1991.* Oregon Convention Center, Portland, OR.

Pigoski, Thomas M. 1997. *Practical Software Maintenance.* New York, NY: John Wiley & Sons.

Pirsig, Robert M. 1974. *Zen and the Art of Motorcycle Maintenance: An Inquiry into Values.* William Morrow.

Plauger, P. J. 1988. "A Designer's Bibliography." *Computer Language*, July, 17–22.

Plauger, P. J. 1993. *Programming on Purpose: Essays on Software Design.* New York, NY: Prentice Hall.

Plum, Thomas. 1984. *C Programming Guidelines.* Cardiff, NJ: Plum Hall.

Polya, G. 1957. *How to Solve It: A New Aspect of Mathematical Method*, 2d ed. Princeton, NJ: Princeton University Press.

Post, Ed. 1983. "Real Programmers Don't Use Pascal," *Datamation*, July 1983, 263–265.

Prechelt, Lutz. 2000. "An Empirical Comparison of Seven Programming Languages," *IEEE Computer*, October 2000, 23–29.

Pressman, Roger S. 1987. *Software Engineering: A Practitioner's Approach.* New York, NY: McGraw-Hill.

Pressman, Roger S. 1988. *Making Software Engineering Happen: A Guide for Instituting the Technology.* Englewood Cliffs, NJ: Prentice Hall.

Putnam, Lawrence H. 2000. "Familiar Metric Management – Effort, Development Time, and Defects Interact." Downloadable from *www.qsm.com*.

Putnam, Lawrence H., and Ware Myers. 1992. *Measures for Excellence: Reliable Software On Time, Within Budget.* Englewood Cliffs, NJ: Yourdon Press, 1992.

Putnam, Lawrence H., and Ware Myers. 1997. *Industrial Strength Software: Effective Management Using Measurement.* Washington, DC: IEEE Computer Society Press.

Putnam, Lawrence H., and Ware Myers. 2000. "What We Have Learned." Downloadable from *www.qsm.com*, June 2000.

Raghavan, Sridhar A., and Donald R. Chand. 1989. "Diffusing Software-Engineering Methods." *IEEE Software*, July, 81–90.

Ramsey, H. Rudy, Michael E. Atwood, and James R. Van Doren. 1983. "Flowcharts Versus Program Design Languages: An Experimental Comparison." *Communications of the ACM* 26, no. 6 (June): 445–49.

Ratliff, Wayne. 1987. Interview in *Solution System.*

Raymond, E. S. 2000. "The Cathedral and the Bazaar," *www.catb.org/~esr/writings /cathedral-bazaar.*

Raymond, Eric S. 2004. *The Art of Unix Programming.* Boston, MA: Addison-Wesley.

Rees, Michael J. 1982. "Automatic Assessment Aids for Pascal Programs." *ACM Sigplan Notices* 17, no. 10 (October): 33–42.

Reifer, Donald. 2002. "How to Get the Most Out of Extreme Programming/Agile Methods," *Proceedings, XP/Agile Universe 2002.* New York, NY: Springer; 185–196.

Reingold, Edward M., and Wilfred J. Hansen. 1983. *Data Structures.* Boston, MA: Little, Brown.

Rettig, Marc. 1991. "Testing Made Palatable." *Communications of the ACM* 34, no. 5 (May): 25–29.

Riel, Arthur J. 1996. *Object-Oriented Design Heuristics.* Reading, MA: Addison-Wesley.

Rittel, Horst, and Melvin Webber. 1973. "Dilemmas in a General Theory of Planning." *Policy Sciences* 4:155–69.

Robertson, Suzanne, and James Robertson, 1999. *Mastering the Requirements Process.* Reading, MA: Addison-Wesley.

Rogers, Everett M. 1995. *Diffusion of Innovations*, 4th ed. New York, NY: The Free Press.

Rombach, H. Dieter. 1990. "Design Measurements: Some Lessons Learned." *IEEE Software*, March, 17–25.

Rubin, Frank. 1987. "'GOTO Considered Harmful' Considered Harmful." Letter to the editor. *Communications of the ACM* 30, no. 3 (March): 195–96. Follow-up letters in 30, no. 5 (May 1987): 351–55; 30, no. 6 (June 1987): 475–78; 30, no. 7 (July 1987): 632–34; 30, no. 8 (August 1987): 659–62; 30, no. 12 (December 1987): 997, 1085.

Sackman, H., W. J. Erikson, and E. E. Grant. 1968. "Exploratory Experimental Studies Comparing Online and Offline Programming Performance." *Communications of the ACM* 11, no. 1 (January): 3–11.

Schneider, G. Michael, Johnny Martin, and W. T. Tsai. 1992. "An Experimental Study of Fault Detection in User Requirements Documents," *ACM Transactions on Software Engineering and Methodology*, vol 1, no. 2, 188–204.

Schulmeyer, G. Gordon. 1990. *Zero Defect Software.* New York, NY: McGraw-Hill.

Sedgewick, Robert. 1997. *Algorithms in C, Parts 1-4*, 3d ed. Boston, MA: Addison-Wesley.

Sedgewick, Robert. 2001. *Algorithms in C, Part 5*, 3d ed. Boston, MA: Addison-Wesley.

Sedgewick, Robert. 1998. *Algorithms in C++, Parts 1-4*, 3d ed. Boston, MA: Addison-Wesley.

Sedgewick, Robert. 2002. *Algorithms in C++, Part 5*, 3d ed. Boston, MA: Addison-Wesley.

Sedgewick, Robert. 2002. *Algorithms in Java, Parts 1-4*, 3d ed. Boston, MA: Addison-Wesley.

Sedgewick, Robert. 2003. *Algorithms in Java, Part 5*, 3d ed. Boston, MA: Addison-Wesley.

SEI 1995. *The Capability Maturity Model: Guidelines for Improving the Software Process*, Software Engineering Institute, Reading, MA: Addison-Wesley, 1995.

SEI, 2003. "Process Maturity Profile: Software CMM®, CBA IPI and SPA Appraisal Results: 2002 Year End Update," Software Engineering Institute, April 2003.

Selby, Richard W., and Victor R. Basili. 1991. "Analyzing Error-Prone System Structure." *IEEE Transactions on Software Engineering* SE-17, no. 2 (February): 141–52.

SEN 1990. "Subsection on Telephone Systems," *Software Engineering Notes*, April 1990, 11–14.

Shalloway, Alan, and James R. Trott. 2002. *Design Patterns Explained*. Boston, MA: Addison-Wesley.

Sheil, B. A. 1981. "The Psychological Study of Programming." *Computing Surveys* 13, no. 1 (March): 101–20.

Shen, Vincent Y., et al. 1985. "Identifying Error-Prone Software—An Empirical Study." *IEEE Transactions on Software Engineering* SE-11, no. 4 (April): 317–24.

Sheppard, S. B., et al. 1978. "Predicting Programmers' Ability to Modify Software." *TR 78-388100-3*, General Electric Company, May.

Sheppard, S. B., et al. 1979. "Modern Coding Practices and Programmer Performance." *IEEE Computer* 12, no. 12 (December): 41–49.

Shepperd, M., and D. Ince. 1989. "Metrics, Outlier Analysis and the Software Design Process." *Information and Software Technology* 31, no. 2 (March): 91–98.

Shirazi, Jack. 2000. *Java Performance Tuning*. Sebastopol, CA: O'Reilly & Associates.

Shlaer, Sally, and Stephen J. Mellor. 1988. *Object Oriented Systems Analysis—Modeling the World in Data*. Englewood Cliffs, NJ: Prentice Hall.

Shneiderman, Ben, and Richard Mayer. 1979. "Syntactic/Semantic Interactions in Programmer Behavior: A Model and Experimental Results." *International Journal of Computer and Information Sciences* 8, no. 3: 219–38.

Shneiderman, Ben. 1976. "Exploratory Experiments in Programmer Behavior." *International Journal of Computing and Information Science* 5:123–43.

Shneiderman, Ben. 1980. *Software Psychology: Human Factors in Computer and Information Systems*. Cambridge, MA: Winthrop.

Shneiderman, Ben. 1987. *Designing the User Interface: Strategies for Effective Human-Computer Interaction*. Reading, MA: Addison-Wesley.

Shull, et al. 2002. "What We Have Learned About Fighting Defects," *Proceedings, Metrics 2002*. IEEE; 249–258.

Simon, Herbert. 1996. *The Sciences of the Artificial*, 3d ed. Cambridge, MA: MIT Press.

Simon, Herbert. *The Shape of Automation for Men and Management*. Harper and Row, 1965.

Simonyi, Charles, and Martin Heller. 1991. "The Hungarian Revolution." *BYTE*, August, 131–38.

Smith, Connie U., and Lloyd G. Williams. 2002. *Performance Solutions: A Practical Guide to Creating Responsive, Scalable Software*. Boston, MA: Addison-Wesley.

Software Productivity Consortium. 1989. *Ada Quality and Style: Guidelines for Professional Programmers*. New York, NY: Van Nostrand Reinhold.

Soloway, Elliot, and Kate Ehrlich. 1984. "Empirical Studies of Programming Knowledge." *IEEE Transactions on Software Engineering* SE-10, no. 5 (September): 595–609.

Soloway, Elliot, and Sitharama Iyengar, eds. 1986. *Empirical Studies of Programmers*. Norwood, NJ: Ablex.

Soloway, Elliot, Jeffrey Bonar, and Kate Ehrlich. 1983. "Cognitive Strategies and Looping Constructs: An Empirical Study." *Communications of the ACM* 26, no. 11 (November): 853–60.

Solution Systems. 1987. *World-Class Programmers' Editing Techniques: Interviews with Seven Programmers.* South Weymouth, MA: Solution Systems.

Sommerville, Ian. 1989. *Software Engineering*, 3d ed. Reading, MA: Addison-Wesley.

Spier, Michael J. 1976. "Software Malpractice—A Distasteful Experience." *Software—Practice and Experience* 6:293–99.

Spinellis, Diomidis. 2003. *Code Reading: The Open Source Perspective.* Boston, MA: Addison-Wesley.

SPMN. 1998. *Little Book of Configuration Management.* Arlington, VA; Software Program Managers Network.

Starr, Daniel. 2003. "What Supports the Roof?" *Software Development.* July 2003, 38–41.

Stephens, Matt. 2003. "Emergent Design vs. Early Prototyping," May 26, 2003, *www.softwarereality.com/design/early_prototyping.jsp*.

Stevens, Scott M. 1989. "Intelligent Interactive Video Simulation of a Code Inspection." *Communications of the ACM* 32, no. 7 (July): 832–43.

Stevens, W., G. Myers, and L. Constantine. 1974. "Structured Design." *IBM Systems Journal* 13, no. 2 (May): 115–39.

Stevens, Wayne. 1981. *Using Structured Design.* New York, NY: John Wiley & Sons.

Stroustrup, Bjarne. 1997. *The C++ Programming Language*, 3d ed. Reading, MA: Addison-Wesley.

Strunk, William, and E. B. White. 2000. *Elements of Style*, 4th ed. Pearson.

Sun Microsystems, Inc. 2000. "How to Write Doc Comments for the Javadoc Tool," 2000. Available from *http://java.sun.com/j2se/javadoc/writingdoccomments/*.

Sutter, Herb. 2000. *Exceptional C++: 47 Engineering Puzzles, Programming Problems, and Solutions.* Boston, MA: Addison-Wesley.

Tackett, Buford D., III, and Buddy Van Doren. 1999. "Process Control for Error Free Software: A Software Success Story," *IEEE Software*, May 1999.

Tenner, Edward. 1997. *Why Things Bite Back: Technology and the Revenge of Unintended Consequences.* Vintage Books.

Tenny, Ted. 1988. "Program Readability: Procedures versus Comments." *IEEE Transactions on Software Engineering* SE-14, no. 9 (September): 1271–79.

Thayer, Richard H., ed. 1990. *Tutorial: Software Engineering Project Management.* Los Alamitos, CA: IEEE Computer Society Press.

Thimbleby, Harold. 1988. "Delaying Commitment." *IEEE Software*, May, 78–86.

Thomas, Dave, and Andy Hunt. 2002. "Mock Objects," *IEEE Software*, May/June 2002.

Thomas, Edward J., and Paul W. Oman. 1990. "A Bibliography of Programming Style." *ACM Sigplan Notices* 25, no. 2 (February): 7–16.

Thomas, Richard A. 1984. "Using Comments to Aid Program Maintenance." *BYTE*, May, 415–22.

Tripp, Leonard L., William F. Struck, and Bryan K. Pflug. 1991. "The Application of Multiple Team Inspections on a Safety-Critical Software Standard," *Proceedings of the 4th Software Engineering Standards Application Workshop*, Los Alamitos, CA: IEEE Computer Society Press.

U.S. Department of Labor. 1990. "The 1990–91 Job Outlook in Brief." *Occupational Outlook Quarterly, Spring.* U.S. Government Printing Office. Document 1990-282-086/20007.

Valett, J., and F. E. McGarry. 1989. "A Summary of Software Measurement Experiences in the Software Engineering Laboratory." *Journal of Systems and Software* 9, no. 2 (February): 137–48.

Van Genuchten, Michiel. 1991. "Why Is Software Late? An Empirical Study of Reasons for Delay in Software Development." *IEEE Transactions on Software Engineering* SE-17, no. 6 (June): 582–90.

Van Tassel, Dennie. 1978. *Program Style, Design, Efficiency, Debugging, and Testing*, 2d ed. Englewood Cliffs, NJ: Prentice Hall.

Vaughn-Nichols, Steven. 2003. "Building Better Software with Better Tools," *IEEE Computer*, September 2003, 12–14.

Vermeulen, Allan, et al. 2000. *The Elements of Java Style*. Cambridge University Press.

Vessey, Iris, Sirkka L. Jarvenpaa, and Noam Tractinsky. 1992. "Evaluation of Vendor Products: CASE Tools as Methodological Companions." *Communications of the ACM* 35, no. 4 (April): 91–105.

Vessey, Iris. 1986. "Expertise in Debugging Computer Programs: An Analysis of the Content of Verbal Protocols." *IEEE Transactions on Systems, Man, and Cybernetics* SMC-16, no. 5 (September/October): 621–37.

Votta, Lawrence G., et al. 1991. "Investigating the Application of Capture-Recapture Techniques to Requirements and Design Reviews." *Proceedings of the Sixteenth Annual Software Engineering Workshop, December 4–5, 1991*. Greenbelt, MD: Goddard Space Flight Center. Document SEL-91-006.

Walston, C. E., and C. P. Felix. 1977. "A Method of Programming Measurement and Estimation." *IBM Systems Journal* 16, no. 1: 54–73.

Ward, Robert. 1989. *A Programmer's Introduction to Debugging C*. Lawrence, KS: R & D Publications.

Ward, William T. 1989. "Software Defect Prevention Using McCabe's Complexity Metric." *Hewlett-Packard Journal*, April, 64–68.

Webster, Dallas E. 1988. "Mapping the Design Information Representation Terrain." *IEEE Computer*, December, 8–23.

Weeks, Kevin. 1992. "Is Your Code Done Yet?" *Computer Language*, April, 63–72.

Weiland, Richard J. 1983. *The Programmer's Craft: Program Construction, Computer Architecture, and Data Management*. Reston, VA: Reston Publishing.

Weinberg, Gerald M. 1983. "Kill That Code!" *Infosystems*, August, 48–49.

Weinberg, Gerald M. 1998. *The Psychology of Computer Programming: Silver Anniversary Edition*. New York, NY: Dorset House.

Weinberg, Gerald M., and Edward L. Schulman. 1974. "Goals and Performance in Computer Programming." *Human Factors* 16, no. 1 (February): 70–77.

Weinberg, Gerald. 1988. *Rethinking Systems Analysis and Design*. New York, NY: Dorset House.

Weisfeld, Matt. 2004. *The Object-Oriented Thought Process*, 2d ed. SAMS, 2004.

Weiss, David M. 1975. "Evaluating Software Development by Error Analysis: The Data from the Architecture Research Facility." *Journal of Systems and Software* 1, no. 2 (June): 57–70.

Weiss, Eric A. 1972. "Review of *The Psychology of Computer Programming*, by Gerald M. Weinberg." *ACM Computing Reviews* 13, no. 4 (April): 175–76.

Wheeler, David, Bill Brykczynski, and Reginald Meeson. 1996. *Software Inspection: An Industry Best Practice*. Los Alamitos, CA: IEEE Computer Society Press.

Whittaker, James A. 2000 "What Is Software Testing? And Why Is It So Hard?" *IEEE Software*, January 2000, 70–79.

Whittaker, James A. 2002. *How to Break Software: A Practical Guide to Testing.* Boston, MA: Addison-Wesley.

Whorf, Benjamin. 1956. *Language, Thought and Reality.* Cambridge, MA: MIT Press.

Wiegers, Karl. 2002. *Peer Reviews in Software: A Practical Guide.* Boston, MA: Addison-Wesley.

Wiegers, Karl. 2003. *Software Requirements,* 2d ed. Redmond, WA: Microsoft Press.

Williams, Laurie, and Robert Kessler. 2002. *Pair Programming Illuminated.* Boston, MA: Addison-Wesley.

Willis, Ron R., et al. 1998. "Hughes Aircraft's Widespread Deployment of a Continuously Improving Software Process," Software Engineering Institute/Carnegie Mellon University, CMU/SEI-98-TR-006, May 1998.

Wilson, Steve, and Jeff Kesselman. 2000. *Java Platform Performance: Strategies and Tactics.* Boston, MA: Addison-Wesley.

Wirth, Niklaus. 1995. "A Plea for Lean Software," *IEEE Computer,* February 1995.

Wirth, Niklaus. 1971. "Program Development by Stepwise Refinement." *Communications of the ACM* 14, no. 4 (April): 221–27.

Wirth, Niklaus. 1986. *Algorithms and Data Structures.* Englewood Cliffs, NJ: Prentice Hall.

Woodcock, Jim, and Martin Loomes. 1988. *Software Engineering Mathematics.* Reading, MA: Addison-Wesley.

Woodfield, S. N., H. E. Dunsmore, and V. Y. Shen. 1981. "The Effect of Modularization and Comments on Program Comprehension." *Proceedings of the Fifth International Conference on Software Engineering,* March 1981, 215–23.

Wulf, W. A. 1972. "A Case Against the GO-TO." *Proceedings of the 25th National ACM Conference,* August 1972, 791–97.

Youngs, Edward A. 1974. "Human Errors in Programming." *International Journal of Man-Machine Studies* 6:361–76.

Yourdon, Edward, and Larry L. Constantine. 1979. *Structured Design: Fundamentals of a Discipline of Computer Program and Systems Design.* Englewood Cliffs, NJ: Yourdon Press.

Yourdon, Edward, ed. 1979. *Classics in Software Engineering.* Englewood Cliffs, NJ: Yourdon Press.

Yourdon, Edward, ed. 1982. *Writings of the Revolution: Selected Readings on Software Engineering.* New York, NY: Yourdon Press.

Yourdon, Edward. 1986a. *Managing the Structured Techniques: Strategies for Software Development in the 1990s,* 3d ed. New York, NY: Yourdon Press.

Yourdon, Edward. 1986b. *Nations at Risk.* New York, NY: Yourdon Press.

Yourdon, Edward. 1988. "The 63 Greatest Software Books." *American Programmer,* September.

Yourdon, Edward. 1989a. *Modern Structured Analysis.* New York, NY: Yourdon Press.

Yourdon, Edward. 1989b. *Structured Walk-Throughs,* 4th ed. New York, NY: Yourdon Press.

Yourdon, Edward. 1992. *Decline & Fall of the American Programmer.* Englewood Cliffs, NJ: Yourdon Press.

Zachary, Pascal. 1994. *Showstopper!* The Free Press.

Zahniser, Richard A. 1992. "A Massively Parallel Software Development Approach." *American Programmer,* January, 34–41.

Index

Symbols and Numbers

* (pointer declaration symbol), 332, 334–335, 763
& (pointer reference symbol), 332
-> (pointer symbol), 328
80/20 rule, 592

A

abbreviation of names, 283–285
abstract data types. *See* ADTs
Abstract Factory pattern, 104
abstraction
  access routines for, 340–342
  ADTs for. *See* ADTs
  air lock analogy, 136
  checklist, 157
  classes for, 152, 157
  cohesion with, 138
  complexity, for handling, 839
  consistent level for class
    interfaces, 135–136
  defined, 89
  erosion under modification
    problem, 138
  evaluating, 135
  exactness goal, 136–137
  forming consistently, 89–90
  good example for class interfaces,
    133–134
  guidelines for creating class
    interfaces, 135–138
  high-level problem domain terms,
    847
  implementation structures,
    low-level, 846
  inconsistent, 135–136, 138
  interfaces, goals for, 133–138
  levels of, 845–847
  opposites, pairs of, 137
  OS level, 846
  patterns for, 103
  placing items in inheritance trees,
    146
  poor example for class interfaces,
    134–135
  problem domain terms, low-level,
    846
  programming-language level, 846
  routines for, 164

access routines
  abstraction benefit, 340
  abstraction, level of, 341–342
  advantages of, 339–340
  barricaded variables benefit, 339
  centralized control from, 339
  creating, 340
  g_ prefix guideline, 340
  information hiding benefit, 340
  lack of support for, overcoming,
    340–342
  locking, 341
  parallelism from, 342
  requiring, 340
accidental problems, 77–78
accreting a system metaphor, 15–16
accuracy, 464
Ada
  description of, 63
  parameter order, 174–175
adaptability, 464
Adapter pattern, 104
addition, dangers of, 295
ADTs (abstract data types)
  abstraction with, 130
  access routines, 339–342
  benefits of, 126–129
  changes not propagating benefit,
    128
  classes based on, 133
  cooling system example, 129–130
  data, meaning of, 126
  defined, 126
  documentation benefit, 128
  explicit instancing, 132
  files as, 130
  guidelines, 130–131
  hiding information with, 127
  instancing, 132
  implicit instancing, 132
  interfaces, making more
    informative, 128
  low-level data types as, 130
  media independence with, 131
  multiple instances, handling,
    131–133
  need for, example of, 126–127
  non-object-oriented languages
    with, 131–133
  objects as, 130

  operations examples, table of,
    129–130
  passing of data, minimization of,
    128
  performance improvements with,
    128
  purpose of, 126
  real-world entities, working with,
    128–129
  representation question, 130
  simple items as, 131
  verification of code benefit, 128
agile development, 58, 658
algebraic identities, 630
algorithms
  commenting, 809
  heuristics compared to, 12
  metaphors serving as, 11–12
  resources on, 607
  routines, planning for, 223
aliasing, 311–316
analysis skills development, 823
approaches to development
  agile development, 58, 658
  bottom-up approaches, 112–113,
    697–698
  Extreme Programming, 58,
    471–472, 482, 708, 856
  importance of, 839–841
  iterative approach. *See* iteration in
    development
  premature optimization problem,
    840
  quality control, 840. *See also*
    quality of software
  resources for, 58–59
  sequential approach, 35–36
  team processes, 839–840
  top-down approaches, 111–113,
    694–696
architecture
  building block definition, 45
  business rules, 46
  buying vs. building components,
    51
  changes, 44, 52
  checklist for, 54–55
  class design, 46
  commitment delay strategy, 52
  conceptual integrity of, 52

Steve McConnell

Steve McConnell is Chief Software Engineer at Construx Software where he oversees Construx's software engineering practices. Steve is the lead for the Construction Knowledge Area of the Software Engineering Body of Knowledge (SWEBOK) project. Steve has worked on software projects at Microsoft, Boeing, and other Seattle-area companies.

Steve is the author of *Rapid Development* (1996), *Software Project Survival Guide* (1998), and *Professional Software Development* (2004). His books have twice won *Software Development* magazine's Jolt Excellence award for outstanding software development book of the year. Steve was also the lead developer of SPC Estimate Professional, winner of a Software Development Productivity award. In 1998, readers of *Software Development* magazine named Steve one of the three most influential people in the software industry, along with Bill Gates and Linus Torvalds.

Steve earned a Bachelor's degree from Whitman College and a Master's degree in software engineering from Seattle University. He lives in Bellevue, Washington.

If you have any comments or questions about this book, please contact Steve at *stevemcc@construx.com* or via *www.stevemcconnell.com*.

Best practices straight from the experts

Code Complete, Second Edition
ISBN 0-7356-1967-0   Suggested Retail Price: $49.99 U.S., $72.99 Canada

Discover timeless techniques and strategies. Widely considered one of the best practical guides to programming, Steve McConnell's original CODE COMPLETE has been helping developers write better software for more than a decade. Now this classic book has been fully updated and revised with leading-edge practices—and hundreds of new code samples—illustrating the art and science of software construction. Capturing the body of knowledge available from research, academia, and everyday commercial practice, McConnell synthesizes the most effective techniques and must-know principles into clear, pragmatic guidance. No matter what your experience level, development environment, or project size, this book will inform and stimulate your thinking—and help you build the highest quality code.

Software Requirements, Second Edition
ISBN 0-7356-1879-8   Suggested Retail Price: $39.99 U.S., $57.99 Canada

Proven practices for requirements engineering—plus more examples, new topics, and sample requirements documents. Discover effective techniques for managing the requirements engineering process all the way through the development cycle. SOFTWARE REQUIREMENTS, Second Edition, features new case examples, anecdotes culled from the author's extensive consulting career, and specific *Next Steps* for putting the book's process-improvement principles into practice. Engineering authority Karl Wiegers amplifies the best practices presented in his original award-winning text—now a mainstay for anyone participating in the software development process.

Writing Secure Code, Second Edition
ISBN 0-7356-1722-8   Suggested Retail Price: $49.99 U.S., $72.99 Canada

Keep hackers at bay with proven techniques from the security experts—now updated with lessons from the Microsoft® security pushes. Learn how to keep the bad guys at bay with the techniques in this entertaining, eye-opening book—now updated with the latest security threats plus lessons learned from the recent security pushes at Microsoft. Easily digested chapters explain proven security principles, strategies, and coding techniques to give you the peace of mind that comes from knowing you've done everything possible to make your code more resistant to attack. Sample code provided to demonstrate the specifics of secure development.

To learn more about Microsoft Press® products for professional Developers, please visit:

microsoft.com/mspress

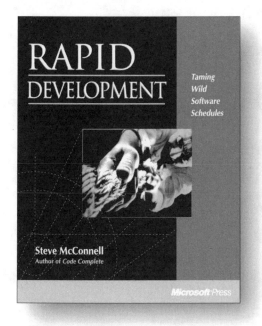

What do you think of this book?
We want to hear from you!

Do you have a few minutes to participate in a brief online survey? Microsoft is interested in hearing your feedback about this publication so that we can continually improve our books and learning resources for you.

To participate in our survey, please visit:
www.microsoft.com/learning/booksurvey

And enter this book's ISBN, 0-7356-1967-0. As a thank-you to survey participants in the United States and Canada, each month we'll randomly select five respondents to win one of five $100 gift certificates from a leading online merchant.* At the conclusion of the survey, you can enter the drawing by providing your e-mail address, which will be used for prize notification *only*.

Thanks in advance for your input. Your opinion counts!

Sincerely,

Microsoft® Learning

Learn More. Go Further.

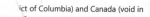